WOODROW WILSON AND
THE AMERICAN DIPLOMATIC TRADITION

Woodrow Wilson and the American Diplomatic Tradition

The Treaty Fight in Perspective

LLOYD E. AMBROSIUS

University of Nebraska–Lincoln

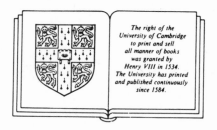

The right of the
University of Cambridge
to print and sell
all manner of books
was granted by
Henry VIII in 1534.
The University has printed
and published continuously
since 1584.

CAMBRIDGE UNIVERSITY PRESS

Cambridge

New York   Port Chester

Melbourne   Sydney

Published by the Press Syndicate of the University of Cambridge
The Pitt Building, Trumpington Street, Cambridge CB2 1RP
40 West 20th Street, New York, NY 10011, USA
10 Stamford Road, Oakleigh, Melbourne 3166, Australia

First published 1987
First paperback edition 1990

Printed in the United States of America

Library of Congress Cataloging-in-Publication Data
Ambrosius, Lloyd E.
Woodrow Wilson and the American diplomatic tradition.
Bibliography: p.
Includes index.
1. World War, 1914–1918 – Peace.   2. Wilson,
Woodrow, 1856–1924.   3. League of Nations.   4. United
States – Foreign relations – 1913–1921.   5. Treaty of
Versailles (1919) I. Title.
D645.A42   1987   946.3'142   86–33347

British Library Cataloguing in Publication Data
Ambrosius, Lloyd E.
Woodrow Wilson and the American diplomatic
tradition: the treaty fight in perspective.
1. Wilson, Woodrow   2. United States –
Foreign relations – 1913–1921
I. Title
327.73   E768

ISBN 0-521-33453-5 hard covers
ISBN 0-521-38585-7 paperback

To my parents
Sterling and Grace Ambrosius
for being who they are

Contents

Preface

World War I demonstrated the interdependence and pluralism of nations in the twentieth century. A global economy had developed, along with world-wide empires. Yet competing nations, and groups within them, continued to pursue their own separate interests. Paradoxically, both centralization and diversity characterized the modern world, which witnessed the simultaneous flourishing of internationalism and nationalism.

Most Americans, including President Woodrow Wilson, possessed only a limited understanding of this world. In 1914 they did not anticipate that the European war would engulf the United States. Wanting to remain isolated from the Old World, they adhered to the traditional American policy of neutrality. Imperial Germany's submarines, however, provoked the United States in 1917 to intervene on the Allies' side. The world was more interdependent than Americans had recognized. The Democratic president subsequently defined his war aims in the Fourteen Points. Placing the League of Nations at the center of his program, he hoped this postwar international organization would preserve peace. Yet the unity he sought failed to materialize at the Paris Peace Conference of 1919. Although the Allies as well as Germany had nominally approved most of his Fourteen Points, they opposed his definition of their national interests. In the United States as well, Wilson's foreign policy encountered resistance. Republicans, led by Senator Henry Cabot Lodge of Massachusetts, rejected the Versailles Treaty. They denounced the Covenant of the new League. Diversity among nations and within the United States continued to shape postwar politics.

Global interdependence and pluralism combined to create a fundamental dilemma for the United States in the twentieth century. This nation could no longer maintain its traditional isolation from the Old World, yet neither could it expect universal acceptance of its own ideals and practices by other nations. Wilson attempted to resolve this dilemma with the League. It promised a global environment in which the United States could protect its vital interests. It would, in his view, permit American control over foreign affairs. By transforming international relations, the League would enable the United States to provide leadership overseas without entangling itself in the Old World's diplomacy and wars. Critics of Wilson's League, on the contrary, saw the danger of foreign influence over the United States. They emphasized the costs of world-wide responsibilities. The resulting conflict between Wilson and the Senate over the peace treaty centered on these issues. It also involved the constitutional question of presidential control of American foreign relations.

Wilson's search for control exemplified a central theme in American history at the beginning of the twentieth century. Robert H. Wiebe examined one of its important facets in *The Search for Order: 1877-1920* (1967),[1] but he overlooked the dynamic quality of the American conception of order. Less interested in order per se than in control at home and abroad, American leaders were willing on occasion to condone and even to foment chaos, war and revolution, although these were inherently disorderly. They subordinated the search for order to their even more characteristic search for control. Wilson's conception of the League, and his attempt to win the Senate's approval of the treaty, demonstrated this central theme. He used presidential power in a vain endeavor to reshape the world. As a progressive, he attempted to resolve the fundamental dilemma of American foreign relations through control over other nations. Although he never fully understood this dilemma, which the combination of interdependence and pluralism posed, the president hoped the League would resolve it. But he failed to realize his vision of collective security. This failure was not Wilson's alone, for it also revealed the limits of American progressive thought. The progressivism that he epitomized furnished unrealistic guidance for the United States in the modern world.[2]

Because of his powerful intellect and dominant personality, Wilson imposed his categories onto the debate over American foreign policy. He claimed the mantle of internationalism and succeeded in placing the derogatory label of isolationism on his critics. He appeared positive or progressive; and they, negative or reactionary. Articulating a new vision, he seemed to herald the future, while they apparently represented the past. This characterization, however, obscures the complexity of the treaty fight. It

1 Robert H. Wiebe, *The Search for Order: 1877-1920* (New York, 1967).

2 For a masterful examination of the dilemmas posed by diversity and centralization in the United States, including the paradoxical relationships between domestic reform and war, nationalism and internationalism, and traditional democratic individualism and industrial centralization, see Barry D. Karl, *The Uneasy State: The United States from 1915 to 1945* (Chicago, 1983). For excellent introductions to the theory and practice of international organizations in modern European and American history, with particular attention to Wilson's conception of collective security and to power in the pursuit of peace, see Inis L. Claude, Jr., *Power and International Relations* (New York, 1962), F. H. Hinsley, *Power and the Pursuit of Peace: Theory and Practice in the History of Relations Between States* (Cambridge, 1963), and Warren F. Kuehl, *Seeking World Order: The United States and International Organization to* 1920 (Nashville, 1969).

ignores the innovative ideas of Republican leaders in foreign affairs, as well as the traditional aspects of the president's own approach.[3]

Some of Wilson's contemporaries criticized his lack of realism. Subsequently, experts on international relations, such as George F. Kennan, Hans J. Morgenthau and Norman A. Graebner, have developed this critique. In their view, his idealism produced an unrealistic response to the World War. Rather than act to preserve the European balance of power and protect the national interest, the president enunciated inappropriate moral or legal principles. In short, his diplomacy exemplified the typical shortcomings of American leadership in the twentieth century.[4]

Reacting to this realist critique, Wilson's defenders have argued that his foreign policy actually served the national interest very well. To scholars such as Edward H. Buehrig, Ernest R. May, Daniel M. Smith and David F. Trask, his decision to intervene in the European war combined force and diplomacy in a commendable fashion. In response to Germany's challenge, he even adopted a balance-of-power policy. From their perspective, his obvious idealism masked a shrewd practice of power politics.[5] Accordingly, as Arthur S. Link has argued, his leadership demonstrated a "higher realism."[6] In the development of this historiography, the concept of realism has lost its original content and gained a Wilsonian meaning. Outstanding historians of Wilson's diplomacy, such as Link, have used the same terminology as Kennan, Morgenthau or Graebner but have given it a substantially different definition.

3   Although David Mervin, "Henry Cabot Lodge and the League of Nations," *Journal of American Studies*, IV (Feb. 1971), 201-14, adhering to the traditional interpretation (e.g., Thomas A. Bailey's), still viewed Lodge as an unprincipled partisan politician, most historians have rejected this negative characterization. John A. Garraty, *Henry Cabot Lodge: A Biography* (New York, 1968), 336-401, offered a somewhat more positive interpretation. Even more favorable assessments of Lodge's leadership during the treaty fight are given by Lloyd E. Ambrosius, "Wilson, the Republicans, and French Security After World War I," *Journal of American History*, LIX (Sept. 1972), 341-52, and William C. Widenor, *Henry Cabot Lodge and the Search for an American Foreign Policy* (Berkeley and Los Angeles, 1979). For a sympathetic treatment of the most extreme Republican opponents of Wilson's League, see Ralph Stone, *The Irreconcilables: The Fight Against the League of Nations* (Lexington, 1970).

4   George F. Kennan, *American Diplomacy, 1900-1950* (Chicago, 1951), 50-65; Hans J. Morgenthau, *In Defense of the National Interest: A Critical Examination of American Foreign Policy* (New York, 1951), 23-33; Norman A. Graebner, ed., *Ideas and Diplomacy: Readings in the Intellectual Tradition of American Foreign Policy* (New York, 1964), 406-17, 487-98.

5   Edward H. Buehrig, *Woodrow Wilson and the Balance of Power* (Bloomington, 1955); Ernest R. May, *The World War and American Isolation, 1914-1917* (Cambridge, 1959); Daniel M. Smith, *The Great Departure: The United States and World War I, 1914-1920* (New York, 1965); Daniel M. Smith, "National Interest and American Intervention, 1917: An Historiographical Appraisal," *Journal of American History*, LII (June 1965), 5-24; David F. Trask, *The United States and the Supreme War Council: American War Aims and Inter-Allied Strategy, 1917-1918* (Middletown, 1961); David F. Trask, *Captains and Cabinets: Anglo-American Naval Relations, 1917-1918* (Columbia, 1972); David F. Trask, "Woodrow Wilson and the Reconciliation of Force and Diplomacy: 1917-1918," *Naval War College Review*, XXVII (Jan./Feb. 1975), 23-31; David F. Trask, "Woodrow Wilson and the Coordination of Force and Diplomacy," The Society for Historians of American Foreign Relations *Newsletter*, XII (Sept. 1981), 12-19.

6   Arthur S. Link, *The Higher Realism of Woodrow Wilson and Other Essays* (Nashville, 1971), 72-139; Arthur S. Link, *Wilson the Diplomatist* (Baltimore, 1957); Arthur S. Link, *Wilson*, Vols. III-V (Princeton, 1960-1965); Arthur S. Link, *Woodrow Wilson: Revolution, War, and Peace* (Arlington Heights, 1979).

The president's own categories have generally dominated assessments of his role at the peace conference and during the treaty fight. In one way or another, critics and defenders from Thomas A. Bailey to Klaus Schwabe have subscribed to the myth of a "Wilson peace."[7] Even New Left historians, such as Arno J. Mayer and N. Gordon Levin, Jr., have tended to accept the president's presuppositions. Sharing his progressive perspective, they have divided the protagonists into two groups, one forward-looking and the other reactionary. Critical of Wilson's liberal-capitalist values, they have reversed his moral judgments without fundamentally rejecting his categories. They have maintained the traditional dichotomy between the Old and New Worlds – or between Old and New Diplomacy – that characterized his belief in American exceptionalism. Their revisionism thus perpetuated the Wilsonian orthodoxy.[8]

In this book, I offer a new interpretation of Wilson's foreign policy, but not from a Wilsonian perspective. Emphasizing the manifold dimensions of the treaty fight, I do not equate the Democratic president and his League of Nations with internationalism, or Republican senators and their alternatives with isolationism. Those categories are inadequate. So, too, are the unqualified concepts of idealism and realism. Both Wilson and Lodge, despite their differences, believed in ideals and engaged in practical politics. On occasion, they both adhered to principle, or resorted to compromise, and both favored American military intervention in the European war. Wilson's statesmanship was indeed unrealistic, but the standards for this judgment are not self-evident.[9]

A redefinition of realism is required to provide a critical perspective on Wilson's particular combination of ideals and practicality. His personality was too complex for simple labels to suffice. Both universalism and unilateralism characterized his conduct of American foreign relations. His conception of the League, which would have involved the United States in global obligations while allowing it alone to define them, included these two typical tendencies. In conventional terminology, Wilson was at once internationalist and isolationist. As alternatives to Wilsonian categories, I

7   Thomas A. Bailey, *Woodrow Wilson and the Lost Peace* (New York, 1944); Thomas A. Bailey, *Woodrow Wilson and the Great Betrayal* (New York, 1945); Klaus Schwabe, *Deutsche Revolution und Wilson Frieden: Die amerikanische und deutsche Friedensstrategie zwischen Ideologie und Machtpolitik 1918/19* (Düsseldorf, 1971); Klaus Schwabe, *Woodrow Wilson, Revolutionary Germany, and Peacemaking, 1918-1919: Missionary Diplomacy and the Realities of Power* (Chapel Hill, 1985). For my critique of the myth of a "Wilson peace," see Lloyd E. Ambrosius, "The United States and the Weimar Republic: America's Response to the German Problem," in Jules Davids, ed., *Perspectives in American Diplomacy: Essays on Europe, Latin America, China, and the Cold War* (New York, 1976), 78-104.
8   Arno J. Mayer, *Political Origins of the New Diplomacy, 1917-1918* (New Haven, 1959); Arno J. Mayer, *Politics and Diplomacy of Peacemaking: Containment and Counterrevolution at Versailles, 1918-1919* (New York, 1967); N. Gordon Levin, Jr., *Woodrow Wilson and World Politics: America's Response to War and Revolution* (New York, 1968).
9   Two notable studies of the interaction between ideals and self-interest in American foreign relations during Wilson's presidency are Robert Endicott Osgood, *Ideals and Self-Interest in America's Foreign Relations: The Great Transformation of the Twentieth Century* (Chicago, 1953), and Kendrick A. Clements, *William Jennings Bryan: Missionary Isolationist* (Knoxville, 1982).

employ the concepts of interdependence and pluralism. Within this framework, I develop the themes of control, universalism and unilateralism. These concepts and themes facilitate a new interpretation of Wilson's contribution to the League's origins and allow a reevaluation of his responsibility for the eventual defeat of the Versailles Treaty in the United States. Because of Wilson's centrality, the concepts and themes that explain his behavior should also illuminate other aspects of the history of American foreign relations. The dual purpose of this book, therefore, is to reinterpret Wilson's peacemaking from this new perspective and to suggest its possibilities for a general reassessment of the American diplomatic tradition.

Acknowledgments

During the years of work on this book, I have benefited greatly from help by many people. Librarians, archivists, other scholars, friends and family have all supported me in numerous ways.

Librarians and archivists generously assisted my research both in the United States and in Europe. I wish to thank them for making available the pertinent manuscripts and documents at the Alabama Department of Archives and History (Montgomery); American Irish Historical Society (New York, New York); Baker Library, Houghton Library and University Archives at Harvard University (Cambridge, Massachusetts); Beaverbrook Library (London, England); British Museum (London); Federal Archives (Koblenz, Germany); Herbert Hoover Presidential Library (West Branch, Iowa); Indiana State Library (Indianapolis); Library of Congress (Washington, D.C.); Massachusetts Historical Society (Boston); Minnesota Historical Society (St. Paul); Nebraska State Historical Society (Lincoln); Political Archives of the Foreign Office (Bonn, Germany); and University of Nebraska Library (Lincoln). The David Lloyd George Papers, now in the House of Lords Record Office, are reproduced by permission of the Clerk of the Records.

Among the many scholars and friends who contributed to my work, a few deserve special mention. Professor Norman A. Graebner, under whose supervision I studied at the University of Illinois, Champaign-Urbana, has continued over the years to provide valuable encouragement and assistance. Among other things, he read an earlier version of the manuscript. Dr. David Reynolds of Cambridge University also read the early chapters of this book and offered suggestions for revision. Professor Larry Andrews of the University of Nebraska–Lincoln, with his reverence for the English language, offered stylistic advice. Professor Erich Angermann of the University of Cologne served as a most gracious host in 1972-1973, when I was doing research in Germany. Professor Klaus Schwabe of the University of Aachen, besides reading the manuscript, stimulated my thinking during several visits. During the final stages of my work, Professor Arthur S. Link of Princeton University provided valuable support. Although none of these scholars is responsible for the interpretation that I offer in this book, I am indebted to them all.

Several research grants and fellowships facilitated my work. The University of Nebraska–Lincoln supported my research and writing in various ways. Its Research Council provided fellowships and research grants to enable me to use the primary sources at archives and libraries in the United States and Europe. Both the Research Council and the College of Arts and Sciences provided free time for writing. A Senior Fulbright Research Grant allowed me to devote a year to research in Germany.

My family participated in different ways in the research for, and writing of, this book. My wife, Margery, offered constructive criticism of various drafts of the manuscript. Over the years she and our sons, Walter and Paul, traveled with me to archives and libraries. All of them undoubtedly heard more about the Wilson era than they ever desired. For their love and indulgence I am most grateful.

Abbreviations

AJB	Arthur J. Balfour	JJP	John J. Pershing
ALL	A. Lawrence Lowell	JPT	Joseph P. Tumulty
DLG	David Lloyd George	NDB	Newton D. Baker
EBW	Edith Bolling Wilson	RL	Robert Lansing
EG	Edward Grey	RSB	Ray Stannard Baker
EMH	Edward M. House	THB	Tasker Howard Bliss
ER	Elihu Root	WGH	Warren G. Harding
HCL	Henry Cabot Lodge	WHT	William Howard Taft
HW	Henry White	WJB	William Jennings Bryan
JD	Josephus Daniels	WW	Woodrow Wilson

CR	*Congressional Record*
FR:Lansing	*Papers Relating to the Foreign Relations of the United States: The Lansing Papers, 1914-1920*
FR1916	*Papers Relating to the Foreign Relations of the United States, 1916. Supplement: The World War*
FR1918	*Papers Relating to the Foreign Relations of the United States, 1918. Supplement 1: The World War*
FR:PPC	*Papers Relating to the Foreign Relations of the United States, 1919: The Paris Peace Conference*
PPWW	*The Public Papers of Woodrow Wilson*
PWW	*The Papers of Woodrow Wilson*

CHAPTER I

Introduction: Wilson's new world

Woodrow Wilson's quest for orderly progress epitomized the modern American search for control. "We have attained," noted John Dewey, the prominent philosopher and educator, in *Quest for Certainty* (1929), "at least subconsciously, a certain feeling of confidence; a feeling that control of the main conditions of fortune is, to an appreciable degree, passing into our own hands."[1] Benefiting from science and technology, Americans had subdued nature. Modern industry and cities had transformed their institutions. As new forms of transportation and communication linked the nation closer together and to the rest of the world, personal relations of traditional rural communities succumbed to bureaucratic patterns. A new corporate or organizational society was reshaping the government's role in both domestic and foreign affairs. Profound social and economic changes prompted Americans to seek what Wilson had called "progressive order" in their democracy.[2] Hoping to manage change so as to avoid uncontrollable chaos or anarchy, progressive Americans preferred reform to revolution. It was in this spirit that Wilson created the League of Nations.

Early in the twentieth century American intellectuals had developed a conscious awareness of what sociologist Edward A. Ross, one of Wilson's former students, described as "social control." Concentrating on the foundations of order in the United States, Ross examined the various means of society's discipline over individuals. In *Social Control* (1901) he only hinted at international implications.[3] But in 1917, after the United States entered

---

1   Helen Everett, "Social Control," in Edwin R. A. Seligman, ed., *Encyclopaedia of the Social Sciences* (New York, 1931), IV, 344-48.
2   "Nature of Democracy in the United States," in Arthur S. Link, ed., *The Papers of Woodrow Wilson*, VI (Princeton, 1969), 238.
3   Edward Alsworth Ross, *Social Control: A Survey of the Foundations of Order* (New York, 1901), 293. For the importance of the idea of social control in sociology, see Morris Janowitz, *The Last Half-Century* (Chicago, 1978), 3-52. Ross did not apply his concept of social control to the League of Nations but later

the World War, the American Sociological Society devoted its annual meeting to this topic. One of its leading members, Charles H. Cooley, expressed a hopeful view of human nature in a paper on "Social Control in International Relations." He emphasized human potential for cooperation. Pointing to the war as evidence that nations were capable of moral development comparable to that in personal relations, he suggested that "perhaps the surest proof that international social control is possible is that nations have shown themselves capable of feeling and acting upon a disinterested indignation at aggression upon other nations, as in the case of Belgium." He looked beyond a balance of power to "an organic international life" in which nations subordinated individuality to their common welfare. Cooley emphasized the transcendent as well as practical functions of a league of nations. In his vision, benevolent social control would supersede brute force: "Force cannot succeed except as the expression of general sentiment, and if we have that it will rarely be necessary." Here he entrapped himself in circular logic. International good will, while crucial for success, would render a league's guarantee of collective security virtually unnecessary. But when its members needed protection, no league could function in the absence of good will. Cooley acknowledged this basic problem when he admitted that "a single powerful nation, whose heart remains hostile to the system, will probably be able to defeat it, and certainly will prevent its developing any spirit higher than that of a policeman." Yet he did not suggest any way to solve the problem.[4]

President Wilson applied the idea of international social control to American foreign relations, promoting collective security to restrain national egoism.[5] Two other social scientists, economist John Bates Clark and

advocated collective security. See Edward Alsworth Ross, *Seventy Years of It: An Autobiography* (New York, 1936), 150-66, and Edward Alsworth Ross, *Principles of Sociology* (New York, 1938), 324-25.

4   "Social Control," *Papers and Proceedings, American Sociological Society*, XII (Chicago, 1918), 207-16; Charles Horton Cooley, *Social Process* (New York, 1918), 255-67. Lloyd C. Gardner, *Safe for Democracy: The Anglo-American Response to Revolution*, 1913-1923 (New York, 1984), 104, raised the crucial problem of the relationship between domestic and foreign affairs, noting that historians need to reconcile Wilson's openness to change abroad and his fear of radicalism at home. The idea of international social control provides the key to reconciling this apparent contradiction and to understanding Wilson's paradoxical response to revolution. As an advocate of "progressive order," the president believed change was essential to prevent chaos or anarchy, which he identified with radicalism. He even welcomed some revolutions (e.g., the March 1917 revolution in Russia and the November 1918 revolution in Germany) as they appeared to expand American influence, while opposing others (e.g., the November 1917 Bolshevik revolution in Russia) which did not. The crucial question for Wilson, both at home and abroad, was whether the change conformed to his ideal of American liberal democracy or threatened it. In other words, he sought a dynamic form of control over both domestic and foreign affairs, or progressive reform, as the antidote to radical revolution. New Left historians, such as Arno J. Mayer with his distinction between the "parties of movement" and the "parties of order," have typically neglected the integral relationship between change and stability in Wilson's thought. To understand the president's idea of collective security, or international social control, and its implications for his response to revolution, it is essential to avoid this false dichotomy. On this point, see Lloyd E. Ambrosius, "The Orthodoxy of Revisionism: Woodrow Wilson and the New Left," *Diplomatic History*, I (Summer 1977), 199-214, and "Woodrow Wilson and the Quest for Orderly Progress," in Norman A. Graebner, ed., *Traditions and Values: American Diplomacy*, 1865-1945 (Lanham, 1985), 73-100.

5   On the Ross-Wilson relationship, see Ross, *Seventy Years*, 40, 87-89, 97-100, 106-07, 110-11,

sociologist Franklin H. Giddings, who also articulated the theme of control, had influenced him in this direction. Clark had offered an argument for curbing the monopolistic power of large American corporations in *The Control of Trusts* (1901). He did not oppose their size, but wanted to prevent them from abusing their power with unfair business practices. Anticipating the economic policies of Wilson's New Freedom, he advocated an active role for the American government to preserve free competition. Economic rivalry among present or potential competitors would force industrial efficiency, thereby benefiting consumers while enabling the United States to capture and dominate foreign markets. For Clark, that was progress.[6] Giddings shared Clark's hope for American hegemony over other countries. In *Democracy and Empire* (1900) he had justified the war against Spain in 1898 and the new imperialism. He viewed the United States as a "democratic empire." Along with Great Britain, which had reconciled democracy with empire, he wanted the United States to extend its rule around the world. Praising Benjamin Kidd's book on *The Control of the Tropics* (1898), Giddings urged "the English-speaking race" to assume the burden of governing "the inferior races of mankind" in order that "the civilized world" could continue "its economic conquest of the natural resources of the globe." A Social Darwinist, he accepted international rivalry as a fact, especially between advanced and backward peoples. Yet he voiced the Christian Social Gospel's hope for a new era of peace. He combined science and religion – or the intellectual traditions of Charles Darwin and Leo Tolstoy – in his conception of the democratic empire.[7]

Like most Americans, Wilson had approved the new imperial role of the United States after the Spanish-American War. He noted the political implications for federal government. In a preface for the fifteenth printing of *Congressional Government* in 1900, he welcomed the growth of executive power resulting from involvement in foreign affairs. For the United States, he affirmed, the president "must utter every initial judgment, take every first step of action, supply the information upon which it is to act, suggest and in large measure control its conduct."[8] He, too, combined the Social Gospel and Social Darwinism to justify involvement overseas. He later drew upon both traditions for his conception of collective security. He called the League's constitution a covenant and advocated the location of its headquar-

245-47, 293-94; WJB to WW, June 2, 1913, *PWW*, XXVII (Princeton, 1978), 492; WW to WJB, June 25, 1913, Mott to WW, July 3, 1913, *PWW*, XXVIII (Princeton, 1978), 4, 22-23; Fairchild to WW, March 17, 1914, *PWW*, XXIX (Princeton, 1979), 352; JPT to WW, Jan. 21, 1915, *PWW*, XXXII (Princeton, 1980), 95-98.

6   John Bates Clark, *The Control of Trusts: An Argument in Favor of Curbing the Power of Monopoly by a Natural Method* (New York, 1901), 55; WW to Clark, Aug. 26, 1887, *PWW*, V (Princeton, 1968), 564-65; Henry Wilkinson Bragdon, *Woodrow Wilson: The Academic Years* (Cambridge, 1967), 178, 222-23; George C. Osborn, *Woodrow Wilson: The Early Years* (Baton Rouge, 1968), 313-14.

7   Franklin Henry Giddings, *Democracy and Empire: Their Psychological, Economic and Moral Foundations* (New York, 1900), v, 284-85, 357; WW to Ellen Wilson, Feb. 11, 1889, *PWW*, VI, 82-83; *Papers and Proceedings*, XII, 201-06.

8   WW, *Congressional Government: A Study in American Politics* (Boston, 1885), xi-xii.

ters in Calvinist Geneva. He used the promise of a postwar community of nations to justify the costs of the World War. Out of conflict and competition would emerge a better world. Like Giddings and Clark, Wilson wanted the United States to provide world-wide leadership in the new League.[9]

Wilson beheld the American presidency as the very fulcrum of change. "One of the greatest of the President's powers," he had asserted in *Constitutional Government in the United States* (1908), was "control, which is very absolute, of the foreign relations of the nation." Taking the initiative, the president could determine the outcome of international diplomacy. Once he had negotiated a treaty, the United States would be "virtually committed," leaving the Senate almost no alternative but to approve.[10] Adhering to this attitude, Wilson failed to secure the Senate's approval of the Versailles Treaty. Republican senators in 1919-1920 refused to play the role assigned them. Despite efforts to influence them through management of public opinion, including a speaking tour of western states, he lost the treaty fight. The Senate demonstrated that the president's power to control American foreign relations was less absolute than Wilson thought.[11]

Other writers had anticipated Wilson's idea of collective security. Herbert Croly had developed the theme of control in both domestic and foreign affairs. In *The Promise of American Life* (1909), a classic statement of progressive thought, he advocated subjection of individual purposes to the national interest. Only by strong national government, he argued, could the United States continue to provide its citizens better economic and social conditions while preserving democratic political institutions. He wanted the nation to employ conscious social control − which he identified as the methods of Alexander Hamilton − to achieve the equalitarian ends of Thomas Jefferson. Linking reform at home and abroad, Croly proposed "a national foreign policy" to promote "the spread of democratic methods and ideas." Claiming not only that the Monroe Doctrine already committed the United States to join Latin America in creating "a stable and peaceful international system," he anticipated the end of American isolation from the Old World. Because of increasing interdependence, Croly expected the United States to join "a world system" to preserve peace. Opposed to involvement in "an exclusively European system," he urged preparation for war to maintain peace.[12]

Walter Lippmann shared Croly's belief in progressive American leadership at home and abroad. A new challenge faced the nation. According to him, "the battle for us, in short, does not lie against crusted prejudice, but against

9   Bragdon, *Woodrow Wilson*, 175, 177, 179-80; John M. Mulder, *Woodrow Wilson: The Years of Preparation* (Princeton, 1978), 229-77.

10   WW, *Constitutional Government in the United States* (New York, 1908), 77-78.

11   Robert C. Hilderbrand, *Power and the People: Executive Management of Public Opinion in Foreign Affairs, 1897-1921* (Chapel Hill, 1981), 93-197.

12   Herbert Croly, *The Promise of American Life* (New York, 1964), 22, 289-314.

the chaos of a new freedom. This chaos is our real problem." The status quo was no longer realistic. Compelled to shape their future either by "drift" or by "mastery," progressive Americans welcomed innovation. "Our time, of course, believes in change," he observed. Americans became progressive to achieve order. "The only possible cohesion now is a loyalty that looks forward," he asserted in *Drift and Mastery* (1914). Lippmann thus recommended a pragmatic method to create progressive order in the chaotic modern world.[13]

As editors of the *New Republic*, Croly and Lippmann initially supported Wilson's foreign policy. They favored intervention in 1917 and advocated a league of nations. Welcoming the president's endorsement of collective security in his 1916 address to the League to Enforce Peace, they used this idea to justify participation in the war. As secretary of the group of experts known as the Inquiry, Lippmann contributed to American preparation for the peace conference. He helped elaborate the principles in Wilson's Fourteen Points. Along with Dewey, who frequently wrote for the *New Republic*, Croly and Lippmann justified American belligerency as a crusade for democracy. To reconcile their liberal idealism with pragmatism, which required them to vindicate the war by its results, they raised their hopes for a world of democracy and peace. Expecting the United States to transform international relations, they inevitably experienced disappointment. The Paris Peace Conference failed to realize their ideals. Croly, Lippmann and Dewey then denounced the Versailles Treaty and opposed obligations in the League to enforce it. This disillusionment resulted from their unrealistic belief that the United States could control the world. That, however, was beyond the capacity of any nation. The reality of competing national interests forced the president to compromise with the Allies and even with Germany. Pluralism limited Wilson's power to redeem the Old World with his particular vision of interdependence.[14]

Like Croly, Lippmann and Dewey, other Americans sought to apply social science to international relations. Giddings had pondered the use of rational discussion to limit national sovereignty, "the ultimate social control." To create conditions conducive to peaceful resolution of conflicts, he favored a balance of power. Political integration of empires had already encompassed most lands. The world's interdependence prevented isolation. Now the problem was to avoid war among the great powers. Like Wilson, Giddings

---

1 3   Walter Lippmann, *Drift and Mastery: An Attempt to Diagnose the Current Unrest* (Englewood Cliffs, 1961), 16-17, 147-48. For Lippmann's ideas and activities throughout the war, see Ronald Steel, *Walter Lippmann and the American Century* (Boston, 1980), 88-170.

1 4   Charles Forcey, *The Crossroads of Liberalism: Croly, Weyl, Lippmann, and the Progressive Era, 1900-1925* (New York, 1961), 221-315; David W. Noble, *The Progressive Mind, 1890-1917* (Chicago, 1970), 53-64, 165-79; Link, *Wilson*, V, 18-19, 23-26, 304, 390-91; EMH to WW, Oct. 29, 1918, Department of State, *Papers Relating to the Foreign Relations of the United States*, 1918, Supplement 1: *The World War* (Washington, 1933), I, 405-13; John C. Farrell, "John Dewey and World War I: Armageddon Tests a Liberal's Faith," *Perspectives in American History*, IX (1975), 299-340; Charles DeBenedetti, *Origins of the Modern American Peace Movement, 1915-1929* (Millwood, 1978), 3-43.

emphasized leadership. Elite leaders, who were "centers of social control," would determine the world's future. "In the final throwing of the dice of fate," he argued, "they are causes of peace and war."[15] The World War challenged Giddings' belief in rationality, but he still affirmed that "the human mind that had mastered nature's way could master and control the ways of man." He acknowledged that obstacles to rational control over human affairs were greater than anticipated. Nevertheless, Giddings persisted in his confidence that the civilized world, especially the English-speaking people, could organize conscience and reason to diminish war. He advocated the federation of nations in a "league of peace." Clark had already reached the same conclusion. In 1915 he saw in the Allies the nucleus for a postwar league of nations. He wanted neutrals like the United States to help form it. To preserve peace, this new international organization would need to fulfill the twofold task of protecting its members from outside attacks and of settling internal disputes between them. Giddings and Clark joined others to establish the League to Enforce Peace. Led by former President William Howard Taft and Harvard's President A. Lawrence Lowell, this bipartisan group became the most effective lobby for the postwar League of Nations.[16] Various others, along with the American Sociological Society, focused on "social control" during the World War.[17]

One of the few Americans to challenge prevailing attitudes was the radical journalist Randolph S. Bourne. Unlike his mentor Dewey, or Croly and Lippmann, he refused to justify involvement in the war with the promise of a league. He observed that the so-called realism and pragmatism of liberals masked their irrational enthusiasm for war. "They wanted a League of Nations," he complained in 1917. "They had an unanalyzable feeling that this was a war in which we had to be, and be in it we would. What more natural than to join the two ideas and conceive our war as the decisive factor in the attainment of the desired end!" Bourne understood that the war generated momentum beyond the control of statesmen. "It is," he continued, "a little unbridled for the realist's rather nice sense of purposive social control." Rejecting the hope for mastery over international relations, he warned that neither Wilson nor anyone else could achieve "any liberal control of events."[18]

The conservative historian Henry Adams shared Bourne's skepticism. He,

15   Franklin H. Giddings, "The Relation of Social Theory to Public Policy," *International Conciliation*, No. 58 (Sept. 1912), 3-13, and *Studies in the Theory of Human Society* (New York, 1922), 209-23.

16   Randolph S. Bourne, ed., *Towards an Enduring Peace: A Symposium of Peace Proposals and Programs, 1914-1916* (New York, [1916]), vii-xi, 135-42; Ruhl J. Bartlett, *The League to Enforce Peace* (Chapel Hill, 1944); Sondra R. Herman, *Eleven Against War: Studies in American Internationalist Thought, 1898-1921* (Stanford, 1969), 55-85; Henry F. Pringle, *The Life and Times of William Howard Taft: A Biography* (Hamden, 1964), 926-50.

17   "Social Control," *Papers and Proceedings*, XII, 1-10, 27-45, 201-32; Franklin Henry Giddings, *The Responsible State: A Reexamination of Fundamental Political Doctrines in the Light of World War and the Menace of Anarchism* (Boston, 1918).

18   Randolph S. Bourne, "A War Diary," *The Seven Arts*, II (Sept. 1917), 535-47, in Carl Resek, ed., *War and the Intellectuals: Essays by Randolph S. Bourne, 1915-1919* (New York, 1964), 36-47.

too, doubted that social scientists could discover laws of human behavior with which to predict and control the future. Adams had searched in vain for some unifying principle to restore order out of chaos. He contrasted twentieth-century multiplicity with thirteenth-century unity under God. "From cradle to grave this problem of running order through chaos, direction through space, discipline through freedom, unity through multiplicity, has always been, and must always be, the task of education, as it is the moral of religion, philosophy, science, art, politics, and economy," he observed in *The Education of Henry Adams* (1918). Unlike Wilson, whose faith in God provided the foundation for his belief in the universality of the world, Adams could not find this principle in religion. Nor could he discover it in science. Despite attempts to apply scientific laws to history, he failed to find any principle that could unite disparate events by explaining cause and effect. Without such a principle the historian could either impose his ideas on the past or admit failure. Adams brilliantly elucidated his own failure. "Historians," he warned, "have got into far too much trouble by following schools of theology in their efforts to enlarge their synthesis, that they should willingly repeat the process in science."[19]

Henry Cabot Lodge evidenced the same skepticism about social control as his friend Adams did. From a conservative philosophical perspective, and not just for reasons of politics, the senator never trusted the promise of Wilson's League. He refused to believe that it could inaugurate a new era of peace. Ironically, Clark and Giddings, who shared Lodge's appreciation for an international balance of power, showed perseverance in advocating the League. They did not succumb to liberal disillusionment. After the war Clark steadfastly favored a "workable" league. Expecting international rivalry to persist, he advocated responsible American participation in the existing international system. Giddings likewise adopted a practical attitude toward the League. He rejoiced that the democratic English-speaking people of the world would exert preponderant power in it. Unlike Croly, Lippmann and Dewey, Clark and Giddings continued to support Wilson throughout the treaty fight.[20]

Political scientists followed Wilson's interpretation, developing the theme of control. Edward S. Corwin, whose career Wilson had promoted at Princeton while serving as its president, emphasized executive prerogatives in *The President's Control of Foreign Relations* (1917). Corwin surveyed the history of war- and treaty-making powers in the United States since the Constitution's adoption, and concluded that "the net result of a century and

19   Henry Adams, *The Education of Henry Adams: An Autobiography* (Boston, 1918), 12, 401.
20   John Bates Clark, "A Workable League," *New York Times* (Nov. 11, 1918), p. 14, and "If This League Fails: The Alternative Is a League for War Dominated by Germany," ibid. (June 1, 1919), sect. 3, p. 2; Franklin H. Giddings, "The United States Among Nations," *The Independent*, XCVIII (June 14, 1919), 399-400, "What the War Was Worth," ibid., IC (July 5, 1919), 16-17, and "What Did It," ibid., CIV (Nov. 20, 1920), 262-64; Statement prepared by Dr. Hamilton Holt and the Committee, List of persons who called on the President, [Oct. 27, 1920], Albert Sidney Burleson Papers, Vol. 26, Library of Congress.

a quarter of contest for power and influence in determining the international destinies of the country remains decisively and conspicuously in favor of the President." The fight between Wilson and the Senate over the Versailles Treaty revived this perennial contest.[21]

Defeat in 1919-1920 did not kill the idea of collective security. The political scientist Quincy Wright, for one, preserved Wilson's legacy through World War II and into the Cold War. In advocating the League of Nations and later the United Nations, he emphasized social control. Analyzing the mandates under the League, he praised them as an alternative to colonialism for supervising "backward peoples." A specialist in international law, he viewed the League as the best hope for peace prior to World War II. He concluded that "in the matter of world organization there is, at least, the possibility that man has means of controlling the future more than in any other enterprise that he had undertaken." In practice, the League had experienced difficulty accomplishing this purpose. Still, he affirmed that, as an instrument for dealing with the problems of the interdependent world, "it must become universal."[22]

After World War II, Wright advocated the United Nations. Combining progress and order, he wanted it to foster "dynamic equilibria" in world affairs. "As civilization advances," he asserted, "methods are discovered and employed for regulating or controlling an increasing proportion of the events which affect human life, and institutions increasingly function as agencies of social control." Fulfillment of this task, he recognized, would require acceptance of certain "universal values" which were "essential to the peaceful coexistence of diverse peoples." Attempting to reconcile this requirement for universality with the world's pluralism, he argued that "acceptance of some universal values does not preclude great diversity in cultures and value systems among different groups."[23] Yet if other nations refused to accept an American definition of these "universal values," he neglected to explain how the United Nations could fulfill its task or what policy the United States should then adopt.

This problem with collective security, for which its advocates never provided a solution, had plagued Wilson. He, too, was entrapped in circular logic. Despite failure after World War I, he remained confident in his vision's ultimate triumph. But it never resolved the persistent dilemma of

2 1   Edward S. Corwin, *The President's Control of Foreign Relations* (Princeton, 1917), 207; Quincy Wright, "The Control of Foreign Relations," and Edward S. Corwin, "Constitutional Law in 1919-1920, II," *American Political Science Review*, XV (Feb. 1921), 1-26, 52-54; Quincy Wright, "Effects of the League of Nations Covenant," ibid., XIII (Nov. 1919), 556-76; Quincy Wright, *The Control of American Foreign Relations* (New York, 1922); Clarence A. Berdahl, *War Powers of the Executive in the United States* ([Urbana, 1921]), 25-42.

2 2   Quincy Wright, *Mandates Under the League of Nations* (Chicago, 1930); Quincy Wright, *The Causes of War and the Conditions of Peace* (London, 1935), 73-104.

2 3   Quincy Wright, *Problems of Stability and Progress in International Relations* (Berkeley, 1954), 5-6, 14-15; Quincy Wright, "Woodrow Wilson and the League of Nations," *Social Research*, XXIV (Spring 1957), 65-86.

American foreign relations. As an alternative to traditional isolationism, it failed. Wilson's League and his legacy of liberal internationalism provided unrealistic guidance for the United States in the interdependent and plural world of the twentieth century.[24]

Accepting the myth of American innocence and virtue, Wilson made a sharp distinction between the Old and New Worlds. He viewed the United States as "a virgin continent." As Lippmann recognized, "Wilson, in spite of the complexity of his character and his mind, was moved by the old American feeling that America is a new land which must not be entangled with Europe."[25] Assuming a polarity, he fluctuated between isolationist and internationalist alternatives. He attempted to maintain neutrality until 1917; then, leading the United States into the European war, he called for a new order under the future League. Hoping either to avoid or redeem the Old World, he never dealt with Europe on its own terms. His response to the World War epitomized the difficulty of the United States in defining a realistic foreign policy in the twentieth century. He failed to overcome the country's inadequate diplomatic tradition. Prior to the war, the United States had attempted to avoid entanglement in the Old World, while maintaining diplomatic, cultural and commercial relations with European countries. For Wilson, as for earlier generations, American independence seemed to require political and military isolation from Europe. At the beginning of the World War he attempted to maintain this tradition. As he developed a new policy, he experienced the difficulty of escaping the American heritage, which proved to be an impossible task for him.

In 1913, when Wilson replaced Taft in the White House, most Americans had forgotten the reasons for American isolation. They simply adhered to this tradition without question. One exception was a member of the diplomatic service, Lewis Einstein, who saw the implications of Anglo-German rivalry. He warned that a German victory against Great Britain in a future war would threaten American security. "Unperceived by many Americans," he explained, "the European balance of power is a political necessity which can alone sanction on the Western Hemisphere the continuance of an economic development unhandicapped by the burden of extensive armaments. At no time, even unknown to the United States, were European politics a matter of indifference to its vital interests. But if hitherto it was impotent to alter their march, a fortunate destiny preserved the

24   Roland N. Stromberg, *Collective Security and American Foreign Policy: From the League of Nations to NATO* (New York, 1963); Roland N. Stromberg, "Uncertainties and Obscurities About the League of Nations," *Journal of the History of Ideas*, XXXIII (1972), 139-54.

25   WW, "The Proper Perspective of American History," *The Forum*, XIX (June 1895), 553; WW, "The Significance of American History," *PWW*, XII (Princeton, 1972), 179; Walter Lippmann, *Men of Destiny* (New York, 1927), 122. For excellent examinations of this myth, see Henry Nash Smith, *Virgin Land: The American West as Symbol and Myth* (Cambridge, 1950) and David W. Noble, *Historians Against History: The Frontier Thesis and the National Covenant in American Historical Writing Since 1830* (Minneapolis, 1965).

existing balance."[26] Recognizing that the United States now possessed the power to take a decisive part in European affairs and that Germany potentially threatened to disrupt the power balance, Einstein concluded that the American government should adopt a new policy. Unlike most of his countrymen, he understood the limits of the American diplomatic tradition.

Without Einstein's understanding, Wilson remained a prisoner of his heritage. He denounced the European balance of power. When he developed a new foreign policy, he projected his conception of American nationalism onto the world. He felt that the closing of the frontier in 1890 – not a shift in the European balance of power – forced the United States to involve itself overseas. He incorporated his version of historian Frederick Jackson Turner's frontier thesis into his rationale for the League. Like him, Wilson attributed the distinctive American character to the influence of the West. Turner had presented his famous paper on "The Significance of the Frontier in American History" to the American Historical Association in 1893. A leading political scientist and historian at that time, Wilson had become the first prominent scholar to endorse the frontier thesis.[27] With the end of free land in the West, he feared, the "complex civilization" of the East, which was "more like the Old World than the New," would engulf the nation. Wilson predicted that "the twentieth century will show another face." The United States, having concentrated on domestic development, must now assume "its special part and place of power" in the world.[28]

The frontier's closing, Wilson thought, had forced Americans to search for "new frontiers for ourselves beyond the seas." Regarding the Spanish-American War of 1898 as the natural consequence of this shift from domestic to foreign expansion, he applauded the willingness of Americans to become "apostles of liberty and of self-government" in Cuba and the Philippines. He believed that because of these countries' lack of progress toward democracy under Spanish rule, the United States needed to contribute to their political education, as England had done to the American colonies. When the Filipinos revolted against this forceful instruction, their behavior seemed to Wilson to demonstrate their ignorance about the necessity for order in a democratic society. He wanted the United States to control them. "They must first take the discipline of law," he stressed, "must first love order and

2 6   Lewis Einstein, "The United States and Anglo-German Rivalry," *The National Review*, LX (Jan. 1913), 736-50, in Graebner, ed., *Ideas and Diplomacy*, 428-34, and *The Living Age* (Feb. 8, 1913), 323-32; C. Vann Woodward, "The Age of Reinterpretation," *American Historical Review*, LXVI (Oct. 1960), 1-19.

2 7   WW, "Mr. Goldwin Smith's 'Views' on Our Political History," *PWW*, VIII (Princeton, 1970), 346-57; WW, *A History of the American People* (New York, 1901), X, 84-90; George C. Osborn, "Woodrow Wilson and Frederick Jackson Turner," *Proceedings of the New Jersey Historical Society*, LXXIV (July 1956), 208-29; Wendell H. Stephenson, "The Influence of Woodrow Wilson on Frederick Jackson Turner," *Agricultural History*, XIX (Oct. 1945), 250-53; Ray Allen Billington, *Frederick Jackson Turner: Historian, Scholar, Teacher* (New York, 1973), 75-76, 187-88, 190; Osborn, *Woodrow Wilson*, 260-61; Bragdon, *Woodrow Wilson*, 193-94, 236-37, 241-43.

2 8   WW, "The Making of the Nation," *Atlantic Monthly*, LXXX (July 1897), 2; WW, "Significance of American History," *PWW*, XII, 184.

instinctively yield to it. . . . We are old in this learning and must be their tutors." Paradoxically, only after they submitted to American rule could they be entrusted with independence. This paternalistic, yet essentially non-colonial, form of American imperialism later became Wilson's model for mandates under the League. In this manner, and without recognizing the irony, he hoped Americans would "seek to serve, not to subdue, the world."[29] He thus rejected the idea of pluralism for other countries, including Cuba and the Philippines. Instead, he advocated American control.

President Wilson projected the American image onto the world during the European war. He continued to believe, as he had affirmed in *The State* (1889), that history moved in a single direction toward the triumph of democracy.[30] His confidence in progress toward democracy, and his interpretation of the frontier's closing in 1890, provided an explanation for involvement in world affairs. He combined these ideas in a new foreign policy during the World War. "It is not by accident," the president proclaimed in 1916, ". . . that only eight years elapsed before we got into the politics of the world. It was in 1898, you remember, that the Spanish war came. . . . We had, as it were, touched a house of cards, and it had collapsed, and when the war was over we found the guardianship of Cuba, the possession of Porto Rico, the possession of the Philippines in our hands. And the frontier which no man could draw upon this continent in 1890 had been flung across the sea 7,000 miles to the untrodden forests of some part of the Philippine Islands. Ever since then we have been caught inevitably in the net of the politics of the world." Wilson nonetheless paid homage to President George Washington's Farewell Address: "You know that we have always remembered and revered the advice of the great Washington, who advised us to avoid foreign entanglements. By that I understand him to mean to avoid being entangled in the ambitions and the national purposes of other nations." Wilson's determination to control foreign affairs enabled him to reconcile the unilateral and universal elements in his diplomacy. He believed Washington's advice did not require strict adherence to traditional neutrality, but it did obligate this nation to preserve its character while becoming involved in foreign affairs. Thus Wilson maintained the Old World – New World polarity, which had shaped the American diplomatic tradition of isolation, even as he concluded that the United States should join a postwar league. He reaffirmed his earlier announcement to the League to Enforce Peace that in looking forward "to the end of this war, we want all the world to know that we are ready to lend our force without stint to the preservation of peace in the interest of mankind." As a consequence of the American frontier's closing, he argued, the United States should adopt this new policy. "What disturbs the life of the whole world is the concern of the whole

29   WW, "The Ideals of America," *Atlantic Monthly*, XC (Dec. 1902), 721-34.
30   WW, *The State: Elements of Historical and Practical Politics* (Boston, 1889), 603.

world," he proclaimed, "and it is our duty to lend the full force of this nation, moral and physical, to a league of nations which shall see to it that nobody disturbs the peace of the world without submitting his case first to the opinion of mankind." The United States should promote democratic international social control. With this rationale for a league, Wilson internationalized his understanding of the American heritage.[31]

His response to the World War alternated between isolationist and internationalist thoughts. He saw no inconsistency in adhering to neutrality until 1917, while developing the idea of collective security. His plan for a league, as Lippmann noted, evidenced "the instinctive American isolationist view of Woodrow Wilson."[32] At the Paris Peace Conference of 1919, while drafting the Covenant, Wilson steadfastly opposed any definite commitment to participate in the Old World's politics or wars. In the form of a veto over the League's future actions, he intended to preserve American independence. His conception of nationalism, embracing the frontier, easily accommodated both universalism and unilateralism. The common element in both tendencies was his desire for the United States to control its own destiny.

Christian faith undergirded Wilson's confidence in progress. He thought God had predestined victory for faithful men and nations. Progress was inevitable for Christians. In the struggle of life between good and evil, continuing despite the certainty of God's ultimate triumph, Wilson looked to the Bible as the source of universal laws of morality and history. He viewed the United States as the epitome of Christianity: "America was born a Christian nation. America was born to exemplify that devotion to the elements of righteousness which are derived from the revelations of Holy Scripture." Religion and patriotism were synonymous, for he recognized no difference between Christianity and Americanism. From his perspective, the United States appeared in the vanguard of world history, leading toward universal progress.[33]

Wilson justified American involvement in the war as a Christian crusade for democracy. George D. Herron, a Social Gospel theologian, became an authentic interpreter of the president's foreign policy. Affiliated with the American legation in Switzerland, he published articles in various European journals. In *Woodrow Wilson and the World's Peace* (1917), a collection of these articles, he proclaimed the kingdom of God on earth as the president's ultimate goal. The theologian explained that "Woodrow Wilson beholds this vision, he follows this faith, because he is both sturdily and mystically Christian in his view of our common life's collective possibilities. The uttermost democracy, the democracy that scales the whole human octave, is to him the certain issue of the idea for which Jesus lived and died. . . . He

---

3 1   Ray Stannard Baker and William E. Dodd, eds., *The Public Papers of Woodrow Wilson: The New Democracy* (New York, 1926), IV, 344-48.

3 2   Lippmann, *Men of Destiny*, 123.

3 3   "The Bible and Progress," *PPWW: College and State* (New York, 1925), II, 291-302; "Religion and Patriotism," *PWW*, XII, 474-78.

believes that the Sermon on the Mount is the ultimate constitution of mankind; and he intends, by hook or crook if you will, by the wisdom of the serpent and the secrecy of the priest, to get this foundation underneath the unaware American nation. He cunningly hopes, he divinely schemes, to bring it about that America, awake at last to her selfhood and calling, shall become as a colossal Christian apostle, shepherding the world into the kingdom of God." Wilson's conception of a league expressed the American mission to redeem the Old World. His purpose was "so revolutionary" that few persons understood it. "His eyes are fixed upon a goal that is far beyond the present faith of nations. His inaugural address before the League to Enforce Peace is perhaps the most pregnant utterance of a national chief in two thousand years."[34] Herron's perception of the ultimate goal of American foreign policy pleased Wilson. To the New York publisher of the theologian's book, the president wrote in 1917: "I have read it with the deepest appreciation of Mr. Herron's singular insight into all the elements of a complicated situation and into my own motives and purposes."[35]

A notable prudence, as well as idealism, characterized Wilson's diplomacy. He personified the competing impulses of the American character that Van Wyck Brooks labeled as "Highbrow" and "Lowbrow."[36] Another radical critic, Harold Stearns, observed that his leadership evidenced "mystical practicality." He was at once idealistic and practical. Emphasizing this duality, Stearns concluded that "in President Wilson we have seen its ultimate culmination in a man who talks like a Transcendentalist and who bargains like any huckster, although even in this extreme case, probably, without conscious hypocrisy."[37] His goals were utopian, but he prepared for the peace conference and displayed skill in the negotiations. The Versailles Treaty incorporated many of his ideas, despite unavoidable compromises. During the drafting of the Covenant, he called for some revisions to meet Republican objections. Yet he never made any compromise that violated his ultimate purpose. At some unpredictable point, the president refused further concessions by appealing to ideals. In the case of the League, which he regarded as the instrument for world redemption through international social control, he rejected substantial changes either at Paris or in the United States.

Wilson's response to the World War expressed the remarkable dualism of

3 4   George D. Herron, *Woodrow Wilson and the World's Peace* (New York, 1917), 68-69, 76-77.

3 5   Mitchell Pirie Briggs, *George D. Herron and the European Settlement* (Stanford, 1932), 249; Charles Howard Hopkins, *The Rise of the Social Gospel in American Protestantism: 1865-1915* (New Haven, 1940), 184-200. See Ernest Lee Tuveson, *Redeemer Nation: The Idea of America's Millennial Role* (Chicago, 1968), for the origins of the myth of the "redeemer nation" and its significance for American warfare. For a brilliant introduction to the particular relationship between religion and foreign policy during Wilson's presidency, see Robert M. Crunden, *Ministers of Reform: The Progressives' Achievement in American Civilization, 1889-1920* (New York, 1982), 225-73.

3 6   Van Wyck Brooks, "America's Coming-of-Age" (1915), in *Three Essays on America* (New York, 1970), 19-20.

3 7   Harold Stearns, *Liberalism in America: Its Origins, Its Temporary Collapse, Its Future* (New York, 1919), 36-37, 53.

the American character. Assuming a polarity between the Old and New Worlds, he alternated between isolationist and internationalist tendencies. He hoped to preserve American innocence either by maintaining neutrality or by redeeming Europe in a crusade for democracy. Viewing the United States as the model, Wilson projected its image to the world. He sought control over foreign affairs. Lacking adequate guidance from the American diplomatic tradition, he internationalized the heritage of his country. From his understanding of science, religion and history, he proclaimed his vision of a league to transform international relations. His belief in progress, based on faith in God, seemed to guarantee the triumph of ideals. Yet the idea of collective security, or international social control, furnished no realistic American policy for the twentieth century. It failed to resolve the fundamental dilemma of interdependence and pluralism. Wilson's contribution to the American diplomatic tradition never overcame its limits.

CHAPTER 2

Origins of Wilson's league of nations idea

Before the outbreak of the World War in Europe, Wilson had developed the themes which would characterize his policy of neutrality. "There is," he said in reference to the Mexican Revolution, "only one possible standard by which to determine controversies between the United States and other nations, and that is compounded of these two elements: Our own honor and our obligations to the peace of the world."[1] From 1914 to 1917 the president attempted to protect American neutral rights, identifying them with national honor and independence. At the same time he hoped to end the war. Twice during the period of neutrality, Wilson's most intimate adviser, Edward M. House, traveled to Europe in search of peace between the Allies and the Central Powers. Out of these attempts at mediation grew the idea of a league of nations. In Wilson's mind, it represented no sharp break from the diplomatic tradition. American mediation and a new league promised world peace, which would protect neutral rights. Neutrality and the league idea reflected his twin desires to isolate the United States and to redeem the Old World. The same conception of the American mission underlay his official neutrality and his emerging conception of collective security.

Throughout the fall of 1914, House attempted in vain to convince the belligerents to accept mediation. With the president's approval, he sought to open negotiations by working through European ambassadors in Washington. Concentrating especially on the British and German ambassadors, Sir Cecil Spring Rice and Count Johann von Bernstorff, House proposed "a durable peace" on the basis of ending militarism and restoring Belgium. Without making any formal commitment, British foreign secretary Sir Edward Grey personally endorsed the general goals of House's proposal. He refused, however, to enter peace negotiations until Germany agreed to evacuate Belgium and pay it an indemnity. Beyond the restoration of Belgian

1   PPWW, III, 71.

independence, he advocated "a durable peace" that would protect the Allies from future German aggression. Beginning to consider American involvement in some form of collective security, Grey instructed Spring Rice in December that "an agreement between the Great Powers at the end of this war with the object of mutual security and preservation of peace in future might have stability if the United States would become a party to it and were prepared to join in repressing by force whoever broke the Treaty." When Spring Rice broached this idea, however, House immediately responded that the United States would approve no such agreement. Neither he nor Wilson intended to entangle the United States in European affairs to that extent. From Germany came a further rejection of American mediation.[2]

Unable to find a way to end the European war, the president began to develop his conception of collective security in the western hemisphere. House encouraged him to take this circuitous approach to peace in Europe. On the eve of war, he had suggested the extension of Wilson's Latin American policy to the Old World as a way to reduce its tensions. This policy, as outlined at Mobile, Alabama, on October 27, 1913, called for "the development of constitutional liberty in the world." The president pledged the United States not to conquer any additional territory from its neighbors but to work with them for their mutual advantage. The opening of the Panama Canal, he anticipated, would produce closer ties between North and South America. In December 1914, House discussed with Wilson the idea of an agreement among these nations "that would weld the Western Hemisphere together." He hoped that it "would serve as a model for the European Nations when peace is at last brought about." Wilson now prepared his own plan for a mutual guarantee of territorial integrity and political independence under republican governments. He also wanted to establish governmental control over the manufacture and sale of munitions. After further consultation with Secretary of State William Jennings Bryan about a Pan-American treaty, the president also included provisions for peaceful settlement of international disputes through diplomacy or arbitration. In January 1915, preparatory to Bryan's formal presentation of the proposed treaty, House shared this plan for Pan-American collective security with the ambassadors of the A.B.C. countries, Argentina, Brazil and Chile. With their anticipated approval, Wilson expected the smaller nations of

2   EMH to WW, Sept. 5, 1914, EMH to Zimmermann, Sept. 5, 1914, *PWW*, XXX (Princeton, 1979), 488-89; Spring Rice to EG, Sept. 8, 20, Oct. 10, Dec. 24, 1914, Gerard to German Foreign Office, Sept. 8, 1914, Jusserand to French Foreign Ministry, Sept. 8, 1914, Page to WJB, Sept. 10, 1914, WJB to WW, Sept. 16, 1914, EMH to WW, Sept. 18, 22, Oct. 8, Dec. 26, 27, 1914, Remarks at a Press Conference, Sept. 21, 1914, EMH Diary, Sept. 28, Dec. 3, 19, 23, 1914, Gerard to WW, Dec. 8, 1914, EG to Spring Rice, Dec. 22, 1914, Zimmermann to EMH, Dec. 3, 1914, *PWW*, XXXI (Princeton, 1979), 13-15, 21-22, 37, 45, 62-63, 76-77, 94-95, 137, 140-41, 384-87, 426-27, 490, 517-20, 522-23, 535, 540-41; EMH to WW, Sept. 5, 6, 1914, EMH to WW, Sept. 16, 18, 19, 20, 22, Oct. 6, 8, 24, Nov. 11, Dec. 26, 27, 31, 1914, Edward M. House Papers, Drawer 49, File 3, Yale University Library; WW to EMH, Sept. 8, 19, Oct. 10, 16, 23, 29, 1914, EMH Papers, 49/15.

Latin America to accept the treaty. The resulting hemispheric solidarity would then provide an example for peacemaking in the Old World.[3]

Despite persistent refusal of the belligerents to welcome mediation, Wilson sent House on another mission to Europe. Going first to London in February 1915, he attempted to initiate peace negotiations. House shared Grey's conviction that the war could not end without the restoration of Belgium and the establishment of an as yet undefined "permanent settlement." The foreign secretary attempted to convince House that the United States should participate in "some general guaranty" of the eventual peace. Evading this suggestion, House proposed a "second convention" at which neutrals and belligerents could determine "the principles upon which civilized warfare should in the future be conducted." At the first convention, or peace conference, the belligerents themselves would settle issues of the war. As the two conventions might be held jointly, House hoped his idea would contribute to peace negotiations. This proposal, which Wilson approved, reflected House's knowledge that neither the Allies nor the Central Powers welcomed American mediation. It also expressed the interest of the United States in protecting "the rights of neutrals" while avoiding entanglement in the Old World. Proceeding to Paris and Berlin, House continued to promote a "second convention." In Berlin he emphasized its potential contribution to freedom of the seas. As Germany was suffering from the British blockade, this sounded appealing. But House failed to obtain any specific commitment. Returning to Paris and London in April, he endeavored to convince the Allies to adopt his idea. Here, too, he failed. Irreconcilable differences between the two sides doomed House's mission.[4]

3   EMH to WW, July 4, 9, Nov. 30, 1914, EMH Papers, 49/3; WW to EMH, Dec. 2, 1914, EMH Papers, 49/15; *PPWW, III,* 64-69; *EMH Diary,* Dec. 16, 1914, *A Draft of a Pan-American Treaty, {Dec. 16, 1914}, PWW,* XXXI, 468-73; EMH Diary, Jan. 13, 1915, *PWW,* XXXII, 63-66; WW to WJB, Jan. 28, 29, 1915, WJB to Argentine, Brazilian and Chilean Ambassadors, Feb. 1, 1915, Department of State, *Papers Relating to the Foreign Relations of the United States: The Lansing Papers,* 1914-1920 (Washington, 1940), II, 471-73. See also Mark T. Gilderhus, "Pan-American Initiatives: The Wilson Presidency and 'Regional Integration,' 1914-17," *Diplomatic History,* IV (Fall 1980), 409-23, and "Wilson, Carranza, and the Monroe Doctrine: A Question in Regional Organization," ibid., VII (Spring 1983), 103-15, and Kurt Wimer, "Woodrow Wilson and World Order," in Arthur S. Link, ed., *Woodrow Wilson and a Revolutionary World,* 1913-1921 (Chapel Hill, 1982), 146-73.

4   WW to EMH, Jan. 5, 16, Feb. 15, 22, 1915, EMH to WW, Jan. 8, 15, 22, Feb. 9, 11, 15, 17, 18, 20, 20, 21, 22, 23, March 8, 9, 9, 14, 20, 22, 26, [29], Apr. 11, 11, 12, 1915, Diary of Chandler P. Anderson, Jan. 9, 1915, EMH Diary, Jan. 13, 25, 1915, Page to WW, Feb. 10, 1915, Zimmermann to EMH, Feb. 4, March 2, 1915, Gerard to EMH, Feb. 15, March 6, 1915, EMH to Gerard, Feb. 17, 1915, EMH to Zimmermann, Feb. 17, 1915, Gerard to WJB, Feb. 19, 1915, Bernstorff to German Foreign Office, Feb. 19, 1915, *PWW,* XXXII, 17-18, 41-42, 44-50, 63-67, 75, 81-82, 107, 119-22, 204-07, 211-15, 220-21, 234, 237-38, 242, 252-56, 262, 264-65, 266-68, 276-78, 340-41, 349-52, 372-75, 402-03, 411, 438-39, 455-56, 504-07, 513-14; EG to EMH, [c. Apr. 15, 1915], EMH to WW, Apr. 17, 18, 30, 1915, *PWW,* XXXIII (Princeton, 1980), 10-14; EMH to WW, Jan. 3, 8, 15, 18, 20, 21, 21, 22, 22, 29, Feb. 8, 9, 11, 11, 12, 13, 15, 17, 18, 20, 20, 21, 22, 23, 24, 27, 27, 28, March 1, 2, 5, 5, 7, 8, 9, 9, 13, 14, 15, 15, 16, 16, 20, 21, 23, 24, 26, 27, 27, Apr. 5, 11, 11, 12, 13, 14, 16, 17, 18, 20, 22, 22, 26, 30, 30, 1915, EMH Papers, 49/4; EMH to WW, May 3, 1915, EMH Papers, 49/5; WW to EMH, Jan. 5, 16, 17, 17, 18, 28, 29, Feb. 13, 15, 20, [22], 25, March 1, 8, 13, [18], 23, Apr. [2], 15, 19, May 4, 1915, Gerard to WJB, Jan. 24, 1915, Page to WJB, Jan. 15, 1915, EMH Papers, 49/16.

Grey fostered the idea of a league of nations with House. In February he had intimated that the British might consider peace short of victory if they could count on the United States to help prevent future aggression. Although House had rejected the idea as a violation of the American diplomatic tradition, Grey reverted to it in April. It offered the obvious advantage of focusing on postwar plans rather than on British violations of neutral rights. He evidenced no interest in peace on the basis of freedom of the seas, a proposal House suggested after visiting Berlin. Only in connection with a postwar league, not in relation to the present war, would he discuss freedom of the seas.[5]

In correspondence during the summer of 1915, Grey nurtured House's conception of collective security. Looking back on the July 1914 crisis, he concluded that prewar negotiations had failed when Germany refused to attend a conference. He hoped to prevent a repetition in the future by creating "some League of Nations that could be relied on to insist that disputes between any two nations must be settled by the arbitration, mediation, or conference of others." The "lesson" of the war was that great powers should organize together to enforce international law with a sanction. Yet he revealed little interest in American mediation. He favored a league only after an Allied victory.[6]

In the autumn of 1915 House responded to Grey's suggestions. On his own initiative in September, he asked him if the president could restore peace on the basis of the prewar status quo and "the elimination of militarism and navalism." Grey answered by proposing a league of nations and poignantly raising the question of American participation. "To me," he explained, "the great object of securing the elimination of militarism and navalism is to get security for the future against aggressive war. How much are the United States prepared to do in this direction?" Besides contemplating the elimination of militarism and navalism only as a future possibility, he rejected House's idea of peace on the basis of *status quo ante bellum*. Evading mediation, he nevertheless encouraged the United States to consider a larger role in European affairs.[7]

House suggested another mission to Europe. Discussing its purpose with Wilson, House noted that "he seemed to think we would be able to keep out of the war."[8] The president showed more interest the world's future peace than in the present war. House shared his reluctance to involve the United States in Europe's disputes over territories and indemnities. Since the sinking of the *Lusitania* on May 7, Bernstorff had encouraged him to focus on

5   Link, *Wilson*, III, 218-19, 229-31; EG to EMH, Apr. 16, 24, 1915, EMH Papers, 9/8; EMH to WW, May 7, 1915, EMH Papers, 49/5.
6   EG to EMH, July 14, Aug. 10, 26, 1915, EMH Papers, 9/8; EMH to WW, Aug. 9, 13, 1915, EMH Papers, 49/5; EMH to WW, Aug. 9, 13, 1915, EG to EMH, July 14, Aug. 10, 1915, *PWW*, XXXIV (Princeton, 1980), 144-46, 186, 370-72.
7   EMH to EG, Sept. 3, 14, 1915, EG to EMH, Sept. 22, 1915, EMH Papers, 9/8.
8   EMH Diary, Nov. 25, 28, Dec. 15, 1915, EMH Papers; EMH Diary, Dec. 15, 1915, *PWW*, XXXV (Princeton, 1980), 355-61.

freedom of the seas. Seeking to improve German-American relations, the ambassador urged the United States to require Great Britain to abide by international law. The Germans wanted the British to lift their illegal blockade. House expanded this idea of freedom to include both land and sea. He hoped to end German "militarism" as well as British "navalism." After Bernstorff indicated his government's interest in such a peace, House advised Wilson that his mission's goal should be to achieve "general disarmament." On this basis he counseled the president to demand an end to the war.[9]

In instructions for House, Wilson combined general disarmament with collective security. Drawing upon Grey's earlier suggestions, he outlined his idea of a postwar league for the first time. By eliminating militarism and navalism and establishing a league, he hoped to prevent aggression and guarantee peace. This long-range purpose seemed more important than specific European conflicts. He approved the use of only "our utmost moral force" to encourage either the Allies or the Central Powers to end the war. Reconciling a postwar league with neutrality during the present war, he thus combined universalism and unilateralism in his foreign policy.[10]

Arriving in London early in January 1916, House linked the league idea with his earlier plan for American mediation. He attempted to overcome British fears regarding freedom of the seas. Yet, under Wilson's instructions, he also urged the British to modify their maritime system. The vagueness of the president's conception of a league caused further doubts about the American role in Europe. Various British officials endeavored unsuccessfully to obtain information about his attitude toward specific issues of the war. "They wanted to know," House reported to Wilson, "how far you would be willing to enter into an agreement concerning European affairs. I thought you would not be willing to do this at all, but you would be willing to come to an agreement with the civilized world upon the broad questions touching the interests and future of every nation." Throughout these discussions he emphasized, moreover, that his plan for mediation and collective security depended upon American neutrality.[11]

House exemplified the typical polarity in American thought about the Old World. At once unilateral and universal, he sought to avoid American entanglement in European affairs while defining a new role for the United States. "The general line of my argument," he reported to Wilson, "was that you had arranged a closer union of the Americas so if it was thought best not to enter a world wide sphere, we could safely lead an isolated life of our own.

9   Bernstorff to EMH, July 10, 27, Sept. 4, Nov. 25, 1915, EMH to Bernstorff, July 12, 28, 30, Nov. 26, 1915, Memorandum, Oct. 30, 1915, RL to Bernstorff, Nov. 24, 1915, Bernstorff to RL, Nov. 25, 1915, EMH Papers, 2/44; EMH to WW, Nov. 10, 11, 19, Dec. 1, 7, 16, 21, 22, 1915, EMH Papers, 49/5; Bernstorff to Bethmann Hollweg, Nov. 23, 1915, EMH to WW, Dec. 22, 1915, *PWW*, XXXV, 240-43, 381-82.
10   WW to EMH, Dec. 17, 24, 1915, EMH Papers, 49/16; EMH to WW, Dec. 26, 1915, EMH Papers, 49/5; EMH Diary, Dec. 24, 1915.
11   EMH to EG, Dec. 7, 1915, EMH Papers, 9/8; EMH to WW, Jan. 11, 15, 16, 1916, EMH Papers, 49/6; EMH to EG, Dec. 7, 1915, *PWW*, XXXV, 383; EMH Diary, Jan. 6, 10, 1916.

If this were decided upon, I told them, we would increase our army and navy and remain within our own hemisphere." The president's proposal for a Pan-American treaty as well as his plans for military preparedness, both of which House had vigorously supported, were designed to enhance this option. "On the other hand," House further reported, "I explained, you believed that in order to fully justify our existence as a great nation, it might be necessary to bring to bear all our power in behalf of peace and the maintenance of it." The president's vision of collective security to preserve "permanent peace among civilized nations" anticipated this other alternative. For both House and Wilson, the same understanding of the American mission in the world expressed itself in both the policy of neutrality and the league idea.[12]

In Berlin, House explored the possibility of peace with Chancellor Theobald von Bethmann Hollweg and at the German Foreign Office. He now recognized that the Imperial German government would settle for nothing short of victory. He also concluded that Germany would soon resort to "an aggressive undersea policy." Extravagant German war aims and prospects of another submarine crisis convinced him that Germany directly threatened the United States.[13]

Under these circumstances, House decided to go beyond his instructions. This initiative, beginning in Paris, culminated in the House-Grey memorandum on February 22, 1916. He used an argument he had earlier employed in discussions with British and German officials. The future might bring the disruption of the Allies rather than the defeat of the Central Powers, he warned the French. He had presented the opposite specter to the Germans. Advocating peace negotiations before such an eventuality, he outlined his plan for mediation. At a critical meeting with Premier Aristide Briand and Jules Cambon of the Foreign Office, House reached what he thought was "a complete understanding." Still, French leaders expressed no immediate desire for mediation.[14]

Returning to London, House concentrated on Grey and Prime Minister Herbert Asquith, and also Arthur Balfour and David Lloyd George, who would succeed them later in the year. He sought to persuade them to accept mediation before the United States entered the war over the submarine issue. But they viewed American intervention without alarm. Grey and Lloyd George frankly told him they would welcome it. Appreciating Anglo-American interdependence, British leaders approved the House-Grey mem-

---

1 2   EMH Diary, Jan. 6, 8, 10, 14-15, 1915; EMH to WW, Jan. 7, 7, 10, 11, 13, 15, 16, 1915, EMH Papers, 49/6; WW to EMH, Jan. 9, 12, 1915, EMH Papers, 49/17.

1 3   EMH to WW, Jan. 30, Feb. 3, 1916, EMH Papers, 49/6; EMH Diary, Jan. 28, 1916; EMH to WW, [Jan. 30, Feb. 1], Feb. 3, 1916, *PWW*, XXXVI (Princeton, 1981), 52, 85, 122-23. Excellent studies of Germany's expansionist war aims are Hans W. Gatzke, *Germany's Drive to the West: A Study of Germany's Western War Aims During the First World War* (Baltimore, 1966), and Fritz Fischer, *Germany's Aims in the First World War* (New York, 1967).

1 4   EMH Diary, Feb. 2, 7, 1916; EMH to WW, Feb. 3, 7, 1916, EMH Papers, 49/6; EMH to WW, Paris, Feb. 3, [7], 1916, *PWW*, XXXVI, 125-26, 138.

orandum. Despite their reluctance to accept mediation, they hoped to prevent total American indifference toward the Old World.[15]

Immediately returning home, House solicited Wilson's endorsement of his plan for mediation. On March 6 he explained the project and gained the president's approval of the House-Grey memorandum. The circumstances surrounding this decision suggested a substantial difference between House's and Wilson's views. Although welcoming a peace conference, the president refused to give any firm commitment which might involve the United States in war. He carefully inserted the word "probably" into the document, thereby avoiding a definite promise of action after an unsuccessful conference. Even if Germany made extravagant demands, he declined to obligate the United States to enter the war on the Allies' side.[16]

Painfully aware of Wilson's reluctance, the Allies fought to achieve their goals without counting on American assistance. Although they would welcome the United States as a belligerent on their side, they did not want interference from Washington with their pursuit of victory. They steadfastly resisted American mediation.[17]

Wilson's attitude during the early months of 1916, expressed both privately and publicly, revealed the significance of the word "probably." Seeking to insulate the western hemisphere from the Old World's problems, he continued to promote Pan-Americanism. Throughout 1915 he and House, along with Bryan and his successor Robert Lansing at the State Department, had endeavored to convince the A.B.C. countries to accept the proposed treaty. They attempted to persuade Latin Americans to join the United States in a partnership to uphold the Monroe Doctrine. After a year of failure, the president decided to publicize his proposal for a Pan-American treaty. He appealed to Latin American nations to unite with the United States "in guaranteeing to each other absolutely political independence and territorial integrity." Addressing the Pan-American Scientific Congress in Washington on January 6, 1916, he advocated "the ordered progress of society" in South as well as North America. The treaty's purpose, he explained, was to achieve "not only the international peace of America but the domestic peace of America." It would, in effect, provide a guarantee against internal revolution as well as external aggression. He claimed that "it is just as much to our interest to assist each other to the orderly processes

15   EMH Diary, Feb. 7-8, 10-11, 14-15, 17, 21-23, 1916; EMH to WW, Feb. 9, 10, 10, 11, 13, 15, 1915, EMH Papers, 49/6; WW to EMH, Feb. 13, 1916, EMH Papers, 49/17; Memorandum, Feb. 22, 1916, EMH Papers, 9/8; EMH to WW, Feb. 9, 10, 10, 11, 11, [13], [15], 25, 1915, WW to EMH, Feb. 12, 1915, *PWW*, XXXVI, 150-51, 166-68, 170, 173, 180, 212.

16   EMH Diary, March 6-7, 1916; Note by E. M. H[ouse], [March] 7, 1916, EMH to EG, March 8, 10, 1916, EMH Papers, 9/8; EMH Diary, March 6-7, 1916, EMH to EG, [March 7, 1916], *PWW*, XXXVI, 262-63, 266-67.

17   Viscount Grey of Fallodon, *Twenty-five Years*, 1892-1916 (London, 1925), II, 126-29; EMH to EG, March 10, 1916, EG to EMH, March 24, 1916, EMH Papers, 9/8; EMH to WW, Apr. 8, 1916, EMH Papers, 49/6; John Milton Cooper, Jr., "The British Response to the House-Grey Memorandum: New Evidence and New Questions," *Journal of American History*, LIX (March 1973), 958-71.

within our own borders as it is to orderly processes in our controversies with one another." This form of international social control, in his view, offered "the hope of the world."[18]

Charles W. Eliot, president emeritus of Harvard University, seized upon the president's advocacy of Pan-Americanism to encourage him to expand the American role in world affairs. From the beginning of the European war, he had identified with the Allies. The American people, he told Wilson, would approve the use of force to protect western civilization despite Washington's traditional advice to keep out of European affairs. By early 1915, he hoped the A.B.C. countries would join the United States in "an American League" to restore order in Mexico, believing it would provide "a suggestive precedent for a European League to keep the peace of Europe." After Wilson's Pan-American address, Eliot urged him to express the same sympathy for France as for Latin America. He did not think the United States should remain aloof as "an umpire or conciliator" between the opposing coalitions. He implored him to expand his Pan-Americanism into a humanitarian proclamation of American ideals for the Old World as well.[19]

Public pressure for some kind of peace initiative increased after the crisis over the March 24, 1916, torpedoing of the *Sussex*. Hamilton Holt, editor of the *Independent* and a founder of the League to Enforce Peace, urged the president to combine mediation with collective security. Unaware that Wilson had already made this linkage in preparing for House's mission earlier in the year, Holt asked him "whether it would be practicable to offer mediation now on the basis of a League to Enforce Peace? Perhaps if the future peace of the world can be guaranteed, the immediate problems will become relatively insignificant and can be easily arranged." Wilson and House had privately reached the same conclusion. They realized, moreover, that rejection of mediation by the Allies would increase tensions between them and the United States now that Germany had given the *Sussex* pledge to abide by cruiser warfare rules in its use of submarines. The American people would increasingly criticize British violations of neutral rights. In view of British and French reluctance to implement the House-Grey memorandum, Wilson decided to publicize his views. He had initially declined an invitation from Taft to speak at the League to Enforce Peace's annual convention, but now welcomed this opportunity.[20]

18 *PPWW*, III, 439-45; WJB to Suarez-Mujica, Apr. 29, 1915, WJB to WW, May 19, 1915, EMH to RL, Oct. 12, 1915, RL to WW, Nov. 11, 1915, Jan. 6, 1916, *FR:Lansing*, II, 482-88, 491-93; EMH to WW, July 19, 25, 1915, EMH Papers, 49/5.

19 Eliot to WW, Aug. 6, 20, 22, 1914, *PWW*, XXX, 353-55, 418-20, 434-35; Eliot to WW, Feb. 19, 1915, *PWW*, XXXII, 263-64; Eliot to WW, Jan. 15, 21, 1916, WW to Eliot, Jan. 18, 1916, *PWW*, XXXV, 486, 500-01, 506-08.

20 Holt to WW, May 11, 1916, Woodrow Wilson Papers, Ser. 4, File 333, Library of Congress; JPT to WW, May 16, 1916, WW to JPT, May 17, 1916, Joseph P. Tumulty Papers, Box 4, Library of Congress; EMH to WW, May 7, 9, 14, 1916, EMH to EG, May 7, 1916, EMH Papers, 49/6; WW to EMH, May 8, 9, 12, 1916, EMH Papers, 49/17; EMH to EG, May 10, 1916, EG to EMH, May 12, 1916, EMH Papers, 9/8; WHT to WW, May 9, 1916, EMH to WHT, May 11, 1916, EMH Papers, 18/32; WHT to WW, Apr. 11, 1916, WW to WHT, Apr. 14, 1916, EMH to WW, May 7, 1916,

Contemplating a future league, Wilson envisaged a partnership to protect small as well as large states against aggression. He thought of it as the extension of Pan-Americanism to the entire world. He expected the United States to exercise the controlling influence in this new structure of peace. His principal advisers shared his ethnocentric perspective. House advised him to emphasize the similarity between private and public morality. Like Wilson, he presupposed that international morality coincided with American liberal values. Secretary of State Lansing approved a league to promote international conciliation and arbitration but opposed any guarantee involving force. "I do not believe," he warned Wilson, "that it is wise to limit our independence of action, a sovereign right, to the will of other powers beyond this hemisphere." He feared that extension of Pan-Americanism throughout the world would permit European powers to violate the Monroe Doctrine. A league of nations, he apprehended, might enable them to interfere in American affairs and entangle the United States in the Old World.[21]

At the League to Enforce Peace convention on May 27, 1916, Wilson first publicly announced his idea of postwar collective security. He proclaimed the views he had privately expressed to House in December 1915. Reconciling a future league with neutrality, he retained his isolationist attitude toward the Old World. Indifferent toward the war's origins and the belligerents' aims, he stated that "with its causes and its objects we are not concerned." Emphasizing global interdependence, he claimed that the war had brought progress toward international unity and universal rights. The United States, he explained, hoped to promote peace now and in the future. Reflecting the dichotomy of his thought, his program combined isolationist and internationalist elements. Affirming that he was interested "only in peace and its future guarantees," he called upon the belligerents to settle "the present quarrel." But he also advocated a "universal association of nations" to maintain freedom of the seas and prevent war, thereby providing "a virtual guarantee of territorial integrity and political independence." Wilson thus united both unilateral and universal tendencies in his new foreign policy.[22] Wilson's address delighted advocates of a league. Holt thought it ranked next to the Declaration of Independence and the Monroe Doctrine. Lippmann agreed, claiming that "in historic significance it is

WW to EMH, May 8, 1916, EMH to EG, May 7, 1916, PWW, XXXVI, 458-59, 481, 631-32, 652-53; WW to EMH, May 9, 1916, WHT to WW, May 9, 1916, EMH to WW, May 9, 1916, EMH to EG, May 10, 1916, WW to WHT, May 18, 1916, JPT to WW, May 19, [1916], Holt to WW, May 11, 1916, WW to JPT, [c. May 19, 1916], PWW, XXXVII (Princeton, 1981), 3, 6-7, 69, 75-76.
2 1   A Memorandum by RSB, [May 12, 1916], WW to EMH, May 18, 1916, EMH to WW, May 21, 1916, A Memorandum, [May 24, 1916], EMH Diary, May 24, 1916, RL to WW, May 25, 1916, PWW, XXXVII, 36-37, 68-69, 88-91, 102-06, 106-09; WW to EMH, May 16, 18, 1916, EMH Papers, 49/17; EMH to WW, May 19, 1916, House's suggestion for Wilson's speech of May 27, 1916, May 21, 1916, EMH Papers, 49/6.
2 2   PPWW, IV, 184-88; An Address in Washington to the League to Enforce Peace, [May 27, 1916], PWW, XXXVII, 113-16.

easily the most important diplomatic event that our generation has known."[23]

Wilson hoped the Allies would see in this promise of collective security an opportunity to end the war short of victory. This would enable the United States to contribute toward peace without abandoning neutrality. Although his address invigorated the League of Nations Society in Great Britain, it generally failed to instill confidence. His indifference toward the causes and objects of the war confirmed doubts in London and Paris about American mediation. Determined to achieve victory, Allied leaders wanted no premature peace conference to end the war in stalemate. His promise that the United States would help guarantee the political independence and territorial integrity of future members of a league went beyond the bounds of credibility in view of his aloofness toward the current plight of Belgium and France. Seeking to counter this negative Allied reaction, House protested in vain that "if we are to take part in maintaining the peace of the world we could hardly be indifferent to the war and its causes and the President never intended to leave such an impression." Despite numerous exchanges with Grey and J. Jules Jusserand, French ambassador in Washington, House failed to satisfy the Allies. They placed little confidence in American mediation or a new league because the United States developed these plans as adjuncts of neutrality.[24]

In his campaign for re-election in 1916, Wilson defended his policy of impartial neutrality and proclaimed his emerging idea of a postwar league. Both of these facets of his foreign policy expressed his Americanism. He emphasized keeping the United States out of the war for the purpose of restoring peace. He believed the United States, as the only disinterested nation in the world, was uniquely qualified to play this dual role of preserving neutrality and reconstructing Europe's peace. It had, as he privately stated, "nothing to gain and nothing to lose" and "certainly . . . nothing to fear" from the war. Although European statesmen failed to appreciate this unique characteristic, belief in American innocence undergirded his twin impulses toward unilateralism and universalism.[25]

23   EMH to EG, May 11, 23, 1916, EMH Papers, 9/8; EMH to EG, May 23, 1916, EMH to WW, May 28, 1916, WW to EMH, May 29, 1916, Holt to WW, May 29, 1916, Lippmann to Hollis, May 29, 1916, *PWW*, XXXVII, 100, 117-18, 120, 166-67.
24   EMH to EG, May 27, June 8, 1916, EMH to EG, July 15, 1916, EG to EMH, May 29, June 28, Aug. 28, 1916, EMH Papers, 9/8; EMH to WW, May 23, 31, 1916, EMH Papers, 49/6; EMH to WW, July 12, 14, 1916, EMH Papers, 49/7; WW to EMH, June 22, 1916, EMH Papers, 49/17; Page to WW, June 1, 1916, EMH to WW, June 9, 14, 25, 27, July 12, 14, 1916, EMH to EG, June 8, July 15, 1916, Page to EMH, May 30, June 2, 1916, Plunkett to EMH, June 7, 1916, Bryce to EMH, June 12, 1916, Gardiner to EMH, June 15, 1916, Lane to WW, July 6, 1916, Buxton to Lane, July 5, [1916], A Memorandum by Noel Buxton, [July 5, 1916], EG to EMH, June 28, 1916, *PWW*, XXXVII, 143-47, 177-80, 225-27, 294-96, 311-13, 370-72, 411-13, 422-24; Buxton to EMH, Aug. 19, 1916, Bryce to EMH, Aug. 26, 1916, EG to EMH, Aug. 28, 1916, *PWW*, XXXVIII (Princeton, 1982), 54-55, 85-86, 89-92.
25   *PPWW*, IV, 275-91; EMH to WW, May 29, June 18, 1916, WW to EMH, July 2, 1916, *PWW*, XXXVII, 121, 265-66, 345-46; A Colloquy with Members of the American Neutral Conference, Aug. 30, 1916, *PWW*, XXXVIII, 108-17.

Promising to keep the United States at peace without sacrificing national honor, the president warned voters that the Republican candidate's election would result in war. Identifying Charles Evans Hughes with prominent Republican advocates of greater military preparedness and closer identification with the Allies, such as ex-President Theodore Roosevelt, elder statesman Elihu Root and Senator Lodge, Wilson defined the choice as peace or war. He reconciled his conception of collective security with Washington's traditional advice, claiming that the United States would still avoid entanglements in the Old World while championing human rights. He described the new global responsibilities of the United States as the culmination of its heritage. Because of the frontier's closing in 1890, this nation had projected itself into the world. The European war demonstrated that it could no longer escape the impact of foreign affairs. As a consequence, he concluded, the United States needed to participate in a postwar league. He thereby harmonized his emerging vision of collective security, or international social control, with his continuing advocacy of neutral rights. Impartial neutrality for the present and a league for the future represented complementary goals. Both expressed his belief in American exceptionalism.[26]

I

After his victory in the November 1916 election, Wilson turned to a new peace overture. This action offered the best hope for keeping the United States out of the war. Unlike Ambassador Walter Hines Page or some prominent Republicans, he refused to identify the interests of the United States with the Allies. British violations of neutral rights as well as Germany's potential resumption of submarine warfare made the international conditions increasingly intolerable. If he could end the war, this would remove the difficulties without sacrificing national honor or neutrality. House's conversations with Bernstorff encouraged the president to believe that Germany might respond favorably to an American initiative. The German ambassador had fostered this belief to gain American assistance in forcing the Allies to open peace negotiations. He hoped thereby to forestall another German-American confrontation over the submarine.[27]

---

26 *PPWW*, IV, 324-36, 344-49, 356-63, 376-82, 384-94; An Address in Omaha, [Oct. 5, 1916], An Address in Indianapolis, [Oct. 12, 1916], A Campaign Address at Shadow Lawn, Oct. 14, 1916, *PWW*, XXXVIII, 343-49, 412-19, 430-38. For Republican positions on the issue of war and peace in 1916, see Merlo J. Pusey, *Charles Evans Hughes* (New York, 1951), I, 350-59, William Henry Harbaugh, *The Life and Times of Theodore Roosevelt* (New York, 1963), 439-68, Philip C. Jessup, *Elihu Root* (New York, 1938), II, 309-52, Garraty, *Henry Cabot Lodge*, 315-35, and Widenor, *Henry Cabot Lodge and the Search for an American Foreign Policy*, 221-65.
27 WW to EMH, Nov. 21, 24, 25, 1916, EMH Papers, 49/17; EMH to WW, Oct. 20, Nov. 20, 1916, EMH Papers, 49/7; Bernstorff to EMH, Oct. 18, 1916, EMH to Bernstorff, Oct. 19, 1916, EMH Papers, 2/45; Memorandum by Colonel E. M. House of a Conversation with the German Ambassador (Bernstorff), Nov. 20, 1916, *FR:Lansing*, I (Washington, 1939), 573; A Memorandum by Walter Hines Page, [Sept. 23, 1916], Memoranda by Walter Hines Page, [c. Sept. 23, 1916], EMH Diary, Sept. 24,

House, in contrast to his earlier optimistic attitude, now believed that prospects for successful peace negotiations were quite meager. He doubted that Germany would approve any terms acceptable to the Allies. He feared that the Imperial German government might, however, agree to attend a peace conference, while still pursuing victory. If the Allies then refused an invitation, the United States would find itself in an embarrassing position. He still hoped, despite his growing distrust of internal British politics, to prevent American alignment with the Central Powers. He discounted Bernstorff's assurances that Germany would welcome participation in a future league to enforce peace of the kind Wilson envisaged. Consequently, House cautioned against hasty action that might alienate the Allies and play into the Germans' hands.[28]

Political considerations overruled House's negative advice. During the campaign, by stressing his determination to avoid war, Wilson had regained Bryan's support. He feared that unless he made some dramatic gesture for world peace, Bryan might again become an active critic, as he had been after his resignation as secretary of state over the handling of the *Lusitania* crisis.[29] The president's peace note, transmitted by the State Department on December 18, 1916, stated explicitly that the United States was not proposing mediation but was merely requesting the Allies and the Central Powers to reveal their war aims. He suggested a universal system of collective security to replace the old alliances and balance of power. His new international order depended upon the current deadlock in the war. For the first time, he showed an interest in specific terms of a European settlement. Yet by minimizing differences between the Allies and the Central Powers, he revealed far more interest in peace per se than in their war aims.[30]

German military and political leaders wanted peace, but without surrendering Allied territory which they had occupied early in the war. Unwilling to express this desire candidly, Bethmann Hollweg decided to reject Wilson's request. Foreign Secretary Arthur Zimmermann informed the

1916, EMH to WW, Oct. 20, 1916, Bernstorff to EMH, Oct. 18, 1916, *PWW*, XXXVIII, 241-59, 494-96; EMH to WW, Nov. 20, 1916, WW to EMH, Nov. 21, 24, 25, 1916, Page to WW, Nov. 24, 1916, A Draft of a Peace Note, [c. Nov. 25, 1916], *PWW*, XL (Princeton, 1982), 4-6, 20-24, 62-67, 70-74. Two outstanding books on Ambassador Page are Ross Gregory, *Walter Hines Page: Ambassador to the Court of St. James's* (Lexington, 1970), and John Milton Cooper, Jr., *Walter Hines Page: The Southerner as American,* 1855-1918 (Chapel Hill, 1977).

2 8   EMH to WW, July 30, Nov. 6, 30, Dec. 3, 1916, EMH Papers, 49/7; Bernstorff to EMH, Nov. 10, 1916, EMH to Bernstorff, Nov. 12, 1916, EMH Papers, 2/45; EMH to WW, Nov. 6, 1916, *PWW*, XXXVIII, 619; EMH to WW, Dec. 3, 1916, *PWW*, XL, 132-35.

2 9   WW to EMH, Dec. 3, 8, 1916, EMH Papers, 49/17; WW to RL, Dec. 9, 1916, A Draft of a Note to Entente Powers, [Dec. 13, 1916], A Draft of a Note to Central Powers, [Dec. 13, 1916], *PWW*, XL, 197-200, 222-29.

3 0   WW to RL, Dec. 17, 1916, Ray Stannard Baker Papers, Ser. I, Box 8, Library of Congress; WW to RL, Dec. 17, 18, 1916, RL to WW, Dec. 17, 1916, An Appeal for a Statement of War Aims, [Dec. 18, 1916], *PWW*, XL, 256-62, 272-76; RL to Page et al., Dec. 18, 1916, Department of State, *Papers Relating to the Foreign Relations of the United States,* 1916. Supplement: *The World War* (Washington, 1929), 97-99; RL to Bernstorff, Dec. 20, 1916, Botschaft Washington, 4A34 (Friedensverhandlungen), Heft 9a, Bd. 1, Politisches Archiv des Auswärtigen Amts, Bonn.

American ambassador in Berlin, James W. Gerard, on December 26. Rather than state their specific objectives, the Germans wanted the United States to press the Allies into accepting their own proposal for direct negotiations. Desiring no American participation except to arrange the peace conference, they hoped to consolidate their previous military gains without the risk that the United States might demand concessions for the Allies' benefit.[31]

Despite Germany's negative response, Wilson continued his search for peace. He quickly endorsed the initiative which House undertook in discussions with Bernstorff. Although previously critical of the president for minimizing differences between the Allies and the Central Powers, House adopted the same tactic to encourage the Germans to reconsider their answer. American willingness to focus on the "permanent peace" of the world rather than on the belligerents' war aims greatly encouraged the German ambassador.[32]

After Wilson approved the position which House had outlined, Bernstorff reported the conversation to Berlin. He recognized the opportunity this new American initiative offered. Since May 27, 1916, when the president had advocated a postwar league, the Germans recognized the advantage of encouraging the United States to concentrate on the world's future peace. In mid-August, Bethmann Hollweg instructed Bernstorff to welcome any American peace initiative as long as it permitted the belligerents to determine the outcome of the war. Acting under these instructions during the October and November discussions with House, the ambassador encouraged the belief that Germany would respond favorably to a new peace overture. Wilson's peace note, by calling for specific war aims, temporarily thwarted the German plan. The situation quickly reversed when House suggested that Germany indicate its willingness to join in preparations for permanent peace. In his report to Berlin, Bernstorff suggested an affirmative statement on the questions of a league of nations, arbitration, and military and naval disarmament. He reminded the Foreign Office that "Wilson lays comparatively little importance on the territorial side of the peace conditions. I am still of the opinion that the chief emphasis should be laid on what are here called the guarantees for the future." Noting the divergence between present and future conditions of peace, he urged his government to exploit this fundamental weakness in American policy toward Europe.[33]

In Berlin, Zimmermann seized the opportunity which House's initiative opened. Although absolutely opposed to American participation in negotiations to end the war, he hoped to convince the Wilson administration of

3 1   Gerard to RL, Dec. 26, 1916, *FR1916*, 117-18; Count Bernstorff, *My Three Years in America* (New York, 1920), 321; Bernstorff to *New-Yorker Staats-Zeitung*, Dec. 24, 1916, Zimmermann to Bernstorff, Jan. 4, 1917, Botschaft Washington, 4A34 (Friedensverhandlungen), Heft 9a, Bd. 1; Gerard to RL, Jan. 2, 1917, *PWW*, XL, 383-84.

3 2   EMH Diary, Dec. 27, 1916; EMH to WW, Dec. 27, 28, 1916, EMH Papers, 49/7; WW to EMH, Dec. 28, 1916, EMH Papers, 49/17; EMH to WW, Dec. 27, 1916, *PWW*, XL, 337.

3 3   Bernstorff, *My Three Years*, 270-325; Bernstorff to German Foreign Office, Dec. 29, 1916, *PWW*, XL, 362-65.

Germany's desire for peace. In accordance with Bethmann Hollweg's policy of keeping "two irons in the fire," the foreign secretary wanted either to use American influence to bring the Allies into direct negotiations or to neutralize the American reaction to the anticipated unrestricted submarine warfare. To convince the president that the Imperial German government genuinely desired peace, he authorized Bernstorff to inform House that Germany would join the United States in a league and reduce military and naval armaments after the war. He even offered an arbitration treaty immediately. At best, if this response satisfied Wilson, the United States might force the Allies to negotiate with the Central Powers on the basis of the German peace note of December 12, 1916. If the Allies still refused, as expected, the president might blame them for continuing the war and, consequently, acquiesce in Germany's unrestricted submarine warfare. By achieving its war aims in negotiations with the Allies or by preventing the United States from entering the war, the German government hoped to profit from discussions about permanent peace. On January 15, 1917, Bernstorff conveyed Zimmermann's answer, temporarily convincing House that Germany desired peace. House, who had been pessimistic, now became positively ecstatic. Wilson, more cautious than his friend, wanted further information. Yet he, too, felt hopeful that the United States had finally discovered the road to peace.[34]

Despite reservations, Wilson thought that Germany now posed less of an obstacle to peace than the Allies. He regarded their war aims, outlined on January 10 in response to his peace note, as an unjustifiable demand for victory. Encouraged by Germany and disheartened by the Allies, the president decided to state his own views. Earlier that month, after House's new initiative evoked a positive response from Bernstorff, Wilson began to draft a "peace without victory" address. After receiving the Allies' answer, he completed this statement of his European policy.[35]

Speaking before the Senate on January 22, 1917, the president outlined the conditions under which the United States would join a postwar league for the preservation of permanent peace. He called for the belligerents to accept the American vision of a "peace without victory." Blaming the balance of power for rivalries in the Old World, he wanted to convert Europe to a new

34 Bernstorff to EMH, Jan. 9, 1917, EMH to Bernstorff, Jan. 17, 1917, EMH Papers, 2/46; EMH to Bernstorff, Jan. 17, 1917, Botschaft Washington, 4A34 (Friedensverhandlungen), Heft 9a, Bd. 1; EMH to WW, Jan. 15, 16, 17, 18, 1917, EMH Papers, 49/8; WW to EMH, Jan. 16, 17, 19, 1917, EMH Papers, 49/18; EMH Diary, Jan. 15, 1917; Bernstorff, *My Three Years*, 325-58; EMH to WW, Jan. 15, 16, 17, 18, 1917, Bernstorff to Bethmann Hollweg, Jan. 16, 1917, WW to EMH, Jan. 17, 1917, *PWW*, XL, 477-78, 493-94, 504-08, 516-17. See also Karl E. Birnbaum, *Peace Moves and U-Boat Warfare* (Stockholm, 1958).
35 EMH Diary, Jan. 3, 11, 1917; WW to EMH, Jan. 19, 1917, EMH Papers, 49/18; EMH to WW, Jan. 19, 1917, EMH Papers, 49/8; Bernstorff to EMH, Jan. 18, 1917, EMH Papers, 2/46, and Botschaft Washington, 4A34 (Friedensverhandlungen), Heft 9a, Bd. 1; EMH Diary, Jan. 3, 11, 1917, RL to WW, Jan. 10, 1917, Grew to RL, Dec. 21, 1916, Sharp to RL, Jan. 10, 1917, WW to RL, Jan. 11, 1917, WW to EMH, Jan. 19, 1917, EMH to WW, Jan. 19, 1917, Bernstorff to EMH, Jan. 18, 1917, *PWW*, XL, 402-05, 428-36, 438-442, 445-47, 524-26.

system of collective security. He called for acceptance of "American principles, American policies." His conception of a league reflected the traditional American aversion to entangling alliances. "There is no entangling alliance in a concert of power," he announced. "When all unite to act in the same purpose all act in the common interest and are free to live their own lives under a common protection." Believing in a universal world order, he had consistently minimized differences between the Allies and the Central Powers. Although he could not ignore conflicts of interest between them and the United States, he disregarded the implications for his idea of collective security. Once the Old World accepted American principles, the problem, presumably, would cease to exist. The league of nations which he envisioned thus represented the Monroe Doctrine's expansion throughout the world. Although Latin American nations had refused to accept his Pan-American treaty, he projected the same idea beyond the western hemisphere. By focusing on conditions of permanent peace, he adopted the very approach which Bernstorff had encouraged. He explicitly left the settlement of specific issues to the belligerents. If the settlement failed to satisfy his sense of justice, he wanted no part in guaranteeing it, although he would not oppose it.[36]

Calling for "peace without victory," Wilson reaffirmed American neutrality as he anticipated a postwar league. He believed that strict neutrality would place the United States in the best position for contributing to peace. On this basis House continued his discussions with the German ambassador. Bernstorff, clearly recognizing the opportunity, urged his government to accept Wilson's offer to arrange negotiations between the belligerents rather than to resort to unrestricted submarine warfare. Bethmann Hollweg and Zimmermann, lacking Bernstorff's perception of the opportunity or the risks, refused to reconsider the decision which had already been made. On January 9, Kaiser Wilhelm II, acting on advice of Generals Paul von Hindenburg and Erich Ludendorff, had decided to authorize the unrestricted use of submarines. Learning of this decision, Bernstorff warned that it would result in war with the United States. He argued unsuccessfully that Wilson's assistance in ending the war would serve Germany's interests far better than the submarine. He realized that the announcement of Germany's new strategy would abruptly terminate discussions with House. Under instructions from Berlin, he informed Lansing on January 31 that Germany would begin unrestricted submarine warfare on the next day. This information shattered House's and Wilson's hope for peace in the near future.[37]

3 6   *PPWW*, IV, 407-14; An Address to the Senate, Jan. 22, 1917, *PWW*, XL, 533-39.
3 7   WW to EMH, Jan. 24, 1917, EMH Papers, 49/18; EMH to WW, Jan. 20, 25, 26, 26, 30-31, 1917, EMH Papers, 49/8; EMH Diary, Jan. 31, Feb. 1, 1917; EMH to Bernstorff, Jan. 19, 1917, Bernstorff to EMH, Jan. 20, 1917, EMH Papers, 2/46; EMH to Bernstorff, Jan. 19, 1917, Bernstorff to EMH, Jan. 20, 1917, Bernstorff to German Foreign Office, Jan. 26, 1917, Botschaft Washington, 4A34 (Friedensverhandlungen), Heft 9a, Bd. 1; EMH to WW, Jan. 20, 1917, Bernstorff to EMH, Jan. 20, 1917, *PWW*, XL, 526-29; WW to EMH, Jan. 24, 1917, EMH to WW, Jan. 25, 26, 26, 1917, RL to WW, Jan. 25, 1917, EMH to RL, Jan. 24, 1917, Bernstorff to Bethmann Hollweg, Jan. 27,

At the White House on February 1, the president listened to House's and Lansing's arguments for sending Bernstorff home. They thought the interests and honor of the United States required immediate termination of diplomatic relations with Germany, probably followed by a declaration of war. Wilson, however, was apprehensive that this course would result in destruction of western civilization. Having no fear for the immediate security of the United States, he seemed willing to sacrifice national honor in order to preserve American strength for restoring Europe after the war.[38] His conception of western civilization included white supremacy. He told Lansing "that he had been more and more impressed with the idea that 'white civilization' and its dominion over the world rested largely on our ability to keep this country intact, as we would have to build up the nations ravaged by the war." In early January he had emphasized to House that "there will be no war. . . . We are the only one of the great White nations that is free from war today, and it would be a crime against civilization for us to go in." At the cabinet meeting on February 2, which he convened to consider the submarine crisis, he reiterated the same theme. He immediately expressed his willingness to consider sacrificing national honor, if necessary, to thwart the Japanese peril.[39]

This justification for inaction apparently convinced none of Wilson's associates. The cabinet overwhelmingly shared Lansing's opinion that the only honorable course for the United States was to break diplomatic relations with Germany immediately. Accepting this advice, the president went before Congress on February 3 to explain his decision. He observed that Germany's new policy directly violated the *Sussex* pledge of May 4, 1916. Because the German leaders had declared their intention to violate their pledge to abide by cruiser warfare rules, the only alternative for the United States was to break diplomatic relations.[40]

Imperial Germany finally forced the United States to declare war. On March 18 news arrived in Washington that German submarines had sunk

1917, Bethmann Hollweg to Bernstorff, Jan. 29, 1917, EMH Diary, Feb. 1, 1917, *PWW*, XLI (Princeton, 1983), 3-4, 17-19, 24-27, 49-52, 59-63, 86-89.

38   RL Diary, I, Dec. 3, 1916, II, Jan. 24, 28, 1917, Robert Lansing Papers, Library of Congress; Memorandum by the Secretary of State, Dec. 1, 1916, RL to WW, Dec. 8, 1916, Jan. 31, Feb. 2, 2, 1917, *FR:Lansing*, I, 227-37, 575-76, 582-84, 591-92; RL to U.S. Ambassadors, Dec. 21, 1916, *FR1916*, 106-07; RL to WW, Jan. 12, 1917, Bernstorff to RL, Jan. 10, 1917, RL to WW, Jan. 17, 23, 1917, Gerard to RL, Jan. 21, 1917, *PWW*, XL, 447-53, 509, 552-53; RL to WW, Jan. 31, Feb. 2, 2, 1917, Bernstorff to RL, Jan. 31, 1917, Bernstorff to EMH, Jan. 31, 1917, EMH Diary, Feb. 1, 1917, *PWW*, XLI, 71-79, 80-82, 86-89, 96-100; Zimmermann to Bernstorff, Jan. 27, 1917, Bernstorff to RL, Jan. 31, 1917, Bernstorff to EMH, Jan. 31, 1917, Botschaft Washington, 4A34 (Friedensverhandlungen), Heft 9a, Bd. 1; Bernstorff to EMH, Jan. 31, 1917, EMH Papers, 2/46; EMH Diary, Feb. 1, 1917.

39   RL Diary, II, Feb. 4, 1917; EMH Diary, Jan. 4, 1917; David F. Houston, *Eight Years with Wilson's Cabinet: 1913 to 1920* (Garden City, 1926), I, 229.

40   RL Diary, II, Feb. 4, 1917; Houston, *Eight Years*, I, 227-31; *PPWW*, IV, 422-26; An Address to a Joint Session of Congress, Feb. 3, 1917, A Memorandum by RL, Feb. 4, 1917, Lane to G. W. Lane, Feb. 9, 1917, *PWW*, XLI, 108-12, 118-25, 183-84; RL to Bernstorff, Feb. 3, 1917, Botschaft Washington, 4A34 (Friedensverhandlungen), Heft 9a, Bd. 1.

three American merchant ships. In view of these overt acts of aggression, Lansing rejoiced that "war is inevitable." He urged Wilson to join the battle in defense of civilization. He explained that "the Entente Allies represent the principle of Democracy, and the Central Powers, the principle of Autocracy, and that it is for the welfare of mankind and for the establishment of peace in the world that Democracy should succeed."[41] The president, however, still hoped to avoid war. On March 19, in separate conversations with Lansing and with Secretary of the Navy Josephus Daniels, he expressed his desire to protect American shipping, if possible, without abandoning neutrality. Lansing, apprehensive that he might fail to act, turned to House for assistance. Sharing this concern, House immediately wrote to Wilson to advocate war. The entire cabinet now agreed that war was inevitable. On March 20 it recommended that he should urge Congress to declare war. By resorting to submarine warfare against neutral as well as belligerent shipping, Germany left the United States no alternative. In view of this unanimity of advice, Wilson made the inescapable decision.[42]

Calling Congress into session on April 2, 1917, the president recommended war against Germany. He summarized the rationale for his emerging European policy. Throughout the period of neutrality, he had hoped to preserve both peace and honor for the United States. Germany's new submarine strategy now forced a choice, which British maritime practices had never done. Abandoning neutrality in favor of belligerency, he still desired a "peace without victory" and a postwar system of collective security. For the first time, the president interpreted the war as a struggle between democracy and absolutism. He endorsed the view which Lansing had previously emphasized, that democracies desired peace while autocracies originated wars. "A steadfast concert for peace can never be maintained except by a partnership of democratic nations," he asserted. "No autocratic government could be trusted to keep faith with it or observe its covenants." Presupposing a direct relationship between democracy and peace, Wilson's policy contained revolutionary implications. He expressed these in welcoming the recent revolution in Russia. "Here," he observed with reference to the new Russian government, "is a fit partner for a League of Honor." In similar fashion, he distinguished between the German people and their autocratic government. "The world must be made safe for democracy," he proclaimed. "Its peace must be planted upon the tested foundations of political liberty." Calling for the Old World's redemption, he internationalized the American heritage. Previously, the reconstruction of Europe

4 1   RL to WW, March 19, 1917, *FR:Lansing*, I, 626-28.
4 2   RL to EMH, March 19, 1917, 12/12; EMH to WW, March 19, 1917, EMH Papers, 49/8; RL to EMH, March 19, 1917, EMH to RL, March 20, 1917, *FR:Lansing*, I, 628-30; RL Diary, II, March 19-20, 1917; EMH Diary, March 19, 22, 1917; E. David Cronon, ed., *The Cabinet Diaries of Josephus Daniels*, 1913-1921 (Lincoln, 1963), 116-18; Houston, *Eight Years*, I, 241-45; RL to EMH, March 19, 1917, Diary of JD, March 19-20, 1917, A Memorandum by RL, March 20, 1917, *PWW*, XLI, 429-30, 436-45.

seemed to require the United States to stay out of the war even at the possible risk of sacrificing national honor. Now, in contrast, he viewed American belligerency as the necessary prelude to a league of nations.[43]

Four days later, on April 6, 1917, Congress voted overwhelmingly to declare war against Imperial Germany. This action seemed to unite most Americans. Even Bryan Democrats, who had favored impartial neutrality, accepted war as the inescapable consequence of Germany's submarine warfare. Wilson's advocacy of a "peace without victory" had captured Bryan's imagination. "The basis of peace which you propose," he told the president, "is a new philosophy – that is, new to governments but as old as the Christian religion, and it is the only foundation upon which a permanent peace can be built." For this purpose he joined the broad bipartisan coalition that now favored war.[44]

Wilson justified the abandonment of neutrality with the promise of a postwar league. Although he had not yet formulated his idea of collective security beyond general principles, it provided the central feature of his new policy. House encouraged this development. He told Jusserand that the president hoped to achieve "a scientific peace." Yet Wilson refrained from endorsing any specific plan. Croly and Lippmann, whose views on the foundations of peace he shared, applauded his emerging policy. The idea of international social control attracted not only these progressives but also leaders of the League to Enforce Peace. Taft concluded that "the lesson of the present situation is the necessity for the political organization of the world to stop the spread of a local war into a general conflagration."[45]

Although the president had successfully fostered a consensus in Congress for war, this did not include his rationale for it. Republicans voted for war without necessarily favoring a league of nations. Lowell had attempted in vain to convince Lodge to accept the program of the League to Enforce Peace. In June 1915, speaking at Union College in New York, the senator had approved the league idea in general terms. "In differences between nations which go beyond the limited range of arbitrable questions," he stated, "peace can only be maintained by putting behind it the force of united nations determined to uphold it and to prevent war. No one is more conscious than I of the enormous difficulties which beset such a solution or such a scheme, but I am certain that it is in this direction alone that we can

43   *PPWW: War and Peace* (New York, 1927), V, 6-16; EMH Diary, March 28, 1917, An Address to a Joint Session of Congress, Apr. 2, 1917, *PWW*, XLI, 496-98, 519-27; EMH Diary, Apr. 2, 1917.
44   JPT to WW, March 24, 1917, *PWW*, XLI, 462-64, and JPT Papers, Box 5; WJB to WW, Jan. 26, Apr. 6, 1917, WW to WJB, Feb. 2, 1917, WW Papers, Ser. 4, File 2400; Link, *Wilson*, V, 390-431.
45   A Report of a News Conference by Charles Merz, Jan. 8, [1917], Remarks at a Press Conference, [Jan. 15, 1917], EMH to WW, Jan. 22, 1917, Croly to WW, Jan. 23, 1917, *PWW*, XL, 421-23, 470-77, 539, 559; Lippmann to WW, Jan. 31, March 11, 1917, A Memorandum by Louis Paul Lochner, Feb. 1, 1917, NDB to WW, Feb. 7, 1917, WHT to NDB, Feb. 6, 1917, EMH to WW, Feb. 19, March 9, 1917, Jusserand to French Foreign Ministry, March 7, 1917, *PWW*, XLI, 83, 89-92, 153-55, 250-51, 354-57, 373-76, 388-90.

find hope for the maintenance of the world's peace and the avoidance of needless wars. Even if we could establish such a union of nations there might be some wars which could not be avoided, but there are certainly many which might be prevented." Within the next year, however, Lodge began to have second thoughts. He approached war with Germany during the winter of 1916-1917 without sharing the president's vision of collective security. He identified American interests with the Allies but refused to commit himself to any plan for a future league. Philosophic as well as personal differences prevented Lodge and Wilson from sharing a common perspective on the American role in world affairs, although they both advocated war against Imperial Germany. These differences, already present, would later profoundly influence American foreign relations.[46]

II

As the United States made the transition from neutrality to belligerency, Wilson defined a new policy. His idea of a league of nations, initially fostered in the context of neutrality, now became a general war aim. Later he gave more substance to this vague idea, but for now the abstract vision served in lieu of a precise definition. His belief in American innocence and uniqueness shaped his approach to peacemaking. He projected his ideals onto the world as the universal basis for permanent peace, thereby internationalizing his conception of American nationalism. Rather than seeking to preserve the balance of power in a plural world, he led the United States in a holy war to redeem Europe.[47]

Randolph S. Bourne, a radical critic of this "war-liberalism," recognized that Wilson's Flag Day address on June 14 marked the collapse of American strategy. The president had previously pursued a negotiated "peace without victory," but now supported the Allies in their desire for the military defeat of the Central Powers. Bourne saw the initiative for peace passing to the Council of Workers' and Soldiers' Deputies in Russia. "The war is pictured in that address," he stated in August 1917, "as a struggle to the death against the military empire of Mittel-Europa. The American role changes from that of mediator in the interest of international organization to that of formidable support to the breaking of this menace to the peace and liberty of Europe." He appreciated the irony of this change in American policy. He understood that if the Central Powers posed such a threat to the United States as to require an all-out response at this time, then the president should have recognized and responded to this danger long before he delivered his war message to Congress. Yet this kind of strategic consideration never

46 Henry Cabot Lodge, *The Senate and the League of Nations* (New York, 1925), 129-30; ALL to HCL, Apr. 28, May 3, Dec. 20, 25, 1916, Jan. 29, Feb. 1, 1917, HCL to ALL, May 1, Dec. 22, 28, 1916, Jan. 30, Feb. 3, 1917, A. Lawrence Lowell Papers, Harvard University Archives; WW to Smith, Dec. 29, 1916, *PWW*, XLI, 354.
47 *PPWW*, V, 2, 22, 53; JPT to WW, March 24, 1917, JPT Papers, Box 5.

troubled Wilson as his reaction to the European war reflected instead his ideological orientation.[48]

With a false sense of national security, Wilson overestimated his capacity to control international affairs. He never recognized American dependence on the Allies. Despite his change of policy in 1917, he remained aloof. In an interview in mid-July with Sir William Wiseman, head of British intelligence operations in the United States, he "pointed out that while the U.S. was now ready to take her place as a world-power, the strong feeling throughout the country was to play a 'lone hand,' and not commit herself to any alliance with any foreign power." With a unilateral approach to wartime diplomacy, he wanted to avoid the complications of Allied secret treaties. Wiseman subsequently observed that Wilson "has the greatest confidence in the future of the Anglo-Saxon race, and believes that the security of the World can best be maintained by an understanding between the democracies of Great Britain and the United States." His liberal crusade enjoyed strong support at home. Yet Americans wanted no alliance. Their attitude toward the Old World expressed an absence of fear about the war's consequences. Wiseman advised that "the American people do not consider themselves in any danger from the Central Powers." American ignorance created difficulties but also an opportunity. Wiseman saw the chance for British leaders to shape the emerging role of the United States in European affairs.[49]

Wilson recognized that the United States still lacked a clear definition of peace terms. Realizing that ideals would eventually need to be translated into more precise guidelines, he asked House to organize the Inquiry for the purpose of gathering data and preparing for the future peace conference. Welcoming this assignment, House began to assemble a group of experts. For now, however, the absence of a policy to direct American military action toward a goal more definite than victory caused no alarm in the Wilson administration.[50]

The Bolshevik revolution in Russia finally stimulated Wilson into defining war aims in greater detail. In his annual message on December 4, 1917, Wilson elaborated his assessment of the war. Although acknowledging the yearning for peace in Russia and throughout the world, he reaffirmed his determination to achieve victory. He denied that the Allied and Associated Powers had any aggressive ambitions. Vaguely defining their aims, he heralded a future league. He intended to exclude the Imperial

---

48   Bourne, "The Collapse of American Strategy," *The Seven Arts*, II (Aug. 1917), in Resek, *War and the Intellectuals*, 22-35; *PPWW*, V, 60-67; EMH Diary, June 13-15, 1917.

49   W. B. Fowler, *British-American Relations, 1917-1918: The Role of Sir William Wiseman* (Princeton, 1969), 243-54; Memorandum on Anglo-American Relations, Aug. 1917, William Wiseman Papers, Drawer 90, File 4, Yale University Library; EMH to DLG, July 15, 1917, EMH Papers, 12/32.

50   EMH to WW, Aug. 24, Sept. 4, 1917, EMH Papers, 49/9; WW to EMH, Sept. 2, 1917, EMH Papers, 49/18; EMH Diary, Aug. 29, Sept. 4-5, 7, 10, 13, 20, 22, 25, Oct. 5-6, 13, 1917; JJP to WW, Oct. 8, 1917, John J. Pershing Papers, Box 213, Library of Congress. For the organization and work of the Inquiry, see Lawrence E. Gelfand, *The Inquiry: American Preparations for Peace, 1917-1919* (New Haven, 1963).

German government from this new community of peaceful nations. "The worst that can happen to the detriment of the German people is this," he explained, "that if they should still, after the war is over, continue to be obliged to live under ambitious and intriguing masters interested to disturb the peace of the world, men or classes of men whom the other peoples of the world could not trust, it might be impossible to admit them to the partnership of nations which must henceforth guarantee the world's peace. That partnership must be a partnership of peoples, not a mere partnership of governments." He thought the Russian people's failure to understand American and Allied aims, as he conceived them, accounted for their desire for peace without victory. The provisional government might not have fallen to the Bolsheviks, he thought, if the Russians had correctly understood the western nations' purposes.[51]

Wilson delivered this unilateral statement in his annual message after the Allies had refused to endorse an American summary of war aims. At the Inter-Allied Conference in Paris, although House and the Allied premiers succeeded in establishing the Supreme War Council to unify military strategy, they failed to agree on terms for an acceptable peace. House reported this outcome to Wilson, who decided to formulate his own pronouncement. Lansing encouraged him to seize this opportunity to increase the German people's dissatisfaction with their government's policies. Using data which House obtained from the Inquiry, the president began preparing his famous Fourteen Points address.[52]

As Wilson completed his preparations, Lloyd George outlined the British Empire's war aims on January 5, 1918. He reversed his government's earlier reluctance to state publicly its minimum objectives and expressed many of the themes Wilson had previously articulated. He asserted that "a just and a lasting peace" would require the restoration of sanctity of treaties, the settlement of territorial disputes on the basis of self-determination, and "the creation of some international organization, to limit the burden of armaments and diminish the probability of war." With this last vague reference, the British prime minister committed his government to a league of nations as an essential condition for peace.[53]

After reading Lloyd George's speech and recognizing the similarity between British and American objectives, the president momentarily hesitated but then delivered his Fourteen Points address to a joint session of

5 1   *PPWW*, V, 128-39.
5 2   DLG to EMH, Sept. 4, 1917, EMH to DLG, Sept. 24, 1917, EMH Papers, 49/9; EMH Diary, Sept. 16, 26, 29, Oct. 13, 21, 24, 29, Nov. 3, 10, 13-14, 16-17, 20-22, 24-25, 27, Dec. 1, 5, 17-18, 22, 31, 1917, Jan. 3-4, 9, 1918; RL to WW, Dec. 25, 1917, The Present Situation: The War Aims and Peace Terms It Suggests, WW Papers, Ser. 5A, Box 2.
5 3   AJB to Cecil, Dec. 29, 1917, Arthur J. Balfour Papers, 49738/183-90, British Museum, London; EMH Diary, Jan. 19, 1918; EMH to WW, Jan. 20, 1918, EMH Papers, 49/10; Page to RL, Jan. 6, 1918, Address of the British Prime Minister Before the Trade Union Conference at London, Jan. 5, 1918, *FR*1918, I, 4-12. An excellent study of British war aims is V. H. Rothwell, *British War Aims and Peace Diplomacy*, 1914-1918 (Oxford, 1971).

Congress on January 8, 1918. Outlining his peace program, he called for "open covenants of peace, openly arrived at" to replace the old diplomacy of secret treaties. He advocated freedom of the seas, equality of trade, and reduction of armaments "to the lowest point consistent with domestic safety." He recommended "absolutely impartial adjustment" of colonial claims, but without specifying how to achieve this goal. For the first time in the American diplomatic tradition, the president suggested guidelines for the settlement of territorial questions in Europe and the Middle East. Despite its previous diplomatic, maritime and commercial relations with European countries, the United States had never before involved itself in the political and territorial issues of the Old World to this extent. In his final point, he reaffirmed his commitment to a postwar league, proclaiming that "a general association of nations must be formed under specific covenants for the purpose of affording mutual guarantees of political independence and territorial integrity to great and small states alike." He offered the prospect of membership for Germany. "We do not wish to fight her either with arms or with hostile arrangements of trade," he pledged, "if she is willing to associate herself with us and the other peace-loving nations of the world in covenants of justice and law and fair dealing." With adoption and implementation of these conditions, he anticipated a new era of peace.[54]

Wilson's address evoked a generally favorable response in Allied countries. Lloyd George conveyed his gratitude that British and American peace policies were "so entirely in harmony." In the French Chamber of Deputies, Foreign Minister Stéphen Pichon endorsed the principles which both Lloyd George and Wilson had proclaimed. He said "a just and durable peace" required the preservation of the "sacred character" of treaties, adherence to self-determination in the adjustment of territorial disputes, and limitation of armaments. This French program coincided closely with the British prime minister's except for placing less emphasis on a league. "As for the society of nations," Pichon stated, "victory alone can bring it to realization." That was something the Allied and Associated Powers could create after they defeated the Central Powers. Wilson appreciated this apparent unity of purpose between the United States and the Allies. Yet Americans were still detached from the realities of war in Europe.[55]

5 4   PPWW, V, 155-62; FR1918, I, 12-17; RL to WW, Jan. 2, 1918, Francis to RL, Dec. 31, 1917, RL, Memorandum on Non-Recognition of a Russian Government, Jan. 6, 1918, WW Papers, Ser. 5A, Box 2.
5 5   Barclay to WW, Jan. 13, 1918, WW to Barclay, Jan. 16, 1918, WW Papers, Ser. 4, File 63; W. H. Page to RL, Jan. 10, 1918, N. Page to RL, Jan. 10, 1918, Sharp to RL, Jan. 10, 14, 1918, FR1918, I, 17-21, 28-31; Wiseman, Notes on Interview with the President, Jan. 23, 1918, Wiseman to Drummond, Jan. 25, 25, 1918, AJB Papers, 49741/2-13; Fowler, British-American Relations, 254-58. An excellent study of French war aims is D. Stevenson, French War Aims Against Germany, 1914-1919 (Oxford, 1982). For British reactions to Wilson, see especially Laurence W. Martin, Peace Without Victory: Woodrow Wilson and the British Liberals (New Haven, 1958), and Sterling J. Kernek, "Distractions of Peace During War: The Lloyd George Government's Reactions to Woodrow Wilson, December, 1916 – November, 1918," Transactions of the American Philosophical Society, New Series, Vol. 65, Part 2 (Philadelphia, 1975).

Wilson's Fourteen Points encountered hostile criticism from Berlin and Vienna. On January 24, German chancellor Georg von Hertling and Austro-Hungarian foreign minister Ottokar Czernin von Chudenitz rejected Wilson's conditions for peace. They suggested that some of these principles, despite their impracticality, might serve as a basis for negotiations. Avoiding any commitment, they voiced minimal interest in a league. "We have sympathy," said Hertling, "with the idea of a league of nations. If proposals are based on the spirit of humanity we shall be ready to study the question." Czernin adopted a neutral stance, announcing only that from Austria-Hungary Wilson would not encounter "any opposition to his proposal regarding the idea of a league of nations."[56]

III

Wilson's ambivalence toward negotiating with the Imperial German government created a real dilemma for him in defining his conception of the future League. His vague references to a new order after the war left open the prospect of a reformed Germany's membership in this community of nations. But if the German people refused to change their government, and the Allied and Associated Powers concluded peace with the existing German rulers, he would face the question of Imperial Germany's inclusion in the League. The Allies easily answered this question by rejecting the possibility. But this solution challenged Wilson's ideal of a universal world community, for it would perpetuate the wartime divisions. It implied the maintenance of a balance of power, or precisely what he hoped to overcome. Either by participating in this postwar balance of power or by imposing a new government onto Germany, the United States would entangle itself in the Old World. One way or another, the very existence of a hostile Imperial German government created a dilemma for the president. The realities of European affairs simply refused to conform to his vision of a league that would enable the United States to exercise controlling influence and yet escape entanglement in Europe. Confronted with this dilemma, he found it exceedingly difficult to define his idea of a league in greater detail than he had in his Fourteen Points address.

Wilson resisted various pressures to develop a specific proposal. In January two key members of the Inquiry, Sidney Mezes and Walter Lippmann, had suggested to House that the president convene a conference of the Allied and Associated Powers in Washington to formulate a league plan. Reflecting Wilson's attitude, House opposed the proposal because a league created during the war would inevitably exclude the Central Powers. While the United States delayed, the British government took the initiative by organizing a committee under the chairmanship of Sir Walter G. F.

56 L Diary, III, Jan. 10, 1918; Garrett to RL, Jan. 24, 1918, WW to RL, Jan. 30, 1918, FR1918, I, 38-42, 54-59.

Phillimore. Representing the Foreign Office, Sir Robert Cecil supervised the Phillimore committee's planning. Through Wiseman and House, he hoped to collaborate with the United States in establishing a league.[57]

The League to Enforce Peace also exerted its influence on the Wilson administration. In the summer of 1917 it had tried to enlist the president's cooperation in developing plans for safeguarding world peace, but he had declined. He was not yet ready to commit himself to any specific outline of a new order. Nor was he willing to encumber himself by too close an association with this particular pro-league lobby. Early in March 1918 the League to Enforce Peace again attempted to encourage Wilson to join in formulating a plan. Theodore Marburg, chairman of its committee on foreign organization, requested the opportunity to discuss with him the views of Lord Bryce, a former British ambassador to the United States. But he declined to meet Marburg. "I do not feel that it is wise to discuss now the formal constitution of a league to enforce peace," the president replied.[58]

To promote its position, the League to Enforce Peace scheduled a convention in May. Fearful that speakers might discuss the future peace treaty, including plans for a league, Wilson attempted to dissuade its leaders from holding the convention. He instructed Bainbridge Colby, a member of the United States Shipping Board, to request Taft to cancel it. Colby's appeal not to embarrass the Wilson administration with a premature discussion of a new international organization failed to persuade Taft, who saw no legitimate reason for the president's anxiety. Convinced that victory over the Central Powers must precede the establishment of any league, Taft resented his attempt to interfere with this "'Win the War' Convention" of the League to Enforce Peace. Sharing this information with Lowell, he complained: "Our President is something of an enigma to a good many people. More than in the action of any man whom I have known to exercise great responsibility, he allows personal consideration to influence him, and I cannot but think that he has some quirk in his mind that the situation is such that he ought to be permitted alone, solemnly closeted with a typewriter in the White House, intuitively to dig out the provisions that ought to enter into a treaty of peace, until he gets stuck and then calls in those eminent statesmen and international jurists, Col. House and Mr. [George] Creel." As Taft observed, Wilson wanted to keep a free hand in planning for peace. He criticized "the folly of these League to Enforce Peace butters-in." Its executive committee

---

57   EMH Diary, Jan. 10, 1918; Drummond to Wiseman, Feb. 9, 1918, Wiseman to Cecil, Feb. 14, 1918, EMH Papers, 20/47. For the origins of the league of nations idea in Great Britain, see the still valuable study by Henry R. Winkler, *The League of Nations Movement in Great Britain, 1914-1919* (New Brunswick, 1952), and the excellent recent monograph by George W. Egerton, *Great Britain and the Creation of the League of Nations: Strategy, Politics, and International Organization, 1914-1919* (Chapel Hill, 1978).

58   EMH Diary, Aug. 25, 1917; Short to McCormick, Aug. 15, 1917, McCormick to Short, Aug. 15, 1917, Questions for Determination, [Aug. 14, 1917], Vance C. McCormick Papers, Drawer 39, File 57, Yale University Library; Marburg to WW, March 5, 1918, WW to Marburg, March 8, 1918, WW Papers, Ser. 4, File 297.

refused his request to cancel the convention, but otherwise Taft and Lowell endeavored to cooperate with him.[59]

Wilson wanted to maintain his control. Seeking to bring others under his influence while postponing consideration of a league, he asked House to arrange an informal meeting with Taft, Lowell and Root. "My own conviction, as you know," he informed his friend, "is that the administrative *constitution* of the League must *grow* and not be made; that we must *begin* with solemn covenants, covering mutual guarantees of political independence and territorial integrity (if the final territorial arrangements of the peace conference are fair and satisfactory and *ought* to be perpetuated), and that the method of carrying those mutual pledges out should be left to develop of itself, case by case." This summary expressed Wilson's organic view of development as well as his preference for broad principles. Although anticipating the mutual obligations of Article 10 of the Covenant, he hesitated to make a commitment to the postwar political and territorial settlement or to any administrative structure. An executive authority under the control of several nations, he feared, would produce "a harvest of jealousy and distrust." Anticipating resistance, he predicted that "the United States Senate would never ratify any treaty which put the force of the United States at the disposal of any such group or body. Why begin at the impossible end when there is a possible end and it is feasible to plant a system which will slowly but surely ripen into fruition?" Preferring to await this development, he hoped to avoid controversy for the moment.[60]

At Wilson's request, House invited Taft, Lowell and Root to a luncheon on April 11 along with Lansing, Mezes and the Archbishop of York, who was active in British planning for a league. Unable to attend, Lansing sent his views to House. He focused on the crucial question of the future League's membership. Believing that universal democracy was the best guarantee of permanent peace, Lansing favored membership only for democratic nations. In his opinion, any league which included both democratic and autocratic governments would be unreliable. "Until Autocracy is entirely discredited and Democracy becomes not only the dominant but the practically universal principle in the political systems of the world," he concluded, "I fear a League of Nations, particularly one purposing to employ force, would not function." Like most Republican leaders, he thought that any viable league must await the defeat of the Central Powers.[61]

House shared the views of Wilson and Lansing with his luncheon guests. He voiced his own skepticism about Lansing's idea of universal democracy as the key to peace, noting that even democratic nations such as Great Britain and France had on occasion engaged in serious conflicts. His Republican

59   WHT to ALL, March 19, 1918, ALL Papers; WW to EMH, March 20, 1918, EMH Papers, Letterbook IV; Memorandum for the President, March 23, 1918, Colby to WW, March 26, 1918, WHT to Colby, March 24, 1918, WHT to JPT, March 24, 1918, WW Papers, Ser. 4, File 156.
60   WW to EMH, March 22, 1918, EMH Papers, Letterbook IV.
61   RL to WW, Apr. 8, 1918, EMH Papers, 12/12, and *FR:Lansing*, II, 118-20.

guests agreed with the secretary's emphasis on military victory, but not with his preference for delay. They were unwilling to entrust the planning for peace to the president. They discussed eventual organization of a conference of nations and a court of arbitration to deal with international disputes which threatened war. Basic to their thought was the idea that any war was a matter of interest to all nations and, consequently, that prudent statesmanship should prepare appropriate international institutions to preserve peace. Unwilling to delay this urgent task, they delegated to Root the responsibility for drafting a memorandum on the subject.[62]

Ignoring Wilson's request for postponement, the League to Enforce Peace proceeded with its planning for an international organization. On April 11, the same day Taft and Lowell attended House's luncheon, its executive committee approved a tentative draft treaty for a league. It proposed various methods to settle disputes, including international inquiry and conciliation, and also arbitration or a judicial hearing. To coerce a recalcitrant state into using these methods, it would obligate the members to employ diplomatic, economic and military force. The draft treaty called for a council of conciliation, a court, and a congress to deal with international law, reduction of armaments, and other matters affecting world peace or "the progress or betterment of human relations." Representation would favor the great powers, whose chief executives would constitute the league's executive body. This body would decide when to employ the prescribed sanctions. Marburg sent this tentative draft to Bryce along with a copy of Wilson's earlier letter urging postponement. Bryce avoided an endorsement of this particular proposal, sharing the president's opinion that it was premature to open a public discussion. He proposed instead a joint Anglo-American committee to study and develop plans for a league. He wanted this work, although done privately, to take place in cooperation with the British and American governments. When Marburg conveyed this proposal to the White House, Wilson again declined to collaborate. He informed Marburg that, despite his respect for Bryce, any such international consultation would become public knowledge and "we would start a discussion of the very thing which ought not now to be discussed, a discussion in the field where jealousy and competitive interest is more likely to block the whole business."[63]

The League to Enforce Peace continued to apply pressure on Wilson. In preparation for its convention in May, the chairman of its organization committee requested a message from him to the five thousand delegates expected to attend. Having failed to persuade Taft and Lowell to cancel this convention, the president showed little enthusiasm for it now. He expressed his interest in the meeting, but refrained from giving any endorsement to the League to Enforce Peace. He stated his "very warm support of the idea of a

---

62   EMH Diary, Apr. 11, 1918.
63   Tentative Draft of a Treaty for a League of Nations, Apr. 11, 1918, McCormick Papers, 39/59; Marburg to WW, May 3, 1918, Bryce to Marburg, [recd. May 1, 1918], WW to Marburg, May 6, 1918, WW Papers, Ser. 4, File 279.

league of nations to preserve and insure the peace of the world" but emphasized that it was "most imprudent" at this time even to discuss a specific constitution.[64]

While Wilson hesitated, British preparations moved ahead. Cecil circulated an interim report of the Phillimore committee to the War Cabinet in May. This report proposed a draft convention for a league of the Allied and Associated Powers. Designed to preserve peace among these wartime partners, this proposal provided for submission of disputes either to arbitration or to a conference of their diplomatic representatives at the new league's seat. After an investigation, this conference would attempt to make a unanimous recommendation. All league members were prohibited from resorting to war without first following this procedure, or against another state which complied with the conference's recommendation. Any violation of this covenant would be regarded *ipso facto* as war, requiring economic and military sanctions against the aggressor. The draft convention opened the possibility of using the same procedures for settling disputes with non-member states. However, it excluded a commitment to mutual defense against external aggression. The Phillimore committee, not wanting to provoke opposition in the United States, refrained from advocating a defensive alliance because the League to Enforce Peace had omitted this provision from its proposal.[65]

At Cecil's request, Wiseman discussed plans for a league with House. He recommended most of the Phillimore committee's interim report, but did not convince him. Following this meeting, House summarized his views in a letter to Cecil. He thought a moral standard for nations equivalent to that for honorable individuals would constitute the most essential feature of any league. Unlike the League to Enforce Peace, he refused to call for a world court, preferring less formal procedures for arbitration. House also opposed an international force to implement any court's decisions. He wanted the diplomatic representatives of the league members in a country such as Switzerland or Holland to serve as peace delegates for the purpose of insisting that potential belligerents settle their disputes by arbitration. If dissatisfied with the results, these nations might then appeal to the league itself. Unless three-fourths of the peace delegates voted to overturn the arbitral award, all league members would be obligated to employ diplomatic and economic sanctions, and possibly physical force, to enforce it. In agreement with his April 11 luncheon guests, House affirmed that "any war, no matter how remote or how insignificant the country involved, is the concern of all nations." Stressing interdependence rather than pluralism, he failed to recognize that all nations were not equally interested in every war. Like Wilson, he proposed that the league members should guarantee each other's

---

64   Macauley to WW, May 14, 1918, WW to Macauley, May 16, 1918, WW Papers, Ser. 4, File 4767; McCormick to EMH, June 5, 1918, EMH Papers, 13/18.

65   Interim Report of the Committee on the League of Nations, March 20, 1918, WW Papers, Ser. 5A, Box 3; David Hunter Miller, *The Drafting of the Covenant* (New York, 1928), II, 3-6.

territorial integrity, thereby anticipating Article 10 of the Covenant. Sharing his views with the president, House urged him to develop a practical plan for a league. He warned him not to hesitate any longer, because others in Great Britain or France, or in the United States, might offer an appealing proposal for postwar collective security and thereby prevent him from gaining credit as "the champion of the idea." Appealing to Wilson's ego, House tried to persuade him to seize the initiative.[66]

Pressure on the president continued from the League to Enforce Peace. Hamilton Holt, a member of its executive committee, spent three months in Europe visiting the western front and discussing the league idea. In England he held long interviews with Balfour and Cecil at the Foreign Office and with a study group of the League of Nations Society. In France he met President Raymond Poincaré and Premier Georges Clemenceau as well as Léon Bourgeois, head of the official commission to develop French plans for a league. Holt also discussed conditions of future peace with King Victor Emmanuel of Italy as well as Premier Vittorio Orlando and Foreign Minister Sidney Sonnino. On the basis of these interviews, he concluded that British and French leaders were ready immediately to organize a league, obviously excluding Germany from membership. He suggested that committees from the United States, England and France, appointed either officially by the governments or unofficially by groups like the League to Enforce Peace, should meet to formulate a joint plan. House attempted to prevent the League to Enforce Peace from endorsing Holt's suggestion. He shared his letter to Cecil with Lowell, expressing the hope that Wilson and Cecil would endorse his own proposal. Despite House's request for delay, the League to Enforce Peace's executive committee adopted Holt's recommendation. Early in July, Lowell requested the president's cooperation in appointing a committee to join with similar Allied committees "to consider the establishment of a League of Nations now." Wilson refused, observing that this was "a question of government policy" and an integral part of relations with the Allies. He urged the League to Enforce Peace not to establish any international connections, which he would consider "very embarrassing."[67]

At this critical stage in the war, Wilson emphasized military victory more than details of a future peace. He delivered a ringing appeal to arms at Mount Vernon on July 4, 1918. Calling for total victory, he said "the settlement must be final. There can be no compromise. No halfway decision would be tolerable." In his summary of the ends of American policy, the president incorporated views of his major advisers. Like Lansing, he

---

66   EMH Diary, June 20, 1918; Wiseman, Memorandum: The League of Nations, June 22, 1918, EMH Papers, 20/47; EMH to Cecil, June 25, 1918, EMH Papers, 4/38; EMH to WW, June 25, 1918, EMH Papers, 49/10.

67   McCormick to Short, May 24, 1918, Short to McCormick, May 23, 1918, Holt to Short, Apr. 27, 1918, McCormick Papers, 39/59; EMH Diary, June 24, 1918; EMH to WW, July 8, 1918, EMH Papers, 49/11A; ALL to WW, July 10, 1918, WW to ALL, July 11, 1918, WW Papers, Ser. 4, File 4767; WW to ALL, July 11, 1918, RSB Papers, Ser 1, Box 9; Holt to WW, July 12, 1918, WW Papers, Ser. 4, File 333.

denounced autocratic governments. He called for settlement of all questions in accordance with self-determination, excluding external mastery of one nation over another. In agreement with House, he wanted all nations to accept "the same principles of honor and respect for the common law of civilized society that govern the individual citizens of all modern states." Reiterating his support for a league, he proposed "an organization of peace which shall make it certain that the combined power of free nations will check every invasion of right and serve to make peace and justice the more secure by affording a definite tribunal of opinion to which all must submit and by which every international readjustment that cannot be amicably agreed upon by the people directly concerned shall be sanctioned." Instead of confronting the hard questions concerning this ideal international community, he merely repeated his vague principles.[68]

As victory approached, Wilson finally proceeded with plans for a league. Forwarding his copy of the Phillimore committee's draft convention, he asked House to revise it in accordance with the views in his letter to Cecil. House welcomed this assignment, but anticipated difficulty on the question of German membership. He favored Germany's eventual inclusion but expected French opposition. Consulting with the lawyer David Hunter Miller as well as Wiseman, he prepared a draft for the president. The purpose of a league, House stated, should be "the maintenance throughout the world of peace, security, progress and orderly government." As the "keystone" of his plan, he again stressed individual honor and morality as the standard for international conduct. To reduce the Allies' resistance to Germany's admission, he sought to abolish espionage. Developing this particular recommendation in consultation with a British intelligence officer was especially ironic. House elaborated the Phillimore committee's plan for a conference. To assist the delegates in making inquiries and preparing reports on international conflicts, he proposed a secretariat. Reversing his earlier position, he now called for a world court to interpret treaties and settle other judicial questions. He continued, however, to favor arbitration as the principal method of resolving disputes. Except for issues settled by diplomacy or the court, House stipulated binding arbitration. To force compliance, he provided for the sanction of a total blockade. Suggesting a league limited to the major powers, he expected the weaker non-member states to comply with the same procedure on an *ad hoc* basis, or suffer the sanction of cessation of all commerce and intercourse.

Despite his willingness to exclude small nations from membership, House envisaged a global instrument for peace. "Any war or threat of war is a matter of concern to the League of Nations," he affirmed. Anticipating Article 10 of the Covenant, he advocated a mutual guarantee of territorial integrity and political independence. Yet he provided for the possibility of

---

68 *PPWW*, V, 231-35; *FR1918*, I, 268-71; Wiseman to Drummond, June 15, 1918, AJB Papers, 49741/89.

territorial changes in accordance with national self-determination. In the balance between enforcement and revision, House affirmed that "the peace of the world is superior in importance and interest to questions of boundary." He justified this revisionist provision by suggesting that Canada and parts of Mexico might sometime desire to join the United States and that he wanted no rigid prohibition of such territorial adjustments. House added another novel feature. He assigned to the league delegates the task of reducing national armaments.[69]

House attempted to muster support for his proposal. He shared parts of it, as well as his letter to Cecil, with Holt, who came to discuss his European trip. Holt criticized the guarantee of territorial integrity until he learned how House proposed to balance enforcement with revision. In contrast to Holt's apparent receptivity, Cecil rejected House's view. Expressing his continuing preference for the Phillimore plan, he questioned the basic precepts of House's draft. He doubted the feasibility of arbitration as the primary method of settling disputes. He persisted in believing that discussion in an international conference, backed by possible sanctions, would offer the best prospect for peace. Although willing to affirm an international code of honor, Cecil refused to rely on it. He sympathized with the French demand for enforcement of the peace conditions, despite his aversion to British involvement in a new Holy Alliance. Fearful of entanglement, he was reluctant to endorse a mutual guarantee of territorial integrity. He hoped to avoid a commitment to a new international status quo. Cecil's response disappointed House, who complained to Wilson that "he would make the League an innocuous affair and leave the world where it is now."[70]

In mid-August, while House was at his summer home in Magnolia, Massachusetts, the president went there to discuss a postwar league. Wiseman, already there, participated in the discussions. Wilson revised House's draft by eliminating the articles dealing with international honor and morality and with a world court. He confined to the preamble his allusion to honor and justice in international relations. Like House, he provided for a body of delegates consisting of ambassadors and ministers at the league's seat. He, too, proposed binding arbitration as the central method for resolving disputes. To enforce this requirement, he was willing to use force to impose a total blockade. Generally, however, Wilson hoped to limit obligations. In his version of the future Article 10, he balanced the guarantee of political independence and territorial integrity with the

6 9   WW to EMH, July 8, 1918, EMH Papers, Letterbook IV; EMH to WW, July 11, 14, 16, 1918, EMH Papers, 49/11A; Murray to Wiseman, July 5, 1918, Wiseman to Murray (EMH to EG), July 9, 1918, EMH Papers, 9/9; EMH Diary, July 9, 13-15, 1918; Viscount Grey, *The League of Nations* (New York, 1918), WW Papers, Ser. 5A, Box 3; Miller, *Drafting of the Covenant*, II, 7-11; Department of State, *Papers Relating to the Foreign Relations of the United States, 1919: The Paris Peace Conference*, I (Washington, 1942), 497-501.

7 0   EMH Diary, July 22, 1918; EMH to Cecil, July 13, 1918, Cecil to House, July 22, 1918, EMH Papers, 4/38; EMH to WW, Aug. 9, 1918, EMH Papers, 49/11A.

possibility of revision. Anticipating territorial changes, he affirmed that "the peace of the world is superior in importance to every question of political jurisdiction or boundary." He nevertheless considered his draft much stronger than the Phillimore plan. "It has no teeth," he told Wiseman. "I read it to the last page hoping to find something definite, but I could not." Wilson wanted to create a league at the peace conference and include its constitution in the peace treaty. "If we formed the league while we were still fighting," he explained, "it would inevitably be regarded as a sort of Holy Alliance aimed at Germany. This would not be the purpose of the American people. Germany should be invited to join the family of nations, providing she will behave according to the rules of the Society." He also sought to avoid criticism by postponing publication of any specific plan. He expected senators such as Lodge to denounce his draft as an excessive commitment to a utopian scheme, while advocates of a league would criticize it for falling short of their expectations. Having completed his first draft, Wilson hoped to retain his freedom in future planning for a postwar league.[71]

While Wilson was at Magnolia, House received the document that Root had, at the April 11 luncheon, promised to prepare. Root combined the consensus of that gathering with some of his own views. He called for universal acceptance of the principle that "an international breach of the peace is a matter which concerns every member of the Community of Nations." The international application of this principle, he stated in agreement with Wilson, would constitute "the enlargement of the Monroe Doctrine to take in the whole world." He advocated a new standard to replace the "old doctrine" which Germany had asserted in July 1914 by rejecting Grey's proposal for an international conference. "The change," he stressed, "involves a limitation of sovereignty, making every sovereign state subject to the superior right of a community of sovereign states to have the peace preserved, just as individual liberty is limited by being made subject to the superior right of the civil community to have the peace preserved." Root recommended "a league of peace." Without offering specific suggestions, he saw the need for appropriate institutions as a compelling "lesson from history." Yet he wanted no commitment which the United States would renounce during a future crisis. "Nothing can be worse in international affairs," he summarized one of his own characteristic themes, "than to make agreements and break them." Aware of the limits of American power, he opposed any excessive or universal promise. Yet he would consider an American obligation which might involve war under particular circumstances. He also suggested disarmament and destruction of the military autocracies of the Hohenzollerns and Hapsburgs. House and Wilson discussed Root's document in detail. The president, however, showed more

71   EMH Diary, Aug. 15, 1918; Wiseman to Reading, Aug. 18, 1918, AJB Papers, 49741/215-17, and David Lloyd George Papers, F/43/1/14, Beaverbrook Library; Fowler, *British-American Relations*, 278-83; WW to EMH, Sept. 7, 1918, EMH Papers, 49/19; Miller, *Drafting of the Covenant*, II, 12-15.

interest in winning Root's endorsement for the league idea than in heeding his admonition about prudent conduct of foreign relations.[72]

After reading Wiseman's report of his discussions with Wilson and House at Magnolia, Cecil agreed to postpone publication of the Phillimore plan. He hoped, however, to generate public support for the league idea to overcome anticipated resistance from British and European bureaucracies. He wanted to create favorable public opinion by appealing to a traditional sentiment. "What is wanted is a great ideal," Cecil informed Wiseman, "and that must be found in the old Hebrew – and let us add, Christian – conception of the reign of Peace." House, too, wished to develop a public constituency for a league. Apprehensive that Wilson's influence with the Allies and in the United States might diminish as victory approached, he expected Lloyd George and Clemenceau as well as Lodge to pose obstacles to a Wilsonian peace. With House's encouragement, the president decided to deliver an address on the future League. The prospect of defeating the Central Powers, arising from military success on the western front during the summer, helped to resolve the dilemma that had hindered him from giving greater clarity to his principles.[73]

Speaking in New York on September 27, Wilson outlined his conception of a league of nations. Despite his earlier ambivalence, he now regarded it as the "indispensable instrumentality" of permanent peace. Calling for its formation at the peace conference, he said "it cannot be formed now. If formed now, it would be merely a new alliance confined to the nations associated against a common enemy. It is not likely that it could be formed after the settlement. It is necessary to guarantee the peace; and the peace cannot be guaranteed as an afterthought." In the transformation of international relations which he envisaged, Wilson advocated the end of discriminatory and special advantages. In pursuit of his ideal of "impartial justice" and the "common interest," he asserted that "there can be no leagues or alliances or special covenants and understandings within the general common family of the League of Nations." He saw no contradiction between the universal and unilateral qualities of his foreign policy. While proposing global involvement of the United States in a postwar league, he reaffirmed the essence of the American isolationist tradition. "We still read Washington's immortal warning against 'entangling alliances' with full comprehension and an answering purpose," Wilson proclaimed. "But only special and limited alliances entangle; and we recognize and accept the duty of a new day in which we are permitted to hope for a general alliance which will avoid entanglements and clear the air of the world for common understandings and the maintenance of common rights." Defeat of the

---

72   EMH Diary, Aug. 18, 1918; ER to EMH, Aug. 16, 1918, EMH to ER, Aug. 23, 1918, EMH Papers, 17/12.
73   Cecil to Wiseman, Aug. 19, 1918, EMH Papers, 20/47; EMH to WW, Sept. 3, 1918, EMH Papers, 49/11A; EMH Diary, Aug. 22, 25, Sept. 9, 24, 1918.

Central Powers, he thought, would allow creation of this new world order.[74]

IV

Wilson's belief in the possibility of transforming international relations after the war expressed his progressive faith. Senator Lodge, with his pessimistic and realistic outlook, refused to endorse this redemptive mission. He saw the genuine tragedy of the war. He could not gloss over it by escaping into the future and embracing the ideal of a new community of nations. He ardently supported the American war effort to achieve victory, but not as the prelude to a league. "For those of us who have passed our lives under the old fabric of civilization," he confided to Root in July 1918, "it is not easy to end it as we are doing in the midst of these horrors and among the wrecks of the world, for it will be a wrecked world when the war ends, however it ends. However, there is nothing to do but fight on and do everything we possibly can to win." Lodge identified with the "philosophy of life" that Henry Adams had expounded. The senator now found relief from the war in editing *The Education* for publication. The conservative philosophy that he shared with Adams, with deep skepticism about progress in human affairs, led him to approach peace from a perspective radically different from Wilson's liberalism.[75]

Lodge shared his views on the future peace with Bryce. Rejecting Lord Lansdowne's appeal for negotiations between the Allied and Associated Powers and the Central Powers, he preferred to fight the war to a victorious end. Like Wilson, he yearned for an enduring peace. But rather than look to a league as the epitome of a new international order, Lodge wanted a balance of power in Europe. He advocated the restoration of Belgium and the return of Alsace-Lorraine to France. He also saw the new nations of Poland, Czechoslovakia and Yugoslavia as vital barriers against Germany's expansion eastward. Approving some of Italy's territorial claims, he favored disruption of the Austro-Hungarian Empire. In contrast, he did not advocate destruction of the German Empire, although he sought to curb its power. He felt confident that Americans would support this peace program. "We have no territory to gain and seek no conquests," he informed Bryce, "but I think the American people are determined on placing Germany in a position where she can never again menace the peace, liberty and civilization of other nations." These peace aims, Bryce assured the senator, would also satisfy the Allies, or at least the British, who wanted a victorious conclusion to the war.[76]

Wilson's conception of a league, in Lodge's view, was irrelevant to the real

---

74   *PPWW*, V, 253-61; *FR*1918, I, 316-21.

75   HCL to ER, July 18, 1918, Henry Cabot Lodge Papers, File 1918 (R-Z), Massachusetts Historical Society.

76   HCL to Bryce, Aug. 2, Sept. 28, 1918, Bryce to HCL, Sept. 4, 1918, HCL Papers, File 1918 (General Correspondence, A-G).

task of peacemaking. Destruction of Germany's capacity for conquest would offer the best prospect for peace. The senator demanded "unconditional surrender." For the future he desired a close relationship between the United States and the Allies. "As to the League to Enforce Peace," he informed Bryce: "There are many very excellent and able men in this country who have favored it. As an abstract proposition it is not well liked in the Senate, and there is a strong feeling just now that it has been caught up by Germany to be used to distract attention from the real issues. One thing I am certain this country will never do, and that is enter into a League to Enforce Peace if Germany is a member of the league. I think it is a matter which can well wait until the termination of the war. We have got a good league now – the Allies and the United States. As Roosevelt said the other day, it is a going concern. Why look for anything else at this moment?" Lodge wanted to concentrate on winning the war and curbing Germany's power before bothering to consider some new international organization.[77]

Early in October, Germany and Austria-Hungary appealed to Wilson for peace on the basis of his Fourteen Points. Before submitting this request to the Allies, he required an explicit acceptance of his principles. He also sent House to Europe to consult the Allies about an armistice, for he wanted to commit them as well to his Fourteen Points. Considering the first three and last of these points as "the essentially American terms" of his peace program, he refused to consider conditions which would represent "only European arrangements of peace." He demanded abolition of secret treaties, freedom of the seas, equality of trade opportunities, and especially establishment of a league. Lloyd George opposed freedom of the seas without qualification because he apprehended potential implications for the British navy. With Wilson's authorization, House threatened a separate peace with Germany and expansion of the American navy unless the Allies accepted the Fourteen Points. But when this threat failed, he compromised with the Allied premiers by approving their reservation on freedom of the seas. He regarded their general acceptance of the president's peace program as "a great diplomatic victory." Wilson endorsed this compromise, thereby preserving essential unity with the Allies in support of his Fourteen Points. All of the belligerents now committed themselves to these conditions for peace.[78]

77   HCL to Bryce, Oct. 14, 1918, HCL to Beck, Sept. 28, 1918, HCL Papers, File 1918 (General Correspondence, A-G).
78   EMH Diary, Oct. 9, 13, 15, 28-31, 1918; Oederlin to WW, Oct. 6, 1918, Ekengren to RL, Oct. 7, 1918, RL to Oederlin, Oct. 8, 1918, Oederlin to RL, Oct. 14, 1918, FR1918, I, 421-27; EMH to WW, Nov. 3 (#38), 3 (#41), 4 (#42), 1918, EMH Papers, 49/11B, WW Papers, Ser. 5C, Box 1, and FR1918, I, 448, 455-57, 460-62; DLG to EMH, Nov. 3, 1918, EMH Papers, 12/32; WW to EMH, c. Oct. 29 (#3), 1918, WW Papers, Ser. 2, Box 186, and FR:PPC, I, 285; WW to EMH, Oct. 30 (#4), 1918, EMH Papers, 49/19, and FR1918, I, 423; WW to EMH, Oct. 31 (#6), 1918, EMH Papers, 49/13, and FR1918, I, 427; WW to EMH, Nov. 4 (#8), 4 (#9), 1918, EMH Papers, 49/19, and WW Papers, Ser. 2, Box 187; EMH to WW, Oct. 30 (#4), 31 (#5), 1918, EMH Papers, 49/11A, and WW Papers, Ser. 2, Box 186; EMH to WW, Nov. 5 (#6), 1918, EMH Papers, 49/11B, and WW Papers, Ser. 2, Box 187; Auchincloss Diary, Oct. 11, 29 – Nov. 4, 1918, Gordon Auchincloss Papers, Drawer 55, Files 83-84, Yale University Library; Geddes to DLG, Oct. 13, 1918, DLG Papers,

When Wilson began to exchange notes with the Imperial German government, Lodge feared that he might compromise with the enemy, thereby losing what had been won on the battlefield. To prevent the president from negotiating an inconclusive peace, Lodge insisted upon "unconditional surrender." "The result must justify the sacrifices," he told the Senate. "Nothing else is possible and nothing will justify those sacrifices but putting Germany where she can not again break out like an armed lunatic upon the world. That will do more than any league of peace. Are we going into a league to enforce peace with Germany as a partner? The way to compel the peace of the world is to break Germany down and make her accept our terms." He affirmed that the Republican party, and the American people as a whole, desired complete victory. Some of Wilson's loyal defenders, such as Senator John Sharp Williams of Mississippi, shared this sentiment. Lodge dreaded the prospect that Wilson would allow Germany to escape defeat in order to leave its power as a counterbalance to the Allies so as to enhance his own personal influence at the peace conference. "He wants," Lodge apprehended, "to be the great world figure in making the peace. If Germany surrenders unconditionally, he will only share in making the peace with the Allies. His hold over the Allies is the German Army in existence, which makes our Army and our alliance indispensable." Insisting on "unconditional surrender," Lodge endeavored to thwart any attempt by the president to increase his own personal power at the expense of the Allies.[79]

Wilson steered a course through the armistice negotiations that failed to confirm Lodge's worst suspicions. On November 5, Lansing notified the Imperial German government that the Allied and Associated Powers were willing to conclude peace in accordance with his principles. Prospects for victory against the Central Powers rapidly improved with the Austro-Hungarian Empire's collapse. With the Allies increasingly dependent upon American supplies and financial assistance, the president determined to fulfill his vision of peace. "America is the leader of the liberal thought of the world," he assured Senator Key Pittman of Nevada, "and nobody from any quarter should be allowed to interfere with or impair that leadership without giving an account of himself, which can be made very difficult." Before the war ended on November 11, 1918, Germany became a republic with Kaiser Wilhelm II's abdication. When representatives of this new republic signed the armistice, House rejoiced that "autocracy is dead." Wilson made a similarly extravagant affirmation to a joint session of Congress. Looking to the future, he projected as the American mission "the establishment of just

F/18/2/23. See also Arthur Walworth, *America's Moment, 1918: American Diplomacy at the End of World War I* (New York, 1977), 1-73.
79   U.S. Senate, 65 Cong., 2 Sess., *Congressional Record*, Vol. 56, 11170-72; HCL to Thayer, Oct. 14, 17, 1918, HCL Papers, File 1918 (R-Z); HCL to Bigelow, Oct. 12, 1918, HCL to Chapman, Oct. 15, 1918, HCL Papers, File 1918 (General Correspondence, A-G); Williams to WW, Oct. 14, 1918, WW to Williams, Oct. 17, 1918, WW Papers, Ser. 2, Box 185.

democracy throughout the world." From his fundamentally different perspective, Lodge felt no such optimism about the future shape of peace. He feared that the president, with his fixation on general principles, might still sacrifice the military victory at the peace conference.[80]

Wilson's idea of collective security expressed his vision of the future. During the armistice negotiations, Wiseman observed that "the American is undoubtedly an idealist. He was never afraid of Germany, or jealous of her. American troops go to Europe with a rather vague idea that they are going to democratize Europe, and put the Kaiser in particular, and all autocrats generally, out of business; an ingenuous notion that they want to make the rest of the world as democratic as they believe their own country to be." Yet Americans combined a practicality with their missionary impulse. The president epitomized this dualistic character. "He is by turns a great idealist and a shrewd politician," Wiseman noted. Wilson approached the peace conference as a practical idealist, not as a realistic statesman seeking a new balance of power.[81]

For the sake of democracy and peace, Wilson expected international social control to protect the world from Bolshevism as well as absolutism. Although he did not adopt Frederick Jackson Turner's suggestion for the creation of international political parties as a check on nationalism, the president shared the historian's desire for the League to counter radicalism. Turner hoped in particular to "keep the Bolsheviki serpent out of the American Eden." By forming international parties in the future League, he thought, the United States could play a constructive role in thwarting the Bolshevik menace to "the existence of Edens anywhere." Both of them expressed their visions of a league in the same religious motif. On his arrival in France, Wilson praised American soldiers and sailors for epitomizing the "true spirit" of their country in "this war of redemption." He anticipated the fulfillment of this missionary task in Paris.[82]

---

8 0   RL to Sulzer, Nov. 5, 1918, EMH to RL, Nov. 11, 1918, *FR*1918, I, 468-69, 494-98; NDB to WW, Oct. 22, 1918, Newton D. Baker Papers, Box 8, Library of Congress; WW to Pittman, Nov. 7, 1918, WW Papers, Ser. 2, Box 187; EMH to WW, Nov. 10 (#9), 11 (#13), 1918, EMH Papers, 49/11B, and WW Papers, Ser. 2, Box 187; *PPWW*, V, 294-302; Announcement by President Wilson, Nov. 11, 1918, EMH to WW, Nov. 11 (#13), 1918, *FR:PPC*, I, 1; HCL to Bryce, Dec. 14, 1919, HCL Papers, File 1918 (General Correspondence, A-G).

8 1   Fowler, *British-American Relations*, 283-96.

8 2   *PPWW*, V, 303, 324-25; Turner, International Political Parties in a Durable League of Nations, WW Papers, Ser. 5A, Box 3.

CHAPTER 3

Drafting of the League of Nations Covenant

At the Paris Peace Conference of 1919, Wilson sought to transform his vision of postwar collective security into an international organization. This process revealed both the idealistic and practical aspects of his character. To achieve his goal, which others regarded as a vague ideal, he engaged in a very practical form of diplomacy. He made concessions, especially to the British, to win their cooperation in drafting the Covenant. During these negotiations and in his conception of the League itself, Wilson expected the United States to play a predominant role. His vision of a new world order, although articulated in universal terms, would allow the United States to continue its unilateral approach in foreign relations. He thought American control over international affairs would benefit other nations as well as his own. From this perspective, he easily reconciled his understanding of American nationalism and his brand of internationalism. Identifying his own country's interests with the world's, the president combined isolationist and internationalist elements in his foreign policy.

Wilson emphasized the future League's redeeming mission in world affairs. In Paris, while awaiting the opening of the peace conference, he outlined his idea of the League as an instrument to prevent absolutism and militarism from again threatening human liberty. He emphasized the function of public opinion in maintaining peace. "My conception of the League of Nations," he proclaimed, "is just this, that it shall operate as the organized moral force of men throughout the world, and that whenever or wherever wrong and aggression are planned or contemplated, this searching light of conscience will be turned upon them and men everywhere will ask, 'What are the purposes that you hold in your heart against the fortunes of the world?' Just a little exposure will settle most questions."[1] This conception of

---

[1] *PPWW*, V, 329-31.

a league placed less emphasis on traditional forms of power in international relations.

Despite his confidence in moral suasion, Wilson recognized the continuing usefulness of military force. In his annual message to Congress on December 2, 1918, he had endorsed Secretary Daniels' naval program for the next three years. He wanted to maintain the building plans which Congress had adopted in 1916. As House had threatened during the armistice negotiations, he apparently hoped to force Great Britain to accept his peace conditions by expanding the American navy. Edward N. Hurley, chairman of the United States Shipping Board, recognized broader implications of this Anglo-American naval rivalry. He informed Wilson that "the British are fearful that under a League of Nations the United States, with its present wealth and commercial power, may get the jump on the markets of the world." He now urged him to alleviate British fears, which had earlier prompted the Allied reservation concerning freedom of the seas.[2]

Wilson's pursuit of an American agenda challenged Allied interests. Both the British and the French governments preferred to settle wartime issues before creating a league. House recognized that this procedure would postpone consideration of those principles which the president had called "the essentially American terms" of his peace program. Before Wilson's arrival in France, House had suggested the way to overcome the Anglo-American dispute. In a discussion with the Earl of Derby, British ambassador to France, he emphasized the president's desire to place top priority on the proposed League. He indicated that if the British cooperated, the United States would reciprocate by adopting a more favorable attitude toward their views on sea power and colonies. Wilson, whom House briefed as soon as he reached Paris, endorsed this suggestion for gaining British support. "The President," the British ambassador reported to Balfour, "is obsessed with the idea that the League of Nations is a panacea for all ills and if we can only get that settled all other matters, such as Freedom of the Seas will at the same time be solved." Apprehensive of possible Franco-American collaboration against his country's maritime power, Derby obtained a promise from Clemenceau to support the British view of freedom of the seas. By the time Wilson and Derby met on December 22, the general outline of an Anglo-American understanding was apparent. The president showed his willingness to consider British control of some former German colonies under the future league's supervision. Conceding that Great Britain as well as the United States needed a large navy, he proposed that these powers cooperate in "the marine policing of the world" through the new League.[3]

2 WW to JD, Nov. 18, Dec. 7, 1918, Josephus Daniels Papers, Box 14, Library of Congress; *PPWW*, 318; Murray to Reading et al., Nov. 25, Dec. 5, 1918, AJB Papers, 49741/235-36; Hurley to WW, Dec. 12, 1918, WW Papers, Ser. 5B, Box 2.
3 AJB to Derby, Nov. 16, 1918, Derby to AJB, Oct. 23, Nov. 18, Dec. 14, 16, 20, 22, 1918, AJB Papers, 49744/130-32, 92, 146-48, 184-90, 195-96, 205-08, 217-19; Wiseman, Memorandum, Dec. 15, 1918, AJB Papers, 49741/116-18; EMH to RL, Nov. 15 (#109), 1918, EMH Papers, 12/12; EMH

By reconciling his vision of a league of nations with traditional British interests, Wilson preserved Anglo-American collaboration. Before his visit to England late in December, the British War Cabinet decided to support his efforts to establish a league at the peace conference. As the president refrained from challenging British views on freedom of the seas and colonies, Anglo-American cooperation became a reality. At a Buckingham Palace dinner, King George V noted the "common ideals" of the British and American peoples and encouraged their joint exertion "to secure for the world the blessings of an ordered freedom and an enduring peace." Wilson responded by calling for Anglo-American hegemony in the world, despite his use of the lofty words "right" and "justice." He considered it the "high privilege" of the United States and Great Britain "not only to apply the moral judgments of the world to the particular settlements which we shall attempt, but also to organize the moral force of the world to preserve those settlements, to steady the forces of mankind and to make the right and the justice to which great nations like our own have devoted themselves the predominant and controlling force of the world."[4]

Wilson advocated a global community under Anglo-American leadership to replace the discredited balance of power among competing nations. Outlining his vision of international relations at the Guildhall in London, he claimed that soldiers had fought the war "to do away with an old order and to establish a new one, and the center and characteristic of the old order was that unstable thing which we used to call the 'balance of power.'" Rather than "an unstable equilibrium of competitive interests" in a plural world, he wanted hegemonial unity through a league. He said, "there must now be, not a balance of power, not one powerful group of nations set off against another, but a single overwhelming, powerful group of nations who shall be the trustee of the peace of the world." He expressed his delight that the British and American governments were in agreement that "the key to the peace was the guarantee of the peace, not the items of it; that the items would be worthless unless there stood back of them a permanent concert of power for their maintenance."[5]

By emphasizing the future League, Wilson hoped to establish extensive American control over world affairs while avoiding entanglement in European politics. This combination of universalism and unilateralism led him to

Diary, Nov. 14, Dec. 14, 1918; Polk to WW, Dec. 2, 1918, Jusserand to RL, Nov. 29, 1918, WW Papers, Ser. 2, Box 189; Auchincloss Diary, Dec. 14, 1918, Auchincloss Papers, 55/86; David Hunter Miller, *My Diary: At the Conference of Paris* (New York, 1924), I, 38; ibid., II, 28-42; EMH to RL, Nov. 15 (#109), 21 (#133), 1918, Miller, Memorandum, Nov. 22, 1918, Davis to Polk, Dec. 19, 1918, *FR:PPC*, I, 344-65, 413-14.

4   Murray to Wiseman, Oct. 10, 1918, EMH Papers, 20/47; EG to EMH, Dec. 19, 30, 1918, EMH to EG, Dec. 26, 1918, EMH Papers, 9/9; EMH to WW, Dec. 25, 1918, EMH Papers, 49/11B; League of Nations Union to WW, Dec. 9, 1918, WW Papers, Ser. 5B, Box 1; EMH to WW, Dec. 25, 1918, The King's Speech, Dec. 27, 1918, WW Papers, Ser. 5B, Box 4; *PPWW*, V, 337-38, 340; Auchincloss Diary, Dec. 24-27, 1918, Jan. 2, 1919, Auchincloss Papers, 55/86; EMH Diary, Dec. 27, 1918; Derby to AJB, Dec. 24, 1918, AJB Papers, 49744/220-21.

5   *PPWW*, V, 341-44; Auchincloss Diary, Dec. 28, 1918, Auchincloss Papers, 55/86.

stress the moral commitment. In Manchester, Wilson explained how he reconciled the American diplomatic tradition of isolation from the Old World with his conception of collective security. "You know that the United States has always felt from the very beginning of her history that she must keep herself separate from any kind of connection with European politics," he recalled, "and I want to say very frankly to you that she is not now interested in European politics. But she is interested in the partnership of right between America and Europe. If the future had nothing for us but a new attempt to keep the world at a right poise by a balance of power, the United States would take no interest, because she will join no combination of power which is not the combination of all of us. She is not interested merely in the peace of Europe, but in the peace of the world. Therefore it seems to me that in the settlement that is just ahead of us something more delicate and difficult than was ever attempted before is to be accomplished, a genuine concert of mind and of purpose."[6]

This transcendent vision of a league, which relegated particular terms of the peace settlement to secondary status, enabled Wilson to compromise on specific issues. By the end of his trip to England, the dispute over freedom of the seas ceased to trouble Anglo-American relations. He refrained from challenging British maritime and colonial policy, while Great Britain cooperated in establishing the League during the peace conference.[7]

Wilson faced a far greater problem in reconciling his ideals with French interests. During his visit to England, Clemenceau delivered a major speech on foreign policy to the Chamber of Deputies, which then gave the premier an overwhelming vote of confidence. He refused to endorse the president's view of a new world order. "There is an old system of alliances called the Balance of Power – this system of alliances, which I do not renounce, will be my guiding thought at the Peace Conference," he affirmed. Although Wilson agreed to exclude Germany from membership during a probationary period, Clemenceau placed little confidence in a league. His blunt summary of French policy evoked widespread criticism in the United States. American newspapers denounced his adherence to the old balance-of-power theory and favored Anglo-American cooperation to counter French influence at the peace conference. The *Literary Digest* reported that the press typically wanted the United States to withdraw from the Old World and return to its traditional policy of isolation unless American and British leaders succeeded in creating a new league.[8] That was the challenge they faced in Paris.

6 *PPWW*, V, 352-56.
7 EMH Diary, Dec. 31, 1918; "British-American Discord," *Literary Digest*, LX (Jan. 4, 1919), 9-11.
8 "Clash of French and American Peace Plans," *Literary Digest*, LX, 9-11; EMH Diary, Dec. 5, 18-19, 30, 1918; Auchincloss Diary, Dec. 15, 1918, Auchincloss Papers, 55/86; Miller, *My Diary*, I, 26; JPT to WW, Dec. 31, 1918, WW Papers, Ser. 5B, Box 5, and JPT Papers, Box 5. For an excellent account of the differences between French and American policies, see David Stevenson, "French War Aims and the American Challenge, 1914-1918," *Historical Journal*, XXII, No. 4 (1979), 877-94.

I

British and American leaders sought to cooperate at the peace conference, but persistent rivalry between them made that task difficult. They wanted to protect their separate as well as common interests. Cecil had earlier summarized his hope for Anglo-American collaboration. "There is undoubtedly a difference between the British and the Continental point of view in international matters," he reminded the War Cabinet. "I will not attempt to describe the difference, but I know that you will agree in thinking that, where it exists, we are right, and the Continental nations are, speaking generally, wrong. If America accepts our point of view in these matters, it will mean the dominance of that point of view in all international affairs."[9]

Fearful of arriving at the peace conference without plans, Cecil had urged Lloyd George during the summer of 1918 to raise the league issue in the War Cabinet. He recommended the Phillimore plan as the basis for discussion. The prime minister, however, preferred to avoid any commitment to a specific plan. In view of Wiseman's report on Wilson's attitude, he rejected Cecil's advice and refrained from what he called "a premature pronouncement that would get us into trouble not merely with the French but with the Americans as well."[10] In the absence of official British action beyond endorsement of the league idea, Cecil regretfully saw the American president seizing control of this issue. He lamented to Lloyd George on the eve of the peace conference that "we have let that eloquent pedagogue 'patent' this question."[11]

Cecil developed his own plan for a league, which emphasized procedures for peaceful resolution of conflicts. He submitted it to the prime minister for circulation to the War Cabinet. This plan called for annual and special conferences of prime ministers and foreign secretaries of the great powers to deal with problems threatening the world's peace. Representatives of minor states would join those of the great powers only for quadrennial meetings. A permanent secretariat at the league's headquarters in Geneva would handle administrative work. Cecil proposed that the league members join in a covenant not to resort to war without first submitting the conflict to a conference or a court of arbitration. They would agree to abstain from belligerent action to overturn a unanimous report from the conference or award by the court. Any nation refusing to abide by these obligations would face immediate war with all other members. States outside the league would also be expected to abide by the same procedures for peaceful resolution of conflicts with league members. The Cecil plan did not absolutely prohibit

9 Egerton, *Great Britain and the Creation of the League of Nations*, 64; Kernek, "Distractions of Peace During War," *Transactions of the American Philosophical Society*, 62.
10 Cecil to DLG, June 26, 1918, DLG to Bonar Law, Aug. 20, 1918, DLG Papers, F/6/5/34, F/30/2/41.
11 Cecil to DLG, Dec. 19, 1918, DLG Papers, F/6/5/53.

warfare, but sought to prevent it by requiring a delay and encouraging public discussion.[12]

General Jan C. Smuts of South Africa simultaneously prepared a similar plan. He shared Cecil's desire for Anglo-American cooperation and later served with him on the commission which drafted the Covenant. Shortly after the armistice, Smuts had outlined for some American newspaper editors his belief that joint efforts of the United States and the British Empire would afford "the best guarantee for the future peaceful development of civilization." He thought "moral idealism" of the British and American peoples, which had sustained them throughout the war, would culminate in a league.[13]

In his "practical suggestion" for world peace, Smuts described the progressive development of civilization from tribes through nation-states to empires, and ultimately to a league of nations. Reconciling British interests with his plan, he viewed the British Empire as the prototype of the proposed League. He elaborated the idea of mandates under the League's auspices but applied it only to the Russian, Austrian and Turkish empires. Smuts explicitly excluded former German colonies from this system, desiring no obstacle to their annexation. Wanting the League to be less powerful than a super-state but more effective than a debating society, he proposed a constitution which would give the prime ministers and foreign secretaries of the great powers the dominant role in its council. The British Empire, France, Italy, Japan and the United States, and perhaps eventually Germany, would enjoy permanent representation on the council, while small states would appoint a minority of four members on a rotating basis. He further recommended a general conference of all league members for the purpose of discussing and endorsing various resolutions and reports submitted to it by the council. Although the council would do the League's real work, the conference would mobilize international public opinion. The Smuts plan, like Cecil's, provided for arbitration and conciliation. The league members would be obligated to submit their disputes either to arbitrators or to the council, and to abide by their decisions. The council's recommendation would be binding unless at least three of its members vetoed it. If any nation violated these obligations, other league members would be required to enforce them through war. In agreement with Cecil, Smuts considered the moratorium on war during the period of conciliation or arbitration as the crucial safeguard of peace, although war was still permissible if these procedures failed to resolve the conflict.[14]

This document greatly influenced Wilson's developing conception of a

---

12   Cecil to DLG, Dec. 17, 1918, WW Papers, Ser. 5B, Box 3; Miller, *My Diary*, III, 85-88.

13   Speech, Nov. 14, 1918 (#857), W. K. Hancock and Jean van der Poel, eds., *Selections from the Smuts Papers* (Cambridge, 1966), IV, 8-16.

14   Smuts to S. M. Smuts, Dec. 17, 1918 (#868), Smuts to Gillett, Dec. 27, 1918 (#872), Hancock and van der Poel, eds., *Smuts Papers*, IV, 30-31, 34; Miller, *Drafting of the Covenant*, II, 23-60; Auchincloss to Polk, Jan. 3, 1919, Frank L. Polk Papers, Drawer 82, File 18, Yale University Library.

league. While reading it, he noted its emphasis on the League's central role in the peacemaking. He, too, wanted the conference to give top priority to the organization of a league. He also gave special attention to the proposed system of mandates and the views on general disarmament in the Smuts plan.[15]

Like Cecil and Smuts, the president reconciled his own country's interests with his advocacy of collective security. Speaking to members of the Inquiry during the voyage to Europe, he had affirmed that Americans would be "the only disinterested people" in Paris. He saw the future League as the Monroe Doctrine's global equivalent. Rejecting a competitive balance among the great powers, he called for their unity in a league. In contrast to the negative covenant of the Cecil and Smuts plans – which would prohibit a nation from resorting to war without first attempting arbitration or conciliation – Wilson favored a positive guarantee of political independence and territorial integrity. He wanted prior authorization for the League to react against aggression, although he, too, intended to decide unilaterally when to exercise this right. He balanced the commitment to enforce the peace treaty with a provision for its revision by providing for "later alteration of terms and alteration of boundaries if it could be shown that injustice had been done or that conditions had changed." He wanted a league to afford both "elasticity and security," but failed to clarify the basis for selecting revision or enforcement. Implicit in his conception of a league, as in the Monroe Doctrine, was the assumption that the United States would decide whether to guarantee the status quo or require changes. His approach to foreign policy was at once unilateral and universal. In accordance with the idea of international social control, Wilson envisaged the preservation of world peace through American hegemony in a league.[16]

Wilson's colleagues in the American Commission to Negotiate Peace shared his desire for Anglo-American collaboration and generally supported his efforts to create a league. Yet they did not altogether approve his conception. Three of them – Secretary Lansing, General Tasker H. Bliss and the career diplomat Henry White – preferred a negative covenant. They found the commitment in the Cecil and Smuts plans to refrain from war, while attempting arbitration or conciliation, more appealing than a positive guarantee of political independence and territorial integrity. Lacking the president's sophistry, they resisted the eventual Article 10 of the Covenant. The other commissioner, House, whose views mirrored Wilson's, attempted to maintain a close working relationship with them. Despite their differences, all five American delegates to the peace conference wanted to achieve a lasting peace with minimal postwar obligations for the United States.

General Bliss considered disarmament as the essential element in a

15 The League of Nations: A Programme for the Peace Conference, Dec. 16, 1918, WW Papers, Ser. 5B, Box 2.
16 Miller, *My Diary*, I, 370-73.

successful league. During the armistice negotiations, he had summarized his position for Holt, sending a copy to House. Bliss affirmed that "the very cornerstone of a League of Nations must be total disarmament." The United States and the Allies, after defeating German militarism, should eliminate militarism in Europe and throughout the world. He advised House that disarmament was the key to future peace.[17] Prewar reliance on armaments appeared to him as the direct cause of the World War. Critical of Clemenceau's old idea of a balance of power, Bliss wanted to replace alliances with a new league. To create a league of disarmed nations, instead of an armed alliance, he hoped for cooperation between Great Britain and the United States. He shared General John J. Pershing's aversion to American entanglement in European diplomacy and his desire for rapid demobilization of the American Expeditionary Forces. Their idea of total victory, which would enable the United States to end its involvement, expressed traditional American aloofness toward the Old World.[18]

Bliss anticipated "a bitter struggle" to accomplish the president's purpose at the peace conference. Expecting "the wiliest and canniest diplomats of Europe" to attempt to embroil the United States in their machinations for material benefit, he hoped American delegates could avoid these problems by adhering to broad principles. "The first object, and naturally so, of our European associates," he advised Lansing, "is to secure certain territorial adjustments. Our first and *only* object is to secure certain principles." Rather than strategic frontiers in anticipation of future wars, Bliss preferred a league with disarmament. In response to European claims for defensible borders, he wanted to reply that "the league of nations is the strategic frontier of every nation which has no other."[19] Like Wilson, he identified American interests with the world's. "Disguise it from ourselves as we may, the basic idea of the League is to begin some form of government for the world in which the ideas of the *best* class of men in the great civilized powers shall dominate," he candidly wrote. And for him, only Americans were fully qualified for this task. Despite this vision of *Pax Americana*, Bliss opposed a positive guarantee of other nations' political independence and territorial integrity. He thought that a solemn promise to respect these rights would suffice. Above all, he emphasized that "disarmament and a League of Nations go hand-in-hand."[20]

1 7   THB to Holt, Oct. 11, 1918, THB to EMH, Oct. 14, 1918, EMH Papers, 3/13; Memorandum, Oct. 28, 1918, Tasker Howard Bliss Papers, Box 69, Library of Congress. See also David F. Trask, "General Tasker Howard Bliss and the 'Sessions of the World,' 1919," *Transactions of the American Philosophical Society*, New Series, Vol. 56, Part 8 (Philadelphia, 1966).

1 8   JJP to March, Nov. 27, 1918, JJP Papers, Box 123; General Bliss' Diaries, Dec. 22, 1918, Jan., 1, 4, 8, 22, Feb. 2, 4, 11, 1919, THB Papers, Box 65; Interview given H. Holt, THB Papers, Box 71; RSB, Notebook, XXII, Dec. 26, 1918, RSB Papers. See also Bullitt Lowry, "Pershing and the Armistice," *Journal of American History*, LV (Sept. 1968), 281-91, and Donald Smythe, *Pershing: General of the Armies* (Bloomington, 1986), 219-22, 230-33.

1 9   THB to March, Nov. 30, 1918, THB Papers, Box 75; THB to RL, Dec. 15, 1918, THB Papers, Box 65.

2 0   THB to Mezes, Dec. 26, 1918, THB Papers, Box 65; THB to RL, Dec. 26, 1918, THB to Mezes, Dec. 26, 1918, *FR:PPC*, I, 521-25.

Despite his profession as an army officer, Bliss envisaged a transformation of international affairs with the abolition of militarism. Secretary of War Newton D. Baker had brought to Wilson's attention the general's view that "the absolute destruction of all militarism" would furnish "the only corner stone" for any league.[21] After the war Baker informed Bliss about the development of a new weapon, which the general then, ironically, used as an additional argument for a league. The secretary reported the perfection of "an aerial bomb," or small unmanned airplane, capable of carrying two hundred pounds of high explosives a distance of fifty to sixty miles with considerable accuracy. Bliss shared this information with his colleagues in the American Commission, observing that this new weapon rendered obsolete the old idea of strategic frontiers.[22] Lansing, too, acknowledged the implications for peacemaking of "this wonderful invention." He also agreed with Bliss that the United States should protect its innocence by avoiding entanglement in the Old World. "We are face to face with jealousies and selfishness which have drawn the map of Europe in the past," he warned.[23]

Viewing the war as a confrontation between autocracy and democracy, Lansing thought that the universal triumph of democracy would afford the best prospect for a peaceful future. This belief rested upon the dubious assumption that "no civilized people on earth desires war." He favored a league of democratic nations, but not an alliance or league to enforce peace. He denounced Clemenceau for advocating a balance of power, which he identified with the pursuit of "world empire ruled by an oligarchy of great powers." Summarizing his central theme, the secretary told Root: "If we can succeed in making democracy the standing political principle of all civilized nations, I believe that we will have gained the most certain guaranty of peace."[24]

Although favoring a league of democratic nations, Lansing opposed a positive guarantee of political independence and territorial integrity. During a conversation on December 8, the president outlined his view of a world organization with such a mutual guarantee. Besides voicing his objections, the secretary resolved to formulate an alternative plan for a league. Convinced that House was responsible for Wilson's scheme, he attempted to persuade him of the undesirability and unconstitutionality of a positive guarantee. He also solicited support from Bliss and White. In preparing his own proposal, Lansing studied an agreement for an association of nations which Miller had drafted for House. He questioned its provision for a positive guarantee because it lacked "sufficient elasticity for natural growth."

---

2 1   THB to NDB, Oct. 9, 1918, WW Papers, Ser. 5B, Box 185; NDB to WW, Oct. 24, 1918, WW Papers, Ser. 5B, Box 186.
2 2   NDB to THB, Dec. 3, 1918, THB Papers, Box 75; THB to RL, Dec. 16, 1918, THB to HW, Dec. 16, 1918, THB Papers, Box 69; THB to EMH, Dec. 16, 1918, EMH Papers, 3/13.
2 3   RL to THB, Dec. 16, 16, 1918, THB Papers, Box 65.
2 4   RL Diary, III, Sept. 30, 1918, IV, Jan. 3, 1919, Appendix to Diary, Dec. 31, 1918; RL to ER, Dec. 3, 1918, RL Papers, Vol. 40.

He offered three primary reasons for objecting to a positive guarantee. A commitment like the future Article 10, he contended, would infringe upon the right of Congress to declare war and regulate commerce. An obligation to use military or economic means to preserve the political independence and territorial integrity of other nations would therefore violate the Constitution. It would also challenge the Monroe Doctrine by opening the possibility that European powers might intervene in American affairs to implement a positive guarantee. While creating this threat to the western hemisphere, it would, finally, entangle the United States in an alliance in Europe. For all these reasons Lansing favored a negative covenant. In his draft for a league of nations convention, he suggested a mutual agreement not to violate territorial integrity or impair political independence without authorization from the league's international council or arbitral tribunal. The international council, consisting of diplomatic representatives of the league's members in a particular country, could permit belligerent action by a three-fourths vote.[25]

Contrary to Wilson's desire, Lansing pursued his own approach to peacemaking. He instructed two assistants, Miller and Dr. James Brown Scott, to prepare a skeleton draft of a peace treaty. He, as well as Bliss and White, whom he consulted, sensed a lack of presidential direction and wanted to provide guidance for the approaching negotiations. All of them found Clemenceau's perspective repugnant and desired the triumph of American principles. During the last days of December, the two assistants completed their work on a skeleton draft, which included a brief reference to an "association of nations." On January 1, 1919, Wilson attended the American Commission's meeting to report on his trip to Great Britain. He informed his fellow delegates of the substantial Anglo-American agreement, including Lloyd George's favorable attitude toward a league. He told them that he was highly impressed with the Smuts plan. In contrast, the president did not react favorably when Lansing gave him a copy of the Miller-Scott skeleton draft. Nevertheless, hoping that he misinterpreted Wilson's reaction, the secretary instructed his assistants to prepare a more detailed version.[26]

Lansing also continued to work on a convention for a league of nations. He viewed Wilson's proposal for a positive guarantee as a victory for Clemenceau

25   RL Diary, III, Oct. 27, Nov. 22, Dec. 18, 1918, Appendix to Diary, Dec. 4, 8, 11, 17, 19-21, 24, 1918; General Bliss' Diaries, Dec. 21, 23, 1918, THB Papers, Box 65; Miller, *My Diary*, I, 50-51; Tentative Draft of an Agreement for an Association of Nations, [Nov. 30, 1918], RL to WW, Dec. 23, 1918, The Constitutional Power to Provide for Coercion in a Treaty, Dec. 20, 1918, Suggested Draft of Articles, Dec. 20, 1918, Suggestions As to an International Council, Dec. 21, 1918, FR:PPC, I, 505-09, 515-19; RL to WW, Dec. 23, 1918, Suggested Draft of Articles, Dec. 20, 1918, WW Papers, Ser. 5B, Box 4.
26   RL Appendix to Diary, Dec. 27, 1918, Jan. 1, 3, 1919; EMH Diary, Jan. 1, 1919; Miller, *My Diary*, I, 60-64; General Bliss' Diaries, Jan. 1, 1919, THB Papers, Box 65; THB to NDB, Jan. 4, 1919, NDB Papers, Box 9; Scott and Miller to RL, Dec. 30, 1918, Skeleton Draft of Peace Treaty, HW to WW, Dec. 31, 1918, WW Papers, Ser. 5B, Box 5.

because its implementation would inevitably establish the great powers' primacy and require their use of military force. Lansing wanted to rely on arbitration instead. If diplomatic methods failed, he wanted potential belligerents to submit disputes to an arbitral tribunal or some other form of arbitration. He wished to empower the international council to require referrals to this tribunal. In short, he recommended compulsory arbitration. But Wilson, as he told Lansing, continued to oppose such a negative covenant.[27]

House joined the secretary of state in this work. He had supplied Lansing with a copy of the president's first draft of the previous summer and seemed now to approve the idea of a self-denying covenant. House endeavored to persuade Clemenceau to abandon his old ideas of a balance of power and military alliances in favor of a new world organization. He depicted the future League as an Anglo-American gift to France. "In the present war," he asserted, "England voluntarily came to France's aid. She was not compelled to do so. The United States did likewise without compulsion. I asked whether or not in the circumstances France would not feel safer if England and America were in a position where they would be compelled to come to the aid of France in the event another outlaw nation like Germany should try to crush her. France, after this peace, under our plan, would be always France as she will stand then. Under the old plan, the shadow and the spectre of another war would haunt her. If she lost this chance which the United States offered through the League of Nations, it would never come again because there would never be another opportunity." House deluded himself into thinking that the French premier was persuaded by this argument to change his perspective.[28]

On their own initiative, House and Lansing attempted to achieve a precise basis for Anglo-American collaboration in creating a league. In a series of meetings with Cecil, they tried to reach an agreement. They urged him to accept compulsory arbitration for the resolution of international conflicts, but he refused because he considered it a threat to national sovereignty. The two Americans eventually conceded the difficulty of gaining international approval for this far-reaching method. When Wilson attended the American Commission's meeting on January 8, Lansing took the occasion to warn that the Cecil and Smuts plans, by establishing a union of the great powers, would entangle the United States in an alliance for the preservation of a postwar balance of power. The president, however, continued to speak favorably of the Smuts plan for a league as the heir to empires. Despite a common desire to give first priority to a league at the peace conference,

---

27   RL Appendix to Diary, Jan. 6-7, 1919; Miller, *My Diary*, I, 66; Draft by the Secretary of State for an International Agreement, [Jan. 7, 1919], Memorandum by the Secretary of State on the Privilege of Becoming an Adherent to the Treaty When Not a Signatory Nation, [c. Jan. 7, 1919], *FR:PPC*, I, 528-32.

28   EMH Diary, Jan. 7, 1919; Derby to AJB, Jan. 6, 1919, AJB Papers, 49744/228-31.

Wilson's colleagues did not agree with him, or with Cecil, on the exact character of this Anglo-American project.[29]

Wilson rejected Lansing's alternative, preferring his own "covenant." Miller and Scott had elaborated their skeleton draft in accordance with the secretary's instructions, and in consultation with House. This new proposal incorporated the main features of Lansing's draft of a league convention, including a negative covenant and compulsory arbitration. On January 10 at an American Commission meeting, the secretary presented the Miller-Scott draft treaty to the president, who immediately denounced it as the product of lawyers. He did not welcome this initiative. He favored instead his own revised covenant, which he gave to the delegates.

Wilson's second draft of a covenant retained the central features of his previous version, while incorporating some major elements from the Smuts plan. As did his first draft, this covenant combined a positive guarantee of political independence and territorial integrity with a provision for revision. The president continued to affirm the premise, which was basic to the interwar appeasement, that "the peace of the world is superior in importance to every question of political jurisdiction or boundary." From the Smuts plan, he adopted the idea of an executive council, which would consist of diplomatic representatives of the great powers plus a minority from small states. Subject to veto by three votes, this council would give the predominant role to the great powers. Wilson wanted to require the nations in the League to submit their disputes either to arbitration or to the executive council for a recommended settlement. Should any nation violate these obligations for peaceful resolution of conflicts, he stipulated that all other members of the League would automatically enter into war with it. These members would then sever all financial, commercial and personal intercourse with that covenant-breaking nation. In this second draft, the president developed his earlier provision for reduction of armaments. He now called for the abolition of conscription or other forms of compulsory military service, and the end of private manufacture of arms and munitions for profit. In supplementary agreements which reflected Smuts' influence, Wilson proposed that the League exercise trusteeship over the territories of Austria-Hungary and Turkey, and also over the German colonies. He wished to avoid annexation of any part of these empires. He wanted the League, as the successor to empires, not only to exercise some jurisdiction over new states created from the Austrian and Turkish empires but also to delegate responsibility for administering the remaining areas. Wilson's system of mandates would require the mandatory states to respect the "open door" policy of equal opportunity for all league members in developing the

29 RL Appendix to Diary, Jan. 8-9, 1919; Auchincloss Diary, Jan. 8-9, 1919, Auchincloss Papers, 55/87; General Bliss' Diaries, Jan. 8, 1919, THB Papers, Box 65; Cecil to EMH, Jan. 8, 1919, EMH Papers, 4/38; Record of interview with Colonel House at Paris, Jan. 9, 1919, Cecil of Chelwood Papers, 51094/206, British Museum; Cecil Diary, Jan. 8-9, 1919, Cecil Papers, 51131; RL, HW, EMH and THB to WW, Jan. 8, 1919, WW Papers, Ser. 5B, Box 7.

economic resources of mandated territories. The president's second draft of a covenant did not satisfy his colleagues in the American Commission. Lansing, Bliss and White shared some of their reservations with him but refrained from outspoken criticism.[30]

Bliss later summarized his critique of Wilson's second draft and offered him his suggestions for possible changes. These suggestions became the major influence on the president's further refinement of the Covenant. Bliss was especially interested in preventing the future League from intervening in a domestic revolution. Persuaded by this recommendation, Wilson limited the guarantee of political independence and territorial integrity with the words "as against external aggression." He also removed the reference to maintaining "orderly government" from the Covenant's preamble. To enable the great powers to compel general disarmament, he shifted responsibility for reducing national armaments from the body of delegates to the executive council. In view of Bliss' concern for the power of Congress to declare war, the president modified the provision for *ipso facto* war with covenant-breaking nations, now affirming only that their violations shall be deemed acts of war. He also accepted the general's suggestion that the executive council or arbitrators should render their decisions within the limit of one year. Finally, he added a provision to require publication of treaties. Wilson did not heed Bliss' warning with regard to mandates that "the sole object of the proposition of General Smuts is to bring the United States into line with Great Britain in exercising supervisory control over certain areas of the earth." Instead, he elaborated his conception of mandates. The president also introduced a provision for freedom of religion in this slightly revised third draft of a covenant.[31]

While Wilson was revising his covenant, a British committee under

3 0   RL Diary, IV, Jan. 11, 1919, Appendix to Diary, Jan. 10-11, 1919; General Bliss' Diaries, Jan. 10-11, 1919, THB Papers, Box 65; THB to NDB, Jan. 11, 1919, NDB Papers, Box 9; Auchincloss Diary, Jan. 10, 1919, Auchincloss Papers, 55/87; Miller, *My Diary*, I, 63-69; Miller, *Drafting of the Covenant*, II, 65-93.

3 1   THB, Suggestions in Regard to the Draft of the Covenant, Jan. 14, 1919, THB to WW, Jan. 15, 1919, WW Papers, Ser. 5B, Box 8; WW to THB, Jan. 17, 1919, WW Papers, Ser. 5B, Box 9; THB to WW, Dec. 15, 1919, WW to THB, Dec. 17, 1919, THB Papers, Box 70; THB, Suggestions in Regard to the Draft of the Covenant, Jan. 14, 1919, THB Papers, Box 71; THB to RL, Dec. 31, 1918, THB Papers, Box 69; General Bliss' Diaries, Dec. 31, 1918, THB Papers, Box 65; Miller, *Drafting of the Covenant*, II, 98-105. Wilson's response to revolutions was ambiguous. Although he intervened – e.g., in Mexico and Russia – against some revolutionary governments, he presupposed that his actions coincided with the people's will and, consequently, that he was not really interfering with the internal affairs of those countries. His willingness to restrict Article 10 to external aggression was therefore consistent with his own understanding of the appropriate American policy toward revolutions, although it conflicted with some of his actions. His ideals and practices were sometimes contradictory. For Wilson's response to the Mexican and Russian revolutions, see George F. Kennan, *Russia Leaves the War* (Princeton, 1956) and *The Decision to Intervene* (Princeton, 1958), Eugene P. Trani, "Woodrow Wilson and the Decision to Intervene in Russia: A Reconsideration," *Journal of Modern History*, XLVIII (Sept. 1976), 440-61, Frederick Katz, *The Secret War in Mexico: Europe, the United States and the Mexican Revolution* (Chicago, 1981), and Lloyd C. Gardner, "Woodrow Wilson and the Mexican Revolution," and Betty Miller Unterberger, "Woodrow Wilson and the Russian Revolution," in Link, ed., *Woodrow Wilson and a Revolutionary World*, 3-104.

Cecil's direction drafted a league of nations convention and accompanying resolutions for the peace conference. He attempted, but without much success, to ascertain the president's views from House. In consultation with Smuts, Balfour, Lloyd George and various advisers from the Foreign Office, Cecil completed the British draft convention and sent copies to Wilson and House. This draft convention, affirming that "the primary object of the League is the preservation of peace among the nations of the world," modified the earlier Cecil and Smuts plans in substantial conformity with the president's position. It included a positive guarantee by requiring the nations in a league to protect as well as respect the territorial integrity of all other members. It balanced this obligation by authorizing the league to recommend revision of boundaries. For the first time, Cecil accepted Wilson's combination of a positive guarantee and revision. Continuing to advocate a preponderant role for the great powers, Cecil wanted them to enjoy exclusive representation in a council, but provided for participation by all states in a general conference. He insisted upon separate membership by British dominions and India in the league rather than a single delegation for the British Empire. He now elaborated plans for an international secretariat under the direction of a chancellor. Procedures for avoidance of war adhered closely to those of previous British plans, including the referral of disputes to an arbitral tribunal or international court for judicial settlement, or to the council or possibly general conference for conciliation. In case of a breach of these procedures, Cecil still called for automatic war involving military, naval and economic sanctions. From the Smuts plan, he took the idea of mandates, giving "the more advanced members of the family of nations" the "duty" to guide the less developed states and territories toward "stable government." Lloyd George generally approved this draft convention, but not officially. He did, however, formally endorse the British committee's accompanying resolutions, which called for a league to enforce the peace treaty.[32]

II

Prospects for establishing a league of nations seemed favorable on the eve of the peace conference. Wilson was now confident that he would succeed. To gain French support, he and Cecil met separately with Léon Bourgeois, whom Clemenceau later appointed, along with Ferdinand Larnaude, to the commission that would draft the Covenant. Bourgeois had earlier attempted to arrange a meeting with Wilson to discuss a league. The

3 2   Cecil to EMH, Jan. 12, 1919, Auchincloss to Cecil, Jan. 13, 20, 1919, EMH Papers, 4/38; Cecil to Auchincloss, Jan. 13, 1919, Auchincloss to Cecil, Jan. 15, 1919, EMH Papers, 4/39; Auchincloss Diary, Jan. 11, 13-16, 1919, Auchincloss Papers, 55/87; Cecil Diary, Jan. 11-18, 1919, Cecil Papers, 51131; Miller, *My Diary*, III, 432-41; Miller, *Drafting of the Covenant*, II, 106-16; Draft Preliminary Resolutions for a League of Nations, Jan. 14, 1919, WW Papers, Ser. 5B, Box 8; Cecil to WW, Jan. 20, 1919, League of Nations, Draft Convention, Jan. 20, 1919, WW Papers, Ser. 5B, Box 10.

French were genuinely interested in collective security. At the peace conference's first plenary session on January 18, 1919, President Poincaré opened formal deliberations by outlining the tasks of peacemaking. In conformity with the last of Wilson's Fourteen Points, he called for "a General League of Nations which will be a supreme guarantee against any fresh assaults upon the right of peoples." Clemenceau expressed the same hope for postwar unity among the victorious powers. "Everything must yield to the necessity of a closer and closer union among the peoples who have taken part in this great war," he emphasized. "The League of Nations is here."[33]

To coordinate British and American plans, Wilson conferred with Cecil and Smuts. Prior to this meeting, House had received a copy of the British draft convention and accompanying resolutions. After studying the British resolutions, he requested Miller to prepare a substitute. Lansing also drafted his alternative resolution, which reaffirmed his idea of a negative covenant. In view of their recommendations, House constructed his own proposal, an abbreviated version of Miller's, submitting it to Wilson along with a copy of the British draft convention. The president ignored this advice, accepting instead the British resolutions with a modification to emphasize that the League Covenant would be an integral part of the peace treaty. On January 19 he presented his draft of a covenant to Cecil and Smuts. They were both impressed with its similarity to previous British plans. Smuts was elated that his plan had been so influential but was terribly anxious because Wilson had altered his conception of mandates to include former German colonies. This alteration threatened South Africa's and Australia's claims, which he and Prime Minister William Hughes advanced. Smuts lamented that Wilson was "entirely opposed to our annexing a little German colony here or there, which pains me deeply and will move Billy Hughes to great explosions of righteous wrath." He had earlier urged Lloyd George to "smooth the way for a conciliatory policy of President Wilson towards our very far-reaching claims." Despite this contentious issue, the president achieved a broad consensus with Cecil and Smuts concerning a league. On January 20 he informed the American Commission about this substantial agreement and shared with them copies of his third draft of a covenant.[34]

Lloyd George was still unwilling to commit his government to a particular

33 WW to Bryce, Jan. 16, 1919, WW Papers, Ser. 5B, Box 9; Poincaré to WW, Dec. 23, 1918, WW to Poincaré, Dec. 24, 1919, EMH, Memorandum for the President, Dec. 24, 1919, WW Papers, Ser. 5B, Box 4; FR:PPC, III (Washington, 1943), 159-70.

34 EMH to WW, Jan. 19, 1919, League of Nations, Draft Convention, Jan. 16, 1919, WW Papers, Ser. 5B, Box 9; EMH to WW, Jan. 19, 1919, EMH Papers, 49/12; Suggested Resolution, Jan. 19, 1919, RL Papers, Vol. 41; RL Appendix to Diary, Jan. 19-20, 1919; THB to NDB, Jan. 21, 1919, NDB Papers, Box 9; Auchincloss Diary, Jan. 19-20, 1919, Auchincloss Papers, 55/87; Miller, My Diary, I, 82-85; ibid., III, 349, 428-29; Cecil Diary, Jan. 19, 1919, Cecil Papers, 51131; Smuts to Gillett, Jan. 14 (#883), 19 (#887), 20 (#889), 1919, Smuts to Clark, Jan. 15, 1919 (#884), Hancock and van der Poel, eds., Smuts Papers, IV, 41-43, 47-50; Smuts to DLG, Jan. 14, 20, 1919, DLG Papers, F/45/9/26, 28.

plan. He was more interested in the general structure of Anglo-American cooperation than in the details of a new league. Smuts regretted that the prime minister was not more enthusiastic about his plan. "I believe the Americans like it more than my British friends; but it has ever been thus with the prophets," he observed with obvious pride of authorship. The prime minister told Cecil he preferred the British draft convention to Wilson's covenant. "However, he did not want to talk about the League of Nations at all, in which he takes no real interest," Cecil regretfully noted.[35]

British and American leaders, despite their differences, collaborated to determine the nature of the future League. In the Council of Ten – heads of government and foreign ministers of Great Britain, France, Italy and the United States, and two delegates from Japan – Lloyd George and Balfour expressed their willingness to accept Wilson's covenant as the basis for discussion. In accordance with the British draft resolutions, they recommended the adoption of general principles and referral to a committee. After this session, apparently with Wilson's encouragement, Lansing prepared his own set of suggested resolutions. For the first time, he now gave tentative endorsement to a positive guarantee. The president, however, supported the British resolutions. The Council of Ten on January 22 officially called for a league of nations – that "should be open to every civilised nation which can be relied on to promote its object" – as "an integral part" of the peace treaty. Lloyd George proposed that the great powers should each appoint two representatives to the drafting commission and jointly select two delegates to represent all small states. Wilson advocated that great powers alone should draft the League Covenant, and only then give small states the opportunity to review it. In contrast, Clemenceau championed the small states' right to full participation. He eventually convinced the British and American leaders to permit small states to select a total of five delegates to serve with ten representatives of the great powers on the commission. To announce these decisions of the Council of Ten, but not to allow any votes or official action, leaders of the five principal Allied and Associated Powers agreed to convene a plenary session of the peace conference. They were clearly determined to maintain control by the great powers.[36]

At the plenary session on January 25, Wilson outlined his league idea. He emphasized that the peace conference's purpose was not only to settle the

35 Smuts to Clark, Jan. 21, 1919 (#891), Hancock and van der Poel, eds., *Smuts Papers*, IV, 51-52; Cecil Diary, Jan. 20, 1919, Cecil Papers, 51131. See also George Curry, "Woodrow Wilson, Jan Smuts, and the Versailles Settlement," *American Historical Review*, LXVI (July 1961), 968-86, George W. Egerton, "The Lloyd George Government and the Creation of the League of Nations," ibid., LXXIX (Apr. 1974), 419-44, Leon E. Boothe, "Anglo-American Pro-League Groups Lead Wilson," *Mid-America*, LI, No. 2 (1969), 92-107, Peter Raffo, "The Anglo-American Preliminary Negotiations for a League of Nations," *Journal of Contemporary History*, IX (Oct. 1974), 153-76, and Herbert G. Nicholas, "Woodrow Wilson and Collective Security," in Link, ed., *Woodrow Wilson and a Revolutionary World*, 174-89.
36 *FR:PPC*, III, 653-54, 668-69, 677-82, 686-90; RL Diary, IV, Jan. 22, 1919, Appendix to Diary, Jan. 21-23, 1919; Suggested Resolutions, Jan. 22, 1919, WW Papers, Ser. 5B, Box 11; Cecil Diary, Jan. 22, 1919, Cecil Papers, 51131.

issues of the recent war but also to lay the basis for lasting peace. He explained that the United States was less interested than other nations in specific terms of the peace settlement because the American people had never feared the war's outcome. It was their ideals that had led them to enter the war and support the future League. Reconciling the isolationist and internationalist aspects of his foreign policy, he stressed the League's importance to the United States. "We regard it," the president asserted, "as the keystone of the whole program which expressed our purpose and our ideal in this war and which the Associated Nations have accepted as the basis of the settlement." In support of Wilson, Lloyd George stated "how emphat-ically the people of the British Empire are behind this proposal." Bourgeois likewise voiced France's "deep enthusiasm" for a league. He observed that local conflicts inevitably threatened the whole world. "There is such an interdependence in all the relations between nations in the economic, financial, moral and intellectual spheres," he stated, "that, I repeat, every wound inflicted at some point threatens to poison the whole organs." Although generally approving the creation of a league, delegates from small states complained about their exclusion from the drafting process. Despite these grumblings, leaders of the great powers asserted their dominance in the peace conference.[37]

This procedure elicited Lansing's strong criticism. Privately, he com-plained that five great powers were running the peace conference like the Congress of Vienna. He said, "the small nations have not more voice in settling the destinies of the world than they had a hundred years ago. . . . Translated into plain terms it will mean that five or six great powers will run the world as they please and the equal voice of the little nations will be a myth." The alienated secretary of state would not play a central role in the peace negotiations. Instead of Lansing, Wilson selected House to serve with himself on the commission that would draft the Covenant. House was more willing to approve the views of Wilson and Lloyd George, both of whom indeed anticipated the great powers' primacy, and especially Anglo-American control, in the future League.[38]

House and Cecil took the initiative to prepare a joint Anglo-American plan for a league. Miller had discussed with Cecil the common characteristics of the British draft convention and Wilson's covenant. Now that the president had modified the provision for automatic war against covenant-breaking states, Miller expressed only one major criticism of the remaining features. He opposed the provision for future revision of boundaries. House instructed him to endeavor to amalgamate British and American plans into a single document. This procedure offered the advantage of avoiding any

37   FR:PPC, III, 177-201; PPWW, V, 395-400.
38   RL Appendix to Diary, Jan. 25, 1919; RL to Polk, Jan. 25, 1919, Polk Papers, 78/8; EMH to WW, Jan. 25, 1919, EMH Papers, 49/12; EMH to DLG, Jan. 25, 1919, EMH Papers, 12/32; EMH to WW, Jan. 23, 25, 1919, WW Papers, Ser. 5B, Box 11; EMH to WW, Jan. 27, 1919, WW Papers, Ser. 5B, Box 12; FR:PPC, III, 694; Auchincloss Diary, Jan. 23-25, 1919, Auchincloss Papers, 55/88.

official American commitment to the resulting joint draft. As long as Lloyd George refused to obligate the British government, House wanted to preserve the same freedom for the president. Taking Wilson's third draft as the basis for discussion, Miller sought British approval with the fewest possible changes. In consultation with Smuts, and with the assistance of Lord Eustace Percy of the Foreign Office, Cecil directed the preparation of British amendments to Wilson's covenant. By January 27 he and Miller agreed on most provisions. At Cecil's request, Miller approved three important alterations so as to allow representation by British dominions and India, to limit membership in the council to the great powers, and to increase the stature of the chancellor's office. The title of this officer was later changed to secretary general. This Cecil-Miller draft resolved most, but not all, of the outstanding differences. Still undetermined were provisions for a permanent court of international justice and a system of mandates. Accompanied by Miller and Wiseman, House and Cecil reviewed this draft. They agreed that the question of mandates was the only major obstacle to complete Anglo-American accord on the future League.[39]

The Council of Ten considered the disposal of Germany's former colonies and the establishment of a mandatory system. It had agreed on January 24 not to restore these colonies to Germany. Lloyd George endorsed the idea of mandates, for which he saw the British Empire as the model. Wanting to protect the British dominions' claims, he committed only Great Britain to this new system. He supported South Africa, Australia and New Zealand in advancing their separate demands for the conquered German colonies in South-West Africa, New Guinea and Samoa. British dominions were not alone in desiring their share of the spoils of war. The Council of Ten heard French claims to the Cameroons and Togoland in central Africa, and also Japanese demands for German islands north of the equator and German rights in the Shantung province of China. During these deliberations, Wilson attempted to convince Allied leaders that trusteeship under a league was preferable to outright annexation. "If any nation could annex territory which was previously a German Colony," he asserted, "it would be challenging the whole idea of the League of Nations." He was afraid that "if the process of annexation went on, the League of Nations would be discredited from the beginning."

As the president firmly opposed the transfer of colonies from one empire to another, Lloyd George and Smuts began to search for a compromise. Despite the reservations of Hughes and, to a lesser extent, of Prime Minister W. F. Massey of New Zealand, Smuts prepared a series of resolutions to establish three classes of mandates. Dividing the conquered parts of the former Turkish and German empires into these classes, the resolution

39   Miller, *My Diary*, I, 86-95; ibid., IV, 16a-c, 163-77, 195-99, 202-04; Miller, *Drafting of the Covenant*, II, 117-41; Auchincloss Diary, Jan. 27, 1919, Auchincloss Papers, 55/88; Cecil Diary, Jan. 21-25, 27, 1919, Cecil Papers, 51131.

distinguished between ostensible levels of development of the affected peoples. The first class included parts of the Turkish Empire, which would enjoy autonomy but not full self-government. Eventual independence was offered as a possibility. The second class encompassed German colonies in central Africa, which the mandatory powers would administer in accordance with principles adopted by the league. The third class of mandates, including German colonies claimed by British dominions, would entail only minimal supervision by the league. After Lloyd George succeeded in gaining the dominions' acceptance of this compromise, Smuts solicited Wilson's approval through House. In accordance with his earlier promise to Derby, House was willing to concede these colonial claims in return for British support for a league. Wilson accepted House's advice. His decision resulted partly from his misplaced confidence in Smuts, who viewed mandates as a veil for annexation. Lloyd George enabled the president to gain a victory for the idea of mandates, while British dominions retained the substance of their colonial claims.[40]

Once the question of mandates was resolved, American and British leaders quickly settled their remaining differences. House and Cecil continued to coordinate joint Anglo-American planning for a league. Although Lloyd George was not enthusiastic about proceeding immediately with this project, he permitted Cecil and Smuts to confer with Wilson, House and Miller on January 31. At this time the president approved the changes that Cecil and Miller had earlier incorporated into their draft. Rather than attempt to agree on elaborate plans for a permanent court of international justice, the conferees decided merely to insert a general provision calling for its later creation. They also agreed, in response to Italy's request, to modify the prohibition of conscription. General Bliss, from whom Wilson had solicited advice, had noted that abolition of conscription would give an unfair advantage to rich nations that could recruit volunteer armies by paying higher wages than poor states could afford. Recognizing that the Cecil-Miller draft, with these additional changes, required polishing, American and British leaders delegated this task to Miller and Cecil J. B. Hurst. These two legal advisers completed their assignment on February 2. In preparing this Hurst-Miller draft, they made one substantial change on their own initiative. They omitted the provision for revision which Wilson and then Cecil had combined with the positive guarantee of political independence and territorial integrity.[41]

40   FR:PPC, III, 718-28, 736-71, 785-817; EMH to WW, Jan. 28, 1919, WW Papers, Ser. 5B, Box 12; EMH to WW, Jan. 28, 1919, Resolutions in Reference to Mandates, Jan. 29, 1919, EMH Papers, 49/12; Auchincloss Diary, Jan. 28-29, 1919, Auchincloss Papers, 55/88; Cecil Diary, Jan. 22, 25, 28-29, 1919, Cecil Papers, 51131; Derby to AJB, Dec. 24, 1919, AJB Papers, 49744/220-21; Smuts to Gillett, Jan. 25 (#895), 29 (#897), 1919, Smuts to Clark, Jan. 31, 1919 (#898), Hancock and van der Poel, eds., Smuts Papers, IV, 55-58.

41   Cecil Diary, Jan. 30-31, 1919, Cecil Papers, 51131; Auchincloss Diary, Jan. 30-31, 1919, Auchincloss Papers, 55/88; EMH Diary, Jan. 31, 1919; THB to EMH, Jan. 31, 1919, EMH Papers, 3/13, and THB Papers, Box 69; Miller, My Diary, I, 100-04, 342-47; ibid., IV, 304a-c, 307-11, 318; Miller, Drafting of the Covenant, II, 142-44; FR:PPC, XI (Washington, 1945), 2.

Wilson now felt hopeful that he could accomplish his goal at the peace conference. But his self-image as a lonely warrior, although justified by Lansing's continued resistance, threatened to destroy the Anglo-American accord that House had fostered in cooperation with Cecil. The president surprisingly denounced the Hurst-Miller draft and began to prepare another draft of a league covenant. Except for allowing representation by small as well as great powers on the executive council, his fourth draft was not substantially different from the Hurst-Miller draft. He even deleted the provision for revision from the positive guarantee of political independence and territorial integrity. Cecil strenuously objected when he learned that the president intended to present his own latest covenant as the basis for deliberations in the drafting commission. With the support of Smuts and House, Cecil succeeded in convincing Wilson to reverse his unilateral decision and preserve Anglo-American collaboration.[42]

Excluded from Anglo-American preparations, French leaders meanwhile had worked for a league of their own liking. At Clemenceau's instigation, Bourgeois invited other national organizations to join the French Association for the Society of Nations for the purpose of developing a common plan. Along with similar groups from Great Britain, Italy, Belgium, Romania, Serbia and China, the League to Enforce Peace participated in this project. Its executive committee had in December 1918 already established a committee in Paris, with Oscar S. Straus as chairman and Hamilton Holt as vice-chairman, to support Wilson's efforts and to advise the New York office. The League to Enforce Peace received no official endorsement or encouragement from the president. Late in January the Paris committee joined similar groups from other countries in unanimously adopting a resolution calling for a powerful league. This resolution, which Bourgeois submitted to Wilson on January 31, proposed an international council to preserve liberty and maintain order. This council would establish a permanent committee on conciliation and also arrange for development of international legislation. The committee on conciliation could mediate any conflict between nations, or refer it either to arbitration or to an international court of justice. The resolution required the settlement of all disputes by peaceful methods. It obligated the league members to use "all means within their power" to prevent any state from resorting to acts of war which would disturb world peace. It also assigned to such a league the responsibility for limiting and supervising the armament of each nation and for prohibiting secret treaties. Only nations which would faithfully fulfill these stringent requirements could be admitted to this proposed league. By endorsing this plan, the League to Enforce Peace showed its willingness to

<hr/>

42 WW to Swope, Feb. 1, 1919, RL to WW, Jan. 31, 1919, Redraft of Resolutions, Jan. 30, 1919, Miller to WW, Feb. 3, 1919, WW to Miller, Feb. 3, 1919, WW Papers, Ser. 5B, Box 13; RL Appendix to Diary, Jan. 29-31, 1919; *FR:PPC*, XI, 3, 7; Miller, *My Diary*, I, 105-06; ibid., IV, 387; ibid., V, 14a; Miller, *Drafting of the Covenant*, II, 145-54; Cecil Diary, Feb. 3, 1919, Cecil Papers, 51131.

support a world organization with greater obligations than Wilson envisaged.[43]

Clemenceau wanted to preserve the wartime coalition and conceived of the League as an alliance against Germany. In the Council of Ten, he repeated his belief that "if, before the war, the Great Powers had made an alliance pledging themselves to take up arms in defence of any one of them who might be attacked, there would have been no war. Today they had not only five nations in agreement but practically the whole world. If the nations pledged themselves not to attack any one without the consent of the members of the League, and to defend any one of them who might be attacked, the peace of the world would be assured. Such an alliance might well be termed a League of Nations."[44] Wilson shared Clemenceau's goal, but not his methods. To the French Senate on January 20, he had related his vision of a league to the security of France: "The whole world is awake, and it is awake to its community of interest. . . . It knows that the peril of France, if it continues, will be the peril of the world. It knows that not only France must organize against this peril, but that the world must organize against it." On February 3, Wilson reiterated this thought to the French Chamber of Deputies. He said, "there shall never be any doubt or waiting or surmise, but that whenever France or any other free people is threatened the whole world will be ready to vindicate its liberty."[45] These assurances, however, did not indicate any intention to establish the future League as a postwar alliance.

The French desire for an anti-German alliance challenged the Anglo-American conception of peace. While Clemenceau sought to restore the balance of power in Europe, Lloyd George and Wilson endeavored to avoid entanglement on the continent. Less concerned about the German problem, they defined their countries' aims in global terms. They identified either British or American interests with universal ideals, while the French concentrated more on the immediate requirements of national security. The ensuing conflict would complicate the negotiations to establish a league. It would, moreover, separate Wilson from some of his opponents at home. Differences between the advocates of a general system of collective security and those of a particular alliance affected not only the peacemaking in Paris but also the treaty fight in the United States.

43   Short to McCormick, Dec. 16, 1918, Taft and Short to McCormick, Dec. 18, 1918, McCormick to Short, Dec. 19, 30, 1919, McCormick Papers, 39/57; Short to McCormick, Dec. 31, 1918, McCormick Papers, 39/56; Miller, *My Diary*, I, 48, 92-93; Cecil Diary, Jan. 26, 1919, Cecil Papers, 51131; Bourgeois to WW, Jan. 31, 1919, WW Papers, Ser. 5B, Box 13; WW to Bourgeois, Feb. 7, 1919, EMH to WW, [Feb. 5, 1919], Holt memorandum, WW Papers, Ser. 5B, Box 14.
44   *FR:PPC*, III, 769; Georges Clemenceau, *Grandeur and Misery of Victory* (New York, 1930), 171-72, 198-99.
45   *PPWW*, V, 392-94, 405-09.

III

Anglo-American cooperation limited French influence during the drafting of the Covenant. At the first meeting of the League of Nations Commission, Wilson presented the Hurst-Miller draft as the basis for deliberation. As agreed, Cecil supported him in overriding the objections of Bourgeois and other delegates that they had not yet had the opportunity even to study this Anglo-American proposal. American and British leaders were determined to maintain their control. By forcing immediate acceptance of the Hurst-Miller draft, they placed other representatives in the difficult position of attempting to achieve their goals for a league through amendments. This procedure immediately thwarted the French initiative to create a powerful international organization to preserve peace.[46]

Foreign Minister Stéphen Pichon belatedly submitted a French plan for a society of nations. Prepared during the spring of 1918 by a commission under Bourgeois' leadership in the Ministry of Foreign Affairs, it provided for military as well as diplomatic, legal and economic sanctions. If conciliation or arbitration failed to resolve a dispute, these sanctions might be employed by an international council against any state that committed aggression. To prepare for military sanctions, the French plan called for the organization of international forces under a permanent staff. Membership in this society of nations would be restricted to states which would loyally fulfill these mutual obligations. This plan provided the basis not only for the resolution that Bourgeois had earlier submitted to Wilson on January 31 but also for subsequent French amendments to the Hurst-Miller draft. Although Bourgeois presented it to the League Commission, the French plan did not enjoy the same official status as the Anglo-American proposal in the ensuing proceedings.[47]

French leaders were not alone in resenting American and British domination of the drafting of the Covenant. When delegates from small states had convened on January 27 to select their five representatives on the League Commission, they began to protest against their subordinate position. They demanded the inclusion of at least four more states out of their total of seventeen. In compliance with the Council of Ten's restriction, the small states elected Belgium, Serbia, Portugal, Brazil and China to the commission. But they also voted for Romania, Poland, Greece and Czechoslovakia as additional choices. In the Council of Ten, which considered the small states' request, Wilson objected to their desire for more representation. He did not want them to enjoy equality with the great powers. On his recommendation, the Council of Ten agreed to refer this question to the

---

46 Miller, *Drafting of the Covenant*, I, 132-35; ibid., II, 230-37; EMH Diary, Feb. 3, 1919; Cecil Diary, Feb. 3, 1919, Cecil Papers, 51131.
47 Pichon to WW, Feb. 4, 1919, Textes Adopté par la Commission, 8 juin 1918, WW Papers, Ser. 5B, Box 13; Miller, *Drafting of the Covenant*, II, 238-46.

League Commission for final decision. Nevertheless, he eventually lost. At its second meeting on February 4, Foreign Minister Paul Hymans of Belgium presented the small states' case. Supported by Bourgeois and the Serbian and Portuguese delegates, he secured a favorable vote in the commission. Despite Wilson's and Cecil's objections, small states gained a larger role in these proceedings.[48]

During subsequent consideration of the Hurst-Miller draft, Hymans and other delegates from small states, aided by Bourgeois and Italian premier Orlando, pressed their demand for membership in the future League's executive council. They generally endorsed the position that Wilson had earlier taken in favor of minority representation by four small states along with the five great powers. Cecil strongly opposed such an alteration but eventually followed the president in making this concession. Nevertheless, with their majority in the executive council and the requirement for unanimity on its vital decisions, the great powers would still retain their primacy in the future League.[49]

In defining the role of great powers in the League, Wilson focused on the positive guarantee of political independence and territorial integrity. This mutual commitment, eventually to emerge from the drafting as Article 10, was, in his opinion, "the key to the whole Covenant." Smuts regarded it as the most far-reaching part of the document. Cecil, who had only reluctantly approved it, now reverted to his earlier preference for a negative covenant. He attempted to remove the positive guarantee from the Hurst-Miller draft, leaving only the obligation for each state in the League to respect other members' political independence and territorial integrity. Cecil's attempt to weaken this article failed as other delegates joined the president in defending it. From Larnaude's French perspective, it was already too weak. This positive guarantee was "only a principle" because it failed to specify the means for its fulfillment. To clarify the procedure for responding to future aggression, Wilson proposed that the executive council should offer advice on the means to fulfill this obligation. After the League Commission approved this amendment, Cecil revived Wilson's earlier idea of periodic revision of international obligations. He later succeeded in inserting it into the Covenant. With this addition, the possibility of revision was again combined with the positive guarantee, as in Wilson's earlier drafts of the Covenant. Article 19 authorized the body of delegates to recommend reconsideration of treaties or other international conditions which might endanger world peace. The net effect of these changes was to leave the positive guarantee as ambiguous as ever. Members of the League would be obligated to protect each other from aggression, but

48 FR:PPC, III, 447-55, 857-58.
49 Miller, Drafting of the Covenant, I, 138-48, 159-63; ibid., II, 256-62, 301-02, 423-26, 470-71; Cecil Diary, Feb. 4-5, 1919, Cecil Papers, 51131; Auchincloss Diary, Feb. 4, 1919, Auchincloss Papers, 55/88.

they would retain the freedom to decide when and how to fulfill this commitment.[50]

Despite their differences over Article 10, British and American leaders alike sought to avoid extensive obligations for their countries. The Hurst-Miller draft would require the league members to submit their conflicts to arbitration or conciliation, if the ordinary processes of diplomacy should fail. Refusal to attempt one of these methods would be regarded *ipso facto* as an act of war, leading to commercial and financial sanctions. On the executive council's recommendation, the League might even use military sanctions. These sanctions were strictly limited to the purpose of forcing the parties to a conflict to submit the issues to arbitration or conciliation. The Hurst-Miller draft did not provide for compulsory arbitration or for enforcement of even the executive council's unanimous recommendations. The key to peace was the cooling-off period for arbitration or conciliation.

Belgium tried to strengthen the Covenant. For any settlement, the Hurst-Miller draft would require a unanimous vote in the executive council, exclusive of the parties to a dispute. Hymans endeavored to remove the power of veto by a single nation in order to permit the executive council to make a recommendation by majority vote. He also wanted to obligate the league members not only to respect but also to enforce a unanimous recommendation. He further sought to empower the League to employ sanctions for the broader purpose of enforcing an arbitral award or a recommendation, rather than only for the limited purpose of requiring submission of disputes to arbitration or conciliation. Sanctions under Article 16 should apply as well to Article 10. Hymans obviously did not wish to rely on a cooling-off period, but favored enforcement of pacific settlement of disputes. All of these Belgian amendments encountered Wilson's and Cecil's opposition, while Bourgeois and various other delegates gave their support. The commission referred this matter to a committee consisting of Hymans, Bourgeois, Cecil and Greek premier Eleutherios K. Venizelos for further study. At its meeting Cecil defeated most of the Belgian amendments. The committee recommended only one change, authorizing the executive council to consider what action to take to enforce its unanimous recommendations. The League Commission approved the amendment, but its decision constituted only a temporary concession. Wilson later successfully reversed this decision, thereby preserving the Hurst-Miller draft's original provisions for pacific settlement of disputes.[51]

Anglo-American control over the drafting limited the League's jurisdiction. Wilson and Cecil prevented what they regarded as excessive obliga-

50   Miller, *Drafting of the Covenant*, I, 168-70, 205; ibid., II, 264, 288-89, 430-31, 457; Cecil Diary, Feb. 6, 1919, Cecil Papers, 51131.
51   Miller, *Drafting of the Covenant*, I, 175-83, 192-95, 290-92, 331; ibid., II, 268-71, 282, 350, 435-38, 449-50; Cecil Diary, Feb. 9-10, 1919, Cecil Papers, 51131; Miller, Memorandum on the Proposed Belgian Amendments, Feb. 7, 1919, Propositions du Délégué Belge, [Feb. 7, 1919], WW Papers, Ser. 5B, Box 14; Miller, *My Diary*, I, 113-15.

tions. "It will be seen," Cecil later wrote, "that there is no provision for the enforcement of any decision by the Council, except so far as the provision goes which lays it down that no State is to be attacked because it carries out the Council's unanimous decision. That was the deliberate policy of the framers of the Covenant. They desired to enforce on the parties a delay of some months before any war took place, believing that during that period some pacific solution would be found. But they did not think that it would be accepted by the nations if there was an attempt to compel them to agree to a solution dictated by the Council." In accordance with this Anglo-American conception of the League, its members would be obligated only to attempt a pacific settlement of conflicts before resorting to war. The purpose of sanctions was merely to enforce a delay, not to impose a settlement. As Cecil noted, "all that the Covenant proposed was that the members of the League, before going to war, should try all pacific means of settling the quarrel."[52]

Clemenceau endeavored to transform this Anglo-American plan into an effective alliance. Through an interview with an Associated Press correspondent, he appealed to the American people "to renounce their traditional aloofness." He cited with approval the president's words of assurance to the Chamber of Deputies that the whole world stood ready to protect the liberty of France and other free nations. Within the League of Nations Commission, Bourgeois and Larnaude attempted to amend the Hurst-Miller draft in conformity with the French plan. Bourgeois offered an amendment, like that of Hymans, which would authorize sanctions against any state that refused to accept an arbitral award or a unanimous recommendation by the executive council. He proposed another amendment to clarify conditions for admission to the League. Beyond its initial members, consisting of the Allied and Associated Powers, he wanted to restrict the League to nations with representative governments that were willing to abide by its principles, including the League's guidelines regarding their military forces. Attempting to amend the Hurst-Miller draft's provision for reduction of national armaments, Bourgeois sought to authorize the executive council to establish control over national military forces and to organize an international force. This was his most important and controversial amendment.

During the ensuing debate, Wilson and Cecil vigorously opposed this French proposal for transforming the future League into a military alliance. The president offered constitutional and political objections to an international force. Placing the American army at the League's disposal, he explained, was incompatible with both the Constitution and public opinion. "Our principal safety," he asserted, "will be obtained by the obligation which we shall lay on Germany to effect a complete disarmament." This

52 Robert Cecil, *A Great Experiment* (New York, 1941), 74-75. On this point, see Lloyd E. Ambrosius, "Wilson's League of Nations," *Maryland Historical Magazine*, LXV (Winter 1970), 369-93, and the criticism of this interpretation in Robert H. Ferrell, *Woodrow Wilson and World War I, 1917-1921* (New York, 1985), 162-67, 275.

argument failed to persuade French delegates. Larnaude countered that "the idea of an international force is bound up with the very idea of the League of Nations, unless one is content that the League should be a screen of false security." In response the president gave his most explicit commitment of American military assistance if required by future circumstances. After Bourgeois continued to press the French case, Wilson further asserted: "All that we can promise, and we do promise it, is to maintain our military forces in such a condition that the world will feel itself in safety. When danger comes, we too will come, and we will help you, but you must trust us. We must all depend on our mutual good faith."[53]

American and British leaders resisted French requests for specific military commitments that would entangle their countries on the continent. Cecil warned a French delegate that "the League of Nations was their only means of getting the assistance of America and England, and if they destroyed it they would be left without an ally in the world." This warning reflected the attitude that House had expressed to Balfour two days earlier. The League Commission referred the French amendments to a committee that it established to review the articles of the Hurst-Miller draft which were already tentatively accepted. When this drafting committee met, Cecil bluntly threatened Larnaude that Great Britain and the United States would form an alliance, excluding France, unless French delegates abandoned their plan for an international force. He described the League as "practically a present to France," and expressed his irritation over French failure to appreciate this Anglo-American gift. As a weak substitute for the French plan, Cecil repeated his offer of the previous day to insert into the Covenant a provision for establishing a permanent commission to advise the League on military and naval affairs. The drafting committee accepted this minor concession as well as the French amendment on requirements for future admission of new members to the League. This committee took no action on the other French amendment concerning sanctions, effectively killing it.[54]

From the French perspective, a viable league would entail specific military obligations. When the League Commission considered the drafting committee's report on February 13, French delegates continued their attempt to strengthen the document, and again failed. Bourgeois explained that "by a thoroughgoing supervision of armaments the League of Nations would discourage any attempt at war." If this international control failed to prevent aggression, French leaders wanted a league capable of responding with sufficient and timely military strength. Coordination of national forces

53   Stone to WW, [c. Feb. 10, 1919], Clemenceau interview, WW Papers, Ser. 5B, Box 16; Amendment to Article VI, Amendment to Article XIV, Amendment to Article VIII, WW Papers, Ser. 5B, Box 15; Eliot to WW, Nov. 17, 1918, WW to Eliot, Nov. 26, 1918, WW Papers, Ser. 2, Box 188; "French Misgivings," *Literary Digest*, LX (Feb. 22, 1919), 18-19; Miller, *Drafting of the Covenant*, I, 206-10; ibid., II, 290-97, 458-66.
54   Cecil Diary, Feb. 11-12, 1919, Cecil Papers, 51131; EMH Diary, Feb. 9, 1919; Miller, *My Diary*, I, 119-21; Miller, *Drafting of the Covenant*, I, 212-20.

would require an international general staff. This French plan continued to encounter British and American rejection. Cecil considered the idea of an international general staff "a perfectly fatuous proposal." He emphatically renounced it, affirming that the future League "could not be considered as an alliance against Germany. Nothing would more quickly imperil peace." As Anglo-American control continued, the commission approved only those changes recommended by the drafting committee. The Covenant would now include Cecil's weak substitute of a permanent advisory commission on military and naval affairs. French leaders failed to transform the Anglo-American plan for a league into an effective alliance for their country's defense.[55]

Japanese delegates did not take an active part in the drafting. In the League Commission on February 13, Baron Nobuaki Makino finally raised the one issue that most interested his country. As an addition to the provision for freedom of religion, he proposed an amendment affirming racial equality. He explained that peoples of various races and nationalities could hardly be expected to assume the responsibilities of the new League unless it affirmed their equality. This Japanese demand challenged the racial prejudice of British and American leaders. Having previously received a copy of the Japanese amendment, House had attempted to prepare an acceptable substitute using language from the American Declaration of Independence. He conferred with Balfour, who rejected the idea that "all men are created equal" as an eighteenth-century proposition. The British foreign secretary said that perhaps all men in a particular nation were equal, but repudiated the notion that black Africans were equal to Europeans. Opposing any amendment that threatened to open the British Empire to Japanese immigration, he denounced as "blackmail" the intimation that Japan might refuse to join the League unless its amendment was accepted. House agreed with this denunciation, but still hoped to find an acceptable compromise. Miller, to whom he assigned the task of drafting a substitute, clearly recognized the difficulty of preparing an amendment which affirmed the principle of racial equality without its having any practical implications. The basic difficulty was that British and American leaders did not believe in this principle. House's efforts were in vain. Rather than adopt any racial equality amendment, the League Commission removed from the Covenant the carefully prepared provision for religious liberty.[56]

Once the League Commission completed its work, Wilson presented the Covenant to the peace conference. His style as well as his words at the plenary session on February 14 exemplified his characteristic combination of

5 5   Miller, *Drafting of the Covenant*, I, 243-60; ibid., II, 303-07, 317-21, 472-79; Cecil Diary, Feb. 13, 1919, Cecil Papers, 51131; Auchincloss Diary, Feb. 11-13, 1919, Auchincloss Papers, 55/88.
5 6   Miller, *My Diary*, I, 116, 118, 121-22; ibid., V, 195, 214-15; Miller, *Drafting of the Covenant*, I, 183-84, 195-96, 267-69; ibid., II, 273-74, 276, 282-83, 307, 315, 323-25, 441, 433-44, 449-52, 486-89; AJB, Conversation with Colonel House on Japanese Claims in Connection with the League of Nations and the Rights of Japanese Immigrants, Feb. 10, 1919, AJB Papers, 49751/177-80.

unilateralism and universalism. He claimed that the League expressed "a common purpose." Although the Covenant was primarily an Anglo-American product, he identified it with all humankind. He ignored dissent from French and Japanese delegates. The League, he claimed, would achieve its goal of maintaining peace by mobilizing the presumed unity of the world. Wilson stressed that "throughout this instrument we are depending primarily and chiefly upon one great force, and that is the moral force of the public opinion of the world." He acknowledged, however, that "the overwhelming light of the universal expression of the condemnation of the world" might not suffice in every case to preserve the new international order. "Armed force is in the background in this programme," he said, "but it is in the background, and if the moral force of the world will not suffice, the physical force of the world shall." What the president did not state explicitly was that the United States and other league members would retain their complete freedom to decide when to offer moral condemnation and when to employ military force. The Covenant reserved this right for each nation. It conformed to the combination of universalism and unilateralism in Wilson's vision of international social control. Announcing that "a living thing is born," he emphasized the League's flexibility. "And yet," he said, "while it is elastic, while it is general in its terms, it is definite in the one thing that we were called upon to make definite. It is a definite guarantee of peace. It is a definite guarantee by word against aggression." Wilson went on to describe the new system of mandates as an altruistic contribution by the advanced countries to the backward peoples of the world. He claimed that this system was in reality not so new, for the Allied and Associated Powers already followed these humane practices in their colonial empires. Nevertheless, he saw the mandatory system, along with the remainder of the Covenant, as a redeeming force in international affairs. "It is practical," Wilson concluded, "and yet it is intended to purify, to rectify, to elevate."[57]

Despite their reservations, European statesmen endorsed the draft Covenant. Cecil, Orlando and Bourgeois praised it for reconciling national sovereignty and world peace. They agreed that the central problem in creating the League was to establish international restraint over states without violating their sovereign rights. There were differences among these delegates over methods. Cecil emphasized, as the Covenant's first principle, the prohibition of war without first attempting arbitration or conciliation. It provided, in his words, "that no nation shall go to war with any other nation until every other possible means of settling the dispute shall have been fully and fairly tried." Giving a somewhat negative interpretation of Article 10, he cited, as the Covenant's second principle, "that, under no circumstances, shall any nation seek forcibly to disturb the territorial settlement to be arrived at as the consequence of this peace or to interfere with the political independence of any of the States in the world." Cecil denounced the idea of

57   FR:PPC, III, 209-15; PPWW, V, 413-29.

the League as an alliance. Like Wilson, he stressed the League's universal character. The Covenant, he thought, provided the foundation for a postwar world in which "the interest of one is the interest of all." Bourgeois, too, noted the common interests of nations throughout the world. But he disagreed with Wilson and Cecil on the appropriate form of organization to express this interdependence. Bourgeois felt strongly that enunciation of principles was not sufficient. He again advocated the French plan for the League's control over national armaments and for an international force. He wished to deter aggression and, should this fail, to prepare in advance for such a contingency. Contrary to the Anglo-American vision of the League, he wanted an effective military alliance. Makino also sounded a dissenting note when he announced that he would later request further consideration by the peace conference of the racial equality amendment. He was obviously unwilling to accept defeat.[58]

Wilson combined internationalist and isolationist elements in the draft Covenant. Other nations should accept Anglo-American rules for international relations, he thought, or the United States should revert to traditional isolation from the Old World. According to his view of interdependence, other nations depended upon the United States, but not the reverse. This country could protect its own vital interests without the new League. Although not necessary for this purpose, the League could facilitate the projection of American influence throughout the world. Yet, by allowing the great powers in the council to determine whether to act during a future crisis, the draft Covenant would permit the United States to make unilateral decisions. It thereby incorporated the features of universalism and unilateralism that characterized Wilson's style of diplomacy. As he interpreted this document, it would authorize a leading American role in the League to maintain peace, and yet it would not entangle the United States in European affairs. This new League of Nations thus embodied his characteristic qualities of idealism and practicality.

58   *FR:PPC*, III, 215-30.

CHAPTER 4

American criticism of Wilson's peacemaking

During the drafting of the Covenant, Wilson's supporters and critics in the United States prepared for the anticipated fight. Despite the Republican victory in the congressional elections of 1918, the Democratic president intended to implement his plans for postwar peace. To a very limited extent, he was willing to recognize the legitimacy of criticism and make revisions in the draft Covenant. He welcomed suggestions from Republicans as well as Democrats, but only on his own terms. He generally dismissed Republican alternatives as partisan and reactionary attacks on his forward-looking vision of a league. Relying on the Democratic party, Wilson expected to take his case to the American people and thereby force the Republican-controlled Senate to approve the peace treaty. He entrusted the future to confrontation rather than compromise. Republican leaders prepared for the confrontation. Unwilling to allow the Senate to play a submissive role, they organized in Washington and throughout the country to force the president to take their views into account. If he ignored them, they would jeopardize his plans for a postwar league.

After presenting the Covenant to the peace conference, Wilson returned to the United States temporarily for the close of the outgoing Congress. On his arrival he was obviously in "a fighting mood."[1] Landing in Boston, he challenged Lodge. All nations were united in their universal desire for a league, the president asserted. "I have come back to report progress," he said, "and I do not believe the progress is going to stop short of the goal." Claiming that the Old World had gone through a process of redemption and now joined the United States in inaugurating "new standards of right" for this "new age" of righteous unity, he explained that "when they saw that America not only held the ideals but acted the ideals, they were converted to America and became firm partisans of those ideals." Wilson used this

[1] Long Diary, Feb. 26, 1919, Breckinridge Long Papers, Box 2, Library of Congress.

supposed unanimity among the nations at the peace conference to pressure domestic opponents into accepting his program. If the United States failed to deliver this promised peace, he warned, disappointment and despair would ensue. The resulting bitterness would foster revolutionary Bolshevism. "All nations will be set up as hostile camps again; men at the peace conference will go home with their heads upon their breasts, knowing they have failed – for they were bidden not to come home from there until they did something more than sign a treaty of peace."[2] As the antidote to radical revolution, the president offered his conception of international social control as embodied in the Covenant.

Wilson's challenge to his Republican critics, proclaimed in Boston on February 24, followed the earlier pattern of his politics. Before the congressional elections of 1918, Homer S. Cummings, soon to become chairman of the Democratic National Committee, had urged a partisan approach to peacemaking. He stressed the importance of victory in those elections.[3] Joseph P. Tumulty, the president's secretary, had also encouraged Wilson to adopt a partisan approach. He repeatedly urged him to appeal for the re-election of a Democratic majority in the Senate and House of Representatives. After consulting Colonel House, Wilson issued an appeal on the eve of the elections. He defined the outcome as a vote of confidence in his leadership. Identifying himself with the national interest, he claimed that "I am asking your support not for my own sake or for the sake of a political party, but for the sake of the nation itself, in order that its inward unity of purpose may be evident to all the world."[4]

Wilson had promised to accept the voters' decision, but the Republican triumph in 1918 caused him to have second thoughts. Rather than acquiesce, he hoped that success at Paris would enable him to overcome opposition in the United States. George Creel, chairman of the Committee on Public Information, encouraged him to continue the struggle to "make the world safe for democracy." He attributed the defeat to the fact that "the reactionary Republicans had a clean record of anti-Hun imperialistic patriotism." To overcome this problem, Creel recommended a concerted campaign through the press. "You will have to give out your program for peace and reconstruction and find friends for it," he advised Wilson. "Otherwise, the reactionary patrioteers will defeat the whole immediate future of reform and progress."[5] Tumulty likewise urged the president not to

2   *PPWW*, V, 432-40; U.S. Senate, 65 Cong., 3 Sess., *CR*, Vol. 57, 4201-03; [speech outline], Feb. 24, 1919, WW Papers, Ser. 5B, Box 17.
3   Cummings to WW, Oct. 22, 1918, WW Papers, Ser. 2, Box 186.
4   Joseph P. Tumulty, *Woodrow Wilson as I Know Him* (Garden City, 1921), 322-34; JPT to WW, June 18, Sept. 18, 1918, JPT Papers, Box 5; JPT to EMH, June 18, July 26, Oct. 7, 1918, JPT to WW, June 18, 1918, Draft by JPT to WW, July 26, 1918, EMH Papers, 19/2; President's appeal, JPT Papers, Box 7. See also Seward W. Livermore, *Woodrow Wilson and the War Congress, 1916-18* (Seattle, 1966), 105-247, and David M. Kennedy, *Over Here: The First World War and American Society* (New York, 1980), 231-45.
5   Creel to WW, Nov. 8, 1918, WW Papers, Ser. 2, Box 188.

compromise. Noting the potential domestic impact of successful international diplomacy, he shared the *Springfield Republican*'s advice: "In its democratic and progressive aspects the lines of the struggle at the peace conference do not follow national lines entirely; they run through the nations themselves. If the president knows how to rally to his support the sympathetic elements in Great Britain, France and Italy, he may neutralize the influences working against him in his own country."[6]

Wilson had recognized his Republican critics, especially Lodge, as formidable opponents. As an alternative to a league of nations, the Massachusetts senator emphasized physical guarantees to preserve the American and Allied victory. He asserted, moreover, the right of Congress to participate in the peacemaking.[7] Although they shared the goal of lasting peace, Wilson felt "genuine anxiety" about Lodge's threat to his leadership, particularly since the senator would become chairman of the Foreign Relations Committee.[8] Because other prominent Republicans posed similar challenges, the president had excluded them from the American delegation to the peace conference. Viewing Root as hopelessly reactionary, he thought "his appointment would discourage every liberal element in the world."[9] Taft and other possibilities were also unacceptable. "I would not dare take Mr. Taft," Wilson declared. "I have lost all confidence in his character."[10] He wanted to overwhelm rather than conciliate his Republican critics.

Believing that Republican leaders were implacable foes, Wilson decided to land in Boston. Various advisers in Washington had proposed the idea. Although refusing to endorse Tumulty's elaborate plans for a formal reception, he agreed to deliver an extemporaneous address.[11] He made this decision despite his earlier request to the Senate Foreign Relations Committee and House Foreign Affairs Committee to dine with him at the White House and, meanwhile, to refrain from debate over the draft Covenant. On his last day in Paris, at House's instigation, the president had issued this invitation.[12] When House later learned through newspaper reports about preparations for an important presidential speech in Boston, he immediately recognized the impropriety. He thought Wilson should extend the courtesy

6 JPT to WW, Dec. 17, 1918, WW Papers, Ser. 5B, Box 3.
7 Anderson to WW, Nov. 14, 1918, "Lodge Warns Against Pacifist Sentimentality in Making Peace Terms," *Boston Evening Transcript* (Nov. 13, 1918), WW Papers, Ser. 2, Box 187.
8 WW to Anderson, Nov. 18, 1918, WW Papers, Ser. 2, Box 188.
9 WW to McAdoo, Nov. 25, 1918, WW Papers, Ser. 2, Box 188; EMH to WW, Nov. 10, 1918, EMH Papers, 49/11B, and WW Papers, Ser. 2, Box 187.
10 WW to Hooker, Nov. 29, 1918, WW Papers, Ser. 2, Box 189.
11 NDB to WW, Jan. 1, 1919, WW Papers, Ser. 5B, Box 5; JPT to WW, Jan. 6, 6 (#2), 1919, WW Papers, Ser. 5B, Box 6, and JPT Papers, Box 6; Gregory to WW, Jan. 14, 1919, WW Papers, Ser. 5B, Box 8; Grayson to JPT, Jan. 23, 1919, JPT to Grayson, Jan. 25, 1919, JPT Papers, Box 1; JPT to WW, Feb. 15, 18, 21, 22, 1919, WW to JPT, Feb. 18, 20, 21, 22, 22, 23, 1919, JPT Papers, Box 6; JPT to WW, Feb. 15, 18, 1919, WW to JPT, [Feb. 21, 22, 1919], WW Papers, Ser. 5B, Box 16; JPT to Grayson, Feb. 20, 1919, WW to JPT, Feb. 20, 1919, WW Papers, Ser. 5B, Box 17.
12 WW to JPT, Feb. 14, 1919, EMH Papers, 49/12, 20; Auchincloss Diary, Feb. 14, 1919, Auchincloss Papers, 55/88; JPT to HCL, Feb. 15, 1919, HCL Papers, File 1919 (Peace, League, Political, I-Z).

of first reporting on the peacemaking to appropriate congressional commit-tees. In a message radioed to the U.S.S. *George Washington*, he advised the president to limit his comments in Boston to generalities.[13] Attempting to avoid an affront to Congress, House compounded the difficulties. He prepared a telegram for Lodge, asserting that newspaper reports about a Boston address were "entirely erroneous." At his request, White dispatched this misleading message to the Republican leader.[14] The result was sheer duplicity in the Wilson administration's relations with Lodge and his congressional colleagues.

In Lodge's opinion, it was "very characteristic" that the president would make a speech in the senator's state after requesting his silence. He complained to White about Wilson's dishonorable action.[15] Despite the circumstances, Governor Calvin Coolidge of Massachusetts encouraged Lodge to remain silent, noting that the existence of pacifist elements made it inadvisable to take a negative stand on the League. He later reported that Wilson had failed to win support for the League because "patriot and pacifist are alike likely to agree about the undesirability of entanglements." Lodge appreciated the governor's report.[16] From other sources as well, he learned that the president's address had not been notably successful.[17]

After practicing the politics of confrontation in Boston, Wilson proceeded to Washington. He hosted the Foreign Relations Committee and Foreign Affairs Committee at the White House on February 26. After dinner he responded to questions about the Covenant, especially from Republican senators Philander C. Knox of Pennsylvania and Frank B. Brandegee of Connecticut. The meeting was amicable, but it did not change any opinions. Lodge was not impressed, noting that "the President answered questions for two hours about the draft of the constitution of the League of Nations, and told us nothing."[18]

Wilson did not rely on his explanation of the Covenant to senators and representatives to gain their endorsement. At a White House luncheon on February 28 for the Democratic National Committee, he called upon these partisan leaders to take the issue to the country. To his fellow Democrats the president said that he was not discouraged by the 1918 congressional elections. Labeling himself as "an uncompromising partisan," he continued

1 3   EMH to WW, Feb. 18, 1919, Auchincloss Papers, 55/88, and WW Papers, Ser. 5B, Box 17.
1 4   HW to HCL, [Feb. 19, 1919], EMH Papers, 12/60; Auchincloss Diary, Feb. 19, 1919, Auchincloss Papers, 55/88; HW to HCL, Feb. 20, 1919, HCL Papers, File 1919 (Henry White).
1 5   HCL to Thayer, Feb. 21, 1919, HCL Papers, File 1919 (Adams-Trevelyan); HCL to HW, Feb. 21, 1919, Henry White Papers, Box 38, Library of Congress.
1 6   Coolidge to HCL, Feb. 22, 24, 1919, HCL to Coolidge, Feb. 24, 26, 1919, HCL Papers, File 1919 (Peace, League, Political, A-H). On the Coolidge-Lodge relationship during the treaty fight, see Donald R. McCoy, *Calvin Coolidge: The Quiet President* (New York, 1967), 105-13.
1 7   HCL to L. A. Coolidge, Feb. 27, 1919, L. A. Coolidge to HCL, Feb. 25, 1919, HCL Papers, File 1919 (Peace, League, Political, A-H).
1 8   HCL, *The Senate and the League of Nations*, 99-100; HCL to Bigelow, Feb. 27, 1919, HCL Papers, File 1919 (Adams-Trevelyan); Polk to Auchincloss, March 1, 1919, Polk Papers, 82/19, Auchincloss Papers, 55/89, and EMH Papers, 16/9.

to look to his party to organize public support for the League. Confident that the politics of confrontation were succeeding, he thought "the magnificent reception" in Boston had forced Lodge to modify his opposition. In his speech earlier that day, the senator seemed to look for a compromise by suggesting amendments to the Covenant rather than outright rejection. Defining the fight over the League as "the real issue of the day," the president said that "the immediate thing that we can do is to have an overwhelming national endorsement of this great plan. If we have that we will have settled most of the immediate political difficulties in Europe." Failure to establish a league would, in contrast, lead to the "utter dissolution of society," and this state of anarchy would promote Bolshevism.

Orderly progress at home and abroad – which Wilson advocated as the alternative to radical revolution – depended upon the future League. He acknowledged that the proposed world organization was not perfect, but thought this form of international social control offered the best hope for peace. Had such a league existed before the World War, it would have deterred Germany's aggression. He absolutely rejected the Republican idea of separating the Covenant from the peace treaty because the League was "the heart of the treaty." In Wilson's view, the world's peoples, unable to depend upon their own governments, looked to Democrats to ensure that the United States would serve in the League as the world's policeman. He wanted his party to prove that "we are ready to put the whole power and influence of America at the disposal of free men everywhere in the world no matter what the sacrifice involved, no matter what the danger to the cause." The president showed nothing but contempt for the league opponents, saying that "of all the blind and little provincial people, they are the littlest and most contemptible." Rejecting Republican alternatives, he called upon Democratic leaders to prepare for the treaty fight.[19]

I

Lodge and his Republican colleagues had anticipated this fight. After the armistice in November 1918, he expressed his doubt to former Senator Albert J. Beveridge that American and Allied delegates to the peace conference could create an effective league. "My own belief is," wrote Lodge, "that when they undertake to make a League to Enforce Peace, they will find the difficulties overwhelming and that there will be very little come out of it except empty words." Nevertheless, Lodge was unwilling to adopt an irreconcilable position.[20] Although skeptical about prospects for a league, he endeavored to make a positive contribution to the peacemaking. He summarized his views in an extensive memorandum, which he gave to White

19   Address of the President to the Democratic National Committee, Feb. 28, 1919, JPT Papers, Box 6.
20   Beveridge to HCL, Nov. 27, 1919, HCL to Beveridge, Nov. 23, Dec. 3, 1918, HCL Papers, File 1918 (General Correspondence, A-G).

on December 2, authorizing him to show it to Balfour and Clemenceau. Offering various specific ideas for "physical guarantees" to ensure a favorable balance of power against Germany, he refused to endorse Wilson's vision of collective security. Linkage of a league with the treaty would not only delay peace, he warned, but also jeopardize the treaty's ratification by the United States.[21]

Knox and Lodge launched their public campaign in the Senate to divide the League from the peace treaty with Germany. On December 3, Knox introduced a resolution calling for postponement of a new league but reaffirming American commitment to "guarantees against the German menace." In the event of future German aggression, he favored a defensive alliance. He outlined "a new American doctrine" on December 18, promising that the United States would join the Allies to protect their freedom and peace against such a menace. Knox reconciled his new doctrine with the Monroe Doctrine. "It entangles us in no way," he claimed, "but it makes us the potential ally of the defenders of liberty whenever a great menace shall arise." In his opinion, the Monroe Doctrine did not prevent the United States from joining a defensive alliance, as it had done during the World War. Desiring to maintain the primacy which the Allied and Associated Powers had achieved with victory, Knox explained that "this league we have stands ready to enforce the conditions of peace." Yet he did not rule out the possibility of a new league sometime in the future. Knox wanted to avoid a vague and unlimited commitment, but he was willing to join Europe for defensive purposes. "If it prove wise for the United States to enter some definite entente, well and good, provided it be a small and natural one, bringing only limited and appropriate obligations," he explained. With this "new American doctrine," and despite his disclaimer, Knox was clearly departing from the American diplomatic tradition of isolation from Europe.[22]

Recognizing that Wilson would not welcome this advice, Lodge nevertheless asserted the Senate's right to offer it. He reminded the president on December 21 that "no treaty can become binding upon the United States or be made the supreme law of the land without the consent of the Senate." Lodge's constitutional position, as Republican senator Robert M. La Follette of Wisconsin reminded his colleagues, differed substantially from Wilson's as summarized in *Constitutional Government in the United States*. In his advice on peacemaking, Lodge distinguished between rhetoric and reality. "We must deal with human nature as it is and not as it ought to be," he warned, "if we are to have any beneficial and effective results or if we are to convert ideals into realities." Desiring an enforceable peace with Germany before considering a league, he offered his suggestions for physical guarantees. Like

21 HCL to WW, Dec. 2, 1918, memorandum, HCL Papers, File 1918 (R-Z); HCL to AJB, Nov. 25, 1918, HCL Papers, File 1918 (General Correspondence, A-G), and AJB Papers, 49742/181-85.
22 CR, Vol. 57, 603-08; HCL to L. A. Coolidge, Dec. 20, 1918, HCL Papers, File 1918 (General Correspondence, A-G).

Knox, Lodge was not expressing an isolationist attitude. Favoring a definite alliance instead of a universal league, he warned that "we ought to be extremely careful that in our efforts to reach the millennium of universal and eternal peace we do not create a system which will breed dissensions and wars." Despite his preference for delaying consideration of a league, he recognized that the initiative lay with the president. Lodge questioned whether Germany would be a member or whether small nations would have voting equality with the major powers. He also wanted to know whose troops would enforce the League's decrees and whether the United States would abandon the Monroe Doctrine or surrender its jurisdiction over immigration and tariffs. All of these potential problems led Lodge to advocate delay in considering a league.[23]

In their campaign to separate the League from the peace treaty, Lodge and Knox followed Roosevelt's recommendation. The former president wanted the United States to continue its coalition with the European Allies but doubted the wisdom of creating a more general league. He thought, however, that Republicans should avoid an absolutely negative response to a new international organization. While endorsing the Knox resolution, Roosevelt added that "the League of Nations may do a little good, but the more pompous it is and the more it pretends to do, the less it will really accomplish. The talk about it has a grimly humorous suggestion of the talk about the Holy Alliance a hundred years ago, which had as its main purpose the perpetual maintenance of peace." He shared his views with Balfour. Writing as a Republican leader, he informed the British foreign secretary that "we feel that each country must have the absolute right to determine its own economic policy, and while we will gladly welcome any feasible scheme for a League of Nations, we prefer that it should begin with our present allies, and be accepted only as an addition to, and in no sense as a substitute for the preparedness of our own strength for our own defense." Roosevelt hoped American delegates in Paris would cooperate with Allied leaders rather than remain aloof. "Above all," he wrote, "we feel that at the Peace Conference, America should act, not as an umpire between our allies and our enemies, but as one of the allies bound to come to an agreement with them, and then to impose this common agreement upon our vanquished enemies."[24]

Other leading Republicans supported Lodge and Knox's strategy. Senator Frank B. Kellogg of Minnesota welcomed the Knox resolution, although he hoped for an acceptable league. He kept an open mind on the kind of league he would favor, explaining that "I shall go as far as possible in sustaining measures necessary to prevent the recurrence of war, provided they do not infringe upon those national rights which I believe all of us deem to be

23   CR, Vol. 57, 723-28.
24   Roosevelt to Knox, Dec. 6, 1918, Roosevelt to AJB, Dec. 10, 1918, Elting E. Morison, ed., The Letters of Theodore Roosevelt, VIII (Cambridge, 1954), 1413-15; HCL to Adams, Dec. 28, 1918, HCL Papers, File 1918 (General Correspondence, A-G); Miller, My Diary, I, 49.

necessary to the future prosperity and happiness of this people." Wanting to preserve American sovereignty, he opposed any "world supergovernment" or "world police." He favored a general arbitration agreement, noting that the Republican administration of President Taft and Secretary of State Knox had successfully negotiated arbitration treaties with Great Britain and France. More optimistic than Lodge or Knox, Kellogg saw progress toward world peace in the destruction of Germany's military autocracy. He thought that democratic nations desired peace. Paraphrasing Abraham Lincoln's view on the irreconcilable conflict between freedom and slavery in the United States, he concluded that peace depended on the triumph of democracy over autocracy in the world.[25]

Efforts by Republican leaders failed to produce a different approach to peacemaking. Knox attempted without success to convince the Foreign Relations Committee to report his resolution to the Senate.[26] Lodge regretted that the president refused to heed Republican senators' advice. During the drafting of the Covenant in February 1919, he lamented the consequent delay in preparing the peace treaty with Germany. He anticipated, however, that Wilson would turn the issue of delay against Republicans by attaching the League to the treaty, and then blaming the Senate for not quickly approving the entire package.[27] Knox and Lodge were frustrated in their attempt to promote alternatives to Wilson's program.

II

Some Republicans outside the Senate were much more enthusiastic about a league of nations. After the armistice in November 1918, Lowell had encouraged Lodge to adopt a positive stance. Reminding him that in May 1916, at a League to Enforce Peace dinner, he had spoken in favor of this idea, Harvard's president invited the senator to address another meeting of this pro-league lobby. He hoped the Republican party would not take a negative position now that Wilson embraced the league idea. Lodge declined the invitation, explaining that the longer he had studied it, the greater the difficulties and dangers of establishing a league appeared. One problem was the question of whether or when Germany should become a member. He felt that at least "a little time must elapse before we can make Germany a full partner with us in such a league." Refusing either to endorse or reject a future league, Lodge wanted to postpone this issue.[28] His refusal to associate

---

25 *CR*, Vol. 57, 73-79.
26 U.S. Senate, Committee on Foreign Relations, *Proceedings of the Committee on Foreign Relations, United States Senate: From the Sixty-third Congress (Beginning April 7, 1913) to the Sixty-seventh Congress (Ending March 3, 1923)* (Washington, 1925), 130; *CR*, Vol. 57, 2420.
27 HCL to Hopkins, Feb. 12, 1919, HCL to Gilmore, Feb. 12, 1919, HCL Papers, File 1919 (Peace, League, Political, A-H).
28 ALL to HCL, Nov. 27, 1918, HCL to ALL, Nov. 29, 1918, HCL Papers, File 1918 (H-Q), and ALL Papers.

with the League to Enforce Peace did not discourage Lowell or Taft. They continued their efforts even though the president, too, in Taft's opinion, seemed to have lost faith in the political feasibility of converting this ideal into reality. They hoped that in Paris Wilson would insist upon a league, including at least the United States and the principal Allies, to enforce the treaty and maintain peace.[29]

Against Republican criticism Taft defended the president's decision to attend the peace conference, and encouraged him to head the League. Repudiating the strategy of Lodge and Knox, the former president insisted that "a treaty of peace can not be made at Paris by which the peace of Europe can be secured and maintained without a league of nations." He argued that an international police force would not be as menacing as its critics claimed. "In most instances," he stated, "no actual force will need to be raised. The existence of an agreement and confidence that the nations will comply with it is all that will be needed." American obligations, in Taft's view, could be limited not only by the League's value as a deterrent but also by the division of the world into spheres of influence. "In the convenient division of the world into zones in which the respective great powers shall undertake the responsibility of seeing to it that members of the league conform to the rules laid down by the treaty," he contended, "it will be unnecessary for any nation to send forces to a distant quarter. The United States can properly take care of the Western Hemisphere and need not maintain in normal times a military establishment more extensive than she ought to maintain for domestic use and the proper maintenance of the Monroe doctrine without such a league."[30] Taft's vision of a league to enforce peace promised global security and peace without any appreciable cost to the United States.

When Wilson and Allied leaders completed the Covenant in February 1919, Taft enthusiastically congratulated him. He saw it as essentially fulfilling the goal of the League to Enforce Peace. Praising the Covenant's "elastic character," he noted that it "does not rigidly maintain the status quo, but makes provision for development and progress among nations." Reconciling Article 10 with the American diplomatic tradition, he asserted that it extended the Monroe Doctrine throughout the world. "The United States is not under this constitution to be forced into actual war against its will," Taft emphasized. "This league is to be regarded as in conflict with the advice of Washington only with a narrow and reactionary viewpoint." To promote the Senate's approval, Taft and Lowell gave their encouragement and assistance to the president. Convinced that public opinion was on their side, they informed him that "the American people will support you in a really effective league." To demonstrate the reality of this claim, the League to Enforce Peace organized a series of nine regional congresses throughout the

29 WHT to Wickersham, Dec. 11, 1918, WHT and ALL to Wickersham, Dec. 11, 1918, ALL to WHT, Dec. 13, 1918, ALL Papers.
30 CR, Vol. 57, 119-20, 1911-12.

country from Boston and New York through Chicago and Minneapolis to San Francisco. Taft and other distinguished speakers addressed these congresses as the League to Enforce Peace endeavored to rally both Republicans and Democrats to the draft Covenant.[31]

These attempts to win bipartisan support for a league encountered strong resistance within the Republican party. Beveridge encouraged various Republican senators to take up this issue. In late January he urged William E. Borah of Idaho to deliver speeches of warning to the country. Disputing the president's claim that a league would fulfill the purpose of American intervention in the World War, Beveridge observed that in any event the voters had repudiated any such mandate in the 1918 elections. He rejected Wilson's and Taft's contention that the United States must join an international organization to guarantee the peace settlement. Borah hardly needed this encouragement. Frustrated that Republican leaders had not taken a position of outright opposition to any league, he responded, "I find most fault just now, Beveridge, with the lack of nerve and vision of our own party." Unlike Knox and Lodge, and in direct contrast to Taft and Lowell, Beveridge and Borah irreconcilably opposed the very idea of a league at any time.[32]

Borah had already launched his campaign against a league. In early December 1918, he called it the most serious proposition to confront the American people since the Constitution's adoption. He denied that a league would have prevented the World War and criticized the vagueness of its proponents' ideas. Disputing their claim that it would ensure peace, the senator asserted that "in its last analysis the proposition is force to destroy force, conflict to prevent conflict, militarism to destroy militarism, war to prevent war." He recognized common interests of the United States with Great Britain and France, but not with eastern Europe or Asia or Africa. He opposed a universal league that would not only entangle the United States throughout the world but also threaten the Monroe Doctrine. Rejecting any infringement upon the sovereign power of the United States, he praised the value of nationalism. "Americanism, the most vital principle in civilization to-day, the hope of the world," Borah concluded, "is not to be compromised, much less abandoned." In January 1919 he turned his criticism against the kind of international organization "based entirely upon the principle of repression" that Taft and the League to Enforce Peace advocated. He feared

3 1   CR, Vol. 57, 3538-39; Short to WW, Feb. 9, 1919, WHT and ALL to WW, Feb. 10, 1919, WHT and Bancroft to WW, Feb. 12, 1919, WW Papers, Ser. 5B, Box 15; WW to Short, Feb. 14, 19, 1919, WW to WHT, Feb. 14, 1919, Short to WW, Feb. 15, 1919, WW Papers, Ser. 5B, Box 16; Osborn et al. to Friends of the League of Nations, [Spring 1919], WW Papers, Ser. 4, File 4767.
3 2   Beveridge to Borah, Jan. 26, 31, 1919, Borah to Beveridge, Jan. 28, 1919, Albert J. Beveridge Papers, Box 214, Library of Congress; Borah to Beveridge, Jan. 28, 1919, Beveridge to Borah, Jan. 31, 1919, William E. Borah Papers, Box 551, Library of Congress. See also John Braeman, *Albert J. Beveridge: American Nationalist* (Chicago, 1971), 258-63, and Robert James Maddox, *William E. Borah and American Foreign Policy* (Baton Rouge, 1969), 50-72.

that the United States would end the war by adopting the very system it had been fighting.[33]

Both privately and publicly, Borah warned about the propaganda campaign against "Americanism" of the League to Enforce Peace. This powerful organization, which enjoyed ample financial resources contributed by wealthy men, seemed to pose a threat of internationalism no less grave than Bolshevism. "With the Bolshevists working away with pick ax and dynamite at one point upon the fabric and the League to Enforce Peace at another point," the senator complained, "it is difficult to tell just how long the real Americans will sit still and permit the infamous propaganda to go on. I have just as much respect for the Bolshevist who would internationalize our whole system from below as I would for the broadcloth gentlemen who would internationalize it from above."[34]

After the completion of the draft Covenant, Borah continued his attack on the proposed League. He saw it as "the most radical departure" from the American diplomatic tradition. Under Article 10's unlimited commitment, he warned, we "are pledging ourselves, our honor, our sacred lives, to the preservation of the territorial possessions the world over and not leaving it to the judgment and sense of the American people but to the diplomats of Europe." Encouraged by Beveridge, the senator now began to focus on anticipated British domination of the League. Observing that Canada, Australia, New Zealand and South Africa as well as Great Britain would vote, he asserted that "this constitution of the league of nations is the greatest triumph for English diplomacy in three centuries of English diplomatic life." Adherence to the traditional policy seemed to offer friendly Anglo-American relations without this League's dangers. Borah sought, above all, to preserve freedom for the United States to make unilateral decisions in foreign affairs.[35]

Like Borah, Senator Miles Poindexter of Washington refused to honor Wilson's request to postpone congressional debate over the proposed League. He thought it was unfair for the president to expect Congress to wait in silence while members of his own administration, as well as the League to Enforce Peace and other proponents such as the Carnegie Endowment for International Peace, were busily promoting it. On February 19, Poindexter opened the Republican attack in the Senate on the draft Covenant. He saw this proposal as a direct threat to American independence. Membership in this League would require the American people to "become a party to all the international complications arising from diversity of race and language and

3 3 *CR*, Vol. 57, 189-97, 1383-87, 1582-84, 2425; Borah to Krogness, Feb. 14, 1919, Borah Papers, Box 551.
3 4 Borah to Babb, Feb. 4, 1919, Borah to Frahm, Feb. 10, 1919, Borah to Gwinn, Feb. 27, 1919, Borah to Kluck, Feb. 28, 1919, Borah to French, March 1, 1919, Borah Papers, Box 550; *CR*, Vol. 57, 2654-56.
3 5 *CR*, Vol. 57, 3911-15; Beveridge to Borah, Feb. 15, 17, 1919, Borah Papers, Box 551, and Beveridge Papers, Box 214.

conflict of interests of the various peoples of Asia, Africa, and Europe." In contrast to Wilson and other advocates of globalism, he recognized that a league would not create unanimity out of the world's existing pluralism. The choice before the United States was, therefore, whether to maintain its diplomatic tradition of isolation or to assume a new role of world policeman. Poindexter opposed such a world-wide obligation and consequently became an irreconcilable foe of Wilson's League.[36]

Not all ardent opponents of the president's foreign policy came from the Republican party. Democratic Senator James A. Reed of Missouri vigorously challenged the premises underlying his conception of peace. Like Poindexter, Reed emphasized the world's diversity. In a plural world, given the inherent evil of men, there were many causes of war, including especially racial conflict. Nations could not depend merely on moral suasion or trust in God for their defense. An effective league would require military force, which would entail obligations that Reed rejected for the United States. He questioned the assumption of Wilson's supporters, such as Senator Williams, that the British and American governments would dominate a league of nations. In any case, Reed did not approve this imperial dream of universal peace. Because the United States was not an appropriate model for all peoples in a plural world, it should refrain from imposing its values and institutions on other civilizations in the Orient. But under Wilson's plan, he observed, "it appears that we are to impose our Christian civilization, our peculiar type of civilization, to some extent upon these races and peoples." He opposed such a mission for the United States. Ignoring Wilson's request for silence, he warned that Americans should not assume they could control this League, which was likely to be "dominated by European monarchs and Asiatic despots." In Reed's opinion, the Covenant would at once destroy the diplomatic tradition and violate the Constitution of the United States by transferring its sovereignty to the new League.[37]

III

In the midst of these attacks on the Covenant, Wilson instructed Senator Gilbert M. Hitchcock of Nebraska, Democratic chairman of the Foreign Relations Committee in the outgoing Congress, on the appropriate response. Hitchcock had asked whether Democrats should remain silent or answer Republicans. The president, despite his request for postponing congressional debate, authorized Democratic senators "to feel at liberty to answer criticisms of the league of nations."[38] While he was encouraging confrontation,

---

36   CR, Vol. 57, 3746-48; Beveridge to Poindexter, Feb. 17, 23, 1919, Poindexter to Beveridge, Feb. 19, 24, 1919, Beveridge Papers, Box 217; Poindexter to Short, March 6, 1919, League to Enforce Peace Papers, Box 11, Houghton Library, Harvard University.

37   CR, Vol. 57, 85-91, 2730-35, 3756-59, 4026-33.

38   JPT to WW, Feb. 19, 1919, WW to JPT, Feb. 21, 1919, JPT Papers, Box 6; JPT to WW, Feb. 19, 1919, WW Papers, Ser. 5B, Box 16.

Hitchcock and Senator Thomas J. Walsh of Montana consulted some Republican senators who favored the proposed League but wanted to offer suggestions for improvement. To take such constructive criticism into account, Walsh invited the president to meet a few Democratic senators, including Hitchcock, for the purpose of reviewing the draft Covenant. Wilson declined this invitation, claiming that "on the whole I think that its reasonable interpretation is clear and that it is a thoroughly workable instrument." He noted the probable difficulty of revising the Covenant in Paris. He wanted outspoken support, not advice, from Democratic senators. Without serious consultation, he expected the Senate's approval of his League.[39]

Various members of the Wilson administration had already begun to speak out. Early in January, when Reed denounced the league idea before the Chamber of Commerce in St. Louis, Third Assistant Secretary of State Breckinridge Long responded with a vigorous, although vague, defense. The president, who subsequently approved Long's action, asked him and others to coordinate with Tumulty their efforts to influence public opinion.[40]

Wilson's supporters failed to serve him well. Democratic proponents of a league frequently resorted to generalities and failed to answer the critics' real questions. Williams, one of Wilson's most ardent defenders, based his hope for peace on God's justice and man's rationality. He assumed that, as the world-wide extension of the Monroe Doctrine, a league would invariably conform to American desires. He foresaw world federalism based on the American model.[41]

In the outgoing Congress the most outspoken protagonist for Wilson's peacemaking was lame-duck Senator J. Hamilton Lewis of Illinois. He viewed a league as a Christian institution, which would rely primarily on public opinion. While not promising that it could guarantee peace, he was unrestrained in his belief that the United States should seek the hegemonial role as humankind's guardian. He dreamed of "America enthroned in her virtues, presiding as the mistress of the fates of the world."[42] Early in January 1919, Lewis charged that Knox, Lodge, Borah and Reed were attempting to undermine Wilson in Paris with the threat that the Senate would not approve the peace treaty. He saw this assault as a Republican conspiracy. He suggested that surely Republicans would not continue to resist the God-given mission of the United States. Hastening to defend the draft Covenant without regard for Wilson's earlier request for delay in the

---

39   Walsh to WW, Feb. 25, 1919, WW to Walsh, Feb. 26, 1919, WW Papers, Ser. 5B, Box 17.
40   Graham to Wilson, Jan. 17, 1919, WW Papers, Ser. 5B, Box 9; Long to WW, Feb. 25, 1919, Long, "The League of Nations," Jan. 8, 1919, WW to Long, Feb. 26, 1919, WW Papers, Ser. 4, File 4767; Gerard to WW, Feb. 27, 1919, WW to Gerard, Feb. 28, 1919, WW Papers, Ser. 4, File 635; Long Diary, Jan. 7, Feb. 25, 27, 1919, Long Papers, Box 2.
41   *CR*, Vol. 57, 84-85, 197-99, 1584; Williams to WW, Dec. 11, 1918, WW Papers, Ser. 5B, Box 2.
42   *CR*, Vol. 57, 79-83, 178-89.

congressional debate, Lewis argued that the proposed League was fully consistent with the American diplomatic tradition.[43]

Hitchcock viewed peacemaking from a similar progressive perspective. Welcoming "the birth of a new world," he castigated Borah for failing to understand that "the old world is dead." The new League would rely primarily on moral suasion. He confidently, but naively, explained that "the power of public opinion in the United States and the power of public opinion throughout the civilized world will be the supreme power, the moral power, which will naturally bring compliance with any agreement duly made." On February 27, after Wilson's dinner for the Senate and House committees, Hitchcock offered the ablest Democratic defense of the draft Covenant in the Senate. He argued that the real choice was peace or war, a league of nations or military preparedness. Because the United States could not escape from foreign affairs, the only question concerned the nature of American participation. "Internationalism has come," he noted, "and we must choose what form the internationalism shall take." He emphasized that in the proposed League the United States would not be bound against its judgment to take action, for each member of the executive council could exercise its veto, and even unanimous decisions were merely advisory. Reconciling the League with the American diplomatic tradition, the senator saw it as the fulfillment of the Monroe Doctrine and the end of entangling alliances. Looking to the future, he proclaimed "a new heaven and a new earth."[44]

IV

Republican senators found these arguments less than compelling. In a discerning critique of the draft Covenant on February 26, Senator Albert B. Cummins of Iowa elucidated one of the fundamental differences between advocates and critics of Wilson's foreign policy. Advocates believed, but critics doubted, that the United States would dominate the proposed League. For the former, this League represented the world-wide expansion of American influence, but for the latter, it constituted a foreign threat to the United States. "The President of the United States," said Cummins, "believes that this compact should be made because he is sincerely of the opinion that the United States can and will control the league of nations and may use it for the government of the earth in the welfare of the people of the earth." Even if that was possible, the senator did not want the United States to undertake such a global obligation. He agreed with Lodge and Knox that the United States should concentrate on the establishment of peace with Germany, but not with Beveridge, who urged him to renounce totally "the Wilson-Taft League of Nations scheme." In agreement with the president,

---

43 *CR*, Vol. 57, 980-93, 1584-85, 4125-35; Lewis to JPT, Jan. 4, Feb. 17, 1919, JPT Papers, Box 13.
44 *CR*, Vol. 57, 2656-57, 4414-18.

Cummins thought that the United States should accept its responsibility in world affairs, affirming that "I am no advocate of isolation." He favored, however, a more limited form of international organization than Wilson's plan for a universal league.[45]

As the debate proceeded in the Senate, Lodge adhered to his intermediate position within the Republican party. He refused to join advocates of Wilson's League, such as Taft, on the one hand, or its uncompromising opponents, such as Borah, on the other. This stance gave Lodge the greatest opportunity to unite Republican senators, which was crucial to their organization of the new Senate and their control of the Foreign Relations Committee. Widespread public sympathy with the league idea, if not with this particular Covenant, made it politically expedient for the party's leadership not to identify with the extreme opponents. In addition to these tactical considerations, genuine conviction led Lodge to adopt his intermediate position. He thought that a responsible foreign policy should avoid the extremes of Wilson's globalism or blind nationalism. He was certainly no stereotypic isolationist. Outlining his conception of the American role in world affairs for Beveridge, who was advocating outright Republican opposition to any league, Lodge explained: "I quite agree with you that we ought not to go into a general, indefinite, unlimited scheme of always being called upon to meddle in European, Asian and African questions; but that is very different from making sure that the barrier states that we shall have to establish in order to fetter Germany are set up, and we ought to give them such help as seems necessary to enable them to do this." In Lodge's view, that kind of temporary involvement in Europe was consistent with Washington's advice to avoid permanent alliances, but a perpetual league of nations with military force would violate the American diplomatic tradition.[46]

Having honored Wilson's request for silence before the White House dinner, Lodge offered his analysis of the Covenant on February 28. He pledged his support for any measure that would contribute to world peace, but not this plan as drafted. Urging the peace conference to heed the Senate's advice, he recommended amendments to clarify the League's obligations. He wanted to avoid ambiguity. Denouncing the draft Covenant as a clear violation of the American diplomatic tradition, Lodge reaffirmed the policy of Washington's Farewell Address and the Monroe Doctrine. That traditional policy was limited in time and space, but the League would constitute a permanent alliance with all nations that became members. He thought that Wilson profoundly misunderstood the Monroe Doctrine when he proclaimed

45 CR, Vol. 57, 4309-10; Beveridge to Cummins, Feb. 20, 1919, Cummins to Beveridge, Feb. 27, 1919, Beveridge Papers, Box 214.
46 Beveridge to HCL, Jan. 28, 28, Feb. 3, 15, 20, 1919, HCL to Beveridge, Jan. 30, Feb. 7, 18, 27, Beveridge Papers, Box 216, and HCL Papers; HCL to Gray, Feb. 4, 1919, HCL to L. A. Coolidge, Feb. 10, 1919, HCL Papers, File 1919 (Peace, League, Political, A-H); HCL to Raymond, Feb. 20, 1919, HCL to Washburn, Feb. 22, 1919, HCL Papers, File 1919 (Peace, League, Political, I-Z).

its world-wide extension in the League. "The real essence of that doctrine," explained Lodge, "is that American questions shall be settled by Americans alone; that the Americans shall be separated from Europe and from the interference of Europe in purely American questions." The claim that this doctrine could apply in the Old World ignored its essentially American character. Article 10, rather than extending the Monroe Doctrine to the entire world, threatened to entangle the United States in limitless obligations. The provision for sanctions in Article 16 would also commit the United States to use military force, however much the League's proponents might obfuscate this reality. Like Cummins, Lodge did not presuppose American control of the League. He feared the loss of sovereignty on matters such as immigration. As a constructive critic, he suggested four possible amendments to the draft Covenant so as to clarify and delimit the League's jurisdiction. The peace conference, he said, should consider amendments that would preserve the Monroe Doctrine, protect exclusive national dominion over questions such as immigration, provide for peaceful withdrawal by any nation, and avoid ambiguous obligations for any international deployment of armed forces. In Lodge's opinion, the United States should not sacrifice American interests by joining a league to preserve peace in the Old World.[47]

Knox generally approved Lodge's conclusions, but offered his own rationale for opposing Wilson's draft Covenant. Shortly after its publication in Paris, he assured Beveridge that "there is small chance for it."[48] He foresaw two possibilities for the proposed League, either that it would encompass "the jurisdiction of the world" or that it would become "a rope of sand." As a global menace or a false hope, depending upon how it functioned in practice, such a league failed to commend itself to the senator. Knox's alternatives reflected his legalistic approach to international cooperation. As one possibility, he suggested a general agreement for compulsory arbitration like the unratified 1911 arbitration treaties with Great Britain and France. As another possibility, he proposed a "strong" alliance with only one or two other major powers. "That we be not thrown into quarrels in which we would have no sympathy," he explained, "we must choose as our allies those powers whose traditions, institutions, ideals, and people are most like our own." As a third possibility, Knox recommended "a true league of nations." By that he meant the cooperation of all nations, including those recently defeated, to outlaw war. He envisioned an international constitution that defined any war for a purpose other than self-defense as a crime and that established an international court to condemn aggressive nations. This court should enjoy the power to call upon the league's members to enforce its judgments with economic and military sanctions. The jurisdiction of the

47   CR, Vol. 57, 4520-28; C. Coolidge to HCL, [Feb.], March 1, 1919, HCL to Coolidge, March 3, 1919, HCL Papers, File 1919 (Peace, League, Political, A-H); HCL to Stockton, Feb. 20, 1919, HCL to Washburn, Feb. 27, 1919, HCL Papers, File 1919 (Peace, League, Political, I-Z).
48   Beveridge to Knox, Jan. 20, Feb. 15, 18, 1919, Knox to Beveridge, Feb. 18, 1919, Beveridge Papers, Box 215.

international court, however, would be restricted so as not to infringe upon American rights of military defense, immigration restriction, and the Monroe Doctrine. Knox saw this kind of league as a future possibility, but he preferred for the present to concentrate on peace with Germany.[49]

Aware that Wilson was deaf to their critiques and alternatives, Republican leaders in the Senate decided to send a message that could be heard across the Atlantic. Brandegee suggested the idea of repudiating the Covenant in a resolution which more than one-third of the senators endorsed. Because any treaty would require approval by two-thirds of the Senate, the president would jeopardize American ratification of the peace treaty if he ignored this so-called round robin. Lodge approved the proposal and joined Brandegee in asking Knox to draft the resolution, which he did. With minor revisions suggested by Cummins, the resolution was circulated among Republican senators and senators-elect. On March 4, with thirty-seven signatures, Lodge introduced the round robin, which rejected the draft Covenant and advised the peace conference to postpone a league while immediately negotiating a treaty with Germany. Because of anticipated Democratic opposition, no vote was taken. Nevertheless, the round robin boldly proclaimed that Wilson's foreign policy lacked crucial support in the United States. With two more signatures, thirty-nine Republicans out of the new Senate's total membership of ninety-six – well over one-third – went on record against the president's League.[50]

V

Wilson refused to listen to this clear Republican message. He chose instead to believe that the American people would ultimately sustain his peacemaking and force the Senate to comply. To give the appearance of bipartisan support for his League, he welcomed Taft to share the platform at a public meeting in New York on the eve of his departure for Europe. Despite his earlier distrust of the former president, Wilson now acknowledged that he was rendering a great service to the League's cause throughout the country. Governor Alfred E. Smith, along with Tumulty, organized this joint appearance at the Metropolitan Opera House on March 4. Taft stressed the League's important role of combating Bolshevism and restoring order in the chaotic postwar world. "Confronted with the chaos and the explosive dangers of Bolshevism throughout all the countries of Europe," he explained, "a League of Nations must be established to settle controversies peaceably and to enforce the settlement." In response to the League's critics, Taft adopted a moderate stance. While denouncing them for failing to suggest any

49   CR, Vol. 57, 4687-94; Beveridge to Knox, [early March], March 6, 1919, Knox to Beveridge, March 3, 1919, Beveridge Papers, Box 215.
50   HCL, The Senate and the League of Nations, 117-21; CR, Vol. 57, 4974.

constructive alternative, he commended Lodge's "useful suggestions" for amendments to the draft Covenant.[51]

Wilson welcomed Taft's support, but not his assessment of Lodge's advice. In New York the president affirmed his uncompromising position. "The first thing that I am going to tell the people on the other side of the water," he said, "is that an overwhelming majority of the American people is in favor of the League of Nations." Denying that it was a partisan issue, he reiterated that "I do not mean to come back until it's over over there, and it must not be over until the nations of the world are assured of the permanency of peace." From his perspective, the only method for achieving this lasting peace was the proposed League. Denouncing the critics' selfish obstruction, Wilson vowed to bind the Covenant to the peace treaty so inextricably that it could never be separated. With this departing challenge, which ignored the political reality in the new Senate, he returned to Paris.[52]

Despite Wilson's determination to force the Senate to approve the Covenant, other Democrats understood the necessity for compromise. Hitchcock advised him that some Republican senators, who had signed the round robin, would vote for the League as part of the peace treaty, but that more of them would approve it with certain amendments. The senator wanted the United States to reserve exclusive national control over domestic issues and the Monroe Doctrine. Moreover, each nation should decide for itself whether to accept a mandate from the League and should enjoy the right to withdraw altogether from membership. Hitchcock also recommended changes in the language of Article 15 to remove the ambiguity concerning the executive council's role in settling disputes, and in Article 8 to provide for national approval of plans for reducing armaments.[53] Bryan, too, counseled revision. While generally praising the draft Covenant, he thought some amendments would improve the future League.[54]

Taft recognized that the Senate would require at least some revision. Beginning in his New York address, he stressed the need for reserving the Monroe Doctrine. He later advised Wilson that this amendment was essential to gain enough Republican votes for approval of the League. He proposed, as an addition to Article 10, that only American states should preserve the independence and territorial integrity of nations in the western hemisphere unless they requested European or non-American assistance. To

51   WW to WHT, Feb. 26, 1919, WW Papers, Ser. 5B, Box 17; WHT to WW, March 1, 1919, WW Papers, Ser. 4, File 156; Burton to JPT, Feb. 24, 1919, WW to JPT, Feb. 26, 1919, Morgenthau to WW, Feb. 26, 1919, WW to Morgenthau, Feb. 26, 1919, WW Papers, Ser. 4, File 4767; JPT to WW, Feb. 26, 1919, JPT Papers, Box 6; Polk to Auchincloss, Feb. 27, 1919, Polk Papers, 82/19; Polk to Auchincloss, March 3, 1919, Polk Papers, 74/7; Theodore Marburg and Horace E. Flack, eds., *Taft Papers on League of Nations* (New York, 1920), 262–80.
52   *PPWW*, V, 444–55.
53   Hitchcock to WW, March 4, 1919, JPT Papers, Box 6, WW Papers, Ser. 5B, Reel 394, Gilbert M. Hitchcock Papers, Vol. 1, Library of Congress, and EMH Papers, 10/27.
54   JD to WW, March 27, 1919, "Bryan Supports League of Nations, Suggests Amendments," WW Papers, Ser. 5B, Reel 397; JD to WW, March 27, 1919, JD Papers, Box 14; Miller, *Drafting of the Covenant*, I, 374–77.

increase the margin of support, Taft suggested other amendments to limit American entanglement in the Old World. He thought any member should be free after ten years to withdraw from the League by giving two years' notice. Reductions in armaments under Article 8 should not continue beyond five years without explicit renewal by the executive council. Decisions of the executive council should require a unanimous vote unless otherwise specified. This amendment would clearly give the United States a veto over any substantial decision. To retain exclusive American control over tariffs and Japanese immigration, Taft also proposed an addition to Article 15 so as to prohibit the executive council or body of delegates from making any judgment concerning domestic issues. Before suggesting these amendments, he ascertained through Tumulty that Wilson was willing to receive them.[55]

In Paris, before Wilson's return, White attempted to maintain liaison with Republican leaders in the United States. He saw little merit in their critique of the draft Covenant. "So far as I have been able to observe, there has been nothing constructive in what has been said on the subject in the Senate," he complained to Root. He viewed the future League as an effective deterrent against aggression and denied that drafting the Covenant was delaying peace with Germany. White cabled Lodge to request the exact amendments which the Senate would require for acceptance of the League. Suspicious of this request, the senator consulted Brandegee, who sent Chandler Anderson, a Republican lawyer, to confer with Root. Root hoped that the opportunity would not be lost to create an acceptable league by amending the draft Covenant. However, he advised against providing amendments to White. He thought that Lodge, as Republican leader in the Senate, should deal only with the president. The Senate, to preserve its dignity as "a co-equal power," should not allow him to flout it publicly while obtaining its views privately. If Wilson wanted the Senate's advice, Root believed, he should have solicited it before the session ended, or should now call a special session. Lodge, while adopting this advice, encouraged Root himself to publish constructive proposals for "a union of nations to promote general peace and disarmament."[56]

55 JPT to WW, March 16, 16, 18, 21, 1919, WW to JPT, March 18, 22, 1919, WHT to JPT, March 18, 1919, JPT Papers, Box 6; JPT to WW, March 18, 21, 1919, WW Papers, Ser. 4, File 156; JPT to WW, March 16 (#15), 16 (#16), 18 (#19), 21 (#24), 1919, WW Papers, Ser. 5B, Reels 395 and 396; JPT to WW, March 18, 1919 (#19), EMH Papers, 49/20; "The Kind of Peace League the Republicans Want," *Literary Digest*, LX (March 15, 1919), 13-16; Karger to WHT, March 19, 1919, WHT to JPT, March 19, 1919, JPT to WHT, March 22, 1919, WHT to WW, [March 21, 1919], ALL Papers.

56 WW to ER, March 7, 12, 1919, HW to HCL, March 9, 1919, HW to HCL, March 11, 1919, Elihu Root Papers, Box 137, Library of Congress; HW to HCL, March 11, 1919, HCL Papers; HW to HCL, March 7, 9, 1919, ER to HCL, March 13, 1919, HCL to ER, March 14, 1919, HCL to HW, March 15, 1919, ER Papers, Box 161, and HCL Papers; HW to ER, March 10, 1919, HW to HCL, March 9, 1919, ER Papers, Box 161; Redmond to HCL, March 10, 12, 1919, Brandegee to HCL, March 12, 1919, HCL to HW, [March 11, 1919], HCL to Redmond, March 14, 1919, HCL Papers, File 1919 (Henry White); Knox to HCL, March 14, 1919, HCL to Knox, March 17, 1919, HCL Papers, File 1919 (Peace, League, Political, I-Z).

Wanting to promote public discussion of the draft Covenant, Lowell invited Lodge to participate in a joint debate in Boston. The senator accepted this invitation, but carefully avoided any commitment. Root's advice for responding to White served as the basis for his position. During the debate on March 19, 1919, Lodge denied that he opposed a league. Noting that Taft had publicly recommended revision of the Covenant in order to remove its obscure language, he endorsed this idea as his first constructive criticism. Specifically, he agreed that the question of a unanimous or majority vote in the executive council needed clarification. He wanted to reserve the Monroe Doctrine, observing that "in its essence it rests upon the proposition of separating the Americas from Europe in all matters political." He also desired to exclude from the League's jurisdiction such international questions as immigration and tariffs, recognizing that these were not merely domestic issues. Like Taft, he suggested a provision for withdrawal. Moreover, the ambiguous responsibility for selecting mandatory powers required clarification. Lodge agreed with Wilson that Article 10 was the most important part of the Covenant, but questioned whether the United States should undertake this extensive obligation. While offering this criticism, he refrained from promising to approve the Covenant even if its defects were removed.

Lodge's refusal to make such a pledge, Lowell emphasized, was the critical difference between them. They both agreed that the Covenant was poorly written. Instead of emphasizing ambiguous points, Lowell wanted to assume that the document meant what it said. He agreed that the League would require its members to assume grave duties, but thought they should. Like Wilson and Taft, he viewed the Covenant not as a threat to the Monroe Doctrine but as its extension throughout the world. As an extra precaution, Lowell recommended an amendment to prohibit foreign powers from acquiring any possession in the western hemisphere. Stressing the League's utility, he argued that "the progress of science" had created an interdependent world in which "the days of American isolation have passed away forever." Lodge refused to promise what Lowell wanted. He voiced his doubt that Wilson would really make the necessary amendments in the draft Covenant. Affirming the Senate's right to advise the president, he challenged him to consult this body. Lodge still avoided any commitment to a league as part of the peace treaty. In conformity with the round robin, he asked for a treaty with Germany as the first priority, and then for consideration of a league. He derided the League's proponents for apparently believing that its appeal in the United States and Europe was so little that it could be realized only as part of the peace treaty. Nevertheless, he affirmed that "I want a League of Nations that will advance the cause of peace on earth, that will make war as nearly impossible as it can be made." More cautious than Lowell, Lodge wanted to preserve the American diplomatic tradition. "I would keep America as she has been – not isolated, not prevent her from joining other nations for these great purposes – but I wish her to be master of her fate," he said.[57]

Reactions to the Lodge-Lowell debate varied according to political perspective. Knox urged Lodge not to assist pro-League propaganda by participating in any other debate. Lodge assured him, and also Senator Joseph Frelinghuysen of New Jersey, that he had adhered to the position of the round robin. He endeavored to reassure these opponents of the president's plan for a league that he had made no real concession.[58] Yet Taft was delighted because he thought he saw a shift in the Republican leader's position. In his opinion, the debate revealed few differences between Lodge and Lowell. The senator seemed to move into the League to Enforce Peace's camp and away from extreme opponents such as Borah, Poindexter, Reed, Knox and Frelinghuysen. Taft congratulated Lowell for achieving this success.[59] From Root's perspective, Lowell made the significant concession by admitting that the draft Covenant needed substantial revision. He congratulated Lodge for his masterful role in bringing Lowell into line in favor of significant amendments.[60]

At the State Department some officials understood the seriousness of Republican opposition. Acting Secretary of State Frank L. Polk reported to Paris that even friendly Democratic senators were troubled by the current confrontation. He endeavored to curb Long's partisan activities and to adopt a conciliatory approach to Republicans. He wanted to give Republicans a face-saving way to accept Wilson's policy. In accordance with this strategy, Assistant Secretary of State William Phillips went to Boston for the Lodge-Lowell debate. The next day he met Lowell and requested him to prepare amendments for submission to Wilson. To assure the Senate's approval of the Covenant, Harvard's president recommended three amendments so as to provide for future withdrawal from the League, reserve the Monroe Doctrine, and exclude domestic affairs such as immigration and tariffs from its jurisdiction. As Phillips and Lowell were both Republicans, this effort at conciliation appeared like a partisan plot to Long, who still preferred to defeat rather than accommodate Lodge. This attempt by Polk and Phillips to reach an understanding with the Republican opposition coincided with Lansing's assessment of the political situation. When Wilson returned to Paris on March 14 and reported overwhelming public support for the League, the secretary was skeptical. He thought the president had lost

5 7   ALL to HCL, March 6, 1919, HCL to ALL, March 8, 8, 1919, HCL Papers, File 1919 (Peace, League, Political, I-Z), and ALL Papers; HCL and ALL, "Joint Debate on the Covenant of Paris," *League of Nations*, II, No. 2 (Apr. 1919), 49-97.

5 8   Knox to HCL, March 20, 1919, HCL to Knox, March 20, 1919, HCL Papers, File 1919 (Peace, League, Political, I-Z); Beck to HCL, March 19, 1919, HCL to Beck, March 24, 1919, HCL to Frelinghuysen, March 24, 1919, HCL Papers, File 1919 (Peace, League, Political, A-H).

5 9   WHT to ALL, March 25, 1919, ALL Papers.

6 0   ER to HCL, Apr. 4, 1919, HCL to ER, Apr. 7, 1919, ER Papers, Box 161, and HCL Papers; HCL to Bigelow, Apr. 7, 1919, HCL Papers, File 1919 (Adams-Trevelyan).

prestige at home and, consequently, would face even greater difficulties with the Allies.[61]

Wilson's rosy account of American public opinion expressed his own analysis and that of Ray Stannard Baker, director of the press bureau for the American Commission to Negotiate Peace. Finding support for the League throughout the political spectrum, Baker exaggerated its popularity. He reported that Republican senator-elect Arthur Capper of Kansas had refused to sign the round robin because the people of his state favored the president's League. What Baker failed to understand was that Capper wanted to amend the draft Covenant before approving it. He also reported the efforts of Dwight M. Morrow, of J. P. Morgan and Company, to promote the League. But Morrow, too, recommended some revision of the proposed Covenant. Public opinion was not as favorable as either Wilson or Baker claimed it was.[62]

VI

Whatever their differences, Republicans united in opposing the draft Covenant. Wilson could not force the Senate to approve his plan for a league. That was the political reality in the spring of 1919, although he and his inner circle of advisers failed to understand. With Lodge and Root, Will H. Hays, chairman of the Republican National Committee, played a central role in defining their party's response to the president's politics of confrontation. Shortly after the draft Covenant's publication, Root spent an evening discussing it with Henry L. Stimson, former secretary of war in Taft's cabinet. On February 18 Stimson shared his ideas with Hays and, at the latter's request, outlined them in a letter. Hays circulated it to all Republican senators. Stimson advised them to avoid a purely negative attitude toward the league idea, although they might criticize certain aspects of the current proposal. He recommended an amendment to prevent the Covenant from superseding the Monroe Doctrine, which conformed to his interpretation of international law. Article 10 appeared to threaten American control of the western hemisphere. At the same time, Article 10's guarantee "against external aggression" failed to perpetuate the Monroe Doctrine's prohibition against peaceful acquisition of American territory by any European power. Stimson saw the draft Covenant's inadequacy with regard

61 RL to Polk, March 14, 1919, Polk to RL, Feb. 10, March 3, 18, 1919, Polk Papers, 78/9; Polk to Auchincloss, March 20, 1919, Polk Papers, 74/7; Polk to Auchincloss, March 18, 1919, Polk Papers, 82/21; ALL to WHT, March 28, 1919, ALL Papers; Emery to Grew, March 20, 1919 (#1208), Polk to American Commission (A.C.N.P.), March 21, 1919 (#1214), WW Papers, Ser. 5B, Reel 396; Long Diary, March 8-9, 21, 1919, Long Papers, Box 2; RL Diary, IV, March 16, 1919; Phillips to RL, March 22, 1919, RL Papers, Vol. 42.
62 RSB to WW, Memorandum, March 6, 1919, Morrow to RSB, March 4, 1919, WW Papers, Ser. 5B, Reel 394; Capper to Boyd, March 21, 1919, Capper to Short, March 21, 1919, Short to Capper, March 22, 1919, League to Enforce Peace Papers, Box 11.

to the Monroe Doctrine as a prime example of its ambiguity. He urged constructive criticism to remove such weaknesses.[63]

Hays set the tone for Republican unity by emphasizing American nationalism. On March 7 he joined Kellogg in St. Paul for a rally of Minnesota Republicans. In his speech he advocated patriotism in the tradition of Lincoln and Roosevelt. No less than Wilson, Hays preached an American civil religion that united God and country. He proclaimed "that the mission of this country in God's scheme of things is being accomplished, and that we have been the instrument under His guidance to go into the unprecedented conflict and save the future of mankind." Hays believed that the Republican party, having contributed toward victory in the World War, should now prepare for peace. In a statement that was widely circulated in newspapers as the keynote of the coming political campaign, he affirmed: "While we seek earnestly and prayerfully for methods lessening future wars, and will go far indeed in an honest effort to that end, and will accomplish very much, we will accept no indefinite internationalism as a substitute for fervent American nationalism."[64]

Although Hays spoke in generalities, Kellogg focused on the League. He, too, emphasized "the spirit of Americanism" but reaffirmed his willingness to approve an acceptable international organization. In agreement with Taft, he thought that a proper league should provide an international court to settle justiciable questions and a procedure for conciliation to recommend compromises on other issues. Yet he wanted to exclude from its jurisdiction all political matters affecting the national interest, such as internal affairs, the Monroe Doctrine and the Panama Canal. He saw Article 10 as an excessive entanglement in the Old World. Kellogg's address pleased both Lodge and Taft. Clearly, differences among Republicans were becoming less distinct as they united against Wilson's League.[65]

In his efforts to assist Lodge in maintaining Republican unity for the treaty fight, Hays turned to Root for an analysis of the proposed League. He wanted their party to contribute "all that can possibly be done toward the maintenance of peace without sacrificing our own supreme nationalism." Responding in a letter on March 29 with a detailed assessment, Root concluded that substantial portions of the draft Covenant promised "great value" but that it suffered from "serious faults." He endorsed the general consensus of Taft, Knox, Lodge and Lowell in favor of important amendments. Under the Constitution it was the Senate's responsibility to discuss

---

63   Stimson to Hays, Feb. 18, 1919, Hays to Bross, Feb. 22, 1919, The Chaney Digest of Scrap Books, Feb. 26, 1919, Will H. Hays Papers, Indiana State Library; Stimson to ER, March 19, 1919, Stimson to Hays, Feb. 18, 1919, ER Papers, Box 137. For Stimson's position, see Kent G. Redmond, "Henry L. Stimson and the Question of League Membership," *Historian*, XXV (Feb. 1963), 200-212.
64   Speech of Will H. Hays, March 7, 1919, Chaney Digest, March 7, 1919, Hays Papers.
65   Speech of Senator Frank B. Kellogg, March 7, 1919, Hays Papers and Frank B. Kellogg Papers, Box 5, Minnesota Historical Society; Kellogg to HCL, March 15, 1919, HCL to Kellogg, March 17, 1919, HCL Papers, File 1919 (Peace, League, Political, I-Z); Short to Kellogg, March 13, 1919, Kellogg to Short, n.d., League to Enforce Peace Papers, Box 11.

and prepare such amendments, but the president failed to convene this body for that purpose. Root divided the causes of war into legal and political categories. To deal with legal disputes over the interpretation of treaties and international law, he advocated compulsory arbitration. In view of the First and Second Hague Conferences in 1899 and 1907, he thought "the world was ready for obligatory arbitration of justiciable questions." In this regard the draft Covenant was deficient. As amendments to Articles 13 and 14, he recommended stronger provisions for arbitration and periodic revision of international law. Following the tradition of Republican administrations in the late nineteenth and early twentieth centuries, Root emphasized legal procedures to preserve peace.[66] For the resolution of political disputes between nations, he favored international conferences. He praised Articles 11, 12, 15 and 16 for prescribing effective methods to deal with this source of wars. Under these, and also Article 10, the United States could contribute toward the maintenance of peace in the Old World. Although the primary American interest was still in the western hemisphere, as defined by the Monroe Doctrine, he observed that "there has, however, arisen in these days for the American people a powerful secondary interest in the affairs of Europe coming from the fact that war in Europe and the Near East threatens to involve the entire world, and the peaceable nations of Europe need outside help to put out the fire, and keep it from starting again. That help to preserve peace we ought to give, and that help we wish to give." Yet in Root's opinion there was no justification for reciprocal European intervention in the New World. He did not want to grant the League authority to interfere with American hegemony in the western hemisphere, protesting that "to submit the policy of Monroe to a council composed chiefly of European powers is to surrender it." Accordingly, he proposed an amendment to exempt purely American questions, including immigration, from the League's jurisdiction.

Regarding the proposed League as essentially the continuation of the wartime coalition, Root approved the obligations of even Article 10 for the immediate postwar years. "Since the Bolsheviki have been allowed to consolidate the control which they established with German aid in Russia," he warned, "the situation is that Great Britain, France, Italy and Belgium with a population of less than 130 millions are confronted with the disorganized but vigorous and warlike population of Germany, German Austria, Hungary, Bulgaria, Turkey, and Russia, amounting approximately to 280 millions, fast returning to barbarism and the lawless violence of barbarous races. Order must be restored." After restoring law and order during a period of reconstruction, the United States and the Allies should not make a perpetual commitment to the status quo. Root thought "it would

66   For excellent accounts of the legalist approach to peace in the Republican tradition, see Calvin DeArmond Davis, *The United States and the Second Hague Peace Conference: American Diplomacy and International Organization, 1899-1914* (Durham, 1975), and David S. Patterson, "The United States and the Origins of the World Court," *Political Science Quarterly*, XCI (Summer 1976), 279-95.

not only be futile; it would be mischievous. Change and growth are the law of life, and no generation can impose its will in regard to the growth of nations and the distribution of power upon succeeding generations." Consequently, he suggested an amendment to Article 10 to allow the League's members to withdraw from this obligation after five years. After that time he also wanted them to have the right of withdrawing altogether from the League. While recommending restrictions on the geographic scope and duration, Root favored a powerful league. Besides compulsory arbitration, he advocated stronger provisions for limitation of armaments. In agreement with the French, he suggested an amendment to grant full power to the permanent commission, established under Article 9, for inspection and verification of military and naval reductions adopted under Article 8. Root thus provided Hays with constructive criticism of the draft Covenant.[67]

Root's letter produced the desired result. Its publication contributed to Republican unity against Wilson's League without committing the party to irreconcilable opposition. "It is really having just the effect we hoped," Hays informed Root. All Republicans, despite their conflicting views on alternatives, could join together in criticizing the draft Covenant. The letter delighted Lowell because it proposed amendments that would make Wilson's plan acceptable to the Senate. By providing such specific suggestions, Root did what Lowell had urged Lodge to do during their debate. Because of his position as Republican leader, Lodge had refused this request from Lowell as well as from White. Root, however, outlined the basis for compromise between the president and Republican senators so that the United States could join the League. By recommending compulsory arbitration, he also endorsed an idea which the League to Enforce Peace had championed.[68]

As Hays worked with Lodge and Root to achieve Republican unity without foreclosing the prospect of American membership in a future league, its irreconcilable opponents began to organize against even that possibility. Beveridge continued to encourage outright Republican opposition to any league. Praising Lodge and Knox for their addresses in the Senate and for the round robin, he urged them to make no concession to Wilson. After Cummings, the Democratic National Committee's new chairman, announced his party's willingness to make a partisan issue out of the League, Beveridge implored Lodge to accept this challenge. He was convinced that public opinion was shifting away from Wilson's vision of collective security. Others such as Frank A. Munsey, publisher of the *New York Sun*, pressed the same advice upon Hays. Brandegee, too, agreed with Beveridge that Republicans should reject any league because it would be either ineffective or dangerous. "Of course," he observed, "these considerations, I suppose, have no influence with the altruistic and the hallelujah band. Many of these would

67   Hays to ER, March 20, 24, 1919, ER to Hays, March 29, 1919, ER Papers, Box 137.
68   ER to Hays, Apr. 1, 1919, Hays to ER, Apr. 4, 1919, ALL to ER, Apr. 2, 1919, ER Papers, Box 137.

sign anything that was labeled League to Insure Peace." Lodge, however, refused to adopt such an irreconcilable stance even under this intense pressure. He informed Beveridge that "I cannot agree with you about taking the ground that we are against any League at all." Lodge stressed that, as Republican leader, he was obligated to adhere to the round robin. "The great and crucial battle is to come when the league, in some form, reaches the Senate," he explained, "and my duty, as I look at it, is to hold such a position that I shall be able to unite the senators behind me." This explanation enabled Lodge to retain Beveridge's and Borah's confidence in his leadership during the developing confrontation with Wilson.[69]

Republican unity under Lodge's leadership did not require all senators to share his views about a future league. Irreconcilable opponents continued their active protest against any such international organization at any time. Borah was already threatening to repudiate his party if it compromised. "It is going to embroil us in every row in Europe," he warned. Appealing to traditional American distrust of the Old World, he claimed that the draft Covenant provided for a league under European control. Whereas Wilson anticipated American control, Borah feared European domination of the proposed League.[70]

To build an anti-League coalition, Borah worked with professional ethnic leaders. He developed a good relationship with Irish-Americans such as Judge Daniel F. Cohalan of New York and the old Fenian John Devoy, editor of the *Gaelic American*. These ethnic leaders combined their advocacy of Irish independence with staunch condemnation of the League, which they saw as a tool of British hegemony. Devoy denounced the draft Covenant as "a British conspiracy against the very existence of these United States as a free, independent, self-governing Nation." Cohalan condemned this proposal for committing the United States to the British Empire's preservation and for preventing it from assisting Ireland. At Cohalan's instigation, the Irish Race Convention in Philadelphia on February 22-23, 1919, adopted resolutions favoring Irish independence and opposing American membership in the League. Hays as well as Borah appreciated the political potential in this ethnic reaction, but the senator took the lead in exploiting it. "I am thoroughly in sympathy with your cause," he proclaimed to Irish-Americans, "and I am against the League of Nations because it is against the

69 Beveridge to Borah, March 26, 1919, Brandegee to Beveridge, March 18, 1919, Beveridge to Brandegee, March 7, 23, 1919, Beveridge Papers, Box 214; Hays to Beveridge, Jan. 2, 1919, Harvey to Beveridge, March 26, 1919, Beveridge to Knox, March 6, 9, 23, 1919, Beveridge Papers, Box 215; Beveridge to HCL, March 6, 9, 18, 23, 27, Apr. 4, 1919, HCL to Beveridge, March 8, 21, Apr. 7, 1919, HCL Papers and Beveridge Papers, Box 216; Beveridge to Borah, Feb. 19, 28, March 13, 25, 1919, Borah to Beveridge, Feb. 25, March 10, 25, 1919, Borah Papers, Box 551, and Beveridge Papers, Box 214; Borah to Hart, March 24, 1919, Borah to Munsey, March 8, 22, 1919, Munsey to Borah, March 18, 19, 1919, Borah Papers, Box 551; Chaney Digest, March 14, 1919, Hays Papers; Cummings, statement, March 12, 1919, WW Papers, Ser. 4, File 4767.
70 Borah to Hodgson, Feb. 20, 1919, Borah Papers, Box 552; Borah to Rudine, March 25, 1919, Borah to Clendening, March 29, 1919, Borah Papers, Box 550.

rights of small nations and the principle of self-determination more aggressively than was Prussianism."[71]

These extreme opponents distorted Wilson's vision of a league. Although he anticipated Anglo-American collaboration in the maintenance of world peace, he certainly did not expect the United States to assist the British Empire in suppressing internal rebellion. Failure of Article 10 to provide an international guarantee against domestic violence was viewed by some, but not by the president, as a weakness. He firmly rejected the suggestion of an amendment to the draft Covenant so as to repeal the right of revolution. He explained that "we must be careful *not* to preclude the right of revolution which most free peoples in common with our own have always held to be a sacred and indefeasible right."[72] In Wilson's opinion, it was not appropriate for the United States to intervene in the British Empire either to promote or to oppose Irish independence. He interpreted Article 10 as neither a threat to Ireland nor an advantage to Great Britain in this dispute, which he regarded as a domestic affair.

Wilson's critics posed a significant challenge to his plan for a league. To succeed with his peace program, he obviously needed to take their objections and alternatives into account. Because Republicans would control the new Senate, he could not expect to secure its endorsement of the peace treaty without accommodating their virtually unanimous insistence upon amendments to the draft Covenant. That task would require him to modify his politics of confrontation and to seek the Allies' approval for important changes. The president's willingness and ability to fulfill this task at the peace conference would determine the fate of the treaty and future League.

71   "Greatest Irish Race Convention Meets To-day," *Gaelic American*, XVI (Feb. 22, 1919), 1; "The League of Nations," ibid., 4; "A Conspiracy Thwarted," ibid. (March 8, 1919), 4; "Cohalan Given Great Ovation in Brooklyn," ibid. (March 15, 1919), 1, 7; "Cohalan's Metropolitan Opera House Speech," ibid. (Apr. 5, 1919), 3; "Let America Stand Bravely for Right of Self-Determination, Says Senator Borah," ibid. (Apr. 12, 1919), 1; "Chicago Irishmen Give Borah Great Ovation," ibid. (Apr. 19, 1919), 10; O'Mahoney to Hays, Special Report, Feb. 26, 1919, Hays Papers; Borah to Mannix, March 29, 1919, Borah Papers, Box 551. See also Charles Callan Tansill, *America and the Fight for Irish Freedom*, 1866-1922 (New York, 1957), 312-39, and F. M. Carroll, *American Opinion and the Irish Question*, 1910-23 (New York, 1978), 139-48.
72   Johnson to WW, March 19, 1919, WW to Johnson, March 20, 1919, WW Papers, Ser. 5B, Reel 396.

CHAPTER 5

Revision of the League of Nations Covenant

Wilson returned to Paris in an uncompromising mood, convinced that a threatening combination of the League's American and European critics awaited him. He resented the French press's coverage of American opposition to the draft Covenant. Encouraged by Tumulty, he decided to thwart the ostensible prospect that the peace conference might conclude a preliminary settlement with Germany without the League. He issued a statement on March 15 reaffirming the earlier decision to establish a league as an integral part of the peace treaty. Neither the round robin nor a preliminary peace was acceptable to him. He wanted to make no concession to the League's opponents.[1]

The Allies, however, often linked their support for the League to his acceptance of their conditions for peace. Wilson misunderstood the idea of a preliminary peace, which was a plan for expediting conference proceedings. It was not directed against the League.[2] Still, he faced a challenge.

---

1   RSB, Notebook, XXII, March 8, 13, 15, 1919; JPT to WW, March 13, 1919 (#8), WW to JPT, [March 18, 1919], WW Papers, Ser. 5B, Reel 395; *PPWW*, V, 457; EMH Diary, March 16, 1919; Cecil Diary, March 16, 1919, Cecil Papers, 51131; Auchincloss Diary, March 16, 1919, Auchincloss Papers, 55/89.

2   EMH Diary, Feb. 14, 19, 27, March 4, 14, 1919; Hankey to EMH, Feb. 19, 1919, Draft Resolutions Proposed by Mr. Balfour, Feb. 19, 1919, EMH Papers, 2/24; *FR:PPC*, IV (Washington, 1943), 85-97, 101-04, 108-09, 195, 214, 315; EMH to WW, Feb. 19, 1919, WW Papers, Ser. 5B, Box 16, and EMH Papers, 49/12; Hankey to DLG, Feb. 23, 1919, DLG Papers, F/23/4/22. According to Inga Floto, *Colonel House in Paris: A Study of American Policy at the Paris Peace Conference, 1919* (Princeton, 1980), 99-214, House's disloyalty in connection with the preliminary treaty precipitated the break between him and Wilson. However, because the president misunderstood the situation in Paris in this instance, the problem was his own (and Ray Stannard Baker's) inaccurate perception. Yet, in general, the egotism, ineptitude and disloyalty of House gave Wilson sufficient justification for ending their intimate friendship and collaboration. For a summary of her generally persuasive analysis of the House-Wilson relationship, see Inga Floto, "Colonel House in Paris: The Fate of a Presidential Adviser," *American Studies in Scandinavia*, VI (1973-74), 21-45. Kurt Wimer correctly questioned the thesis, which had originated from Baker, that Wilson returned to Paris to confront a plot to sidetrack the League with a preliminary treaty. However, his argument that Wilson was seeking to conclude an executive agreement

Clemenceau wanted a more tangible guarantee of French security. He feared that the United States would revert to "traditional aloofness" and leave France vulnerable to a potentially resurgent Germany. In his opinion, the League, even when combined with German disarmament, would not afford adequate protection. Consequently, he sought to separate the Rhineland from Germany and to maintain Allied and American occupation of this territory. Because neither Wilson nor Lloyd George favored this policy, Clemenceau endeavored to win their approval without disrupting the victorious coalition, the maintenance of which he regarded as even more essential to France's security. André Tardieu, the premier's closest political associate in the French delegation, insisted upon military control of the Rhine. Marshal Ferdinand Foch, commander in chief of the Allied and American armies during the war, urged Wilson to accept this strategic assessment. He argued that the proposed League needed a military frontier on the Rhine to achieve its purpose.[3]

Clemenceau wanted military security for France. In view of Bourgeois' failure to win British or American approval for the French conception of the League as an alliance, he insisted upon a defensible frontier. Yet British and American leaders opposed French policy toward the Rhineland as an unwarranted violation of Germany's territorial integrity and sovereignty. The ensuing deadlock prompted Lloyd George to search for an alternative. He originated the idea of an Anglo-American guarantee of immediate military assistance to France in the event of unprovoked German aggression. Wilson approved Lloyd George's proposal. This special alliance seemed justifiable as a particular example of Article 10's general guarantee of territorial integrity and political independence. On March 14 they offered this alternative to Clemenceau on the condition that he abandon his plans for permanent separation and occupation of the Rhineland. To obtain the security treaty, he needed to sacrifice perpetual military control of the Rhine.[4]

to start the League immediately, but was stymied by its opponents, is not well founded. For his argument, see Kurt Wimer, "Woodrow Wilson's Plans to Enter the League of Nations Through an Executive Agreement," *Western Political Quarterly*, XI (Dec. 1958), 800-12.

3   "French Misgivings," *Literary Digest*, LX (Feb. 22, 1919), 18-19; André Tardieu, *The Truth About the Treaty* (Indianapolis, 1921), 147-67; Great Britain, "Papers Respecting Negotiations for an Anglo-French Pact," Cmd. 2169, *House of Commons Sessional Papers*, Vol. 26 (London, 1924), 25-57; Rhine Question, [Feb. 26, 1919], WW Papers, Ser. 5B, Box 17; Foch to WW, March 14, 1919, Memorandum, Jan. 10, 1919, WW Papers, Ser. 5B, Reel 395; [Foch], Memorandum, [Jan. 10, 1919], WW Papers, Ser. 5B, Box 7; EMH Diary, Feb. 23, March 2, 1919; Auchincloss Diary, Feb. 25, March 11, 1919, Auchincloss Papers, 55/89; Hankey to DLG, Feb. 24, 1919, DLG Papers, F/23/4/24. See also Lloyd E. Ambrosius, "Wilson, Clemenceau and the German Problem at the Paris Peace Conference of 1919," *Rocky Mountain Social Science Journal*, XII (Apr. 1975), 69-79, Robert McCrum, "French Rhineland Policy at the Paris Peace Conference, 1919," *Historical Journal*, XXI, No. 3 (1978), 623-48, and Walter A. McDougall, *France's Rhineland Diplomacy, 1914-1924: The Last Bid for a Balance of Power in Europe* (Princeton, 1978).

4   Cecil to EMH, March 8, 1919, EMH Papers, 4/38; EMH Diary, March 12, 1919; David Lloyd George, *Memoirs of the Peace Conference* (New Haven, 1939), I, 265-66; Tardieu, *Truth About the Treaty*, 176-78.

Clemenceau welcomed the Anglo-American proposal for a security treaty, but he also wanted at least temporary occupation of the Rhineland. To ensure its demilitarization after the period of occupation, he proposed a permanent commission for inspection. He demanded the right to reoccupy the Rhineland if Germany violated the conditions for demilitarization or disarmament. In the security treaty as well, Clemenceau wanted the British and American governments to recognize that Germany's introduction of troops into the Rhineland would constitute aggression and require their response.[5]

In the American delegation, only House joined Wilson in approving a security treaty. Lansing thought the proposed League had already taken on too much the character of a quintuple military alliance. A special alliance to guarantee French security would reduce even further the League's value. The new nations in eastern Europe could not be expected to depend upon the League if France refused. "All the old evils of a 'concert of powers' and the 'balance of power' are being swallowed without protest," he lamented.[6] Bliss wanted to avoid any definite American commitment to protect France or any other European nation from aggression. He advised the president that the "growing democratic feeling" of Germany and the League would provide better security for France than "harassing" military control.[7] White, too, denounced the idea of a security treaty. Hoping to avoid American entanglement in European affairs, he interpreted the round robin as proof that the Senate would never approve a special alliance. He denounced it to Lodge as another French effort to entangle the United States permanently in Europe. Lansing, Bliss and White opposed any security treaty with France.[8]

White ignored the advice he had repeatedly received from Lodge. He failed to perceive that the Senate might approve a specific commitment in western Europe, while opposing the universal obligations of Wilson's League. White denounced France and favored a league as the first step toward peace, but Lodge reversed the priorities. He praised France and advocated peace with Germany before considering a new league. In response to White's criticism of the proposed security treaty, Lodge asserted, "I cannot share with you your views about France." His advice failed to convince White that the Senate, despite its criticism of the draft Covenant, might approve a defensive alliance. Apparently incapable of comprehending how Lodge could favor an alliance with France and Great Britain, while

5   Clemenceau to WW, March 17, 1919, WW Papers, Ser. 5B, Reel 395; Clemenceau to EMH, March 17, 1919, Note sur la Suggestion Présenté le 14 Mars, EMH Papers, 5/4; "Negotiations for an Anglo-French Pact," Great Britain, Sessional Papers, Vol. 26, 69-76; Tardieu, Truth About the Treaty, 177-82; Clemenceau, Grandeur and Misery, 232-37; Auchincloss Diary, March 16, 1919, Auchincloss Papers, 55/89.
6   RL Diary, IV, March 7, 20, 1919.
7   THB to A.C.N.P., Feb. 26, 1919, THB Papers, Boxes 65 and 75, and NDB Papers, Box 9; THB to WW, March 14, 1919, THB Papers, Box 70, and WW Papers, Ser. 5B, Reel 395.
8   HW to HCL, March 19, 1919, ER Papers, Box 161; FR:PPC, XI (Washington, 1945), 124-26, 130; EMH Diary, March 20, 1919; Miller, My Diary, I, 192-93.

opposing the president's global vision of collective security, this career diplomat missed the opportunity to serve as an effective liaison between Wilson and Republican senators.[9]

Both Wilson and Lloyd George sought to guarantee French security without entangling their countries on the European continent. The British prime minister emphasized the danger of revolution in the postwar world. To prevent Bolshevism from spreading to the heart of Europe, he advocated moderate peace terms for Germany in accordance with the principle of national self-determination. He viewed the League as the most viable "alternative to Bolshevism." While repeating his promise of a security treaty, Lloyd George opposed French policy toward the Rhineland. He rejected not only its separation from Germany but also its occupation even temporarily. He approved the left bank's demilitarization, but not French proposals for military control of the Rhine. If Germany sent troops into this demilitarized zone, France should rely on the security treaty with Great Britain and the United States.[10]

In the Council of Four, Wilson endorsed Lloyd George's assessment. Of the French proposals, he approved only the provision for demilitarization of the Rhineland, but without a permanent commission for inspection. He opposed American and Allied occupation of this territory even to prevent its remilitarization by Germany. In the event of such violations, the president wanted no obligation under the security treaty for British or American military assistance to France. Clemenceau charged that Lloyd George and Wilson were seeking to appease Germany at France's expense. He thought this approach to peace was doomed to failure because Germany would demand more than the Allied and Associated Powers could grant.[11]

Clemenceau correctly discerned the British shift toward appeasement of Germany. Even Balfour rejected the French policy toward the Rhineland, although he understood why the French refused to trust the proposed League and German disarmament as guarantees of peace. He concluded that "a change in the international system of the world" was "the only radical cure" to this problem.[12] Cecil cautioned Lloyd George not to allow the future League to become a new Holy Alliance permanently directed against Germany. Instead, he anticipated eventual German membership after "a genuine repentance." He also favored general disarmament as a sequel to

9   HCL to HW, Jan. 11, Feb. 1, March 4, 1919, HW to HCL, Jan. 14, 24, Feb. 10, 20, Apr. 3, 1919, HCL Papers, File 1919 (Henry White); HW to HCL, Feb. 10, 20, 1919, ER Papers, Box 161; HCL to HW, Apr. 8, 1919, HW Papers, Box 41, and HCL Papers.
10   Some Considerations for the Peace Conference, March 25, 1919, WW Papers, Ser. 5B, Reel 397; DLG, *Memoirs*, I, 266-73; "Negotiations for an Anglo-French Pact," Great Britain, *Sessional Papers*, Vol. 26, 76-85.
11   Paul Mantoux, *Les Délibérations du Conseil des Quatre: 24 mars-28 juin* 1919 (Paris, 1955), I, 39-51; DLG to Bonar Law, March 31, 1919, DLG Papers, F/30/3/40.
12   Curzon to AJB, Feb. 28, March 2, 1919, AJB to Curzon, March 1, 1919, AJB Papers, 49734/64-66; Memorandum by Mr. Balfour, March 18, 1919, AJB Papers, 49751/230-33.

German disarmament.[13] Smuts advised the prime minister that Europe could be saved from Bolshevism only by cooperating with Germany. Rather than accept the French strategic assessment, he recommended Germany's inclusion in the League. He openly counseled a policy of "appeasement" which recognized Germany as "the *dominant factor* on the Continent of Europe."[14]

Despite anti-French attitudes of some American and British advisers, Wilson and Lloyd George remained faithful to their promise of a security treaty. The president ignored the warning of Lansing, Bliss and White that "an alliance would be extremely unfortunate, and absolutely fatal to the success of the League of Nations." Like House, Wilson hoped to reconcile an alliance with the League. On March 28 he approved the demilitarization of the Rhineland, labeling possible German violations as "hostile acts." Pledging the United States to assist France against any unprovoked German aggression, he linked the proposed security treaty to the League. This assistance would require approval of the League's executive council. Moreover, the security treaty would remain in force only until the League itself could provide adequate protection.[15]

Welcoming the president's linkage between the proposed alliance and League, Clemenceau endeavored to strengthen these methods of enforcing the peace treaty. He wanted to expand the demilitarized zone to include an area east of the Rhine. In his view, any German violation of conditions for disarmament, and not just for demilitarization, should be regarded as "an hostile act." The League's executive council should immediately investigate all such alleged violations. The security treaty should clearly obligate the United States and Great Britain to protect France against all potential acts of aggression. Clemenceau sought to retain Allied and American military control over the Rhine. Wilson rejected these changes. He saw no reason to expand the demilitarized zone or to give the League's executive council specific authorization to investigate German violations of military, naval, and air terms of the peace treaty. Refusing to acknowledge that eventual German rearmament might constitute a threat, he omitted it from the security treaty's definition of aggression. Wilson warned that he and Lloyd George had offered "the maximum of what I myself deem necessary for the safety of France or possible on the part of the United States."[16]

House bluntly told Tardieu that French plans for a strong military defense

13 Cecil to DLG, March 10, 1919, DLG Papers, F/6/6/17.
14 Smuts to DLG, March 26, 1919, DLG Papers, F/45/9/29, and Hancock and van der Poel, eds., *Smuts Papers*, IV, 83-87.
15 *FR:PPC*, XI, 133; EMH Diary, March 20, 27, 1919; Note for Colonel House, [March 20, 1919?], WW Papers, Ser. 5B, Reel 395; Proposal, March 28, 1919, WW Papers, Ser. 5B, Reel 398; Auchincloss Diary, March 19-22, 26-27, 1919, Auchincloss Papers, 55/89-90.
16 WW to EMH, Apr. 13, 1919, Amendments Proposed by France, Apr. 2, 1919, WW, Memorandum on the Amendments Proposed by France, Apr. 12, 1919, EMH Papers, 49/20; WW to EMH, Apr. 12, 1919, Memorandum on the Amendments Proposed by France, Apr. 8, 1919, WW Papers, Ser. 5B, Reel 400; EMH Diary, Apr. 2-4, 1919; Mantoux, *Délibérations*, I, 144-45; Auchincloss Diary, March 29, Apr. 3, 1919, Auchincloss Papers, 55/90; Tardieu, *Truth about the Treaty*, 138, 205.

against Germany were unacceptable. Clemenceau offered to compromise if the president would consent to temporary occupation of the Rhineland. With House's encouragement, Wilson reluctantly agreed. On April 20 the president and premier approved a draft of the security treaty and plans for the Rhineland occupation. When Lloyd George returned to Paris after a brief trip to London, he endorsed this compromise. It represented less of a commitment to French security than Clemenceau desired, but more than either Wilson or Lloyd George had initially intended to give. They had preferred the League's vague promises, which would facilitate Anglo-American control over international affairs without entangling their countries on the European continent. When White learned that Wilson had agreed to a security treaty with France, he again cautioned that it would stir up opposition in the United States. Supporters of the League would regard it as an indication of the Covenant's inadequacy, while critics would view it as a violation of the American diplomatic tradition against "entangling alliances." To minimize this opposition, he advised, the United States and Great Britain should conclude separate bilateral treaties with France instead of a tripartite agreement. Wilson adopted this advice about the form, but discounted White's broader concern. He attempted to reassure him that, "as you know, all that I promised is to try to get it." Clearly, the president himself was not very enthusiastic about the French security treaty.[17]

Both Wilson and Lloyd George interpreted the French security treaties as involving minimal commitments. Before presenting the peace treaty to Germany at Versailles on May 7, 1919, Clemenceau requested from them a written confirmation and public announcement of these bilateral treaties. Balfour prepared a letter, which he and Lloyd George would sign, summarizing the compromise concerning the Rhineland and French security. This letter carefully qualified British obligations by excluding the dominions, unless their parliaments approved the security treaty, and by making its ratification even by Great Britain conditional upon that of the United States. Wilson agreed that he and Lansing would sign a similar letter for Clemenceau. Although these letters referred to demilitarization of the Rhineland, the president refused to include any such reference in the public announcement. He wanted to avoid any mention of possible German remilitarization of the Rhineland as an act of aggression.[18]

1 7   EMH Diary, Apr. 12, 14-15, 19, 1919; Auchincloss Diary, Apr. 14, 1919, Auchincloss Papers, 55/90; HW to WW, Apr. 16, 1919, WW to HW, Apr. 17, 1919, Stipulations to Be Embodied in the Treaty, Apr. 20, 1919, WW Papers, Ser. 5B, Reel 401; *FR:PPC*, V (Washington, 1944), 113-14, 117-18; Mantoux, *Délibérations*, I, 318-19; DLG, *Memoirs*, I, 280-81; Tardieu, *Truth About the Treaty*, 139-40, 186; Treaty Between France and the United States, Apr. 20, 1919, AJB Papers, 49750/16.
1 8   *FR:PPC*, V, 474-75, 485-86, 494-95; Miller, Memorandum for the President, May 6, 1919, announcement, May 6, 1919, WW Papers, Ser. 5B, Reel 404; Draft by Mr. Balfour for 'Council of Three' of suggested Treaty between England and France, May 5, 1919, AJB Papers, 49750/17-18; DLG and AJB to Clemenceau, May 5, 1919, DLG Papers, F/51/1/22; WW and RL to Clemenceau, May 6, 1919, EMH Papers, 5/4; Miller, *My Diary*, I, 293-95; Auchincloss Diary, May 6, 1919, Auchincloss Papers, 55/91.

Political considerations in the United States and the British Empire encouraged Wilson and Lloyd George to limit their commitments to French security. From Washington, Tumulty warned that news about the alliance was stimulating widespread criticism in the press. Wilson attempted to assure him that the security treaty was fully consistent with the proposed League.[19] South African prime minister Louis Botha, upon recieving a copy of the French security treaty, voiced his concern. On Smuts' advice, he underscored the qualifications that allowed Great Britain to escape any obligation to protect France against Germany if the United States declined to ratify its security treaty, and that excluded British dominions unless they consented. Lloyd George assured Botha as well as the prime ministers of Canada, Australia and New Zealand that British dominions were clearly exempted from the alliance. He emphasized, moreover, that it would not entangle Great Britain in a European war which France provoked.[20]

Despite French attempts to transform the League into an anti-German alliance and to retain permanent military control of the Rhine, the Anglo-American conception of international relations prevailed. The compromise involving the security treaties and temporary Rhineland occupation limited British and American obligations to protect France. Wilson and Lloyd George successfully reconciled these with their understanding of the Covenant. Only overt German aggression against France would require the United States and Great Britain to respond under the security treaties, and Article 10 already contained that promise. In both the League and the alliance they reserved American and British freedom to decide whether to repel alleged aggression.

I

Maintaining Anglo-American control over drafting of the Covenant, Wilson, House and Cecil met privately in March to consider possible amendments. The president consistently opposed any substantial change in the future League. Despite his reluctance even to appear to compromise, he recognized widespread American sensitivity on questions such as the Monroe Doctrine. Encouraged by House, Cecil took the initiative in preparing amendments. They agreed to stipulate that decisions of the executive council and the body of delegates would require unanimity unless otherwise specified. This wording coincided with their earlier interpretation of the League's procedures. Anticipating Germany's admission to the League,

---

19   JPT to WW, Apr. 19, 1919 (#66), WW Papers, Ser. 5B, Reel 401; JPT to WW, Apr. 22, 1919 (#72), WW Papers, Ser. 5B, Reel 402; WW to JPT, [May 9, 1919], WW Papers, Ser. 5B, Reel 402; JPT to WW, Apr. 22, May 7, 1919, WW to JPT, May 9, 1919 (#43), JPT Papers, Box 6; JPT to Forster, Apr. 24, 1919, WW Papers, Ser. 4, File 470.
20   DLG to Bordon, Massey, Hughes and Botha, May 10, 1919, Botha to DLG, May 15, 1919, DLG to Botha, June 26, 1919, DLG Papers, F/5/3/56, F/5/5/9, 14; Botha to DLG, May 6, 15, 1919, DLG to Botha, May 10, 1919, Hancock and van der Poel, eds., *Smuts Papers*, IV, 150-51, 155, 158-59.

which Lloyd George favored, they wanted to empower the executive council to expand its membership. This provision for eventually including Germany among the great powers reflected the Anglo-American vision of a universal league rather than an alliance. In other ways as well, British and American leaders sought to limit national commitments under the Covenant. They altered Article 8 to clarify that the League could not adopt any plan for disarmament without each government's approval. They also specified that the League could not assign a mandate to a state without its consent. At Wilson's instigation, they omitted from Article 15 the executive council's obligation to recommend measures for implementing its own unanimous decisions, even if a disputing party refused to comply with the proposed settlement. Cecil suggested an amendment, which Sir Robert Borden, prime minister of Canada, had strongly advocated, to remove Article 10's guarantee of territorial integrity and political independence; but he did not press for its acceptance. Wilson, House and Cecil also discussed possible amendments to exempt the Monroe Doctrine and domestic affairs from the League's jurisdiction and to reserve the right of each nation to withdraw from the organization at some future time. Reaching no agreement on these questions, they postponed them for later consideration.[21]

In their determination to control the drafting of the Covenant, British and American leaders refused to consider seriously other statesmen's proposals for revision. With Clemenceau's acquiescence and Wilson's authorization, Cecil and House arranged a meeting between a committee of the League Commission and representatives of twelve neutral countries. At this meeting, delegates of the Allied and Associated Powers gave these representatives the opportunity to suggest amendments to the draft Covenant. But as Cecil clearly stated, the general principles of the proposed League were not subject to reconsideration. The meeting itself was unofficial. Six members of the commission, including Cecil, House and Bourgeois, merely received various amendments from the neutrals. Although these nations, especially from Europe and Latin America, would be invited to join the League as original members, they lacked any real influence over its inception.[22]

Neither France nor the neutrals succeeded in revising the Covenant. When the League Commission reconvened to consider amendments, only Wilson and Cecil achieved their desired changes. Bourgeois attempted to strengthen

---

21 Miller, *My Diary*, I, 162-63, 172, 176-89; Cecil Diary, March 16, 18, 1919, Cecil Papers, 51131; EMH Diary, March 16, 18, 1919; Auchincloss Diary, March 18, 1919, Auchincloss Papers, 55/89; McCall to WW, Feb. 26, 1919, WW to McCall, Feb. 28, 1919, WW Papers, Ser. 4, File 4767; Miller, *Drafting of the Covenant*, II, 580-91; Bordon to WW, March 14, 1919, The Covenant of the League of Nations: Memorandum by Sir Robert Bordon, March 13, 1919, WW Papers, Ser. 5B, Reel 395; *FR:PPC*, XI, 123-24.

22 Cecil Diary, Feb. 16-17, March 5, 1919, Cecil Papers, 51131; Auchincloss Diary, March 19-21, 1919, Auchincloss Papers, 55/89; Miller, *Drafting of the Covenant*, II, 592-645; Cecil to WW, March 19, 1919, Hymans to WW, March 19, 1919, EMH to WW, March 22, 1919, Amendments to the Draft of the Covenant proposed by the Neutral Powers, March 20-21, 1919, WW Papers, Ser. 5B, Reel 396; Cecil to EMH, Feb. 25, March 8, 9, 1919, EMH Papers 4/38.

the League's jurisdiction over military affairs, again proposing amendments that British and American delegates had previously rejected. Under Article 8 he wanted to empower the executive council or a special commission to investigate and verify the level of military preparedness by the League's members. Wilson objected to this verification as a violation of national sovereignty. Bourgeois also endeavored to establish a "permanent organism" to prepare for military and naval operations so that the executive council could take immediate and effective action in response to aggression. Wilson and Cecil again refused to expand the permanent commission's functions under Article 9. They also declined to broaden the scope of sanctions in Article 16. Opposing Hymans' recommendation to restrict the League's original membership to the Allied and Associated Powers, Wilson explained that he wished "to avoid giving the League the appearance of an alliance." It should instead be "a world league." He defended the neutral nations' right to join the League. He also secured an amendment to Article 15 to exempt domestic affairs from the League's jurisdiction. His final amendment, which would allow any state to withdraw from the League after ten years on one year's notice, encountered French criticism. Larnaude noted that a reference to ten years would give a temporary appearance to the League. To protect a nation's right to withdraw without giving this implication, Italian Premier Orlando suggested a compromise. With Wilson's and Bourgeois' approval, the commission adopted his amendment to permit any member that had fulfilled its obligations under the Covenant to withdraw at any time on two years' notice. The president reserved his right to introduce a Monroe Doctrine amendment at a later time. Cecil and Balfour had attempted to draft such an amendment, but had not obtained either Lloyd George's or Wilson's approval. On other issues, where British and American leaders had agreed, they prevailed in writing their changes into the Covenant.[23]

Their failure to devise an acceptable Monroe Doctrine amendment stemmed from the serious Anglo-American naval rivalry. Lloyd George had decided to force the United States to conclude an agreement on naval policy as a condition for his final approval of the League. Recognizing American sensitivity over the Monroe Doctrine, he selected this issue as the best way to coerce Wilson into accepting a compromise. In this situation the president had refrained from introducing his own Monroe Doctrine amendment in the League Commission. He was fully aware of the seriousness of this impasse. If Wilson expected the Senate to approve American membership in the League, he needed to preserve the Monroe Doctrine. Lodge advised White: "In some form or other the Monroe Doctrine will be protected in any League

23   Miller, *Drafting of the Covenant*, II, 336-60; Cecil Diary, March 22, 24, 26, 1919, Cecil Papers, 51131; EMH Diary, March 24, 1919; Miller, *My Diary*, I, 191, 198-206; Auchincloss Diary, March 22, 24, 26, 1919, Auchincloss Papers, 55/90; Bourgeois, Organisme permanent (Art. 9), EMH Papers, 4/16; AJB and Cecil, Monroe Doctrine amendment, [March 19, 1919], EMH Papers, 49/12, and WW Papers, Ser. 5B, Reel 403; Smuts to Gillett, March 27, 1919, Hancock and van der Poel, eds., *Smuts Papers*, IV, 88-89; *FR:PPC*, XI, 133.

that is made." Yet Lloyd George refused any amendment for this purpose unless he first achieved a naval agreement.[24]

Lloyd George's tactic of linking the Monroe Doctrine and naval questions was especially powerful because of the Republican position. Congress had refused to pass the naval bill before adjourning on March 4, thereby depriving the president of authority to engage in a naval race with Great Britain. Lodge saw no justification for Anglo-American naval rivalry but insisted upon excluding the Monroe Doctrine from the League's jurisdiction.[25] Politically vulnerable at home on both the Monroe Doctrine and naval policy, Wilson needed to accommodate Lloyd George in order to salvage the League. They delegated the negotiations for a naval agreement to Secretary of the Navy Daniels and Admiral William S. Benson, Chief of Naval Operations, for the United States, and Colonial Secretary Walter Long and Admiral Sir Rossalyn Wemyss, First Sea Lord and Chief of the Naval Staff, for Great Britain. Both sides refused to compromise. Daniels and Benson wanted to expand the American navy as authorized in the Naval Appropriations Act of 1916. They thought the new League's success depended upon a balance between American and British naval strength. The United States, they contended, required a navy equal to the British navy to achieve its goals throughout the world.[26]

This American claim for parity was precisely what Long and Wemyss opposed. Aware of the Republicans' friendly attitude, Long wanted to force the Wilson administration to acquiesce in "the supremacy of the seas" by Great Britain. To him it appeared contradictory for the president to advocate both the League and a larger American navy. Long warned Lloyd George that Wilson was trying "to make England play second fiddle" at the peace conference and that British representatives should do everything possible to prevent him from seizing first place. With the prime minister's approval, Long urged Daniels to reduce the American naval program by three battleships, leaving Great Britain with thirty-three battleships to twenty for the United States. The British navy would also have thirteen battle cruisers

24   DLG to Bonar Law, March 31, 1919, DLG Papers, F/30/3/40; DLG, *Memoirs*, I, 266-73; "Negotiations for an Anglo-French Pact," Great Britain, *Sessional Papers*, Vol. 26, 76-85; Lamont to WW, March 19, 1919, WW Papers, Ser. 5B, Reel 396; WW to Lamont, March 24, 1919, Some Considerations for the Peace Conference, March 25, 1919, WW Papers, Ser. 5B, Reel 397; JPT to WW, March 28 (#39), 28 (#41), Apr. 2 (#48), 1919, WW to JPT, March 31, 1919, WW Papers, Ser. 5B, Reel 398; Clagett to JPT, Apr. 3, 1919, WW Papers, Ser. 4, File 331; JPT to WW, March 28, 1919, WW Papers, Ser. 4, File 156; WW to EMH, Paris, March 31, 1919, JPT Papers, Box 1, and EMH Papers, 49/20; Polk to ER, Apr. 1, 1919, HW to ER, March 28, 1919, HW to HCL, March 25, 1919, ER Papers, Box 137; HCL to HW, March 5, 1919, HCL Papers, File 1919 (Henry White); HCL to HW, Apr. 8, 1919, HW Papers, Box 41, and HCL Papers.
25   HCL to Bryce, Jan. 16, Feb. 3, March 4, 25, Apr. 8, 1919, HCL Papers, File 1919 (Adams-Trevelyan); HCL to Finch, March 17, 1919, HCL Papers, File 1919 (Peace, League, Political, A-H).
26   JD to Close, March 27, 1919, WW Papers, Ser. 5B, Reel 397; Benson to WW, Apr. 9, 1919, U.S. Naval Advisory Staff, Paris, Memorandum No. 25, Apr. 7, 1919, WW Papers, Ser. 5B, Reel 399; JD to WW, March 4, 4, 30, 1919, Benson to JD, Feb. 22, 1919, JD Papers, Box 14; JD to WW, March 4, 4, 1919, WW Papers, Ser. 5B, Reel 394.

to six for the United States. By limiting the American fleet's size to sixty percent of Great Britain's, the British navy could remain equal to the combined naval strength of the United States and France. Lloyd George's argument that new American ships were superior in firepower failed to convince Daniels to accept numerical inferiority. Negotiations remained deadlocked.[27]

Cecil and House regretted that Anglo-American naval rivalry endangered the League's prospects. They hoped to remove this obstacle, but neither of them intended to make any real concession. Cecil protested to Lloyd George that Long and Wemyss, by the confrontational method they were using, were most likely to antagonize Americans without reaching an agreement. He expressed keen disappointment that the prime minister seemed to have abandoned the future League. Rather than pursue this dangerous course, he wanted to separate naval policy from the Monroe Doctrine. Cecil warned Balfour that "the Prime Minister intends to use the League of Nations as a stick to beat the President with until he agrees with him about the Navy. Such a plan may succeed, but I am personally very doubtful of it." By alienating Americans, this tactic might cost Great Britain the political and especially economic assistance the United States might otherwise supply. It might also undermine Lloyd George's government if Parliament learned about its "fantastic" view of the American navy as a threat. Implicit in this assessment was the warning that Cecil himself might resign from the cabinet in protest over Lloyd George's lack of commitment to Anglo-American cooperation in the League. "I feel his policy to be exceedingly hazardous for the whole success of the League," concluded Cecil. ". . . It can only work with the hearty cooperation of the British and Americans."[28]

Lloyd George, by now aware of the dangers of this impasse, authorized Cecil to negotiate a compromise with House. In their exchange of letters on April 8 and 9, which outlined the terms of an Anglo-American naval agreement, these two removed the controversy over naval policy as an obstacle to the League. Cecil reiterated the British contention that American naval expansion was inconsistent with the league idea. To avoid an arms race and promote friendship, he asked the American government to abandon its new naval program after signing the peace treaty. He also wanted assurances that in future years the United States would consult Great Britain about their respective naval programs. With Wilson's approval, House accepted these conditions but carefully excluded from the definition of a new naval program the American fleet as authorized by the Naval Appropriations Act of 1916. Lloyd George desired a further promise that the United States would not build under the existing program any new ships that were not already under construction. Without making a commitment, House indicated American

2 7   Long to DLG, Feb. 16, March 7, Apr. 8, 1919, DLG Papers, F/33/2/13, 22, 31; JD to WW, Apr. 7, 1919, JD Papers, Box 14.
2 8   Cecil to DLG, Apr. 4, 1919, DLG Papers, F/6/6/25, and Cecil Papers, 51076/35-36; Cecil to AJB, Apr. 5, 1919, Cecil Papers, 51094/210-11.

willingness to discuss this curtailment and the relative strengths of the two fleets after concluding peace. He especially stressed the president's determination to prevent a naval race with Great Britain. Although Lloyd George preferred a more explicit agreement, he now withdrew his opposition to a Monroe Doctrine amendment to the Covenant. After all, expansion under the current program would still leave the American navy less than two-thirds the size of the British fleet. The naval agreement preserved Anglo-American collaboration in creating the League.[29]

New amendments to the Covenant produced more controversy in the League Commission. Reconvening to review the report of its drafting committee, it readily approved this committee's recommendation to change the name of the body of delegates to "the assembly," and that of the executive council to simply "the council." Problems arose when Bourgeois proposed French as the League's official language, with the French text of the Covenant as the binding version. Wilson ruled this amendment out of order. Both he and Cecil were determined that the English draft should be the Covenant's official text. As an addition to Article 10, the president introduced his amendment that international engagements, such as arbitration treaties or regional understandings like the Monroe Doctrine, would remain valid. This Monroe Doctrine amendment, he argued, would not prevent the League from acting in American affairs, nor would it prevent the United States from participating in European affairs. "The Covenant," he explained, "provided that the members of the League should mutually defend one another in respect of their political and territorial integrity. The Covenant was therefore the highest tribute to the Monroe Doctrine. It adopted the principle of the Monroe Doctrine as a world doctrine." Larnaude and Bourgeois voiced their fear that this amendment might allow the United States to refrain from joining other League members to stop aggression. It might, in effect, divide the League between the Old and New Worlds. Wilson passionately rejected this interpretation. He claimed that the Monroe Doctrine had provided "a successful barrier against the entrance of absolutism into North and South America." Now the United States sought to join other nations in extending "the movement of liberty" throughout the world. To alleviate French fears, Cecil suggested separating the Monroe Doctrine amendment from Article 10. Larnaude and Bourgeois eventually acquiesced in this arrangement, although they still preferred even greater assurances. The Monroe Doctrine amendment was adopted as the president desired.[30]

29   Cecil Diary, Apr. 3, 8, 10, 1919, Cecil Papers, 51131; EMH Diary, March 10, Apr. 8-10, 1919; Miller, *My Diary*, I, 229-37; Auchincloss Diary, March 31, Apr. 3, 9-10, 1919, Auchincloss Papers, 55/90; Cecil to EMH, Apr. 8, [10], 1919, EMH to Cecil, Apr. 9, 1919, Cecil to [DLG], Apr. 10, 1919, EMH Papers, 4/38; Miller, Memorandum for Colonel House, Apr. 9, 1919, draft letter from EMH to Cecil, n.d., EMH Papers, 14/16; EMH to DLG, Apr. 8, 1919 [not sent], EMH Papers, 12/32; Cecil to DLG, Apr. 10, 1919, Cecil Papers, 51076/37; Cecil to EMH, Apr. 8, 10, 10, 1919, EMH to Cecil, Apr. 9, 1919, Cecil to [DLG], Apr. 10, 1919, Cecil Papers, 51094/212-18.

30   Miller, *Drafting of the Covenant*, II, 360-87, 658-82; Miller, *My Diary*, I, 207, 212, 215-18, 223, 238-44; EMH Diary, Apr. 11-12, 1919; Auchincloss Diary, Apr. 3, 10-11, 1919, Auchincloss Papers,

British and American leaders also prevailed in the choice of Geneva as the location for the League's headquarters. At the commission's previous meeting, Wilson had appointed a committee to consider this question. Naming Orlando, Smuts, Makino and House, he had excluded any French or Belgian advocates of Brussels. The committee selected Geneva, Orlando now reported, because of Switzerland's tranquility and neutrality. Cecil defended this choice, arguing that the League should be located in a cosmopolitan country but not in a capital city. Expressing his preference for Geneva instead of Brussels, the president said "the antipathies of the war should be set aside; otherwise it might be thought that the League was a mere coalition of Allies moved by the hatreds born of the war. Our object was to bring about friendly relations between all peoples." The arguments of Hymans and Larnaude in favor of Brussels were offered in vain. Behind the choice of Geneva lay Wilson's appreciation of its traditions. George D. Herron had earlier conveyed to him the invitation of the President of the Council of State of the Republic of Geneva to locate the League there. Herron commended Geneva's traditions of religious liberty and political democracy and its contributions, especially from John Calvin, to the Scottish Covenanters and English Puritans, and subsequently to the United States. These were persuasive arguments for the Scotch-Irish Presbyterian president, who had determined to call the League's constitution a Covenant. Ignoring Belgian and French pleas for Brussels, he successfully advocated Geneva.[31]

II

At the League Commission's final meeting on April 11, Japanese delegates again raised the question of racial equality. By this time Wilson was well aware of its importance for Japan.[32] Baron Makino and Viscount Sutemi Chinda were willing to introduce an amendment to the draft Covenant in a form acceptable to British and American leaders. They had consulted Smuts, Cecil and House. Smuts played the leading role in seeking a compromise

55/90; Miller to WW, Apr. 4, 5, 1919, Drafting Committee, The Covenant of the League of Nations, Miller, Memorandum on the Text of the Covenant to Be Reported by the Drafting Committee, Apr. 4, 1919, WW Papers, Ser. 5B, Reel 399; Miller to WW, Apr. 12, 1919, The Covenant of the League of Nations, WW Papers, Ser. 5B, Reel 400; EMH to Hitchcock, Apr. 4, 1919, EMH Papers, 10/27.

3 1 Miller, *Drafting of the Covenant*, II, 365-68; Herron to WW, March 20, 1919, Edward to Herron, March 20, 1919, Gignoux to Herron, March 19, 1919, WW to Mar, March 20, 1919, Calonder to WW, March 24, 1919, WW to Herron, March 26, 1919, Hymans to WW, March 26, 1919, WW Papers, Ser. 5B, Reel 397; Herron to WW, Apr. 14, 1919, Gignoux to Herron, Apr. 14, 1919, Stovall to WW, Apr. 14, 1919, Ador to WW, Apr. 13, 1919, WW Papers, Ser. 5B, Reel 400; WW to Gignoux, May 2, 1919, WW Papers, Ser. 5B, Reel 404; Auchincloss Diary, Feb. 21, March 29, Apr. 3-4, 10, 1919, Auchincloss Papers, 55/89-90; Cecil Diary, Feb. 16, March 22, 1919, Cecil Papers, 51131.

3 2 Long to WW, March 4, 1919, WW Papers, Ser. 5B, Reel 394; Polk to A.C.N.P., March 20 (#1200), 22 (#1248), 1919, WW Papers, Ser. 5B, Reel 396; Phillips to A.C.N.P., Apr. 4, 1919 (#1440), WW Papers, Ser. 5B, Reel 399; Polk to A.C.N.P., Apr. 10, 1919 (#1514), WW Papers, Ser. 5B, Reel 400. See also Paul Gordon Lauren, "Human Rights in History: Diplomacy and Racial Equality at the Paris Peace Conference," *Diplomatic History*, II (Summer 1978), 257-78.

acceptable to his colleagues in the British Empire. All of them except Hughes of Australia approved Borden's formula for a Japanese amendment. Rather than accept Borden's suggestion to recognize the principle of equality of nations and "just treatment" of nationals in the Covenant's preamble, Hughes threatened to denounce the League. None of the British or American leaders was willing to call his bluff. They were all more interested in appeasing Hughes than the Japanese. His intransigence consequently prevented British and American representatives from supporting the Japanese amendment. In Smuts' absence, Cecil found himself in a difficult position as Makino introduced the amendment in the form Borden had earlier suggested. Makino asserted that "the principle of equality of nations and the just treatment of their nationals should be laid down as a fundamental basis of future relations in this world organisation." He argued that the League's success would depend upon adhering to such "noble ideals." It was difficult for Cecil to oppose these arguments. He responded that the Japanese amendment, if it was more than a vague and insignificant principle, would result in interference by the League in the domestic affairs of nations. Unwilling to approve such a potential infringement of national sovereignty, he persisted in his opposition even after Chinda emphasized that the amendment would not affect immigration. Except for Wilson, only Roman Dmowski of Poland supported Cecil's position, arguing that no principle, even one as acceptable as racial equality, should be included in the preamble unless it would be enforced under the Covenant. Other representatives, including Orlando, Bourgeois and Larnaude, as well as V. K. Wellington Koo of China, advocated the Japanese amendment. When Wilson called a vote, eleven of the seventeen members at this meeting favored the amendment. The president, however, arbitrarily ruled that it was defeated because the vote was not unanimous. This ruling clearly demonstrated his determination to maintain Anglo-American control. It also reflected racial prejudice in the British Empire and the United States. Wilson appreciated the explosiveness of issues relating to Japanese immigration on the west coast. Among others, Democratic Senator James D. Phelan of California had alerted him to vehement opposition in that state to the principle of racial equality. Sharing rather than challenging the racial attitude of white supremacy, the president chose to alienate the Japanese by rejecting their amendment.[33]

Despite this defeat, Japanese delegates continued to advocate the principle of racial equality. They raised the issue on April 28 at the plenary session of

33   Miller, *Drafting of the Covenant*, II, 387-92; Cecil Diary, March 24-25, 29, Apr. 11, 1919, Cecil Papers, 51131; Smuts to Gillett, March 31, 1919, Hancock and van der Poel, eds., *Smuts Papers*, IV, 94-96; Cecil to DLG, Apr. 15, 1919, DLG Papers, F/6/6/29; Auchincloss Diary, March 29, 31, Apr. 3, 10-11, 13, 17, 1919, Auchincloss Papers, 55/90; Miller, *My Diary*, I, 343-45; Phelan to A.C.N.P., March 24, 1919, WW Papers, Ser. 5B, Reel 397; Phelan to WW, Apr. 4, 1919, Phelan to JPT, Apr. 4, 1919, Beck to RL, Apr. 5, 1919 (#719), WW to Phelan, Apr. 7, 1919, Dunnigan to A.C.N.P., Apr. 7, 1919 (#751), WW Papers, Ser. 5B, Reel 399.

the peace conference, which convened to consider the revised Covenant. Makino reviewed the previously unsuccessful attempts to write the Japanese amendment into the Covenant. Having attempted to compromise, but still failing to win British and American approval, he now introduced the original amendment. "It was solely and purely from our desire to see the League established on a sound and firm basis of good-will, justice, and reason that we have been compelled to make our proposal," he explained. Nevertheless, Makino acquiesced in the inevitable defeat of the Japanese amendment. The delegates approved the Covenant as drafted by the League Commission. They also ignored Bourgeois' final plea for the previously defeated French amendments to Articles 8 and 9. His arguments in favor of strengthening the League's powers to verify the level of armaments and to plan for joint military defense fell on deaf ears. The Anglo-American conception of the League prevailed. Yet the unanimous vote for the Covenant masked serious dissension. Besides the continuing Japanese and French criticism, Italian delegates were noticeably absent from this plenary session. The principal Allied and Associated Powers were obviously not in total agreement.[34]

Because of concessions on Shantung, Japanese delegates refrained from pressing for their racial equality amendment. Prior to the plenary session, Balfour had negotiated a compromise providing for the transfer to Japan of German rights in this Chinese province, including a leasehold at Kiaochow, iron and coal mines, and a railway. Promising to restore political and territorial sovereignty to China, the Japanese claimed these economic concessions not only as a result of military victory but also under two Sino-Japanese treaties in 1915 and 1918. Supported initially by Wilson, Chinese delegates demanded full restoration of Shantung to their country. Under an Anglo-Japanese agreement in 1917, Lloyd George sided with Japan. The president tried to persuade Japanese delegates that with the League's creation and recognition of the "open door" principle, Japan would not need special rights in China. The Japanese, however, wanted a more precise definition of their rights in Shantung. During this dispute in the Council of Four, Chinda clearly warned that his government would not permit Japanese delegates to sign the peace treaty unless it transferred Germany's claims to Japan. After Orlando and Sonnino departed from Paris for Rome, this warning took on even greater significance. The possibility that two of the great powers might reject the treaty and refuse to join the League threatened to destroy prospects for peace. Emphasizing Shantung's

---

34 *FR:PPC*, III, 285-332; Miller, *Drafting of the Covenant*, II, 695-719; *FR:PPC*, XI, 158-59; Auchincloss Diary, Apr. 15, 28, 1919, Auchincloss Papers, 55/90; Cecil Diary, Apr. 26, 1919, Cecil Papers, 51131; Miller, *My Diary*, I, 278; EMH Diary, Apr. 28, 1919; Notes passed at Plenary Conference, Apr. 28, 1919, EMH Papers, 49/20; EMH to WW, Apr. 28, 1919, EMH Papers, Letterbook IV; *PPWW*, V, 469-73; Report of the Commission on the League of Nations, [Apr. 28, 1919], WW Papers, Ser. 5B, Reel 400; Cecil to WW, Apr. 21, 1919, WW Papers, Ser. 5B, Reel 401; Miller, Memorandum of Important Changes Made in the Covenant Reported to the Plenary Conference, Apr. 28, 1919, The President, at the 5th Plenary Session, Apr. 28, 1919, WW Papers, Ser. 5B, Reel 403.

importance to Japan, especially in view of the racial equality amendment's rejection, Balfour extracted Wilson's consent. Although this compromise would alienate the Chinese, resulting in their refusal to sign the peace treaty, the president approved the Shantung settlement to keep Japan in the future League. Aware that it would be unpopular in the United States, he prepared to defend this decision.[35]

III

Wilson refused to compromise with Italy over Fiume. In the Council of Four, Orlando had outlined Italy's territorial claims in the Alps and along the Dalmatian coast. In accordance with the Treaty of London of 1915, Lloyd George and Clemenceau supported most Italian demands, but not for the city of Fiume. Wilson rejected this treaty's validity and quickly escalated the confrontation into an intractable dispute over principles. "To put Fiume inside Italy would be absolutely inconsistent with the new order of international relations," he asserted. He affirmed that the League would provide the best guarantee of Italy's interests, and that the United States would make its contribution toward that end. A skeptical Sonnino protested that the League would face difficulties as a new institution and, moreover, would lack military forces under its direct control. This argument coincided with Clemenceau's doubts about the League as a guarantor of French security. Seeking a compromise, Lloyd George suggested an Italian sphere of influence in the form of mandates in Turkey. Wilson persisted in opposition, claiming to represent the aspirations not only of Americans but also of Allied peoples. Under this delusion, he published on April 23 a statement affirming the principles that he wanted to govern the Italian-Yugoslav settlement. In response to this appeal over their heads to the Italian people, Orlando and Sonnino withdrew from the peace conference and went to Rome. During the crisis both Lloyd George and Clemenceau remained faithful to the Treaty of London. They privately warned the Italians not to expect Fiume and not to exclude Italy from great-power status as a member of the League council, which their absence from Paris would entail. Their failure to sign the peace treaty with Germany would, moreover, terminate British and French obligations to Italy under the Treaty of London. Under this pressure, Orlando and Sonnino returned to Paris, but only after the Italian Parliament had given them a vote of confidence. Although failing to

35   FR:PPC, V, 109-111, 123-34, 138-48, 222-23, 227-28, 245-47, 249-50, 316-18, 325-35, 389, 460; FR:PPC, IX, 168-69; RL Diary, IV, Apr. 28, May 1, 1919; EMH to WW, Apr. 29, 1919, WW to JPT, Apr. 30, 1919, WW Papers, Ser. 5B, Reel 403; WW to JPT, Apr. 30, 1919, JPT to Grayson, May 4, 1919, JPT Papers, Box 6; PPWW, V, 474-75; AJB to Makino, Apr. 28, 30, 1919, AJB to WW, Apr. 29, 1919, WW to AJB, Apr. 30, 1919, AJB to Curzon, May 8, 1919, AJB Papers, 49751/186-94, 197-205. See also Russell H. Fifield, Woodrow Wilson and the Far East: The Diplomacy of the Shantung Question (Hamden, 1965).

obtain Fiume, they demonstrated that they, rather than Wilson, were the real spokesmen for Italy.

Despite their agreement with Wilson concerning Fiume, Lloyd George and Clemenceau preferred secret diplomacy and refused to announce their position publicly. The president protested that "public opinion in the United States was intensely interested. It could not understand why the United States was apparently left in isolation. United States public opinion was much more important than Italian. If the United States again became isolated it would break up the whole scheme on which the Peace Conference was working." Lloyd George, despite his keen awareness of the importance of unity between the United States, Great Britain and France, refused to agree. "It must not be forgotten," he bluntly reminded Wilson, "that there was a growing feeling that Europe was being bullied by the United States of America. In London this feeling was very strong and that matter had to be handled with the greatest care. Any such rift would be the saddest possible ending to the present Conference. It would put an end to the League of Nations." The president, still not convinced, retorted that "he was sure of the fact that the so-called bullying was recognized by the common man as based on the principles which inspired the Peace." Accordingly, he expected Great Britain and France to support the United States against the "troublesome" Italians.[36]

This crisis ended when Italy's delegates returned to the peace conference, but it clearly demonstrated the limits of Wilson's international leadership. His endeavor to create a new world order based on his principles produced dissension instead. He succeeded in revising the Covenant, but at a high price. Allied leaders approved his amendments, but forced him to make real concessions. He granted a security treaty to France, a naval agreement to Great Britain, and a transfer of German rights in Shantung to Japan. While denying Fiume to Italy, he still acquiesced in most Italian claims as defined in the Treaty of London. The unity that remained between the United States and the Allies resulted from a series of diplomatic compromises, not from the reformation of international affairs that Wilson had envisaged. The reality of interdependence among these nations was profoundly different from his global vision of a postwar league. Although the Covenant embodied the Anglo-American conception of a league, even Lloyd George was not enthusiastic.[37] French, Italian and Japanese leaders, too, obviously placed little confidence in this new system of collective security. Wilson had failed to transform international relations in accordance with his ideals. This failure resulted less from the inadequacy of his diplomatic skill than from the impossibility of the task. No statesman could achieve the democratic

36   FR:PPC, V, 80-101, 106-09, 135-37, 149-51, 202-03, 210-27, 353-54, 390-92, 407-16, 420, 426-36, 452-59, 465-69, 482-83; FR:PPC, XI, 157, 163, 167, 171; PPWW, V, 465-68; Auchincloss Diary, Apr. 2-3, 15, 23-24, 1919, Auchincloss Papers, 55/90; RL Diary, IV, March 29, Apr. 24, 1919; Page to Wilson, March 18, 1919, WW Papers, Ser. 5B, Reel 396; Cecil Diary, May 6, 1919, Cecil Papers, 51131.
37   Cecil Diary, May 3, 1919, Cecil Papers, 51131.

redemption of the Old World. That unrealistic goal exceeded the means available to the United States. The limits of its power, even in 1919 at a time of preeminence, prevented the American president from fulfilling his ideals. From the beginning, his promise of world peace far surpassed the new League's real potential for resolving conflicts and preventing war. Failing to account for the world's pluralism as well as its interdependence, the new Covenant evidenced this fundamental problem in Wilson's conception of international relations.

IV

At Versailles on May 7, 1919, Premier Clemenceau, as president of the peace conference, submitted the treaty to the German delegates. Germany's foreign minister, Count Ulrich von Brockdorff-Rantzau, read a statement. Demanding a "Peace of Justice," he called for Germany's immediate admission into the League. To prevent a postwar economic collapse, he contended that "both victors and vanquished" must recognize "the economic and social solidarity of peoples" by joining together in "a free and comprehensive League of Nations." Praising this international organization as "the greatest advance in human progress," he insisted that "if the slain in this war are not to have died in vain, then the portals of the League of Nations must be thrown open to all peoples of good will."[38]

Brockdorff-Rantzau's avowed interest in a league represented a new development in Germany. Throughout the war the Imperial German government had shown no desire to join a postwar international organization. But in the face of military defeat during the summer of 1918, a Wilsonian peace became more appealing. The initiative came from leaders of the Social Democratic, Center and Progressive Peoples' parties, which constituted a majority in the Reichstag. In mid-September, Matthias Erzberger, a Center party leader who had previously sponsored the Reichstag's peace resolution of July 19, 1917, once again played the key role. In interparty meetings he argued that Germany needed to achieve peace during the autumn, and for that purpose it must establish a credible government and demonstrate a genuine willingness to join a postwar league. Other party leaders agreed that Germany should place the league idea in the forefront of its approach to peace. To prepare a German proposal for a league, they appointed Erzberger as chairman of a committee, which also included Friedrich Ebert and Georg Gothein, respectively, of the Social Democratic and Progressive Peoples' parties.[39]

---

38 *FR:PPC*, III, 413-20; Rede des Herrn Reichsministers des Auswärtigen Grafen Brockdorff-Rantzau, May 7, 1919, Deutsche Friedensdelegation in Versailles, Pol 13, Bd. 1, Politisches Archiv des Auswärtigen Amts, Bonn.

39 Interfraktionelle Sitzung, Sept. 12, 1918, Interfraktionelle Sitzung, Sept. 13, 1918, Matthias Erzberger Papers, Nr. 21, Bundesarchiv (Federal Archives), Koblenz; M. Erzberger, *Erlebnisse im Weltkrieg* (Stuttgart, 1920), 305-07.

Erzberger favored an inclusive league, which would embrace all states that subscribed to its basic principles. The members should accept the obligation of submitting all disputes to the league for peaceful settlement, if they failed to resolve them through diplomacy. They should all agree to the mutual reduction of arms and to economic and legal equality for all states. In particular, they should terminate economic warfare and preserve the "open door." They should maintain freedom of transportation, including freedom of the seas. In the future, the league should develop international standards for the rights of labor. This program, which Erzberger prepared for the committee, leaders of the majority parties adopted at their meeting on September 30. They had not yet gained the Imperial German government's approval.[40]

Only after the Supreme Command of the German Army recognized its desperate need for an armistice were Wilson's Fourteen Points embraced officially in Berlin as a favorable basis for peace. The Kaiser's appointment of Prince Max of Baden as chancellor, and the opening of armistice negotiations on October 3, inaugurated a shift in German policy. The new foreign secretary, Wilhelm Solf, now began to cooperate tentatively with advocates of a postwar league. Various members of the Reichstag, government officials, university professors, commercial leaders, editors and lawyers joined to develop plans for propagandizing the league idea in Germany. Out of these efforts emerged the German Society for a League of Nations (Deutsche Liga für Völkerbund). Officially sponsored and financed by the Foreign Office, this pro-league society became active only after the end of the war. Its belated appearance gave it a substantially different character from the League to Enforce Peace in the United States or its counterparts in Allied countries. German interest in a postwar league was essentially a product of military defeat and did not represent a genuine conversion to Wilson's Fourteen Points.[41]

On the eve of the armistice, Solf finally directed his subordinates in the Foreign Office to plan for peace on the basis of Wilson's principles. Earlier preparations had anticipated a German victory or at least a stalemate in the war. After Wilhelm II's abdication, the new republican government, expecting peace negotiations, began to define its interpretation of Wilson's Fourteen Points. Erzberger, who headed the German armistice commission, continued to direct the planning for a league even after Brockdorff-Rantzau replaced Solf.[42]

40   Interview, Sept. 13, 1918, Erzberger Papers, Nr. 14; [Programm], Sept. 24, 1919, [Aufzeichnung], Sept. 27, 1918, Interfraktionelle Sitzung, Sept. 25, 1918, Interfraktionelle Besprechung, Sept. 30, 1918, Erzberger Papers, Nr. 21; Erzberger, *Erlebnisse*, 307-13.
41   Franke to Solf's Geheimrat, Oct. 9, 1918, [Anlage], Oct. 9, 1918, Wilhelm Solf Papers, Nr. 56, Bundesarchiv, Koblenz; Preuss to Schücking, Oct. 14, 1918, Walther Schücking Papers, Nr. 88, Bundesarchiv, Koblenz; Bericht über die Umfrage wegen Errichtung einer "Deutschen Völkerbund-Liga," Schücking Papers, Nr. 92; Christoph M. Kimmich, *Germany and the League of Nations* (Chicago, 1976), 15.
42   Solf to Undersecretaries and Directors, Nov. 8, 1918, Weltkrieg, WK 30, Bd. 1, Politisches

The draft Covenant that Wilson presented to the peace conference on February 14, 1919, disappointed the Germans. They resented their exclusion from the League and their loss of colonies. Both Erzberger and the Foreign Office expected revisions to allow Germany to join the League and to recieve mandates on an equal basis with its former enemies. At a public meeting of the German Society for a League of Nations, Erzberger criticized the Covenant for failing to fulfill the wartime promise of "a durable peace" based upon "the principle of justice among equals." Article 10 appeared to threaten a disarmed Germany. Denouncing the article on mandates, Erzberger claimed that "Germany has an indisputable moral right to colonial possessions." In his opinion, the proposed League was merely a disguise for violence. He called for a league that would protect German interests. Offering his alternative, he stated that "in such a League of Nations there can be no discrimination other than that which acknowledges the principle of right and which opposes the principle of might."[43]

Hoping to escape its diplomatic isolation, the new Weimar Republic endeavored to exploit a direct connection with Wilson. Colonel Arthur L. Conger, a military intelligence officer in Pershing's general staff, had convinced his German counterpart, Walter Loeb, that he could provide this link. Consequently, the German cabinet under Chancellor Philipp Scheidemann decided on March 28, 1919, to authorize Erzberger and Brockdorff-Rantzau to use this channel of communication with the president. In accordance with their instructions, Loeb submitted a statement of "Peace Conditions Acceptable to Germany" to Conger. This statement, which Wilson received but without knowing its source, reiterated that "if the League of Nations is formed, Germany must become a member, with equal rights." These rights included the maintenance of an army and navy unless Germany's neighbors also disarmed, and the retention of colonies. Wilson paid little attention to this statement or to Erzberger's address, a copy of which he also received. The Conger-Loeb connection provided no opportunity to reconcile differences between the draft Covenant and the German view of a league.[44]

Archiv des Auswärtigen Amts; Besprechung in der Reichskanzlei über die Friedens-Verhandlungen, Jan. 27, 1919, Richtlinien für die deutschen Friedensunterhändler, Akten der Reichskanzlei, R43I/1, Bundesarchiv, Koblenz; Einverständnis zwischen Rantzau und Erzberger, Feb. 21, 1919, Handakten des Unterstaatssekretär Toepffer, 8, Politisches Archiv des Auswärtigen Amts.

43 Trautmann to Foreign Office, Feb. 16, 1919, Weltkrieg, WK 30, Bd. 23; Fehrenbach to Rantzau, March 1, 1919, A. A. Weimar, IV. 2, Politisches Archiv des Auswärtigen Amts; Roediger to Prussian War Ministry, Feb. 18, 1919, Reinhardt to Foreign Office, Feb. 12, 1919, A. A. Weimar, IV. 9; Loeb to Roediger, Feb. 19, 1919, Roediger to Loeb, Feb. 20, 1919, A. A. Weimar, V. 9; Loeb, Bericht über den Aufenthalt im amerikanischen Hauptquartier in Trier am 23. Febr. 1919, Feb. 24, 1919, Otto Landsberg Papers, Kleine Erwerbungen 328-3, Bundesarchiv, Koblenz; Press Review, March 29, 1919, WW Papers, Ser. 5B, Reel 398.

44 Loeb to Foreign Office, March 28, 1919, Loeb, Peace Conditions Acceptable to Germany, [March 30, 1919], Weltkrieg 30 Geh., Bd. 1, Politisches Archiv des Auswärtigen Amts; Reichsminister to Ebert, March 28, 1919, Loeb Telegramm, March 28, 1919, Akten der Reichskanzlei, R43I/1; Hagen Schulze, ed., Akten der Reichskanzlei, Weimarer Republik: Das Kabinett Scheidemann, 13. Februar bis 20. Juni 1919 (Boppard, 1971), 109-16; Nolan to THB, March 31, 1919, Nolan, Memorandum for General

By the time the German delegation went to Versailles, a broad consensus had formed in Germany concerning the future League. On April 10 the National Assembly resolved to reject any treaty that failed to offer a peace of reconciliation. In the name of Wilson's principles, it demanded equality for all nations in self-determination, disarmament, colonial questions, and membership in a league. President Ebert reaffirmed this position in a public statement.[45] The Foreign Office's guidelines for its delegates likewise stipulated that Germany must immediately become a league member. The draft Covenant was unacceptable because it assigned the dominant role to the five principal Allied and Associated Powers. Such an exclusive league would jeopardize German interests, notably with regard to colonies. Moreover, Germany should refuse to disarm unless its former enemies reciprocated. In short, the guidelines interpreted the Fourteen Points from a distinctively German perspective, which differed substantially from either the Allied leaders' or Wilson's own understanding of his principles.[46] Aware of this significant difference, Ebert repeatedly emphasized that the Allies needed to abandon their belligerent attitudes and welcome Germany into the League. He expected the president to share the German interpretation and to prevail upon the Allies to accept it as well.[47]

Because of their unrealistic expectations, German leaders were naturally disappointed by the Versailles Treaty. President Ebert and Scheidemann's cabinet issued a statement to the German people on May 9 denouncing these conditions of peace as a contradiction to the promised Fourteen Points. They labeled this treaty as "unbearable" and "unfulfillable." The revised Covenant that it contained obviously failed to satisfy the German desire for an inclusive league. The German government asserted that "the world must abandon all hope for a league of nations that would liberate and reconcile peoples and secure peace."[48]

What these leaders wanted was a peace that spared Germany the consequences of military defeat. The treaty, including the Covenant, obviously fell short of this goal, which they had identified with Wilson's Fourteen Points. Ebert concluded that in the negotiations with the Allies,

Bliss, No. 5, March 31, 1919, WW Papers, Ser. 5B, Reel 398. For contrasting views of Conger's role in German-American relations, see Lloyd E. Ambrosius, "Secret German-American Negotiations During the Paris Peace Conference," *Amerikastudien/American Studies*, XXIV, No. 2 (1979), 288-309, and Schwabe, *Woodrow Wilson, Revolutionary Germany, and Peacemaking*, 1918-1919, 299-394.

4 5   Fehrenbach to Scheidemann, Apr. 10, 1919, Akten der Reichskanzlei, R43I/1; Ebert to Scheidemann, Apr. 12, 1919, Abschrift, Apr. 15, 1919, Büro des Reichspräsidenten, R54/190, Bundesarchiv, Koblenz.

4 6   Simons to Albert, Apr. 20, 1919, Erzberger to Chancellor's Office, Apr. 28, 1919, Simons to Albert, Apr. 22, 1919, Richtlinien für die deutschen Friedensunterhändler, Akten der Reichskanzlei, R43I/2.

4 7   Frankfurter to Geheimrat, March 16, 1919, Anlage, [Statement], March 29, 1919, Naumann to Nadolny, Apr. 7, 1919, Anlage, Büro des Reichspräsidenten, R54/192.

4 8   An das deutsche Volk, May 9, 1919, Büro des Reichspräsidenten, R54/190; Scheidemanns Rede im Friedensausschuss, May 8, 1919, Akten der Reichskanzlei, R43I/2; "The German National Assembly and the Peace-Conditions of the Entente," (Berlin, 1919), Akten der Reichskanzlei, R43I/3; Tagebuch, May 12, 1919, Erich Koch-Weser Papers, Nr. 16, Bundesarchiv, Koblenz.

either Wilson had failed to realize his principles or he had never intended to fulfill his promise. In either event, the American president had betrayed Germany's confidence. From Ebert's perspective, the Covenant would establish a new Holy Alliance of the victorious powers. Rather than accept the conditions offered by the Allied and Associated Powers, he called for a genuine league that would provide equal membership for Germany. Advocating the previously published German proposal for such an international organization, he asserted that "our goal is no more special alliances, but a true, just and inclusive league of nations."[49]

At Versailles the German delegation attempted to achieve this goal through revision of the peace treaty. Brockdorff-Rantzau protested that no nation could endure or implement such harsh terms. He immediately submitted the German proposal for a league, spelling out in detail the ideas Erzberger had earlier developed. It affirmed that "the League of Nations is constituted for the purpose of founding a permanent peace between its members by obligatory settlement of international differences." All disputes not resolved by diplomacy were to be settled by arbitration or mediation. Every member must agree to extensive disarmament on land and sea and in the air. Although each state would reserve its right of self-defense, the German proposal emphasized the members' mutual responsibility to guarantee their respective territories and to refrain from interfering in other nations' internal affairs. This plan differed significantly from the Covenant by stipulating that the league would include all wartime belligerents. Brockdorff-Rantzau stressed this difference in his note to Clemenceau. He asked whether, and on what conditions, Germany would receive an invitation to membership. Wilson quickly prepared the initial American and Allied response, which rejected the German contention that the treaty departed from the promised conditions of peace. It noted that the Covenant included a procedure for admitting new members. At Wilson's request, Cecil convened a committee to study the German proposal for a league. The Council of Four subsequently approved the committee's expected conclusion that the Covenant was preferable. In their reply to Brockdorff-Rantzau, American and Allied leaders happily noted that Germany favored a league to preserve peace. Agreement in principle, however, still left a gulf between their conditions, on one side, and Germany's self-serving expectations on the other.[50]

4 9 Zussammenfassung: Interview mit dem Herrn Reichspräsidenten Ebert, May 15, 1919, Interview mit dem Reichspräsidenten Ebert, Nadolny to Dehn-Schmidt, June 3, 1919, I. Teil, Büro des Reichspräsidenten, R54/192; Dresel to A.C.N.P., Apr. 24, 1919, WW Papers, Ser. 5B, Reel 402. German leaders stressed the integrationist theme in Wilson's Fourteen Points, but other factors also shaped his handling of the question of Germany's membership in the League. For a good summary of these factors, see Klaus Schwabe, "Woodrow Wilson and Germany's Membership in the League of Nations, 1918-19," *Central European History*, VIII (March 1975), 3-22.
5 0 Bernstorff to Peace Delegation, May 8, 9, 10, 13, 1919, Rantzau to Foreign Office, May 8, 9, 10, 12, 1919, Rantzau to Clemenceau, May 9, 9, 1919, Clemenceau to Rantzau, May 10, 1919, Bernstorff to Rantzau, May 11, 1919, Rantzau to Scheidemann, May 12, 13, 1919, Deutsche Friedensdelegation

Desiring to revise the treaty, the Germans at first expected Wilson to support their interpretation of the Fourteen Points. Assuming that his weakness in the Allied negotiations had resulted in the harsh terms, they hoped to strengthen his position by firmly resisting the Versailles Treaty. This approach reflected a profound misunderstanding of the American president's role at Paris. He did not share the German view of his principles and did not favor extensive revision of the treaty. Shortly before the United States and the Allies presented it to the German delegation at Versailles, a discouraged Herron complained to Wilson that, because his principles had been badly compromised, "nothing now can save European civilization from utter disintegration." He wanted the United States at least to avoid entrapment in this Old World "pit." Repudiating the theologian's pessimistic outlook, Wilson responded that "it is undoubtedly true that many of the results arrived at are far from ideal, but I think that on the whole we have been able to keep tolerably close to the lines laid down at the outset." Before the end of May 1919, a copy of this letter arrived in Berlin at the Foreign Office, where it possibly contributed to the growing German suspicion that Wilson had not intended to work for the peace terms that Germany claimed in the name of his principles.[51]

Still hopeful of achieving revision, Brockdorff-Rantzau submitted the German delegation's counterproposal to Clemenceau on May 29. He again complained that the Allied and Associated Powers planned to exclude Germany from the League. Only as a member would the German government approve the treaty's terms for disarmament, and then only as a first step toward general disarmament. Germany also expected to receive mandates for its former colonies. This counterproposal emphasized the ostensible contradiction between Wilson's Fourteen Points and the Versailles Treaty. "A new spirit was to emerge from this peace and become embodied in a League of Nations, of which Germany was likewise to become a member," it claimed. For the treaty to fulfill this promise, revision was obviously necessary. Emphasizing advantages for the American and Allied countries, the counterproposal argued that an inclusive league would constitute "the most powerful guarantee of the faithfulness to Treaties of every German Govern-

in Versailles, Pol 13, Bd. 1; Clemenceau to Rantzau, May 22, 1919, Deutsche Friedensdelegation in Versailles, Pol 13, Bd. 2; *FR:PPC*, V, 559, 563-64, 756, 767-69; *FR:PPC*, VI (Washington, 1946), 765-78; Vorschläge der Deutschen Regierung für die Errichtung eines Völkerbundes, Akten der Reichskanzlei, R43I/483; Miller, *Drafting of the Covenant*, II, 744-61; Grew to Close, May 12, 1919, Rantzau to Clemenceau, May 9, 9, 1919, Clemenceau to Rantzau, May 10, 1919, WW Papers, Ser. 5B; Reel 405; WW to Cecil, May 14, 1919, Cecil to WW, May 17, 1919, WW Papers, Ser. 5B, Reel 406; Cecil Diary, May 16, 1919, Cecil Papers, 51131.

5 1   Herron to WW, Apr. 21, 1919, WW Papers, Ser. 5B, Reel 402; WW to Herron, Apr. 28, 1919, WW Papers, Ser. 5B, Reel 403; Langwerth to Peace Delegation, May 3, 1919, Rantzau to Langwerth, May 8, 1919, Langwerth to Rantzau, May 12, 1919, Deutsche Friedensdelegation in Versailles, Pol 13, Bd. 1; Langwerth to Rantzau, May 18, 1919, Deutsche Friedensdelegation in Versailles, Pol 13, Bd. 2; Minister to Foreign Office, May 27, 1919, Deutsche Friedensdelegation in Versailles, Pol 13, Bd. 31; Boetticher to Erzberger, May 6, 1919, Erzberger to Boetticher, May 8, 1919, Erzberger Papers, Nr. 46.

ment." Somehow, it presupposed, the conciliatory gesture of welcoming Germany into the League would transform international relations and render unnecessary the peace treaty's other methods of control. This would enable former enemies to live together in a peaceful world with political, military and economic equality.[52]

The Germans initially expected Wilson to show a more positive attitude than any of the Allied leaders toward their demands for revision. That inaccurate assessment reflected their false understanding of his real position. The British delegation, instead of the president, provided the greatest impetus for appeasing Germany. A month before the Allied and Associated Powers submitted the treaty to Brockdorff-Rantzau at Versailles, Wiseman had told House about the emerging British policy toward Germany. The alternatives, he said, were either a punitive peace, which the French favored, or a moderate peace, which Wilson had promised. He identified the president's principles with the appeasement of Germany. Wiseman doubted that the Allies could satisfy their national aspirations and still allow Germany to recover. He hoped, with some dramatic gesture that would force the Allies to adhere to the Fourteen Points, Wilson could enable the peace conference to escape this dilemma. An exaggerated fear of Bolshevism helped foster this new British attitude.[53]

After Germany began to protest against the treaty's conditions, British leaders from throughout the political spectrum urged Lloyd George to seek an accommodation. Arthur Henderson of the Labour party favored immediate German admission to the League. His Labour colleague in the British delegation in Paris, George N. Barnes, conveyed Henderson's advice to the prime minister, adding that he, too, wanted Germany in the League, but perhaps not until after its first organizing session. Smuts emerged as a prominent critic of the Versailles Treaty and advocate of "drastic revision." He recommended discussions with the Germans to amend the territorial, military and reparation clauses. While denouncing the treaty's punitive features and calling for immediate German membership in the League, he carefully protected South Africa's interest in former German colonies. Willing to make concessions at the expense of the European Allies, Smuts absolutely refused to countenance German retention of colonies. In agreement with Barnes and Smuts, Winston Churchill, the British war secretary, advised the prime minister to seize the current opportunity for negotiations. "On every ground, therefore," he concluded, "I strongly urge settling up

52   Aufzeichnungen, May 13, 1919, Moritz Julius Bonn Papers, Nr. 3, Bundesarchiv, Koblenz; Sitzung der Abordnung des Kabinetts und der Versailler Delegation in Spa am 23. Mai 1919, Erzberger Papers, Nr. 14; Rantzau to Bernstorff, May 14, 1919, Bernstorff to Peace Delegation, May 13, 1919, Deutsche Friedensdelegation in Versailles, Pol 13, Bd. 1; Bernstorff to Rantzau, May 21, 1919, Deutsche Friedensdelegation in Versailles, Pol 13, Bd. 2; Rantzau to Scheidemann, May 29, 1919, Bernstorff to Leinert and Rantzau, May 28, 1919, Deutsche Friedensdelegation in Versailles, Pol 13, Bd. 3; Rantzau to Clemenceau, May 29, 1919, Die Friedensbedingungen: Antwort der Deutschen Delegation, Deutsche Friedensdelegation in Versailles, Pol 13, Bd. 3a; FR:PPC, VI, 795-901.
53   Wiseman to EMH, Apr. 5, 1919, EMH Papers, 20/48.

with the Germans now. Now is the time, and it may be the only time, to reap the fruits of victory." Under this political pressure, Lloyd George convened a series of meetings with the British delegation and members of his cabinet in late May and early June. He then informed Wilson and Clemenceau of the British consensus that had formed in favor of revision. In his summary of desirable amendments, the prime minister included the German-Polish border, military occupation of the Rhineland, reparations, German membership in the League, and so-called pin-pricks. On all these issues, he now advocated concessions to Germany.[54]

Sharing Smuts' disillusionment with the treaty, Cecil joined his efforts to gain Wilson's approval for revision. Welcoming the German counterproposal, Smuts denounced the treaty. He endorsed the German claim to "a Wilson Peace" in the name of the Fourteen Points. Cecil suggested empowering the League to revise any part of the treaty after a definite period of not more than five years. This procedure for later revision would grant the League much greater responsibility for making changes in the peace settlement than Article 19, which authorized the assembly only to offer advice concerning the reconstruction of treaties or other international conditions that endangered the world's peace. Although House apparently endorsed this British proposal, Wilson quickly rejected it. He thought such a provision in the peace treaty, by encouraging dissatisfied nations to bring their grievances to the League, would result in continuing instability. At this stage of the peace conference, he was simply unwilling to consider extensive changes in the treaty. The president explained to Smuts that "the Treaty is undoubtedly very severe indeed. I have of course had an opportunity to go over each part of it, as it was adopted, and I must say that though in many respects harsh, I do not think that it is on the whole unjust in the circumstances, much as I should have liked to have certain features altered." Wilson simply rejected the German thesis, which was gaining credence in the British delegation, that the Versailles Treaty deviated substantially from the Fourteen Points. Adhering to the view he had earlier expressed to Herron, he added that Germany, by its attack on civilization, deserved "the most severe punishment."[55]

Wilson's colleagues in the American delegation generally shared his reluctance to revise the treaty. Lansing thought it required some substantial changes, but confided his suggestions only to his diary. "Even the measure

54   Barnes to DLG, May 18, 1919, Henderson to Barnes, May 16, 1919, DLG Papers, F/4/3/16; Smuts to DLG, May 5, 14, 22, June 2, 4, 1919, DLG to Smuts, June 3, 1919, DLG Papers, F/49/9/33, 34, 35, 39, 40, 41; Smuts to DLG, May 14, June 2, 4, 1919, DLG to Smuts, June 3, 1919, Smuts to Gillett, May 14, 19, June 1, 2, 3, 1919, Hancock and van der Poel, eds., Smuts Papers, IV, 156-58, 171-72, 211-13, 215-21; Churchill to DLG, May 20, 1919, DLG Papers, F/8/3/55; Cecil Diary, May 30-31, 1919, Cecil Papers, 51131; FR:PPC, VI, 139-46.
55   Smuts to WW, May 14, 1919, WW to Smuts, May 16, 1919, WW Papers, Ser. 5B, Reel 406; Smuts to WW, May 30, 1919, WW to Smuts, May 31, 1919, WW Papers, Ser. 5B, Reel 408; Smuts to Wilson, May 14, 30, 1919, WW to Smuts, May 16, 31, 1919, Hancock and van der Poel, eds., Smuts Papers, IV, 157-58, 160-61, 208-10; Cecil Diary, May 20, 25, June 1, 1919, Cecil Papers, 51131; EMH to Wiseman, May 31, 1919, Wiseman to EMH, n.d., EMH Papers, 20/48; EMH Diary, June 1, 1919.

of idealism, with which the League of Nations was at the first impregnated," he lamented, "has, under the influence and intrigue of ambitious statesmen of the Old World, been supplanted by an open recognition that force and selfishness are primary elements in international cooperation." Rather than the United States transforming the Old World, the Old World had overwhelmed Wilson and reduced him to dealing with European statesmen on their terms. The resulting League, merely a quintuple alliance of the principal Allied and Associated Powers, could not succeed in its task of preserving the peace settlement and preventing wars.[56] Lansing revealed his bitter criticism to Polk. "The League of Nations," he reported, "has become a veritable millstone about our necks." He had joined Bliss and White in applauding Wilson's stand on Fiume and opposing his compromise on Shantung, but otherwise exerted no real effort to shape developments in Paris. By now the secretary's influence on the president was nil, but he lacked the initiative even to resign. Bliss was far more forthright in presenting his moderate criticism and recommendations. Unlike Lansing, he welcomed the opportunity to express his views to Wilson at a meeting of the American Commission on June 3. In response to the German counterproposal, he advocated German membership in the League after a temporary probation. The general argued that "Germany will be far less a menace to the peace of the world if she is inside rather than outside the League." Less favorable toward revision, White expected Germany to accept the treaty with only minor modification. Although he, too, had condemned the Shantung settlement, he defended most of the treaty.

House, ever the chameleon, reacted to the German counterproposal with typical inconsistency. Privately with Lloyd George and Cecil, he endorsed the British – and also German – contention that the treaty deviated from the Fourteen Points; but with Clemenceau and Tardieu, he supported the French position that the Allied and Associated Powers should require Germany to sign it without major changes. The egotistical House reconciled these contradictory attitudes by lamenting that American and Allied leaders had neglected to follow his advice, which would have enabled them to draft a treaty acceptable to Germany. Because they had failed to do this, it was now too late to consider extensive revision. The only modification that he advocated was Germany's admission into the League in the near future. Otherwise, he remained silent at the June 3 meeting, waiting for the president to define the American response to the German counterproposal. None of Wilson's colleagues in the American delegation advised extensive revision of the treaty.[57]

---

56 RL Diary, IV, May 5, 6, 8, 1919.
57 RL Diary, IV, May 19, June 1, 5, 1919; RL to Polk, May 1, 1919, Polk Papers, 78/10; RL to Polk, June 4, 1919, Polk Papers, 78/11; THB to WW, Apr. 29, June 6, 1919, THB Papers, Box 70; THB to WW, Apr. 29, 1919, WW Papers, Ser. 5B, Reel 403; THB to WW, June 6, 1919, HW to WW, June 5, 1919, WW Papers, Ser. 5B, Reel 409; HW to HCL, May 13, 26, 1919, HCL Papers and ER Papers, Box 161; EMH Diary, May 28, 30, June 1, 1919; FR:PPC, XI, 190, 197-222.

At the American Commission's meeting, Wilson clearly expressed his opposition to revision for the sake of securing a German signature. He ridiculed the British reaction to Germany's protest. "They ought to have been rational to begin with," he asserted with reference to British leaders who now advocated appeasement, "and then they would not have needed to have funked at the end." The president readily acknowledged the stringency of the peace conditions, but thought Germany deserved them. He refused to consider revision unless someone could show him that the terms violated his Fourteen Points. He was willing to anticipate German membership in the League after a period of probation. But he refused to specify a date. In response to Lansing's question, Wilson explained, "I think it is necessary that we should know that the change in government and the governmental method in Germany is genuine and permanent. We don't know either of them yet."[58]

Wilson reiterated in the Council of Four his position on Germany's admission to the League. Regarding this as the most important issue other than Upper Silesia for the Germans, he wanted to assure them that they could join the League after probation. "It was," he said, "a question of whether they were to be pariahs, or to be admitted into the League of Nations." He agreed with Lloyd George that one argument for admission was that "Germany could be better controlled as a member of the League than outside it." After clarifying that the Covenant's procedures for admitting new members would apply to Germany, Clemenceau accepted Wilson's position. The Council of Four decided to deny Germany's demand for immediate membership in an inclusive league, but to offer possible admission after probation.[59]

A committee under Cecil's direction prepared this part of the reply to the German counterproposal. While the French and Italian members acquiesced, House endorsed the British desire for revision. The committee's proposed reply promised Germany not only membership in the League "within a few months" but also reconsideration of the financial, economic and communications clauses of the treaty at that time. It further indicated that German disarmament would hasten "a general reduction of armaments" with the prospect of "substantial progress" toward this goal by the first meeting of the League's assembly in the autumn of 1919. Finally, the draft offered the League's protection for educational, religious and cultural rights of German minorities living in territories lost to Germany as a consequence of the war. The report of Cecil's committee provoked a vigorous reaction in the Council of Four. Even Lloyd George refused to promise German membership in the League "within a few months." Clemenceau voiced "the gravest doubt" about other aspects as well. Privately, he notified Wilson of French

58 *FR:PPC*, XI, 215-22; HW to HCL, June 3, 1919, ER Papers, Box 161; EMH to Clemenceau, June 3, 1919, EMH Papers, 5/4.
59 *FR:PPC*, VI, 157-58.

repudiation of this draft. Clemenceau complained to House, who characteristically shifted responsibility to Cecil, that the committee exceeded its jurisdiction by dealing with economic and military questions. Tardieu also attacked the Council of Four's apparent willingness to revise the peace treaty. "Have they supposed," he asked, "that this draft of conditions should gratify Germany?" Especially critical of the British, Tardieu pleaded with House for American support. Before the Allied premiers and Wilson approved their last reply to the German proposal for a league, they substantially modified the Cecil committee's draft. In its final form, it offered Germany only the possibility of admission to the League "in the early future" and the hope of "a general reduction of armaments." This reply rejected the German request for a different league. Rather than accommodate the Germans, as the British desired, it substantially affirmed the president's position. Accordingly, Germany's possible admission to the League would depend upon future German behavior.[60]

Clemenceau officially notified Brockdorff-Rantzau that the Allied and Associated Powers rejected the German request for admission to the League. "The German revolution," he explained on June 16, "was postponed to the last moment of the war and there is as yet no guarantee that it represents a permanent change." If the Germans faithfully fulfilled the terms of the Versailles Treaty, Clemenceau stated, "it will be possible at an early date to complete the League of Nations by the admission of Germany." Their postwar behavior would determine whether that possibility became a reality.[61]

This reply shattered the German government's expectations. To escape from its status as a defeated enemy, it wanted discussions about the peace conditions. Immediate membership in the League would also symbolize equality for Germany with the other nations of the world. But Wilson and Allied leaders now demanded German approval of the peace treaty with only minor modifications. Refusing to accept this treaty, Brockdorff-Rantzau regarded the German counterproposal as the only possible basis for agreement. Ebert and Scheidemann agreed. Preparing for the contingency that the Allied and Associated Powers might refuse to negotiate, the German cabinet authorized its delegation to depart from Versailles. Once he received the negative reply, Brockdorff-Rantzau withdrew from the peace conference. This serious action was not merely a diplomatic ploy. To avoid responsibility for signing the treaty, both Scheidemann and Brockdorff-Rantzau resigned. The resulting political crisis in Germany ended only after Ebert appointed another Social Democrat, Gustav Bauer, as chancellor. With Erzberger's assistance, Bauer formed a new cabinet which recognized that accepting the

60 Ibid., VI, 246, 251-52, 324-27, 330-42, 370; Cecil Diary, June 7, 9, 1919, Cecil Papers, 51131; Cecil to DLG, June 7, 1919, DLG Papers, F/6/6/51; Auchincloss Diary, June 7, 9, 1919, Auchincloss Papers, 55/92; Clemenceau to WW, June 7, 1919, WW Papers, Ser. 5B, Reel 409; EMH Diary, June 8, 1919; Tardieu to EMH, June 10, 1919, EMH Papers, 18/34.
61 FR:PPC, VI, 926-96.

treaty was Germany's only realistic option. Further resistance could only prolong the war and result in greater losses. The previous strategy for revising the treaty had certainly failed. The new foreign minister, Hermann Müller, a Social Democrat, and one of his colleagues in the cabinet from the Center party, Johannes Bell, went to Versailles to sign the treaty. Although it violated the German interpretation of the Fourteen Points, the overwhelming power of the victorious countries forced Germany to accept their conditions of peace. At a plenary session of the peace conference on June 28, 1919, delegates from Germany as well as the Allied and Associated Powers officially signed the Versailles Treaty, including the Covenant.[62]

Despite this moment of apparent triumph, Wilson had clearly failed to transform the Old World. Neither the Allies nor Germany shared his global vision of a new international order, although they now accepted the League of Nations. A series of diplomatic compromises, reflecting the limits of any nation's power in the interdependent and plural world, produced this outcome. Practicality rather than idealism prevailed. Disregarding this reality, the president continued to pursue foreign-policy goals that exceeded the means available to the United States or any nation. He prepared to return home to proclaim the Versailles peace as the fulfillment of the redemptive American mission in world affairs.

62   Bernstorff to Peace Delegation, June 4, 6, 1919, Langwerth to Rantzau, June 5, 6, 1919, Rantzau to Langwerth, June 6, 1919, Rantzau to Foreign Office, June 9, 11, 12, 1919, Rantzau to Naumann, June 10, 1919, Rantzau to Toepffer, June 12, 1919, Deutsche Friedensdelegation in Versailles, Pol 13, Bd. 4; Bauer to Haniel, June 21, 21, 21, 21, 1919, Müller to Haniel, June 22, 22, 22, 22, 23, 1919, Haniel to Müller, June 22, 22, 23, 23, 23, 1919, Brecht to Haniel, June 23, 1919, Haniel to Foreign Office, June 23, 1919, Moltke to Foreign Office Weimar, June 23, 1919, Deutsche Friedensdelegation in Versailles, Pol 13, Bd. 6; Albert to Cabinet Members, June 28, 1919, Akten der Reichskanzlei, R43I/5; FR:PPC, III, 421-23.

CHAPTER 6

The question of control at home and abroad

Once Germany signed the Versailles Treaty, Wilson returned to the United States to urge the Senate to approve it. Continuing his politics of confrontation, he chose to fight rather than conciliate critics of his peacemaking. He wanted to defeat his opponents, not compromise with them.[1] The question of control divided Americans in two different ways during the treaty fight. The president believed that the League of Nations would enable the United States to exercise its benevolent influence over other countries. While controlling foreign affairs, the American government could still avoid entanglement in the Old World's politics and wars. The League would inaugurate a "new order" of international relations to replace the old system of alliances and balances of power. Wilson's critics, in contrast, saw in the League a threat to American independence. Not only would it entangle the United States in perpetual conflict around the globe, it would also allow foreign powers to meddle in this country's domestic affairs and violate the Monroe Doctrine. It would subject the nation to foreign control. This question of control constituted the central issue in the treaty fight. Advocates and critics disagreed basically over the question of whether the League would enable the United States to control the world, or the world to control the United States. This dispute related to another controversy over decision-making. Wilson viewed the conduct of American foreign relations as primarily a presidential function, but Lodge and his Republican colleagues asserted the rights of Congress. This executive-legislative conflict, involving the Constitution's interpretation, raised the issue of appropriate separation of powers between the White House and Congress. It constituted another aspect of the question of control at home and abroad.

When the president submitted the treaty to the Senate on July 10, 1919, he emphasized the redeeming influence of American intervention in the

---

[1] EMH Diary, June 29, 1919.

European war. He viewed the League not only as a means to implement the treaty but as an end in itself. It epitomized the new order of international relations. Through it the United States would provide "moral leadership" as a world power. Wilson called on the Senate to accept this new responsibility as the God-given destiny for the nation: "It has come about by no plan of our conceiving, but by the hand of God who led us into this way. We cannot turn back. We can only go forward, with lifted eyes and freshened spirit, to follow the vision. It was of this that we dreamed at our birth. America shall in truth show the way."[2]

Wilson's determination to compel the Senate to approve the treaty encountered widespread Republican resistance. Lodge resolutely rejected the president's vision of a "new order." In his judgment, the revised Covenant did not meet the Senate's earlier objections. The new provision for withdrawal from the League was inadequate. Exclusion of domestic questions from the League's jurisdiction failed to reserve American control over immigration, for the council would determine whether an issue was international or domestic. Likewise, the Monroe Doctrine amendment was unsatisfactory. "It is wholly worthless as a protection of that doctrine, which is a policy of the United States and not a regional understanding or an international engagement." The Senate, he avowed, would reserve for the American people the exclusive right to interpret the doctrine. Moreover, the revised Covenant still included Article 10. Lodge also criticized the president's stand on Fiume, arguing that the United States should not interfere in this "purely European question." While criticizing Wilson's reluctance to compromise in this instance, Lodge condemned his willingness to approve Japan's demands in Shantung. He thought the Japanese had raised the issue of racial equality only as a method of extracting concessions in Shantung. Nevertheless, he expected swift approval of the peace treaty. His real objection focused on the League. He preferred the French security treaty. "If there had been no League and no Article 10," he concluded, "I think it would have stood a very good chance. What its future will be now, I cannot say."[3]

To limit the president's mastery of American foreign relations, Lodge had established Republican control in the new Senate. Republicans enjoyed only a slim majority with forty-nine seats, two more than the Democrats. Appealing to all factions, he endeavored to prevent internal differences over the League from disrupting the party. He turned to Root, observing that "your position is very essential to our holding control of the Senate and of the vote in regard to the treaty." Noting that Wilson had failed to revise the

2   CR, Vol. 58, 2336-39; PPWW, V, 527-52.
3   HW to HCL, Apr. 22, 1919, HCL Papers and ER Papers, Box 161; HW to HCL, Apr. 14, 1919, HCL to HW, Apr. 30, May 6, 20, 29, 1919, HCL Papers, File 1919 (Henry White); HCL to Trevelyan, March 25, Apr. 30, 1919, HCL to Bryce, Apr. 30, May 27, June 10, 1919, HCL to Morse, May 2, 1919, HCL to Frewan, June 23, 1919, HCL Papers, File 1919 (Adams-Trevelyan).

Covenant as Root had recommended, Lodge requested his help in securing "necessary amendments."[4]

Root agreed with Lodge's assessment of Wilson's diplomacy. He continued to criticize the president's refusal to consult the Senate and especially his misunderstanding of the Monroe Doctrine. When Lowell had tried to convince him that the revised Covenant incorporated all of his proposed amendments except for compulsory arbitration of justiciable questions by a permanent court, Root remained unconvinced. His concept of the League differed substantially from Wilson's. He viewed it as "a continuance of the present alliance against the Central Powers for the purpose of the reconstruction which must necessarily follow the War." Root welcomed the League as an instrument for enforcing the peace in the real context of European diplomacy, not as a way of transcending the "old order" of alliances and balances of power. He saw the League as a method of American control over foreign affairs, but he declined to disguise that purpose in idealistic language or to deceive himself by believing it would enjoy universal acceptance.[5]

Lodge's strategy for amending the Covenant depended upon Republican unity in the Senate. He had feared especially that Borah might defect and deprive him of the leadership. To prevent that debacle, Lodge persuaded Beveridge to impress upon the Idaho senator the importance of party unity. Although he remained adamantly opposed to the League even with amendments, Borah shared with Lodge a common interest in defeating the president. On April 29 they reached a tactical agreement. Borah accepted Lodge's leadership and acquiesced in his plan for amendments. When the Congress convened for a special session on May 19, all Republicans joined Lodge to organize the Senate. With that achievement he determined the membership of committees. In that task he collaborated with Brandegee, whom he appointed to the Committee on Committees. For the Foreign Relations Committee, Lodge selected hard-line opponents of the League, such as George H. Moses of New Hampshire and Harry S. New of Indiana, passing over others, such as Kellogg, who were more favorable toward it. He wanted to avoid any risk of losing control of this committee to a coalition of pro-League Republicans and Democrats.[6]

This tactical agreement to unite against Wilson's League left Borah free to advocate rejection of even an amended Covenant. He felt he had at least

4 HCL to ER, Apr. 29, 1919, ER Papers, Box 161.
5 ER to ALL, Apr. 29, 1919, ALL to ER, May 1, 1919, ALL to ER, May 1, 1919, ER to Storey, March 20, 1919, Strong to ER, Apr. 25, 1919, ER to Strong, Apr. 28, 1919, ER to HW, June 5, 1919, ER Papers, Box 137; ER to HW, June 5, 1919, HW Papers, Box 43.
6 HCL to Beveridge, Apr. 30, 1919, Beveridge Papers, Box 216, and HCL Papers; Brandegee to HCL, Apr. 7, 1919, HCL to Brandegee, May 19, 1919, HCL to Cummins, Apr. 30, 1919, HCL Papers, File 1919 (Peace, League, Political, A-H); Kellogg to HCL, May 27, 31, 1919, Kellogg to Brandegee, May 27, 1919, HCL to Kellogg, May 28, 1919, HCL to Williams, May 13, 19, 1919, HCL Papers, File 1919 (Peace, League, Political, I-Z); Beveridge to Borah, Apr. 27, 1919, Borah Papers, Box 551, and Beveridge Papers, Box 214; Borah to Dewey, May 6, 1919, Borah Papers, Box 550; Beveridge to New, Feb. 17, March 7, 1919, New to Beveridge, Feb. 19, March 8, June 7, 1919, Beveridge Papers, Box 217; Beveridge to Moses, Apr. 29, 1919, Moses to Beveridge, May 5, 1919, Beveridge Papers, Box 216.

prevented the Republican leadership from drifting toward acceptance of the president's project. American membership in the League, he believed, would undoubtedly result in foreign control over the United States. "It is," he asserted, "a deliberate attempt to sell our country to the domination of foreign powers." Once the American people became aware of the stakes, Borah expected them to reject the League and also the French security treaty. He regarded this special alliance as an admission that the League could not fulfill its avowed purpose of protecting its members. He intended to defeat any alliance with European powers, either in the guise of the League or the treaty with France.[7]

Other opponents joined Borah in attacking the League's threat to American independence. Reed emphasized the racial peril of this "colored league of nations." Observing that its initial membership included only fifteen white nations but seventeen of "black, brown, yellow, and red races," he feared that these nations would use their majority to the detriment of "civilized government." He denounced them as high in illiteracy, "low in civilization" and "steeped in barbarism." He appealed to other Democratic senators from the South, where black Americans were prohibited from voting by Jim Crow laws, not to allow the United States to succumb to this international racial peril. Hitchcock tried to answer this contention by arguing that non-white nations, even with a majority, could not endanger the United States, for "the league has very little to do." This claim exposed a fundamental contradiction in the pro-League argument, which Reed hastened to exploit. "All you have argued thus far," he countered, "is that your league is an innocuous thing because it is powerless, and yet you tell us it is to save the world!"[8]

Senator Lawrence Y. Sherman of Illinois denounced the Covenant as "a revolutionary document." The dream of creating "a sinless world" violated his view of human nature. The goal of establishing the kingdom of God on earth, which Herron had identified as the ultimate purpose of Wilson's foreign policy, seemed wholly unrealistic. The senator warned that the League could prevent war only by superior armed forces. Given the diversity in the world, any endeavor to achieve Wilson's ideal of a universal community would inevitably require the United States to pay a high price. By joining the League the United States would entangle itself in the Old World. The danger that Sherman most feared came from the Vatican. He stressed that the League would include seventeen Catholic nations but only eleven Protestant nations and four of other faiths. Consequently, the Pope would control a majority of the members. How-

7   Borah to Rea, June 19, 1919, Borah to Ketcham, May 3, 1919, Borah to Saunders, May 5, 1919, Borah to Dunn, May 17, 1919, Borah to Dudley, May 3, 1919, Borah Papers, Box 550; Borah to Dunne, May 22, 1919, Borah to Munsey, Apr. 19, 29, 1919, Borah Papers, Box 551; Beveridge to Borah, Apr. 19, 1919, Borah to Beveridge, Apr. 22, 1919, Borah Papers, Box 551, and Beveridge Papers, 214.
8   CR, Vol. 58, 235-46.

ever unintentionally, the Presbyterian president appeared as an accomplice of the Vatican.[9]

Preliminary skirmishing in the Senate dealt with publication of the treaty. Senator Hiram W. Johnson of California introduced a resolution requesting the secretary of state to release the full text that had been delivered to the Germans at Versailles. During the debate he offered his critique of Wilson's peacemaking. He recognized the limits of American isolation, but wanted to adhere to the traditional policy of no entanglement in the Old World. The United States could exercise its humanitarian influence in the world without assuming the Covenant's obligations. He viewed Article 10 as a reactionary commitment to the status quo. From his progressive perspective, Johnson did not want the American nation to preserve the British Empire or guarantee the possessions of France, Italy and Japan, including "the rape of China." Like Borah, he viewed the French security treaty as an argument against the League. If, as Wilson claimed, the alliance with France only specified the obligations intended by the Covenant, Johnson wanted no such commitment on a global scale. "It means," he concluded, "the halting and betrayal of New World liberalism, the triumph of cynical Old World diplomacy, the humiliation and end of American idealism."[10]

As the Senate debated the Johnson resolution, Wilson reiterated his earlier decision not to publish the treaty. He had agreed with Lloyd George and Clemenceau to release only a summary so as to minimize the difficulty in making changes in response to German criticism.[11] The controversy over publication became explosive on June 3, when Borah charged that certain New York interests already had the treaty in their possession. While the Senate and the American people were asking to see it, the treaty was available only to a privileged few. Lodge then confirmed that he had seen one of the copies in New York on the previous day.[12]

At first on the defensive, Democratic senators soon seized the initiative. Hitchcock introduced a resolution calling for a Foreign Relations Committee investigation of Borah's allegation. By voice vote on June 6, the Senate approved both this resolution and Johnson's. Neither of them produced any dramatic results. The president persisted in withholding the treaty, while the investigation threatened to embarrass the Republicans. Thomas W. Lamont had given a copy of the treaty to Henry P. Davison, one of his partners in J. P. Morgan and Company, who was in Paris as head of the American Red Cross. He had authorized Davison, upon returning to New York, to share it with Root as well as Morrow, another Morgan partner. Lamont never expected public disclosure. Root used his influence with

9   CR, Vol. 58, 164-71, 1435-38.
10   CR, Vol. 58, 501-09.
11   FR:PPC, V, 469-70; Polk to A.C.N.P., May 16, 1919 (#2005), WW Papers, Ser. 5B, Reel 406; WW to RL, May 21, 24, 1919, Polk to RL, May 22, 1919 (#2057), JPT to WW, May 22, 1919 (#138), WW to JPT, May 24, 1919, WW Papers, Ser. 5B, Reel 407.
12   CR, Vol. 58, 558-61.

Lodge and other Republican senators to limit the investigation and prevent the whole controversy over publication of the treaty from destroying the credibility of their leadership. In the final analysis, the investigation, as Tumulty informed Wilson, amounted to nothing more than "a tempest in a tea-pot."[13]

Having failed to force the Wilson administration to submit the treaty to the Senate, Republicans decided to publish an unofficial copy. On June 9 they passed Borah's motion to print a copy that he had received from a *Chicago Tribune* correspondent. This vote evoked a bitter response from Hitchcock, who accused Republicans of collaborating with Germans "for the purpose of throwing a monkey wrench into the negotiations." The debate now descended to the lowest level of charge and countercharge. The Democratic leader asserted that "the majority of the Senate of the United States is deliberately cooperating with the German Government" to interfere with the peace negotiations so as to secure better terms for Germany. Without mentioning Hitchcock's name, Poindexter retorted that the very senators who now accused others of pro-German activity had themselves been least supportive of war measures earlier. Vice President Thomas Marshall attempted unsuccessfully to stop this acrimonious exchange by reminding the senators that their rules prohibited them from using such language. Brandegee suggested that Hitchcock had surely not intended to charge senators with "being pro-German and cooperating with our enemies," but he refused to retract his previous statement. Thereupon Brandegee asserted that "the Senator is crazier, then, than I thought he was." In this exchange of insults Hitchcock condemned Republicans for acting like Bolsheviks. "The Senate of the United States," he said, "is putting itself in the attitude of a Bolshevik organization, running amuck here in the treaty negotiations." Publication of the treaty, he reiterated, constituted a betrayal of the Allies and collaboration with the enemy.[14]

In the midst of this acrimony, Hitchcock announced the inflexible Democratic decision to resist any amendments to the treaty. He told Republicans that "if this league is defeated there will be no league at all."

1 3   CR, Vol. 58, 635-36, 673-82, 733-35; U.S. Senate, *Proceedings of the Committee on Foreign Relations*, 136-38; RL to WW, June 4, 6, 7, 7, 8, 1919, Polk to RL, June 4 (#2180), 4 (#2189), 5 (#2196), 6 (#2224), 6 (#2219), 1919, Polk to A.C.N.P., June 4 (#2192), 6 (#2217), 1919, JPT to WW, June 4 (#162), 5 (#164), WW to JPT, June 7, 1919, WW Papers, Ser. 5B, Reel 409; Polk to A.C.N.P., June 9, 1919 (#2247), Lamont to WW, June 10, 1919, WW to RL, June 10, 1919, Emery to Grew, June 11, 1919 (#2265), RL to WW, June 13, 1919, RL to Polk, June 13, 1919 (#2250), JPT to WW, June 13, 1919 (#189), WW Papers, Ser. 5B, Reel 411; JPT to WW, June 4, 13, 1919, WW to JPT, June 7, 1919, JPT Papers, Box 7; PPWW, V, 508; Polk to RL, June 5, 1919, Polk Papers, 78/11; F. L. P[olk], Memorandum, June 4, 1919, Polk to Hitchcock, May 28, 1919, Polk Papers, 78/28; Polk to RL, May 19 (#2018), 22 (#2057), June 5 (#2196), 7 (#2227), 1919, Polk Papers, 88/22; Polk Diary, June 4, 1919, Polk Papers, 88/16; Auchincloss Diary, June 10, 1919, Auchincloss Papers, 55/92; ER to HCL, June 6, 1919, ER Papers, Box 161, and HCL Papers; ER to Brandegee, June 8, 1919, Murphy to ER, May 26, 1919, ER Papers, Box 137; Anderson Notes, June 11, 1919, Chandler P. Anderson Papers, Box 4, Library of Congress; HCL to HW, June 12, 1919, HCL Papers, File 1919 (Henry White).
1 4   CR, Vol. 58, 781-89.

Asserting that "the issue is this league or none," he castigated Republicans for stacking the Foreign Relations Committee in order to embarrass the president. He denounced the Republican leadership for seeking "to kill the league of nations, if possible, and to kill it by indirection." He claimed to have greater respect for Borah because he openly avowed his intention. Lodge, the obvious target of this attack, refrained from public comment, but his private view was just as unflattering of Hitchcock as of Wilson.[15]

In his announcement of the uncompromising Democratic position, Hitchcock followed the president's direction. Earlier, the senator had recommended a conciliatory approach. As a way of gaining enough Republican votes for the treaty's ratification, he thought the Democrats should acquiesce in some modifications of the Covenant. Wilson vehemently rejected this advice. Especially sensitive about Republican criticism of Article 10, he asserted that: "Without it, the Covenant would mean nothing. If the Senate will not accept that, it will have to reject the whole treaty." The president clearly intended to fight for the League until he achieved victory or suffered defeat. "It is manifestly too late now," he further explained to Lansing, "to effect changes in the Covenant, and I hope that Polk will urge Hitchcock and all our friends to take a most militant and aggressive course, such as I mean to take the minute I get back." Lansing relayed Wilson's instructions through Polk to Hitchcock.[16]

Williams followed Hitchcock in assaulting Republicans. He denounced them for appealing to ethnic and racial prejudice. Castigating Lodge and Borah for pandering especially to Irish-Americans, he argued that Wilson "represents the American people and his opponents represent all of the hyphenates in America – all of the enemy hyphenates in America." Instead of appealing for toleration, the Mississippi senator engaged in a vicious form of ethnic politics. He thought the president should have taken more opportunities to expose the disloyalty of hyphenated Americans. An advocate of the Jim Crow system in the South, he wanted to preserve the United States as "a white man's country." Yet he rejected Reed's claim that the League presented an international racial peril, for he assumed that the American government could either control enough votes to dominate it or veto undesirable proceedings. He saw the League as the hope of civilized man against savage and barbarous nations. Because his world was neatly divided between good and evil, or white and black, or civilization and barbarism, Williams could practice a most divisive style of politics while criticizing others for doing so. His ethnic prejudice had led the senator earlier, on June 6, to cast the only dissenting vote against Borah's resolution, which urged the American delegation to secure a hearing for Irish representatives at the

---

1 5   *CR*, Vol. 58, 790-92; HCL to Morse, June 7, 1919, HCL Papers, File 1919 (Adams-Trevelyan).
1 6   Polk Diary, May 15, 1919, Polk Papers, 88/15; Polk to RL and EMH, May 17, 1919 (#2014), Polk Papers, 88/22; Polk to RL, May 24, 1919, RL to Polk, May 26, 1919 (#2276), WW Papers, Ser. 5B, Reel 407; F.L.P., Memorandum, June 4, 1919, Polk to Hitchcock, May 28, 1919, Polk Papers, 78/28.

peace conference. A coalition of sixty Republican and Democratic senators had overwhelmingly endorsed that appeal for Ireland against Great Britain. Both parties were obviously playing ethnic politics.[17]

Lodge and Borah welcomed the support of hyphenated Americans in the treaty fight. Although the Massachusetts senator justified his criticism of Wilson's handling of the Fiume controversy on foreign-policy grounds, he certainly appreciated its political value among Italian-Americans in his own state and throughout the country. However, he left to Borah the principal task of working with ethnic leaders, particularly among Irish-Americans. In developing the strategy for his Irish resolution, the Idaho senator had cooperated with Judge Cohalan. During his earlier trips around the country to rally the American people against the League, Borah had spoken on several occasions under the auspices of Irish-American organizations. He championed the cause of Irish self-determination and American independence, condemning the British Empire for denying the one and endangering the other. He claimed that unless Ireland gained independence before the establishment of the League, it could never achieve that goal. "I not only take this position because of my deep sympathy with Ireland," Borah explained to one Catholic archbishop, "but I have long entertained it because of my sympathy for subject nationalities everywhere and in the interest of human progress and human liberty." In his effort to attract Catholic support, Borah attempted, unsuccessfully, to convince Sherman not to attack the Vatican as the power behind the League.[18]

Implications of the Irish question for the treaty fight produced ever increasing anxiety for Democrats. As early as March 1919 five senators – three of whom were Irish-Americans – had warned the president that the peace conference's failure to deal with self-government for Ireland would jeopardize the League in the United States. Wilson acknowledged their concern but saw no way to heed their advice. By late May, Tumulty, himself an American of Irish Catholic origins, saw the prospects of a general ethnic revolt against the League. Dissatisfaction among the Irish, Jews, Poles, Italians and Germans, he alerted the president, might tempt Republicans to take a rigid stance against the League to attract these voters. British statesmen also began to observe this danger. Bryce expressed his concern to White, while the British ambassador, Lord Reading, raised the issue with Polk. He told the acting secretary of state that Republicans were threatening to join Irish extremists for the purpose of defeating the president. He feared that many Republicans, although previously sympathetic, were now turning against Great Britain because of their resentment over the close collaboration

1 7   CR, Vol. 58, 728-33; U.S. Senate, *Proceedings of the Committee on Foreign Relations*, 135-36.
1 8   Borah to Cohalan, May 29, 1919, Borah to Smith, May 31, 1919, Borah to Peterson, June 24, 1919, Borah Papers, Box 551; Borah to Christie, May 1, 1919, Borah Papers, Box 552; Cohalan to Borah, June 5, 10, 1919, Daniel F. Cohalan Papers, American Irish Historical Society; "Irish United Against the League," *Gaelic American*, XVI (May 10, 1919), 4; "Borah Resolution Passed by Senate 60 to 1," ibid., XVI (June 14, 1919), 1.

between Lloyd George and Wilson. Polk promptly sent this news to Paris. Despite these various warnings, the president persisted in his refusal to place the Irish question on the peace conference's agenda. He blamed the Irish-Americans who had come to Paris to lobby for a hearing for Irish representatives, claiming that they had so inflamed the issue that he could not raise it productively with British delegates. [19]

After the Senate passed Borah's Irish resolution, Wilson still refused to submit this request to the Allies, ignoring the advice of the four other members of the American Commission. Unwilling to disturb Anglo-American relations at this time, he suggested that the League would provide a forum for dealing with the Irish question in the future. He ignored Tumulty's repeated pleas to speak up on this issue. Bryce adopted a similar attitude. He appreciated that the League, far from enjoying the universal appeal that Wilson claimed for it, lacked widespread approbation in countries other than the United States and Great Britain. Consequently, he recognized that the Irish question threatened not just American membership in the League but the long-range success of the League itself. Still refusing to confront this risk, he, too, recommended a stoic silence. Bryce himself was playing politics. He evidently wanted, above all, to steer Wilson away from the Irish question. [20]

I

After raising tangential issues, Republican senators launched a direct attack on the League. On June 10, Knox introduced a resolution calling for separation of the Covenant from the Versailles Treaty. It demanded this separation to give the United States time to consider the League without delaying peace with Germany. Affirming that the Senate was "a coequal part of the treaty-making power," it rejected Wilson's insistence upon the Senate's accepting the League to remain faithful to American war aims. Noting that no treaty could amend the Constitution, the resolution implied that the Covenant entailed such a violation. Knox offered his "new American doctrine" as an alternative to both traditional isolationism and Wilsonian

---

19   Gerry, Walsh, Pittman, Kendrick and Walsh to WW, March 28, 1919, WW Papers, Ser. 5B, Reel 398; WW to Gerry, Apr. 17, 1919, WW Papers, Ser. 5B, Reel 401; Bryce to HW, May 19, 1919, RL to WW, May 23, 1919, JPT to WW, May 26, 1919, WW Papers, Ser. 5B, Reel 407; WW to JPT, June 7, 1919, WW Papers, Ser. 5B, Reel 409; Polk Diary, Apr. 26, 1919, Polk Papers, 88/15; Polk to RL, Apr. 16, 1919, Polk Papers, 78/9; Polk to RL, May 7, 1919, Polk Papers, 78/11; Polk to Auchincloss, May 5, 1919, Polk Papers, 74/8; JPT to WW, May 26, 1919, JPT Papers, Box 6; JPT to Grayson, June 7, 1919, JPT Papers, Box 7.
20   JPT to WW, June 9, 1919 (#173), RL, HW, EMH and THB to WW, June 10, 1919, WW to RL, June 10, 1919, RL to WW, June 12, 1919, WW Papers, Ser. 5B, Reel 411; JPT to WW, June 18, 1919 (#196), Bryce to HW, June 12, 1919, WW Papers, Ser. 5B, Reel 412; JPT to EMH, June 25, 1919, JPT to WW, June 25, 1919 (#211), WW to JPT, June 27, 1919, WW Papers, Ser. 5B, Reel 413; JPT to WW, June 25, 1919, WW to JPT, June 27, 1919, JPT Papers, Box 7; JPT to EMH, June 25, 1919, EMH to JPT, June 28, 1919, JPT Papers, Box 1; Bryce to ER, June 6, 1919, ER Papers, Box 137.

internationalism. The fifth section of the Knox resolution proclaimed that if any power or coalition threatened Europe's freedom and peace, the United States would again join the Allies to remove this menace and defend civilization.[21]

In the Foreign Relations Committee the Knox resolution ran into difficulty. With the fifth section in it, two Republicans as well as the Democrats opposed the resolution. Aware that this coalition could prevent the committee from reporting it to the Senate, Lodge, with Knox's concurrence, moved to delete the fifth section. That proposal at first encountered resistance from Porter J. McCumber of North Dakota and Albert B. Fall of New Mexico, two Republicans who strongly favored Knox's "new American doctrine." They joined the Democrats to defeat Lodge's motion. However, Fall then called for reconsideration and switched to the Republican side to provide a majority for deleting the fifth section. That same majority subsequently approved the amended resolution for submission to the entire Senate. Only McCumber voted with the defeated Democratic minority.[22]

Defending his resolution in the Senate, Knox stressed that it would only delay a decision about the League. Nevertheless, his hostility toward the League was quite evident. He contended that certain provisions of the Covenant were unconstitutional. He condemned Article 10 for seeking to maintain an international status quo. "As the Covenant is now framed," Knox said, "it contains the pernicious provisions embodied in article 10, which are designed to fix through all time – and merit is made of this purpose of the provision – the boundaries set up by the treaty of peace." He considered it inappropriate for the United States to attempt to exercise that kind of control throughout the world. If the League enjoyed such a global jurisdiction, it might, as Wilson claimed, deal with the Irish question, but it might also consider the Negro question in the United States. Noting such contradictions in pro-League arguments, Knox observed that the League could not be at once so weak as not to endanger the United States and so strong as to establish "a great world state which was to compel the obedience not only of its constituent members, but of all others who might be outside and beyond the pale." He regarded the revised Covenant as worse than the original draft. Its reference to the Monroe Doctrine as an international engagement or regional understanding seemed particularly inappropriate because this doctrine was "merely a policy" of the United States, and one which he did not intend to surrender to international control. He urged caution in considering membership in the League.[23]

2 1   CR, Vol. 58, 894; JPT to WW, June 10, 13, 1919, JPT Papers, Box 7; Beveridge to Knox, June 12, 13, 1919, Knox to Beveridge, June 14, 1919, Philander C. Knox Papers, Box 30, Library of Congress; Beveridge to Knox, Apr. 19, June 12, 13, 1919, Knox to Beveridge, Apr. 24, June 14, 1919, Beveridge Papers, Box 215.

2 2   U.S. Senate, Proceedings of the Committee on Foreign Relations, 138-41; Knox to Spence, June 13, 1919, Knox Papers, Box 30; JPT to WW, June 13, 1919, JPT Papers, Box 7; CR, Vol. 58, 1373.

2 3   CR, Vol. 58, 1216-22.

McCumber took his fight against the amended Knox resolution to the floor of the Senate. Acknowledging his support for Knox's "new American doctrine," he affirmed that "I would be satisfied if that section 5, without elimination or addition, should be the only compact between the great nations of the world." Because of the fifth section's deletion, the North Dakota senator strongly denounced the Knox resolution. He now began to emerge as the foremost Republican advocate of the League in the Senate. He had earlier advised Wilson not to permit its separation from the peace treaty. Contrary to the signers of the round robin, he had seen in the draft Covenant no surrender of American sovereignty, no threat to American jurisdiction over purely domestic affairs, and no danger to the Monroe Doctrine. He had encouraged the president, however, to amend the Covenant so as to avoid any misunderstanding. The subsequent revisions in Paris seemed to McCumber to remove these alleged faults. He now argued that the United States had the "moral duty" to provide leadership in the League. To furnish the legal basis for this global responsibility, he urged acceptance of the Covenant with the treaty. In his view of interdependence, the Old World depended upon the United States, but this nation did not depend upon Europe. The League, he contended, would outlaw war. He favored Article 10, for it applied only to "external aggression" and not to internal revolution or rebellion. Criticizing efforts to incite hyphenated Americans over Great Britain's voting power, he argued that the United States faced no danger from this source because of its own power to control the council or assembly. Likewise, the League would not jeopardize American jurisdiction over domestic matters such as immigration. In agreement with Wilson, McCumber saw the League as the world-wide extension of the Monroe Doctrine, not as a threat to it. Refusal by the United States to play its leading role in this international system, he warned, would inevitably result in more wars of aggression.[24]

White congratulated McCumber for his able defense of the League. He reported that the entire American delegation, including Lansing and Bliss, believed that the League was essential to prevent another war. He expressed this same viewpoint to Lodge and Root. In his correspondence with Lodge, however, White refrained from criticizing the Knox resolution. "As regards the League of Nations," he confided, "I have for some time past decided to leave it to fight its own battles at home."[25]

Democratic senators joined McCumber in denouncing the Knox resolution. Charles S. Thomas of Colorado, who would later vote against the treaty, now condemned the resolution as another unwarranted attempt by the Senate to interfere with the American delegation's task of negotiating a

24   CR, Vol. 58, 1264-76; McCumber to WW, March 13, 1919, WW Papers, Ser. 5B, Reel 395; WW to McCumber, Apr. 15, 1919, WW Papers, Ser. 5B, Reel 400.
25   HW to McCumber, June 23, 1919, HW Papers, Box 43; HW to ER, June 30, 1919, ER Papers, Box 137; HW to HCL, June 12, 19, 1919, ER Papers, Box 161, and HCL Papers.

peace treaty. Like the round robin, it was a partisan Republican effort to infringe upon the president's treaty-making power. Morris Sheppard of Texas delivered, in Wilson's subsequent opinion, an "excellent speech." Noting that the peace conference had approved the Covenant, he castigated the Knox resolution as "a repudiation of the combined judgment of the civilized world." He defended the League as "the most effective instrument for the maintenance of peace and the prevention of war the heart and brain of man have yet produced." Aware that it was not perfect and that it could not offer an absolute guarantee of peace, he still regarded it as a major step in the right direction. Developing Sheppard's argument, Henry F. Ashurst of Arizona addressed the phobias of Sherman, Reed and Borah. He denied that the Vatican, or non-white races, or Great Britain would dominate the League. "Whether we like it or not," he argued, "we must either face a league of nations or face constant warfare."[26]

With one exception, probably Reed, Democratic senators closed ranks against the Knox resolution, but Republicans experienced disarray. Various Republicans such as Lodge, Hays and Beveridge praised Knox for his address, but his resolution still failed to unite the party. Approximately ten Republican senators opposed the resolution, leaving only a minority of about forty votes in its favor. That was more than one-third of the Senate, enough to signal that the League faced formidable opposition, but far less than a majority. Beveridge urged Knox to resist pressures for compromise, observing that "if your resolution gets a heavy vote – more than one-third – and after it becomes clear to everybody that the men who voted for it will stand firm and fast against this Covenant, or even against the Treaty if they are not separated, the fight is won." Fearful that Republicans might weaken, he warned other senators as well to guard against any attempt to adopt the League with reservations. Johnson agreed that ratification of the treaty with the Covenant, even with reservations, "was really tantamount to a surrender." Borah challenged Hays and the Republican party to take an unequivocal position either for or against the League, while contending that the only stance consistent with nationalism was opposition. Earlier, Brandegee had pointedly warned Root not "to bend in the middle or truckle to Wilson & Taft" under the pressure of international banks and newspapers. The desperation of these irreconcilables, except Knox, stemmed from their apprehension, later confirmed, that the Republican leadership was searching for an alternative to the Knox resolution. As Republicans fought this internecine battle, Wilson prudently decided not to make any public announcement about the Knox resolution, confident that it would fail.[27]

2 6   CR, Vol. 58, 1372-79, 1431-35, 1444-50; WW to Sheppard, Aug. 8, 1919, WW Papers, Ser. 4, File 4767.

2 7   Hays to Knox, June 17, 1919, HCL to Knox, June 17, 1919, Beveridge to Knox, June 17, 1919, Knox to Beveridge, June 18, 1919, Knox Papers, Box 30; Beveridge to Johnson, June 16, 1919, Johnson to Beveridge, June 18, 1919, Knox to Beveridge, June 18, 1919, Beveridge to Knox, June 20, 1919, Beveridge Papers, Box 215; Beveridge to HCL, June 12, 1919, Beveridge Papers, Box 216; Beveridge

From their strongly nationalist viewpoint, Borah and Johnson perceived the risk of control not only by foreigners but also by international bankers. They saw the League as a tool of Wall Street to protect overseas investments. The prominence of Lamont and Morrow of J. P. Morgan and Company among the League's advocates seemed more than coincidental. So, too, did the financial contributions of "big business" to the League to Enforce Peace. It appeared, as Borah told the Senate, that "these men are in a conclave or a combination to exploit the natural resources of Europe, to gather their untold and uncounted millions, as they did from 1914 to 1916 from the distressed and exigent conditions of Europe, and to have this Nation underwrite their investment and American boys guarantee the mortgage they will have upon the energies of the people of Europe." If the League could establish American control over the Old World, it was not of the variety Borah would approve. It might serve the financial interests of international bankers for the American government to guarantee the territorial integrity and political independence of other nations, as Article 10 provided, but not those of the American people as a whole.[28]

With Republicans in disarray, Lodge summoned Hays and Root to Washington to assist him in developing a consensus. The national chairman played a key role in consulting a variety of senators to determine their views on the treaty. With this information Root and Lodge drafted a letter that analyzed the peace treaty and proposed reservations to the Covenant. They then conferred with Knox to ensure his endorsement of the letter. All four of these Republican leaders approved Root's letter to Lodge of June 19. Four days later Lodge published it in the *Congressional Record*. In this letter Root recalled that he had recommended amendments to the draft Covenant in his March 29 letter to Hays, but that subsequent revisions in Paris had only partially addressed his concerns. The Covenant still failed to provide for a system of arbitration and codification of international law. It also retained the potentially limitless obligations of Article 10. "The people of the United States," Root explained, "certainly will not be willing ten years or twenty years hence to send their young men to distant parts of the world to fight for causes in which they may not believe or in which they have little or no interest." Acceptance of responsibilities under this article, moreover, would likely exacerbate ethnic tensions in the United States. Root noted that,

to Borah, June 16, 1919, Borah Papers, Box 551, and Beveridge Papers, Box 214; *CR*, Vol. 58, 1502-05; Brandegee to ER, June 9, 9, 1919, ER Papers, Box 137; WW to JPT, June 16, 1919, JPT Papers, Box 7; Emery to Grew, June 12 (#2287), 14 (#2308), 1919, WW Papers, Ser. 5B, Reel 411; Miller to Auchincloss, June 13 (#103), 14 (#104), 1919, WW to JPT, June 16, 1919, WW Papers, Ser. 5B, Reel 412.

28   *CR*, Vol. 58, 2063-67; Beveridge to Borah, July 19, 1919, Beveridge Papers, Box 214; Beveridge to Johnson, July 19, 1919, Johnson to Beveridge, July 21, 1919, Beveridge Papers, Box 215; Borah to Born, May 5, 1919, Borah to Dunne, June 26, 1919, Borah to Zimmerman, June 10, 1919, Borah to Jenness, July 7, 1919, Borah to Evans, Aug. 31, 1919, Borah Papers, Box 550; Borah to Rainey, June 20, 1919, Beveridge to Borah, July 19, 1919, Borah Papers, Box 551. See also Howard A. DeWitt, "Hiram W. Johnson and Economic Opposition to Wilsonian Diplomacy: A Note," *Pacific Historian*, XIX (Spring 1975), 15-23.

according to the 1910 census, thirty-five percent of the American people were of foreign birth or foreign parentage. Anticipating that constant American involvement in foreign quarrels would produce greater dissension and even disloyalty among these persons, he remembered the wisdom of Washington's Farewell Address.

Root emphasized, while proposing three reservations, that he wanted to preserve the League's positive benefits. As his first reservation, he recommended exclusion of Article 10. He also criticized the new provision for withdrawal from the League after two years' notice because it failed to stipulate that each nation could determine for itself whether its obligations under the Covenant were fulfilled. To ensure that the United States could withdraw without other members of the League complaining that it had not fulfilled all its obligations, he proposed a second reservation to clarify this ambiguity. As his third reservation, Root recommended exclusion of all "purely American questions" from the League's jurisdiction. In this category he included the Monroe Doctrine as well as issues such as immigration. The changes that Wilson had made in the Covenant had failed to meet Root's earlier criticism because, by their ambiguity, they would allow the council to decide whether these American questions were strictly American or international in character. Root wanted to remove any doubt. While expecting European powers to refrain from interfering in American affairs, he thought the United States should reciprocate. He endorsed the Knox resolution, but he also advocated American membership in the League with reservations.

Root stressed that the United States might appropriately make definite and limited commitments to western European security, although not of the vague and universal variety of Article 10. "If it is necessary for the security of western Europe that we should agree to go to the support say of France if attacked," he explained, "let us agree to do that particular thing plainly, so that every man and woman in the country will understand the honorable obligation we are assuming. I am in favor of that. But let us not wrap up such a purpose in a vague universal obligation, under the impression that it really does not mean anything likely to happen." With this affirmation Root recommended an alternative to traditional isolationism.[29]

Root's letter signaled the failure of the Knox resolution but posed an equally serious threat to Wilson's uncompromising position. It provided a basis for consensus among Republicans. Because more than one-third of the senators, by their approval of the Knox resolution, had indicated their reluctance to accept the Covenant as it existed, those Republicans who favored the League could endorse reservations as the only way to secure the

29   HCL to Bigelow, June 23, 24, 26, 1919, HCL Papers, File 1919 (Adams-Trevelyan); HCL to Hopkins, June 23, 1919, HCL Papers, File 1919 (Peace, League, Political, A-H); ER to HCL, June 19, 1919, HCL Papers, File 1919 (Peace, League, Political, I-Z), and ER Papers, Box 161; Knox to Beveridge, June 21, 1919, Beveridge Papers, Box 215; Chaney Digest, June 19-23, 1919, Hays to Goodrich, June 21, 1919, Hays Papers; CR, Vol. 58, 1545-50.

necessary two-thirds majority. Root himself shared this viewpoint. Other Republicans who irreconcilably opposed the League could nevertheless support reservations as a method for eliminating at least some of its worst features, although they might still vote against the Covenant even with these reservations. Whether for positive or negative reasons, Republicans could join together in favor of reservations. This new strategy produced an immediate reaction from Wilson. "My clear conviction," he notified Tumulty, "is that the adoption of the Treaty by the Senate with reservations would put the United States as clearly out of the concert of nations as a rejection. We ought either to go in or to stay out. To stay out would be fatal to the influence and even to the commercial prospects of the United States, and to go in would give her the leadership of the world." Wilson wanted to force the senators to choose between these extreme alternatives of internationalism or isolationism by accepting or rejecting the entire treaty. He was in no mood to compromise even for the purpose of assuring American membership in the League. He authorized Tumulty, at his discretion, to publish this message. After consulting Hitchcock and other Democratic senators, Tumulty decided not to release it. A few days earlier the Democratic leader had already thrown down the gauntlet in the Senate. "If the Republicans defeat this treaty, it will be thrown into the next election," he had announced. He hoped, however that "independent Republicans" would eschew partisan politics and join the Democrats in voting for the League, thereby avoiding the necessity for taking this issue to the people in 1920.[30]

Wilson's and Hitchcock's intransigence, by eliminating options for bipartisan accommodation, helped the Republicans achieve unity on the basis of Root's reservations. Under these increasingly partisan circumstances, the emerging Republican consensus jeopardized the League's future. "In my opinion," Lodge informed White about the impact of Root's letter, "it is more disastrous to the League than any statement that has been made by anyone. It has consolidated feeling in the Senate. It is obvious that it is producing an immense effect upon public opinion throughout the country." The Senate, he confidently affirmed, would not approve the treaty without "very strong reservations" like Root's. The only serious reluctance among Republicans to embrace strong reservations came from senators who either wanted milder reservations or hoped to kill the League altogether. To convince irreconcilables to follow his leadership, Lodge now argued that reservations would accomplish the same purpose as amendments. "I think you are wrong about reservations as attached to treaties," he told Beveridge. "They have precisely the same effect as amendments." Beveridge still

30 JPT to WW, June 20, 21, 23, 25, 25, 1919, WW to JPT, June 25, 1919, message, June 25, 1919, JPT Papers, Box 7; JPT to WW, June 21, 1919 (#206), WW Papers, Ser. 5B, Reel 412; WW to JPT, June 23, 1919, JPT to WW, June 23 (#208), 25 (#215), 25 (#216), 25 (#217), 1919, Strauss and Miller to Auchincloss, June 23, 1919 (#107), Miller to Auchincloss, June 23, 1919 (#109), WW Papers, Ser. 5B, Reel 413; CR, Vol. 58, 1505-07.

preferred an all-out fight against the League, and so did Borah. But rather than break the tactical agreement with Lodge, the Idaho senator vented his frustration on Hays, who had refused to take a stand against the League. "Such miserable, cowardly, white livered, contemptible crawling in the midst of a great fight," Borah exploded, ". . . is incomprehensible to me. . . . Treason is just the same to me whether it comes under the name of Democrat or Republican."

By the beginning of July, despite misgivings of both extremes in the party, Lodge achieved nearly unanimous Republican support for all of Root's reservations. He counted all forty-nine Republican senators as proponents of the second and third reservations on the right of withdrawal and the exclusion of American questions from the League. All but McCumber and Charles L. McNary of Oregon also endorsed the reservation to Article 10. Two Democrats, Reed and Thomas P. Gore of Oklahoma, assured Lodge of their support for this reservation, thereby providing a majority for all three. The Wilson administration counted votes in a different way. As the Republican majority consolidated, the president requested a list of senators opposing the League. Tumulty responded that only thirty-two senators, including six irreconcilables, would require reservations. This excessively optimistic report implied that Wilson could find the votes to defeat any reservation and even enough to provide the required two-thirds majority for the treaty without any changes.³¹

II

Tumulty's inaccurate analysis of the situation in the Senate exemplified his general failure to face the reality of the treaty fight. On previous occasions he had assured the president that Republican opposition was collapsing and that the Senate would eventually accept the entire peace treaty. To achieve this goal, he had recommended effective use of public relations. Even before American and Allied delegates presented the treaty to the Germans, Tumulty began to prepare for a campaign to sell it to the country. He advised Wilson, in presenting the treaty to the Senate, to address Congress and then undertake an extensive tour throughout the nation to rally public support. He urged him to take the offensive by defining the issue as an all-or-nothing choice. "In other words," Tumulty explained in a long memorandum in early June, "the President should make the issue before the Senate and the country one of War or Peace. It is either the League of Nations

---

31   HCL to WW, June 23, July 2, 1919, HCL Papers, File 1919 (Henry White); HCL to Beveridge, June 23, 1919, Beveridge Papers, Box 216; Harvey to Beveridge, June 28, 1919, Beveridge to Harvey, June 30, 1919, Beveridge Papers, Box 215; Borah to Beveridge, June 27, 1919, Beveridge to Borah, July 2, 1919, Borah Papers, Box 551; Hays to ER, July 1, 1919, ER Papers, Box 137; ER to HCL, July 3, 1919, HCL to ER, July 7, 1919, ER Papers, Box 161, and HCL Papers; Grayson to JPT, July 2, 1919, JPT to Grayson, July 2, 1919, JPT Papers, Box 1; JPT to Grayson, July 2, 1919, WW Papers, Ser. 5B, Reel 413; Kohlsaat to Polk, June 19, 1919, Kohlsaat to WW, June 20, 1919, Polk to Kohlsaat, June 20, 1919, Polk Papers, 74/101.

or another final war." He advocated a defense of the League as an essential part of postwar reconstruction at home and abroad, emphasizing that American participation was crucial as a check against Bolshevism. Ignoring evidence of extensive opposition to the League in the Senate, he continued to believe that the president could work some sort of miracle with good publicity.

At first Tumulty did not even plan for Wilson to spend time in Washington, after returning from Paris, to discuss the treaty with senators. Only at the urging of Virginia's Claude A. Swanson, second-ranking Democrat on the Foreign Relations Committee, was the provision for two or three weeks of consultation in Washington included in the president's schedule. The senator recognized the need for serious discussion and even compromise to ensure the treaty's ratification. Tumulty also prepared for a public reception in New York when Wilson landed, thereby beginning the demonstration of popular support. All of these plans, which the president approved, were designed to force senators to accept the League despite their desire for amendments or reservations. Upon Wilson's arrival in the United States, he, too, shared the fantasy that he could dominate the Senate through management of public opinion.[32]

On the morning of July 10, just before he presented the treaty to the Senate, Wilson held a press conference. Telling the reporters that he expected approval of the entire treaty, he questioned the Senate's right to adopt reservations by less than a two-thirds majority. He suggested that even innocuous reservations would require the reopening of negotiations at Paris. Announcing his intention to delay the French security treaty's submission to the Senate, he emphasized that it presupposed the League's existence. This treaty, a specific instance of the obligation that the United States would undertake under the Covenant, depended upon the council's approval. This commitment would not, he further claimed, involve any legislative surrender of war powers to the executive, for Congress would still retain its right to declare war or not. In the event of German aggression, the president would advise Congress, but Congress could exercise its own judgment regarding a military response. With his answers to the reporters' questions

3 2   JPT to WW, Apr. 29, May 1, 8, 26, 1919, WW to JPT, May 2, 1919, JPT Papers, Box 6; WW to JPT, June 16, 27, 1919, JPT to WW, June 1, 4, 16, 17, 20, 28, 1919, JPT Papers, Box 7; JPT to WW, Apr. 29, 1919 (#84), WW Papers, Ser. 5B, Reel 403; JPT to WW, May 1, 1919 (#87), WW Papers, Ser. 5B, Reel 404; JPT to WW, May 8, 1919 (#108), WW Papers, Ser. 5B, Reel 405; JPT to WW, June 1, 1919 (#153), RL to WW, June 2, 1919, Polk to RL, May 31, 1919 (#2151), WW Papers, Ser. 5B, Reel 408; JPT to WW, May 26, 1919 (#144), WW Papers, Ser. 5B, Reel 407; JPT to WW, June 4, 1919, WW Papers, Ser. 5B, Reel 409; JPT to WW, June 9, 1919, WW Papers, Ser. 5B, Reel 411; WW to JPT, June 16 (#194), 17 (#195), 1919, WW Papers, Ser. 5B, Reel 412; JPT to WW, June 23 (#207), 25 (#210), 28, 1919, Suggestions of Mr. Tumulty, [c. June 4, 1919], WW Papers, Ser. 5B, Reel 413; Swanson to Burleson, June 25, 1919, JPT to Burleson, June 25, 1919, Burleson Papers, Vol. 24; Notes, June 10, 13, 1919, Polk Papers, 88/16; Burleson to JPT, June 25, 1919, Swanson to Burleson, June 25, 1919, WW Papers, Ser. 4, File 4767. For a somewhat less critical view of Tumulty during the treaty fight, see John M. Blum, *Joe Tumulty and the Wilson Era* (Boston, 1951), 200-18, 223-39.

Wilson appealed through the press to the country, but for now he intended to remain in Washington. He divulged no information about his anticipated trip through the western states.[33]

Although Wilson adamantly resisted compromise, other advocates of the League began to shift toward reservations. Taft became increasingly aware that the only way to gain a two-thirds majority was by accepting reservations. Earlier, immediately after adoption of the revised Covenant in Paris, he had expressed his approbation in the *Philadelphia Public Ledger*. He then denounced the Knox resolution, especially after the Foreign Relations Committee deleted its fifth section under Borah's influence. Taft deplored the "demagogic appeals" of irreconcilable senators. In the *Washington Post*, he rejected their arguments that the League would grant "universal dominion" to Great Britain, or place "the white people of the world under the scheming and cooperating dominion of the black, yellow, and brown races," or allow the Pope to restore the Roman Catholic Church's temporal power over the world. Responding to Root's letter, Taft announced disappointment over his new position on Article 10. He doubted that the Allies would accept it without further negotiations. "I do not agree with him," stated the former president, "that article 10 would involve us in remote wars." Seeking to prevent any changes in the Covenant, he argued that the Root reservations were equivalent to amendments, and consequently would create obstacles to the treaty's ratification. He expected the French, because of their anxiety over future German aggression, to object to any weakening of Article 10. Their desire to reinforce this commitment with the security treaties with Great Britain and the United States seemed to demonstrate Article 10's importance as a deterrent. Taft also criticized Root for willingness to allow hyphenated Americans to influence the nation's foreign policy. Instead of fearing domestic repercussions of global involvement, he preferred "a more complete Americanization of our foreign-born citizens."[34]

Taft's strategy for assisting Wilson depended on an ill-defined group of senators known as mild reservationists. These Republicans favored the League but recognized the political necessity of adopting reservations. Taft turned at first to Kellogg to lead this group. Although he, too, opposed amendments, the senator shunned this assignment. He declined to associate too closely with any faction. On his own, he notified Lodge that he preferred reservations. Kellogg wanted the United States to undertake no military or naval action without approval of Congress, but otherwise defended Article 10. With Kellogg pursuing his own course, Taft relied primarily on three other pro-League senators, McCumber, McNary, and LeBaron B. Colt of Rhode Island. He maintained contact with these mild reservationists, and also with Hitchcock, not only directly but also through Gus J. Karger, a

33 Newspaper Interview, July 10, 1919, WW Papers, Ser. 2, Box 190; I. H. Hoover Diary, July 10, 1919, Edith Bolling Wilson Papers, Box 57, Library of Congress.
34 Marburg and Flack, eds., *Taft Papers*, 312-31; *CR*, Vol 58, 1430-31, 1550-51, 2586; Public Ledger, July 9, 1919, William Howard Taft Papers, Ser. 3, Box 451, Library of Congress.

Washington, reporter for the *Cincinnati Times-Star*. All of these senators recognized the political imperative for compromise to save the League, but Hitchcock, under Wilson's constraint, refrained from endorsing any reservations.[35]

Taft anticipated that the moment for compromise would arrive after the coalition of Democrats and mild reservationist Republicans defeated the amendments or equivalent reservations which he expected from the Foreign Relations Committee. He counted on McCumber, McNary and Colt to join forty-five Democratic senators to prevent any serious weakening of the League. Defeating amendments or reservations would not, however, secure American membership, for that would require a broader coalition. To achieve that goal, McCumber indicated his willingness to accept a reservation to Article 10. Yet, unlike Root, he refused to scrap this article altogether.[36] McNary agreed with McCumber. In the Senate he defended Article 10 as "purely a moral obligation." Like Wilson, he argued that it would impose no legal duty on the United States to protect the League's members, thereby leaving Congress complete freedom to decide whether to declare war against a future aggressor. Although the United States and other nations would retain the right to decide whether to take any military action, McNary claimed that the League would provide an effective deterrent. Some of its features caused doubts in his mind. He shared his concern about Article 11 with Root, whom he credited with contributing to improvements in the revised Covenant. Because that article authorized the League to intervene in any war-threatening situation, he feared it might permit interference in domestic affairs. It might allow the League to deal not only with the Irish question but also with Japanese immigration. Root responded that he, too, desired a clearer division between domestic and foreign affairs. Like McCumber and McNary, Colt advocated American membership in the League as an essential contribution to "the restoration of peace and order." But he, too, kept an open mind about possible reservations to Article 10.[37]

The ubiquitous Hays, persistently working to unite the Republican party, encouraged Taft to prepare reservations. Believing that the national chairman shared his desire to save the League, Taft entrusted his ideas to him as well as to McCumber, McNary, Colt and Hitchcock. He sought to conform as closely as possible to Root's reservations, while moderating them. On a confidential basis, he revealed his strategy for defeating amendments and reaching a compromise. Secure in the knowledge that even Taft had shifted toward the consensus that Lodge and Root had fostered, Hays announced on

---

35 WHT to Kellogg, Apr. 30, 1919, WHT to Kellogg, June 10, 1919, Kellogg Papers, Box 5; Kellogg to WHT, July 21, 1919, WHT Papers, Ser. 3, Box 452, and Kellogg Papers; Karger to WHT, July 1, 2, 1919, WHT Papers, Ser. 3, Box 451; Kellogg to HCL, July 7, 1919, HCL Papers, File 1919 (Peace, League, Political, I-Z); Kellogg to ER, June 18, 1919, ER Papers, Box 137.
36 McCumber to WHT, July 2, 1919, WHT Papers, Ser. 3, Box 451.
37 McNary to ER, May 5, 1919, ER to McNary, June 18, 1919, ER Papers, Box 137; *CR*, Vol. 58, 2721-22, 2983-85; Colt to WHT, July 18, 1919, WHT Papers, Ser. 3, Box 452; WHT to Colt, July 24, 1919, WHT Papers, Ser. 3, Box 453.

July 15 that Republicans demanded "effective reservations." Taft summarized his views in two letters on July 20. In the first letter to Hays, he criticized both extremes in the treaty fight. He blamed Wilson for his partisan refusal to accommodate moderate Republicans, and irreconcilables for their deliberate distortion of issues such as Shantung. Taft proposed six reservations to the Covenant, or, as he preferred to call them, five interpretations and one reservation. His interpretations were designed to clarify that the right of withdrawal would not cancel earlier obligations during the period of League membership, that the British Empire could have only one vote in the council, that Congress could determine American obligations under Article 10, that issues of immigration and tariffs were domestic except as stipulated otherwise in treaties, and that the United States could still unilaterally interpret the Monroe Doctrine under international law. Taft's only so-called reservation related to Article 10. It sought to limit the American commitment under this article to ten years unless the president and two-thirds of the senators affirmatively decided after that period to keep the United States in the League. In his second letter Taft requested Hays not to reveal his interpretations and his reservation to Root or Lodge or other opponents of the League. He did not want to weaken the bargaining position of mild reservationists by a premature disclosure. But unfortunately for him, Hays had already conveyed Taft's reservations directly to Lodge and Root. Moreover, someone released both of his letters to the press. With this unauthorized publication, Taft's willingness to compromise on the League became public knowledge.[38]

In his continuing efforts to achieve a Republican consensus, Hays also encouraged Charles Evans Hughes to announce his support for reservations. During the earlier debate over the draft Covenant, the 1916 Republican candidate had voiced his general approval, but insisted upon amendments. He praised especially Article 11 because "it gives voice to the lesson of the great War. It provides the machinery for consultation, mediation and conciliation." Yet it involved no specific commitment for action. In his proposed amendments Hughes called for deletion of Article 10. "I regard this guaranty as a trouble-breeder," he said, "and not a peace-maker." He wanted the United States to assume no legal or even moral obligation to defend other League members.

3 8   H. Taft to WHT, July 2, 9, 1919, WHT Papers, Ser. 3, Box 451; WHT to Hays, July 13, 16, 17, 19, 20, 20, 23, 1919, Hays to WHT, July 21, 1919, WHT to Colt, July 15, 17, 20, 1919, WHT to McCumber, July 17, 19, 20, 23, 1919, McCumber to WHT, July 18, 1919, WHT to McNary, July 17, 19, 20, 1919, WHT to Hitchcock, July 21, 1919, WHT to Karger, July 15, 17, 20, 1919, Karger to WHT, July 17, 19, 23, 1919, H. Taft to WHT, July 16, 21, 1919, WHT to H. Taft, July 16, 1919, Hilles, Confidential Memorandum, July 17, 1919, WHT to Hilles, July 20, 1919, Hilles to WHT, July 22, 22, 23, 1919, WHT Papers, Ser. 3, Box 452; WHT to Hays, July 24, 1919, WHT Papers, Ser. 3, Box 453; WHT to Hitchcock, July 21, 1919, Hitchcock Papers, Vol. 1; Chaney Digest, July 15, 23-25, 1919, "The Republican Attitude," *St. Louis Globe-Democrat* (July 17, 1919), "American Independence Is Saved," *Harvey's Weekly* (July 26, 1919), Hays Papers; Hays to ER, July 17, 19, 1919, WHT to Hays, July 17, 1919, ER Papers, Box 137; Hays to HCL, July 17, 19, 22, 1919, WHT to Hays, July 17, 1919, HCL Papers, File 1919 (Peace, League, Political, I-Z).

Because the revised Covenant still contained this undesirable feature, Hughes continued to favor changes. He told Root that he completely agreed with his June 19 letter to Lodge. Root shared this information with Hays, who collaborated with Senator Frederick Hale of Maine to obtain a public statement from Hughes. Hale wrote to Hughes requesting his suggestions for reservations that would permit the United States to join the League without surrendering its sovereignty or traditional policies. In reply on July 24, Hughes advocated American membership in the League with reservations on the right of withdrawal, domestic matters, the Monroe Doctrine and Article 10. He reiterated his objection to a prior commitment that Congress might or might not fulfill during a later crisis. "Article 10," he wrote, "is objectionable because it is an illusory engagement." Hughes proposed that the United States should assume no obligation under this article which would bind Congress to take military action. Hale released this correspondence with Hughes in the Senate, while Hays arranged for wider distribution throughout the country.[39]

Both Lodge and Root appreciated the political significance of Taft's and Hughes' advocacy of reservations. Although unwilling to accept the particular versions that either of them recommended, they welcomed their contributions to Republican unity. For that purpose, Lodge began to shift toward accommodation with mild reservationists. He asked Kellogg to ascertain the basis for a possible compromise. During late July, Kellogg consulted not only McCumber and McNary but also Hale, Cummins, Irvine L. Lenroot of Wisconsin and Selden P. Spencer of Missouri. In this search for acceptable reservations, McCumber actively participated. Kellogg formulated four reservations that apparently expressed the consensus, and on August 7 he addressed the Senate to present them. In a belated public response to Knox, Kellogg offered a strong defense of the League's constitutionality. Recalling the Franco-American alliance of 1778, he argued that the Constitution allowed the United States to conclude treaties of alliance and to guarantee political independence and territorial integrity of other nations. Although the League was both desirable and constitutional, he nevertheless wanted the United States to retain complete freedom in areas vital to its interests. All of Kellogg's reservations, relating to withdrawal, Article 10, internal affairs and the Monroe Doctrine, were designed to protect the unilateral right of this country to delimit its obligations in the League. His views closely followed Root's. On Article 10, agreeing that the United States should avoid a global commitment, he sought to reserve the right of Congress to decide what action, if any, to undertake on the League council's recommendation. Kellogg argued that with his reservations the

39 "The Proposed Covenant for a League of Nations," Address of Charles E. Hughes, March 26, 1919, Charles Evans Hughes Papers, Box 172, Library of Congress; ER to Hays, July 5, 1919, ER Papers, Box 137; Hays to Hughes, July 22, 1919, Hughes Papers, Box 4A; CR, Vol. 58, 3301-03.

United States would face no greater prospect of costly entanglement than it had experienced during the recent war before the League's existence.

As mild reservationists moved toward accommodation with their Republican colleagues, Hitchcock tried pathetically to convince them that reservations were not necessary. He interjected that "there is not a word in the constitution of the league anywhere which justifies any nation in calling upon any other for protection." This defense of the Covenant, including Article 10, reduced the League to a mirage. Ironically, Republicans who favored reservations took it more seriously.[40]

Taft's reservations created conflict in the League to Enforce Peace. His brother, Henry W. Taft, and William H. Short, secretary of the League to Enforce Peace, presented his strategy for building a bipartisan coalition to a meeting of its executive committee on July 22. In attendance, besides Lowell, were prominent Republicans George W. Wickersham and Oscar S. Straus as well as Democrats Vance McCormick, chairman of the War Trade Board, and William G. McAdoo, former secretary of the treasury. The executive committee temporarily resolved its internal turmoil by accepting Henry Taft's suggestion to postpone any action. But once President Taft's letters to Hays were published, the League to Enforce Peace faced renewed pressure to disclose its current position. After consulting Lowell and Wickersham, Short announced that it continued to favor ratification of the treaty without amendments or reservations. To avoid embarrassment to this pro-League lobby, Taft immediately offered his resignation as its president. Lowell, however, withheld his letter of resignation from the executive committee when it reconvened on July 31. At this meeting McAdoo prevailed in defining the issue in the treaty fight as a clear-cut choice for or against the League. He had denounced the League's opponents for seeking to maintain the traditional American policy of "splendid isolation." He praised the League as the way to overcome horrors of war which resulted from balances of power, secret diplomacy and competitive armaments. The executive committee approved McAdoo's resolution calling for unqualified ratification of the treaty and opposing any amendments or reservations. Wilson welcomed this inflexible position of the League to Enforce Peace.[41]

40   HCL to Hays, July 19, 1919, HCL Papers, File 1919 (Peace, League, Political, I-Z); ER to HCL, July 24, 1919, HCL to ER, July 28, 1919, ER Papers, Box 161, and HCL Papers; McCumber to WHT, July 24, 31, 1919, WHT to McCumber, July 27, 1919, McNary to WHT, July 24, 1919, WHT to McNary, July 27, 1919, WHT to Kellogg, July 27, 1919, WHT to Karger, July 27, 1919, Karger to WHT, July 31, 1919, Colt to WHT, July 29, 1919, WHT Papers, Ser. 3, Box 453; Kellogg to WHT, Aug. 11, 1919, WHT Papers, Ser. 3, Box 454; WHT to Kellogg, July 25, 1919, Kellogg to WHT, July 28, 1919, Kellogg Papers, Box 5; *CR*, Vol. 58, 3680-91.
41   WHT to Short, July 18, 1919, Short to WHT, July 22, 1919, H. Taft to WHT, July 22, 1919, WHT Papers, Ser. 3, Box 452; Short to WHT, July 24, 31, 1919, WHT to ALL, July 27, 1919, WHT Papers, Ser. 3, Box 453; McCormick to WW, July 17, 1919, WW Papers, Ser. 2, Box 190; McAdoo to WW, July 31, 1919, WW to McAdoo, Aug. 1, 1919, WW Papers, Ser. 2, Box 191; McAdoo to WW, May 12, 1919, WW Papers, Ser. 5B, Reel 405; McAdoo to JPT, May 27, 1919, Address of W. G. McAdoo, May 26, 1919, WW Papers, Ser. 4, File 331; Resolution Adopted by Executive Committee, League to Enforce Peace, July 31, 1919, WW Papers, Ser. 4, File 4767.

Yet even the president recognized the need to win votes of Republican as well as Democratic senators. For that purpose he adopted a conciliatory manner in dealing with them, while still refusing to compromise. Throughout July and into August he held private interviews with a total of forty-nine senators, beginning with Democrats and then turning to Republicans. He invited a variety of Republican senators to the White House, but focused primarily on mild reservationists. Most accepted his invitations, but the irreconcilable George W. Norris of Nebraska declined, reminding him of the official method for ascertaining the Senate's position on the treaty.[42] During these interviews Wilson gave the impression that he would accept some reasonable reservations, but carefully avoided any definite promise. He told Wiseman that he would accept an interpretive resolution from Republicans, but not amendments or reservations to the treaty. He was willing to clarify the Covenant's meaning relative to the right of withdrawal, Article 10 and the Monroe Doctrine, but not as part of the resolution of ratification. He bitterly complained that Taft was weakening in his support for the League. Once the country learned about Taft's shifting position, Tumulty urged the president to announce his willingness to approve an interpretive resolution. He thought a public statement of this sort would at once limit the damage incurred by publication of Taft's reservations and draw a line between advocates of unqualified ratification and proponents of reservations.

Seeking polarization rather than compromise, Tumulty encouraged Wilson's own inclination to appear conciliatory while rejecting reservations as well as amendments. The president employed a version of this tactic during an interview with Lowell, McCormick and Straus on August 6. Despite recent adoption and publication of the McAdoo resolution by the League to Enforce Peace's executive committee, Lowell agreed with Taft that some reservations were required to save the League. Privately, he encouraged Colt to continue his work toward this goal. At the White House interview Wilson indicated his willingness to accept interpretations like Kellogg's reservations. The senator, at his earlier interview with Wilson, had urged him to approve them. The crucial difference between the president and these reservationists, however, concerned the method of acceptance. He discussed with officials of the League to Enforce Peace the possibility of an exchange of letters, whereas even mild reservationists expected to include their views in the legally binding resolution of ratification. This substantial gulf between Wilson and mild reservationists lessened the possibility of creating a bipartisan coalition. His unwillingness to commit himself or to allow reservations in the resolution of ratification left the burden with Republicans to seek a compromise. After conferring with Wilson, Swanson challenged McNary to find twenty Republican senators who supported Taft's reservations, suggesting that Democrats might join them to provide a two-thirds

---

42   For Norris' views on peacemaking, see Richard Lowitt, *George W. Norris: The Persistance of a Progressive,* 1913-1933 (Urbana, 1971), 107-23.

majority. There were, according to Taft's count, only eleven mild reservationists seeking such an accommodation. The president's persistent intransigence, despite his conciliatory demeanor, reduced the incentive for Republican senators to pursue such a course.[43]

III

Wilson kept the simple issue of accepting or rejecting the League at the forefront of the controversy. Although unable to determine the ultimate outcome, he succeeded in setting the agenda for the national debate. Other parts of the Versailles Treaty received relatively little attention from either Democratic or Republican senators as they focused on the Covenant's merits or dangers. They rarely mentioned specific conditions of peace with Germany. The same fate befell the French security treaty. Although the president delayed its submission to the Senate, some newspapers discussed its implications for American foreign policy. Significantly, divisions over this alliance were not the same as over the League. In a review of this press coverage, the *Literary Digest* observed that "the French treaty has at least as many journalistic friends as foes, and they include both supporters and critics of the League Covenant." One defender of this alliance, who irreconcilably opposed the League, was George Harvey. In *Harvey's Weekly* he vehemently criticized Wilson for neglecting to send this special treaty to the Senate. Brandegee, too, repeatedly demanded its submission. The treaty itself stipulated that it should be presented to the Senate at the same time as the peace treaty, a point that Lodge made in a resolution he introduced to request its transmission. The president finally complied on July 29. In his message to the Senate he explained the relationship between the League and the French security treaty. The alliance, he stated, would obligate the United States to provide "immediate military assistance to France" against unprovoked German aggression. In this particular case, the League council

43   I. H. Hoover Diary, July-August 1919, EBW Papers, Box 57; Wiseman to AJB, July 18, 18, 1919, Wiseman to EMH, July 19, 1919, Wiseman to Murray, July 23, 1919, Wiseman Papers, 90/7; Wiseman to AJB, July 18, 1919, Wiseman to EMH, July 19, 19, 1919, EMH Papers, 20/48; WFJ to WW, July 18, 1919, WW to Dyke, July 17, 1919, JPT to WW, July 25, 1919, JPT Papers, Box 7; JPT to WW, July 18, 23, 25, 1919, Norris to WW, July 21, 1919, WW Papers, Ser. 2, Box 190; Yost to WW, July 7, 1919, WW to Yost, July 15, 1919, Kohlsaat to WW, July 19, 1919, WW to Kohlsaat, July 31, 1919, WW Papers, Ser. 4, File 4767; H. Taft to WHT, July 18, 1919, WHT Papers, Ser. 3, Box 452; Karger to WHT, July 24, 28, 1919, Capper to WHT, July 29, 1919, WHT Papers, Ser. 3, Box 453; Karger to WHT, Aug. 11, 1919, ALL to WHT, Aug. 1, 7, 1919, ALL to Short, Aug. 1, 1919, ALL to Colt, Aug. 1, 1919, WHT to Karger, Aug. 15, 1919, WHT to Short, Aug. 15, 1919, WHT Papers, Ser. 3, Box 454; ALL to Colt, Aug. 1, 1919, ALL Papers; Notes, July 30, 1919, Anderson Papers, Box 4. According to Kurt Wimer, "Woodrow Wilson Tries Conciliation: An Effort That Failed," *Historian*, XXV (Aug. 1963), 419-38, Wilson genuinely sought to conciliate senators in the summer of 1919. But this argument overlooked the president's earlier decision to persevere in his all-or-nothing stance and, consequently, confused his conciliatory method with his uncompromising purpose. Although his appearance was conciliatory, he steadfastly refused to make real concessions. Even Wimer conceded that "the President was not ready to yield" to Republican senators.

would not need to offer advice under Article 10. "It is to be an arrangement, not independent of the League of Nations, but under it."[44]

Subordination of the alliance to the League was precisely what Lodge found most objectionable. He favored the guarantee of French security, but not as a particular example of a general obligation in the League. He had earlier told White that, were it not for this connection, he thought the Senate would certainly approve this commitment to France. Rejecting Beveridge's advice to oppose the alliance as well as the League, Lodge summarized his position: "If there had been no proposition such as is included in Article 10, but a simple proposition that it would be our intention to aid France, which is our barrier and outpost, when attacked without provocation by Germany, I should have strongly favored it for I feel very keenly the sacrifices of France and the immense value her gallant defense was to the whole world. But they have made the French treaty subject to the authority of the League, which is not to be tolerated. If we ever are called upon to go to the assistance of France as we were two years ago, we will go without asking anybody's leave. It is humiliating to be put in such an attitude and not the least of the mischief done by the League is that Article 10 will probably make it impossible to do anything for France as Root recommends and as many of our Senators desire. That would be a distinct and separate thing which we could well afford to do. When it is already wrapped up in that unending promise to go to the assistance of anybody it becomes intolerable."[45]

By early August, Lodge felt fairly confident that Republican senators would unite behind Root's reservations. Wilson was failing to woo them to his side with the interviews, while Taft and Hughes were now contributing to this emerging Republican consensus. Lodge counted nearly forty votes for effective reservations. He could defeat the League unless Wilson accepted these. He warned irreconcilables, however, that their pursuit of the League's total rejection might erode support for strong reservations to less than one-third of the Senate, thereby possibly resulting in unqualified ratification of the peace treaty. By threats and promises Lodge endeavored to keep both irreconcilables and mild reservationists in line behind his leadership. He informed Louis A. Coolidge, an organizer for the League for the Preservation of American Independence, that "such reservations as we should adopt would take the United States out of the treaty entirely on all the points where we wish to refuse obligations." George W. Pepper and Henry Watterson had established the League for the Preservation of American Independence during the spring of 1919 as a counter to the League to Enforce Peace. Although he

44   "That 'Entangling Alliance' with France and England," *Literary Digest*, LXII (July 19, 1919), 12; *CR*, Vol. 58, 3075-83, 3235-36, 3310-12; *PPWW*, V, 555-57; Hays to HCL, July 22, 1919, HCL Papers, File 1919 (Peace, League, Political, I-Z); Beveridge to Harvey, May 13, 1919, Beveridge Papers, Box 215; Beveridge to Munsey, Aug. 8, 1919, Beveridge Papers, Box 216.
45   HCL to HW, June 23, 1919, HCL Papers, File 1919 (Henry White); Beveridge to HCL, Aug. 9, 1919, HCL to Beveridge, Aug. 11, 1919, Beveridge Papers, Box 216, and HCL Papers.

avoided any affiliation with this anti-League lobby, Lodge encouraged its work. Yet he consistently resisted its advocacy of an irreconcilable position. Lodge adhered to this intermediate position throughout the treaty fight.[46]

Extreme opponents of the League only reluctantly acquiesced in Lodge's search for reservations. Borah told the Senate that "I am not interested in any form of interpretations or amendments or reservations. No amendments or reservations which leave us in an alliance or league with European or Asiatic powers will satisfy me." Johnson likewise protested to Beveridge that "it doesn't make any difference whether we are finally to be betrayed with reservations. I think we ought to get out just the same and make plain to our people the infamy of the League of Nations." Both of these irreconcilables remained in Washington, declining opportunities to speak elsewhere at this time, to exert their influence against the League. Yet they continued to operate within the framework of the tactical agreement that Borah and Lodge had concluded before this session of Congress. Political necessity forced irreconcilables to collaborate with Lodge, despite their preference for a decisive vote for or against the League. In their desire for such a showdown, if on nothing else, they agreed with Wilson.[47]

At the core of Borah's argument lay the question of control. Throughout the debate he stressed that both the Covenant and the French security treaty would sacrifice American independence and involve the United States in war. He called attention to the observation of Andrew Bonar Law, Conservative leader in the British House of Commons, that there were twenty-three different wars still in progress in Europe. Under these conditions, the League would escalate local conflicts into global wars. He argued that "the whole world will be called to act under article 10 at just the same moment any particular nation is called upon to act under article 10, and instead of localizing a war, instead of circumscribing its activities, any controversy will immediately spring into a world conflict." Senator Thomas Walsh, denying that a local war would inevitably escalate into a world war, introduced the distinction between moral and legal obligations. The United States would retain the legal right not to become involved even if the League council so advised. But Borah rejected this distinction as a ruse. Senator Peter G. Gerry of Rhode Island defended the League's potential for controlling war. "The

---

46   Beveridge to HCL, July 31, Aug. 8, 1919, HCL to Beveridge, Aug. 4, 1919, Beveridge Papers, Box 216; Beveridge to HCL, Aug. 8, 1919, HCL Papers; HCL to Coolidge, July 30, Aug. 2, 7, 1919, Coolidge to HCL, July 31, 1919, HCL to Beck, July 29, 1919, HCL Papers, File 1919 (Peace, League, Political, A-H); HCL to Weeks, July 31, 1919, Pepper to HCL, March 9, 10, 1919, Powers to HCL, March 7, 1919, Powers to Pepper, Apr. 5, 1919, HCL to Pepper, Apr. 11, 1919, HCL to Powers, Apr. 7, 1919, HCL Papers, File 1919 (Peace, League, Political, I-Z); HCL to Bigelow, July 19, 1919, HCL to Bryce, Aug. 9, 1919, HCL Papers, File 1919 (Adams-Trevelyan). See also Sheldon M. Stern, "Henry Cabot Lodge and Louis A. Coolidge in Defense of American Sovereignty, 1898-1920," *Massachusetts Historical Society Proceedings*, LXXXVII (1975), 118-34.

47   *CR*, Vol. 58, 3441-42; Borah to Beveridge, Aug. 4, 1919, Beveridge Papers, Box 214; Beveridge to Johnson, June 21, July 31, 1919, Johnson to Beveridge, Aug. 7, 1919, Beveridge to Knox, July 15, 31, 31, 1919, Beveridge Papers, Box 215; Borah to Roberts, Aug. 5, 1919, Borah Papers, Box 550; Borah to Reed, July 16, 1919, Borah to Benson, Aug. 13, 1919, Borah Papers, Box 551.

real question," he stated, "is whether we believe that it is not better for the United States to have a say in European matters and thus try to prevent another horrible war or to keep our hands off and wait until the world is aflame and then endeavor to assert our might to protect our rights." He saw in the League an opportunity for positive American influence over Europe, while Borah apprehended the danger of foreign control. Wanting to avoid any moral or legal obligations, the irreconcilable senator opposed the alliance with France for the same reason.[48]

Lodge also concentrated on the question of control. He summarized his criticism in a major address on August 12. Drawing upon his knowledge of history, he argued that Wilson's scheme repeated the errors of the past. Like the Holy Alliance, the League would entangle its members in both external and internal conflicts. Noting that any revolution or insurrection could endanger world peace, he anticipated that the League would become an instrument for repression. Lodge did not wish to place the United States under the control of any international organization that could legitimately require it to assist in this task or to protect all countries against external aggression. If the United States joined the League without reservations, he saw no escape in good faith from either of these roles, for he rejected the distinction between legal and moral obligations. He reiterated his refusal to allow the League to establish its jurisdiction over domestic questions, such as tariffs and immigration, or over the Monroe Doctrine. Instead of joining a new Holy Alliance, he wanted the United States to maintain its traditional Monroe Doctrine. "It is," Lodge said, "as important to keep the United States out of European affairs as to keep Europe out of the American Continents." He criticized the British delegates for trying to bring the Monroe Doctrine under the League's jurisdiction and for seeking to entangle the United States in their empire's defense. To preserve the independence and safety of his own country, he demanded the absolute right of withdrawal from the League. Lodge advocated prudent involvement: "Nobody expects to isolate the United States or to make it a hermit Nation, which is a sheer absurdity. But there is a wide difference between taking a suitable part and bearing a due responsibility in world affairs and plunging the United States into every controversy and conflict on the face of the globe." The question of control, not isolationism versus internationalism, was the central issue in the treaty fight.

Avoidance of unnecessary entanglement abroad, according to Lodge, was also important for the assimilation of American immigrants and their children. The reality of ethnic politics suggested to him, as well as to Root, the wisdom of restraint in foreign relations. Not only practical considerations of American politics but also an element of idealism characterized Lodge's

48   CR, Vol. 58, 1737-49, 2054-58, 3143-45; Borah to Truitt, July 3, 1919, Borah Papers, Box 550; Borah to The World, May 8, 1919, Beck to Borah, July 22, 1919, Borah to Beck, July 23, 1919, Borah Papers, Box 551; "The War Not Over," Literary Digest, LXII (July 12, 1919), 9-12.

advocacy of reservations. "The United States is the world's best hope," he proudly asserted, "but if you tangle her in the intrigue of Europe, you will destroy her power for good and endanger her very existence."[49]

IV

Meanwhile, the Foreign Relations Committee began its official consideration of the treaty. After devoting two weeks to reading the treaty, it opened hearings at the end of July. Lansing, one of the first witnesses, appeared before the committee on August 6 and 11. The dilemma that he faced arose from the necessity of publicly defending a peace settlement that he privately questioned. By the time the peace conference had finished the Versailles Treaty, he felt thoroughly alienated. He had not contributed much to it. In his view, Wilson and Allied leaders had failed to create the new order of international relations they had promised. Self-interest rather than justice governed the policies of other nations but not those of the United States. He continued to regard his own country as an innocent and virtuous land. Expecting other governments to pursue their selfish interests even in the League, he doubted that it could achieve the unanimity that the Covenant required for effective international action. Therefore, he concluded, "the future foreign policies of the United States should be formulated on the assumption that the League of Nations cannot properly function." In his opinion, Wilson had suffered a serious loss of prestige by failing to transform the Old World. Yet even Lansing refused to acknowledge the limits of American power or sacrifice the dream of American control over foreign affairs. He found a simpler explanation for failure in the president's decision to lead the American delegation rather than to leave that task to the secretary himself. "It was," he believed, "a great calamity that the President ever came to Europe. In Washington he could have dictated a just peace. In Paris he had to bow to the will of others."[50]

Lansing decided not to make a strong case for the League in his testimony to the committee. Aware of the hostility engendered by the treaty fight, he chose not to jeopardize bureaucratic interests of the State Department by antagonizing Lodge and his colleagues. He made a pathetic appearance as he declined to answer questions about the Covenant's origins. Not only did he deny any knowledge about the so-called American plan for the League, he even responded to Johnson that he did not know who had conceived the idea for Article 10. He gave more information about the Shantung settlement, shifting responsibility for it to Wilson. He denied, however, that the president made this compromise to ensure Japan's membership in the League. The secretary also refused to clarify Wilson's statements about the

49   *CR*, Vol. 58, 3778-84.
50   U.S. Senate, *Proceedings of the Committee on Foreign Relations*, 145-59; RL Diary, V, June 9, 29, Aug. 7, 1919.

relationship between the French security treaty and the League. He likewise avoided Knox's requests for an explanation of the difference between moral and legal obligations and a definition of "aggression" with reference to Article 10. Brandegee also tried in vain to pin Lansing down on commitments under the Covenant, arguing that either it imposed real obligations on the League members to use military force or it offered a false promise. None of these Republican inquiries evoked any clear defense of the League by the secretary.[51]

Rather than pressing for the treaty's unqualified ratification, Lansing urged the president to compromise. He thought his refusal to accommodate even mild reservationists would kill the treaty. The secretary gave this unwelcome advice to Wilson on August 11, but failed to persuade him. Instead, as Lansing recorded this encounter, "his face took on that stubborn and pugnacious expression which comes whenever anyone tells him a fact which interferes with his plans." Given the political situation, the secretary saw no prospect for the treaty without reservations. "The way I see it," he noted, "the President is 'riding to a fall' and a pretty bad one too. His uncompromising attitude and his unwillingness to confer with anyone who disagrees with him in the slightest particular will, I believe, force the Republican 'moderates' into the ranks of the radicals who oppose ratification of any sort or ratification without reservations so drastic as to destroy the Covenant. This impolitic policy of the President's will, if it continues, defeat the Treaty in all probability, and will certainly do so if he decides to make his western trip and appeal to the people, because the 'moderates' will feel personally insulted by this going over their heads." Despite his pathetic ineffectiveness as secretary of state, Lansing at least understood that the only hope for the treaty depended upon Wilson's acceptance of reservations.[52]

After its failure to elicit a clear explanation of the League from Lansing, the Foreign Relations Committee turned to others with more knowledge about the drafting of the Covenant. David Hunter Miller provided some additional information but failed to satisfy Republican senators. The committee consequently decided to request a conference with the president himself. Wilson responded by inviting them to the White House on August 19. In an opening statement he presented his case for early ratification of the treaty without any changes. He disparaged their continuing doubts about the League, claiming that the Covenant now contained all the revisions which they had suggested when they had last met with him. It now expressly recognized the Monroe Doctrine, excluded domestic matters, guaranteed the right of withdrawal, and reserved the right of Congress to declare war or preserve peace. Wilson emphasized that Article 10 left the United States

51   U.S. Senate, Committee on Foreign Relations, *Treaty of Peace with Germany: Hearings*, Document No. 106 (Washington, 1919), 139-378; RL to Polk, July 26, 1919, Polk Papers, 78/11; RL to Polk, July 31, 1919 (#2678), Polk Papers, 82/1; RL to Stebbins, July 31, 1919, RL Papers, Vol. 45.
52   RL Diary, Aug. 2, 11, 1919. See also Dimitri D. Lazo, "A Question of Loyalty: Robert Lansing and the Treaty of Versailles," *Diplomatic History*, IX (Winter 1985), 35-53.

completely free to determine what response, if any, to make to alleged aggression. He explained this unilateral decision-making within the League by contrasting moral and legal obligations. Article 10, he said, "constitutes a very grave and solemn moral obligation. But it is a moral, not a legal, obligation, and leaves our Congress absolutely free to put its own interpretation upon it in all cases that call for action. It is binding in conscience only, not in law." This explanation raised as many questions as it answered. Even McCumber suggested the wisdom of including reservations in the resolution of ratification so as to avoid any misunderstanding. The president reiterated his opposition to such reservations, in contrast to a separate resolution of interpretations which he would accept. Denying the distinction between amendments and reservations that Lodge cited under international law, he claimed that any reservation would require further negotiations with the Allies and also with Germany. He added to the confusion with his interpretation of the French security treaty. He conceded that this alliance involved both moral and legal obligations, but still viewed it as a particular case under the general guarantee of Article 10, which he nevertheless persisted in regarding as only a moral commitment.

This casuistry failed to convince Republican skeptics. Senator Warren G. Harding of Ohio pressed the issue by observing that Article 10 either did or did not impose a binding obligation on the United States to prevent aggression. If it did, this country would not enjoy the unilateral right of decision-making that Wilson claimed; if not, the League would not serve as the effective deterrent that he also promised. When the senator posed this dilemma, the president obfuscated. "When I speak of a legal obligation," he replied, "I mean one that specifically binds you to do a particular thing under certain sanctions. . . . Now a moral obligation is of course superior to a legal obligation, and, if I may say so, has a greater binding force; only there always remains in the moral obligation the right to exercise one's judgment as to whether it is indeed incumbent upon one in those circumstances to do that thing." Rejecting this ruse, Brandegee argued that "the distinction between a moral obligation and a legal one seems to me to be not of great importance, because we are obligated in any event." Harding agreed as he continued to insist that the League could not provide an effective deterrent against aggression and yet leave its members totally free to determine their own responses. Doubting that the League could achieve agreement among major powers during any real crisis, he noted that "the conscience of any nation in Europe, for example, may be warped by its prejudices, racial, geographical, and otherwise. If that be true and any nation may put aside or exercise its judgment as to the moral obligation in accepting any recommendation of the league, really what do we get out of this international compact in the enforcement of any decree?" Harding's question emerged from his view of a divided world, but Wilson's answer reflected his vision of global unanimity. "We get," he answered, "the centering upon it generally of the definite opinion of the world, expressed through the authoritative organs of the responsible governments." The Ohio senator countered that if such universality of opinion existed among foreign governments in the League, then it could subject the United States to its judgment. The president denigrated this threat of foreign control by rejecting the assumption that "the United States will not concur in the general moral judgment of the world." In those rare instances when American and global opinion diverged, this country could pursue its own course; but in those more typical cases, he wanted the American government to exert its influence through the League to prevent war. This defense of Article 10 expressed Wilson's basic presupposition that his own conception of collective security enjoyed universal acceptance, and that public opinion in the United States and other democratic nations would support American leadership in world affairs. Despite his experience in Paris and with the Senate, he still refused to adjust his definition of foreign policy to the reality of pluralism at home and abroad.

Wilson endeavored to explain the treaty. He insisted that reservations, such as Root, Hughes and Taft advised, were not necessary as "the meaning of the wording is plain." He traced the Covenant's origins to various British and American documents, and in the case of Article 10 to his own earlier Latin American policy. Answering numerous questions about the Shantung settlement, he conceded that Japan would probably not join the League without this concession. He refused, however, to answer Johnson's inquiry about his stance on the Japanese proposal for racial equality, claiming that secrecy would best contribute to international amity. He also largely side-stepped the controversy over six British votes in the League assembly, failing to clarify which matters would affect the whole British Empire and which would affect only Great Britain or one of the dominions or India. On conditions of peace with Germany, including the Rhineland occupation, reparations and the Polish-German border, the president gave more explicit answers. As in the general debate, however, this major part of the Versailles Treaty received relatively little attention at the White House conference. In his summary of American relations with the Old World, Wilson affirmed his desire to "keep free from European affairs." He saw no contradiction between this traditional American attitude and his new vision of collective security. With his distinction between moral and legal obligations, he hoped to reconcile the potentially contradictory themes of unilateralism and universalism in his policy. He wanted the United States to assume global responsibilities in the League, establishing its control over foreign affairs, but without sacrificing American independence or paying a high price.[53]

By his rigid refusal to accept reservations in the resolution of ratification, Wilson ignored both legal and political evidence that contradicted his

53   U.S. Senate, *Treaty of Peace with Germany: Hearings*, 499-556; HCL, *The Senate and the League of Nations*, 297-379; *PPWW*, V, 574-80; U.S. Senate, *Proceedings of the Committee on Foreign Relations*, 162-63.

position. Earlier, one of his staunch supporters in the Foreign Relations Committee, Pittman, had offered an analysis of the law and politics of peacemaking. The Nevada senator argued that any amendments, reservations or interpretations in the resolution of ratification would require the reopening of negotiations, but that fortunately a coalition of pro-League senators could be built with the adoption of "interpretive reservations" in a separate resolution. He thought this approach would satisfy mild reservationists. The State Department's solicitor had analyzed Pittman's legal argument and concluded that, contrary to his contention, only amendments would necessitate further negotiations. Although Lansing had brought the solicitor's report to Wilson's attention, he ignored its conclusion. The president told the Foreign Relations Committee that reservations as well as amendments would require renewed negotiations. By mid-August, Pittman had recognized a growing tendency among Democratic senators to favor reservations as the best way to prevent the treaty's defeat. He warned Wilson that Kellogg's reservations might win a majority, leaving the die-hard loyalists who supported unqualified ratification in the embarrassing position of delaying a vote or voting against the treaty. Consequently, he urged the president to indicate his willingness to accept an interpretive resolution, which he finally did at the White House conference. Tumulty had offered the same advice to preempt the possibility that Republicans might suggest this form of compromise and take the initiative from Wilson. This recommendation reflected Tumulty's totally unfounded fear about Republican behavior. More to the point, Pittman's warning had alerted the president to the deteriorating situation on the Democratic side of the Senate.[54]

Beyond signaling his approval for an interpretive resolution, Wilson made no effort at accommodation. On his own initiative, Pittman introduced a separate resolution on August 20 with his interpretations of the procedure for withdrawal, the obligations of Article 10, the exclusion of domestic affairs, and the preservation of the Monroe Doctrine under the treaty. Rather than attracting mild reservationists, the actions of Wilson and Pittman hardened partisan divisions in the Senate. Even McCumber, McNary and Colt rejected the idea of a separate interpretive resolution. Aware of this gulf, Hitchcock still expressed the forlorn hope that enough Republicans might eventually abandon their insistence on reservations and join Democrats to approve the treaty. He admitted to Taft, however, that he could not foresee how to create such a bipartisan coalition. All he could do, as he operated under Wilson's constraint, was to repeat the president's argument against reservations, although he appreciated that votes, not arguments, would determine the outcome of the treaty fight.[55]

54   For Pittman's role during the treaty fight, see Fred L. Israel, *Nevada's Key Pittman* (Lincoln, 1963), 34-41.
55   *CR*, Vol. 58, 3130-35, 4035-39; J. A. M[etzger] to RL, July 29, 1919, WW Papers, Ser. 2, Box 190; Pittman to WW, Aug. 15, 1919, JPT to WW, Aug. 15, 1919, WW Papers, Ser. 2, Box 191;

Wilson's inflexibility aided Lodge in his search for reservations that could unite Republican senators. The White House conference sharpened differences between the parties and virtually eliminated the possibility for a bipartisan compromise. As Wilson and Lodge led their parties in different directions, the Foreign Relations Committee became an arena for conflict instead of conciliation. The Republican majority considered various amendments and reservations, which Democrats opposed. While this work proceeded in private, the hearings provided Republican senators a public forum for criticism. They encouraged spokesmen for several nationalities to voice their grievances against the peace conference and the resulting treaty. For his part, Wilson made final preparations for his western trip. Gathering information for this speaking tour, he solicited reports from his cabinet on consequences of failure to ratify the peace treaty. Both sides hoped to win the battle for public opinion in their efforts to determine the treaty's fate.[56]

Much of the testimony at the Foreign Relations Committee's hearings displayed an anti-British or anti-Japanese bias. Irish-Americans condemned the British Empire for denying self-determination and seeking perpetual imperial control through the League. Cohalan claimed the mantle of the American diplomatic tradition as he championed the cause of republican government in Ireland. "We Irish," he affirmed, using that term ambiguously for his people on both sides of the Atlantic, "think that there should be no abandonment of the policy laid down by Washington in his Farewell Address of keeping away from permanent entangling alliances with any of the countries of the Old World." This statement sounded isolationist, but his real concern was just the opposite. He feared that Article 10 would prevent the United States from intervening in the Anglo-Irish conflict on Ireland's side. Rather than opposing entanglement, he objected to the alignment of the United States with Great Britain in the League. It would be, in Cohalan's view, "un-American" for the United States to assume an obligation that would prevent it from assisting Ireland in the same way that France had helped the thirteen colonies achieve their independence from England during the American Revolution. Lodge agreed that Article 10 would prohibit the United States from giving military assistance to Ireland, but he never advocated such a role. He remained somewhat aloof from ethnic leaders of this sort, while Borah maintained his close contact with Cohalan.[57]

Karger to WHT, Aug. 21, 1919, Hitchcock to WHT, Aug. 29, 1919, WHT Papers, Ser. 3, Box 455; Knox to Beveridge, Aug. 21, 1919, Beveridge Papers, Box 215.

56 HCL to L. A. Coolidge, Aug. 20, 1919, HCL Papers, File 1919 (Peace, League, Political, A-H); HCL to Stearns, Aug. 30, 1919, HCL Papers, File 1919 (Peace, League, Political, I-Z); U.S. Senate, *Proceedings of the Committee on Foreign Relations*, 161-70; Glass to WW, Aug. 13, 1919, Houston to WW, Aug. 13, 1919, WW to Glass, Aug. 14, 1919, WW Papers, Ser. 2, Box 191; Glass to WW, Aug. 13, 1919, WW to Glass, Aug. 14, 1919, Carter Glass Papers, Box 8, University of Virginia Library; RL Diary, V, Aug. 25, 1919.

57 U.S. Senate, *Treaty of Peace with Germany: Hearings*, 757-94; HCL to Walsh, Aug. 14, 1919, HCL Papers, File 1919 (Peace, League, Political, I-Z); Cohalan to Borah, July 11, 1919, Borah to Cohalan, July 14, 1919, Cohalan Papers; Borah to Cohalan, July 14, 1919, Borah Papers, Box 551.

After Cohalan completed his testimony, the committee heard three Irish-Americans who had gone to Paris on the futile mission of trying to persuade Wilson and Allied leaders to give a hearing to the delegation from Ireland. Frank P. Walsh articulated his disillusionment with Wilson's diplomacy. As a member of the League to Enforce Peace, he had once believed that creation of an international organization would promote national self-determination. But the peace conference's failure to recognize this right for Ireland led him to view the League of Nations as an instrument for repression instead of freedom. Under British domination, it would serve the cause of monarchy rather than republicanism. Walsh rejected as a false promise Thomas Walsh's argument that the League offered the best hope for Ireland. Michael J. Ryan and Edward F. Dunne reinforced this criticism with their comments. Various other Irish-Americans also contributed to this litany of condemnation before the Foreign Relations Committee.[58]

Spokesmen for India and Egypt expressed similar grievances against the British Empire. A prominent Irish-American, Dudley Field Malone, testified on India's behalf. Asserting that the unofficial Indian National Congress actually represented the Indian people, he denounced British rule as "an absolute despotism." Under these circumstances, India's vote in the League would only strengthen the power of the government in London. He urged senators to amend the Covenant to promote the "humanitarian purpose" of fostering self-government. Joseph W. Folk appeared as counsel for the Egyptian legislative assembly's commission that had attempted to gain a hearing in Paris. He protested against the "masked annexation" of Egypt by Great Britain under the peace treaty, noting that this seizure would make the status of Egypt an internal question of the British Empire. "The people of Egypt," he affirmed, "want a league of nations to protect their independence, not to destroy their independence." The people of India and Egypt, according to Malone and Folk, wanted the League to foster national self-determination rather than to perpetuate British imperialism. They desired the United States to promote that purpose, not to assist the British Empire in maintaining its imperial control around the globe.[59]

Japan ranked next to Great Britain as a target of criticism in the hearings. John C. Ferguson, an American adviser to China's president, testified against Japanese acquisition of German rights in Shantung, although he conceded under McCumber's questioning that Japan had not obtained sovereignty over that province. Professor Edward Thomas Williams of the University of California, a technical adviser to the American delegation in Paris, agreed with Ferguson that the German rights should have been returned to China. They saw no legitimate reason for Japan to expand its influence in Asia to the point of threatening to control China.[60]

---

58   U.S. Senate, *Treaty of Peace with Germany: Hearings*, 794-933; *CR*, Vol. 58, 3222-29; "Wilson's Alliance With Lloyd George," *Gaelic American*, XVI (Sept. 13, 1919), 1.
59   U.S. Senate, *Treaty of Peace with Germany: Hearings*, 651-78, 750-54.
60   Ibid., 557-649.

Although anti-British and anti-Japanese themes dominated the hearings, the Foreign Relations Committee heard spokesmen for a variety of European nationalities. American ethnic leaders defended the sometimes conflicting claims of their ancestral homelands, except that no German-American appeared to voice Germany's grievances against the treaty. The political climate would not permit German-Americans to protest in the way that Representative Fiorello H. La Guardia of New York criticized the treaty for prohibiting Italy from annexing Fiume. Leaders of ethnic organizations spoke not only for Ireland and Italy but also for several new nations that had emerged from the Russian, German and Austro-Hungarian empires. Afro-Americans also told the committee their concerns. William Monroe Trotter, secretary of the National Equal Rights League, proposed an amendment to the treaty to include the promise of racial equality, stressing "the great need of the protection of life and of equality of rights for the colored American minority." Far from fearing foreign control, he welcomed an international guarantee of equality for all races. While he was primarily interested in protecting rights of all American citizens, representatives of the National Race Congress of America focused on Africa. They advocated that the United States should accept a mandate for a former German colony in Africa. "We submit that a backward people can only gain actual knowledge of government by experience," explained Charles Sumner Williams of Indianapolis. "The development of the Philippines and Cuba are shining examples of what might occur if America would consent to act as a trustee for these African colonies. The United States has the advantage of a large number of Americans of color, and this would make it easy for this Government, through sympathetic agencies, to aid the peoples of Africa to self-government on the highways of civilization." For this purpose he favored the League. Unlike most witnesses, he shared Wilson's vision of international social control. The League, he believed, could serve as an instrument for benevolent American influence in foreign countries. But these ethnic and racial concerns, unlike those relating to the British and Japanese empires, received only marginal attention from the committee.[61]

The treaty fight concentrated on the question of control at home and abroad. In the conflict between the president and Republican senators, the hearings served primarily as a method for publicizing critical commentary on the treaty and especially on the Covenant. The Foreign Relations Committee used the hearings as an appeal to public opinion, not as a source of new ideas. Except for the prominence of anti-British and anti-Japanese themes, the testimony gave no indication of the content of the committee's amendments and reservations. Crucial to the committee's entire proceedings, however, was the question of control. Wilson persisted in demanding the treaty's

61   Ibid., 679-749, 934-1011, 1054-86, 1098-1159. See also Joseph P. O'Grady, *The Immigrants' Influence on Wilson's Peace Policies* (Lexington, 1967), and Frederick C. Luebke, *Bonds of Loyalty: German-Americans and World War I* (DeKalb, 1974), 309-34.

unqualified ratification so that the United States could exercise global influence through the League, while Lodge and his Republican colleagues wanted to protect American interests by adopting amendments or reservations. The gulf between Democrats and Republicans clearly doomed prospects for ratification even before Wilson left on his western trip or the committee reported the treaty to the Senate. His vision of global interdependence failed to gain universal acceptance even though he identified the League with the God-given destiny of the United States. Despite his ability to define the agenda in the politics of peacemaking, the president alone could not control the modern world. Pluralism at home as well as abroad limited his power to shape American foreign relations.

CHAPTER 7

The Versailles Treaty in the Senate

Neither Wilson nor his Republican foes evidenced any willingness to compromise their fundamental differences. The question of control continued to separate them as the Senate undertook formal action on the Versailles Treaty. The Foreign Relations Committee recommended amendments and reservations, but the president rejected any changes. Ironically, the rigidity of his all-or-nothing stance reflected his growing awareness that the United States could not influence the myriad patterns of international relations in the way he hoped. Voicing his despair to Lansing, he revealed that he was considering withdrawal of the United States from the League because of the selfish conduct of other nations. Wilson asserted that "when I think of the greed and utter selfishness of it all, I am almost inclined to refuse to permit this country to be a member of the League of Nations when it is composed of such intriguers and robbers. I am disposed to throw up the whole business and get out."[1] Becoming increasingly aware of the limits of American power in the postwar world, he adjusted to this reality by holding more inflexibly to his ideals. Rather than attempt to define a constructive, but inherently frustrating, foreign policy that might win the Senate's support and contribute to postwar reconstruction, he preferred his dream of global leadership. He held firmly to his vision of collective security and refused to accept a more limited, but definite, role for his country in the interdependent and plural world.

After the White House conference on August 19, Lodge intensified his efforts to prepare a set of reservations that all Republican senators would approve. He also endorsed amendments, but doubted that the Senate would accept them. Some Republicans as well as Democrats opposed textual changes in the treaty. He confidently expected, however, to unite a majority in favor of strong or effective reservations in the resolution of ratification.

[1]   RL Diary, V, Aug. 20, 1919.

Wilson's actions at the meeting with the Foreign Relations Committee, especially his "ignorance and disingenuousness" and "his slippery evasions on the moral obligations," had weakened his position. Republican senators, Lodge emphasized, while still sympathetic toward the Allies, intended to protect American rights and independence.[2]

Voting in the Foreign Relations Committee registered a sharp partisan division in late August, when it recommended amendments. All Republicans except McCumber supported Lodge's Shantung amendment, while the Democratic minority opposed it. Although he expected the amendment's defeat in the Senate, Lodge wanted to record his desire to return Germany's rights in Shantung to China. He resisted American complicity in their transfer to Japan, although the Republican administration of President William McKinley had not protested in 1898 against Germany's acquisition of these concessions. During McCumber's absence, the committee voted along strictly partisan lines for Fall's amendments to prohibit American membership on various commissions established by the treaty. Only the Reparation Commission, on which Fall wanted American representation under certain restrictions, was exempted. On this amendment, McCumber joined Democratic senators against the Republican majority. The same pattern characterized the adoption of amendments by Johnson and Moses to equalize the votes of the United States and the British Empire in the League. Johnson's amendment stipulated that the United States should have the same number of votes in the assembly or council as any other country plus its self-governing dominions or colonies. Because the British Empire would have a total of six votes in the assembly, this amendment would effectively increase American votes to the same number. The Moses amendment required that all self-governing dominions and colonies as well as the mother country could not vote in the assembly if any one of them was involved in a dispute with another League member. In the event, for example, that the United States became embroiled in a conflict with Great Britain, Canada, South Africa, Australia, New Zealand or India, none of these countries could cast a vote in the assembly.[3]

The Foreign Relations Committee next adopted Lodge's four reservations as part of the resolution of ratification. These dealt with Root's concerns, but in a way more acceptable to mild reservationists. The first one protected the "unconditional right" of the United States to withdraw from the League. The second reservation stipulated that the United States would not assume any obligations under Article 10, or any other article, except with

---

2 HCL to Bigelow, Aug. 25, 1919, HCL to Trevelyan, Sept. 9, 1919, HCL Papers, File 1919 (Adams-Trevelyan); HCL to HW, July 5, Aug. 7, 19, 1919, HCL Papers, File 1919 (Henry White); HCL to Hobbs, Aug. 20, 1919, HCL Papers, File 1919 (Peace, League, Political, A-H); HCL to Williams, Aug. 5, 1919, HCL Papers, File 1919 (Peace, League, Political, I-Z); Notes, Aug. 22, 1919, Anderson Papers, Box 4.
3 U.S. Senate, *Proceedings of the Committee on Foreign Relations*, 164-68; HCL to Bigelow, Aug. 1, 1919, HCL Papers, File 1919 (Adams-Trevelyan); HCL to L. A. Coolidge, July 30, 1919, HCL to Beck, Aug. 23, 1919, HCL Papers, File 1919 (Peace, League, Political, A-H).

congressional approval. It was designed to prevent the president alone from undertaking military action or using economic measures against foreign nations in case of either external aggression or internal conflict, or from accepting a mandate from the League. At issue was the split between the White House and Congress over the power to control future policy. The third reservation, almost identical with Kellogg's earlier proposal, affirmed the exclusive American right to determine which questions were domestic and, consequently, outside the League's jurisdiction. The fourth reservation similarly removed the Monroe Doctrine from the League's domain, thereby preserving its interpretation as an exclusively American prerogative. As on the amendments, voting on these reservations followed partisan divisions, with two notable exceptions. McCumber opposed the first two reservations, but especially the one on Article 10. He recognized, however, that Lodge had moved closer to mild reservationists. On the Democratic side, John K. Shields of Tennessee defected. This Irish-American senator abstained on the Article 10 reservation but joined Republicans on the others. Despite the committee's endorsement on September 4 of all his reservations, Lodge had not yet united Republicans or attracted many Democrats, especially with his Article 10 reservation. But he had achieved considerable success, while Wilson's support among Democratic senators was beginning to erode.[4]

Claiming falsely that all Republican senators approved the committee's reservations, Hays challenged the president to accept them. His statement angered Taft, who felt betrayed. Taft suspected that Knox had drafted the Article 10 reservation as a way of killing the League. He reiterated his willingness to approve his own or Hughes' reservation to Article 10, but not the committee's, as it would totally delete American obligations. Taft's protest exerted little impact on Hays.[5]

The Republican majority and Democratic minority in the Foreign Relations Committee submitted separate reports to the Senate. Lodge reported the committee's amendments and reservations on September 10. Expressing the "most vital objection" to Article 10, he rejected "any legal or moral obligation upon the United States to enter into war or send its Army and Navy abroad" or "to impose economic boycotts on other countries" without the "unfettered" approval of Congress.[6] Faithful to the president, the Democrats on the committee, except Shields, submitted a minority report. They labeled the amendments and reservations as "equivalent to rejecting the treaty" and defended Wilson's League as "the only plan proposed to redeem the world from war, pestilence and famine." Paradoxi-

4   U.S. Senate, *Proceedings of the Committee on Foreign Relations*, 170-74; HCL to Harvey, Sept. 5, 11, 1919, HCL Papers, File 1919 (Peace, League, Political, I-Z); Harvey to HCL, Sept. 9, 1919, HCL Papers, File 1919 (Peace, League, Political, A-H).
5   Chaney Digest, Sept. 7, 1919, statement, Sept. 6, 1919, WHT to Hays, Sept. 10, 1919, Hays to WHT, Sept. 22, 1919, Hays Papers; Hays to WHT, Sept. 22, 1919, WHT Papers, Ser. 3, Box 457.
6   U.S. Senate, *Proceedings of the Committee on Foreign Relations*, 173-78; *CR*, Vol. 58, 5112-14; HCL to Beveridge, Sept. 9, 1919, Beveridge Papers, Box 216, and HCL Papers.

cally, for senators claiming that the League could exert such a benevolent influence in the world, they presupposed American weakness vis-à-vis Germany. The Democrats opposed any change that might reopen negotiations with the defeated enemy. Their report essentially endorsed Wilson's all-or-nothing stance in the treaty fight.[7]

Dissatisfied with both reports, McCumber delivered his own views to the Senate. He defended the treaty for seeking to establish in international relations a code of morality like that which governed civilized people in their internal affairs. To protect American interests without defeating the treaty, he recommended six reservations, but opposed all amendments. Except for minor changes, McCumber endorsed the committee's reservations on domestic affairs and the Monroe Doctrine. He modified the committee's affirmation of the American right of withdrawal so as to require the United States to fulfill its international obligations, as it defined them, before leaving the League. He strenuously objected to the committee's Article 10 reservation because it would effectively destroy this "most important" part of the Covenant. He offered a substitute that would accept Article 10's obligations but leave the United States complete discretion as to methods for fulfilling them. In particular, this reservation stipulated that the use of military or naval forces or of economic sanctions would require congressional approval. In place of Lodge's Shantung amendment, McCumber preferred a reservation. He criticized the Johnson amendment for seeking to give the United States an unfair advantage by increasing its votes in the assembly. If the British Empire should not enjoy such an advantage, then neither should the United States. Defending the British dominions' right to be in the League, McCumber sought to resolve the problem of voting equality with a reservation affirming that a dispute with any part of the British Empire involved the whole empire and, consequently, that neither Great Britain nor its self-governing dominions or colonies could vote. He hoped these six reservations would provide the basis for a two-thirds majority for the treaty.[8]

Wilson made final preparations for his western trip, hoping for a political miracle through management of public opinion. McCumber and Phelan urged him to address the Irish and Japanese questions, the two sources of a variety of particular issues. McCumber traced controversies over six British votes in the assembly, British acquisition of German colonies, and an alleged requirement for the United States to aid Great Britain against rebellion in Ireland, Egypt or India, to the "most bitter opposition" of "Sinn Fein followers." Phelan warned of potential Irish-American defection from the Democratic party because of the anti-revolutionary interpretation of Articles 10 and 11. American hostility toward the Japanese appeared, as McCumber noted, in the Shantung dispute and, as Phelan stressed, closer to home in the controversy over immigration. Anti-British and anti-Japanese sentiments,

---

7   U.S. Senate, *Proceedings of the Committee on Foreign Relations*, 178–81.
8   Ibid., 181–88.

they advised, jeopardized the treaty's prospects. Sharing their concern, the president promised to deal with these questions in his speeches.[9]

Wilson combined unilateralism and universalism in his uncompromising defense of the treaty. On September 4 he began his speaking tour in Ohio, Harding's home state. Acknowledging the treaty's severity on Germany, but denying any injustice, he argued that the League would prevent another war without using arms. By its unanimity of purpose, it would provide an effective deterrent against aggression. The president carried his fight to Indiana, whose two Republican senators, New and James E. Watson, favored strong reservations. He justified Article 10 as the "essential safeguard" against another war. Denying any partisanship in his position, he depicted himself as a true American. Just as Americans had defended their liberty during the Revolution, so now would they spread it throughout the world. He asserted that "we are ready to insist that everywhere men shall be champions of liberty." He interpreted the Covenant as authorization under international law for this global projection of American ideals. "In other words," Wilson proclaimed, "at present we have to mind our own business. Under the Covenant of the League of Nations we can mind other peoples' business, and anything that affects the peace of the world, whether we are parties to it or not, can by our delegates be brought to the attention of mankind."[10]

From this perspective, Wilson denied any distinction between nationalism and internationalism. In St. Louis, where the wavering mild reservationist Spencer lived, he affirmed that "the greatest nationalist is the man who wants his nation to be the greatest nation, and the greatest nation is the nation which penetrates to the heart of its duty and mission among the nations of the world." He defined the essence of world politics as the progressive fulfillment of this mission under the guidance of Divine Providence. He went on to explain how the United States could achieve such an exalted purpose through the League without using military force. Noting provisions for economic sanctions, he viewed the embargo on food as a powerful weapon. "That is the League of Nations," concluded the president, "an agreement to arbitrate or discuss, and an agreement that if you do not arbitrate or discuss, you shall be absolutely boycotted and starved out." This argument reflected his firm conviction that the United States could enter the League as the "senior partner." Contending that American membership would serve the United States as well as others, Wilson avowed that "the financial leadership will be ours. The industrial primacy will be ours. The commercial advantage will be ours. The other countries of the world are looking to us for leadership and direction." In short, the United States could control the world through the League.[11]

9　McCumber to WW, Aug. 29, 1919, Phelan to WW, Aug. 31, 1919, WW to Phelan, Sept. 1, 1919, WW Papers, Ser. 2, Box 192.
10　PPWW, V, 590-620; Watson to Strong, June 25, 1919, League to Enforce Peace Papers, Box 11.
11　PPWW, V, 620-45; Spencer to WHT, July 12, 1919, WHT Papers, Ser. 3, Box 452.

As Wilson's endeavor to mobilize public opinion failed to force the Senate to conform to his desires, he became increasingly desperate. He began to escalate charges against his political opponents. At first subtly but later directly, he accused them of serving the purposes of Bolshevism and Germanism. He identified the League with Christian civilization, claiming that the alternative was a chaotic world. In Kansas City, Reed's home, after referring to Russian affairs, the president challenged the treaty's foes to propose a better substitute. "Opposition is the specialty of those who are Bolshevistically inclined," he charged. He argued that all the world's "great peoples," except Germans, would participate in the League, and Germany, too, could later join after a period of probation. Failure of the United States to ratify the treaty would obviously isolate it from other great nations. In Iowa, represented by two moderate ¡Republican senators, Cummins and William S. Kenyon, Wilson developed this argument. "The isolation of the United States is at an end," he asserted, "not because we chose to go into politics of the world, but because by the sheer genius of this people and the growth of our power we have become a determining factor in the history of mankind, and after you have become a determining factor you cannot remain isolated, whether you want to or not." In Nebraska, Norris' residence, the president offered a systematic review of the Covenant. He tried to explain why there was no need for changes to protect American interests. He also began to defend the Shantung settlement. After taking the high road here, he switched to the low road in South Dakota. Although that state's Republican senator, Thomas Sterling, was a mild reservationist, Wilson sharpened his rhetoric as he called for "a fundamental choice" between the "old system" of international relations and the "new system" of the League. Charging that the "pro-German element" had begun to reassert itself, he told his audience that "your choice is between the League of Nations and Germanism." He thus tried to identify the League's critics with Bolshevism or Germanism.[12]

The president appealed to both American ideals and prejudices. In the tradition of Ralph Waldo Emerson and John L. O'Sullivan, major contributors to the concept of "manifest destiny" in the nineteenth century, he depicted the United States as the land of the future. "America does not march," he observed, "as so many other peoples march, looking back over its shoulder. It marches with its eyes not only forward, but with its eyes lifted to the distances of history, to the great events which are slowly culminating, in the Providence of God, in the lifting of civilization to new levels and new achievements. That is what makes us Americans." As he developed this conception of American nationalism, Wilson emphasized both its positive and negative aspects. The new League, he claimed, would embody the integral relationship of liberty, order and progress that had long character-

12 *PPWW*, VI, 1-57; Short to WHT, July 10, 1919, Kenyon to Secor, June 30, 1919, WHT Papers, Ser. 3, Box 451.

ized the United States. "Liberty," he proclaimed in St. Paul, Minnesota, "is a thing which is rooted and grounded in character, and the reason I am so certain that the leadership of the world, in respect of order and progress, belongs to America is that I know that these principles are rooted and grounded in the American character." By the same token, anyone opposing Wilson's project appeared less than patriotic. He now began to attack hyphenated Americans as the source of opposition to the League. He asserted that "the most un-American thing in the world is a hyphen." If ethnic groups wanted to remember their ancestral homes with fondness, Wilson did not object; but if they obstructed his purpose for the future, he condemned such actions as a conspiracy. He focused on German-Americans. Their disloyal purpose, he claimed, was to keep the United States out of the League so as to align it with Germany. These direct charges against hyphenated Americans, made in a state with a large ethnic population, obviously distorted political reality. During the treaty fight, Minnesota's Kellogg and Knute Nelson ranked next to McCumber as two Republican senators giving the greatest support to the president. But that reality failed to deter him from seeking scapegoats to explain his failure in the all-or-nothing confrontation with the Senate. This negative aspect followed logically from his complete identification of the League with American nationalism. [13]

Proceeding westward to the Pacific coast, the president repeated familiar themes of his earlier addresses. In McCumber's home state of North Dakota, also represented by irreconcilable Senator Asle J. Gronna, he defended American participation in the League as the inescapable consequence of modern interdependence. In Montana on September 11, the same day the Democratic minority in the Foreign Relations Committee submitted its report to the Senate, he reiterated his refusal to compromise. "It is either this treaty or a lone hand," he asserted, "and the lone hand must have a weapon in it." He defended the League as the alternative to Bolshevism that was threatening to spread from Russia across western Europe to the United States. Contributing to the Red Scare, Wilson claimed that "there are apostles of Lenin in our own midst." Alluding to the race riots and the Boston police strike, he urged his countrymen not to forget that "the pride of America is that it can exercise self-control." He wanted them to utilize this same quality in "the organization of the world for order and peace." In Borah's Idaho he continued to warn against the dual threat of Germanism and Bolshevism, reasserting that "the pro-German propaganda has started up in this country coincidently with the opposition to the adoption of this treaty." He likened Bolshevism to an infectious poison spreading from Russia through Europe, and cautioned that even the United States was not immune. Depicting the alternatives with such extreme rhetoric, Wilson rejected all amendments or reservations to the treaty. He claimed that any qualification in the resolution of ratification would reopen negotiations with

13 *PPWW*, VI, 57-89.

the Weimar Republic as well as the Allies. Conceding only the possibility of adopting interpretations in a separate resolution, he had not shifted his position since the White House conference.[14]

In the Pacific coast states Wilson turned more explicitly to the Irish and Japanese questions. Republican senators, who were targets of his campaign to influence public opinion here, ranged from Oregon's mild reservationist McNary to California's irreconcilable Johnson. Between them were Poindexter and Wesley L. Jones of Washington, who favored strong reservations. Eventually Poindexter joined the irreconcilables as an all-out foe of the League. The president defended the peace conference's decision to allow British dominions to participate as full members in the assembly. He argued that the single vote of the United States would equal the British Empire's six votes because any action by the League would require unanimity. Moreover, distinguishing between the council as the agency of action and the assembly as a forum for debate, he contended that the United States would enjoy complete equality with the British Empire where it really counted. He conveniently ignored the possibility of a British dominion's election to one of the council's temporary seats. He also denied that any member of the British Empire could vote in the assembly on a dispute involving another part of the empire. In short, although the British might have six votes, they could never use them in any way that would adversely affect the United States. "That settles that matter," Wilson emphasized in San Francisco, a city with a large Irish-American constituency, "and even some of my fellow countrymen who insist upon keeping a hyphen in the middle of their names ought to be satisfied with that." He also defended the Shantung settlement. Summarizing the history of Germany's exploitation of this province since 1898, when McKinley was in the White House, he contended that China lost nothing by the transfer of German rights to Japan. On the contrary, the Versailles Treaty promised new protection for China's sovereignty. If Japan failed to abide by its commitments, China could turn to the League.

Throughout this trip the president repeatedly demanded the Senate's approval of the treaty without any change. Not only did he reject amendments and reservations, he even opposed interpretations that might differ from his own. He left no doubt that in his opinion the Versailles peace depended upon the League exactly as prescribed in the Covenant. Rather than seeking accommodation, he continued to condemn Republican senators for serving Germany's purpose by advocating a policy of American isolation from the Old World. Wilson's despair apparently increased as his trip produced no favorable results back in Washington. To sustain himself he entrusted the League's fate to God. He told one audience that "I believe in Divine Providence. If I did not, I would go crazy. If I thought the direction of the disordered affairs of this world depended upon our finite intelligence,

14 PPWW, VI, 89-150; WW to Shaffer, Aug. 27, 1919, WW Papers, Ser. 2, Box 192.

I should not know how to reason my way to sanity, and I do not believe that there is any body of men, however they concert their power or their influence, that can defeat this great enterprise, which is the enterprise of divine mercy and peace and good will." Even if God was on his side in the treaty fight, the president still needed Republican votes in the Senate. Adopting Tumulty's suggestion for a new approach, he began to identify prominent Republicans with the League. He quoted earlier statements by Roosevelt and Lodge favoring the league idea, and suggested that Republicans had shifted their position out of sheer partisanship. The president challenged them to abandon their current negative stand or face the consequences in the 1920 elections. Attempting to bludgeon his Republican adversaries into accepting the treaty, he was not seeking a genuinely bipartisan foreign policy. Identifying the peace settlement with God's will, and its critics with Germanism or Bolshevism, left no room for compromise. The paranoid style of Wilson's politics reinforced the rigidity of his all-or-nothing stance in the treaty fight.[15]

I

Lodge looked beyond the Foreign Relations Committee to the voting in the Senate. To ensure adoption of strong or effective reservations, as he defined them, he needed all factions in the Republican party. That political reality dictated an accommodation with mild reservationists. He had moved in that direction within the committee with his four reservations, but McCumber's report signaled the necessity for further negotiations. In mid-August, before the committee had taken any action on amendments or reservations, he had initiated the process that would eventually lead to agreement. He enlisted Root's aid in persuading mild reservationists to cooperate in this Republican search for a consensus. Root warned Kellogg of the danger of too many reservations. He complied with his request to draft a reservation to replace the Shantung amendment, after the senator agreed to work toward a common set of reservations. For his approach to Colt, Root focused on Wilson's distinction between moral and legal obligations under Article 10. "To my mind," he reported his persuasive argument to Lodge, "the proposition that a moral obligation leaves room for the exercise of judgment as to whether the thing agreed upon shall be done or not while a legal obligation leaves no such opportunity is false, demoralizing and dishonest." He regarded the president's distinction as casuistry, and Colt agreed. Colt later made this point on the floor of the Senate. For now, however, he warned Root about the dire consequences of a Republican defeat of the treaty. Republican leaders, he feared, were determined to kill the treaty.

15 *PPWW*, VI, 150-326; JPT to WW, Sept. 12, 19, 20, 1919, JPT Papers, Box 7; JPT to WW, Sept. 19, 20, 1919, WW Papers, Ser. 2, Box 193.

Obviously, it would not be easy to prepare reservations that satisfied the entire party.[16]

Taft appreciated, as did Lodge, that mild reservationists could make a critical difference in the treaty fight. As long as Democratic senators remained faithful to Wilson, this small group of Republicans held the balance. They might determine what reservations the Senate included in the resolution of ratification. Taft hoped they could become the Republican nucleus of a bipartisan coalition to provide a two-thirds majority. This plan's success, as he fully recognized, depended upon the president's willingness to approve some reservations. Taft urged Kellogg to play a leading role in building this coalition. He feared that irreconcilables might seize control of the situation through the Foreign Relations Committee and defeat the treaty. In his contacts with mild reservationists, and also with Hitchcock and the White House, Taft promoted the Hughes reservations. He thought these would clearly protect American interests without jeopardizing the League's real value. Moreover, if Wilson endorsed the 1916 Republican candidate's suggestions, he could escape the appearance of partisanship. The Hughes reservations, however, lacked any real appeal for either him or Republican senators. The president preferred to plead his case for the treaty on the western trip, while Republicans turned their attention to the competing Lodge and McCumber reservations. McCumber secured a pledge from McNary, Colt, Nelson and Kellogg to adhere to their earlier mild reservations and to oppose any changes that would reopen the negotiations. He recognized, however, that they would need to make some concessions to expand the size of their group. The reservations that McCumber offered a few days later were his attempt to broaden the appeal of the mild reservationist alternative.[17]

Wilson's intransigence made some Democrats increasingly restless. Although Hitchcock and Pittman faithfully adhered to his position, two other Democratic members of the Foreign Relations Committee, in addition to Shields, began to consider compromising with Republicans on reservations. Swanson, the committee's second-ranking Democrat, continued to favor a conciliatory approach. He was especially critical of the sycophants surrounding the president and encouraging his inflexibility. Atlee Pomerene of Ohio now agreed with Swanson that Wilson should cooperate with mild reservationists while the opportunity still existed. When the rumor began to

16 HCL to ER, Aug. 15, Sept. 3, 1919, ER to HCL, Aug. 28, Sept. 10, 1919, ER Papers, Box 161, and HCL Papers; ER to Colt, Aug. 28, 1919, Colt to ER, Sept. 3, 1919, ER to Kellogg, Aug. 19, Sept. 8, 1919, Kellogg to ER, Aug. 21, 30, Sept. 6, 11, 1919, ER Papers, Box 137; CR, Vol. 58, 6925-26.
17 Colt to ALL, Aug. 11, 1919, Kellogg to ALL, Aug. 18, 1919, WHT to ALL, Aug. 14, 1919, ALL Papers; WHT to Kellogg, Aug. 15, 1919, Kellogg to WHT, Aug. 20, 1919, WHT Papers, Ser. 3, Box 454, and Kellogg Papers; Karger to WHT, Aug. 26, 28, 1919, WHT to Karger, Aug. 23, 24, 1919, WHT to Kellogg, Aug. 23, 1919, Kellogg to WHT, Aug. 29, 1919, McCumber to WHT, Aug. 30, 1919, WHT Papers, Ser. 3, Box 455; WHT to Kellogg, Aug. 23, 1919, Kellogg to WHT, Aug. 30, 1919, Kellogg Papers; Karger to WHT, Sept. 3, 1919, WHT to Hitchcock, Sept. 2, 1919, WHT Papers, Box 456.

circulate in mid-September that McCumber and Lodge had reached a compromise, Pomerene urged the president not to delay in reaching an accommodation with mild reservationists. Other Democratic senators such as Gore, Thomas, David I. Walsh of Massachusetts and Hoke Smith of Georgia appeared ready to join Shields in supporting at least some Lodge reservations. If enough Democrats defected, Lodge might secure a majority without mild reservationists, thereby denying them their pivotal role. Postmaster General Albert S. Burleson warned that even senators from cotton states of the South, which would provide Wilson's most solid bloc of votes during the treaty fight, were threatening to bolt. To prevent that possibility, Burleson applied pressure on them through cotton producers. He sent out the message that the treaty's prompt ratification could alone provide stable conditions in Europe for industrial recovery. Only then would American credits, primarily private but perhaps also from Washington, become available to finance the sale of cotton to Europe. Meanwhile, the surplus of this product would lower the price in the United States. Burleson enlisted cotton producers to lobby their senators to support the treaty as the quickest way to peace and their own economic prosperity. Also advising Wilson to woo Shields back into the Democratic fold rather than attack him for supporting three of Lodge's reservations, Burleson implicitly acknowledged how desperately the administration needed votes. Hitchcock and Oscar W. Underwood of Alabama, who shared the Democratic leadership in the Senate, both concurred in that advice.[18]

Underwood's stance exemplified the South's sensitivity to the cotton issue. He had not shown a great deal of interest in the League, but hoped to restore peace as soon as possible for the benefit of the American economy. Aware that the president had not adequately conferred with the Senate and that the treaty included some objectionable provisions, he nevertheless advocated its ratification as quickly as possible. After all, the United States could later withdraw from the League. In mid-July, during Hitchcock's absence, Underwood had faced a potential test vote on the treaty in the Senate. He met this challenge from Fall by agreeing to terminate enforcement of the Trading with the Enemy Act in exchange for removal of all references to the treaty from Fall's motion. Underwood readily made this concession because he, too, desired the early lifting of restrictions on American trade with other countries, noting the "vast importance" to the South of exporting cotton. The ensuing deadlock between Wilson and his Republican foes over the treaty troubled him as it threatened to postpone peace. He was more concerned about the consequences of delay for his region than with the League's fate. Although Underwood publicly praised the League, he

1 8   Forster to JPT, Sept. 8, 1919, WW Papers, Ser. 2, Box 192; Burleson to WW, Sept. 13, 22, 1919, NDB to JPT, Sept. 15, 1919, WW Papers, Ser. 2, Box 193; Burleson to WW, [Sept. 13, 22, 1919], Burleson Papers, Vol. 24; Karger to WHT, Sept. 5, 13, 1919, WHT to Karger, Sept. 8, 1919, WHT Papers, Ser. 3, Box 456; Miller to EMH, Sept. 16, 1919 (#3146), EMH Papers, 14/16.

privately acknowledged the cotton trade as a key factor in his determination to secure the Senate's prompt approval of the treaty.[19]

Wilson ignored all advice to compromise on reservations, choosing instead to insist that Democratic senators adhere to his all-or-nothing stance. On September 19, Vance McCormick sent him the ominous report that Lodge and mild reservationists were reaching agreement on a reservation to Article 10. He had previously informed the president that the Lodge reservations, or similar ones, might well pass and that the treaty could not attract the required two-thirds majority without reservations in the resolution of ratification. McCormick hoped the western tour would strengthen the president's position, but clearly implied that he should reconsider his options. Wilson immediately responded by rejecting any reservation to Article 10. Such a compromise, he insisted, amounted to total rejection of the Covenant.[20]

This inflexibility shattered Taft's hope for a bipartisan coalition. The president managed to keep the support of most Democratic senators, but at a tremendous cost. By preventing them from joining mild reservationists in a compromise, he weakened this one group of Republicans who were most desirous of establishing the League. He left them no option but to seek an agreement with their fellow Republicans as the only prospect for creating a two-thirds majority. He bore, in Taft's judgment, the primary blame for polarization between the parties. Taft certainly did not welcome this outcome, for he thoroughly distrusted Lodge's leadership. He considered the Foreign Relations Committee's report as "a flagrant exhibition of national selfishness, vanity and brutal disregard for the rest of the world." But his characterization of Wilson was even less flattering. "He is obstinate, egotistic, with a vanity so thick that it can not be penetrated, and a self love that exceeds almost that of anyone living," Taft privately confided. As mild reservationists negotiated with Lodge on a reservation to Article 10, Taft sought to strengthen them so as to preserve the real value of American membership in the League. He simultaneously endeavored to limit the influence of irreconcilables, who appeared to follow a "pro-German" course.[21]

19   Emery to Grew, March 19, 1919 (#1192), WW Papers, Ser. 5B, Reel 396; Lang to Underwood, May 23, 1919, Underwood to Lang, May 17, 1919, Gilmer to Underwood, June 11, 1919, Underwood to Gilmer, June 13, 1919, Kenna to Underwood, June 21, 1919, Underwood to Kenna, June 23, 1919, Carmichael to Underwood, July 18, 1919, Underwood to Carmichael, July 21, 1919, Ellison to Underwood, July 16, 1919, Underwood to Ellison, July 21, 1919, Bishop to Underwood, July 22, 1919, Underwood to Bishop, July 24, 1919, Smith to Underwood, Sept. 18, 1919, Underwood to Smith, Sept. 20, 1919, Oscar W. Underwood Papers, Alabama Department of Archives and History; *CR*, Vol. 58, 2600-02.

20   Forster to JPT [McCormick to WW], Sept. 18, 1919, WW to Forster, Sept. 19, 1919, WW Papers, Ser. 2, Box 193, and Hitchcock Papers, Vol. 1; McCormick to Forster, Sept. 8, 11, 1919, Forster to JPT, Sept. 12, 1919, WW Papers, Ser. 4, File 3211.

21   Karger to WHT, Sept. 8, 8, 10, 1919, WHT to Karger, Sept. 10, 1919, WHT Papers, Ser. 3, Box 456; WHT to Edwards, Sept. 16, 1919, WHT to Karger, Sept. 16, 1919, WHT to H. Taft, Sept. 16, 1919, WHT to Yost, Sept. 16, 1919, WHT Papers, Ser. 3, Box 457.

Partisan polarization produced serious tensions in the League to Enforce Peace. While continuing as its president, Taft felt increasingly dissatisfied with this organization's direction. Wanting it to advocate mild reservations, he thought it remained too subservient to Wilson. In his opinion, Democrats such as McAdoo and McCormick exerted too much influence on its decisions. Taft sharply criticized its secretary, William H. Short, for circulating a petition over his signature but without his authorization. This petition, which Short had distributed after the White House conference, essentially endorsed the president's position. It called for early ratification without amendments and with, at most, only interpretive reservations. It ignored the question of whether the reservations might be included in the resolution of ratification. Despite Taft's objections, the League to Enforce Peace collected signatures in thirty-nine states and submitted the petition to the Senate. Taft declined to attend a meeting of the executive committee on September 20, but through Lowell, Holt and Short, he urged it to call for mild reservations in the resolution of ratification. He hoped thereby to strengthen McCumber and his cohorts in their search for the best possible compromise. Wilson's idea of a separate interpretive resolution, Taft fully understood, was totally irrelevant. Lowell shared Taft's view that mild reservations offered the only realistic hope for ratification. The executive committee, however, decided not to publish any new statement, which might appear to weaken its advocacy of the League. It agreed, instead, to support mild reservationists privately. The executive committee of the League to Enforce Peace thus accepted its Washington bureau's advice, which followed McCumber's assessment that this course would fortify his position in the negotiations on an Article 10 reservation. Taft unhappily acquiesced.[22]

Wilson's refusal to seek a bipartisan coalition with mild reservationists assisted Lodge in unifying the Republican party. By rejecting all reservations in the resolution of ratification, the president forced mild reservationists to turn to Lodge in their desire to build a two-thirds majority. For his part, Lodge wanted to accommodate this group of senators in order to gain a majority for his reservations. The unanswered question was whether a compromise on an Article 10 reservation would most resemble Lodge's or McCumber's. Lodge wanted to remove both legal and moral obligations, while McCumber desired to leave the moral obligation. Both agreed that Congress, not the president alone, should decide when the United States would take military action or impose economic sanctions under Article 10 in

22   Short to Houston, Aug. 19, 1919, WHT Papers, Ser. 3, Box 454; Short to WHT, Aug. 21, 22, 23, 27, 1919, WHT to Short, Aug. 21, 23, 24, 25, 29, Sept. 10, 14, 1919, ALL to WHT, Sept. 12, 1919, WHT to ALL, Sept. 15, 1919, WHT Papers, Ser. 3, Box 456; ALL to WHT, Sept. 20, 1919, Minutes, Meeting of the Executive Committee, League to Enforce Peace, Sept. 20, 1919, WHT to Short, Sept. 19, 23, 25, 1919, WHT to ALL, Sept. 20, 28, 1919, Short to WHT, Sept. 22, 1919, WHT Papers, Ser. 3, Box 457; WHT to ALL, Sept. 10, 15, 20, 1919, WHT to Short, Sept. 14, 1919, WHT to Holt, Sept. 14, 1919, ALL to WHT, Sept. 20, 1919, ALL Papers; Auchincloss to EMH, Sept. 20, 1919, EMH Papers, 2/4; CR, Vol. 58, 5363-65.

response to external aggression. In mid-September, with McCumber's cooperation, Kellogg and McNary drafted a reservation to Article 10 for Lodge's consideration. He responded with a counterproposal, which mild reservationists accepted with one change. McCumber insisted upon this minor change so as, in his opinion, to preserve the moral obligation. On September 22, Lodge approved this compromise with mild reservationists, a group of six senators including McCumber, Kellogg, McNary, Nelson, Colt and Lenroot. The ambiguity of the compromise left doubts about American obligations. Whether the reservation would remove them altogether, or merely leave their interpretation to Congress, was the real question, as Lowell noted. McCumber admitted the ambiguity, but thought the compromise embodied Lowell's second alternative. In any event, he saw no other option for securing a two-thirds majority for the League.[23]

As Wilson continued his western tour across Nevada, he learned about the compromise between Lodge and the mild reservationists. He promptly responded after receiving a copy from Assistant Secretary Long, who had obtained it. On the next day, in Salt Lake City, Wilson denounced this reservation to Article 10. "That is a rejection of the Covenant," he proclaimed. He saw no ambiguity, but only total repudiation of his League. Not only did he condemn this particular reservation, he also ruled out all reservations as equivalent to amendments. He argued that any such qualification would require the approval of Germany as well as the Allies or, in other words, the reopening of peace negotiations. He tried to persuade his audience, and through them Republican senators such as Utah's Reed Smoot, that no reservation was necessary. Under the Covenant, he contended, the League council would never call upon the United States to halt aggression in some remote area such as the Balkans, unless a local war escalated into a global conflict. In that case, the United States would become involved regardless of the League. He promised benefits of world-wide leadership at a very modest cost to the United States. Renouncing the proposed Republican compromise, the president adhered to his all-or-nothing stance. In his view, a "final choice" confronted the American people: "Either we are going to guarantee civilization or we are going to abandon it." He wanted the United States to join the League and accept "the leadership of the world." Questioning the patriotism of his political adversaries, Wilson charged that "the only popular forces back of serious reservations" to the treaty were coming from pro-German sources. He warned that Germany

23   HCL to Williams, Sept. 6, 1919, Kellogg to HCL, Aug. 21, 1919, HCL Papers, File 1919 (Peace, League, Political, I-Z); Short to WHT, Sept. 15, 1919, Williams to WHT, Sept. 15, 1919, Kellogg-McNary Proposal, c. Sept. 14, 1919, WHT Papers, Ser. 3, Box 456; Karger to WHT, Sept. 17, 18, 1919, McCumber to Kellogg, Sept. 16, 1919, [HCL] reservation to Article 10, Williams to WHT, Sept. 19, 1919, Warner, Memorandum for Mr. Rickey, Lodge's counter-proposition to McCumber, Williams to WHT, Sept. 22, 1919, memorandum, Sept. 22, 1919, WHT to Short, Sept. 16, 1919, Short to WHT, Sept. 22, 1919, WHT Papers, Ser. 3, Box 457; Williams to ALL, Sept. 22, 1919, memorandum, Sept. 22, 1919, Lodge reservation to Article 10, ALL to McCumber, Sept. 23, 1919, McCumber to ALL, Sept. 26, 1919, McCumber-Lodge reservation to Article 10, ALL Papers.

might gain in the Senate what it had failed to win by war, if Republicans isolated the United States from the Allies.[24]

The choice, as Wilson defined it, was between unqualified approval and total rejection of the Versailles peace. He made this "extraordinary pronouncement" in Salt Lake City, but Tumulty, who accompanied him on his western tour, doubted that the audience fully understood. So he advised the president to dramatize his decision not to accept any reservations. In the remaining addresses through Wyoming and Colorado, Wilson attempted to follow Tumulty's advice. He reduced the treaty fight to "a show-down" between two absolutist alternatives. The Republican reservation to Article 10, he reiterated, would remove the moral obligation and consequently amount to rejection of the treaty. Because he would not proceed with the treaty's ratification with that reservation, its adoption would result in a separate peace with Germany. The United States faced the choice of "adoption or rejection," insisted the president. "We must either go in or stay out." He noted, quite correctly, that except for the Shantung settlement the principal criticism of the treaty focused on the League. He again offered his most persuasive arguments to explain why the Covenant would provide the best "insurance against a barbaric reversal of civilization" without endangering the United States. But he also reiterated his charges against hyphenated Americans. In the last address before his illness, on September 25, Wilson reasserted that organized propaganda against the League originated from that traitorous source. Actually, hyphenated Americans exerted only a marginal influence on the treaty fight. Precisely because of their weakness, ethnic minorities served as convenient scapegoats for his own failure.[25]

After his last address in Pueblo, Colorado, the exhausted president cancelled the remainder of his tour. On his physician's advice, he returned to Washington, where he suffered a tragic stroke on October 2. Before his collapse he had targeted primarily Republican senators, such as Wyoming's Francis E. Warren and Colorado's Lawrence C. Phipps. He had never expected his speeches in Missouri, for example, to force the Democratic irreconcilable Reed to become a League supporter. Of course, he hoped his appearance would assist Democratic senators, such as Phelan of California, in defending the treaty in their home states. In Colorado, Wilson was just beginning the phase of his tour that was directed more toward wavering Democrats such as Thomas. From there he had planned to travel through Kansas into Oklahoma, Arkansas, Tennessee and Kentucky. Democratic senators in these southern states, especially Shields, would have become the primary targets of Wilson's persuasion. Because his illness forced the cancellation of that part of his tour, his efforts to coerce the Senate through public opinion were chiefly aimed at Republicans, including mild and

2 4   Long Diary, Sept. 24, 1919, Long Papers, Box 2; Long to JPT, Sept. 22, 1919, Mason to JPT, Sept. 22, 1919, Forster to JPT, Sept. 22, 1919, WW Papers, Ser. 2, Box 193; *PPWW*, VI, 326-65.
2 5   JPT to WW, Sept. 24, 24, 1919, JPT Papers, Box 7; *PPWW*, VI, 365-416.

strong reservationists as well as irreconcilables. Refusing to compromise with any of them, the president had attempted to win the treaty fight by managing public opinion.[26]

Wilson's western tour totally failed to achieve its objective. Before his departure, General Leonard Wood had informed Lodge that sentiment in the West seemed to be running against the treaty and in favor of strong reservations. Concurring in that assessment at the time, Lodge saw no reason to change it as a consequence of the president's speeches. He concluded that Wilson had failed to rally public opinion or gain any support in the Senate for the treaty. Political bias apparently did not distort Lodge's perception, for Hitchcock had reached the same conclusion. Just before Wilson's illness, the Democratic leader reported to him that "the situation has not materially changed since you left here." That analysis directly challenged false optimism of the president and his entourage. Believing in rationality, he thought that if only he could explain the League to the American people and counter the misinformation emanating from its critics, he could win the treaty fight. His failure to manage public opinion toward that end perhaps contributed to his physical and emotional collapse.[27]

Members of Wilson's cabinet agreed with Lodge and Hitchcock that the western tour had failed. Secretary of War Baker recognized the difference between the president's popular reception in the West and the impact on the Senate. "He seems to have been received with very great enthusiasm and to have had every evidence given him of the popularity of the treaty and the covenant," Baker informed Ambassador Hugh C. Wallace in Paris, "but I do not believe, so far as I can discover from the talk here, that his work among the people has had any effect one way or the other upon the Senate." Baker himself had loyally supported the president despite his own misgivings about the treaty. In June, Lippmann had condemned the harsh conditions which it imposed on Germany, expressing his doubt that the League could moderate them. Preferring revision rather than enforcement, he consequently opposed any American commitment to the status quo in either the League or the alliance with France. Baker had conceded that "there is a distinct variance in some of these matters, both from what we all expected and even from what we would now desire as making for a permanent readjustment on harmonious lines of world relationships." But, as he explained to Lippmann, he continued to hope that the League could foster "the spirit of accommodation" and correct the treaty's shortcomings. As the fight over the League intensified during the summer of 1919, he sharply criticized Taft for

26 "Wilson's Appeal to the West," *Literary Digest*, LXII (Sept. 13, 1919), 14-15; Forster to JPT, Sept. 25, 1919, JPT to McCormick, Sept. 25, 1919, WW Papers, Ser. 4, File 3211.

27 Wood to HCL, Aug. 15, 1919, HCL to Wood, Aug. 18, 1919, HCL Papers, File 1919 (Peace, League, Political, I-Z); HCL to Berry, Sept. 11, 1919, HCL Papers, File 1919 (Peace, League, Political, A-H); HCL to Bigelow, Sept. 15, 1919, HCL Papers, File 1919 (Adams-Trevelyan); HCL to HW, Sept. 30, 1919, HCL Papers, File 1919 (Henry White); WW to Kohlsaat, Aug. 27, 1919, WW to Lamont, Aug. 29, 1919, WW Papers, Ser. 2, Box 192; WW to Lamont, Sept. 19, 1919, Hitchcock to JPT, Sept. 24, 1919, WW Papers, Ser. 2, Box 193; Hitchcock to JPT, Sept. 24, 1919, Hitchcock Papers, Vol. 1.

recommending reservations. Loyally supporting the president, Baker nevertheless recognized the political reality in Washington.[28]

Failure of Wilson's western tour came as no surprise to Lansing. He had advised the president to compromise, and continued to see this course as the only way to save the treaty. Trying to find some face-saving procedure for him to use in approaching Republicans, Lansing suggested that he might promise to support amendments to the Covenant after the League's establishment, or offer to accept reservations of a purely interpretive character. The secretary saw accommodation, instead of the confrontation that Wilson practiced on his western tour, as the appropriate method of gaining Republican votes. This advice fell on deaf ears, especially after William C. Bullitt gave his testimony to the Foreign Relations Committee on September 12. A former employee of the State Department in the Division of Western European Affairs, Bullitt had served in Paris during the peace conference in the Current Intelligence Section. He had frequently met with the American delegates to give them briefings before he resigned in protest against the Versailles Treaty. Summoned to testify by the Republican majority, he revealed not only documents on the Covenant's origins and other aspects of the peace settlement but also confidential conversations. Most devastating of all were his revelations of Lansing's criticism of the League. "I consider that the League of Nations at present is entirely useless," Bullitt quoted the secretary from a May 19 conversation. "The great powers have simply gone ahead and arranged the world to suit themselves." According to Bullitt, Lansing had then commented on the treaty's prospects in the Senate. "I believe," he allegedly said, "that if the Senate could only understand what this treaty means, and if the American people could really understand, it would unquestionably be defeated, but I wonder if they will ever understand what it lets them in for." Because of the accuracy of Bullitt's testimony, Lansing made no public attempt to discredit it. This silence, combined with his lukewarm endorsement of the League in a speech to the American Bar Association earlier in September, gave Wilson little justification for believing the secretary's private assurance that he favored the treaty without reservations. His advice that the president should seek a compromise with Republicans also pointed to the opposite conclusion. This evidence of Lansing's attitude contributed to the alienation between him and Wilson. Despite the accuracy of his assessment of the treaty's fate in the Senate if the president persisted in his rigid stance, the secretary lacked the ability to persuade Wilson to change.[29]

28 Lippmann to NDB, June 9, 1919, NDB to Lippmann, June 13, 1919, NDB to Peabody, July 30, 1919, NDB Papers, Box 10; NDB to Westhaver, June 15, 1919, WHT to NDB, July 8, 1919, Wallace to NDB, July 1, 1919, NDB to Wallace, Sept. 27, 1919, NDB Papers, Box 11; NDB to WW, July 24, 1919, WW Papers, Ser. 2, Box 190.
29 RL to Polk, Sept. 2, 1919, Polk to RL, Sept. 22, 1919, Polk Papers, 78/14; RL to Polk, Oct. 1, 1919, Polk Papers, 78/15; RL Diary, IV, May 19, 1919; Phillips to Polk, Sept. 4, 11, 18, 26, 1919, Polk Papers, 78/97; HW to HCL, Sept. 19, 1919, ER Papers, Box 161, and HCL Papers; HCL to HW, June 12, Oct. 2, 1919, HCL Papers, File 1919 (Henry White); HCL to Bennett, Aug. 18, 1919, HCL

Nevertheless, irreconcilables feared that Wilson might compromise to save the treaty. To promote his failure, the League for the Preservation of American Independence used its resources to influence public opinion. It sponsored speaking tours by Senators Johnson, Borah and Reed. Their rallies attracted substantial attendance, causing anxiety for some of Wilson's associates. McAdoo, who shared Tumulty's generally optimistic view of the president's tour, worried that the League's opponents seemed more active than its proponents. The competing campaigns to shape public opinion contributed to a stalemate. Although pleased with the popular response at anti-League rallies, Borah concluded that irreconcilables had not yet achieved their objective. He still anticipated the treaty's ratification with reservations. That outcome, of course, would depend upon the president's willingness to compromise. The possibility that he might seek an accommodation with Lodge and mild reservationists was the nightmare that haunted irreconcilables. These extremists could prevent Wilson from monopolizing the management of public opinion, but they, too, lacked the power to determine the League's fate. He might still obtain the Senate's approval of the treaty if he abandoned his own extremist position. Although he could not by himself control foreign relations, by cooperating with the Senate he might lead the United States into the League. The postwar role of the United States in world affairs therefore depended upon Wilson's choice between maintaining or compromising his all-or-nothing stance in the treaty fight.[30]

II

As the Senate prepared to vote on various amendments and reservations, the Versailles Treaty clearly lacked a two-thirds majority. Democrats, however, preferred to ignore this reality. Anticipating defeat of the Foreign Relations Committee's amendments and possibly even its reservations, they focused on these immediate questions rather than on building a bipartisan coalition of sixty-four votes. Wilson's intransigence left his supporters no room to maneuver in the politics of peacemaking. Hitchcock informed him that the Fall and Shantung amendments would definitely fail, and that Johnson's would probably experience the same fate. Senators Joseph T. Robinson of Arkansas and Thomas Walsh offered even more optimistic assessments as they predicted

Papers, File 1919 (Peace, League, Political, A-H); RL to WW, Sept. 5, 1919, WW Papers, Ser. 4, File 4767; RL to WW, Sept. 17, 1919, WW Papers, Ser. 2, Box 193; Auchincloss to EMH, Sept. 15, 1919, EMH Papers, 2/4; U.S. Senate, *Proceedings of the Committee on Foreign Relations*, 161, 188; U.S. Senate, *Treaty of Peace with Germany: Hearings*, 1161-1292.

30 L. A. Coolidge to HCL, Sept. 5, 1919, HCL Papers, File 1919 (Peace, League, Political, A-H); Reed to Carpenter, Aug. 18, 1919, WHT Papers, Ser. 3, Box 454; Clark to ER, Sept. 20, 1919, ER Papers, Box 137; Knox to Beveridge, Sept. 10, 1919, Beveridge Papers, Box 215; McAdoo to JPT, Sept. 30, 1919, Beveridge Papers, Box 215; McAdoo to JPT, Sept. 30, 1919, WW Papers, Ser. 4, File 331; Borah to Coffin, Sept. 27, 1919, Borah to Williams, Sept. 9, 1919, Wood to Borah, Sept. 6, 1919, Borah Papers, Box 551; Borah to Paul, Sept. 30, 1919, Borah Papers, Box 550; Beveridge to Reed, [Sept. 1919], Reed to Beveridge, Sept. 24, 1919, Beveridge Papers, Box 217.

defeat of Lodge's reservations as well. The president welcomed especially this fanciful news. Avoiding such fantastic predictions, Hitchcock and Underwood soberly recognized that most senators wanted some reservations. Because Wilson was unwilling to accept this political reality, before as well as after his stroke, these Democratic leaders refrained from urging a compromise prior to the voting in the Senate. They entrusted the treaty to future developments despite their awareness that his western tour had not forced the Republican majority, or even all Democrats, to accept the treaty without qualifications.[31]

Wilson's defiant attitude toward reservations failed to deter the Republican leadership. Root advised Lodge that if the president persisted in his stance, thereby preventing the treaty's ratification, the Senate should declare an end to the war by a joint or concurrent resolution. The prospect that Wilson might kill the treaty caused Lodge no anxiety. Like Root, he saw him as "an awful bluffer" and expected him eventually to compromise. Anticipating that contingency, Lodge wanted strong reservations to protect American interests and also to create the opportunity for ratification. He did not want to bear responsibility for the treaty's defeat. As the voting pattern on amendments and reservations would reveal, he correctly understood his colleagues' views. Given the attitudes of Republican senators, Lodge offered the only real hope for American ratification. Despite his deep personal and political hostility toward Wilson, he provided the best opportunity for the United States to join the League.[32]

Lodge endorsed amendments as well as reservations, but he did not regard them as a necessity. This attitude governed his stance during the controversy over the platform at the Massachusetts Republican convention on October 4. In cooperation with Louis A. Coolidge, he effectively controlled the drafting of the plank dealing with the treaty. Before the Senate had voted on any amendments, he recommended a plank stipulating only the necessity for effective reservations. At the convention ex-Senator Murray Crane and other proponents of the League insisted upon adding the words "without amendment" to the plank's call for prompt ratification. Lodge acquiesced in this change, although he told the convention he would not be bound by it. He would continue supporting amendments. Pro-League advocates such as Taft regarded Crane's success as a significant triumph over Lodge, while anti-League critics such as Knox and Beveridge viewed it as a serious defeat. In fact, it was neither. Lodge conceded this change in the plank to preserve harmony within the Republican party in order to ensure re-election of Calvin Coolidge as governor of Massachusetts. Moreover, the revised plank did not

3 1   Forster to JPT, Sept. 23, 24, 1919, Hitchcock to JPT, Sept. 24, 1919, Robinson to WW, Sept. 25, 1919, WW to Robinson, Sept. 25, 1919, Treaty Poll As Per "S," [Sept. 1919], WW Papers, Ser. 2, Box 193; Forster to JPT, Sept. 24, 1919, WW Papers, Ser. 4, File 4767; Hitchcock to JPT, Sept. 24, 1919, Hitchcock Papers, Vol. 1; Treaty Poll As Per "S," [Sept. 1919], Hitchcock Papers, Vol. 2; JPT to WW, Sept. 30, 1919, JPT Papers, Box 7; Poole to Underwood, Sept. 29, 1919, Underwood to Smith, Oct. 4, 1919, Underwood Papers.
3 2   ER to HCL, Sept. 26, 1919, HCL to ER, Sept. 29, 1919, ER Papers, Box 161, and HCL Papers.

substantially alter Lodge's original recommendation but simply made explicit what he had implied. Whether or not the Senate amended the treaty, he favored its ratification. He demanded only effective reservations.[33]

Lodge's position at the state convention anticipated his role in the Senate during the voting on the treaty. He supported amendments but concentrated his efforts primarily on strong reservations. To ensure a majority for them, he needed to preserve harmony among all factions of the Republican party. By the time the Senate began to vote, partisan polarization created a sharp division between Republicans and Democrats with few exceptions. Voting on almost all amendments, reservations and procedural questions, as well as on the treaty itself, followed a general pattern, as shown by a Guttman scale analysis of all roll-call votes relating to the treaty. Except for Reed, Shields, Gore and David Walsh, all Democratic senators voted solidly as a bloc. Republicans were less cohesive. From La Follette at one extreme to McCumber at the other, they ranged from irreconcilables through strong reservationists to mild reservationists. Yet these different groups did not represent distinct voting blocs. Irreconcilables, as defined by their opposition to the treaty either with or without reservations, generally favored the most extreme changes in the treaty. They provided the greatest support for substantial amendments and reservations. But in the ranking of senators on the basis of all roll calls, there was no clear-cut division between irreconcilables and strong reservationists. Nor was there a sharp distinction between those who demanded strong reservations before approving the treaty and those who wanted only mild reservations. Different factions within the Republican party blended together in a continuum during the voting. At the irreconcilable end of this continuum, senators demanded the most extreme amendments and reservations without necessarily favoring the treaty even with these changes; at the other end, mild reservationists opposed amendments and preferred more moderate qualifications. In the middle, Republican senators generally endorsed amendments, but did not regard them as essential conditions for approving the treaty. They approved its ratification with strong reservations. As Republican leader, Lodge faced the difficult task of maintaining sufficient unity to provide a majority for the Foreign Relations Committee's reservations, thereby forcing Wilson to ratify the treaty with those reservations or bear responsibility for killing it.[34]

33   Crocker to HCL, Oct. 15, 1919, HCL to Crocker, Oct. 18, 1919, HCL to Bird, Oct. 8, 1919, HCL to Bernard, Oct. 10, 1919, C. Coolidge to HCL, Oct. 6, 1919, HCL to C. Coolidge, Oct. 8, 1919, L. A. Coolidge to HCL, Sept. 15, 22, 26, 30, Oct. 1, 1919, HCL to L. A. Coolidge, Sept. 19, 23, 27, 29, Oct. 20, 1919, HCL to Hatch, Oct. 10, 1919, HCL Papers, File 1919 (Peace, League, Political, A-H); WHT to McCumber, Oct. 5, 1919, WHT Papers, Ser. 3, Box 458; Beveridge to Knox, Oct. 6, 1919, Knox to Beveridge, Oct. 7, 1919, Beveridge Papers, Box 215; Beveridge to HCL, Oct. 6, 1919, Beveridge Papers, Box 216, and HCL Papers; Hooker to JPT, Oct. 3, 1919, Lynch to JPT, Oct. 4, 1919, WW Papers, Ser. 4, File 4767; Beveridge to Hays, Oct. 5, 1919, Hays Papers.
34   Observations about the Senate's voting pattern are based on a Guttman scale analysis of all roll calls relating to the Versailles Treaty, including amendments, reservations and procedural questions, in all three sessions of the 66th Congress.

Beginning on October 2, the Senate first disposed of the Fall amendments. After the White House conference Fall had submitted a list of questions to Wilson. The president's answers failed to convince him that the United States should assume major responsibilities for enforcing the treaty. Consequently, he advocated amendments as the most effective way of excluding American participation from the various commissions designed to implement the treaty. The Senate voted first on an amendment to strike the provision associating the United States with the Allies in determining the precise boundaries between Germany and Belgium. This amendment's purpose, Fall told his colleagues, was "to see that the United States has nothing to do with boundary lines and does not pledge herself to a moral or legal obligation hereafter to send her troops and stand them across those lines to preserve them eternally." Other Republican members of the Foreign Relations Committee voiced similar unwillingness to undertake continuing responsibilities in the Old World. "I do not see," Brandegee asserted, "why the United States must be a member of these 35 commissions to determine these European questions, about which we know nothing and in which we are most remotely interested." Lending his support, Lodge sounded more isolationist now than ever before during the treaty fight: "I have as little desire to interfere in the boundaries of the European countries, beyond maintaining the decisions of the conference as they are agreed to at this time, as I have to have them interfere in ours." These arguments failed to persuade a majority to accept this amendment. A bipartisan coalition of Democrats and mild reservationist Republicans voted against it. Three more of the Fall amendments suffered the same defeat. One of them would have excluded American representation from the governing commission for the Saar Basin, which the League would appoint. Another would have cancelled any American responsibility for requiring Czechoslovakia to conclude a treaty with the Allies in which that new nation promised to protect the interests of its racial, linguistic and religious minorities. The other amendment would have prohibited American representation on the international commission for Upper Silesia and excluded American troops from occupying that region. After defeating these four amendments by substantial majorities, the Senate disposed of the remaining Fall amendments without roll calls. Although these amendments were the least popular of the Foreign Relations Committee's recommendations, they received more than one-third of the votes on the roll calls. Because the treaty would require a two-thirds majority, their appeal among Republican senators heralded the treaty's eventual fate unless Wilson made significant concessions.[35]

Rejection of the Fall amendments bolstered Hitchcock's confidence that the Senate would defeat all the Foreign Relations Committee's amendments. Yet this expected action only slightly discouraged Borah as he anticipated

35   Fall, list of questions, [Aug. 19, 1919], WW to Fall, Aug. 20, 1919, WW Papers, Ser. 4, File 5033; CR, Vol. 58, 6133-43, 6265-81.

greater support for the Shantung and Johnson amendments, which he regarded as more important. Moreover, he pursued the primary goal of defeating the entire treaty. Like other irreconcilables, he preferred its clear-cut rejection. In contrast, Lodge advocated amendments as well as reservations to broaden the treaty's appeal. He gave the greatest personal endorsement to the Shantung amendment, which he had introduced in the committee. In his view, Japan was "the coming danger to the world" as it followed the German example of aggression. Nevertheless, wanting to avoid war, he ruled out any military action to restore Shantung to China. "I am not going into an argument as to whether or not we ought to interfere in Shantung," Lodge asserted, "although I draw a distinction between Asia, where we are an Asiatic power, holding the Philippines, and Europe, where we have no interests whatever." He hoped either to force Japan to surrender its gains in Shantung to China or to escape any American complicity in the peace treaty which sanctioned them.[36]

Norris voiced the strongest denunciation of the Shantung settlement. Like Lodge, he condemned the president for giving "our official sanction to the robbery." He accused him of missing the opportunity at Paris to return Shantung to China without war. In his opinion, Wilson could have mobilized public opinion throughout the world so as to force Japan to acquiesce. If the United States approved the treaty without amendment, Norris claimed, it would assist Japan in achieving mastery over China, as it already had over Korea, and this "will put the clock of civilization back a thousand years." He shared Wilson's progressive philosophy but applied it in a fundamentally different way. He advocated the amendment or rejection of the treaty to serve "the cause of freedom, of liberty, of Christianity, and of an advancing civilization."[37]

Most Democrats, including Wilson's strongest defenders, remained silent during the debate over Shantung. McCumber responded to his Republican colleagues by emphasizing the risk of a strong anti-Japanese position. He contended that the only certain way for the United States to halt Japanese influence over China was by resorting to war. Unless Americans were prepared to pay that price, which he did not favor, he argued that the League would provide the best method for protecting China. Shields lacked McCumber's enthusiasm for the League, but similarly focused on the Shantung amendment's false promise. By adopting it, the United States would interfere in the conflict between China and Japan, whereas the avowed purpose of the Article 10 reservation was to avoid such foreign entanglement. This appeared to the Tennessee senator as a contradiction. He was no

36   NDB to Hitchcock, Oct. 14, 1919, Hitchcock Papers, Vol. 1; Hitchcock to NDB, Oct. 14, 1919, NDB Papers, Box 10; Phillips to Polk, Sept. 9, 1919, Polk Papers, 82/2; RL to A.C.N.P., Oct. 14, 1919, Polk Papers, 82/3; Borah to Parkhurst, Oct. 9, 1919, Borah to Hodgins, Oct. 11, 1919, Borah to Dunne, Oct. 9, 1919, Borah Papers, Box 550; HCL to Chanler, Aug. 18, 1919, HCL to Forbes, Aug. 9, 1919, HCL Papers, File 1919 (Peace, League, Political, A–H); CR, Vol. 58, 6872-80, 6952.
37   CR, Vol. 58, 6788-6826.

more desirous of assuming obligations to protect China than other weak countries around the globe. Democrats and mild reservationist Republicans combined to defeat the Shantung amendment on October 16. Lodge then tried to eliminate the treaty's provisions relating to Shantung. This new amendment answered Shields' objections and gained his vote, but still failed on November 4 by a similar margin. These Shantung amendments were scarcely more acceptable to the Senate than Fall's.[38]

Considerably more appealing were the Foreign Relations Committee's recommendations to guarantee voting equality between the United States and the British Empire. The Johnson amendment, in effect, would change the Covenant to give the United States six votes in the League assembly. It neglected the possibility of a dispute between the United States and Great Britain, or one of its dominions or colonies. In that case, the American government could not vote, but other parts of the British Empire might use their five votes. To prevent that possibility, the Moses amendment would prohibit either the mother country or any dominion or colony from voting in the League on a dispute involving any of them. Both amendments enjoyed Lodge's formal, if not enthusiastic, endorsement. He thought the prominent British role in drafting the Covenant had produced anxiety among Americans about the League. British interference with the Monroe Doctrine further exacerbated Anglo-American relations. This gave an opportunity to the American Irish, which they exploited with the nearly unanimous adoption of Borah's Irish resolution. Lodge himself did not share intense anti-British or pro-Irish attitudes that characterized many of his colleagues. He saw no justification for excluding Canada, Australia, New Zealand or South Africa from voting in the League, although he was dubious about India's inclusion.[39]

Irreconcilables concentrated their attack on the League by focusing on voting equality. They feared that Great Britain would control the League. Beveridge asked Lodge to allow ample time to consider the Johnson amendment in order to arouse the American people. The Republican leader complied with this request, but this delay also allowed pro-League senators to test their strength on the less popular Fall and Shantung amendments.[40]

Reed had intensified this controversy on September 22 with a dramatic disclosure. He revealed to the Senate a letter to Sir Robert Borden, Canada's prime minister, from Clemenceau, Wilson and Lloyd George, affirming the right of self-governing dominions to be elected to the League council. At the peace conference Borden had insisted that British dominions should enjoy

3 8 CR, Vol. 58, 6880-83, 6934-36, 7012-13, 7941-42.
3 9 HCL to Charnwood, July 2, 1919, HCL Papers, File 1919 (Peace, League, Political, A-H).
4 0 Notes, Aug. 23, 1919, Anderson Papers, Box 4; Beveridge to Cummins, Sept. 22, 1919, Beveridge Papers, Box 214; Beveridge to Johnson, Sept. 24, 1919, Beveridge Papers, Box 215; Beveridge to HCL, Sept. 20, 1919, HCL to Beveridge, Sept. 22, 1919, Beveridge Papers, Box 216, and HCL Papers; New to Beveridge, Sept. 17, 1919, Beveridge Papers, Box 217; Williams to WHT, Sept. 27, 1919, WHT Papers, Ser. 3, Box 457.

the same opportunity as other League members to fill the rotating seats in the council. Because of the Covenant's ambiguity, he had requested a clarification and succeeded in extracting the letter on May 6. Recently released in Ottawa, this letter appeared to Reed to confirm the British Empire's dangerous control over the League. It seemed like a startling contradiction to the president's assurances during his western tour that the United States would suffer no disadvantage vis-à-vis the British Empire despite its six votes in the assembly. The threat to American sovereignty, Reed asserted, bordered on "the edge of treason." From his perspective, Wilson's claim that the League could exert significant influence throughout the world, yet not endanger the United States, was clearly contradictory.[41]

In the wake of Reed's disclosure, Johnson advocated his amendment. Preaching his "doctrine of Americanism," he insisted that his purpose was not anti-British, but pro-American. Against the evidence of the Borden letter and the nationalist appeals of irreconcilables, two of Wilson's loyal defenders, Williams and Pittman, offered pitiable responses. Despite the documentation, they claimed that British dominions could not be elected by the assembly to the council. Thomas Walsh suggested a more plausible explanation by reminding senators that, regardless of the number of British votes, the United States could veto any decision for action by the League council. Unable to convince irreconcilables, Williams resorted to scapegoating by blaming hyphenated Americans. He denounced ethnic minorities for retaining their ancestral loyalties and hatreds. This search for scapegoats replaced rational debate.[42]

Mild reservationists reeled under the impact of Reed's disclosure of the Borden letter. Even Taft, who earlier had learned about it from Canada's prime minister, stiffened his position. Initially inclined to accept Borden's interpretation, he reversed himself in the furor over Reed's revelation and pressed his own reservation as a better alternative to the Foreign Relations Committee's amendments. His reservation would limit the British Empire to one seat on the League council and prohibit all parts of it from voting in the assembly if either Great Britain or a self-governing dominion or colony was involved in a dispute. Kellogg angrily reacted to the Borden letter. In view of Wilson's duplicity, he considered voting for the Johnson amendment. McCumber appealed to Taft to come to Washington to prevent other mild reservationists from reacting that same way. Early in October, Taft visited several senators and corresponded with others to oppose the Johnson amendment. Mild reservationists, including Kellogg, soon rallied against the Foreign Relations Committee's amendments, but not in favor of Taft's reservation. Instead, they generally turned to Lenroot's reservation, which stipulated that the United States would not be obligated by any decision of the League council or assembly if any other power plus its self-governing dominions and colonies cast more than one vote. By promising to support this reservation, mild reservationists hoped to defeat the amendments. They feared, however, that enough Democrats might defect to provide a majority for the Johnson amendment. Not all Republican senators whom Taft lobbied responded as he desired. Charles E. Townsend of Michigan, whom he tried to convince by playing ethnic politics, refused to commit himself against the Johnson amendment. [43]

Root contributed his influence to shift the Senate from amendments to reservations. At the request of Senator Walter E. Edge of New Jersey, he analyzed the difference between these two forms of qualification. Although carefully avoiding any criticism of senators who favored amendments, he stated his preference for reservations. Proposing a reservation to deal with the British Empire's votes in the League, he clearly implied his opposition to the amendments. Edge used Root's letter to encourage Republican senators to oppose the Johnson amendment. [44] Root's position differed only slightly from Lodge's. During the debate, the Republican leader announced his intention to vote for the Foreign Relations Committee's amendments, but simultaneously indicated his willingness to approve the treaty without them. [45]

Prepared to accept defeat of the Johnson and Moses amendments, Lodge left their fate to others. Ironically, the only Democratic senator to offer an extensive argument against them was Thomas, who later voted against the treaty because of its labor provisions. Emphasizing the common heritage of the United States and the British Empire, he preferred a reservation to protect his country from the slight danger of six British votes. As most Democrats remained silent, the debate raged primarily within the Republican party between irreconcilables and mild reservationists. McCumber argued repeatedly that six British votes posed no threat to the United States. He claimed that no British dominion could become a member of the League council. Like Williams and Pittman, he rejected the contrary evidence of the Borden letter. He also denied that Great Britain could control the

4 3   WHT to Yost, July 29, 1919, WHT Papers, Ser. 3, Box 453; WHT to McCumber, Aug. 15, 1919, WHT Papers, Ser. 3, Box 454; WHT to Karger, Aug. 31, 1919, WHT Papers, Ser. 3, Box 455; Karger to WHT, Sept. 23, 24, 28, 1919, Williams to WHT, Sept. 23, 1919, WHT to Kellogg, Sept. 24, 1919, Kellogg to WHT, Sept. 25, 1919, McCumber to WHT, Sept. 25, 1919, McNary to WHT, Sept. 26, 1919, WHT to Karger, Sept. 29, 1919, WHT Papers, Ser. 3, Box 457; WHT to Colt, Oct. 5, 1919, WHT to Kellogg, Oct. 5, 1919, WHT to ALL, Oct. 5, 1919, WHT to McCumber, Oct. 5, 1919, WHT to McNary, Oct. 5, 1919, Karger to WHT, Oct. 6, 1919, WHT to Townsend, Oct. 7, 11, 1919, McNary to WHT, Oct. 9, 1919, Townsend to WHT, Oct. 9, 1919, WHT to Kellogg, Oct. 11, 1919, WHT to Capper, Oct. 12, 1919, WHT to Yost, Oct. 13, 1919, WHT Papers, Ser. 3, Box 458; Karger to WHT, Oct. 17, 1919, WHT to Karger, Oct. 21, 1919, Colt to WHT, Oct. 25, 1919, Kellogg to WHT, Oct. 27, 1919, Karger to WHT, Oct. 29, 1919, WHT Papers, Ser. 3, Box 459; WHT to Kellogg, Oct. 3, 5, 11, 1919, Kellogg to WHT, Sept. 25, Oct. 27, 1919, Kellogg Papers, Box 5; Boyd to JPT, Sept. 23, 1919, WW Papers, Ser. 2, Box 193; Notes, Oct. 1, 1919, Anderson Papers, Box 4.
4 4   Edge to ER, Sept. 26, Oct. 3, 8, 1919, ER to Edge, Oct. 1, 7, 1919, ER Papers, Box 137.
4 5   CR, Vol. 58, 7488-91.

dominions' votes. Restrictions on the League's powers, including the requirement for unanimity for any action, provided further protection for the United States. Moreover, McCumber based his confidence on American power to shape international relations. "Our position," he said, "will always make us a dominant power." Other mild reservationists joined McCumber in the debate with irreconcilables over the committee's amendments. Unlike Thomas, Republican irreconcilables stressed the danger of British domination of the League and defined the issue of voting equality as a test of American loyalty. In a typical accusation, Senator Medill McCormick of Illinois charged that "in the course of this debate Senators have become more royalist than kings and more English than the English themselves."[46]

Despite passionate appeals to American nationalism, advocates of the Johnson and Moses amendments failed to convince a majority. By a narrow margin of two votes the Senate defeated Johnson's on October 27. A coalition of forty Democrats and mild reservationist Republicans voted against this most popular amendment; eight more senators abstained but indicated their opposition to it. Two days later, by a larger margin, the same bipartisan coalition rejected the Moses amendment as well as a substitute for it offered by Shields. Recoiling from these defeats, Johnson immediately proposed a new amendment that combined features of the Foreign Relations Committee's two amendments to guarantee voting equality, but it experienced the same fate.

Democrats and mild reservationists again united to defeat La Follette's amendment. It was designed to preserve complete freedom for the United States to formulate its own labor policy by eliminating Part XIII from the treaty. That part provided for establishment of an International Labor Organization and uniform standards to improve working conditions. A few Democratic senators criticized these labor provisions for posing the threat of international socialism. Henry L. Myers of Montana claimed that the proposed organization "would provide a nursery for the germination, sprouting, and dissemination of socialistic and bolshevistic doctrines." Reed, Thomas and David Walsh also favored the amendment. Reed agreed that Part XIII would introduce "the principle of Bolshevism" by allowing organized labor "to control the destiny of the world." These anti-Bolshevik diatribes failed, however, to secure a majority for the La Follette amendment.[47]

Two amendments appealed to fewer than one-third of the senators, mostly at the irreconcilable end of the spectrum. Calling the treaty a "Godless document" and the peace conference a "Godless body of men," Sherman offered his amendment to remedy this deficiency. Using Abraham Lincoln's closing words in the Emancipation Proclamation, the Illinois senator sought to "invoke the considerate judgment of mankind and the gracious favor of

46 *CR*, Vol. 58, 6326-38, 6439-46, 6588-90, 6925-26, 7320-28, 7355-73, 7436-39, 7491-7504.
47 *CR*, Vol. 58, 7431-36, 7548-82, 7677-80, 7683-92, 7762, 7797-7812, 7957-69.

Almighty God." As the best means of achieving this same goal, Gore sought to democratize the League. His amendment called for an advisory vote of the people before the governments could resort to war. By democratizing the decision-making, he hoped to prevent or at least reduce the chances of war. "The voice of the people," the Oklahoma Democrat proclaimed, "is the nearest approach to the voice of God." As if to parody Wilson, these two amendments appealed to democracy and Divine Providence, both of which the president had repeatedly invoked in defending the treaty. Their resounding defeat indicated that most senators considered them inappropriate. By rejecting all amendments, a bipartisan majority demonstrated its reluctance to insist upon changes in the treaty itself. Yet over one-third of the senators, more than enough to kill the treaty, voted for every amendment except Sherman's and Gore's. This voting pattern clearly indicated that Wilson and Democratic senators needed to accommodate strong reservationist Republicans if they wanted to ensure the Versailles Treaty's ratification. Even with nine mild reservationists who consistently opposed all amendments, Democrats lacked the votes for a two-thirds majority.[48]

III

Democrats refused to seek an accommodation with Republicans. Early in October, while encouraging mild reservationists to oppose the Johnson amendment, Taft implored Hitchcock and Underwood to seek a compromise with them. He hoped his own reservations might serve as the basis for a Democratic counterproposal. Although Tumulty had confirmed the president's openness to "clarifying reservations," Democrats refused to negotiate with their most likely Republican allies. While Hitchcock remained noncommittal, Underwood revealed political considerations for this refusal. Forty Democratic senators, he explained, were firmly committed to the treaty without amendments or reservations. But several of them actually desired some reservations. Consequently, any attempt by Democratic leaders to compromise with mild reservationists might result in their loss of control as other Democratic senators might offer their own additional reservations. In this precarious situation, Hitchcock saw no realistic alternative other than advocating the treaty's ratification without qualification. He also defended this tactic as the best way to avoid delay. Even Swanson, who had consistently favored a compromise, now agreed. Wilson's adherence to the politics of confrontation foreclosed all prospects for serious bipartisan attempts at conciliation.[49]

48   CR, Vol. 58, 6703, 7680-83, 7953-57, 8011-13.
49   Karger to WHT, Sept. 30, 1919, WHT Papers, Ser. 3, Box 457; WHT to ALL, Oct. 5, 1919, WHT to Hitchcock, Oct. 7, 1919, WHT to Underwood, Oct. 7, 11, 1919, WHT to Karger, Oct. 8, 1919, Underwood to WHT, Oct. 9, 1919, WHT Papers, Ser. 3, Box 458; WHT to ALL, Oct. 5, 1919, ALL Papers; WHT to Hitchcock, Oct. 7, 1919, Hitchcock Papers, Vol. 1; Swanson to Churchill, Oct. 10, League to Enforce Peace Papers, Box 11.

With no opportunity for a bipartisan compromise, mild reservationists and their Republican colleagues worked together to formulate a common set of reservations. Toward that end, Lodge made major concessions to mild reservationists. Once it became apparent that the Senate would reject all amendments, he reconvened the Foreign Relations Committee and introduced a preamble and twelve reservations as a substitute for the four it had previously adopted. He had originally achieved agreement on reservations dealing with withdrawal, domestic affairs and the Monroe Doctrine. Through subsequent intraparty negotiations, he had also prepared an Article 10 reservation. All Republicans in the committee, from McCumber to irreconcilables, united to approve new versions of these four crucial reservations. Except for Shields, who also supported them, Democrats offered futile resistance. Hitchcock introduced substitute reservations concerning Article 10, internal affairs, the Monroe Doctrine and also Shantung, but the committee defeated each of them. Even some Democratic senators besides Shields defected.

The committee adopted all of Lodge's reservations and two others from Shields. Some of Lodge's new reservations, including one withholding American approval of the Shantung settlement and retaining full liberty for American action toward a Sino-Japanese conflict, replaced the amendments which the Senate had defeated. Several of them, including some from other Republicans, were designed to protect congressional prerogatives in foreign affairs. Kellogg had urged one reservation, which Chandler Anderson had originally proposed. It stipulated that Congress would retain the right to provide by law for American representation in the League and other international bodies and that any American representative's appointment would require the Senate's approval. Another reservation, which Anderson had prepared, would exempt the United States from contributing to help pay the expenses of implementing the treaty, including the League's costs, unless Congress appropriated the funds. Under two other Lodge reservations, Congress would retain its discretion regarding acceptance of mandates from the League, and of regulations from the Reparation Commission relative to American trade with Germany. Another reservation would allow the United States to increase its armaments in case of invasion or war, regardless of whether it had earlier accepted a limitation as proposed by the League council under Article 8. Two other reservations would safeguard rights of American citizens. According to one, if the League subjected a state to a boycott under Article 16, Americans could still maintain economic and other relations with its nationals in the United States or elsewhere outside that state. This proviso would, it was hoped, prevent a foreign dispute from creating ethnic conflict within the United States by clarifying that the boycott would apply only to the covenant-breaking state, not to immigrants. Under the other, Americans would retain their right to challenge any decision of the Alien Property Custodian in the courts of the United States. One of Shields' reservations stipulated that the United States would renounce any responsibility for Germany's former overseas possessions. The other one, originally proposed by Reed to the committee, provided that the United States would retain the exclusive right to decide what questions affected its honor and vital interests and that these questions could not be submitted to arbitration or to the League council or assembly. With the committee's approval of the preamble and these fourteen reservations, Lodge reported them to the Senate on October 24. Although mild reservationists were not fully satisfied, he had achieved substantial unity among Republicans with this new set of reservations.[50]

Mild reservationists focused their criticism on the preamble and the Reed reservation. The other reservations, although not altogether desirable, seemed an acceptable price to achieve ratification. McCumber and Kellogg led the fight to modify the preamble. In the committee McCumber had attempted unsuccessfully to delete its requirement for three of the four principal Allies to accept the reservations. Upon further reflection, he saw in it "a covert purpose to destroy our ratification entirely." He anticipated that Japan would refuse to acquiesce in the reservations because of Shantung, and Italy because of Fiume. Even France and Great Britain might withhold their approval. Refusal by any two of these powers would invalidate American ratification. He therefore urged the eight other stellar mild reservationists – Kellogg, Nelson, McNary, Colt, Hale, Sterling, Edge and Henry W. Keyes of New Hampshire – to oppose this stringent requirement. They did not accept this assessment. Kellogg, McNary and Hale foresaw a greater risk in the Senate's possible rejection of the treaty unless the preamble demanded some indication of the Allies' consent to the reservations. Kellogg and Lenroot explored with Lodge some modification of the preamble which would keep the requirement and yet facilitate compliance by the Allies. Lodge suggested a simple exchange of diplomatic notes. Kellogg then brought Lowell into these discussions for the dual purpose of persuading Lodge to revise the preamble and committing the League to Enforce Peace to the reservations. After consulting several mild reservationists, Lowell approved Lodge's suggestion. Accordingly, Lodge incorporated this minor modification in the preamble to the Foreign Relations Committee's reservations, which he formally introduced in the Senate on November 6. All mild reservationists except McCumber now accepted the preamble. By accommo-

50   U.S. Senate, *Proceedings of the Committee on Foreign Relations*, 189-99; *CR*, Vol. 58, 7417-18; HCL to Hays, Oct. 20, 1919, HCL Papers, File 1919 (Peace, League, Political, A-H); Kellogg to HCL, July 22, 1919, Anderson to Kellogg, July 4, 1919, C. P. A[nderson], reservations, Oct. 1, 1919, Kellogg to HCL, Sept. 9, Oct. 3, 1919, HCL to Kellogg, Oct. 9, 1919, HCL Papers, File 1919 (Peace, League, Political, I-Z); Kellogg to Anderson, Sept. 27, 1919, Brandegee to Anderson, Oct. 16, 1919, Anderson to HCL, Oct. 22, 1919, Anderson Papers, Box 4; Cummings to ALL, Oct. 31, 1919, McCumber to Crocker, Oct. 29, 1919, ALL to Cummings, Nov. 1, 1919, ALL Papers; WHT to McNary, Sept. 20, 1919, WHT to Karger, Sept. 21, 1919, WHT Papers, Ser. 3, Box 457; memorandum, Oct. 22, 1919, WHT to McCumber, Oct. 22, 23, 1919, WHT to Colt, Oct. 23, 1919, McCumber to WHT, Oct. 24, 24, 1919, WHT to Yost, Oct. 27, 1919, McNary to WHT, Oct. 28, 1919, WHT to H. Taft, Oct. 29, 1919, WHT Papers, Ser. 3, Box 459.

dating mild reservationists, Lodge once again succeeded in uniting his party.[51]

As Republicans rallied behind the Lodge reservations, Hitchcock and Underwood prepared for confrontation. Knowing that they could count on only some forty Democratic votes, Hitchcock formulated a plan that could, they hoped, transform defeat into victory. In accordance with Wilson's desire, he intended to oppose the Lodge reservations to the bitter end. He realized that Democrats could not prevent their adoption by a majority. After denying a two-thirds majority for the Republican resolution of ratification, he hoped to secure reconsideration and offer a Democratic resolution for unqualified ratification, which he also expected to fail. At that point of stalemate, he planned to propose interpretive reservations as the basis for compromise. He promised no real concessions to Republicans but hoped somehow miraculously to create a two-thirds majority. In accordance with Hitchcock's plan, Underwood stated the issue before the Senate as total acceptance or rejection of the Versailles Treaty. Lodge defined the crucial question in a different way. The Senate could either approve the treaty with his reservations or defeat it. "If these reservations are put on the treaty," he pledged, "it will be ratified; and it will not be ratified, in my judgment, in any other way."[52]

Hitchcock's plan appeared to Taft and others in the League to Enforce Peace to condemn the treaty to defeat. "The Democrats are playing the fool," Taft concluded at the beginning of November 1919. "If they were to appoint a committee to deal with the mild reservationists, who are now increased to nine, I should think they might control the situation; but if they wait and defeat the resolution of ratification, the wrath of the country will be poured on them and not the Republicans." When Hitchcock persisted in his plan after meeting Wilson at the White House, the League to Enforce Peace's executive committee began preparations for shifting its public position. Having previously advocated unqualified ratification, it now prepared to call for ratification with the Lodge reservations. Lowell agreed with Taft that this option offered the only realistic possibility for achieving American membership in the League. This conclusion emerged from a growing realization that Wilson's intransigence foreclosed a bipartisan compromise between mild reservationists and Democrats. Attributing this outcome to his "egotism"

51   Kellogg to ALL, Oct. 31, 1919, ALL to Kellogg, Nov. 1, 1919, McCumber to ALL, Nov. 1, 1919, McCumber to [Colt, Nelson, McNary, Kellogg, Hale, Edge, Keyes and Sterling], Nov. 1, 1919, ALL to McCumber, Nov. 3, 1919, ALL to WHT, Nov. 1, 1919, WHT to ALL, Nov. 3, 1919, ALL Papers; WHT to Kellogg, Oct. 29, 1919, Kellogg Papers, Box 5; Short to WHT, Oct. 23, 1919, WHT to Colt, Oct. 29, 1919, WHT to McNary, Oct. 29, 1919, Williams to WHT, Oct. 31, 1919, Williams, Memorandum, Oct. 29, 1919, WHT Papers, Ser. 3, Box 459; ALL to WHT, Nov. 1, 1919, WHT to Williams, Nov. 1, 1919, WHT to Yost, Nov. 1, 1919, WHT to ALL, Nov. 3, 1919, Karger to WHT, Nov. 3, 6, 1919, WHT to Karger, Nov. 5, 1919, WHT Papers, Ser. 3, Box 460; Kellogg to ER, Oct. 31, 1919, ER to Kellogg, Nov. 12, 1919, ER Papers, Box 137; CR, Vol. 58, 8022-27, 8057-58, 8066-74.
52   CR, Vol. 58, 7882-86, 8017-22; Hitchcock to EMH, Oct. 22, 1919, EMH to Hitchcock, Oct. 25, 1919, EMH Papers, 10/27; Phillips to Polk, Nov. 10, 1919, Polk Papers, 82/5.

and "personal vanity," Taft felt it "shows how hollow is his real desire for a League of Nations, except as he may be the author and promoter of it and may have it his way." Taft now anticipated that irreconcilables would combine with Democrats to defeat the treaty. Despite the contrary views of some members, such as McAdoo, the executive committee decided to change its policy. Hitchcock made belated appeals to Taft and Lowell for their continued acquiescence in his plan. He criticized especially the preamble and the Article 10 reservation. But his argument against the Lodge reservations failed to persuade. Announcing the executive committee's decision on November 18, the Washington bureau called for "the immediate ratification of the treaty, even with its reservations," but with a change in the preamble to permit the "silent acquiescence" of the Allies. This statement noted that the Reed reservation, which the executive committee opposed, had already been defeated by the Senate.[53]

Adhering to Hitchcock's plan, the Democrats lacked the votes to prevent adoption of most of the Foreign Relations Committee's reservations. By November 15, acting as a committee of the whole, the Senate approved all twelve reservations which Lodge had introduced in the committee. Four Democratic senators, Reed, Gore, David Walsh and Hoke Smith, consistently aligned with Republicans to provide a solid majority. Additional Democrats defected and supported some of the more popular reservations, including those relating to domestic affairs, the Monroe Doctrine and mandates. Almost without exception, mild reservationists voted with their Republican colleagues. Only three of them attempted further modifications of the Lodge reservations. Hale introduced an amendment to the reservation concerning domestic affairs in order to include disputes over American boundaries and overseas possessions. Shattering the unity of both parties, this proposal attracted a bipartisan majority which included both Lodge and Hitchcock. Nevertheless, at Lodge's instigation, Hale later withdrew this amendment. In contrast, Nelson and McCumber failed to win the votes of other Republicans for their changes. As only Democrats joined them, the Senate rejected Nelson's amendment to the withdrawal reservation, so as to require a joint instead of a concurrent resolution, and McCumber's substitute for the Shantung reservation. McCumber then opposed Lodge's Shantung reservation, but otherwise all Republican senators voted solidly for the twelve Lodge reservations.

This pattern of uniform Republican support did not apply to the committee's reservations originating from Shields and Reed. On November

53   Williams to WHT, Oct. 1, 1919, WHT to Short, Oct. 12, 1919, WHT Papers, Ser. 3, Box 458; WHT to Vandenberg, Oct. 21, 1919, McAdoo to WHT, Oct. 23, 1919, WHT Papers, Ser. 3, Box 459; WHT to Karger, Nov. 1, 8, 11, 1919, Williams to WHT, Nov. 4, 1919, Short to WHT, Nov. 6, 10, 15, 1919, ALL to WHT, Nov. 8, 1919, ALL to Short, Nov. 8, 1919, Karger to WHT, Nov. 10, 1919, WHT to McCumber, New Haven, Nov. 10, 1919, Hitchcock to WHT, Nov. 12, 1919, WHT Papers, Ser. 3, Box 460; Hitchcock to ALL, Nov. 15, 1919, ALL Papers; WHT to Hitchcock, Nov. 15, 1919, Hitchcock Papers, Vol 1; *CR*, Vol. 58, 8773-74.

17 various Republicans joined Democrats to overwhelm the Shields reservation by more than a two-thirds majority, while mild reservationists and Democrats aligned together against the Reed reservation, as they had earlier done to defeat the amendments. McCumber and the League to Enforce Peace successfully organized against the Reed reservation, which they regarded as the most destructive. After these two reservations from Democratic senators failed, the prevailing Republican majority added two others. On November 18 the Senate passed McCumber's reservation stipulating that the United States would withhold its assent to Part XIII of the treaty unless Congress authorized American representation in the International Labor Organization. It also adopted a reservation to ensure voting equality for the United States with the British Empire. Because the Senate had not yet defeated the Johnson and Moses amendments when the Foreign Relations Committee reconvened to consider reservations, Lodge had not proposed one on this subject. During the fight over those amendments, Republicans had generally agreed on the Lenroot reservation as a substitute. Accordingly, rejecting the alternative proposals of Johnson and McCumber, they united behind the Lenroot reservation.

All other proposals for reservations failed. The Republican majority that Lodge had forged defeated various attempts by Democratic senators to offer amendments to or substitutes for his reservations. It also rejected all additional reservations, including five from La Follette to require the United States to withdraw from the League unless other nations conformed to his strict standards, and one to prohibit the United States from helping Great Britain to crush a rebellion in Ireland, India, Egypt, or elsewhere, or from assisting any other country such as Japan to exploit weaker people. As Lodge had anticipated and desired, the Senate passed only his twelve reservations and the two of McCumber and Lenroot. With the preamble, these fourteen reservations constituted the Republican majority's conditions for ratifying the Versailles Treaty.[54]

Of all these reservations, the one relating to Article 10 created the greatest

54 *CR*, Vol. 58, 8074-80, 8121-40, 8192-8218, 8271-96, 8365-73, 8413-37, 8546-71, 8617-44, 8699-8760; RL to Polk, Nov. 14, 1919 (#3769), Polk Papers, 82/6; WHT to Karger, Nov. 7, 1919, WHT to Williams, Nov. 7, 1919, WHT to Yost, Nov. 7, 1919, McCumber to WHT, Nov. 15, 1919, WHT Papers, Ser. 3, Box 460; WHT to McCumber, Nov. 16, 1919, WHT to Short, Nov. 16, 1919, WHT to Capper, Nov. 17, 1919, WHT to Hale, Nov. 17, 1919, WHT to Kellogg, Nov. 17, 1919, Kellogg to WHT, Nov. 17, 1919, WHT to Keyes, Nov. 17, 1919, Keyes to WHT, Nov. 17, 1919, WHT to ALL, Nov. 17, 1919, WHT to Smoot, Nov. 17, 24, 1919, WHT to Sterling, Nov. 17, 1919, WHT to Townsend, Nov. 17, 1919, Townsend to WHT, Nov. 17, 1919, WHT to Warren, Nov. 17, 1919, Warren to WHT, Nov. 17, 1919, Smoot to WHT, Nov. 18, 1919, WHT Papers, Ser. 3, Box 461; WHT to Kellogg, Nov. 17, 1919, Kellogg to WHT, Nov. 17, 1919, Kellogg Papers; WHT to Lowell, Nov. 17, 1919, Colt to ALL, Nov. 18, 1919, ALL to Hale, Nov. 17, 1919, ALL to McNary, Nov. 17, 1919, ALL to Colt, Nov. 17, 1919, ALL to Kellogg, Nov. 17, 1919, ALL to McCumber, Nov. 17, 1919, McCumber to ALL, Nov. 15, 1919, ALL Papers; HCL to Bigelow, Nov. 12, 1919, HCL to Adams, Nov. 17, 1919, HCL Papers, File 1919 (Adams-Trevelyan); HCL to Hobbs, Nov. 10, 1919, HCL Papers, File 1919 (Peace, League, Political, A-H); HCL to Washburn, Nov. 15, 1919, HCL Papers, File 1919 (Peace, League, Political, I-Z); HCL to Beveridge, Nov. 15, 1919, Beveridge Papers, Box 116, and HCL Papers.

obstacle to compromise. Both Republicans and Democrats focused on its future implications for American foreign policy and for executive-legislative relations. Irreconcilables wanted to avoid altogether any American obligation under Article 10. They opposed not only this commitment to other nations but also the delegation of authority to the president to determine when to fulfill it. If approved, they argued, it would allow the president to deploy American armed forces anywhere in the world without a declaration of war by Congress. Introducing a substitute for the Lodge reservation to Article 10, Borah attempted to prevent the United States from accepting either legal or moral obligations. This irreconcilable alternative attracted only eighteen votes as most Republicans, including Lodge, joined Democrats to defeat it by more than a two-thirds majority. This roll call, which did not fit the typical pattern, demonstrated the potential for defeating irreconcilables if Democrats could unite with both strong and mild reservationist Republicans.

Republicans defeated all Democratic attempts to change their Article 10 reservation. In the debate Thomas Walsh made two revealing assertions. Claiming that the United States could defend itself, he affirmed that it did not need the League for its national security. This affirmation that Americans could unilaterally protect their own interests expressed a consensus that Wilson's loyal supporters and the irreconcilables shared. The League appeared to both groups as an altruistic American contribution to the world. Disagreement between them concerned whether to make the gift. Walsh contended, moreover, that Article 10 would impose no legal or moral obligation to accept the League council's advice during a future crisis. It would empower the nations to unite against war, yet leave them free to determine their own actions. In short, the extent of future American contributions would depend upon the United States. Stressing the limits of Article 10, Walsh's advocacy of the League failed to assuage Republicans. Unwilling to weaken the Lodge reservation to this article, they rejected Thomas' attempt to substitute the alternative which McCumber had proposed in his report on September 15. The Democratic minority, despite having shown no interest at that time, now preferred McCumber's reservation to Lodge's. But even mild reservationists, including McCumber himself, recognized that the Lodge reservation offered the only realistic prospect for ratification. Consequently, all Republican factions voted against this belated Democratic endorsement of McCumber's milder alternative. Expressing their distrust of future presidential action as commander in chief, they also opposed Walsh's attempt to delete the constitutionally dubious assertion in the Lodge reservation that Congress had the sole power to authorize employment of American military and naval forces. In frustration, Walsh offered an addition to the Lodge reservation that would cancel all obligations under Article 10. "The Walsh amendment," Pittman proclaimed, "is simply a declaration to those who do not understand that the existing reservation is a fraud." Only La Follette and Norris joined Walsh and Pittman in a strange coalition in favor of this declaration. Most Republican senators adhered to the Lodge reservation, while Democrats generally refused to abandon their hopes for Article 10.[55]

Democratic senators failed to alter or defeat the Lodge reservation to Article 10. Hitchcock opposed the reservation by emphasizing both the importance and the limits of Article 10. Because of this article, he argued, the League could effectively deter German aggression against the new nations of Poland, Czechoslovakia and Yugoslavia. Yet the United States would retain its freedom to accept or reject the council's advice for fulfilling this moral obligation during a future crisis. Meanwhile, he saw no necessity for maintaining American armies in Europe. In short, he interpreted Article 10 as an effective, yet inexpensive, deterrent. Robinson denounced supporters of the Lodge reservation for seeking "to preserve the United States in a condition of isolation." Denying this charge, Lodge reaffirmed the position he had advocated in December 1918. He still wanted to assist Germany's neighbors as barriers against its aggression. "But when I held that opinion," he explained, "I never for a moment contemplated that we were to be handed out a document which bound us for all time, without any possible limitation anywhere." Lodge would approve specific commitments of a limited variety, but not the vague and indefinite obligations of Article 10. This fundamental difference between his perspective and the Wilsonian idea of a moral obligation, not just the political importance of Republican unity, led Lodge to reject piecemeal efforts of Democratic senators to address some of his concerns. Under his leadership, Republicans opposed Thomas' amendment to his reservation to limit Article 10's obligations to five years. They also defeated attempts of Walsh of Montana and Kenneth McKellar of Tennessee to specify those obligations to Poland, Czechoslovakia and Yugoslavia, and to France in Alsace-Lorraine, for five years. The prevailing Republican majority also rejected Hitchcock's substitute for the Lodge reservation that affirmed the right of Congress to accept or reject the League council's advice under Article 10, and a similar substitute by Robert L. Owen. It defeated, moreover, Hitchcock's attempt to add the deleted fifth section of the Knox resolution to the Lodge reservation. After resisting all efforts to change it, Republicans approved this reservation on November 13. Only thirty-three Democrats voted against it as the president desired. On the crucial question of Article 10, Lodge triumphed over Wilson in the Senate.[56]

Hitchcock's substitute for Lodge's Article 10 reservation was one of a series of five reservations that he proposed to the Senate. Before leaving Washington on his western tour early in September, Wilson had secretly shared with the Nebraska senator his suggestion for the correct interpretation

---

55   CR, Vol. 58, 8193-8214, 8420-21; Adee to Polk, Oct. 17, 1919 (#3464), Polk Papers, 82/4; Borah to Schmidt, Nov. 6, 1919, Borah Papers, Box 550; McCumber to WHT, Nov. 8, 1919, WHT to Yost, Nov. 12, 1919, WHT Papers, Ser. 3, Box 460.
56   CR, Vol. 58, 8214-18, 8271-96, 8365-73, 8422-37; Williams to WHT, Nov. 11, 1919, WHT Papers, Ser. 3, Box 460.

of the Covenant on the controversial issues of withdrawal, Article 10, domestic affairs and the Monroe Doctrine. Using the president's suggestion as a model, Hitchcock prepared four interpretive reservations to cover these issues and a fifth to deal with voting equality. Without revealing Wilson's contribution, he offered these five reservations on November 13 to replace Lodge's. Hitchcock attempted to substitute his reservations on domestic affairs and the Monroe Doctrine for the Foreign Relations Committee's, but with no more success than in the case of Article 10. Subsequently, on November 19, he endeavored to win the Senate's approval of all five reservations, but the Republican majority steadfastly resisted. As alternatives to Lodge's, Hitchcock's reservations appealed to only forty-one Democrats. Attracting no Republican votes, and not even a presidential endorsement, they provided no basis for a bipartisan compromise. The willingness of Democratic senators to vote without Wilson's approval for the Hitchcock reservations and other alternatives, however, demonstrated that the president was the principal obstacle to compromise. Although Hitchcock offered his substitutes too late to entice even mild reservationists, his actions showed a flexibility unmatched by the White House.[57]

As the final vote on the Versailles Treaty approached, Hitchcock attempted to implement his plan. For its success, he needed both to prevent Democrats from defecting and to bring Republicans into negotiations for a bipartisan compromise. Working through Mrs. Wilson, he tried to convince the president to assist in this dual task. He drafted a letter from Wilson to himself, urging Democratic senators to defeat the Lodge reservations as a prelude to "a possible compromise agreement on a resolution that will make ratification possible." Tumulty encouraged the president to adopt this approach. But Underwood worked against Hitchcock by advising Wilson to insist that Democrats vote against the Lodge resolution and then for the treaty's unconditional ratification. He promised that this procedure would enable the president "to dictate the terms of settlement between the different forces in the Senate." Although Mrs. Wilson jealously guarded her husband, Hitchcock went to the White House on November 17 to see him again. At this meeting Wilson remained intransigent. He was in no mood to compromise with Republicans, and certainly not with Lodge. He firmly rejected their reservation to Article 10. Declining even to endorse Hitchcock's interpretive reservations, he acquiesced only in the senator's desire to contact Republicans in search of a possible basis for accommodation. Determined to retain his own complete freedom, the president wanted them to make the first overture. He still insisted on dealing with Republicans on his own terms. Learning about this meeting from Tumulty, Lansing recognized the futility of this course, which could only consolidate

57   Hitchcock to EBW, Nov. 13, 1919, Proposed Substitute Reservations, WW Papers, Ser. 2, Box 193; Suggestion, [Sept. 1919], Hitchcock Papers, Vol. 1; Hitchcock, Nebraska, the World War and the World Peace, 1925, Gilbert M. Hitchcock Papers, Nebraska State Historical Society; CR, Vol. 58, 8433, 8800.

the opposition. He realized that the most favorable time for a bipartisan compromise had already passed and that Republicans would not now offer concessions. "The President," Lansing informed Polk, "is with his back to the wall and means to go down rather than surrender."

Hitchcock searched for a way to break the deadlock. On November 18 he approached Lodge with a proposal on procedure. Both of them expected Lodge's resolution of ratification to receive less than a two-thirds majority. After that failure Hitchcock wanted to reconsider the treaty and then to introduce a resolution of ratification with his interpretive reservations. The two sides could then attempt to reach a compromise. During the consideration of this proposal, he refused to indicate what kind of compromise Democrats might approve as he could speak for neither the president nor the senators of his party. Under these conditions, after consulting his Republican colleagues, Lodge declined the proposal. Hitchcock appreciated that the only person who could break this deadlock was Wilson. He now appealed to the president to accept the Republican reservation to Article 10 in order to save the treaty. He forwarded to the White House a letter from Thomas Walsh advocating acceptance of this reservation as a reasonable price to preserve all of the League's benefits. In his effort to persuade, Hitchcock informed the president that many Democratic senators agreed with Walsh. The choice that Wilson now faced, as Hitchcock and Walsh clearly presented it, was whether to save most of the treaty by compromising with Republicans or to sacrifice it altogether by insisting upon unqualified acceptance.[58]

Before the final vote, other Republican and Democratic senators explored possible ways to compromise, but the president destroyed any chance of success. Kellogg and Charles Curtis urged Hitchcock to take the initiative, but he hesitated to act without Wilson's permission. Pomerene sought to persuade McCumber to present a resolution as the basis for bipartisan agreement. Swanson appealed for delay to allow time for a compromise. All these efforts failed as the president denounced any action by the Senate other than unqualified approval of the treaty. Editing Hitchcock's suggested draft, he prepared a letter to the senator outlining his advice. He called upon Democrats to defeat Lodge's resolution of ratification with reservations, denouncing it as "the nullification of the treaty." Deleting the section of Hitchcock's draft referring to "a possible compromise agreement on a resolution that will make ratification possible," he expected instead "a genuine resolution of ratification." With this letter Wilson destroyed Hitchcock's plan for a bipartisan compromise, leaving him in a very

58   Hitchcock to EBW, Nov. 15, 17, 18, 1919, A Suggestion, [Nov. 17, 1919, for WW to Hitchcock], Walsh to Hitchcock, Nov. 18, 1919, JPT to EBW, Nov. 11, 1919, JPT to WW, Nov. 11, 1919, WW Papers, Ser. 2, Box 193; JPT to WW, Nov. 11, 17, 1919, JPT Papers, Box 7; JPT to EBW, Nov. 17, 1919, JPT Papers, Box 3; RL to Polk, Nov. 17, 1919, Polk Papers, 78/16; Phillips to Polk, Nov. 17, 1919, Polk Papers, 78/97; Hitchcock, Nebraska, the World War and the World Peace, 1925, Hitchcock Papers, Nebraska State Historical Society; Williams to WHT, [Nov. 17, 1919], WHT Papers, Ser. 3, Box 461; HCL to ER, Dec. 3, 1919, ER Papers, Box 161, and HCL Papers.

awkward position. In the morning of November 19 the senator read the letter to his colleagues in the Democratic conference. Lodge obtained a copy from the press and brought it to the entire Senate's attention in the afternoon. Hitchcock still talked about a possible compromise, but his words were hollow. He could not offer even his own interpretive reservations with the assurance that the president would accept them. At first he tried to disavow them, but then presented his reservations for official action. Under these conditions he could not win support of a single mild reservationist.

Mild reservationists preferred Lodge's leadership to Wilson's. Defending the Lodge reservations, Lenroot asserted: "These reservations do nothing more nor less than to Americanize this treaty so far as it affects us." With reference to the Article 10 reservation, Kellogg reminded senators that "it was drawn by the friends of the treaty who did not wish, in the face of our Constitution, to agree to make war in defense of the territorial integrity of every country on the face of the earth without a vote of the Congress." McCumber placed the responsibility squarely on Democratic senators for killing the treaty if they complied with Wilson's request to defeat Lodge's resolution of ratification.[59]

With Wilson's help, irreconcilables succeeded in preventing the Senate from approving the treaty either with or without reservations. Mild reservationists aligned with strong reservationists in favor of Lodge's resolution of ratification, but Democrats, except Gore, Shields, Hoke Smith and David Walsh, refused to join them. On a second vote, three more Democrats – Myers, Owen and Pomerene – defected. But most Democrats, adhering to the president's position, formed a coalition with Republican irreconcilables to defeat the resolution. Irreconcilables had feared that Democrats would eventually approve reservations, possibly even Lodge's, as a way of saving the treaty. Instead of pursuing that course, Democratic senators enabled the irreconcilables to achieve their goal of keeping the United States out of the League. After defeat of his resolution by votes of 39 to 55 and 41 to 50, Lodge permitted Underwood to introduce a resolution of unqualified ratification. Irreconcilables continued their opposition, now rejoining the Republican majority against the treaty. Five Democrats supported this negative majority of fifty-three votes, while only McCumber crossed the partisan division the other way. Even with him the Democratic leadership could muster only thirty-eight votes for unqualified ratification. The Versailles Treaty failed to win even a simple majority. As Wilson forced a choice between total approval or rejection of the League, the Senate now selected the option of defeating the treaty.[60]

59   Herbert F. Margulies rightly emphasized the contribution of mild reservationists to the so-called Lodge reservations in *Senator Lenroot of Wisconsin: A Political Biography*, 1900-1929 (Columbia, 1977), 261-309.
60   Warren to WHT, Nov. 17, 1919, Karger to WHT, Nov. 17, 20, 1919, WHT to Karger, Nov. 18, 1919, WHT to H. Taft, Nov. 18, 1919, Edge to WHT, Nov. 19, 1919, WHT Papers, Ser. 3, Box 461; WW to Hitchcock, Nov. 18, 1919, Hitchcock Papers, Vol. 1, WW Papers, Ser. 4, File 5033, and

Republicans felt confident that the political responsibility for the treaty's defeat would rest with Democrats, and especially with Wilson. Referring to him, Harding asserted that "there was but one man in the United States of America who did not know that this treaty could never be ratified without reservations." He foresaw no difficulty for Republicans in the 1920 elections as a consequence of the Senate's actions. Root praised Lodge for his skillful handling of the treaty, noting that he had given, but Wilson had rejected, the only chance for its ratification. Lodge agreed that "it was killed by Wilson." Mild reservationists had contributed to Lodge's success, as Hays gratefully acknowledged. Taft shared the Republican consensus that the president played a destructive role, but he also blamed Lodge. "The whole world," he lamented, "has suffered through the bitter personal antagonism, vanity and smallness of two men, Henry Cabot Lodge and Woodrow Wilson."[61]

Wilson's loyal defenders from the South exonerated him and placed blame elsewhere. "Unfortunately," Underwood observed, "last night the Republicans finally defeated the treaty of peace." Treasury Secretary Carter Glass condemned Lodge and his fellow Republicans for using hyphenated Americans to defeat the treaty. Seeking scapegoats, he found them in the Irish-Americans, Italian-Americans and Afro-Americans. "Instead of being a real American," Glass concluded, "what Lodge has done has been to array every racial group in the United States against real Americans." He rebuked these opponents for disloyalty to Wilson's standard of American nationalism.[62]

Some professional ethnic leaders claimed credit for their contributions to the treaty's defeat. But that, too, was a false claim. Only three of the five Democratic senators of Irish ancestry had refused to support Wilson. Gore, Shields and David Walsh rejected presidential leadership in the treaty fight, but Phelan and Thomas Walsh conformed to it despite their inclinations to approve some reservations. Irish-Americans had accounted for most Democratic defections in the Senate, but their three negative votes made no real difference. Although Borah congratulated this particular ethnic group on its significant contribution, he recognized that their fight against the League was largely to influence public opinion outside the Senate. Within the Senate he credited Knox as chief architect of the treaty's defeat.[63]

HCL Papers, File 1919 (Peace, League, Political, A–H); WW to Hitchcock, [undated copy in EBW's hand], JPT Papers, Box 3; Johnson to Beveridge, Nov. 14, 1919, Beveridge Papers, Box 215; *CR*, Vol. 58, 9767-9804.

61 *CR*, Vol. 58, 8791-92; ER to HCL, Dec. 1, 1919, HCL to ER, Dec. 3, 1919, ER Papers, Box 161, and HCL Papers; Hays to HCL, Nov. 22, 1919, HCL to Harvey, Nov. 20, 1919, HCL Papers, File 1919 (Peace, League, Political, I–Z); HCL to Chanler, Nov. 20, 1919, HCL Papers, File 1919 (Peace, League, Political, A–H); WHT to Warren, Nov. 18, 1919, WHT to Yost, Nov. 18, 1919, WHT to Karger, Nov. 23, 1919, WHT Papers, Ser. 3, Box 461.

62 Underwood to Ellis, Nov. 20, 1919, Underwood Papers; Glass to Haislip, Nov. 28, 1919, Glass Papers, Box 138.

63 "Senate's Action a Splendid Vindication of Americanism," *Gaelic American*, XVI (Nov. 29, 1919), 1; "Victory For America and Ireland," ibid., 4; Phelan to Short, Sept. 19, 1919, League to Enforce Peace

The irreconcilables' nightmare about American entanglement in world affairs failed to materialize because of Wilson's refusal to compromise with Lodge. Rather than demonstrating the influence of ethnic groups or even of irreconcilable senators, the treaty's defeat had resulted from failure of the president's politics of confrontation. His all-or-nothing stance left him with nothing as the Senate adjourned without approving the Versailles Treaty under any conditions. The United States now refused to join the League of Nations.

Papers, Box 11; Borah to Cohalan, Nov. 22, 1919, Borah Papers, Box 551; Borah to Knox, Nov. 21, 1919, Knox Papers, Box 30.

CHAPTER 8

American rejection of the Versailles peace

Wilson's intransigence forestalled any compromise between Democratic and Republican senators, thereby preventing them from approving the Versailles Treaty. His all-or-nothing stance resulted in American rejection of the League and failure of the French security treaty. In the spring of 1920, the Senate again refused to accept the peace treaty. Lodge's Republican majority persisted in demanding reservations which Wilson opposed. This executive-legislative stalemate contributed to estrangement between the United States and the Allies. Clinging to his ideal of the League, the president sacrificed real possibilities for constructive involvement in the postwar world, including the Anglo-American alliance with France. Unable to establish his new order, he retreated from active American participation in Europe. He denounced the Allies as he abandoned them. Wilson's isolationist reaction expressed the reverse side of his internationalism, for he had consistently endeavored to redeem or avoid the Old World. He chose to forsake the League, except as an ideal, rather than acquiesce in the Lodge reservations. Vainly pursuing his dream of collective security, he refused to adjust to the realities of interdependence and pluralism. This serious failure led to the final American rejection of the Versailles peace.

Wilson sacrificed the French security treaty to the League, obviously preferring Article 10's universal, but vague, commitment. After belatedly submitting the bilateral treaty to the Senate in late July 1919, he had ignored it. Throughout his western tour Wilson never mentioned this treaty. He refrained from urging the Foreign Relations Committee to recommend its approval, or from encouraging any senator to promote it. Only one Democratic senator, on his own initiative, defended it. Responding to questions, Thomas Walsh reported the Judiciary Committee's conclusion, upholding the constitutionality of this proposed alliance. Yet even he abstained from advocating the treaty as he, too, was primarily concerned about the League's fate.[1]

Republicans showed far greater interest in the French security treaty. Root as well as Lodge favored its ratification, but not in conjunction with the League. White reminded them that Clemenceau depended upon an American guarantee to defend France against German aggression. Through either the League or the special alliance, or preferably both arrangements, French leaders looked to the United States for assistance in maintaining the postwar balance of power. Root urged Lodge to take the initiative. In view of the civil war in Russia he feared that Germany and Japan might combine to dominate that country. To prevent Germany's resurgence from threatening western Europe, he advocated the Anglo-American alliance with France. "I hope to the Lord," Root advised Lodge on November 1, "you are going to consent to the French treaty, striking out of course the provision for submission to the League Council." He preferred this alliance to Article 10. "With regard to all these things," he noted, "it seems to me that it is desirable to accompany the opposition which you are making to the vague and indefinite commitments of the League Covenant with an exhibition of willingness to do the definite certain specific things which are a proper part of true American policy, and which are necessary to secure the results of the War upon which America has expended so much life and treasure." Lodge agreed, reiterating that "I am in favor of the French treaty with the provision referring to the League Council out. With that in it could not possibly get through." He informed Root that, according to Lenroot's assessment, there were too few votes in the Senate to approve the treaty. Nevertheless, he promised to work for its passage.[2]

Once the Senate rejected the Versailles Treaty on November 19, some Republican irreconcilables feared that it might turn to the French security treaty as an alternative. "Our true course is to stand firmly for our traditional policy of no political alliance whatever with any foreign country," Beveridge advised Brandegee. He feared that France and Great Britain would dominate the alliance and entangle the United States in the Old World. "At best," he warned Moses, "it is nothing but a trap to make us a part of a new European balance of power – a balance of power too, in which the other members have identical interests and work in complete harmony and therefore would control the alliance at all times and on all questions." Regarding it as a dangerous threat of foreign control over the United States and a violation of the American diplomatic tradition, Beveridge implored Cummins to oppose it. He urged Republican senators to resist the alliance as they had the League.[3]

1 Walsh to WW, Aug. 12, 1919, WW Papers, Ser. 2, Box 191; *CR*, Vol. 58, 5677-79.
2 HW to ER, Aug. 5, 1919, ER Papers, Box 137; HW to HCL, June 6, Sept. 10, 19, Oct. 11, 1919, ER to HCL, Nov. 1, 1919, HCL to ER, Nov. 3, 1919, HCL to Chanler, Oct. 14, 1919, HCL Papers, File 1919 (Peace, League, Political, A-H).
3 Beveridge to Brandegee, Nov. 24, 1919, Beveridge to Johnson, Nov. 22, 1919, Beveridge to Knox, Nov. 22, 1919, Beveridge Papers, Box 215; Beveridge to HCL, Nov. 21, 1919, Beveridge to

Irreconcilables such as Johnson and Borah shared Beveridge's anxiety. Recognizing the security treaty's appeal among Republicans, they welcomed his active opposition. "Believing our foreign policy should remain unchanged," Johnson responded, "I could not vote for the French-British-American Alliance. I fear, however, very many of the Senators have been carried away with the idea, first of doing this for France, and, secondly with adopting a course, which they foolishly thought might avoid a league of nations." Borah agreed that they had not yet won this battle. He anticipated that international bankers, who had invested in Europe and wanted American soldiers to protect their money, would continue to press the Senate. To prevent it from approving either the League or the alliance, he, too, intended to remain vigilant. Other Republican irreconcilables, in contrast, showed greater understanding of the problem of French security. To satisfy France, Brandegee had suggested adoption of the fifth section of Knox's resolution, which affirmed his "new American doctrine." It promised cooperation with the Allies for defense against any power or coalition that threatened the freedom and peace of Europe. Knox kept an open mind toward the French security treaty. But Brandegee perceived why it would not be ratified, despite its appeal to many Republicans. He noted that "Wilson is doing nothing whatever to urge the Senate to pass the French-American Treaty which he promised to France" because he preferred to keep French pressure on Republicans to approve the peace treaty.[4]

By subordinating it to the League, Wilson forfeited potential Republican support for the French security treaty. Lord Grey, who had arrived in Washington in late September on his special mission, observed the alliance's appeal even to some irreconcilables. "I hear some Senators, irreconcilable to Covenant and Treaty, are saying that if these are finally killed in the Senate they will agree to the passage of [the] Franco-American Treaty with omission of reference to the League of Nations and for a term of five years," he reported on November 26. "It remains to be seen whether the President will agree to this." Although Lord Curzon, the new British foreign secretary, instructed Grey not to encourage this treaty's adoption as an alternative to the League, the special ambassador continued to expect its ratification by the United States. Curzon thought an American delay would benefit Great Britain by inducing France to adopt "a more moderate attitude," although Grey anticipated the opposite result. Lloyd George's government, like Wilson, sought to maximize its control and minimize its obligations in continental Europe by emphasizing the general League instead of the specific alliance. Of

Moses, Nov. 24, 1919, Beveridge Papers, Box 216; Beveridge to New, Aug. 10, 1919, Beveridge Papers, Box 217; Beveridge to Smoot, Apr. 23, Nov. 24, 1919, Beveridge Papers, Box 218; Beveridge to McCormick, Nov. 24, 1919, Beveridge to HCL, Nov. 21, 1919, HCL Papers, File 1919 (Peace, League, Political, A-H); Beveridge to Borah, Nov. 24, 1919, Borah Papers, Box 551, and Beveridge Papers, Box 214.

4 Brandegee to Beveridge, Dec. 9, 1919, Borah to Beveridge, Nov. 28, 1919, Beveridge Papers, Box 214; Johnson to Beveridge, Nov. 24, 1919, Knox to Beveridge, Nov. 24, 1919, Beveridge Papers, Box 215; Borah to Beveridge, Nov. 28, 1919, Borah Papers, Box 551; CR, Vol. 58, 8777.

course, if the United States failed to ratify the treaty with France, its Anglo-French counterpart would never go into effect.[5]

Lodge blamed Wilson for the alliance's anticipated failure. Aware of justifiable apprehension of the French over their future defense, he conveyed his assurance that the United States would assist them regardless of the outcome in the Senate. Deadlock over the League prevented action on the French security treaty. As Lodge recognized, the alliance's approval by the Senate, or even the Foreign Relations Committee, would require a bipartisan coalition. Yet, he lamented in mid-December, Democratic senators were still awaiting the president's direction. In this situation Lodge refrained from even attempting to report the French security treaty out of the committee. "The treaty," he explained, "has received no support from the President and I have not even been able to find out whether he would allow the Democrats to vote for it now. If the Democrats would vote for the treaty I think we could ratify it. If they will not, of course ratification will be out of the question." Indifference of the Democratic president and senators, even more than opposition from some Republicans, killed this alliance. It died in the Foreign Relations Committee by the end of 1919.[6]

This treaty's demise exemplified the emerging postwar pattern of American relations with Europe. The Senate's adjournment on November 19 without approving the Versailles Treaty already undermined the Allies' confidence in the United States. The French desperately wanted American help to enforce the peace conditions against a recalcitrant Germany, and the British desired it to moderate French demands. Despite their differences, European powers favored the involvement of the United States in the Old World. While the Senate was considering the peace treaty, Clemenceau had announced his hope for American ratification. Speaking in the Chamber of Deputies on September 25, he appealed to the United States to ratify the treaty and join the League. "Fundamentally," he explained, "so far as the League of Nations itself is concerned, our ardent desire is to see America, as a result of whose initiative it came into being, make the enterprise a success." He then directed his appeal to Republican senators: "If the Republican statesmen who are campaigning against the President, and who express at every opportunity such warm sentiments of friendship for France, could hear our voice, I would send them this one message: 'Make haste; ratify the Covenant of the League of Nations. It will be a great success, a great triumph for the cause of humanity.'" Clemenceau emphasized that France continued to rely on the United States. Larnaude, who had represented

---

5 EG to Curzon, Nov. 26 (#413), Dec. 11 (#435), 1919, Curzon to EG, Dec. 2, 1919 (#423), E. L. Woodward and Rohan Butler, eds., *Documents on British Foreign Policy, 1919-1939*, First Series, V (London, 1954), 1039-40, 1051, 1060-61.
6 Berry to HCL, Oct. 27, 1919, HCL to Berry, Dec. 1, 1919, HCL to Hale, Dec. 13, 1919, HCL Papers, File 1919 (Peace, League, Political, A-H); Tucker to HCL, Dec. 14, 1919, HCL to Tucker, Dec. 17, 1919, HCL Papers, File 1919 (Peace, League, Political, I-Z); HW to HCL, Nov. 1, 13, 1919, ER Papers, Box 161, and HCL Papers; Notes, Dec. 10, 1919, Anderson Papers, Box 4.

France in the commission that had drafted the Covenant, published an open letter to President Wilson in mid-October as his way of encouraging the United States to join the League. The Senate's subsequent refusal to approve the treaty shocked French leaders. They felt betrayed by Republicans as well as Democrats. White reported the French panic and British dismay to Lodge and Root, observing that "the rejection of the Treaty has impaired our prestige among the Allies." Although White himself welcomed the imminent departure of the remaining American delegates from Paris, that prospect underscored for the Allies the implications of the Senate's action.[7]

Under the leadership of Frank Polk, who had replaced Lansing in Paris, the American delegation prepared to depart. The secretary of state agreed that it would find itself in an anomalous position if the Senate rejected the Versailles Treaty. When that occurred, acting on the president's authority, he instructed Polk, White and Bliss to leave the peace conference. Clemenceau and Lloyd George immediately apprehended the ominous impact on Europe of this withdrawal. The French appealed to the United States to reverse this decision. Polk suggested that Bliss might remain in Paris so that at least one American delegate would continue. Wilson, however, rejected the request. He conceded only a slight delay in the date of departure, and the appointment of Ambassador Wallace as unofficial observer. To the Allies' disappointment, the American delegation left Paris on December 9. John W. Davis, American ambassador in London, lamented that the executive-legislative stalemate over the treaty in the United States had led to this consequence. He preferred ratification with the Lodge reservations to total rejection. "This action," he confided to Polk, "would at least show Germany that America stood with the Allies on the substantive portion of the Treaty regardless of the League of Nations." But Wilson had consistently opposed such a compromise. "It looks to me," Polk explained to Davis, "as if the President is going to pull out of the whole thing in order to demonstrate to the American people what we will look like in case the Treaty is not ratified. It is a dangerous game as they may not give a damn how they look." Wilson maintained his all-or-nothing stance, ignoring the fact that Republicans such as Lodge had not called for the delegation's departure from Paris. If he could not force the Senate to accept the League without reservations, the president intended to curtail American participation in European affairs regardless of the impact on the Allies.[8]

---

7   Phillips to WW, Oct. 2, 1919, Wallace to RL, Sept. 26, 1919 (#1435), WW Papers, Ser. 2, Box 193; HW to Polk, n.d., [extracts of Clemenceau's speech], Wallace to RL, Sept. 26, 1919 (#1435), Polk Papers, 74/107; Polk to RL, Sept. 29, 1919, Polk Papers, 82/12; Kennaday to JPT, Oct. 14, 1919, Larnaude to WW, n.d., WW Papers, Ser. 4, File 4767; HW to ER, Nov. 28, Dec. 5, 1919, HW to HCL, Dec. 5, 1919, ER Papers, Box 137; HW to HCL, Nov. 21, 28, 1919, ER Papers, Box 161; HW to HCL, Nov. 21, 28, Dec. 5, 1919, HCL Papers.
8   RL to Polk, Nov. 14, 1919, RL Papers, Vol. 49; RL to EG, Dec. 8, 1919, RL Papers, Vol. 50; Polk to RL, Nov. 7, 1919, Polk Papers, 78/16; RL to A.C.N.P., Nov. 27, 1919 (#3906), Polk Papers, 82/7; RL to A.C.N.P., Dec. 6, 1919 (#3985), Polk Papers, 82/8; Polk to RL, Nov. 12, 1919, Polk Papers, 82/15; Polk to RL, Nov. 29, 1919, Polk Papers, 82/16; Polk to RL, Dec. 1, 2, 4 (#5554), 5,

I

Wilson stood virtually alone in his adamant refusal to compromise with Republicans to save the Versailles Treaty. All other former members of the American Commission favored ratification even with strong reservations. Lansing privately blamed both political parties but refrained from attempting to break the deadlock. He acknowledged his total incapacity to shape American foreign policy. House, too, now enjoyed no real influence. He had remained in Europe to assist the initial organization of the League, experiencing a kind of political exile. After finishing that work and returning to the United States in October, he continued to lack access to the sick president. Mrs. Wilson delayed telling her husband about House's arrival and poor health, explaining that "we keep everything from him . . . which would annoy or distress him," except the "important" matters requiring his advice. House immediately perceived that Wilson was more seriously ill or more deeply disturbed over the colonel's unauthorized return than anticipated. The intimate friendship between them no longer existed. Consequently, using the only means still available, House sent two letters to the president recommending a compromise with Lodge. "To the ordinary man," he bluntly stated, "the distance between the Treaty and the reservations is slight." He suggested that Wilson authorize Hitchcock to negotiate with the Republican majority. House recognized that the price for success would be reservations similar to Lodge's, although Hitchcock should attempt to moderate them. If the Allies refused to accept these American conditions, then at least Wilson would not bear responsibility for blocking the treaty's ratification. But if, as House expected, the Allies acquiesced, the League could begin to function. In either event the president would avoid failure and personify the ideal of the League.[9]

Assuming that the only legitimate reason for Wilson's refusal to accept the Lodge reservations was his belief that the Allies would object, Bliss drafted an "imaginary letter" to Lloyd George and Clemenceau. He emphasized that American ratification was crucial to Europe's peace. "The continuance of that peace," he argued, "is surely of far more vital interest to you than the meaning and effect of most of the fourteen reservations can possibly be." This view reflected the general's conviction that other parts of the Versailles

6, 9, 1919, RL to Polk, Dec. 8, 1919 (#3997), Polk Papers, 82/7; Confidential Diary, Dec. 4, 1919, Polk Papers, 88/18; RL to WW, Dec. 2, 1919, EBW to [RL], Dec. 2, 1919, Polk Papers, 89/125; RL to EBW, Dec. 7, 1919, EBW Papers, Box 23; Davis to Polk, Dec. 4, 1919, Polk to Davis, Dec. 8, 1919, Polk Papers, 73/121; HCL to Trevelyan, Dec. 8, 1919, HCL Papers, File 1919 (Adams-Trevelyan); Curzon to DLG, Dec. 6, 1919, [Curzon] to Derby, Dec. 4, 1919, [Curzon] to Crowe, Dec. 4, 1919, DLG Papers, F/12/2/9; Curzon to EG, Dec. 2, 1919 (#424), Crowe to Curzon, Dec. 3, 1919 (#425), EG to Curzon, Dec. 4, 1919 (#426), Woodward and Butler, eds., *Documents on British Foreign Policy*, First Series, V, 1051-54.
9   RL Diary, V, Nov. 22, Dec. 9, 27, 1919; Notes, Dec. 4, 1919, Anderson Papers, Box 4; EBW to Mrs. EMH, Oct. 17, 1919, EBW to EMH, Nov. 18, 1919, EMH Papers, Letterbook IV; EMH to WW, Nov. 24, 27, 1919, EMH Papers, 49/13; EMH to EBW, Oct. 22, 1919, EMH to WW, Nov. 24, 27, 1919, WW Papers, Ser. 2, Box 193.

Treaty were more important for the Allies than the Covenant. He regarded reservations, or even the League's temporary postponement, as an acceptable concession to save the remainder of the treaty. He imagined that if the Allied leaders would impress this point upon Wilson, who was the principal obstacle to a compromise, they might break the deadlock in Washington.[10]

Conflict over the treaty, pitting Republicans against Democrats, caught White in the middle. Like Lansing, House and Bliss, he concluded that compromise was preferable to the treaty's defeat. As a career diplomat, he endeavored to remain faithful to the president. He confided to the secretary of state, rather than to his fellow Republicans, that he could see no basis for objecting to "a few harmless reservations." Once he returned to the United States, White attempted to reconcile differences between the White House and the Senate. Except for the preamble, he saw no reason to oppose the Lodge reservations. His efforts, however, were totally inadequate to convince either Wilson or Lodge to make significant concessions.[11]

Other prominent members of the earlier American delegation to the peace conference agreed that Wilson should compromise rather than sacrifice the treaty. Herbert Hoover, chairman of the American Relief Administration, urged him to accept the Lodge reservations, except for the preamble. He argued that Europe's economic reconstruction required exports and credits from the United States, while American producers needed European markets. Moreover, resumption of commerce depended upon ratification. Hoover's advocacy of the League emphasized its pacific rather than military functions. Because, in his view, there was "no obligation for the United States to engage in military operations" under the Covenant, the French had requested the separate Anglo-American guarantee of their defense.[12]

Hoover's emphasis on ratification for economic recovery coincided with the assessment of other financial experts. Thomas W. Lamont, the Wall Street banker, had exerted his influence throughout the year to promote the League. He had fought against separating the Covenant and advocated ratification without any reservations that would require renegotiation in Paris. Yet by mid-November, as a way of avoiding the Lodge reservations, Lamont concluded that Wilson and the Senate should compromise on the Knox resolution. The United States could then promptly ratify the treaty except for the Covenant.[13]

---

10   THB to Polk, Dec. 3, 1919, THB to DLG and Clemenceau, Dec. 4, 1919, Polk Papers, 74/35; THB to Polk, Dec. 3, 1919, THB Papers, Box 69; [THB to DLG and Clemenceau, Dec. 4, 1919], THB Papers, Box 71.

11   HW to RL, Aug. 26, 1919, HW Papers, Box 44; HW to RL, Oct. 23, 1919, HW Papers, Box 45; EBW to HW, Dec. 22, 1919, HW to Bowman, Dec. 31, 1919, HW Papers, Box 23; HW to HCL, Dec. 24, 1919, HCL Papers, File 1919 (Henry White).

12   Hoover to WW, Nov. 19, 1919, WW Papers, Ser. 2, Box 193, Herbert Hoover Pre-Commerce Papers, Box 32, Herbert Hoover Presidential Library, and EMH Papers, 10/37; CR, Vol. 58, 6402-03. See also David Burner, *Herbert Hoover: A Public Life* (New York, 1979), 147-50.

13   Lamont to Morrow, Feb. 24, 1919, Thomas W. Lamont Papers, Box 165, Baker Library, Harvard

Democratic leaders in the Senate also attempted to convince Wilson to compromise. In a conference with Tumulty on November 21 and a subsequent letter to the president, Underwood outlined his twofold plan. He suggested that senators from both political parties, excluding irreconcilables, might still reach a compromise. But if Republicans insisted on a reservation to Article 10 that would threaten the League's integrity, he recommended Democratic resistance. Expecting the Republican majority to propose a compromise, the senator wanted to preserve the prerogative of Democrats to decide whether to accept. Aware that this aspect of his plan might well fail, he advised as an alternative that the president call upon the Senate to approve the Versailles Treaty exclusive of the Covenant. By eliminating this part altogether, the United States could achieve peace with Germany without adopting reservations that would emasculate the League. The issue of American membership in the League with "its full integrity" could then be fought in the next election. Although Wilson never endorsed Underwood's plan, the senator proceeded with the first phase of it by appealing on December 11 to Republicans to propose a compromise. Two days later he also revived Pomerene's idea of a bipartisan committee of conciliation. As he emphasized, the economic situation at home and abroad required resumption of international trade, which depended upon credits and consequently on peace. With his proposal for breaking the deadlock, the Alabama senator endeavored to serve the economic interests of his state, while appearing to maintain his uncompromising support for the League. Unreservedly endorsing the ideal of collective security, he nevertheless would postpone American membership in the real League. Deftly attempting to avoid alienating Wilson while removing the League as an obstacle to peace, Underwood solicited his cooperation.[14]

Hitchcock refused to accept the current deadlock as permanent defeat. He explained to Wilson in two letters in late November that he still wanted to arrange a bipartisan compromise. He hoped to elicit cooperation of nineteen Republican senators who would join the Democrats to provide a two-thirds majority. This strategy would require Democratic flexibility. Its success, Hitchcock told Wilson, would depend upon a mutually acceptable reservation to Article 10. He began to consider new alternatives to the Lodge reservation. Although the president did not respond favorably, the senator persisted. On December 5, at the Foreign Relations Committee's request, Wilson received Hitchcock and Fall in the White House to discuss the Mexican situation. Hitchcock apparently used even this occasion to urge a compromise.[15]

University; Lamont Diary, July 5, 1919, Lamont Papers, Box 164; Lamont to EMH, Oct. 17, 27, 29, 1919, Lamont to JPT, Nov. 17, 1919, EMH Papers, 12/8; Davis to JPT, Dec. 1, 1919, WW Papers, Ser. 2, Box 193.
14 Underwood to WW, Nov. 21, 1919, WW Papers, Ser. 2, Box 193; CR, Vol. 59, 401-02, 531-33; CR, Vol. 58, 8799-8800; Underwood to Jenkins, Dec. 17, 1919, Underwood Papers.
15 Hitchcock to WW, Nov. 22, 24, 1919, WW Papers, Ser. 2, Box 193; JPT to EBW, Dec. 1,

Despite Wilson's negative response, Hitchcock still persevered. In the Senate on December 13 he blamed Lodge for rejecting Pomerene's proposal of a committee of conciliation. Referring to his own interpretive reservations, he claimed that Democrats had not blocked a compromise. They still wanted to meet Lodge in "a give-and-take committee" to reach an agreement. "We hold out the olive branch," he reaffirmed. By suggesting Democratic concessions and making this overture to Republicans, Hitchcock risked his own personal relationship with Wilson for the treaty's sake.[16]

Except in the White House, advocates of the peace treaty increasingly viewed the president as the chief obstacle to ratification. Leaders of the League to Enforce Peace now favored compromise. Otherwise, as Taft and Lowell clearly recognized, their work would end in failure. The executive committee of this pro-League lobby convened on November 23 to determine its future activities in the aftermath of the Senate's refusal to approve the treaty. Long-time proponents of international organization such as John Bates Clark, Hamilton Holt, Theodore Marburg, and Oscar S. Straus attended this meeting. Hoover, who had begun to collaborate with them, also participated. The executive committee unanimously decided to urge Wilson to accept the Lodge reservations, except the preamble. They combined this private appeal, which Lansing had offered to deliver to the White House, with a public statement and a nation-wide publicity campaign. Seeking to save the treaty, the League to Enforce Peace called upon the Senate to pass a resolution of ratification that would facilitate acquiescence of other signatories. Although willing to accept reservations, these leaders reaffirmed their support for the Covenant. "The League of Nations," they announced, "gives the promise of a world cooperating for the purposes of peace and protecting itself by concerted action against war and the threat of war. The ideal is American." They sought to convert this ideal into reality, not to preserve its purity as a mere symbol of a potentially new era of international relations.[17]

Now that Taft and the League to Enforce Peace advocated the treaty's ratification with the Lodge reservations other than the preamble, they fully endorsed the mild reservationists' position. These Republican senators had already indicated their willingness to vote for these reservations. After the Senate reconvened in December, they still hoped to form a bipartisan coalition. Mild reservationists such as Lenroot, Colt and McNary communicated their assessment that twenty Republicans were ready to join

1919, JPT Papers, Box 3; U.S. Senate, *Proceedings of the Committee on Foreign Relations*, 203-04; RL Diary, V, Dec. 4-5, 1919; Hitchcock, Nebraska, the World War and the World Peace, 1925, Hitchcock Papers, Nebraska State Historical Society; Rickey to Short, Dec. 8, 1919, WHT Papers, Ser. 3, Box 462.

1 6   [Address], Dec. 10, 1919, Hitchcock Papers, Vol. 1; *CR*, Vol. 59, 534-36.

1 7   ALL to Calkins, Dec. 6, 1919, WHT to ALL, Nov. 23, 1919, ALL Papers; WHT to Yost, Oct. 29, 1919, WHT Papers, Ser. 3, Box 459; ALL to WHT, Nov. 20, 1919, Short to WHT, Nov. 22, 25, 1919, Minutes, Meeting of the Executive Committee, League to Enforce Peace, Nov. 23, 1919, Statement Adopted by the Executive Committee of the League to Enforce Peace, Nov. 23, 1919, WHT Papers, Ser. 3, Box 461.

forty-five Democrats to approve the treaty. They insisted, however, on reservations essentially like those bearing Lodge's name, but with a modification of the preamble and possible changes in terminology. Expecting Democrats to initiate a compromise, they recognized that successful accommodation would depend upon the president. Hitchcock was undoubtedly aware of their conditions when, on December 13, he publicly called for compromise. By signaling his desire for accommodation, he risked not only Wilson's ire but also loss of his own leadership of Democrats in the Senate, for they were deeply divided. Some of them, including Pomerene, who had so stated in a frank letter to the president, had concluded that the only way to save the treaty was "to accept the substance of the Lodge reservations." He thought that even with the Article 10 reservation the League could fulfill most of its valuable functions. Although Pomerene believed they should have engaged in serious negotiations with mild reservationists long ago, other Democratic senators continued to resist. Williams, an early member of the League to Enforce Peace, condemned it for approving any concessions beyond "interpretative reservations." These divisions among Democrats made it extremely difficult for Hitchcock to initiate a compromise.[18]

Republicans retained their basic unity in favor of the Lodge reservations. Not even Taft expected ratification without these conditions in some form. Root praised Lodge for forming this consensus and thereby offering the best opportunity for the treaty. Yet, favoring some flexibility, he suggested three possible modifications in the reservations. Like the League to Enforce Peace, he recommended removal from the preamble of the requirement for an exchange of notes. In the reservation concerning withdrawal from the League, he wanted to substitute a provision for a joint instead of a concurrent resolution of Congress. Seeking to avoid any unnecessary challenge to the presidential prerogative in foreign affairs, he also proposed a rewording of the reservation providing for appointment of American representatives to the League so as to reaffirm congressional authority rather than prohibit the president's. Lodge appreciated Root's approval of his leadership, but showed less willingness to accommodate the Democrats. Except for the preamble, he preferred to maintain the existing reservations. Blaming Wilson for killing the treaty, he reaffirmed that "he can have the treaty ratified at any moment if he will accept the reservations and if he declines to do so we are not in the least afraid to meet him at the polls on that issue." Lodge insisted that Democrats must initiate any compromise, but did not expect one from the sick president.[19]

18   WHT to Edge, Nov. 24, 1919, WHT Papers, Ser. 3, Box 461; Rickey to Short, [Dec. 11, 1919], Short to Rickey, Dec. 12, 1919, Williams to Short, Dec. 11, 1919, WHT Papers, Ser. 3, Box 462; Pomerene to WW, Nov. 22, 1919, WW Papers, Ser. 4, File 5033; Phelan to Hitchcock, Dec. 12, 1919, Hitchcock Papers, Vol. 2.
19   ER to HCL, Dec. 1, 1919, HCL to ER, Dec. 3, 1919, ER Papers, Box 161, and HCL Papers; HCL to Blake, Dec. 3, 1919, HCL Papers, File 1919 (Peace, League, Political, A-H); HCL to Morse, Dec. 2, 1919, HCL Papers, File 1919 (Adams-Trevelyan); ER to Damrosch, Dec. 2, 1919, ER to Gray, Dec. 1, 1919, ER Papers, Box 137.

Irreconcilables feared that the pressures for accommodation might shatter the Republican consensus. Brandegee warned Lodge to guard against Democratic attempts to attract mild reservationists. He sought to counter the influence of the League to Enforce Peace and international bankers on these senators. He resented Root's intrusion, as well as Taft's and Lowell's, into the Senate's deliberations. Along with other irreconcilables such as McCormick, he wanted Hays to make the Lodge reservations into a partisan issue so as to encourage mild reservationists to remain faithful to the Republican majority. Of course, he intended to oppose the treaty even with these reservations, for he saw in the League the danger that Congress would totally lose control over American foreign relations.[20] Borah thought they now faced "the most critical period of the fight." He encouraged Oswald Garrison Villard of the *Nation* and Frank Munsey of the *New York Sun* to remain vigilant against international bankers' efforts to protect their investments by imposing their own particular conception of interdependence. He advocated defeat of "the Wilson-Hoover-Lamont plan to exploit and control the whole world."[21]

Adhering to his intermediate position, Lodge sought to preserve the Republican consensus. In the Senate on December 13 he reminded Hitchcock that he had consulted primarily mild reservationists in preparing his reservations. Yet he also rejected Underwood's attempt to revive Pomerene's proposal for a committee of conciliation, noting that Democrats could present at any time whatever modifications in the reservations the president would accept. Unless Wilson indicated a genuine desire to compromise, Lodge saw no reason to establish a bipartisan committee. "If the President desires to present to the Senate any modifications or concessions from his position," he explained, "it is open to him to do it." The Republican majority refused to offer further concessions, leaving any initiative to Democrats.[22]

Wilson responded quickly and defiantly to Lodge's challenge. On the next day, December 14, the White House issued a statement reiterating the president's unwillingness to modify his position. He still refused to accept any of the Lodge reservations. "He has no compromise or concession of any kind in mind," the statement affirmed, "but intends, so far as he is concerned, that the Republican leaders of the Senate shall continue to bear the undivided responsibility for the fate of the treaty and the present condition of the world in consequence of that fate." Wilson was obviously more concerned with shifting blame for American rejection of the Versailles

20 Brandegee to HCL, Nov. 27, 1919, HCL Papers, File 1919 (Peace, League, Political, I-Z), and Cohalan Papers; Brandegee to Cohalan, Nov. 26, 1919, Cohalan Papers; Beveridge to Brandegee, Dec. 2, 1919, Brandegee to Beveridge, Nov. 28, 1919, Beveridge Papers, Box 214; McCormick to Beveridge, Nov. 28, 1919, Beveridge Papers, Box 222.
21 Borah to Munsey, Nov. 21, Dec. 12, 1919, Borah to Villard, Nov. 28, 1919, Borah Papers, Box 551; Borah to Carusi, Dec. 3, 1919, Borah to Shumake, Dec. 8, 1919, Borah Papers, Box 550.
22 *CR*, Vol. 59, 533-40.

peace than with the effects of this action on Europe. His reaction was personal and political, not appropriate for a responsible statesman. Because of his stroke, he probably experienced greater difficulty than before in changing his mind in the midst of a fight. But Wilson's instransigence on the treaty did not stem from his illness. He had adopted his all-or-nothing stance before his stroke and now simply adhered to it.[23]

Wilson's close associates, although not suffering from the same neurological problems, evidenced a similar mentality. Tumulty, who was apparently absent from the White House on the Sunday when the presidential statement was issued, welcomed it as "a body blow" to "our enemies" and "indifferent friends" who were willing to consider modifications in the League. Calling the issuance of the statement "a brave, audacious thing to do," he asked Mrs. Wilson to convey his opinion to her husband that "it will cleanse and purify the murky atmosphere which has surrounded the whole situation." At a cabinet meeting on December 16 Treasury Secretary Glass and Postmaster General Burleson likewise denounced Republicans and defended the president's statement. When Lansing and Interior Secretary Franklin K. Lane suggested that he should at least reconfirm his support for interpretive reservations in order to escape unnecessary blame for obstinacy, Glass angrily

---

2 3   For a different view of the impact of Wilson's stroke on the treaty fight, see Edwin A. Weinstein, *Woodrow Wilson: A Medical and Psychological Biography* (Princeton, 1981), 363, and John Milton Cooper, Jr., *The Warrior and the Priest: Woodrow Wilson and Theodore Roosevelt* (Cambridge, 1983), 339-42. Scholars have reached no consensus on Wilson's psychological and physical condition in 1919-1920 and its effect on his political leadership. Sigmund Freud and William C. Bullitt, *Thomas Woodrow Wilson: A Psychological Study* (Boston, 1966), offered a crude analysis of the president, tracing his psychological problems in dealing with Senator Lodge and the Versailles Treaty to his childhood relations with his father and to his moral collapse during the peace conference. A more sophisticated Freudian interpretation had already been published by Alexander L. George and Juliette L. George, *Woodrow Wilson and Colonel House: A Personality Study* (New York, 1964). James David Barber, *The Presidential Character: Predicting Performance in the White House* (Englewood Cliffs, 1972), 17-142, accepted the Georges' interpretation of Wilson, while categorizing him as one of the active-negative presidents. Edwin A. Weinstein presented an alternative to these Freudian interpretations in "Woodrow Wilson's Neurological Illness," *Journal of American History*, LVII (Sept. 1970), 324-51, and in his later book. He argued that a series of little strokes and then the massive stroke in October 1919 were the source of Wilson's rigidity during the treaty fight. In other words, Wilson's psychological problems resulted from his physical ailment rather than from his childhood experience. Edwin A. Weinstein, James William Anderson, and Arthur S. Link, "Woodrow Wilson's Political Personality: A Reappraisal," *Political Science Quarterly*, XCIII (Winter 1978), 585-98, criticized especially the Georges' interpretation. They argued that Wilson's stroke in 1919 caused personality changes which significantly contributed to the treaty's defeat. On this crucial point, but not on all questions, Juliette L. George and Alexander L. George offered a persuasive reply in "*Woodrow Wilson and Colonel House*: A Reply to Weinstein, Anderson, and Link," *Political Science Quarterly*, XCVI (Winter 1981-1982), 641-65. They emphasized the element of continuity in Wilson's position before and after his October 1919 stroke. Along with Michael F. Marmor, "Wilson, Strokes, and Zebras," *New England Journal of Medicine*, CCCVII (Aug. 26, 1982), 528-35, they also raised serious medical questions about Weinstein's diagnosis of Wilson's illness. For the best synthesis of these conflicting interpretations, see Jerrold M. Post, "Woodrow Wilson Re-examined: The Mind-Body Controversy Redux and Other Disputations," comments by Juliette L. George and Alexander L. George, Edwin A. Weinstein, and Michael Marmor, and Post's reply, *Political Psychology*, IV, No. 2 (1983), 289-331. For a good summary of the controversy, see Thomas T. Lewis, "Alternative Psychological Interpretations of Woodrow Wilson," *Mid-America*, LXV (Apr.-July 1983), 71-85. For a critique of the scholarship on this issue, see Lloyd E. Ambrosius, "Woodrow Wilson's Health and the Treaty Fight, 1919-1920," *International History Review*, IX (Feb. 1987), 73-84.

criticized their recommendation. Secretaries Baker and Daniels sided with Glass and opposed any attempt to explain Wilson's statement. Reflecting on this meeting, Lansing accused Glass of displaying the same self-centered attitude that characterized the president: "It was perfectly evident that he was willing to sacrifice the interests of this country and of the world rather than recede one step in the political battle going on in the Senate." The people surrounding Wilson in the White House, and his faithful cabinet, refusing to bring him bad news, chose to reinforce the barriers that isolated him from political reality.[24]

Hitchcock and Underwood nevertheless persisted in their efforts to arrange a compromise. They both informed the League to Enforce Peace of their continuing desire to break the deadlock. Interpreting the president's statement as an indication of his refusal to participate in formulating a compromise, but not as an absolute rejection of a bipartisan agreement, Hitchcock expected him to accept the senator's own interpretive reservations. On this basis he hoped to open negotiations with mild reservationists. He refused, however, to consider reservations that Wilson would definitely reject, for that would not contribute to ratification. To circumvent this stalemate, Underwood wanted to separate the Covenant from the remainder of the treaty. In the Senate on December 13 he had already expressed his personal willingness to approve the Knox resolution in order to conclude immediate peace with Germany, while postponing the League for future consideration. He was most interested in reviving the export trade on which his state depended. Through Tumulty and Mrs. Wilson, Hitchcock sought to ascertain whether his interpretation of the president's statement was accurate. He wanted to determine "whether the President would look with favor upon any effort on his part to make an adjustment with the mild reservationists by which to soften the Lodge reservations and thus avoid splitting the Democratic party." He knew that some Democratic senators were increasingly rebellious against Wilson's leadership. On December 19, one day after Tumulty relayed Hitchcock's question, he received his answer. The president emphatically told Hitchcock not to intimate any inclination to compromise with Republicans but to await concessions from them. He opposed any reservations dealing with the treaty's substance but would accept "interpretations" that merely restated his own position as previously expressed to the Foreign Relations Committee. In short, Wilson refused to compromise with Lodge and also denounced attempts by Democratic senators to form a coalition with mild reservationists.[25]

---

24 Short, Report on Treaty Situation in Washington and the Senate with Reference to the Policies and Work of the League to Enforce Peace, Short to WHT, Dec. 18, 19, 1919, WHT Papers, Ser. 3, Box 463; JPT to EBW, Dec. 16, 1919, JPT Papers, Box 3; RL Diary, V, Dec. 16, 1919. For an excellent study of Mrs. Wilson's role in isolating the president, see Judith L. Weaver, "Edith Bolling Wilson as First Lady: A Study in the Power of Personality, 1919-1920," *Presidential Studies Quarterly*, XV (Winter 1985), 51-76.
25 Short, Report on the Treaty Situation in Washington, [Dec. 18, 1919], WHT Papers, Ser. 3, Box 463; *CR*, Vol. 59, 540-44; JPT to EBW, Dec. 18, 1919, JPT Papers, Box 3; JPT to EBW, Dec. 18,

In view of the president's steadfast refusal, Knox reintroduced his resolution to end the war between the United States and Germany. By removing the League from consideration, it offered the prospect of ending the stalemate. In the Foreign Relations Committee, to which it was referred, Knox presented a modified version as a substitute. This new Knox resolution provided for peace on the condition that Germany would concede to the United States all of the Versailles Treaty's benefits. Moreover, it reaffirmed the 1916 act of Congress, which had proposed an American policy for settling international disputes through mediation and arbitration, and called for an international conference to establish a court of arbitration and address the question of disarmament. The Foreign Relations Committee decided by a strictly partisan vote to recommend Knox's resolution. With this joint resolution, if the House of Representatives would join the Senate, Lodge hoped to achieve peace by circumventing the controversy over reservations. If Wilson refused to accept it, he would clearly bear the responsibility. Lodge foresaw no danger for the Republican party in leaving the League as an unresolved issue for the campaign. Democratic senators, including Hitchcock, Williams and Pomerene, who voted against the resolution in the committee, rejected Knox's proposal. Even Underwood, despite his willingness to accept the resolution as a last resort, reiterated his preference for compromise. He introduced a plan for a bipartisan committee of ten senators to prepare a resolution of ratification capable of attracting a two-thirds majority. Some mild reservationist Republicans as well as Democrats rallied against the Knox resolution. On December 21, McNary, Colt, Kellogg, Cummins, Hale and Edge notified Lodge of their "strong opposition" to it and urged instead a bipartisan compromise. This group, to Taft's delight, effectively killed the Knox resolution and forced Lodge to consider a possible agreement on reservations. Given Wilson's attitude, the result was continuing stalemate as the year ended. Like all other options in 1919, the Knox resolution failed to bridge the gulf between Republicans and Democrats, despite its appeal for senators as different as Brandegee and Underwood. The Versailles Treaty remained in the Senate for further action in the new year.[26]

II

A compromise between Wilson and Lodge offered the only prospect for American ratification of the treaty, but neither of them was inclined to make real concessions. As almost everyone except the president understood,

1919, EBW to Hitchcock, Dec. 19, 1919, WW Papers, Ser. 2, Box 194; EBW to Hitchcock, Dec. 19, 1919, Hitchcock Papers, Vol. 2; Hitchcock to Cummings, Dec. 17, 1919, ALL Papers.

26 CR, Vol. 59, 737-39, 956-61; U.S. Senate, *Proceedings of the Committee on Foreign Relations*, 211-12; HCL to Adams, Dec. 17, 1919, HCL Papers, File 1919 (Adams-Trevelyan); HCL to Williams, Dec. 20, 1919, HCL Papers, File 1919 (Peace, League, Political, I-Z); Notes, Dec. 18-20, 1919, Anderson Papers, Box 4; McNary to WHT, Dec. 22, 1919, WHT to McNary, Dec. 24, 1919, WHT to Kellogg, Dec. 24, 1919, WHT Papers, Ser. 3, Box 463.

Democratic senators needed to accept reservations if they wanted to form a two-thirds majority. Recognizing this reality, both Hitchcock and Underwood continued to seek an agreement with various Republican senators in late December 1919 and early January 1920. Lowell lobbied to break the deadlock over Article 10 in order to preserve the benefits of other parts of the Covenant. He urged Democratic senators to sacrifice this most controversial article. But neither his arguments nor other actions of pro-League advocates outside the Senate could produce a compromise. More clearly than Lowell, Taft appreciated the impotence of outsiders. Lamont hoped to gain access to Wilson to persuade him to compromise, but he never received an invitation to the White House. Bernard Baruch, head of the War Industries Board, attempted to use his influence in Washington for the same purpose, but without notable results. The president's steadfast refusal to permit any reservations in the resolution of ratification severely limited Hitchcock and Underwood, especially since they were simultaneously vying for election to succeed the late Thomas Martin as Democratic leader in the Senate. They dared not alienate Wilson or Democratic senators who remained loyal to him. McNary attempted to mediate between Lodge and Hitchcock. Lodge revealed his willingness to modify some of his reservations. Like Root, he welcomed a change in the preamble. He refused, however, to consider substantial alteration of his reservations, or purely verbal changes for the sake of apparent conciliation. He would consider modifications in phraseology only if these did not weaken the Republican reservations. As he assured irreconcilables, who opposed any changes whatsoever, Lodge intended to adhere to these minimal conditions for ratification. He shared the general Republican consensus that, if anyone made concessions, it should be Democrats. Yet he could not decline to discuss a possible compromise, for that kind of intransigence, although appealing to irreconcilables, might alienate mild reservationists. These Republicans, Lodge recognized, might then join Democrats in a bipartisan coalition in favor of reservations somewhat milder than his own. The remaining Republicans would then bear responsibility for the treaty's defeat. To avoid that political liability, Lodge worked diligently to maintain the confidence of all Republican senators. With a unified party, he could force Democrats to choose either to accept his reservations or kill the treaty.[27]

27   Tucker to Underwood, Dec. 20, 1919, Underwood to Tucker, Dec. 22, 1919, Underwood to Williams, Dec. 22, 1919, White to Underwood, Dec. 31, 1919, Underwood to White, Jan. 6, 1920, Underwood Papers; Hale to Calkins, Dec. 2, 1919, ALL to Underwood, Dec. 31, 1919, ALL to Hitchcock, Dec. 31, 1919, Jan. 7, 1920, ALL Papers; Anderson to HCL, Dec. 3, 1919, HCL to Anderson, Dec. 6, 1919, Anderson Papers, Box 4; HCL to Adams, Dec. 30, 1919, HCL Papers, File 1919 (Adams-Trevelyan); Beveridge to HCL, Jan. 1, 1920, HCL to Beveridge, Jan. 3, 1920, HCL to L. A. Coolidge, Jan. 1, 1920, HCL Papers, File 1920 (A-G); HCL to Beveridge, Dec. 31, 1919, Beveridge Papers, Box 216, and HCL Papers; HCL to Beveridge, Jan. 3, 1919, Beveridge Papers, Box 221; New to Beveridge, Dec. 6, 1919, Beveridge Papers, Box 217; Watson to Cohalan, Dec. 1, 1919, Cohalan Papers; Borah to Johnson, Dec. 29, 1919, Borah to Johnesse, Dec. 29, 1919, Borah Papers,; Box 550; Beveridge to Borah, Dec. 3, 1919, Borah Papers, Box 551, and Beveridge Papers, Box 214; Lamont to ER, Dec. 18, 24, 1919, ER to Lamont, Dec. 23, 1919, ER to Bacon, Dec. 17, 1919, ER Papers, Box

Wilson refused to consider any compromise on reservations even to secure American participation in the League. On January 5, Mrs. Wilson conveyed his request to Hitchcock to return the memorandum which outlined the president's suggestion for interpreting the treaty. Before departing on his western tour in September 1919, Wilson had given this document to the senator, who had subsequently used it as the basis for the first four of his own interpretive reservations. Hitchcock had based his fifth reservation on a conversation with the president. Furthermore, Mrs. Wilson urged Hitchcock not to show this document to anyone else. Wilson apparently wanted to avoid any association with Hitchcock's interpretive reservations, which he had not yet endorsed. The senator used this opportunity to inform the president through Mrs. Wilson about the necessity for concessions. He noted that twelve, and perhaps as many as fifteen, Republican senators wanted compromise. Because there were too few of these mild reservationists to create a two-thirds majority with the Democrats, they would not abandon fellow Republicans in a futile attempt to approve the treaty, thereby achieving nothing except to shift the political responsibility for its defeat to their party. At the other end of the Republican spectrum, Hitchcock observed, some fifteen irreconcilables would follow Borah out of the party if Lodge weakened his position. Under these circumstances, Democrats could not reasonably expect Lodge to shift his stance unless they offered real concessions to entice about twenty Republicans into a bipartisan coalition. Hitchcock regretted that he had received "little encouragement" from Wilson to make concessions, which he thought public opinion favored, to achieve ratification.[28]

Wilson resisted Hitchcock's advice. Rather than accommodate even mild reservationists, he acted to sharpen partisan differences. Ignoring political realities, the isolated president rigidly called for unqualified ratification. Within the White House, Tumulty urged Mrs. Wilson to encourage her sick husband not to surrender. Wilson gave his response to Hitchcock's counsel in the partisan setting of the Democratic party's celebration of Jackson Day on January 8, 1920. In a letter to the Democratic national chairman, he reaffirmed his all-or-nothing stance. Cummings read this letter to the Democrats attending the Jackson Day banquet. Claiming that the United States had enjoyed "the spiritual leadership of the world" before the Senate's refusal to approve the treaty, Wilson reiterated his commitment to cooperation with the Allies in "the concert of progressive and enlightened nations." The world had been made safe for democracy, he contended, but American

137; WHT to Short, Dec. 15, 1919, WHT to Yost, Dec. 15, 1919, WHT Papers, Ser. 3, Box 462; WHT to Karger, Dec. 17, 1919, Karger to WHT, Dec. 31, 1919, WHT to Kopald, Dec. 17, 1919, ? to Baruch, Dec. 22, 1919, Nugent to WHT, Dec. 30, 1919, WHT Papers, Ser. 3, Box 463; WHT to Karger, Jan. 1, 1920, WHT to King, Jan. 1, 1920, WHT to Nugent, Jan. 1, 1920, WHT to Short, Jan. 2, 1920, WHT to H. Taft, Jan. 2, 1920, WHT to Yost, Jan. 2, 1920, Karger to WHT, Jan. 3, 1920, WHT Papers, Ser. 3, Box 465; Edith Bolling Wilson, *My Memoirs* (Indianapolis, 1938), 296.
28 EBW to Hitchcock, Jan. 5, 1920, Hitchcock to EBW, Jan. 5, 1920, Hitchcock Papers, Vol. 2; Hitchcock to EBW, Jan. 5, 1920, Suggestion, [Summer 1919], WW Papers, Ser. 2, Box 195.

leadership was still necessary to achieve "a happy, settled order of life" and "political liberty." In other words, international social control would require the active involvement of the United States in the League. "The maintenance of the peace of the world and the effective execution of the treaty," Wilson argued, "depend upon the whole-hearted participation of the United States." Unless the Senate conformed to his will, he wanted to resolve the issue in a partisan manner in the 1920 election. Urging Democrats not to compromise with Republicans, he called instead for "a great and solemn referendum" on the treaty.[29]

At the Jackson Day banquet Bryan delivered a very different message. He advised Democrats against making the League the central issue in 1920. He thought they should compromise even on Article 10. Rather than quibbling over reservations, he wanted Democrats to join Republicans in approving the treaty. In that way the League's real benefits could be achieved, while difficulties of focusing a presidential campaign on a foreign-policy question, such as Bryan himself had experienced in 1900, could be avoided.[30]

Bryan expressed the mood of Democratic senators better than Wilson did. They continued their informal attempts to reach an agreement with Republican colleagues despite the president's opposition. His control over the party was clearly slipping, although most Democrats were not yet ready openly to reject his leadership. Their recognition that he could kill the treaty by refusing to ratify it, even if a bipartisan coalition gave it a two-thirds majority, circumscribed their inclination toward accommodation. In that case, Democratic senators would have succeeded only in placing the political responsibility for defeat on the head of their own party. Competition between Hitchcock and Underwood for Democratic leadership in the Senate further complicated these political considerations. Democratic senators, evenly divided between these two candidates, failed to elect either one in the vote that was finally held on January 15. Hitchcock had attempted to gain a presidential endorsement, but Wilson refused to support him or Underwood. The two rivals subsequently agreed to postpone the choice, while continuing to divide the duties of leading the minority. Hitchcock retained primary responsibility for the treaty, while Underwood handled domestic affairs. This division and unresolved rivalry curtailed the discretion of both senators in their pursuit of compromise on the treaty.[31]

29   JPT to EBW, Jan. 6, 1920, JPT Papers, Box 3; WW to Cummings, Jan. 8, 1920, JPT Papers, Boxes 7 and 14; *CR*, Vol. 59, 1249; *PPWW*, VI, 453-56.
30   *CR*, Vol. 59, 1250-51; Long Diary, Jan. 8, 1920, Long Papers, Box 2.
31   Short to WHT, Jan. 6, 10, 1920, Warner to Short, Jan. 5, 1920, McNary to WHT, Jan. 8, 1920, Karger to WHT, Jan. 10, 1920, Report of W. H. Short on Treaty Situation in Washington, Jan. 8-9, [1920], WHT Papers, Ser. 3, Box 465; Hitchcock to EBW, Jan. 13, 1920, EBW to Hitchcock, Jan. 13, 1920, WW Papers, Ser. 2, Box 195, and Hitchcock Papers, Vol. 2; McDowell to Underwood, Dec. 8, 1919, Underwood to McDowell, Dec. 11, 1919, Johnson to Underwood, Nov. 22, 1919, Jan. 21, 1920, Underwood to Johnson, Nov. 25, 1919, Jan. 16, 1920, Scott to Underwood, Jan. 29, Feb. 26, 1920, Underwood to Scott, Jan. 31, March 1, 1920, Miller to Scott, Feb. 26, 1920, Palmer to Underwood, Feb. 16, 1920, Underwood to Palmer, Feb. 19, 1920, Hoke Smith to Underwood, Jan. 26, 1920, Underwood Papers; *CR*, Vol. 59, 1250-51.

Outside the Senate, pro-League organizations continued their futile efforts to convince politicians to settle differences for the sake of peace. By now the League to Enforce Peace had fallen on hard times. Advocating unqualified ratification throughout the fall of 1919, it had alienated Republicans and become increasingly dependent upon Democratic members. When the executive committee then endorsed reservations in November, it began to lose support among Democrats. As a consequence, the League to Enforce Peace enjoyed less influence not only in Washington but throughout the country. It now experienced acute difficulty raising funds. Aware of these problems, its leaders saw the necessity for collaborating with other organizations. Taft encouraged cooperation with the Chamber of Commerce, which might provide money for pro-treaty activities. The executive committee, however, turned to organized labor. Joining Samuel Gompers of the American Federation of Labor, it invited leaders of other national organizations to a meeting in Washington on January 13, 1920. Representatives of twenty-six organizations responded to this invitation to indicate their desire for ratification of the treaty with the Covenant. To achieve this goal immediately, they appealed to Wilson and the Senate to compromise on reservations. This position, which the League to Enforce Peace had previously adopted, leaders of labor, farm, peace, church, education and women's organizations now jointly embraced. The unity among these twenty-six organizations, including the National Grange, Federal Council of Churches, National Education Association, and National Women's Christian Temperance Union, reflected weakness instead of strength. Even Taft, Lowell and Gompers failed to attend this meeting. The League to Enforce Peace and the American Federation of Labor, conscious of their inability to shape events in Washington, were desperately attempting to increase their influence by creating a broad national coalition.[32]

In 1920 the only hope for compromise depended upon the Senate. Given Wilson's intransigence, the one strategy that might break the deadlock would require pro-League Republican and Democratic senators to take the initiative. If they could agree on reservations acceptable to a two-thirds majority, this might force the president to ratify the treaty with reservations so as to avoid the political responsibility for defeat. Lodge shared Wilson's reluctance to offer concessions. For this reason, Taft encouraged mild reservationists to force Lodge's hand by seeking compromise with Democrats. McNary and Colt were actively pursuing this goal. Taft also counseled Democrats such as Senator Furnifold Simmons of North Carolina to continue

3 2   Houston to Short and WHT, Dec. 10, 1919, WHT Papers, Ser. 3, Box 462; Williams to Short, Dec. 25, 1919, ALL to WHT, Dec. 24, 1919, WHT to ALL, Dec. 25, 1919, WHT to Short, Dec. 25, 1919, Short to WHT, Dec. 27, 29, 1919, Short to ALL, Dec. 27, 29, 1919, WHT Papers, Ser. 3, Box 463; Short to WHT, Jan. 5, 7, 1920, WHT to Karger, Jan. 5, 1920, WHT to Short, Jan. 8, 1920, WHT Papers, Ser. 3, Box 465; Short to WHT, Jan. 16, 1920, Minutes of the Conference of National Organizations Favorable to Immediate Ratification of the Treaty of Peace with Germany Held in the City of Washington, D.C., Jan. 13, 1920, WHT Papers, Ser. 3, Box 466.

their work for an acceptable compromise, including a reservation to Article 10. Out of these informal efforts emerged the bipartisan conference, which convened for its first meeting on January 15. Lodge agreed to participate as the best way to maintain unity among Republican senators. While steadfastly refusing to concede the substance of his reservations, he wanted to demonstrate his willingness to consider Democratic proposals and thereby avoid alienating mild reservationists. Irreconcilables, he knew, adamantly opposed any weakening of his reservations, which they already regarded as inadequate. They preferred simply to pass the Knox resolution or some other resolution to end the war. Although he did not oppose this eventual outcome, Lodge appreciated that mild reservationists would not support a peace resolution until the Senate had first exhausted all possibilities for approving the treaty. As a demonstration of his good faith to mild reservationists, he explored conditions for a compromise in the bipartisan conference. An adroit political leader, Lodge combined flexibility in tactics with firmness on principles, for he intended to resist any concessions on crucial issues such as Article 10.[33]

For the bipartisan conference both Lodge and Hitchcock selected a few colleagues to join them. Excluding irreconcilables, Lodge picked New, Lenroot and Kellogg. Although McNary and Colt were not included, mild reservationists were well represented by Lenroot and Kellogg. Hitchcock, however, viewed New and even Lenroot as nearly as irreconcilable as Lodge, and only Kellogg as more reasonable. Excluding intractable opponents of reservations, such as Williams, Hitchcock invited Owen, McKellar, Simmons and Thomas Walsh to participate in this last attempt at conciliation. These senators began to consider the Lodge reservations one after another. By this procedure Democrats implicitly acknowledged the necessity for accepting reservations to the peace treaty. They recommended modifications in some reservations, but generally acquiesced in them. Lodge demonstrated his flexibility by indicating willingness to change the preamble and the first reservation concerning American withdrawal from the League. Republicans also favorably considered Walsh's substitute for the seventh reservation authorizing Congress to regulate by law American representation in any body established by the treaty. Equally conciliatory, Simmons presented his substitute for Lodge's reservation to Article 10, and McKellar offered his suggestion for its slight modification. Both of these Democratic alternatives underscored the role of Congress in determining whether the United States would use military power to preserve territorial integrity and political independence of other nations, thereby accepting the essence of the

33   WHT to McNary, Jan. 6, 11, 14, 1920, McNary to WHT, Jan. 13, 1920, ALL to WHT, Jan. 9, [1920], WHT to Karger, Jan. 12, 1920, WHT to White, Jan. 12, 1920, WHT to Simmons, Jan. 14, 1920, WHT Papers, Ser. 3, Box 465; Moses to Beveridge, Dec. 1, 1919, Beveridge Papers, Box 216; HCL to Beveridge, Jan. 13, [1920], Beveridge Papers, Box 221; HCL to Bigelow, Jan. 15, 1920, Beveridge to HCL, Jan. 10, 1920, HCL to Beveridge, Jan. 13, [1920], HCL Papers, File 1920 (Personal, A-G); Borah to Heinneman, Jan. 16, 1920, Borah Papers, Box 552.

Republican reservation. Hitchcock dutifully reported this progress to Tumulty. As the four Republican and five Democratic senators moved toward an agreement on a revised Article 10 reservation, Hitchcock notified Wilson himself on January 22 about the imminent prospect for successful compromise. It appeared that the deadlock would soon end.[34]

At this moment of apparent success, extremists on both sides intervened. Republican irreconcilables, disturbed by rumors of compromise, asked Lodge and New to leave the bipartisan conference on January 23 in order to meet them in Johnson's office. Borah, Brandegee, Moses, Knox, Mc-Cormick, Poindexter and Johnson served notice that they would not tolerate any retreat from the previous reservations. Lodge and New attempted to allay their fears. "The trouble is," New explained to Beveridge the next day, "that the fourteen Republicans who are irreconcilable had a brainstorm yesterday over something which didn't exist." Whether it was real or not, Borah continued to perceive danger. He warned Lodge that he would break from the Republican party if it compromised. Unless Democrats were actually giving up the fight, while seeking cosmetic changes in the Lodge reservations to save face, he feared that compromise would involve Republican concessions. Borah wanted no part of either a charade to help Democrats or a Republican betrayal of vital American interests. Given the thin margin of the Republican majority, Lodge dared not ignore Borah's warning. If even a few other irreconcilables joined him in bolting, the Republicans would lose control of the Senate. Vigorous reaction of the irreconcilables against possible compromise severely restricted Lodge's freedom to maneuver in subsequent sessions of the bipartisan conference.[35]

On the other extreme, the president reacted negatively to possible compromise. On January 15, the day of the bipartisan conference's first meeting, Tumulty sounded the alarm. Warning Mrs. Wilson that the senators might reach an agreement, he recommended that the White House seize the initiative to forestall this ominous prospect. If the Senate agreed on reservations, Tumulty anticipated, the American people would expect Wilson to accept these conditions and ratify the treaty, or they would blame him for killing it. To avoid either of these undesirable alternatives, the president needed to intervene. He could appear conciliatory, while actually blocking compromise. By forcing the Senate to approve the treaty on his terms or to reject it, he would either achieve victory or place the responsibility for defeat on Lodge's Republicans. Either outcome would strengthen the Democrats as they took the League into the 1920 election.

34   Hitchcock to JPT, Jan. 16, 17, 1920, Hitchcock to WW, Jan. 22, 1920, WW Papers, Ser. 2, Box 195; Williams to Hitchcock, Jan. 9, 1920, revised reservation to Article 10, Hitchcock to WW, Jan. [22], 1920, Hitchcock Papers, Vol. 2.

35   Moses to Beveridge, Jan. 23, 27, 1920, Beveridge Papers, Box 222; New to Beveridge, Jan. 24, 1920, Beveridge Papers, Box 223; Borah to HCL, Jan. 24, 1920, HCL Papers, File 1920 (Personal, A-G), and Borah Papers, Box 550; memo on Dec. 1919-Jan. 1920 bipartisan negotiations [by Kenneth McKellar], Hitchcock Papers, Vol. 2; HCL, *The Senate and the League of Nations*, 193-94.

Accordingly, Tumulty drafted a letter for the president to send to Hitchcock at the right "psychological moment" when the bipartisan conference approached an agreement.

Before Wilson acted on this proposal, Tumulty circulated his draft to a few cabinet members. Baker and Secretary of Agriculture David Houston offered suggestions for minor revision but generally endorsed this summary of the president's interpretation of the treaty. Lansing also gave his perfunctory approval. Privately, however, he agreed with Bliss and White that the failure now to achieve a bipartisan basis for ratifying the treaty would inevitably lead to adoption of a peace resolution by Congress or a separate peace with Germany. The all-or-nothing stance that Tumulty was urging Wilson to maintain, Lansing understood, would lead to the result preferred by irreconcilables, not to presidential victory in the treaty fight. Wilson accepted Tumulty's advice, but prepared his own letter to Hitchcock. In this letter, which Mrs. Wilson delivered to the senator on January 26, the president retreated only slightly from his earlier position. For the first time he endorsed Hitchcock's interpretive reservations. But these reservations were no longer under serious consideration by even Democratic senators in the bipartisan conference, for they were now negotiating on the basis of the Lodge reservations. In effect, Wilson notified Hitchcock not to proceed with compromise involving strong reservations as part of the resolution of ratification. By this negative reaction, he consolidated his tacit coalition with irreconcilables to kill the treaty.[36]

Despite resistance from Wilson and irreconcilables, the bipartisan conference continued for the next few days to seek compromise. For the moment, both Lodge and Hitchcock ignored these extremists. While Taft and Lowell hoped for a successful outcome, Borah worried that moderate Republican and Democratic senators might still agree on reservations. Unfortunately, from his perspective, the irreconcilables' warning to Lodge and his threat to bolt from the Republican party had not halted the bipartisan conference. Borah began to relax only after the president's intervention finally doomed these negotiations. On January 28, at her husband's request, Mrs. Wilson asked Burleson to ascertain from Hitchcock and Underwood which senators were obstructing and which were supporting ratification. Wilson obviously intended to hold each senator accountable. Because of Underwood's illness,

36   JPT to EBW, Jan. 15, 17, 1920, JPT's draft of WW to Hitchcock, EBW's draft of WW to Hitchcock, n.d., WW to Hitchcock, Jan. 26, 1920, WW Papers, Ser. 2, Box 195; WW to Hitchcock, Jan. 26, 1920, E. B. W[ilson], note, [Jan. 26, 1920], Hitchcock Papers, Vol. 2; JPT's draft of WW to Hitchcock, n.d., WW Papers, Ser. 4, File 5191; RL to JPT, Jan. 15, 1920, JPT's draft of WW to Hitchcock, JPT Papers, Box 2; JPT to EBW, Jan. 15, 16, 17, 1920, JPT Papers, Box 3; Houston, memo, n.d., JPT Papers, Box 7; JPT's draft of WW to Hitchcock, Jan. 14, 1920, Memorandum by Secretary Houston, n.d., NDB's notations on JPT's draft of WW to Hitchcock, n.d., Hitchcock to JPT, Jan. 26, 1920, JPT Papers, Box 14; THB to RL, Jan. 21, 1920, THB memorandum, Jan. 21, 1920, RL Papers, Vol. 51; THB to HW, Jan. 21, 1920, HW to THB, Jan. 23, 1920, THB Papers, Box 69; THB memorandum, Jan. 21, 1920, THB Papers, Box 71; THB to HW, Jan. 21, 1920, THB memorandum, Jan. 21, 1920, HW to THB, Jan. 23, 1920, HW Papers, Box 23; *PPWW*, VI, 460-61.

Burleson conferred only with Hitchcock, who exonerated all Democratic senators except Reed. The Nebraskan blamed Republicans, from irreconcilables to mild reservationists, for the treaty's fate. He labeled mild reservationists as actually "Lodge Reservationists," which meant they were more concerned with the Republican party's welfare than the treaty's passage. Forced to employ the president's own categories for evaluating loyalty of senators, Hitchcock lost his remaining freedom to proceed in the bipartisan conference.

Wilson was obviously unwilling to consider a compromise originating in the Senate or to propose one himself. Consequently, Hitchcock and Lodge announced on January 30 the bipartisan conference's unsuccessful conclusion. By that time the conferees had reached tentative agreement on a revised preamble and eight reservations. Democratic senators had accepted four of the original Lodge reservations, while Republicans had conceded minor changes in phraseology in four others. They failed, however, to overcome differences on six reservations. These disputed reservations dealt with American rights and obligations relative to withdrawal from the League, Article 10, the Monroe Doctrine, the League's expenses, sanctions under Article 16, and British votes in the League. For Lodge the two principal obstacles were Article 10 and the Monroe Doctrine. Steadfastly refusing any moral or legal commitment under Article 10, he rejected all Democratic proposals that might limit the discretion of Congress in deciding whether to authorize American armed forces to protect another nation. As a last resort in the final session on January 30, Democrats had proposed Taft's reservation, but to no avail. Lodge likewise resisted any curtailment of unilateral American interpretation of the Monroe Doctrine. Although flexible on minor points, he and his Republican colleagues in the bipartisan conference never intended to surrender on these key issues.[37]

Wilson's rigidity threatened to destroy what he had apparently sought to accomplish at the peace conference. Some of his closest associates at Paris now saw this danger. Ray Stannard Baker feared that the deadlock would prevent the United States from reorganizing the world. The American people, he thought, would still respond to a moral appeal for the League, but only if petty disputes over apparently insignificant differences in reservations could be avoided. He delicately urged Mrs. Wilson to encourage her

37   Borah to Dunne, Jan. 26, 1920, Borah to Babb, Jan. 31, 1920, Borah Papers, Box 550; Borah to Mulchaey, Jan. 27, 1920, Borah Papers, Box 551; WHT to Yost, Jan. 20, 1920, WHT to Karger, Jan. 21, 1920, ALL to WHT, Jan. 21, 1920, WHT to ALL, Jan. 21, 1920, WHT to McCumber, Jan. 21, 1920, WHT to H. Taft, Jan. 21, 1920, WHT to Boardman, Jan. 28, 1920, Karger to WHT, Jan. 19, 31, 1920, WHT Papers, Ser. 3, Box 466; EBW to Burleson, Jan. 28, 1920, Burleson to EBW, Jan. 28, 1920, WW Papers, Ser. 2, Box 195; EBW to Burleson, Jan. 28, 1920, Burleson to EBW, Jan. 28, 1920, EBW to Burleson, [c. Jan. 29, 1920], Burleson Papers, Vol. 25; EBW to Burleson, Jan. 28, 1920, Burleson to EBW, Jan. 28, 1920, RSB Papers, Ser. I, Box 3; CR, Vol. 59, 2285-87; HCL, The Senate and the League of Nations, 194-205; HCL to Bigelow, Jan. 30, 1920, Beveridge to HCL, Jan. 29, 1920, HCL Papers, File 1920 (Personal, A-G); HCL to L. A. Coolidge, Feb. 2, 1920, HCL Papers, File 1920 (A-G); HCL to Wardwell, Jan. 29, 1920, HCL Papers, File 1920 (Personal, H-Z).

husband to compromise. House shared Baker's anxiety that the treaty fight would destroy any possible American effectiveness in the League. "I doubt whether the League can ever recover," he confided to Secretary Baker. The dream of benevolent American leadership, which they had once identified with the League, was now rapidly fading.[38]

Lippmann observed a greater danger from Wilson's leadership than American rejection of the treaty, for he no longer believed in the redemptive role of the United States in the League. He saw the terrible irony that the president, who had promised to make the world safe for democracy, was now responsible for the Red Scare in the United States. "Well it was possible to fail in those hopes," Lippmann lamented to Secretary Baker. "It was credible that the wisdom and the strength to realize them would be lacking. But it is forever incredible that an administration announcing the most spacious ideals in our history should have done more to endanger fundamental American liberties than any group of men for a hundred years." Wilson's search for American control at home and abroad, rather than benefiting other countries, produced "a reign of terror" in the United States. Instead of saving the world, his liberalism failed even in this country. Responding to Lippmann's criticism, Secretary Baker expressed his confidence that the current hysteria would eventually pass away. What he most regretted was that the United States was missing "the opportunity to seize and hold the spiritual leadership of the world." Despite even its negative consequences in the Red Scare at home, he continued to affirm Wilson's global vision of the American mission, while Lippmann had lost his faith. For the president and his loyal followers, adherence to his creed for the world's redemption was more important than its practical realization.[39]

III

Wilson's leadership during the treaty fight vitally affected other countries. The British government had closely observed American developments, aware of their world-wide implications. In August 1919, Lloyd George had decided to send Lord Grey to Washington as special ambassador. The president, because of his illness, never received him in the White House. After three frustrating months, Grey returned to Great Britain at the end of the year. On January 31, 1920, in a letter to *The Times* of London, he expressed his views on the impasse between Wilson and the Senate. Although unofficial, Grey's letter aroused favorable and critical responses

3 8   RSB to EBW, Jan. 25, 1920, EBW Papers; EMH to NDB, Jan. 29, 1920, NDB Papers, Box 12.
3 9   Lippmann to NDB, Jan. 17, 1920, NDB to Lippmann, Jan. 20, 1920, NDB Papers, Box 12. For the Red Scare in the United States, see Robert K. Murray, *Red Scare: A Study in National Hysteria*, 1919-1920 (New York, 1964), Stanley Coben, *A. Mitchell Palmer: Politician* (New York, 1963), 196-245, and Stanley Coben, "A Study in Nativism: The American Red Scare of 1919-20," *Political Science Quarterly*, LXXIX (March 1964), 52-75.

from Americans. They welcomed or denounced it, depending upon whether they thought it strengthened or weakened their positions in the treaty fight.[40]

Before Grey's appointment, British observers in Washington had reported on American politics. Wiseman, after serving as chief adviser on American affairs in the British delegation at the peace conference, had returned to the United States. Early in July 1919 he noted the anti-British character of Republican criticism of the League. Although some Republicans, including Lodge and Knox, were "reluctantly anti-British," others such as Borah and Johnson were "violently anti-British and anti-European generally." Wiseman still believed the president could force the Senate to approve the treaty without amendments or reservations, but feared the influence of Irish-Americans. The recent arrival in the United States of Eamon De Valera, president of the self-proclaimed Irish republic, Wiseman regarded as an ominous event. He expected German-Americans to exploit the Sinn Fein movement as an effective way to disrupt Anglo-American cooperation. By advocating American isolation and attacking British imperialism, German propaganda in the guise of promoting Irish independence might adversely influence the treaty fight.[41]

To prevent American policy from shifting in an anti-British direction, Lloyd George decided to send Grey on his special mission to Washington. Announcement of this appointment in the House of Commons caught the State Department by surprise. Various British leaders, including the prime minister and Grey himself, had consulted House in London, but the Foreign Office had neglected to check with the State Department. The unofficial link between Wiseman and House continued to operate outside of regular channels, despite the estrangement between House and Wilson. Nevertheless, Lansing assured the Foreign Office that the United States would welcome Grey, although it would prefer a permanent ambassador. In accordance with the president's desire, the secretary instructed House to remain in Europe rather than accompany Grey to the United States. Despite his contribution to the initiation of Grey's mission, House no longer played a pivotal role in Anglo-American relations.[42]

---

4 0   For an excellent account of Grey's mission, see George W. Egerton, "Britain and the 'Great Betrayal': Anglo-American Relations and the Struggle for United States Ratification of the Treaty of Versailles, 1919-1920," *Historical Journal*, XXI, No. 4 (1978), 885-911, and also Leon E. Boothe, "A Fettered Envoy: Lord Grey's Special Mission to the United States, 1919-1920," *Review of Politics*, XXXIII (Jan. 1971), 78-94.

4 1   Wiseman to Malcolm, July 1-2, 1919, Wiseman Papers, 90/7, House Papers, 20/48, and Woodward and Butler, eds., *Documents on British Foreign Policy*, First Series, V, 980-85; Lindsay to Curzon, Aug. 21 (#352), 21 (#343), 22 (#354), 1919, ibid., V, 988-92.

4 2   EMH to Wiseman, July 4, 1919, Wiseman to EMH, July 8, 11, 1919, EMH Papers, 20/48; EG to EMH, statement, [Aug. 11, 1919], EMH Papers, 9/9; RL to EMH, Aug. 28, 1919, EMH Papers, 49/20; EMH to WW, July 30, 1919, Aug. 8, 11, 1919, EMH Papers, 49/13; EMH to WW, Aug. 11, 1919, WW Papers, Ser. 2, Box 191; EMH to WW, Sept. 3, 1919, WW Papers, Ser. 2, Box 192; Tyrrell to Wiseman, Aug. 18, 1919, Wiseman to Tyrrell, Aug. 25, 1919, Wiseman Papers, 90/25; Lindsay to Curzon, Aug. 16 (#347), 20 (#350), 20 (#351), 1919, Curzon to Lindsay, Aug. 19

In Grey's instructions Curzon focused on three outstanding issues in Anglo-American relations. He stressed the British government's desire to cooperate with the United States in the League to fulfill their common ideals. He also wanted Grey to allay American suspicions about the British ship-building program. Expansion of the British navy, he emphasized, related to world-wide threats to the British Empire, not to the American navy's size. The British did not reckon the United States as an enemy. Curzon instructed Grey, while preventing a naval race, also to neutralize the Irish question in American politics. But Lloyd George's cabinet refused to recognize Irish independence as an acceptable price for harmonious Anglo-American relations. Although anticipating some measure of home rule for Ireland, the British government intended to retain control over foreign policy as well as military and naval affairs for that country. In short, the British Empire's strategic interests remained more important than even American ratification of the treaty. It welcomed American membership in the League, but interpreted its ideals in accordance with traditional British interests.[43]

Arriving in Washington after Wilson's stroke, Grey immediately experienced difficulty. Unable even to present his credentials to the president, he lacked formal status as British ambassador. He continued to confer with House, who had finally come back to the United States, but quickly perceived his diminished position. Grey noted the pervasive effect of the Irish question on relations between London and Washington. As a way of isolating the "extreme Sinn Feiners" who advocated independence, he advised the British government to announce a policy of self-government for Ireland, but it refrained from taking this step. Another source of anti-British sentiment in the United States, he observed, came from the Covenant's provision for six British votes in the League. He hoped to assure Americans that no part of the British Empire would vote in the assembly if it was in any way involved in a controversy. He asked Curzon for permission to confirm this interpretation and also for the official view of representation by the British dominions on the council. Before the Senate narrowly defeated the Johnson amendment, both Lansing and Hitchcock urged Grey to clarify British policy. Curzon endorsed Grey's interpretation regarding British votes in the League assembly, but denied him permission to announce it. The foreign secretary also opposed any restriction on eligibility of British dominions or India for election to the League council, recalling the promise of Clemenceau, Wilson and Lloyd George in the letter to Borden. Pending consultation with the dominions, Curzon cautioned Grey not to make any public statement on British voting in the League. This response prevented

(#348), 19 (#349), 1919, Woodward and Butler, eds., *Documents on British Foreign Policy*, First Series, V, 997-1000.
43   Curzon to EG, Sept. 9, 1919 (#360), ibid., V, 997-1000.

Grey from removing this issue as a major source of conflict in the treaty fight.[44]

British silence failed to allay American suspicions. Although the Senate defeated all amendments, including Johnson's, the issue of British voting reappeared in Lenroot's reservation. The British government responded to Grey's repeated requests for an official view by consulting the dominions. Borden approved Grey's interpretation of the Covenant, but the prime ministers of South Africa and Australia refused. Fearful that they would contradict the kind of public statement Grey wanted to make, thereby stirring up even more anti-British sentiment in the United States, Curzon instructed him not to risk this consequence. Nevertheless, Grey shared his personal opinion of the Lenroot reservation with Lansing. In a letter on November 19, he accepted its assertion that the United States would not be bound by any decision of the League assembly or council in a dispute with the British Empire if any if its parts voted. He objected, however, to the reservation's denial of all American obligations in the League if any empire, including its dominions or colonies, cast more than one vote. This qualification, Grey insisted, violated the Borden letter's promise to the dominions. It would cause serious obstacles to the League's success, for the British government would not tolerate their disfranchisement. Unable to resolve such outstanding differences in Anglo-American relations, Grey wanted to return home, aware that he could never accomplish the goals of his mission. Besides his unauthorized letter to Lansing, which he allowed him to share with Hitchcock, Grey hesitated to involve himself in the debate over reservations before the Senate completed voting in November 1919. In view of the potential American veto of any decision by the League council, he told Lansing that the anxiety expressed in these reservations seemed unwarranted. However, as he explained to Curzon, the "real difficulty is that the Senate assumes the existence of a President instructing the American Representative on the Council of the League to pursue a policy obnoxious to the Senate and Congress." This executive-legislative conflict over the control of American foreign relations superseded the particular points of disagreement over reservations. Obviously, constitutional discord within the United States as well as the British Empire made Grey's mission exceedingly difficult.[45]

Lloyd George had begun to worry about implications of American

44 EG to DLG, Oct. 5, 17, 1919, EG to Curzon, Oct. 27, 1919, DLG Papers, F/60/3/7, 10, 14; EG to Curzon, Oct. 4 (#366), 4 (#367), 4 (#368), 7 (#371), 9 (#373), 11 (#375), 15 (#376), 16 (#377), 24 (#379), 1919, Curzon to EG, Oct. 6 (#369), 8 (#372), 22 (#378), 24 (#380), 24 (#381), 1919, Woodward and Butler, eds., *Documents on British Foreign Policy*, First Series, V, 1003-12.
45 Thornton to Davies, Nov. 10, 13, 1919, Milner to Governors-General of Canada, South Africa, Australia and New Zealand, Nov. 8, 1919, Buxton to Milner, Nov. 11, 1919, Ferguson to Milner, Nov. 14, 1919, DLG Papers, F/39/1/46, 47, 48; EG to RL, Nov. 19, 1919, RL Papers, Vol. 49, and EMH Papers, 9/9; EG to DLG, Nov. 11, 1919, [Curzon] to EG, draft copy, Dec. ?, 1919, DLG Papers, F/60/3/18, 20, 23; EG to Curzon, Oct. 29 (#385), Nov. 1 (#387), 6 (#389), 7 (#391), 13 (#394), 14 (#395), 17 (#396), 21 (#400), 25 (#409), 25 (#410), 1919, Curzon to EG, Oct. 31 (#386), Nov. 12 (#393), 18 (#397), 1919, Curzon to Watson, Nov. 22, 1919 (#401), Woodward and Butler, eds., *Documents on British Foreign Policy*, First Series, V, 1013-14, 1017-23, 1029-31, 1036-37.

reservations for the British position in the League. If the United States ratified the treaty with reservations, it would enjoy an advantage. On the other hand, if the president refused to ratify the treaty with reservations, the Allies would assume their obligations without American assistance. Through his secretary, Philip Kerr, the prime minister requested the Foreign Office's assessment. He wanted the opinion of legal adviser Hurst on the effect of reservations on the peace treaty, and the advice of Curzon on the desirability of British ratification while Americans were still considering reservations. "The question that is exercising the Prime Minister's mind at present," Hurst learned from Kerr, "is that the Covenant of the League of Nations imposes considerable obligations upon all the members, particularly upon the Great Powers and most of all upon the British Empire with its world-wide interests. The one element which made the representatives of the Great Powers at Paris accept the scheme without exhaustive consideration of the obligations which the League would entail was the fact that all the nations of the world and especially all the Five Great Powers would be, so to speak, in the same boat and would share the burden in common." Hurst recognized the vital importance of American participation in the League, noting that "the existing League will not work unless it comprehends practically the entire universe." Nevertheless, he thought the British government should proceed with ratification whether the United States did or not. It should, however, refuse all American reservations. If the United States declined to ratify the treaty without qualification, Hurst agreed with Kerr, the British government could announce its withdrawal from the League in two years. Lord Hardinge, permanent undersecretary in the Foreign Office, concurred in Hurst's advice to resist American reservations. After reviewing their recommendations, Curzon agreed that the British government should not delay ratification of the peace treaty much longer. In his report to Lloyd George, he also endorsed the idea of possible British withdrawal from the League if the United States failed to join.[46]

Lloyd George agreed with the Foreign Office that the British government should oppose American reservations. Kerr asked Wiseman to notify House about this negative decision. British leaders hoped the Senate would drop its reservations and approve the entire treaty. At the prime minister's request, Curzon circulated Hurst's memorandum on American reservations to the cabinet on November 19. American failure to ratify the treaty on the basis of common obligations, Hurst argued, would undermine the League and return international relations to the old system. Opposing the Article 10 reservation, he claimed that "the President is probably right in saying that the effect of this reservation is to cut the heart out of the Covenant." Other reservations were equally unacceptable. He thought the British Empire

46 Curzon to DLG, Nov. 7, 1919, Hurst to Curzon, Nov. 4, 1919, Kerr to Campbell, Oct. 30, 1919, Hurst, note, Nov. 2, 1919, Hurst to Campbell, Nov. 4, 1919, Hurst to Hardinge, Nov. 5, 1919, DLG Papers, F/12/2/3.

should not acquiesce in them even to ensure American membership in the League and avoid an Anglo-American naval race.[47]

House refused to regard this British position as irrevocable. He told Grey he hoped the State Department might consult him and the French ambassador about a compromise. For this eventuality, in response to Grey's request for instructions, Curzon reiterated British policy. If the United States adopted reservations, he explained, Great Britain might announce its withdrawal from the League. Deep fear of overcommitment, if Anglo-American cooperation failed to materialize in the League, accounted for this negative British attitude toward reservations. For its own reasons, Lloyd George's government adopted an all-or-nothing stance comparable to Wilson's.[48]

After November 1919, British policymakers adhered to their uncompromising position. Both Lloyd George and Curzon expressed to Polk in London their desire for American ratification. They declined, however, to consider any reservations to achieve this outcome. Under these circumstances, the prime minister feared the renewal of Anglo-American naval rivalry. Grey adopted a more conciliatory attitude on both the League and naval policy. After consulting various Republicans, including Lodge and Root, he was convinced that the Senate would never accept the treaty without reservations. Except for the preamble, he expected Republicans to adhere to all their reservations. He saw no prospect of their abandoning the Lenroot reservation. Acceptance of all the Lodge reservations, Grey finally concluded, would be better than total American rejection of the treaty. Failing to persuade the British government to change its policy, and lacking any opportunity to see Wilson, Grey decided to return home to explain the treaty fight to the British public.[49]

Grey's letter to *The Times* of London on January 31, 1920, expressed his personal opinion. He urged British acceptance of the Lodge reservations to gain American participation in the League. Defending the Senate, he recognized that the executive-legislative conflict involved fundamental questions rather than merely partisan politics. "There is in the United

47 Wiseman to N. G. T. [for EMH], Nov. 12, 1919, Wiseman to EMH, Nov. 20, 1919, EMH Papers, 20/48; [Wiseman to EMH], Nov. 12, 1919, EMH Papers, 12/41; Memorandum by Mr. Hurst, Nov. 18, 1919 (#399), Woodward and Butler, eds., *Documents on British Foreign Policy*, First Series, V, 1024-28.

48 EG to Curzon, Nov. 23, 1919 (#405), Curzon to EG, Nov. 27, 1919 (#414), ibid., V, 1034, 1040-42.

49 Polk to RL, Nov. 29, 1919, Polk Papers, 82/16; Interview with the Press, Nov. 26, 1919, Polk Papers, 82/24; HCL to Trevelyan, Oct. 25, 1919, HCL Papers, File 1919 (Adams-Trevelyan); Notes, Nov. 27, 1919, Anderson Papers, Box 4; RL to JPT, Dec. 15, 1919, JPT to EBW, Dec. 18, 1919, WW Papers, Ser. 2, Box 194; JPT to EBW, Dec. 18, 1919, JPT Papers, Box 3; Curzon to EG, Nov. 25 (#411), 27 (#415), Dec. 8 (#430), 24 (#440), 1919, EG to Curzon, Nov. 26 (#412), 28 (#418), 28 (#419), 28 (#420), Dec. 10 (#432), 11 (#433), 11 (#434), 11 (#435), 12 (#436), 12 (#437), 16 (#438), 24 (#441), 1919, Watson to Curzon, Dec. 6, 1919 (#428), Curzon to Watson, Dec. 8, 1919 (#429), Campbell to EG, Dec. 29, 1919 (#443), Woodward and Butler, eds., *Documents on British Foreign Policy*, First Series, V, 1037-39, 1042-49, 1054-65.

States," he reported, "a conservative feeling for traditional policy, and one of those traditions, consecrated by the advice of Washington, is to abstain from foreign, and particularly from European entanglements." He believed the United States, even with reservations, could make a crucial contribution in the League to maintain peace. It was therefore in the British interest, Grey concluded, to accept even Lenroot's reservation to enable the United States, which would in practice cooperate with the British Empire, to join the League.[50]

Reactions to Grey's letter varied according to political persuasion. Although Lodge immediately brought it to the Senate's attention, the White House responded negatively. In a press release, the president denounced it, stating that he would have demanded Grey's recall if he were still in Washington. In the State Department, where opinions varied, Long shared this revulsion. Suspecting Lansing of disloyalty, he blamed him for encouraging Grey to take this rash action. But Polk, expecting a "peevish" response from Wilson, welcomed the letter's potential contribution to compromise. Now that the Allies seemed ready to accept reservations, Republicans might force the president to acquiesce. Taft likewise saw Grey's letter as confirmation of British willingness to accept reservations and corroboration of his own advocacy of compromise. Irreconcilables, however, interpreted it as proof of their very different position. Grey's claim that the Lodge reservations would not in practice impede American participation in the League appeared to verify their contention that even strong reservations would not protect the United States. Borah and Reed consequently continued to oppose concessions. Professional Irish-American leaders shared the irreconcilables' fear that Grey's letter would lead to compromise. Urging Borah to remain vigilant, Cohalan hoped that Wilson's stubbornness and vanity would save them from this great danger. All of these reactions to Grey's letter reflected the previously established attitudes of protagonists in the treaty fight. Extremists, from the president to irreconcilables, did not welcome Grey's attempt to improve Anglo-American relations. Only proponents of the League with reservations appreciated his advocacy of compromise.[51]

In the wake of Grey's letter Hitchcock decided to publicize Wilson's most conciliatory statement of his position. On February 7 the senator released the president's letter of January 26, which contained his first endorsement of Hitchcock's interpretive reservations. Lacking an explicit rejection of any

50 CR, Vol. 59, 2335-36.
51 JPT to EBW, [Feb. 3, 1920], "Taking Account of Stock," Springfield Republican (Feb. 3, 1920), press release, [Feb. 6, 1920], WW Papers, Ser. 2, Box 195; Long Diary, Feb. 17, 21, 1920, Long Papers, Box 2; Polk to EMH, Feb. 10, 1920, EMH Papers, 16/9; WHT to McNary, Dec. 24, 1919, WHT Papers, Ser. 3, Box 463; WHT to Karger, Feb. 2, 1920, Karger to WHT, Feb. 5, 1920, WHT Papers, Ser. 3, Box 467; Borah to Chandler, Jan. 19, 1920, Borah to Pope, Feb. 9, 1920, Borah Papers, Box 550; Borah to Owen, Jan. 23, 1920, Borah Papers, Box 551; CR, Vol. 59, 2352-60; Cohalan to Borah, Feb. 2, 1920, Cohalan Papers; "Wilson, Grey and the Peace Treaty," Gaelic American, XVII (Feb. 14, 1920), 4.

other reservation to Article 10, it specifically repudiated only the negative form of the bipartisan conference's draft. Publication consequently conveyed the impression of greater flexibility in the White House than actually existed. Taking advantage of this apparent sign of openness, pro-League lobbyists again urged compromise. Representatives of the twenty-six national organizations which had earlier met in Washington reconvened for a second meeting on February 9. Despite Taft's absence, the League to Enforce Peace continued to provide leadership. Straus served as chairman and Short as secretary of the conference. Attending as a World Peace Foundation delegate, Lowell introduced a resolution which the conference unanimously adopted. It called for bipartisan compromise, proclaiming that the American people favored the treaty's ratification with reservations. Regarding differences between the Lodge and Hitchcock reservations as "insignificant," it placed higher priority on saving the treaty than on partisanship. Leaders of the national organizations appealed to Wilson and the Senate in the hope of promoting American membership in the League.[52]

Outside the White House, advocates of the peace treaty recognized that ratification depended upon bipartisan conciliation. Even Glass, who had faithfully defended the president's position in the cabinet before accepting appointment as Virginia's new senator, now found arguments for compromise compelling. His constituents encouraged him in that direction. He urged Wilson during a rare personal interview on February 6 to accept Taft's reservation to Article 10, while opposing the Lodge reservations generally. After subsequently gaining Hitchcock's and Underwood's concurrence, he reiterated his rationale in a letter. If Democrats endorsed the Taft reservation, Glass contended, that would pose a real dilemma for Republicans. The Republican majority might accept it, but would then face Borah's and Johnson's defection. More likely, Lodge would reject it to prevent the revolt of irreconcilables, but would then bear responsibility for defeating the treaty. In both cases Democrats would benefit, either by securing the treaty's ratification on acceptable terms or by demonstrating the Republicans' inclination "to wreck the world to satiate their hatred of a Democratic President." Wanting to seize the political initiative, Glass implored Wilson to signal his willingness to accept the Taft reservation. But Wilson absolutely refused to approve this strategy. At his direction Mrs. Wilson informed Glass that he wanted Democrats "to force the Republicans to take or reject the Treaty as it stands, or to propose some other course with regard to it." But Taft's alternative was not acceptable: "Article 10 is the backbone of the Covenant and Mr. Taft's proposed reservation is not conceived in good faith." Even in utmost confidence the president would not inform Glass, one of his staunchest supporters, what reservations he might allow as part of the

5 2   "Wilson Insists Obligation Must Be Assumed by U.S.," Feb. 7, 1920, JPT Papers, Box 7; *CR*, Vol. 59, 2622; Short, Minutes of the Second Conference of National Organizations Favorable to Immediate Ratification of the Treaty of Peace with Germany, Feb. 9, 1920, WHT Papers, Ser. 3, Box 467.

resolution of ratification. If Republicans proposed some course other than unqualified approval, he intended to retain his unquestioned right to oppose it. This uncompromising stance left Democratic senators no freedom to maneuver with any assurance that he would accept even the mildest reservation. As the Senate prepared to reconsider the Versailles Treaty, Wilson instructed Democrats that "absolute inaction on our part is better than a mistaken initiative." He remained intransigent, disregarding pressures toward compromise.[53]

IV

Despite the failure of all previous attempts to reach an agreement, the Senate refused to abandon the peace treaty. Lodge proposed its reconsideration on February 9 in order to preserve his leadership. He seized the initiative to prevent mild reservationists from forming a coalition with Democrats. Except for some irreconcilables, senators from both parties approved. Lodge intended to force the Democratic senators and president to accept his reservations or kill the treaty. If they accepted them, the United States could still join the League. This risk troubled irreconcilables such as Borah and Brandegee, who feared that Democrats might acquiesce. Success for irreconcilables depended upon Wilson's continuing intransigence. Lodge now offered him a new opportunity to save the treaty.[54]

A growing number of Democratic senators wanted to take advantage of this opportunity. Hitchcock experienced great difficulty in keeping their loyalty. He informed Wilson on February 24 that only fifteen to eighteen of them would remain faithful, while the remainder wished to accept the Lodge reservations. This meant that the tacit coalition between irreconcilables and Wilson's loyal followers might not prevent a two-thirds majority. Glass and Robinson gave an equally bleak report to Tumulty, explaining that senators were under pressure from their constituents to achieve peace without regard for the precise nature of reservations. All three senators advised the president to issue a public statement to rally Democrats against the Lodge reservations. Other prominent Democratic senators such as Underwood and Pomerene wanted to end the treaty fight by accepting them. Even Tumulty began to waver. He thought the president should postpone a statement, while

53   Glass to WW, Feb. 8, 1920, [EBW to Glass], Feb. 11, 1920, Glass Papers, Box 8; Glass to Ensley, Dec. 19, 1919, Glass to Hardy, Jan. 15, 1920, Turner to Glass, Feb. 5, 1920, Glass to Turner, Feb. 6, 1920, Richmond Rotary Club to Glass, Feb. 8, 1920, Glass to Richmond Rotary Club, Feb. 11, 1920, Glass Papers, Box 143.

54   HCL to L. A. Coolidge, Feb. 11, 1920, Beveridge to HCL, Feb. 12, 1920, HCL to Beveridge, Feb. 16, 1920, HCL Papers, File 1920 (Personal, A-G); Borah to Marsters, Feb. 7, 1920, Borah to Dunn, Feb. 24, 1920, Borah to Cohalan, Feb. 9, 1920, Borah Papers, Box 551; Beveridge to Brandegee, Feb. 18, 1920, Brandegee to Beveridge, Feb. 27, 1920, Beveridge Papers, Box 219; Beveridge to HCL, Feb. 12, 1920, HCL to Beveridge, Feb. 16, 1920, Beveridge Papers, Box 221; Beveridge to New, Feb. 9, 1920, New to Beveridge, Feb. 12, 1920, Smoot to Beveridge, Feb. 17, 1920, Beveridge Papers, Box 223; CR, Vol. 59, 2627-37.

awaiting the outcome in the Senate. Tumulty hoped to protect him against the political liability of refusing to ratify the treaty if two-thirds of the Senate approved it. In that event, he even contemplated Wilson's ratification of the treaty with reservations, accompanied by a reiteration of his rationale for having preferred unqualified ratification. Glass and Hitchcock understood that the president would not compromise under any circumstances. Knowing that he would rather kill the treaty than acquiesce in Lodge's reservations, they sought to avoid a resolution of ratification that he would reject. Hitchcock appealed to Democratic partisanship to curb defections. He asked his colleagues to imagine how they could possibly explain why they had reversed themselves between the fall of 1919 and the spring of 1920, while the president had not. Capitulation to the Republican majority would severely embarrass the Democratic party but would not secure the treaty's ratification. Now convinced that Wilson would never compromise, and that Republicans would not surrender, Hitchcock worked to salvage a credible position for Democrats in the coming campaign.[55]

Wilson's handling of Lansing's resignation further discredited his leadership. He accused the secretary of state of attempting to usurp presidential authority, especially by convening the cabinet during his illness. This unsubstantiated charge of disloyalty failed to provide a plausible justification for requiring Lansing to leave the State Department. There were substantial reasons for Wilson to select a new secretary. The two men had long disagreed over fundamental aspects of foreign policy. The president had not entrusted Lansing with an important part in the negotiations at the peace conference. Yet he had relied upon him during the summer of 1919 before Bullitt gave his damaging testimony. Following the Bullitt affair and Wilson's stroke, Lansing lost the small measure of effectiveness that he still possessed. For the sake of American foreign relations, he should have followed his inclination to quit, or the president should have replaced him. When he finally resigned on February 12, 1920, Lansing benefited from a favorable public reaction. In the correspondence they released to the press, Wilson's disingenuous explanation for desiring Lansing's departure appeared mean and petty. It did not enhance the president's reputation for rational leadership during this critical stage of the treaty fight.[56]

55   Hitchcock to WW, Feb. 24, 1920, JPT to WW, Feb. 27, 1920, JPT Papers, Box 7; Glass to WW, Feb. 12, 1920, Glass Papers, Box 8; Allen to Underwood, Feb. 8, 1920, Underwood to Allen, Feb. 12, 1920, Underwood Papers; Miller to EMH, Feb. 19, 1920, Miller to Hitchcock, Feb. 17, 19, 1920, Hitchcock to Miller, Feb. 18, 1920, EMH Papers, 14/16; Short, Conference with Senator Hitchcock, Feb. 29, 1920, ALL Papers.
56   WW to RL, Feb. 11, 1920, RL to WW, Feb. 12, 1920, WW Papers, Ser. 2, Box 195; RL Diary, V, Dec. 10, 1919, VI, Jan. 2, 7, Feb. 9, 13, 20, 22-23, 1920; HCL to RL, Feb. 16, 1920, RL Papers, Vol. 52; HCL to RL, Feb. 16, 1920, RL to HCL, Feb. 18, 1920, HCL Papers, File 1920 (H-O); Karger to WHT, Feb. 20, 1920, WHT Papers, Ser. 3, Box 467; Long Diary, Feb. 2-3, 11, 13-14, 16, 1920, Long Papers, Box 2; HW to RL, Feb. 14, 1920, HW Papers, Box 23. See also Clifford W. Trow, "Woodrow Wilson and the Mexican Interventionist Movement of 1919," *Journal of American History*, LVIII (June 1971), 46-72, and Joyce G. Williams, "The Resignation of Secretary of State Robert Lansing," *Diplomatic History*, III (Summer 1979), 337-43.

As the Senate began to reconsider reservations, Democratic weakness became apparent. Hitchcock repeatedly urged presidential action to prevent a total collapse. He reported that only twenty-two Democratic senators would definitely oppose the Lodge reservations. Although more than his previous estimate, that number was still less than half of the Democrats. Noting that Simmons was already discussing a compromise on Article 10 with Senator Watson, Hitchcock advised Wilson to invite him to the White House for a conference. He also continued to urge the issuance of a statement. Now endorsing this request, Tumulty began to suggest ideas for the president to use in a public letter to Hitchcock. He wanted Wilson to denounce Grey's unwarranted interference in American politics. Claiming that Article 10 marked the end of European imperialism, Tumulty counseled him to contrast this achievement with the Lodge reservation's reversion to the "old system." In view of current discussions in the Senate over Article 10, Burleson also encouraged Wilson to clarify his interpretation and indicate what kind of compromise he might accept.[57]

The president defined the central issue in the treaty fight in absolutist terms. Rejecting any thought of compromise, he gave his definitive response in a letter to Hitchcock on March 8. Opposing any qualification of Article 10, he argued that the United States could not escape its "moral obligations." By neglecting these responsibilities, he claimed, Americans would sacrifice the "new conception of justice and peace" and fail "to redeem the world from the old order of force and aggression." The reservations under consideration in the Senate were "virtual nullifications" of the Covenant. "The choice," he asserted, "is between two ideals: on the one hand, the ideal of democracy, which represents the rights of free peoples everywhere to govern themselves, and on the other hand, the ideal of imperialism which seeks to dominate by force and unjust power, an ideal which is by no means dead and which is earnestly held in many quarters still. Every imperialistic influence in Europe was hostile to the embodiment of Article X in the Covenant of the League of Nations, and its defeat now would mark the complete consummation of their efforts to nullify the treaty. I hold the doctrine of Article X to be the essence of Americanism. We cannot repudiate it or weaken it without at the same time repudiating our own principles." Developing this theme as Tumulty had suggested, Wilson proclaimed that Article 10 had forced Great Britain, Japan, France and Italy to abandon "the old pretensions of political conquest and territorial aggrandizement" and "the old balances of power." Appealing to ideals, he refused to consider any reservations even to ensure American membership in the League. Universalism and unilateralism characterized his attitude. "Either we should enter the league fearlessly, accepting the responsibility and not fearing the role of leadership which we now enjoy, contributing our efforts towards establishing

57   JPT to EBW, March 1, 7, 1920, Burleson to JPT, March 5, 1920, JPT Papers, Box 3; Hitchcock to WW, [March ?, 1920], JPT to EBW, March 7, 1920, WW Papers, Ser. 2, Box 195.

a just and permanent peace," Wilson argued, "or we should retire as gracefully as possible from the great concert of powers by which the world was saved." He reiterated his threat to withdraw the United States from active collaboration with the Allies unless he alone could control the conditions for its participation.

During the controversy over the Adriatic settlement involving Fiume, the president had already threatened to abandon the Old World unless Europeans implemented his principles as he desired. "The Adriatic issue as it now presents itself," Wilson notified the British and French on February 10, "raises the fundamental question as to whether the American Government can on any terms cooperate with its European associates in the great work of maintaining the peace of the world by removing the primary causes of war." If the "old order" prevailed, he warned, the United States would refuse to entangle itself in European affairs. He wanted either to control international relations or to withdraw, but not to participate in the inherently difficult and frustrating compromises of the interdependent and plural world. Clinging to his ideals, he rejected concessions either abroad or at home. Only extreme internationalist or isolationist alternatives were conceivable to him as he repudiated the option of ratifying the treaty with reservations. "I hear of reservationists and mild reservationists," he told Hitchcock, "but I cannot understand the difference between a nullifier and mild nullifier." The embattled president saw all American advocates of reservations, like the Allies, as representatives of the "old order" which he intended to defeat.[58]

Publication of Wilson's letter to Hitchcock caused what Ambassador Wallace described as "a tremendous sensation in France." In Washington, Ambassador Jusserand protested to Acting Secretary of State Polk against the president's assertion that the "militaristic party" had gained control in Paris. But Wilson refused to retract this statement, choosing instead to expand upon it. Polk dutifully complied with his order to elaborate this critical characterization of the French government in a private session with Jusserand. Personally, Polk regretted the letter. Marking the treaty's final defeat, it signaled American refusal to collaborate with the Allies. Blaming Wilson for this outcome, Lodge reiterated his desire for close Franco-American relations. "I do not think that France is in the least militaristic," he told the Senate. "I think she desires to have protection against the repetition of such sufferings as she has endured, and I think that is a feeling which we all must share." Polk desperately hoped to prevent the treaty's defeat, sharing with Hoover a preference for its ratification with reservations. But they could not find an effective way to convince the president. He chose to keep the United States out of the League rather than accept reservations. The French also found this choice deeply disappointing. On March 1, Jusserand had told Polk that the French government hoped the president

58   WW to Hitchcock, March 8, 1920, JPT Papers, Box 7; *CR*, Vol. 59, 3545-53, 4051-52; *PPWW*, VI, 462-79.

would ratify the treaty with reservations. Official French policy coincided with the Republican majority's position rather than Wilson's. Both his refusal to compromise and his accusation of French militarism produced serious tensions in Franco-American relations. Ironically, while pursuing his ideal of international cooperation, he actually generated unnecessary dissension at home and abroad.[59]

Wilson's letter to Hitchcock impressed his staunch supporters but failed to convince those, like Bryan, who favored a compromise. Many Democratic senators, according to Glass and Burleson, still hoped that Wilson would eventually acquiesce in Lodge's reservation to Article 10. This impression, which Simmons continued to promote, fostered disunity among Democrats. Glass and Hitchcock knew that the president would never compromise, but they could not totally convince their colleagues to abandon this hope. Having declined to invite Simmons to the White House, Wilson now accepted Tumulty's advice to appeal for his support. In a letter on March 11, the president reaffirmed the attitude he had earlier shared with Glass and Hitchcock. He told Simmons that his position on Lodge's reservation to Article 10 was "unalterable" because it would nullify "the very heart of the Treaty itself." This letter, demonstrating that Wilson's public and private positions were identical, ended remaining expectations among Democrats that Wilson might abandon his all-or-nothing stance. The treaty was now dead, as subsequent votes would merely confirm.[60]

Republicans dominated proceedings in the Senate. As numerous Democrats deserted the president, Lodge formed a substantial majority for reservations. He and his associates introduced some modifications in conformity with the bipartisan conference's tentative agreement. Beginning on March 4 the Senate altered the form, but not the substance, of some reservations. Lodge proposed deletion of specific references to China and Japan in the Shantung reservation. He also introduced the substitute which Thomas Walsh had proposed in the bipartisan conference for the reservation regarding American representation in the League or other agencies created by the treaty. When Hitchcock now denounced it, Lodge withdrew his motion, thereby forcing Walsh to offer his own substitute. Kellogg introduced a change in the reservation prohibiting the United States from paying the League's expenses without specific appropriations from Congress in order to

59 Wallace to Polk, March 11, 1920, Polk Papers, 74/91; Polk to WW, March 13, 15, 1920, WW to Polk, March 15, 1920, Polk Papers, 89/130; Polk to WW, March 13, 1920, Jusserand to Polk, March 11, 1920, WW to Polk, March 15, 1920, WW Papers, Ser. 2, Box 196; Polk to EMH, March 9, 1920, EMH Papers, 16/9; Hoover to JPT, March 19, 1920, JPT Papers, Box 7, and Hoover Pre-Commerce Papers, Box 32; Confidential Diary, March 1, 11, 15, 1920, Polk Papers, 88/20; CR, Vol. 59, 4051.
60 JPT to WW, March 11, 1920, JPT Papers, Box 7; JPT to EBW, March 5, 11, 1920, WW to Simmons, March 11, 1920, JPT Papers, Box 3; NDB to WW, March 9, 1920, WW Papers, Ser. 2, Box 195; WW to Simmons, March 11, 1920, WW Papers, Ser. 2, Box 196; WW to Simmons, March 11, 1920, Crenshaw to Glass, March 10, 13, 18, 1920, Glass to Crenshaw, March 12, 17, 1920, Glass Papers, Box 8; Hitchcock to WW, [March 11?, 1920], WW to Hitchcock, n.d., Hitchcock Papers, Vol. 2; CR, Vol. 59, 4054-55.

exempt the secretary general's salary and office expenses. New proposed his substitute for the reservation on limitation of armaments under Article 8. It would guarantee the Congress' right to act on any plan of the League council for arms limitation and would preserve the discretion of the United States to increase its armed forces when threatened by invasion or engaged in war. Lodge called for two changes in the Lenroot reservation. One recommended an amendment to the Covenant to provide equality of voting for the United States in the League. Another waived this reservation in cases where the Congress had previously given its consent. The Senate approved all these modifications by large majorities. Walsh's substitute, attracting the least support, passed by a margin of 37 to 32. Approval of Lodge's change in the Shantung reservation was nearly unanimous.[61]

Article 10 continued to pose the greatest obstacle to bipartisan agreement. On February 9 a group of mild reservationists had met with Lodge to persuade him to modify his reservation. Hoping to entice Democratic senators to compromise, they proposed and Lodge accepted a change in its wording. Based on earlier conversations with McKellar and with Josiah Wolcott of Delaware, they expected this new form to attract Democrats. Lenroot attempted to win Hitchcock's endorsement, but without any success. His refusal convinced Lenroot that Hitchcock was more interested in protecting his party for the upcoming election than in ratifying the treaty. Although failing to fulfill the mild reservationists' hope for bipartisan compromise, this revised reservation helped Lodge to preserve Republican unity. He wanted to demonstrate his genuine desire for ratification without sacrificing the essential Republican conditions. Root, whom Kellogg and Watson consulted, agreed that the revised reservation amply protected the United States. After Lodge introduced it on March 12, Borah suggested a slight alteration to clarify its meaning. As this change was acceptable to Lenroot and other mild reservationists, Lodge quickly incorporated it. His flexibility enabled him to keep all Republicans working together under his leadership, and even to attract some Democrats. On March 15 the Senate gave a two-thirds majority of 56 to 24 to substitute this Article 10 reservation for Lodge's earlier one.[62]

All attempts to change or replace this new reservation failed. Senator William Kirby of Arkansas offered two alternatives that Democrats had proposed in the bipartisan conference. As a substitute for Lodge's reservation, he introduced one affirming that the United States would assume no

61 CR, Vol. 59, 3839-47, 3857-63, 3939-49, 3955-58, 4004-06, 4010-21, 4050-62.

62 Karger to WHT, Feb. 6, 11, 1920, WHT Papers, Ser. 3, Box 467; Karger to WHT, March 4, 9, 1920, WHT Papers, Ser. 3, Box 468; Short to ALL, March 9, 1920, Substance of an Interview with Senator Lenroot, Feb. 29, 1920, ALL Papers; HCL to ER, March 6, 13, 1920, ER to HCL, March 11, 1920, ER Papers, Box 161; ER to Kellogg, March 13, 13, 1920, Kellogg to ER, March 12, 18, 1920, ER Papers, Box 138; HCL to L. A. Coolidge, March 13, 17, 1920, HCL Papers, File 1920 (Personal, A-G); ER to HCL, March 11, 1920, HCL to ER, March 6, 13, 1920, HCL to Williams, March 13, 1920, ER to Kellogg, March 13, 1920, HCL Papers, File 1920 (Personal, H-Z); CR, Vol. 59, 4120-29, 4170-77, 4208-23, 4262-85, 4332.

obligation to use military or naval force or an economic boycott under Article 10, or military or naval force for any purpose under any other article, unless Congress approved in the particular case. This reservation, which was under discussion when the bipartisan conference had reached a stalemate, would not prohibit an economic boycott as a sanction under Article 16. As his other alternative, which Democrats had also offered in the bipartisan conference, Kirby proposed the Taft reservation. It stated that the United States would assume no legal obligation under Article 10 or other articles of the Covenant to use military or naval force, but left Congress free to decide what moral obligation it should assume in any particular case. Against a united Republican majority, Kirby's two alternatives suffered overwhelming defeat. Only thirty-one Democrats voted for the first substitute, and thirty for the Taft reservation. After these votes on March 15, Simmons introduced his substitute. Unlike Lodge's reservation, it would commit the United States to offer friendly offices under Article 10 to settle political and territorial disputes and prevent external aggression, while excluding the use of American armed forces or economic resources for this purpose without congressional approval in a particular case. Only twenty-seven Democrats supported this substitute. Three days later Simmons renewed his attempt to modify the Lodge reservation, hoping that Wilson would then accept it. He thought the "chief trouble" with it was "the fact that it contains the broad proposition that this Government shall not interfere in any way whatsoever with controversies between other nations unless Congress so provides." But Simmons failed to persuade a majority. Lodge easily mustered enough votes to defeat all proposals for changing his reservation, whether from Democrats or Republican irreconcilables. Only twenty-six Democrats opposed this reservation on each of the two final roll-call votes. More than twice that number of senators, including some Democrats as well as Republicans, accepted Lodge's Article 10 reservation.[63]

Voting on this reservation followed the same pattern as on Lodge's other reservations. Between February 21 and March 9 the Senate had already approved them by substantial margins, ranging from a high of 68 to 4 to a low of 44 to 28. Senators were nearly unanimous in prohibiting the United States from accepting a mandate without congressional consent. They gave the least support to the reservation that would restrict sanctions under Article 16 to a foreign state, while preserving the right of Americans to maintain economic and other relations with its nationals in the United States or elsewhere outside of that state. Hitchcock attempted in vain to amend or offer substitutes for the Lodge reservations. Receiving at most thirty-six votes, his proposals failed to attract several Democrats. In adopting Lodge's reservations and rejecting Hitchcock's, and on other alternatives as well, the alignment of senators in roll-call votes in the spring of 1920 followed the same general pattern as in the fall of 1919, with one notable difference:

---

63   *CR*, Vol. 59, 4317-33, 4532-36.

Democratic defections now resulted in larger majorities for the Lodge reservations. Eight passed by over a two-thirds majority as moderate Democrats joined Republicans. By their votes these senators overwhelmingly rejected the president's control of American foreign relations. While Democrats were in disarray, no longer united under Wilson's or Hitchcock's leadership, all Republicans still insisted upon the Lodge reservations. [64]

The voting pattern on Lodge's fourteen reservations did not continue when the Senate dealt with the Irish question. On March 18, Peter Gerry introduced a reservation reaffirming the principle of self-determination and Borah's Irish resolution of June 6, 1919, and calling for prompt admission of Ireland to the League as soon as it achieved self-government. The sweeping affirmation of the principle of national self-determination in this reservation drew Lodge's criticism, but he could not muster enough votes to delete it or limit it only to Ireland. Kellogg, too, opposed Gerry's reservation, noting that its adoption would alienate Great Britain and consequently prevent ratification. He saw no justification for such American interference with internal affairs in the British Empire. Although this argument appeared persuasive to Underwood, it did not convince Hitchcock, who endorsed the reservation. The Senate, while proclaiming the principle of self-determination, refrained from applying it to any country other than Ireland. It defeated Thomas' attempt to name Korea as well. Support for the Gerry reservation came from a strange bipartisan coalition primarily of irreconcilable Republicans and northern Democrats. All five Irish-American senators – Gerry, Phelan, Shields, David Walsh and Thomas Walsh – favored it, while reservationist Republicans and southern Democrats opposed. There was no correlation between this pattern of voting and that for the Lodge reservations. Producing crosscurrents, the Irish question shattered the alignment of senators that generally characterized the votes throughout the treaty fight. If the influence of Irish-Americans culminated in the Gerry reservation, then it had not been a decisive factor in the Senate's overall response to the treaty. Contrary to the claims of professional Irish-Americans and the accusations of Wilson and other advocates of the League, ethnic politics exerted only a marginal impact. With their votes senators made a substantial distinction between the Gerry reservation and the fourteen Lodge reservations. [65]

After completing the consideration of reservations, the Senate prepared to vote on the resolution of ratification on March 19, 1920. Lodge introduced it with a revised preamble, which would permit the Allies to acquiesce in the

64   CR, Vol. 59, 3229-43, 3500-21, 3564-82, 3611-26, 3692-3701, 3733-48, 3792-808, 3838-64, 3885-3906, 3939-58, 4004-21, 4050-67.
65   HCL to Carroll, March 22, 1920, HCL Papers, File 1920 (A-G); Lyons to Underwood, March 22, 1920, Underwood to Lyons, March 26, 1920, McMahon to Underwood, March 23, 1920, Underwood to McMahon, March 26, 1920, Underwood Papers; CR, Vol. 59, 4499-4532; "The League of Nations Beaten," "The Senate's Action on Ireland" and "Senator Shield's Fine Record," Gaelic American, XVII (March 27, 1920), 4.

fifteen reservations by silence rather than by exchange of notes. Lenroot appealed to Democrats, observing that all reservations except Gerry's were supported by "the friends of the treaty." He hoped Wilson's followers would not combine with irreconcilables to kill the treaty. Claiming that the Allies would accept reservations, he misrepresented the situation. Lenroot mistakenly believed that Grey had expressed official British policy. The British Empire actually opposed the Lodge reservations, and would undoubtedly resent Gerry's. By its public silence, however, Lloyd George's government left the impression that Grey spoke for it. In contrast, the French government had already conveyed its willingness to acquiesce in Lodge's reservations. Despite his error, Lenroot correctly perceived the president as the most immediate obstacle to ratification. Some Democrats agreed. Pomerene and Hoke Smith observed that differences between Lodge's Article 10 reservation and Democratic alternatives to it were too insignificant to justify the treaty's defeat. Thomas Walsh argued that the League could still serve its primary purpose even with this reservation. But such arguments failed to persuade. On the final vote, most Democratic senators joined irreconcilables to defeat the treaty. A bipartisan, although predominantly Republican, majority of forty-nine senators favored the resolution of ratification, while Wilson's loyal followers and irreconcilables cast thirty-five negative votes. The Versailles Treaty received a simple majority, but not the required two-thirds.[66]

This outcome disappointed Hitchcock, but not Wilson. Preventing even more Democratic senators from surrendering to the Republican majority had required the Nebraskan to exert the "most energetic efforts." He could not accomplish more in the Senate than to avoid the treaty's approval with Lodge's reservations. "Certainly you have nothing to reproach yourself with in connection with the defeat of the treaty," Wilson assured him. Abstractions of national or personal honor and world peace were more important to the president than the reality of American foreign relations. Having identified the League with God's will for the United States in the modern world, he absolutely refused to compromise. Lodge had presented him the alternatives of accepting reservations or killing the treaty, and he selected the latter. He gave irreconcilables a victory they could not win for themselves. The League to Enforce Peace and other advocates of bipartisan compromise had failed to persuade him to abandon his all-or-nothing stance. Wilson's intransigence eventually convinced Democratic senators such as Hitchcock, Underwood, Glass and Simmons of the futility of attempting to save the treaty. As Glass explained to Marburg shortly before the final vote, "the President will positively not exchange ratifications if the treaty is sent to him with the Lodge amendment to Article 10 attached." Given this reality, these senators fell into line and attempted to salvage a credible position for their party. Otherwise, more Democrats would probably have voted for the resolution of ratification with the fifteen reservations. "Wilson's greatness," Taft bitterly concluded, "is oozing out, as it ought to. He will live in history as a man with great opportunities which were not improved, but which were wrecked by his personal egotism, selfishness, vanity and mulishness."[67]

In his effort to control American foreign relations at home and abroad, the president had failed. Diversity of opinion within the United States prevented him from forcing the Senate to approve the peace treaty exactly as he presented it. Refusing to accept any Republican alternatives, he preferred to withdraw the United States from active involvement in European affairs. Adhering to his ideal of collective security, he stopped the United States from joining the real League. Although he made this choice, Wilson blamed Republicans. His inability to prevail at home coincided with his lack of control over foreign affairs, as the controversy over the Adriatic question had demonstrated. Unless he could dominate, which was clearly impossible in the plural world of conflicting views and interests, he wanted to abstain from entanglement in international relations. Both universalism and unilateralism characterized Wilson's peacemaking. If leaders in other countries or senators in the United States rejected his particular conception of global interdependence, as they did, the president denounced them for preventing the United States from playing a constructive role in the world. Yet he was the person most responsible for American rejection of the Versailles peace.

67   Hitchcock to WW, March 20, 1920, WW to Hitchcock, March 23, 1920, WW Papers, Ser. 2, Box 196; WW to Hitchcock, March 23, 1920, Hitchcock Papers, Vol. 2; HCL to Bigelow, March 15, 1920, HCL Papers, File 1920 (Personal, A-G); HCL to Trevelyan, March 23, 1920, HCL Papers, File 1920 (Personal, H-Z); Borah to Kearney, March 22, 1920, Borah Papers, Box 550; Cohalan to Borah, March 8, 1920, Cohalan Papers; Marburg to Glass, March 16, 1920, Marburg to Hitchcock, March 16, 1920, Glass to Marburg, March 17, 1920, Glass Papers, Box 143; WHT to H. Taft, March 23, 1920, WHT Papers, Ser. 3, Box 468; ALL to Ayer, March 16, 1920, ALL to Walsh, March 15, 1920, ALL Papers.

CHAPTER 9

The aftermath of Wilson's peacemaking

Twice defeated in the Senate, the Versailles Treaty lacked any realistic prospect for ratification by the United States. Wilson's intransigence had sacrificed the opportunity for American membership in the League. Rather than make any concession to achieve this goal, he looked to the 1920 election as a "solemn referendum" on the treaty. Insisting that the nation faced a choice between internationalism and isolationism, he hoped it would endorse his uncompromising stance. Republicans welcomed this challenge. The president's extreme position enabled them to unite for the campaign. They felt confident that American voters would sustain the Senate's refusal to approve the treaty without reservations. Opposition to Wilson's League united all Republicans from irreconcilables to mild reservationists. As long as Democrats followed their ailing leader in the White House, Republicans knew they could not lose the treaty fight. Regardless of the presidential election's outcome, the Senate would remain substantially unchanged. Even Democratic victories in all senatorial races in 1920 would fail to provide a two-thirds majority for the treaty in the new session. In short, the "solemn referendum" could not possibly vindicate Wilson's leadership in international affairs. He had lost touch with political reality in his vain search for control of American foreign relations.

Adhering steadfastly to his all-or-nothing stance, the president refused to take any action that might save the treaty. His new secretary of state, Bainbridge Colby, informed him about Hitchcock's views on possible initiatives. Not wanting to consider a compromise, Wilson preferred the current stalemate. "At present," he explained to Colby, "the dead treaty lies very heavy on the consciences of those who killed it and I am content to let it lie there until those consciences are either crushed or awakened."[1] Rather than reconsider his own position, he desired either to force his opponents to change or to defeat them. But he could not manage public opinion to

[1] Colby to WW, Apr. 1, 1920, WW to Colby, Apr. 2, 1920, WW Papers, Ser. 2, Box 196.

produce this outcome. The American people, now even less than in the previous year when he had undertaken his western tour, evidenced little enthusiasm for Wilson's leadership at home or abroad. As Lodge clearly understood, the treaty fight had generated an American reaction against entanglement in the Old World. "The fact is," he informed Bryce, "the protracted debate on the League both inside and outside the Senate has wrought a great change in public opinion and the feeling is growing constantly stronger against the United States involving itself in quarrels of Europe at all." This general reaction would, he anticipated, prevent the United States from accepting a mandate for hapless Armenia.[2] The unresolved deadlock over the League prevented the United States from participating as the president desired in world affairs. His methods thwarted the fulfillment of his goals.

The treaty's defeat led inevitably to a separate peace between the United States and Germany. Lodge had anticipated this eventuality. Mild reservationists, he knew, would acquiesce in a peace resolution only as a last resort. That time arrived after the March 1920 votes. Root accepted this political reality, although he regretted the failure of the United States to become "an associate with the powers who have entered into the League of Nations." Aware that even Knox offered a positive alternative, he repudiated Wilson's negative characterization of Republicans. Rejecting his categories of internationalism versus isolationism, Root argued that "the Senate's refusal to ratify the Treaty of Versailles does not mean a policy of isolation."[3] Taft blamed Wilson for polarizing the politics of peacemaking. He saw no escape before the election. Doubtful that a peace resolution could resolve the impasse, he expected the treaty fight to continue throughout the campaign.[4]

Republicans in the House of Representatives took the initiative to terminate the war by a joint resolution. Some of the president's fellow delegates at Paris now assisted in this effort to end the deadlock. Lansing offered his encouragement and advice to Stephen G. Porter of Pennsylvania, author of the congressional peace resolution. White worked with John Rogers of Massachusetts, conveying to him Root's suggestions for modifying the earlier Knox resolution in order to attract greater support. He told Bliss, who opposed a separate peace with Germany, that the treaty's defeat in the Senate left no other viable alternative. He explained that Lodge shared this conclusion. Like Taft, however, White doubted that a peace resolution could overcome the president's opposition.[5]

2   HCL to Bryce, Apr. 20, 1920, HCL Papers, File 1920 (Personal, A-G).
3   HCL to L. A. Coolidge, Jan. 28, 1920, HCL Papers, File 1920 (A-G); ER to Wilcox, March 26, 1920, ER Papers, Box 138.
4   WHT to ALL, March 22, 1920, ALL Papers; WHT to H. Taft, March 23, 1920, WHT Papers, Ser. 3, Box 468.
5   Porter to RL, March 25, 1920, Memorandum of Conversation over the Telephone with Representative Stephen G. Porter, March 26, 1920, RL Papers, Vol. 52; HW to Rogers, March 26, 1920, HW to Johnson, March 15, 1920, HW Papers, Box 23; THB to HW, March 9, 1920, HW to THB, March 11, 1920, THB Papers, Box 69.

With the Democrats in disarray, Republicans proceeded with their plan to end the war. On April 8, Porter introduced his joint resolution, which provided for termination of war and resumption of trade between the United States and Germany. He defended the House of Representatives' right to participate in peacemaking. Rogers elaborated this point, asserting the constitutional right of Congress to end the legal status of war without a treaty.[6] Democrats challenged this interpretation. Cordell Hull of Tennessee offered both constitutional and political arguments to denounce the peace resolution. Defending Wilson's leadership, he blamed the Republican majority in the Senate for the "temporary deadlock." Denying the House's right to infringe upon the president's treaty-making power, which was subject only to the Senate's approval, he interpreted the Porter resolution as merely a partisan ploy.[7]

Polarization in the politics of peacemaking generated extreme interpretations from both political parties. While Hull and other Democrats ardently defended Wilson, several Republican representatives used very strong language to denounce him. Calling him "our imperial President" whose League would threaten American sovereignty, Thomas D. Schall of Minnesota supported Porter's resolution.[8] Nicholas Longworth of Ohio denounced Wilson as the "one insurmountable obstacle in our path toward peace." Like John Maynard Keynes, the British Treasury official who had criticized Wilson in *The Economic Consequences of the Peace* (1920), Longworth thought the Old World diplomats had overwhelmed the president in Paris. To extricate the United States from this deplorable situation, he saw the peace resolution as the only remedy.[9] The opposite view prevailed among Democrats. Henry D. Flood of Virginia, ranking Democratic member of the House Committee on Foreign Affairs, summarized their objections to Porter's resolution. Beyond constitutional questions, he emphasized its damage to future American relations with other nations. He contended that the United States needed to join the League to secure its goals overseas. He continued to profess his faith in the potentially positive influence of Wilson's League.[10]

At the conclusion of debate, Flood attempted to recommit the peace resolution to the Foreign Affairs Committee with instructions to replace it with a simple resolution to repeal wartime legislation. Without actually restoring peace, this would end the emergency powers authorized by Congress for the war's duration. By a substantial partisan majority of 222 to 171, the House rejected this motion. Only two Republicans approved, while five Democrats opposed it. The House then proceeded on April 9 to adopt

6   JPT to EBW, March 24, 1920, JPT Papers, Box 3; *CR*, Vol. 59, 5346, 5358-67.
7   *CR*, Vol. 59, 5411-12.
8   *CR*, Vol. 59, 5436-40.
9   *CR*, Vol. 59, 5467-68.
10   *CR*, Vol. 59, 5473-76.

the Porter resolution by an even larger margin of 242 to 150. Twenty Democrats joined the predominantly Republican majority. With this minimal bipartisan support, Republicans seized the initiative from loyal Democrats. They offered the Porter resolution as an alternative to the treaty for ending the war. [11]

Republicans in the Senate continued to take the offensive. In the Foreign Relations Committee, which reviewed the Porter resolution, they decided to substitute a revised resolution prepared by Knox. It declared an end to war between the United States and Germany, while carefully protecting certain American interests. It provided for retention of seized German property in the United States to guarantee Germany's payment of outstanding American claims for wartime losses. It also reserved all rights and privileges of the United States under not only the armistice but also the Versailles Treaty. In other words, it outlined conditions for separate peace with Germany. Knox's resolution, moreover, proclaimed the end of war between the United States and the Austro-Hungarian Empire. By a strictly partisan vote, the committee reported this resolution to the Senate. [12] Knox opened debate on his resolution in the Senate on May 5. He accused the president of seeking to retain his extraordinary war powers, while refusing to allow any modification of the peace treaty. Given Wilson's determination to conclude peace only on his own terms, Knox intended to strip him of the legal right to wage war and also of his domestic war powers. He wanted to reduce the president's authority and restore peace without the League. [13]

McCumber pursued his own course without following either the Democratic president or the Republican majority. Aware of the futility of a "solemn referendum," he asserted that "you can not make the League of Nations the real issue in this campaign." Although most critical of Wilson, he refused to support the Knox resolution. Because it would require the president's signature, or a two-thirds majority over his veto, it offered no realistic solution to the deadlock. Proposing his own substitute resolution, which simply provided for resumption of commercial relations between the United States and Germany while leaving the settlement of other questions to a new treaty, McCumber attempted to overcome the current impasse. But this substitute attracted no support from his fellow Republicans or Democrats. [14]

Democratic senators continued to affirm the president's leadership of American foreign relations. Denying the House's right to participate in peacemaking, Hitchcock asserted that "it is manifest that the foreign affairs of the United States are placed in the sole and only control of the Executive. The Constitution specifically places in him the sole power to negotiate treaties and settle foreign affairs, and the only restriction upon him is that in

11   CR, Vol. 59, 5349-52, 5479-81.
12   U.S. Senate, Proceedings of the Committee on Foreign Relations, 232-36.
13   CR, Vol. 59, 6556-66.
14   CR, Vol. 59, 6852-57.

making treaties he must have the consent of two-thirds of the Senators present and voting." A joint resolution, whether Porter's or Knox's, was therefore clearly unconstitutional. Hitchcock also reaffirmed Wilson's decision to take the "great issue" of the peace treaty into the election.[15] Republicans welcomed this opportunity. Against dangers of "presidential dictation," Harding defended the role of Congress in restoring "a popular representative government" in the United States. "I think," he proclaimed, "the significance of the passage of this resolution lies in its reestablishment of the constitutional powers of the American Congress." He concluded that "it would be well for us to put America in order before we assume to run the remainder of the world."[16]

Voting on the Knox resolution on May 15 followed the same pattern that had characterized the Senate's earlier roll calls on amendments and reservations to the Versailles Treaty. The continuing deadlock still produced a sharp division between political parties. Republicans furnished all forty-three votes for the resolution, while Democrats cast all but one of the thirty-eight negative votes. In McCumber's absence, only Nelson broke from his Republican colleagues. No Democratic senator demonstrated comparable independence by favoring the peace resolution.[17]

Partisanship also continued to characterize the House. Introducing the Knox resolution on May 21, Porter defended it as an acceptable substitute. It would accomplish substantially the same purpose as his own earlier resolution. While Republicans generally agreed, most Democrats still resisted. Unique among his Democratic colleagues, George Huddleston of Alabama openly criticized the president for making the League into a partisan issue. He deplored Wilson's recent telegram to G. E. Hamaker, chairman of the Democratic committee in Multnomah County, Oregon, which reaffirmed his refusal to compromise. This kind of stubbornness did not impress Huddleston, who thought it would be fatal to the Democratic party. But most Democrats acquiesced in Wilson's leadership by voting against the joint resolution; only twenty-one of them favored it. They lost, however, as Republican representatives, except for two, overwhelmingly approved the Knox resolution, which passed by a substantial majority of 228 to 130. With few exceptions, politicians on both sides were willing to continue the confrontation as the election approached.[18]

Wilson rigidly adhered to his position in the treaty fight. In the telegram to Hamaker on May 9, which he had sent at Tumulty's instigation, he called upon his fellow Democrats to continue their crusade for the Versailles Treaty without the Lodge reservations. "It is time," he stated, "that the party should proudly avow that it means to try, without flinching or turning at any time away from the path for reasons of expediency, to apply moral and

15 CR, Vol. 59, 6895-99.
16 CR, Vol. 59, 7098-99.
17 CR, Vol. 59, 7101-02.
18 CR, Vol. 59, 7423-30.

Christian principles to the problems of the world." He entertained no doubt that these principles required the United States to accept the Covenant as he had drafted it. "The League of Nations," he reaffirmed, "is the hope of the world." He completely identified this form of collective security with the American heritage. By its decision to intervene in the European war, he claimed, the United States had promised the global application of American principles – a promise now fulfilled by the Covenant. Wilson's understanding of American nationalism furnished his international ideals; his internationalism expressed the global extension of his national principles. For him there was no conflict between nationalism and internationalism.[19]

Wilson's decision to make the treaty into a partisan issue in the approaching election pleased some, but not all, Democrats. House had intended to make a final appeal to him to allow Underwood and Hitchcock to save the treaty by compromising with Republicans. The exact wording of the Covenant, he thought, was less important than actual establishment of the League. But with publication of the Hamaker telegram, House abandoned this futile effort. Underwood, who had defeated Hitchcock in late April to become the new minority leader in the Senate, privately regretted the president's course. Advocates of bipartisan accommodation, such as former Secretary Lansing, welcomed his election as leader. Underwood still favored a compromise. But, as he explained to Straus, who wanted the United States in the League, there was nothing to gain by the Senate's approval of reservations which Wilson would reject. Desiring an end to this deadlock before the campaign, Underwood finally reconciled himself to the hopelessness of the situation only after the Hamaker telegram's publication. He now understood that the president's implacable determination to take the issue to the country would preclude any constructive action in Washington. In contrast to Underwood's conciliatory approach, Glass steadfastly opposed the Lodge reservations. He denounced the Knox resolution for its allegedly unconstitutional method of peacemaking. On the other hand, he saw no constitutional obstacles to American participation in the League. Advising Wilson to seize the opportunity to clarify the misunderstanding by the American people on this point, Glass urged him to persevere with his hard line.[20]

The president reiterated the themes of his Hamaker telegram to justify his

19 JPT to WW, May 7, 1920, WW Papers, Ser. 2, Box 196; JPT to WW, May 7, 1920, Hamaker to WW, May 6, 1920, WW to Hamaker, May 9, 1920, JPT Papers, Box 7; *PPWW*, VI, 483-84.
20 Note by E. M. House, May 10, 1920, EMH to WW, May 8, 1920 [not sent], EMH Papers, 49/13; Skeggs to Underwood, Jan. 18, 1920, Underwood to Skeggs, Jan. 21, 1920, Underwood to Lemoine, Apr. 28, 1920, RL to Underwood, Apr. 28, 1920, Underwood to RL, Apr. 30, 1920, Straus to Underwood, Apr. 28, 1920, Underwood to Straus, Apr. 30, 1920, Null to Underwood, May 5, 1920, Underwood to Null, May 8, 1920, Underwood to Percy, May 18, 1920, Moore to Underwood, May 21, 1920, Underwood to Moore, May 27, 1920, Underwood Papers; Glass to Munford, March 18, 1920, Glass to Mosby, March 31, 1920, Glass to Golub, Apr. 23, 1920, Glass to Meddee, Apr. 14, 1920, Glass to Kirk, March 29, 1920, Glass to Goodloe, March 30, 1920, Glass Papers, Box 143; Glass to WW, May 18, 1920, Glass Papers, Box 145.

veto of the Knox resolution. Denouncing it in his May 27 message to Congress, he claimed that it would sacrifice the very purpose for which the United States had declared war in 1917. "We entered the war most reluctantly," he observed. "Our people were profoundly disinclined to take part in a European war, and at last did so only because they became convinced that it could not in truth be regarded as only a European war, but must be regarded as a war in which civilization itself was involved and human rights of every kind as against a belligerent government." Only by ratifying the Versailles Treaty, he argued, could the United States protect those rights and achieve its goal of preventing Germany from again violating the freedom of other nations.[21] Republican representatives attempted to override his veto. On May 28, joined by eighteen Democrats, they registered another majority of 228 to 152 for the joint resolution. No Republican opposed it. Falling far short of the required two-thirds, the Knox resolution failed to resolve the executive-legislative impasse.[22] As Taft and McCumber had anticipated, it offered no solution to the continuing deadlock.

Democrats and Republicans were not fighting over internationalist and isolationist alternatives. In his veto message, the president himself reiterated his reluctance to entangle the United States in European affairs. Yet he also continued to emphasize the League's role in transforming the Old World through the application of American principles. He combined unilateralism and universalism. On the other extreme, the irreconcilables denied that they intended to isolate the United States. For them, as for Wilson, the crucial issue was control of American foreign relations. Borah agreed with Knox that the United States could no longer isolate itself, although they opposed American membership in the League. After voting for the Knox resolution, Borah explained: "I wish to pursue a little further the idea that because we are opposed to surrendering the control of our affairs to a European tribunal, therefore we either have pursued or will pursue a policy of isolation. It is not isolation. It is simply retaining the power upon the part of this Republic to judge for itself in every emergency, as the facts are presented and as they arise, what it shall do." The United States, he emphasized, would not abandon the Old World. "Europe need have no fear, if Europe will put her house in order and do those things which Europe can do – settle down and go to work instead of continuing war over boundary lines and conditions which do not concern us at all – that undoubtedly the people of the United States will lend every assistance possible."[23]

Republicans anticipated American involvement in foreign affairs but wanted to avoid the entanglements of Wilson's League. This attitude characterized their approach to Armenia. As chairman of a subcommittee of the Foreign Relations Committee, Harding prepared a resolution which the

---

21   PPWW, VI, 492-94; CR, Vol. 59, 7747-48.
22   CR, Vol. 59, 7805-09.
23   CR, Vol. 59, 7280.

Senate approved on May 13 to advise the president on policy toward this new nation. In view of the massacres and other atrocities suffered by the Armenian people, and "the deplorable conditions of insecurity, starvation, and misery now prevalent in Armenia," it endorsed the president's decision to recognize the Republic of Armenia. The Senate expressed its hope that this country might soon enjoy "stable government, proper protection of individual liberties and rights, and the full realization of nationalistic aspirations." Moreover, Harding's resolution requested the president to dispatch a warship with marines to the port of Batum for the purpose of protecting American lives and property. It articulated Republican approval for limited American commitments overseas. Wilson welcomed this resolution as an indication that the Senate might approve even greater involvement in Armenia. On May 24 he asked Congress for authority to accept a League mandate for Armenia as requested by the Allies. He regarded this role of assisting the "Christian men and women" of that country as "a sacred trust for civilization." But Republican senators were not persuaded. The Foreign Relations Committee approved a resolution, which Knox had prepared, declining to accept a mandate. On June 1 the Senate passed this resolution by the decisive margin of 52 to 23. Eleven Democrats joined the Republicans, while no Republican favored a mandate. This bipartisan, although predominantly Republican, majority considered a League mandate too great an obligation for the United States. A majority in the Senate shared Wilson's desire to assist Armenia but rejected his method as too costly and too entangling. This decision reflected the pattern of disagreement that had prevailed throughout the treaty fight. While most Democrats supported their president, Republicans generally sought to limit the global commitments of the United States. They disagreed over the goals and methods of American foreign policy, but neither Wilson nor his Republican adversaries believed that the United States could totally ignore foreign affairs.[24]

I

As the political parties approached their national conventions in the summer of 1920, their leaders endeavored to handle divisive issues of foreign policy so as to gain public support at home. The consequences vitally affected other nations as well. The new British ambassador, Sir Auckland Geddes, observed that Wilson was still seeking to secure American ratification of the peace treaty, which Lloyd George's government desired. But the president also appeared to welcome the opportunity to bedevil Republicans. His recommendation for an American mandate in Armenia seemed to Geddes to exemplify this pattern as it forced Lodge and his colleagues into a negative

24   U.S. Senate, *Proceedings of the Committee on Foreign Relations*, 236-40; *PPWW*, VI, 487-91; *CR*, Vol. 59, 8070-73; HCL to Gerard, May 14, 1920, HCL to Barton, June 4, 1920, HCL Papers, File 1920 (A-G).

stance. This complex mixture of external and internal politics complicated the ambassador's job. The British government shared the Democratic administration's desire for the United States to participate fully in the League. Toward this end Geddes worked closely with Secretary Colby. Yet the British officially refrained from repudiating Grey's letter, thereby alienating some loyal Democrats by leaving the impression that they favored the Lodge reservations. The Democratic party, moreover, included various ethnic groups, such as Irish-Americans, who were hostile toward the British Empire. To neutralize this ethnic factor in American politics, Geddes advised Lloyd George to discredit the Irish quest for freedom by identifying it with Bolshevism. He hoped thereby to exploit the intense antipathy toward Bolshevism in the United States. To prevent German-American voters from opposing closer Anglo-American relations, he also recommended that the British government should announce its desire for cooperation with Germany in the economic reconstruction of postwar Europe. Recognizing that Anglo-Saxons were in the minority in American politics, especially in the Democratic party, he wanted to divide and conquer the ethnic groups. Geddes hoped in this way to promote Anglo-American cooperation and, if possible, to bring the United States into the League. But, as he recognized, this assignment was not easy. Neither he nor Colby, who confided in him, knew how deeply Americans were committed to "the Wilsonian ideals" or whether this commitment would counterbalance their "bitter personal hostility to the President." Aware that the election would determine the future policy of the United States, the ambassador did not know what to anticipate or how to shape the outcome except in marginal ways.[25]

Wilson failed to comprehend the limits of his control over the politics of peacemaking. By forcing a choice between unqualified acceptance or rejection of the League, he steered Republicans into a negative role in the treaty fight. He thwarted their attempts to offer positive alternatives. Lodge lamented that the United States could not adopt a more constructive European policy, although he saw political advantages for his party. Given the president's extreme stance, Lodge clearly understood, the American people would reject his internationalism. By demanding unqualified acceptance of the Covenant's potentially unlimited obligations, Wilson had generated a negative reaction against foreign entanglement. He denounced Republicans for courting this sentiment, but could not prevent them from exploiting it. Although he had defined the choices, he could not control the selection which voters ultimately made.[26]

For Lodge the crucial issue in 1920 transcended the controversy over American membership in the League. At stake was the extent of presidential powers both at home and abroad. He challenged not only the content of Wilson's foreign policy but also his right to define it. "Underlying the whole

---

25 Geddes to DLG, June 8, 1920, Geddes to Curzon, June 29, 1920, DLG Papers, F/60/4/2, 4.
26 HCL to Charnwood, June 16, 1920, HCL Papers, File 1920 (Personal, A-G).

question of the treaty," Lodge had concluded, "is the determination to put an end to executive encroachments and to reestablish the legislative branch of the Government and its proper Constitutional power." The fundamental question of control appeared in both its external and internal dimensions in the treaty fight. Republicans under Lodge's leadership resisted Wilson's League not only because they wanted to retain the unquestioned right of the United States to determine its role in foreign affairs, but also because they intended to restrict the president's prerogatives in this field. Lodge viewed this apparently negative stance in positive terms as he identified himself with the historic legacy of the Founding Fathers. The Constitution as well as the American diplomatic tradition of Washington's Farewell Address and the Monroe Doctrine, he contended, found their authentic expression in the Republican party's position, not in Wilson's. [27]

Turning a potential liability into an asset, Lodge welcomed the opportunity to unite the Republican party against Wilson's League. All Republicans agreed that the United States should refuse to join the League on the president's terms, despite their serious disagreements over appropriate alternatives. Preparing for the Republican national convention, Lodge hoped to unite the party by concentrating on this negative consensus, which mild reservationists as well as irreconcilables shared. He expected, if successful, to witness in the election results a final vindication of Republican opposition to the president's leadership. [28]

Lodge collaborated with Hays in preparing the plank on American foreign policy for the Republican party's platform. He had approved the Republican National Committee's plan to appoint an Advisory Committee on Policy and Platform in preparation for the national convention. In response to Hays' request, he agreed to serve on it and also named Moses, Lenroot and Watson. Senator Boies Penrose of Pennsylvania, Smoot and Kellogg joined it as three of the National Committee's twelve representatives. The Advisory Committee also included Capper, Fall, Knox and New. Besides these eleven senators and members of the National Committee, more than one hundred men and women representing various groups and interests throughout the country participated in the effort to form a consensus on major issues. Their assignment was to prepare recommendations for the Resolutions Committee of the national convention. Under the leadership of Ogden L. Mills of New York, the Advisory Committee at first concentrated on domestic issues while awaiting the outcome of the treaty fight. [29]

2 7   HCL to Charnwood, Jan. 24, Feb. 25, Apr. 16, 1920, HCL Papers, File 1920 (Personal, A-G).
2 8   Beveridge to HCL, May 11, 1920, HCL to Beveridge, May 14, 1920, HCL to C. Coolidge, May 10, 1920, HCL Papers, File 1920 (Personal, A-G); HCL to Bird, May 5, 1920, HCL Papers, File 1920 (A-G); HCL to Harvey, May 25, 1920, HCL Papers, File 1920 (Personal, H-Z).
2 9   Hays to HCL, Dec. 17, 1919, HCL to Hays, Dec. 18, 1919, HCL Papers, File 1919 (Peace, League, Political, I-Z); Chaney Digest, Dec. 12, 1919, Policy and Platform Committee, Jan. 29, 1920, Hays, Statement of Republican National Committee Relative to Advisory Committee on Policies and Platform, Jan. 28, 1920, Republican National Committee, "Tentative Plan of Work, Topics of Inquiry,

Meanwhile, Hays promoted Root's ideas within the Republican party. He distributed thousands of copies of the address which Root had delivered at the New York Republican state convention on February 19. On that occasion Root noted economic interdependence between the United States and Europe. He favored American ratification of the Versailles Treaty, but only on the condition that the president accept the Republican reservations. New York Republicans endorsed Root's position in their platform. Denouncing Article 10 and reaffirming the Monroe Doctrine, the New York platform rejected Wilson's internationalism.[30]

As the Senate continued to deal with the peace treaty, the Advisory Committee completed its work on domestic issues. Mills prepared to present the conclusions at a meeting of its executive committee that Hays scheduled in Lodge's office on May 18-19. This session would include the senators and representatives who served on the committee along with the chairmen of its various subcommittees. In anticipation of this meeting, Lodge attempted to reach an agreement among these Republican senators on a foreign-policy plank. Curtis actively assisted him and Hays in this process, and by early May Lodge had prepared a draft that most of them approved. However, mild reservationists such as Lenroot and Kellogg wanted a positive endorsement of the peace treaty with reservations, not merely a defense of the Senate's previous actions as he preferred. Like Root, they favored American membership in the League with those reservations. Lacking their full approbation, Lodge sent his draft to Hays for the Indiana Republican state convention. Hays planned to use it for the guidance of Republicans in his home state, hoping that the Indiana platform could then serve as a model for the national convention.[31]

Lodge's draft denounced Wilson's League and his refusal to accept the Senate's reservations, blaming him for sacrificing the treaty and delaying peace with Germany. But it refrained from promising that Republicans would ratify the treaty with reservations if they won the presidential and senatorial elections. In a paragraph that Cummins had written, the draft affirmed only that they favored "an association of nations to promote the clarification and codification of international law and for discussion and consultation respecting non-justiciable controversies before war begins." While advocating establishment of a world court and reduction of arma-

and Assignment of Topics to Members of the Advisory Committee on Policies and Platform," Feb. 2, 1920, Hays to HCL, Feb. 13, 1920, HCL to Hays, Feb. 16, 1920, Hays Papers.
3 0   Address by Elihu Root as Temporary Chairman of New York Republican State Convention, Feb. 19, 1920, Hays to ER, Feb. 20, 1920, Platform Adopted at the New York Republican State Convention, Feb. 20, 1920, Hays Papers.
3 1   Hays to HCL, Apr. 17, 1920, HCL to Hays, Apr. 17, May 10, 1920, HCL to Hays, May 9, 9, 12, 1920, HCL Papers, File 1920 (H-O); Hays to Penrose, Apr. 7, 1920, Hays to White, Apr. 17, 1920, Hays to Sub-Committee Chairmen, Apr. 17, 1920, Hays to the members of the General Committee who are members of the Senate or House, Apr. 17, 1920, HCL to Hays, Apr. 17, May 9, 9, 12, 1920, Hays to HCL, Apr. 19, 26, 1920, Curtis to Hays, Apr. 18, May 7, 1920, Mills to Hays, May 6, 1920, Hays Papers.

ments, it opposed any league that infringed upon exclusive control by the United States over its military and naval forces and its domestic affairs, or that abridged the Monroe Doctrine. The concluding paragraph of Lodge's draft reiterated the "new American doctrine" that Knox had outlined in his original resolution. It affirmed that if any great power or coalition, like the Central Powers in 1914, threatened Europe's freedom and peace, the United States would again join other nations to defend civilization as it had done in 1917. Avoiding any commitment to the League, Lodge once more recommended Knox's alternative to traditional isolation.[32]

After consulting Kellogg and Lenroot, Hays revised Lodge's draft slightly and then secured the Indiana Republican state convention's endorsement. As adopted on May 13, it called for "an association of nations to promote the peace of the world." Except for this somewhat more positive affirmation of the idea of collective security, the Indiana platform stated exactly what Lodge had proposed. Hays then distributed copies to various Republican senators to elicit interest. He obviously hoped to use the Indiana platform to form a consensus within the Republican party prior to the national convention. But the work of Hays and Lodge failed to accomplish the desired result in time for the May 18-19 meeting.[33]

Mild reservationists continued to urge Hays and Lodge to resist the danger of committing the Republican party to the irreconcilables' position. President Nicholas Murray Butler of Columbia University, who had earlier encouraged Hays to promote the New York platform, now welcomed the positive tone of the Indiana platform.[34] Other mild reservationists were less satisfied with the Indiana platform because it did not promise American membership in the League. Taft had already called upon Root to use his influence to encourage Lodge to adopt a more positive approach. Root sent a strong letter to Lodge, warning against the irreconcilables' attempt to write their plank into the Republican platform or to force a compromise. He advocated affirmation of the Republican majority's role in the Senate in favor of the treaty with reservations. At stake was the Republican record on this foreign-policy issue and also on the related constitutional question. He warned that retreat from that policy in the Republican platform would give the impression that the Senate had approved reservations as a devious method of defeating the treaty.[35]

3 2   [HCL's draft of platform for Indiana state convention, May 9, 1920], Hays Papers.
3 3   Memorandum, by Lenroot and Kellogg, May 10, 1920, Peace [Hays' handwritten copy of Indiana platform], n.d., [Indiana platform], May 13, 1920, Hays to WGH, May 14, 1920, Hays to Elkins, May 14, 1920, Hays to Frelinghuysen, May 14, 1920, Hays to Johnson, May 14, 1920, Hays to Knox, May 14, 1920, Hays to McCormick, May 14, 1920, Hays to Moses, May 14, 1920, Hays to Nelson, May 14, 1920, Hays to New, May 14, 1920, Hays to Penrose, May 14, 1920, Hays to Phipps, May 14, 1920, Hays to Smoot, May 14, 1920, Hays to Spencer, May 14, 1920, Hays to Kellogg, May 14, 1920, Hays to HCL, May 14, 21, 1920, Hays to Lenroot, May 21, 1920, Hays to Mills, May 21, 1920, Hays Papers; Hays to HCL, May 14, 21, 1920, HCL Papers, File 1920 (H-O).
3 4   Butler to Hays, Feb. 21, May 7, 18, 1920, Hays Papers.
3 5   Root to HCL, May 14, 1920, HCL Papers, File 1920 (P-Z), and ER Papers, Box 161; WHT to ALL, May 16, 1920, WHT to ALL, June 7, 1920, ALL Papers.

In response to Root's letter, Lodge persuasively presented his strategy. He reiterated his desire to defend the Senate's past record, but without promising that the Republican party would approve the treaty with reservations. He wanted to keep open all options for a new Republican president. Irreconcilables, he assured Root, were not insisting that the platform should endorse their views by excluding the option of American membership in the League; but neither did they want it to proclaim a pro-League position. Lodge commended the Indiana platform for offering a basis on which to unite all factions of the party. Although he would welcome endorsement of the reservations bearing his name, the senator explained, "I am much more interested in getting the whole party to fight together against Wilson and the League as he brought it home than I am in myself or anything else, and I have been trying to bring about some sort of statement which would enable us all to go in together, every man fighting along the line he preferred provided he fights against Wilson's League." This negative consensus, Lodge argued, would enable all Republicans to join a unified campaign against the Democrats by postponing the question of future policy.[36]

These arguments persuaded Root that this was the correct position for the Republicans. Once more he used his immense prestige to help Lodge and Hays create a consensus within the party. At the instigation of ex-Senator Crane of Massachusetts, Lowell attempted unsuccessfully to convince Root to advocate a plank in the Republican platform favoring the Versailles Treaty's ratification with proper reservations. Declining this request, Root refused to take any further action of that sort. Irreconcilables, he now confidently predicted, would not succeed in writing their extreme position into the platform. But, he concluded, the question of American ratification would have to await the election of a new Republican president. As he prepared to depart for Europe at the invitation of the League council to assist in preparing a plan for the Permanent Court of International Justice, Root aligned himself with Lodge and Hays in supporting the party's emerging negative consensus. All three of them were seeking to avoid a fight among Republicans over the League that might jeopardize prospects for victory in the fall elections.[37]

These Republican leaders prevailed at the national convention in Chicago. Hays had sent Mills to consult Root about the platform shortly before his departure. At this meeting on May 29, Root drafted a League plank which summarized the Republican critique of Wilson's peacemaking and promised an association of nations to prevent war. Lodge, with whom Mills shared this draft, doubted that irreconcilables would approve it. He still hoped to unite all factions of the party on the basis of the Indiana platform, but reached no

---

36   HCL to ER, May 17, 1920, ER Papers, Box 161, and HCL Papers, File 1920 (P-Z).
37   Crane to ALL, May 21, 1920, ALL to ER, May 22, 1920, ER to ALL, May 27, 1920, ALL Papers; ALL to ER, May 22, 1920, ER to ALL, May 27, 1920, ER Papers, Box 138.

agreement prior to the convention. He presented his case directly to the delegates in his keynote address on June 8. Welcoming the opportunity, as temporary chairman of the convention, to deliver this address, Lodge used the occasion to defend the Senate's record and condemn Wilson's leadership. The League, he argued, threatened to entangle the United States in unwise military obligations, for Article 10 "rests entirely upon naked force." It would produce war rather than peace. Moreover, the League would interfere with American domestic affairs and the Monroe Doctrine. To preserve American independence, he observed, the Senate had insisted upon genuine reservations instead of Wilson's wholly unsatisfactory interpretive reservations. Carefully stating the negative consensus he was fostering, Lodge called upon Republicans in Chicago to endorse the Senate's record. He emphasized that rejection of Wilson's League did not commit the Republican party to an isolationist policy. "We hear the timid cry that America will be isolated," he explained. "Have no fear. The United States cannot be isolated. The world needs us too much. We have never turned a deaf ear to the cry of suffering humanity and we never shall but we must do it in our own way, freely and without constraint from abroad." Although the convention affirmed his leadership by electing him permanent chairman, Lodge failed to persuade mild reservationists to accept the Indiana platform. Crane, Lenroot, Kellogg, Hale and Stimson, among others, still endeavored to write a plank favoring the League with reservations. They abandoned this attempt only after Mills showed them Root's plank, which they agreed to accept. After consulting Crane and Hays, Mills then submitted it to McCormick and Borah, who also approved. Agreement between these mild reservationists and irreconcilables broke the deadlock in the Resolutions Committee. On June 10 it recommended, and the convention quickly approved, Root's plank.[38]

The Republican platform denounced Wilson's League. The Covenant he had drafted in Paris, it claimed, violated the American diplomatic tradition. The League plank applauded the Senate for exercising its constitutional responsibility by refusing to acquiesce in the president's dictatorial demand for unqualified ratification. While condemning Wilson's role in clear language, Republicans vaguely endorsed "an international association." They stated that "the Republican party stands for agreement among the nations to preserve the peace of the world." Except for this obscure alternative, the Republican platform summarized the negative consensus against Wilson's League that Lodge and Hays, with Root's timely assistance, had carefully developed. It left open the option of American membership in some unspecified international organization, possibly the League under

3 8   Chaney Digest, June 8-10, 13, 1920, HCL, [address] at Convention, June 8, 1920, Mills to Hilles, June 18, 1920, Hays Papers; HCL to Hill, June 22, 1920, HCL Papers, File 1920 (Personal, H-Z); HCL to L. A. Coolidge, Apr. 17, 1920, HCL to Cabot, June 15, 1920, HCL Papers, File 1920 (A-G); HCL to Harvey, May 1, 1920, HCL to Hopkins, July 15, 1920, HCL Papers, File 1920 (H-O); WHT to Yost, June 19, 1920, WHT Papers, Ser. 3, Box 471.

acceptable conditions, but avoided any specific commitment. It gave all factions of the party, from mild reservationists to irreconcilables, a basis for common opposition to Democrats, while postponing difficult decisions about American involvement in world affairs.[39]

Ambassador Geddes observed that the Republicans had failed to take a definite stand on the major issue of American foreign relations. "What their plank on the League of Nations may be supposed to mean I am not sure," he reported to Lloyd George, "but as Senator Johnson can stand on it and Murray Butler also finds a foothold I do not think it can have any meaning at all." He thought they were really awaiting the choice of a presidential candidate before determining their position.[40]

The Republican party was as deeply divided over the nomination as over the League plank. To some extent these divisions coincided, although other factors also shaped the contest. General Leonard Wood and Governor Frank Lowden of Illinois, as expected, emerged as the two leading contenders during the early balloting at the convention. Lodge supported Wood, although he voted twice for Massachusetts' favorite son, Governor Coolidge, before switching to Wood. Root also favored Wood but had played an even less active role than Lodge in promoting him. Taft placed his hope on Lowden, who had assured him that he approved the Republican majority's stance during the treaty fight. Although Lowden avoided promises for the future, Taft viewed him as the best prospect for leading the United States into the League with reservations. The former president, like Root, refrained from any active campaigning for his choice. In contrast, Borah, who threatened to bolt the party if either Wood or Lowden won, vigorously promoted Johnson. For the past year, he had looked to the California senator as the candidate most qualified to lead the Republican party in a campaign against Wilson's League. But not even all irreconcilables shared this assessment. Moses and Beveridge supported Wood, while McCormick and Sherman favored the governor of their home state of Illinois.

On the early ballots Wood and Lowden came in first and second, respectively, followed by Johnson in third place. Lowden took a slight lead on the fifth ballot, but could not hold it. The deadlock continued in Chicago. Both Wood and Lowden received their highest votes on the seventh ballot, by which time Johnson was beginning to decline. Harding, who now moved into third place, began to erode the strength of the two leading contenders and subsequently succeeded on the tenth ballot in winning the presidential nomination. Acceptable to all factions in the party, the Ohio senator triumphed on June 12 as a safe compromise. Breaking the deadlock by turning to him, Republicans maintained the unity of their party. As in the adoption of the League plank, they chose an option that would promote

---

39   Donald Bruce Johnson and Kirk H. Porter, eds., *National Party Platforms*, 1840-1972 (Urbana, 1975), 231.
40   Geddes to DLG, June 11, 1920, DLG Papers, F/60/4/3.

harmony. Harding had carefully avoided making enemies within the party, unlike Wood, Lowden and Johnson. The convention then selected Coolidge, another champion of party unity, as its candidate for vice president. The nomination of the Harding-Coolidge ticket finally enabled the Republican convention to adjourn.[41]

Although not the first choice of most delegates, Harding skillfully united all factions of the party behind his candidacy. Loyally supporting the Republican majority in the Senate during the treaty fight, while nurturing good personal relations with all his colleagues, he had made himself an indispensable alternative to other presidential contenders. Working with Harry M. Daugherty, his campaign manager, he had carefully handled divisive issues such as the League by avoiding any extreme stands. His personality and political style sharply contrasted with Wilson's. He promised to return the country "Back to Normal." Rejecting Wilson's conception of "super-government," he offered a different kind of peace, which would preserve both the independence and the world markets of the United States. He believed that all peoples, like Americans, aspired to express their nationality and develop their commerce. "Knowing that these two thoughts are inspiring all humanity, as they have been since civilization began," he concluded, "I can only marvel at the American who consents to surrender either." With this kind of innocuous rhetoric, Harding used his masterful oratorical and political skills to capture the Republican nomination. Contrary to the impression of American journalists such as George Harvey, and of even the British ambassador, this outcome was not the result of a decision by Lodge and other senators in a "smoke-filled room" at the convention. It was instead the accomplishment of a talented but self-effacing politician, Harding, who now became the Republican party's new leader.[42]

Wilson welcomed these developments. The League plank in the Republican platform delighted him. He thought it would sharpen the distinction between the two parties on "the dominant issue of the campaign."[43] Wanting the election to serve as a "solemn referendum," the president

41 Chaney Digest, June 11-12, 1920, New to Hays, Apr. 8, 1920, Hays Papers; C. Coolidge to HCL, Dec. 1, 13, 20, 1919, HCL to C. Coolidge, Dec. 3, 15, 23, 1919, HCL to Foley, Dec. 8, 1919, HCL to Pound, Jan. 14, 1919, HCL Papers, File 1919 (Peace, League, Political, A-H); HCL to James, May 8, 1920, HCL to Watson, July 1, 1920, HCL to Wood, June 15, 1920, HCL to Wister, June 14, 1920, HCL Papers, File 1920 (Personal, H-Z); ER to Godkin, Jan. 12, 1920, ER Papers, Box 138; WHT to ALL, May 16, 1920, Carter to WHT, May 13, 1920, WHT to ALL, June 7, 1920, ALL Papers; WHT to Karger, Feb. 7, 1920, WHT Papers, Ser. 3, Box 467; WHT to H. Taft, June 7, 1920, WHT to Karger, June 19, 1920, WHT Papers, Ser. 3, Box 471; The Bulletin to Borah, June 14, 1919, Borah to The Bulletin, June 16, 1919, Borah to Levison, Feb. 16, 1920, Borah to Benson, May 18, 1920, Borah Papers, Box 550.

42 Daugherty to WGH, Apr. 2, July 3, Sept. 6, 1919, WGH to Daugherty, Apr. 4, July 11, 1919, Warren G. Harding Papers, Box 85 (Roll 28), Ohio Historical Society; Daugherty to WGH, Dec. 26, 1919, WGH Papers, Box 86 (Roll 28); "Back to Normal," May 14, 1920, WGH Papers, Box 838 (Roll 238); Chaney Digest, June 12, 1920, Hays Papers; Geddes to DLG, June 30, 1920, DLG Papers, F/60/4/4.

43 NDB to WW, June 11, 1920, WW to NDB, June 14, 1920, WW Papers, Ser. 2, Box 197; WW to NDB, June 14, 1920, NDB Papers, Box 13.

exerted his continuing influence to distinguish the Democratic party as the League's steadfast champion. He sought to control not only the drafting of its platform but also the selection of its candidate. As his two principal spokesmen in this endeavor, he selected the Democratic national chairman, Cummings, and Senator Glass. One of his most loyal supporters, Glass still advocated the League and staunchly defended Wilson. "The wretched talk about the 'obstinacy' of the President over the Peace Treaty," he explained to a Roanoke judge, "is purely an invention of adversary politicians, acquiesced in by a species of Democrat which has never sympathized with Mr. Wilson's ideals or his policies. The President has not evinced one particle of obduracy about the Treaty."[44]

So intent was Wilson on controlling the Democratic campaign, he even hoped the national convention would nominate him for a third term in order that he could personally lead the fight. A year earlier, while he was still at the peace conference, Wilson had contemplated running again for the presidency. At that time he had asked Tumulty to consult Cummings, Secretaries Glass and Baker, and Secretary of Labor William B. Wilson about this prospect. Advising against the idea without consulting them, Tumulty foresaw potential political danger in a premature announcement. He thought the president should give the impression that he might seek a third term without actually committing himself. This implicit threat might strengthen his ability to secure the Senate's approval of the treaty. This ploy did not work. By the spring of 1920, after the Senate had twice rejected the treaty, Tumulty concluded that Wilson should withdraw his name from further consideration. Failure to do so, he reasoned, would enable Republicans to claim that the president had refused to compromise on reservations in order to create an issue on which to run for a third term. By withdrawing, Wilson could demonstrate that his commitment to the League was based on principle rather than on personal ambition. But this advice he refused to accept.[45]

Wilson's reluctance to announce either his candidacy or his withdrawal left other Democratic candidates in a quandary. Even his closest associates did not know his intentions. His son-in-law, William G. McAdoo, experienced the greatest difficulty. Trying to avoid an open challenge to the president while seeking to win delegates for his own nomination, McAdoo publicly announced that he was not a candidate but privately indicated that he would accept a draft. Despite this handicap, he emerged as the front-runner on the eve of the convention. Aware of the burden he was imposing on McAdoo, Wilson nevertheless refused to step aside. On June 19 he shared his views with Glass at a private meeting in the White House.

44   Glass to Jackson, March 28, 1920, Glass Papers, Box 4; Glass to Hilt, May 12, 1920, Glass Papers, Box 119.
45   WW to JPT, June 2, 1919 (#43), JPT to WW, June 3, 1920, JPT Papers, Box 7; JPT to EBW, March 23, 1920, JPT Papers, Box 3; WW to JPT, June 2, 1919, JPT to WW, June 3, 1919 (#158), WW Papers, Ser. 5B, Reel 408.

From Dr. Cary Grayson, the president's physician, the senator had learned that poor health would prevent him from enduring another campaign. Grayson as well as Tumulty urged Glass to discourage him from seeking the nomination. But the senator hesitated to deliver such bad news with unmistakable clarity. While expressing his regret that Wilson was not physically able to fight for the League by running for a third term, Glass also told him, "I would rather follow the President's corpse through a campaign than the live bodies of some of the men mentioned for the nomination." Apparently pleased with this affirmation of loyalty, Wilson still hoped the convention would turn to him. He agreed with Glass that Attorney General A. Mitchell Palmer, McAdoo's principal rival, would make a good president but could not win the election. As for Governor James M. Cox of Ohio, Wilson considered his possible nomination "a fake." He found none of these leading contenders acceptable as his successor in the White House.[46]

Glass collaborated with Wilson in preparing their party's platform. At Tumulty's suggestion, the president approved the strong pro-League statement that Glass had written for the Virginia platform in late May. It applauded the League as the best method of achieving "permanent peace" and fulfilling "American ideals." Moreover, criticizing Republicans for their partisan and personal opposition to Wilson and his League, it condemned their advocacy of the Knox resolution. The president, sharing his suggestions for other planks with Glass, asked him on June 12 to seek the chairmanship of the Resolutions Committee at the San Francisco convention. He wanted him to transform the Virginia platform, with these additions, into the national position of the Democratic party.[47]

Not all Democrats wanted their party to continue Wilson's politics of confrontation. Underwood recognized the necessity of endorsing his leadership but wanted to avoid any embarrassment for Democratic senators, like himself, who had favored compromise on the treaty. Obviously desiring the president not to run for a third term, the minority leader in the Senate preferred the nomination of Palmer or possibly Cox. He decided, however, not to attend the convention. Despite his private concerns, Underwood wanted to avoid an open rift in the party.[48]

At the Democratic national convention in San Francisco, Wilson's

46 McAdoo to Whitford, March 24, 1920, WW Papers, Ser. 4, File 331; NDB to WW, June 10, 1920, WW to NDB, June 11, 1920, WW Papers, Ser. 2, Box 197; NDB to Whitlock, Apr. 4, 1920, WW to NDB, June 11, 1920, NDB Papers, Box 13; Memorandum, June 10, 1920, Memorandum, June 16, 1920, Memorandum, June 17, 1920, Memorandum, June 18, 1920, Memorandum, June 19, 1920, Glass Papers, Box 3; Rixey Smith and Norman Beasley, *Carter Glass: A Biography* (New York, 1939), 205-08.

47 JPT to WW, May 17, 1920, JPT Papers, Box 7; Glass to WW, May 27, 1920, WW to Glass, May 28, 1920, WW Papers, Ser. 2, Box 196; WW to Glass, June 11, 14, 1920, Glass to WW, June 12, 1920, WW Papers, Ser. 2, Box 197; Memorandum, June 12, 1920, Memorandum, June 19, 1920, Glass Papers, Box 3; Glass to WW, May 27, June 12, 1920, WW to Glass, May 28, 1920, Glass Papers, Box 8; Glass to WW, May 27, 1920, WW to Glass, May 28, 1920, Virginia Platform [1920], Burleson Papers, Vol. 26.

48 Underwood to Taylor, May 24, 1920, Underwood to Sanders, June 6, 1920, Underwood Papers.

political allies were prepared to dominate the proceedings. Cummings delivered an uncompromising keynote address which he had previously cleared with the president. They had met in the White House on May 31 to review this address and plan their strategy. To facilitate secret communication between San Francisco and Washington, they had arranged a special code. As planned, Glass won the chairmanship of the Resolutions Committee. However, Wilson's choice for permanent chairman of the convention, Colby, failed to obtain this position in a race against several contenders. Senator Robinson, one of the president's most consistent supporters during the treaty fight, eventually emerged as the choice. In the Resolutions Committee on July 1, Colby aided Glass in securing adoption of a platform with an acceptable League plank. Bryan had attempted unsuccessfully to amend it by calling for acquiescence in any reservation necessary to achieve the Senate's approval. In sharp conflict with Wilson, he advocated bipartisan compromise. But he lost as the president's associates managed to control the drafting of the platform, except for minor modifications.[49]

The Democratic platform, as adopted, vigorously defended Wilson's peacemaking. It committed the party to "the League of Nations as the surest, if not the only, practicable means of maintaining the permanent peace of the world and terminating the insufferable burden of great military and naval expenditures." The treaty, proclaimed this plank, fulfilled not only "American ideals" but also "the aspirations of civilized peoples everywhere." Denouncing Lodge, the platform approved the president's all-or-nothing stance during the treaty fight. Rejecting the Knox resolution, it applauded Democrats in Congress for opposing a disgraceful separate peace. The platform endorsed Wilson's contention that only interpretive reservations were acceptable. No other reservations were necessary, it concluded, to preserve American independence, including the right of Congress to declare war before the United States used armed forces to fulfill obligations under the Covenant.[50]

Adoption of this platform by the Democratic national convention delighted Wilson. As he desired, the two parties now appeared to represent diametrically opposite positions. The choice for voters in 1920, he thought, was between Republican isolationism and Democratic internationalism. "While our opponents are endeavoring to isolate us among the nations of the world," he announced in a congratulatory message to the convention, "we are following the vision of the founders of the republic who promised the world the counsel and leadership of the free people of the United States in all matters that affected human liberty and the justice of law. . . . This is a conquering purpose and nothing can defeat it."[51]

49 Cummings memorandum, May 31, 1920 [Jan. 18, 1929], Cummings to WW, July 1, 1920, RSB Papers, Ser. I, Box 3; Colby to WW, June 18, 1920, WW to Colby, June 19, 1920, Cummings to WW, June 30, July 1, 1920, WW Papers, Ser. 2, Box 197.
50 Johnson and Porter, eds., *National Party Platforms*, 213-14.
51 WW to Cummings, July 2, 1920, JPT Papers, Box 7.

Although their platform approved the president's leadership, Democrats in San Francisco did not nominate him for a third term. On July 2, as the convention faced a deadlock among the leading contenders, Colby conceived a plan to suspend the rules and place Wilson's name in nomination. Without consulting anyone else, he requested his permission to implement the plan. The president apparently welcomed this dramatic move, but his other close associates did not. They recognized that it would most likely fail, resulting only in considerable embarrassment. At a conference which Cummings convened, Glass and McCormick strongly opposed Colby's plan. The others in attendance – including Robinson, Hull, Ray Stannard Baker, Daniels and Burleson – agreed with this negative assessment. They forced Colby to convey this bad news to the president, who then acquiesced in their decision not to seek his nomination. This finally ended Wilson's vain hope for a third term. The convention itself eventually broke the deadlock that had continued for forty-four ballots. After both McAdoo and Palmer had failed to achieve the required two-thirds majority, Cox finally won the nomination on July 6. He selected Assistant Secretary of the Navy Franklin D. Roosevelt from New York for his running mate, a choice readily approved by the convention. The responsibility for defending Wilson's record during the campaign now shifted to this new Democratic team.[52]

II

Presidential politics during the campaign of 1920 focused on Wilson's leadership and especially his League of Nations. Despite his inability to control the final choice, he still shaped the debate between Republicans and Democrats. Cox and Roosevelt, soon after their nomination, went to the White House on Sunday, July 18. By their presence as well as their words, they promised to continue the president's fight. At the conclusion of this meeting, he issued a statement praising Cox for his dedication to the League. Although Wilson had not favored Cox's nomination, he now looked to him as the champion of his great cause.[53]

Cox affirmed his loyalty to Wilson and his commitment to the League. Some political advisers, including the manager of his bid for the nomination at San Francisco, Edmond H. Moore, had warned him to avoid this identification and even to stay away from the White House. Unlike both McAdoo and Palmer, who had served in Wilson's cabinet, Cox had not previously suffered from the political liability of too close an association with the president, which had been one of his assets at the Democratic

52   Colby to WW, July 2, 1920, WW Papers, Ser. 2, Box 197; JPT to EBW, July 4, 1920, JPT Papers, Box 3; Cummings memorandum, July 3-4, 1920 [Jan. 18, 1929], RSB Papers, Ser. I, Box 3; James M. Cox, *Journey Through My Years* (New York, 1946), 225-33; JPT, *Woodrow Wilson*, 492-99; Wesley M. Bagby, *The Road to Normalcy: The Presidential Campaign and Election of* 1920 (Baltimore, 1962), 102-22; Frank Freidel, *Franklin D. Roosevelt: The Ordeal* (Boston, 1954), 51-69.
53   Cox, *Journey*, 241-42; EBW, *My Memoirs*, 306.

convention. But he chose to ignore this prudent advice. He fully endorsed Wilson's stance during the treaty fight in a statement to the press which he prepared at the White House. Regardless of the consequences, Cox decided to wage his campaign for the presidency by embracing Wilson's legacy.[54]

Cox's visit to the White House helped to sharpen partisan differences. Accompanied by Roosevelt, Cox gave his statement to the newspaper correspondents at the White House and informed them about his determination to campaign for the League. One critical observer at the press conference, who had not expected Cox to subordinate himself so fully to Wilson, reported this surprising news to Lodge. The close identification between Cox and Wilson delighted the senator. On the basis of this private report as well as Cox's published statement, Lodge rejoiced: "We have now got him tied not only to the League but to Wilson and it makes our campaign." He recognized the potential benefits for the Republican party from the White House meeting and appreciated Harding's quick response to exploit this opportunity.[55]

Harding had already begun to unite Republicans behind his candidacy by emphasizing their common antipathy toward Wilson's League. Hays and other Republican leaders had decided soon after the Democratic convention to focus on the League as the "paramount issue" in 1920. Prominent spokesmen from all factions of the party congratulated their candidate and pledged their support. Within the negative consensus toward Wilson's League, each of these Republican factions hoped to persuade Harding to embrace its own position as the basis for future policy. The most immediate problem for him was to attract the active participation of irreconcilables without alienating mild reservationists. Consequently, both he and Lodge rejoiced when Johnson publicly announced his loyalty to the Republican ticket. The California senator, in his statement on July 7, had focused on the League as the crucial issue between the parties. Reaffirming his commitment to the American diplomatic tradition, Johnson hoped to preserve independence from the Old World by keeping the United States outside the League.[56]

Mild reservationists as well as irreconcilables loyally endorsed the Repub-

54   JPT, *Woodrow Wilson*, 499-500; Cox, *Journey*, 242-43; Geddes to DLG, July 8, 1920, DLG Papers, F/60/4/5.
55   Groves to HCL, July 24, 1920, HCL to Groves, July 26, 1920, HCL to Gillett, July 19, 1920, HCL Papers, File 1920 (Personal, A-G).
56   Randolph C. Downes, *The Rise of Warren Gamaliel Harding*, 1865-1920 (Columbus, 1970), 565-66; Chaney Digest, July 6-7, 1920, Hays Papers; WGH to WHT, June 14, 1920, WHT Papers, Ser. 3, Box 471; WGH to Hughes, June 15, 1920, Hughes to WGH, June 25, 1920, Hughes Papers, Box 4A; Knox to WGH, June 12, 15, 1920, WGH to Knox, June 14, 1920, Knox Papers, Box 30; Beveridge to WGH, July 6, 10, 1920, WGH to Beveridge, June 18, 1920, WGH to Beveridge, July 8, 20, 1920, Beveridge Papers, Box 221, and WGH Papers, Box 126 (Roll 40); Beveridge statement, n.d., Beveridge to Johnson, July 17, 20, 1920, Beveridge Papers, Box 221; Johnson to WGH, June 13, 1920, WGH to Johnson, June 22, 1920, WGH to Johnson, July 8, 1920, WGH Papers, Box 102 (Roll 34); WGH to HCL, July 6, 1920, HCL to WGH, July 8, 1920, HCL Papers, File 1920 (Personal, H-Z), and WGH Papers, Box 144 (Roll 45).

lican ticket. Although Harding assiduously avoided any promise of future American membership in the League even with reservations, its foremost Republican advocates saw no realistic alternative but to support him. Before Cox's nomination, Taft and Lowell had decided to prevent the League to Enforce Peace from aligning itself with the Democratic candidate. They sought to maintain this organization by keeping it out of the campaign. Expecting a Republican victory, they hoped to preserve their credibility with Harding. To promote the League of Nations with the Lodge reservations, Lowell appealed to Root for assistance. Because Root had drafted the League plank in the Republican platform, Taft, too, expected him to use his immense influence on behalf of membership in the League. Meanwhile, Taft advised Harding to attack the Democrats by concentrating on Article 10. If he adopted this strategy, by focusing on the past instead of the future, he could force Cox to defend Wilson's record. He could thereby place the burden on Democrats for failing to accept the Republican majority's reservations. This strategy would, moreover, preserve the option of joining the League with reservations. Above all, Taft sought to prevent Harding from abdicating to "the Bitter Enders" by committing himself unequivocally against the League.[57]

Harding designed his acceptance speech to take into account the recommendations from various Republican factions. On July 22 a Republican delegation, headed by Lodge, called at his home in Marion, Ohio, to inform him officially of his nomination. Hoping to satisfy irreconcilables and mild reservationists alike, Harding emphasized potential costs of Wilson's League. Lodge, like Taft, had encouraged him to focus on the dangers of Article 10. Accepting this advice, Harding proclaimed his opposition to Wilson's plan for a "world super-government." Reiterating the Republican party's negative consensus, he avoided any explicit statement about his alternative to Wilson's League. He rejoiced that the Senate had demanded reservations to preserve American independence. Although primarily concerned about his country, Harding regretted the treaty fight's consequences for the Old World. He denied that Republicans were seeking to isolate the United States. "The world will not misconstrue," he insisted. "We do not mean to hold aloof. We do not mean to shun a single responsibility of this Republic to world civilization." Both unilateralism and universalism thus characterized Harding's view of international affairs. Despite his criticism of Wilson's League, he, too, combined these two typical American tendencies.[58]

57   ALL to WHT, June 15, 21, 23, 23, 1920, ALL Papers; ALL to ER, July 14, 1920, ER Papers, Box 138; ALL to WHT, June 15, 23, 23, 1920, WHT to ALL, June 19, 22, 1920, WGH to WHT, June 30, 1920, WHT Papers, Ser. 3, Box 471; WHT to WGH, July 12, 14, 16, 18, 1920, WGH Papers, Box 351 (Roll 112).

58   HCL to WGH, July 9, 1920, WGH to HCL, July 16, 1920, HCL Papers, File 1920 (Personal, H-Z), and WGH Papers, Box 144 (Roll 45); HCL to Hays, July 10, 1920, HCL Papers, File 1920 (Personal, H-Z); WGH, Speech of Acceptance, July 22, 1920, Hays Papers; Acceptance Speech, July 22, 1920, WGH Papers, Box 839 (Roll 238).

Harding's acceptance speech delighted irreconcilables. Although he had obfuscated, his remarks sounded like a total rejection of the League even with reservations. Lodge interpreted the speech that way. "What he did was to throw the present League and the reservations overboard," Lodge explained to Moses, "and he then said that we would go to work and make a proper agreement with foreign nations." Expecting a "great fight" in the campaign "against Wilsonism," Lodge congratulated Harding for clarifying the differences between the parties.[59]

Privately, Harding identified himself with an irreconcilable interpretation of the League plank in the Republican platform. While attempting to reconcile the competing factions in the Republican party, he considered the remarks about the League in his acceptance speech as merely an elaboration of Johnson's earlier statement. "I think you could well understand," Harding assured the California senator, "that in the making of this speech I was seeking to perform a party service in making it possible for the divergent elements of the party to come together, with the assurance of preserved nationality, on the one hand, and a readiness to participate in performing a recognized duty to world civilization, on the other. However, I did not mean to add to the interpretation which you have already made quite correctly and which will stand as the official utterance on our international relationship." Harding revealed his future intention by endorsing Johnson's statement as the "official" Republican position.[60]

Harding exploited Cox's visit to the White House. "The only possible inference is that Governor Cox is maintaining the same attitude toward Article 10 that President Wilson has long maintained," he announced.[61] He sought to force the Democrats to defend Wilson's League. While avoiding any public clarification of his own alternative, Harding endeavored to unite the Republican party by reiterating its negative consensus. This strategy led him as well as Lodge closer to the irreconcilable position. Yet even when he privately approved Johnson's statement as the "official" interpretation of the Republican platform, Harding preserved freedom to advocate American participation in some kind of association of nations. The United States, he insisted, would fulfill its responsibilities to civilization by fostering peace and justice without sacrificing independence.

Cox as well as Harding emphasized the differences between their parties over the League. In his acceptance speech in Dayton, Ohio, on August 7, the Democratic candidate reaffirmed his loyalty to Wilson. He had previously

59   Johnson to Beveridge, July 24, 27, 1920, Beveridge to Johnson, July 31, 1920, Beveridge Papers, Box 221; HCL to Moses, July 26, 1920, HCL Papers, File 1920 (Personal, H-Z); HCL to Lyman, July 28, 1920, HCL Papers, File 1920 (H-O); HCL to WGH, July 26, 1920, HCL Papers, File 1920 (Personal, H-Z), and WGH Papers, Box 144 (Roll 45); WGH to HCL, July 29, 1920, WGH Papers, Box 144 (Roll 45).

60   WGH to Johnson, July 27, 1920, WGH Papers, Box 102 (Roll 34); Beveridge to WGH, July 26, 1920, WGH to Beveridge, July 28, 31, 1920, Beveridge Papers, Box 221, and WGH Papers, Box 126 (Roll 40).

61   WGH, statement, July 31, 1920, Hays Papers.

submitted to Tumulty, who relayed it to Mrs. Wilson for the president, the part of this address relating to the League. Moreover, Cox accepted Tumulty's recommendation for an additional section in his speech. This revision strengthened his affirmation of the Democratic party's promise to lead the United States into the League. Cox denounced the Lodge reservations as the work of "the present senatorial cabal" to destroy the Versailles peace. Republicans, he claimed, intended to abandon the League and conclude a separate peace with Germany. Their proposal of an association of nations, in his opinion, was wholly unrealistic inasmuch as other nations were already operating in the League. Noting Johnson's public endorsement of Harding's acceptance speech, Cox accused the Republican party and its candidate of capitulating to the irreconcilables. "In short," he asserted, "principle, as avowed in support of the Lodge reservations, or of the so-called mild reservations, has been surrendered to expediency." Yet he refused to accept Republican reservations as a satisfactory basis for securing the Senate's approval of the treaty. Instead, he vigorously defended Article 10, contending that it was essentially the same as the Monroe Doctrine. What that doctrine had accomplished in Central and South America, he argued, the League would achieve throughout the world. Without explaining how he expected to find the necessary votes in the Senate, Cox promised that as president he would ratify the peace treaty as his first duty.[62] He courageously championed the League and avoided the equivocation that had characterized Harding's acceptance speech. But, as Lippmann observed, there was "an atmosphere of unreality" about Cox's treatment of this central issue.[63]

III

Within the Republican party, advocates and opponents of the League continued their efforts to persuade Harding to endorse their conflicting positions. His obfuscation failed to satisfy them. Leaders of the League to Enforce Peace, including Lowell and Straus, wanted him to call for ratification with reservations. As Harding seemed to abandon the treaty, Hoover took the initiative to convince him that the United States should not conclude a separate peace with Germany. On the contrary, he argued, it should enter the League and take a constructive part in European affairs. Although he, too, opposed Article 10, Hoover urged Harding to reject the irreconcilable position by renouncing Johnson's interpretation of the Republican platform. As he also explained to Hays, he appreciated Harding's concern for harmony among Republicans, but not at the cost of a separate peace with Germany and abandonment of the League.[64]

---

62 JPT to EBW, Aug. 1, 1920, [Cox's speech], WW Papers, Ser. 2, Box 197; Suggestion for insert in Gov. Cox's Speech of Acceptance on 7th of Aug., Aug. 4, 1920, JPT Papers, Box 14; Cox, *Journey*, 265-66.
63 Lippmann to NDB, Aug. 10, 1920, NDB Papers, Box 12.
64 ALL to ER, Aug. 17, 1920, ER Papers, Box 138; Straus to Hoover, July 28, 1920, Hoover

Irreconcilables encouraged Harding and Hays to continue attacking the League. Unlike Hoover, who cautioned against the political liability, they thought the Republican party would benefit from this negative stance. Johnson advised Harding to resist demands for details about his plan for an association of nations. "You are on safe and high ground," he insisted, "when you say you will first declare a state of peace to exist, and then leisurely and reflectively take up with the nations of the world, the questions of disarmament and prevention of war through international cooperation." Johnson wanted Harding, instead of revealing his own future policy, to focus on "the real issue" of Wilson's League. The new Republican administration, he expected, would refuse to join. "We will scrap the Wilson League of Nations," he told Harding, "declare a state of peace as you indicate in your speech of acceptance, and thereafter, as you have clearly put it, we will perform in our own way our recognized duty to world civilization." Welcoming Johnson's advice, Harding assured him that he intended to remain on "perfectly safe ground."[65]

After reviewing Cox's acceptance speech, Harding and Hays decided to continue campaigning against Wilson's record. Lodge agreed that their best strategy was to discuss the League and constitutional government as the foremost issues in the election rather than to focus on Cox himself. By identifying him with the president, Republicans could maintain their negative consensus against Wilsonism. Nevertheless, under pressure from both mild reservationists and irreconcilables, Harding decided to elaborate his position on the League.[66] On August 28 he contrasted the differences between Democrats and Republicans over foreign policy. If the United States had joined Wilson's League, he told a delegation visiting his home as part of his front-porch campaign, it would now find itself embroiled in the European war between Poland and Russia. Under Article 10, Poland would surely have requested American military assistance against Soviet Russia's aggression. The distinction which Wilson had attempted to make between moral and legal obligations would not excuse the United States from the promise to protect other nations. As a member of the League, Harding argued, this nation would now face the choice between sacrificing its honor, if it reneged on its commitment, or involving itself in the Soviet-Polish war. This situation, in his view, demonstrated the Senate's wisdom in rejecting

Pre-Commerce Papers, Box 28; Hoover to WGH, Aug. 3, 1920, Hoover Pre-Commerce Papers, Box 7, and WGH Papers, Box 102 (Roll 34); Hoover to Hays, Aug. 11, 1920, Hoover Pre-Commerce Papers, Box 7; WGH to Hoover, Aug. 5, 1920, WGH Papers, Box 102 (Roll 34); WGH to Hoover, Aug. 7, 1920, Hoover Pre-Commerce Papers, Box 24, and WGH Papers, Box 102 (Roll 34); Gay to Hoover, Aug. 4, 1920, Hoover to Hays, Aug. 21, 1920, Hoover Pre-Commerce Papers, Box 24.

65 Johnson to WGH, Aug. 9, 1920, WGH to Johnson, Aug. 16, 1920, WGH Papers, Box 102 (Roll 34); Knox to Hays, Aug. 5, 1920, Robins to Hays, Aug. 11, 1920, Johnson to Hays, Aug. 23, 1920, Hays Papers; Beveridge to WGH, Aug. 21, 1920, Beveridge Papers, Box 221, and WGH Papers, Box 126 (Roll 40).

66 Chaney Digest, Aug. 10, 1920, WGH to Hays, Aug. 16, 1920, Hays to HCL, Aug. 19, 20, 1920, Hays Papers; HCL to WGH, Aug. 21, 1920, WGH Papers, Box 252 (Roll 81), and HCL Papers, File 1920 (Personal, H-Z).

the League without reservations. While defending the Republican record during the treaty fight, Harding refused to approve the League even with reservations. He contended that "the conditions have changed. Experience has brought enlightenment. We know now that the league constituted at Versailles is utterly impotent as a preventive of wars." Harding advocated a different form of international relations. Distinguishing between Democratic and Republican alternatives, he repudiated Wilson's internationalism for establishing "an offensive and defensive alliance of great powers, like that created at Versailles, to impose their will upon the helpless peoples of the world." Republicans, he claimed, wanted the United States to exercise "world leadership" through "an association of free nations" without sacrificing its nationality. He depicted this Republican alternative as the best hope for the future.[67]

Harding sought to satisfy all factions in the Republican party by denouncing Wilson's League and advocating an association of nations. He rejoiced at Johnson's approval of his August 28 speech and assured him that he expected "complete accord" between them in the future. Harding's first priority was to win the election. He was therefore quite willing to postpone divisive questions. But one point was now clear. He did not intend for the United States to join Wilson's League.[68]

Lodge approved completely Harding's handling of the League issue. On August 28 in Boston, where he delivered an address on world peace, the Massachusetts senator criticized Cox by identifying him with Wilson. In greater detail than Harding, he defended the Senate's record. The issue in 1920, he concluded, was whether or not the United States should join Wilson's League. Cox favored this action, while Republicans opposed it. Instead of "a political alliance," they advocated an association of nations which would establish a world court, codify international law, and reduce armaments. Lodge insisted that this Republican alternative to Wilson's internationalism would not sacrifice American independence. Focusing on the underlying question of control, he proclaimed that "we are nationalists and not internationalists. We stand for America first. It will be no benefit, but utter calamity to the rest of the world, if the United States should fail. The best hope of the world is here. Therefore, we must not impair our strength or allow ourselves to be led or controlled by others." Lodge wanted to protect the United States from the threat of foreign control inherent in Wilson's League. To accomplish that goal, he desired the election not only of Harding but also of Republican senators. He explained to Daugherty that "it is almost as important to control the Senate as it is to control the Presidency." Sharing this concern, Daugherty assured him that the expected

67   Address to Indianapolis Delegation, Aug. 28, 1920, WGH Papers, Box 839 (Roll 239); WGH, A Free People: Speech on the Wilson League of Nations, Delivered Before the Indiana Delegation at Marion, Ohio, Aug. 28, 1920, Hays Papers.
68   Johnson to WGH, Aug. 31, 1920, WGH to Johnson, Sept. 6, 1920, WGH Papers, Box 102 (Roll 34).

"landslide" for Harding would improve Republican prospects in close senatorial races. In Lodge's view, the internal and external aspects of control of American foreign relations were at stake in the election.[69]

Within their understanding of American nationalism, Republicans welcomed various ethnic groups. They hoped to attract voters whom Wilson had alienated by his attitudes or policies toward their ancestral lands. Hays had begun early in 1920, in accordance with the plans he had previously outlined for the Republican National Committee, to implement a strategy for winning the so-called foreign vote. He appointed A. B. Messer of New York to organize this effort throughout the country. Under his direction, Republicans formed committees in the states, particularly where ethnicity was politically significant. "We are not only making our plans for the cultivation of the foreign born vote for 1920," Messer explained, "but to try to interest them in the real principles of the Republican party." In Chicago, after the national convention, Senator McCormick joined him to provide leadership in this campaign for ethnic votes. They focused on Americans of German, Irish, Italian and Greek birth and parentage. Recognizing that not all of them would abandon the Democratic party, or vote for the Republican ticket even if they did, Republicans hoped at least to gain some additional support from these groups.[70]

Both Lodge and Harding actively participated in this Republican effort to attract ethnic votes. In an open letter in the *Boston Herald* on August 26, the Massachusetts senator defended his party's record on the Irish question. He noted the Republican contribution to the passage of Borah's Irish resolution in 1919. Yet, because of his desire to assimilate immigrants and their children in this country, Lodge emphasized the avoidance of entanglement in the Old World's politics. To prevent divisiveness at home, he urged all of his fellow citizens to "be Americans first."[71] Harding emphasized the same theme in welcoming the endorsement of some German-Americans. Because of his opposition to the League and his desire for peace with Germany, the German American National Conference had, at its meeting in Chicago on August 17-18, decided to favor his candidacy. One of its leaders, George

69   HCL, The Road to World Peace, Aug. 28, 1920, Hays Papers; Address of Senator Lodge, Aug. 28, 1920, HCL Papers, File 1920 (A-G); [address, Aug. 28, 1920], HCL Papers, File 1920 (H-O); HCL to WGH, Aug. 30, 1920, WGH to HCL, Sept. 1, 1920, HCL Papers, File 1920 (Personal, H-Z); HCL to WGH, Sept. 2, 3, 1920, WGH to HCL, Sept. 6, 10, 1920, HCL Papers, File 1920 (Personal, H-Z), and WGH Papers, Box 252 (Roll 81); Daugherty to HCL, Aug. 29, Sept. 5, 1920, HCL to Daugherty, Sept. 2, 1920, HCL Papers, File 1920 (Personal, A-G).

70   Hays to Republican National Committee, [1919], Messer to Smith, Jan. 10, 1920, Messer to Stratton, Jan. 13, 1920, Messer to Welsh, Jan. 13, 1920, Messer to Benjamin, Jan. 14, 1920, Messer to Roraback, Jan. 14, 1920, Messer to Clark, Jan. 24, 1920, Messer to Baker, Feb. 2, 1920, Messer to Sollitt, Apr. 13, 1920, Bone to McCormick, July 13, Sept. 2, 1920, Welliver to Bone, July 24, 1920, McCormick to Messer, July 29, 1920, HCL to Hays, Aug. 12, Sept. 2, 1920, Hays to Stokes, Aug. 18, 1920, Messer to Hilles, Aug. 26, 1920, Messer to Stokes, Aug. 27, 1920, Messer to HCL, Aug. 30, 1920, HCL to Messer, Aug. 31, 1920, HCL to Weeks, Sept. 2, 1920, Cassavetes to [WW], Aug. 30, 1920, Bone to HCL, Sept. 3, 1920, Hays to HCL, Sept. 7, 1920, Hays Papers; Hays to HCL, Sept. 7, 1920, HCL Papers, File 1920 (H-O).

71   HCL to WGH, Sept. 3, 1920, "America First, Lodge's Slogan," *Boston Herald* (Aug. 26, 1920).

Sylvester Viereck, informed him about this action. Harding indicated his willingness to accept support from all American citizens. He encouraged German-Americans to vote for the Republican ticket, but did not promise them anything in return. Like Lodge, he expected them to conform to his conception of Americanism.[72] "We are unalterably against any present or future hyphenated Americanism," he bluntly told several delegations of "foreign born" voters. He warned against the "un-American policy" of "meddling" in European affairs, which would threaten to divide American society along ethnic lines. The Republican candidate thereby cautioned against the potentially disruptive consequences of ethnicity while skillfully playing ethnic politics for his advantage.[73]

In contrast to Harding's masterful campaign, Cox experienced considerable difficulty. At his headquarters the leadership of Representative George White of Ohio, who became the Democratic National Committee's new chairman after the convention, failed to match that of Hays. Poor coordination and limited funds characterized the Democratic effort. Although Wilson personally contributed some money to the campaign, other Democrats did not readily follow his example. Cox himself valiantly pursued the presidency by traveling and speaking throughout the western states during August and September. Convinced that "the people want the League," he expected to carry several of these states. Blaming the Republicans and their newspapers for confusing the voters, he thought the Democrats could win by "getting the gospel to the people." He assured Secretary Baker, who had urged him not to compromise on Article 10, that he would not sacrifice it. Others were less optimistic than Cox. McAdoo warned Tumulty that prospects for the Democratic ticket were not encouraging. Nevertheless, he actively supported it by undertaking a speaking tour across the nation, especially to defend the League. Aware of Cox's troubles, Tumulty assisted him by providing information about the treaty fight. He urged him to expose the contradictions in Harding's position on the League resulting from his attempt to mollify different Republican factions. Tumulty also endeavored to involve the president directly in the campaign. As a way of focusing national attention on the issues, particularly the League, he tried to convince him to release a statement to the American people during each week of the last month before the election. Assisted by Creel, Tumulty prepared a document to prove that Wilson had accepted Taft's suggestions for revising the Covenant during the peace conference. He thought this proof of the League's bipartisan character would be "a knockout." The president, however, refused to participate in

---

7 2 Viereck to WGH, Aug. 31, Sept. 5, 1920, Resolutions, adopted at the German American National Conference, Chicago, Aug. 17-18, [1920], WGH to Viereck, Sept. 6, 1920, WGH Papers, Box 182 (Roll 57).

7 3 Address to Foreign Born, Sept. 18, 1920, WGH Papers, Box 840 (Roll 239); Downes, *Rise of Harding*, 481-82.

this way in the campaign against Harding. He allowed Tumulty only to provide information for Democratic speakers.[74]

Instead of issuing weekly statements as Tumulty advised, Wilson decided to make a single appeal to the country. On October 3 he called upon American voters to make the final decision about the League's fate. Tumulty and Creel had attempted to persuade Wilson not to stake everything on the election because of the difficulty of focusing it on a single issue and the possibility of defeat. But he rejected this advice. He asked the American people to decide whether the United States should ratify the Versailles Treaty and enter the League. Denouncing the "Americanism" of Republicans for its kindred spirit to "Prussianism," he accused them of abandoning the historic role of America as "the light of the world" and of pursuing "the policy of isolation." Yet he also reaffirmed: "There is nothing in the Covenant which in the least interferes with or impairs the rights of Congress to declare war or not declare war, according to its own independent judgment, as our Constitution provides." As before, he emphasized both universal and unilateral qualities of the League. Continuing to stress its potential for benevolent American influence over other nations, he discounted Republican fears that the League would establish foreign control over the United States.[75]

Wilson's all-or-nothing stance promoted unity within the Republican party. By identifying Cox with the president, Harding retained the loyalty of most pro-League Republicans despite his shift toward the irreconcilables. Taft, for example, was satisfied with his August 28 speech. To most Republicans, Harding's promise of an association of nations seemed like a better alternative than the uncompromising commitment of "the Wilson-Cox alliance" – in Hays' words – to the existing League. Advocates of the League with reservations hoped that Harding would fulfill his promise by eventually accepting their position, while its irreconcilable opponents expected him to abandon the League altogether. For the moment, these differences among Republicans were somewhat obscured by their negative consensus against Wilson's League. After Harding's speech of August 28, journalist W. H. Crawford of the *New York Times* attempted to clarify its real meaning by submitting some questions to him. In his response Harding reiterated that as president he would undertake to negotiate a "new covenant" rather than ask the Senate to approve the League with reservations. Rejecting the Democratic program of "a super-government of the world," he identified himself as the champion of independence.[76]

74   JPT to WW, Sept. 16, 1920, JPT to Cox, Sept. 23, 1920, JPT to WW, Sept. 26, 1920, WW to JPT, n.d., Cox to WW, Sept. 27, 1920, JPT Papers, Box 7; JPT to Cox, Sept. 16, 29, 1920, Cox to JPT, Sept. 25, 1920, Cox to JPT, Sept. 30, 1920, Pittman to JPT, Sept. 22, 1920, JPT Papers, Box 14; NDB to Cox, Sept. 7, 1920, Cox to NDB, Sept. 19, 1920, NDB Papers, Box 11; McAdoo to JPT, Sept. 17, Oct. 2, 1920, WW Papers, Ser. 4, File 331; WW to Marsh, Sept. 17, 1920, WW Papers, Ser. 4, File 4612; Cox, *Journey*, 238-39, 266-70.
75   *PPWW*, VI, 503-05; JPT to WW, Oct. 1, 1920, WW to JPT, n.d., JPT Papers, Box 7.
76   WHT to Hilles, Sept. 7, 1920, WHT to H. Taft, Sept. 10, 1920, WHT Papers, Ser. 3, Box 474;

Harding's position troubled some pro-League Republicans. Early in September, George Wickersham, former attorney general in Taft's cabinet, visited the candidate in Marion to urge him not to repeat his intention to scrap the League. He received a friendly reception, but no promise. Lowell sought to apply public pressure on Harding. He prepared a petition asking him to commit himself to the League with reservations. Hoping to gather signatures of Republican advocates of the League, Lowell wanted to convince Harding to accept their position in order to secure their votes. He also contemplated using the League to Enforce Peace to persuade him that the existing League provided the best foundation for creating the association of nations to which the Republican party was committed. Taft, however, refused to approve Lowell's proposals for coercing Harding. He did not want the League to Enforce Peace to participate in the campaign. Keenly aware of the weakness of pro-League Republicans, he thought they should quietly implore Harding to espouse the League with Lodge's reservations. Convinced that Cox was "a demagogue" who would lose the election, Taft saw no option but to support the Republican ticket. He explained to his brother that "the only hope of League friends was in Harding because he was going to be the next President, League or no League." Taft's loyalty pleased the Republican candidate, who appreciated his understanding of the political necessity for uniting the party's divergent elements.[77]

Despite growing evidence of Harding's antipathy toward the League, most pro-League Republicans persevered in their increasingly contradictory hopes. For the purpose of promoting the League through Harding's election, President Jacob Gould Schurman of Cornell University took the initiative to assemble a group of prominent Republicans. Working with Hays, he invited other presidents of leading colleges and universities and some additional proponents of the League to convene at the University Club in New York on September 18. Those attending this meeting delegated to Schurman, Lowell and Hoover the task of preparing a public statement of their position. While Lowell wanted to urge Harding to approve the League with reservations, Schurman preferred a less explicit commitment to an association of nations. Hoover continued to expect that, as president, Harding would fulfill his promise of an international association by ratifying the Versailles Treaty with a revised Covenant. Like Lowell, he wanted particularly to eliminate Article 10. Hoover thought an economic boycott and public opinion were better methods than military force for preventing aggression. "In any event," he had already concluded, "the great and solemn referendum on the League or

Hays' statement, Aug. 29, 1920, Bone to New, Aug. 31, 1920, WGH to Hays, Sept. 6, 1920, W. H. Crawford, "Harding Amplifies His Views on League," *New York Times* (Sept. 6, 1920), Hays Papers.
7 7   Wickersham to Hoover, Aug. 29, 1920, Hoover Pre-Commerce Papers, Box 29; ALL to WHT, Sept. 9, 1920, [ALL et al.] to WGH, n.d., Wickersham to H. Taft, Sept. 7, 1920, WHT to Ullman, Sept. 13, 1920, WHT to H. Taft, Sept. 17, 1920, ALL to WHT, Sept. 22, 1920, WGH to WHT, Sept. 25, 1920, WHT Papers, Ser. 3, Box 474; WHT to Hays, Sept. 9, 1920, Hays to WHT, Sept. 13, 1920, Hays Papers; ALL to WHT, Sept. 9, 1920, WHT to ALL, [Sept. 1920], WHT to ALL, Sept. 15, 1920, ALL Papers.

no League of our Democratic friends has failed to materialize and the issue itself has become a question of 'a' league or 'the' league." Interpreting Harding's August 28 speech and his subsequent interviews with the *New York Times* and Wickersham in this hopeful way, Hoover denied that a Republican victory would prevent the United States from joining a revised League. Before completing their assignment, Schurman, Lowell and Hoover decided to consult Root, who had just returned from Europe, where he had assisted in drafting plans for the Permanent Court of International Justice. They wanted to promote the League, but without disrupting their party or jeopardizing Harding's election.[78]

Republican irreconcilables endeavored to keep the United States totally outside the League or any similar international organization. Publication in mid-September of plans for the Permanent Court of International Justice deeply concerned several of them. Because of Root's prominent identification with it, they feared that Harding might approve the world court and eventually involve the United States in the League through the "back door." Knox and Beveridge warned him to avoid this trap; Brandegee appealed to Lodge to keep Root from pressuring Harding by joining other pro-League Republicans. Sharing the irreconcilables' concern, Lodge advised Harding to oppose the world court because of its connection to the League. The League assembly and council would elect its judges. Although in principle the Republicans favored a world court, Lodge counseled, they should resist this one along with Wilson's League. Accepting Lodge's advice, Harding assured anxious irreconcilables that the world court would not affect his stand on the League. Republicans might approve a world court by itself or as part of a new association of nations, but he promised steadfastly to resist any attempt to bring the United States even indirectly into Wilson's League.[79]

Contrary to the wishful thinking of Republican proponents, Harding definitely opposed American membership in the League. Johnson correctly represented his position when he, in agreement with Wilson, interpreted the election as a "solemn referendum" on this issue. The choice between Cox and Harding, he proclaimed in San Francisco on September 20, was between

7 8   Schurman to Hoover, Sept. 10, 1920, Hoover to Schurman, Sept. 13, 1920, ALL to Hoover, Sept. 22, 1920, Schurman to Hoover, Sept. 24, 29, Oct. 1, 1920, ALL to Hoover, Sept. 28, 29, Oct. 1, 1, 1920, Hoover to ALL, Sept. 29, 30, Oct. 1, 1920, Herter to Schurman, Sept. 30, 1920, Hoover Pre-Commerce Papers, Box 10; Hoover to Robinson, Sept. 15, 1920, Hoover Pre-Commerce Papers, Box 27; Hoover to Hays, Sept. 7, 1920, Hays Papers.
7 9   Beveridge to Borah, Sept. 3, 1920, Borah to Beveridge, Sept. 6, 1920, Borah Papers, Box 551, and Beveridge Papers, Box 219; Beveridge to Brandegee, Sept. 18, 1920, Brandegee to Beveridge, Sept. 20, 1920, Brandegee to Borah, Sept. 21, 1920, Beveridge Papers, Box 219; Beveridge to WGH, Sept. 16, 1920, Beveridge Papers, Box 221; Beveridge to WGH, Sept. 16, 1920, WGH to Beveridge, Sept. 10, 20, 1920, Beveridge Papers, Box 221, and WGH Papers, Box 126 (Roll 40); Beveridge to Munsey, Sept. 18, 1920, Beveridge Papers, Box 222; Brandegee to HCL, Aug. 10, Sept. 15, 20, 24, 1920, HCL to Brandegee, Sept. 17, 28, 1920, HCL Papers, File 1920 (Personal, A-G); HCL to WGH, Sept. 17, 1920, WGH to HCL, Sept. 20, 1920, HCL Papers, File 1920 (Personal, H-Z), and WGH Papers, Box 252 (Roll 81); HCL to WGH, Sept. 28, 1920, HCL Papers, File 1920 (Personal, H-Z); Knox to WGH, Sept. 16, 18, 1920, WGH to Knox, Sept. 25, 1920, WGH Papers, Box 215 (Roll 69).

going into and staying out of the League. While adamantly opposing Wilson's League, Johnson insisted that Republicans wanted the United States to play a constructive role in world affairs. Despite Democratic accusations, they were not advocating a policy of "aloofness and selfish isolation." Hays, too, defined the alternatives with equal clarity. "Make your choice," he told an Indiana audience. "It is Covenant or Constitution; the League or the United States."[80]

Although obscuring his plans for an alternative, Harding clearly stated his intention to abandon the League. At Des Moines, Iowa, on October 7, he reaffirmed his decision to "scrap" it. In fact, he explained, Wilson had already "scrapped" it by stubbornly refusing to accept any of the Senate's reservations. The opportunity for approving the peace treaty with reservations had now passed. "I do not want to clarify these obligations," he asserted. "I want to turn my back on them. It is not interpretation, but rejection, that I am seeking." Outside of the League, Harding wanted the United States to provide "moral leadership" to promote international cooperation. Unlike Wilson's League, any plan that he might approve for an international association would safeguard sovereignty. In the name of "America First," he repudiated not only Wilson's foreign policy but also his threat to "constitutionalism" within the United States.[81]

Before Harding delivered his Des Moines address, pro-League Republicans had become increasingly anxious about his future intentions regarding the Versailles Treaty. They worried about his apparent identification with irreconcilables. If he fully accepted the position of the Johnson-Borah wing of the party, Lowell expected not to vote for him. He hoped Harding was only appearing to adopt an irreconcilable attitude for the sake of political expediency, observing that "his object must be to appear frank and remain evasive." In any case, he thought Wilson's entire record, rather than merely the League, was at stake in the election. Although Hoover agreed that the election would not depend solely upon the League, he implored both Hays and Harding to avoid alienating the Republicans who favored some kind of international association. He did not expect Harding openly to repudiate Johnson's interpretation of his own position, but urged him to express a more positive attitude toward the League. On October 4, Hoover and Schurman warned Hays that they could not proceed with their plans for a public statement by pro-League Republicans unless Harding assured them that he still favored an international association. He appeared, from their perspective, to have recently endorsed the irreconcilable position of Johnson and Borah. Hays and Harding conferred in Marion about this concern. Harding immediately telegraphed Schurman that there was "no change" from the position he had taken in his August 28 speech. He asked these

80   Johnson, Speech, Sept. 20, 1920, Hays, Speech, Sept. 17, 1920, Chaney Digest, Sept. 17, 1920, Hays Papers.
81   Speech in Des Moines, Oct. 7, 1920, WGH Papers, Box 841 (Roll 239).

pro-League Republicans to await his Des Moines speech for confirmation that there would be "no change" in the future. In his response to Hoover, Harding noted that Wilson's uncompromising statement on October 3 demonstrated "the utter impossibility of anything being worked out through a Democratic administration." Whether they liked it or not, pro-League Republicans could not turn to the Democrats as a realistic option.[82]

A superb politician, Harding skillfully retained the loyalty of most pro-League Republicans despite his intention to abandon the League. Without misrepresenting his position, he gave them the assurance they desired. He honestly informed them that his stance had not changed since his August 28 speech. Committed only to some kind of international association, he allowed them to hope that this Republican alternative would be realized through revision of the existing League. But Harding himself had never endorsed this interpretation of the Republican platform. On the contrary, he approved Johnson's. Nevertheless, for a variety of reasons, most prominent pro-League Republicans accepted his assurances at face value. Schurman appreciated his continuing commitment to an association of nations. Hoover, like Lowell, viewed the League as only part of the broader question facing the voters. "The solemn referendum is not on the League," he explained, "it is on the failure of the Democratic party." Paradoxically, while sharing Wilson's conception of social control, Hoover criticized the president's leadership for failing in practice to exemplify this standard of "party responsibility." In a democratic government, Hoover explained, compromise was essential to facilitate "orderly change" and avoid "the violence of revolution." By refusing to cooperate with Republicans during the treaty fight, Democrats had revealed their "failure of statesmanship." Consequently, in Hoover's view, the Republican party offered the only viable option.[83]

These proponents of the League now proceeded with their plans for a public statement. They collaborated with New York attorney Paul D. Cravath, who prevailed upon Root to write it. During its preparation, Schurman and Cravath cooperated closely with Hays. Although they rejected most of his suggestions for revising Root's draft, they shared his dedication to Republican unity. Both Hays and Harding appreciated the importance of this appeal to the pro-League wing of the party. They were concerned about the widespread perception, which the New York newspapers expressed, that Harding had definitely taken an isolationist stance in his Des Moines speech. Seeking to counter this impression, Stimson urged Harding to repeat his

82 Hoover to Hays, Sept. 20, 1920, Chaney Digest, Oct. 5, 1920, Hays Papers; Hoover to WGH, Sept. 27, 1920, WGH Papers, Box 173 (Roll 54), and Hoover Pre-Commerce Papers, Box 7; ALL to Hoover, Oct. 2, 1920, Hoover Pre-Commerce Papers, Box 10; WGH to Hoover, Oct. 4, 1920, Hoover Pre-Commerce Papers, Box 24, and WGH Papers, Box 173 (Roll 54); Schurman and Hoover to Hays, Oct. 4, 1920, WGH to Schurman, Oct. 5, 1920, Hoover Pre-Commerce Papers, Box 24.

83 Hoover to Burdette, Sept. 29, 1920, Speech by Herbert Hoover, Oct. 9, 1920, Schurman to Rhees, Oct. 13, 1920, Hays Papers; Speech by Herbert Hoover, Oct. 9, 1920, Hoover Pre-Commerce Papers, Box 10; Hoover to Burdette, Sept. 29, 1920, Hoover Pre-Commerce Papers, Box 27.

positive commitment to an association of nations. Accepting this advice, which closely coincided with Hoover's, Harding assured Cravath that, in this election, "it is not an issue between the League and no League, but it is an issue between the President's League on the one hand and America's participation in the world with preserved sovereignty on the other hand." He told Stimson there was "no change" in his position. "While I am unalterable in my opposition to Article X of the Wilson league," he asserted, "I never fail to make a constructive suggestion and say that America cordially favors a full association of nations." Yet he still did not explain what he meant by this alternative.[84]

After collecting thirty-one signatures of prominent Republicans, the pro-League group published on October 15 their statement in support of Harding for president. Fifty-five advocates of international cooperation for peace, including Root, Hoover, Schurman, Lowell, Cravath and Stimson, eventually endorsed this appeal. Although Taft's name was conspicuously absent, his brother Horace as well as Straus and Wickersham included theirs. So did Charles Evans Hughes. Several university presidents, including Butler of Columbia and John Grier Hibbin of Princeton, joined this attempt to persuade their fellow Republicans. The statement emphasized Harding's reaffirmation in his August 28 speech of the Republican platform's positive commitment to an international association. "The question accordingly is not between a league and no league," these Republicans affirmed, "but is whether certain provisions in the proposed league agreement shall be accepted unchanged or shall be changed. The contest is not about the principle of a league of nations, but it is about the method of most effectively applying that principle to preserve peace." Signing this statement, these Republicans affirmed their delusive hope that Harding would approve the League with reservations.[85]

Throughout the remainder of the campaign, these pro-League Republicans, such as Root, Hoover and Hughes, continued to support Harding. Seeking to counter the impression that he had joined the irreconcilables, they endeavored to assure voters that his election would not result in an American policy of isolation. In New Haven on October 23, Hughes emphasized that "the real issue" was instead more narrowly focused on Article 10. "Mr. Wilson and Mr. Cox stand for the obligation and are merely willing to state the methods by which our obligations are fulfilled," he contended. "The

8 4   Cravath to ER et al., n.d., Cravath to Hays, Oct. 8, 1920, Stimson to Hays, Aug. 8, 14, 1920, Hays to Cravath, Oct. 11, 1920, WGH to Hays, Oct. 12, 1920, WGH to Cravath, Oct. 12, 1920, WGH to Stimson, Oct. 12, 1920, WGH to Stoddard, Oct. 12, 1920, Hays to Stimson, Oct. 12, 16, 1920, Hays to WGH, Oct. 16, 1920, Hays Papers; Cravath to Hoover, Oct. 5, 1920, Cravath to Hoover's Secretary, Oct. 11, 1920, ER to Cravath, Oct. 9, 1920, Hoover Pre-Commerce Papers, Box 10; Barnes to Hoover, Oct. 11, 1920, Hoover Pre-Commerce Papers, Box 22; Cravath to ER, Oct. 11, 13, 1920, ER Papers, Box 138; ER to Cravath, Oct. 9, 1920, Cravath to ER et al., n.d., Root's paper, Oct. 12, 1920, Hughes Papers, Box 4A.
8 5   Statement in Support of Harding for President, [Oct. 15, 1920], Statement, Oct. 15, 1920, Hays Papers.

Republican Party stands against the obligation as one which we cannot assume in accordance with the principles of our institutions." Although Republicans absolutely refused to commit the United States to potentially unlimited global responsibilities as the world's policeman, they would not ignore foreign affairs.[86]

Some Republican advocates of international organization found even these assurances inadequate. They wanted more than vague promises. Hoover alerted Hays that "there is a perfect landslide of people of intellectual insight towards Mr. Cox." To halt these defections, he hoped Harding would publicly endorse the pro-League Republicans' statement as an accurate interpretation of his position. But Harding remained silent. He did not dispute Johnson's claim that he intended to reject the League altogether. Hays likewise refused to give any explicit promise as he reiterated the negative consensus among Republicans. On the eve of the election, he called upon the American people to decide between Democratic "Internationalism" and Republican "Americanism." He expected them to repudiate "Wilsonism," which Cox represented, by casting their ballots for Harding.[87]

As the election approached, Wilson generally refused to participate in the campaign. Tumulty urged him to respond to Harding's Des Moines speech with a press release, but he declined. After the pro-League Republicans published their statement, Wilson did not want to take any official notice of it. He denied Tumulty's request for permission to have Secretary Colby answer Root's speech in favor of the Republican ticket. He did, however, react to Harding's statement that "spokesmen" from France had approached him to indicate their desire for the United States to take the initiative in establishing an association of nations. Concerned about possible interference either by the French government in the election or by Harding in the conduct of American diplomacy, he demanded explanations from them on October 18. The French embassy immediately denied that any authorized representative of France had approached the Republican candidate, and Harding assured Wilson that his contacts with French citizens were strictly informal and unofficial. These explanations quickly ended this minor episode before it could possibly hurt Republicans. Because of the president's reluctance to allow his administration to participate directly in the campaign, he curbed his secretary's efforts to involve the White House. Unable to play a more active role in exposing the contradictions in Harding's position so as to exacerbate the differences among Republicans over the League, Tumulty provided Cox more encouragement than assistance.[88]

86   Brookings to ER, Oct. 11, 1920, Brookings to WGH, Oct. 11, 1920, ER to Brookings, Oct. 23, 1920, ER Papers, Box 138; Hoover to Bacon, Oct. 20, 1920, Hoover Pre-Commerce Papers, Box 22; Bacon to Hoover, Oct. 18, 1920, Hoover to Cooke, Oct. 20, 1920, Hoover Pre-Commerce Papers, Box 23; Speech of Charles E. Hughes, Oct. 23, 1920, Hays Papers.
87   Hoover to Hays, Oct. 23, 1920, Statement of Hiram W. Johnson, Oct. 23, 1920, Hays to Hoover, Oct. 26, 27, 1920, Hays, press release, Oct. 18, 1920, Statement by Will H. Hays, Nov. 1, 1920, Hays Papers.
88   JPT to WW, Oct. 6, 7, 19, 1920, WW to JPT, n.d., WW to JPT, n.d., JPT Papers, Box 7;

On one more occasion, however, Wilson agreed to help Cox. In response to the Democratic candidate's request, which Tumulty relayed, the president decided to invite a small group of pro-League Republicans to the White House on October 27. Coming from New York and other eastern cities, these fifteen Republicans placed their commitment to the League above partisan politics. In this group were long-time advocates of collective security such as Hamilton Holt, John Bates Clark and Theodore Marburg. Speaking for them, Holt praised Wilson for his unique contribution to peace among nations: "It was you who first focused the heterogeneous and often diverse aims of the war on the one ideal of pure Americanism, which is democracy. It was you who suggested the basis on which peace was negotiated. It was you, more than any man, who translated into practical statesmanship the age-old dreams of the poets, the prophets and the philosophers by setting up a League of Nations to the end that cooperation could be substituted for competition in international affairs."[89] Responding to this praise, Wilson expressed his determination to persevere in the treaty fight. Giving his first formal address since his stroke a year earlier, Wilson repeated familiar themes of his hard-line defense of the League. He told his Republican guests that the United States had entered the war for the purpose not merely of defeating Germany but also of preventing future wars. The existing League with Article 10, he affirmed, was the only feasible method for achieving this purpose. The great issue before the American people was whether to sustain the "real Americanism" of his League or succumb to "the spirit of imperialism."[90]

Wilson's arguments for the League failed to salvage Cox's candidacy. Only a minority of pro-League Republicans abandoned their party, not nearly enough to compensate for Democratic vulnerability. Aware of the odds against him, Cox resorted to a final desperate measure at the close of the campaign. Shifting from high idealism to low politics, he attempted to discredit Harding by identifying him with both the recently defeated enemy and hyphenated Americans. Tumulty had earlier encouraged Cox to employ this divide-and-conquer technique for smearing Republicans – a technique which Wilson had adopted on his secretary's advice in 1916 with apparent success. Noting that German-Americans such as Viereck had endorsed Harding, Tumulty had advised Cox to proclaim the Republican candidate's guilt by association. "Harding's cry of isolation for America," he counseled, "is as dangerous to this country as Germany's cry of Germany over all was fatal to herself." At first Cox hesitated to employ this divisive tactic. Using

JPT to Cox, Oct. 12, 25, 1920, JPT to WGH, Oct. 17, 1920, JPT Papers, Box 14; Davis to Wilson, Oct. 18, 1920, WGH to WW, Oct. 18, 1920, WW to Davis, Oct. 19, 1920, WW Papers, Ser. 2, Box 198; Borah to HCL, Oct. 18, 1920, HCL to Borah, Oct. 21, 1920, HCL Papers, File 1920 (A-G).
89   JPT to WW, Oct. 22, 1920, WW Papers, Ser. 2, Box 198; Statement by Dr. Hamilton Holt and the Committee, [Oct. 27, 1920], List of persons who called on the President, [Oct. 27, 1920], Holt, speech, Oct. 27, 1920, Burleson Papers, Vol. 26.
90   Statement by the President, Oct. 27, 1920, Burleson Papers, Vol. 26; PPWW, VI, 506-10.

more positive methods, he attempted to keep the loyalty of Irish-Americans and other ethnic groups within the Democratic party. But on the eve of the election, the despairing candidate succumbed, announcing that: "Every traitor in America will vote tomorrow for Warren G. Harding."[91] Cox attempted to exploit the American people's lingering wartime prejudice against German-Americans as well as Germany. Like Wilson before, he did not rely solely on their rational judgment to decide this election and the League's fate.

IV

When the American people returned their verdict on November 2, they gave a landslide victory to Republicans. Harding received 16,143,407 votes and carried thirty-seven states, while only 9,130,328 voters and eleven states favored Cox. Democrats also failed in most senatorial races. Although all Democratic senators running for re-election, except Underwood, had abandoned Wilson in the treaty fight on at least one of the Lodge reservations, that did not give them immunity in 1920. Republicans captured ten of the seventeen contested seats previously held by Democratic senators, while retaining their own fifteen. This outcome increased Republican predominance in the Senate from a thin margin of two to an overwhelming majority of twenty-two. The Democratic party succeeded only in the South, where it re-elected seven senators and provided Cox with the only electoral votes he won. Elsewhere in the country, Republicans triumphed in the "solemn referendum." Their success resulted from a general reaction against the Wilson administration and the Democratic party. This shift in the electorate encompassed, but was not restricted to, some ethnic groups. Although both parties had focused either positively or negatively on hyphenated Americans, the ethnic factor was not decisive. The election demonstrated the widespread desire of Americans for new leadership.[92]

This Republican victory appeared to Lodge as a final repudiation of the president. "We have won the fight," he exulted. "We have destroyed Mr.

9 1   JPT to Cox, Sept. 17, Oct. 12, 1920, JPT Papers, Box 7; Cox to JPT, Oct. 8, 1920, Cox to JPT, Oct. 10, 1920, Pittman to JPT, Oct. 21, 1920, JPT Papers, Box 14; Cox, *Journey*, 272-76; Bagby, *Road to Normalcy*, 145; Tumulty, *Woodrow Wilson*, 214; John F. Duff, "German-Americans and the Peace, 1918-1920," *American Jewish Historical Quarterly*, LIX (June 1970), 424-44.

9 2   Bureau of the Census, *Historical Statistics of the United States: Colonial Times to 1957* (Washington, 1960), 682-84; Karger to WHT, March 20, 1920, WHT Papers, Ser. 3, Box 468; *CR*, Vol. 59, 9377-88; HCL to Frewen, Nov. 24, 1920, HCL Papers, File 1920 (Personal, A-G); HCL to Trevelyan, Dec. 28, 1920, HCL Papers, File 1920 (Personal, H-Z); HCL to Phillips, Nov. 26, 1920, HCL Papers, File 1920 (P-Z). Historians such as Bailey, *Woodrow Wilson and the Great Betrayal*, 22-30, and Selig Adler, *The Isolationist Impulse: Its Twentieth Century Reaction* (New York, 1957), 73-89, criticized the hyphenates for helping to defeat the treaty. That traditional interpretation greatly exaggerates the ethnic factor in the treaty fight both in the Senate and in the 1920 elections. See Lloyd E. Ambrosius, "Ethnic Politics and German-American Relations After World War I: The Fight over the Versailles Treaty in the United States," in Hans L. Trefousse, ed., *Germany and America: Essays on Problems of International Relations and Immigration* (New York, 1980), 29-40, and Rhodri Jeffreys-Jones, "Massachusetts Labour and the League of Nations Controversy, 1919," *Irish Historical Studies*, XIX (Sept. 1975), 396-416.

Wilson's League of Nations and, what is quite as important, we have torn up Wilsonism by the roots." The voters, in his view, decided not only to keep the United States out of the League but also to reject the entire Democratic administration. "The League played a very large part," he explained, "but underneath it all was the determination on the part of the American people to get rid of Wilsonism and everything connected with it."[93]

Although both parties had emphasized their differences during the campaign, they had not presented a clear-cut choice between international-ism and isolationism. Democrats, following Wilson, used those categories to interpret the two alternatives, but Republicans saw other possibilities for American involvement in foreign affairs. Soon after the election, Lodge reiterated for Harding's benefit that the central issue was merely Wilson's League, not the entire Versailles Treaty: "It does not follow because we abandon Mr. Wilson's text of the League of Nations that we are going to undertake to remake the treaty with Germany." While rejecting the League, Lodge wanted the United States to play a constructive role in the Old World. He advised Harding to accept the Knox resolution, including the original fifth section which stated the "new American doctrine." Once again Lodge sought to assure Europe, and especially France, that the United States would not return to its traditional isolation. But he wanted no part of Wilson's League as the foundation for involvement. Harding agreed with Lodge's analysis, although he still avoided any precise statement about his alterna-tive. The president-elect continued to anticipate American participation in some kind of international association, but definitely not in the existing League.[94]

Despite the overwhelming Republican victory at the polls, Wilson maintained his all-or-nothing stance on the peace treaty. He refused to accept this election as the final verdict of the American people. Although he had called for a national referendum on the League, he chose to disregard the Democratic defeat. Praising Cox for his faithful dedication to this great cause throughout the campaign, he, too, intended to keep the faith and continue the fight. Colby, disappointed by the election, relayed to the president the suggestion that he should resubmit the treaty to the Senate and offer to accept the Lodge reservations. But Wilson emphatically rejected this proposal, reiterating that the Republicans had never desired a compromise on that basis. They had, he still believed, offered their reservations for the sole purpose of nullifying the treaty.[95]

93   HCL to McCormick, Nov. 13, 1920, HCL Papers, File 1920 (Personal, H-Z); HCL to Chanler, Dec. 1, 1920, HCL Papers, File 1920 (A-G).
94   HCL to WGH, Nov. 10, 1920, HCL to WGH, Dec. 24, 1920, Jan. 4, Feb. 14, 1921, WGH to HCL, Dec. 29, 1920, WGH to HCL, Jan. 10, 1921, WGH Papers, Box 252 (Roll 81); WGH to HCL, Nov. 5, 1920, WGH to HCL, Nov. 16, 1920, HCL to WGH, Nov. 10, 1920, HCL to WGH, Dec. 23, 1920, HCL Papers, File 1920 (Personal, H-Z).
95   WW to Cox, Oct. 29, 1920, WW Papers, Ser. 2, Box 198; Colby to WW, Nov. 3, 1920, WW to Colby, Nov. 20, 1920, WW Papers, Ser. 2, Box 199; Anderson to Colby, Nov. 16, 1920, Colby to

During the last months of his presidency, Wilson remained as reluctant as Harding or Lodge to consider any bipartisan compromise to enable the United States to join the existing League. The tacit alliance between Wilson and irreconcilables, whose position on the League these Republican leaders now shared, continued to the end. He refused, moreover, to allow even unofficial participation by American representatives in the League's activities. Rather than adjust to the political reality of his limited power at home as well as abroad, the president adhered to his idealistic vision of the League. Unable to control American foreign relations, he preferred to isolate the United States from the Old World. Withdrawing the nation from active involvement in the ongoing process of peacemaking in Europe, Wilson blamed the Republicans for this consequence. His bitterness toward Lodge and his own conception of the American role in world affairs prevented him from considering any Republican alternative to the League. Wilson ended his second term in the White House still rigidly clinging to his ideals, despite his failure in the treaty fight and Cox's defeat in 1920. Contrary to his hope, the League of Nations began to function in the Old World without American leadership. The United States refused to join Wilson's League to preserve peace through international social control.[96]

WW, Nov. 18, 1920, WW to Colby, Nov. 20, 1920, Bainbridge Colby Papers, Box 3B, Library of Congress.
96   Davis to WW, Dec. 4, 1920, Glass to WW, Dec. 8, 1920, WW to Glass, Dec. 11, 1920, WW to Davis, Dec. 9, 1920, WW Papers, Ser. 2, Box 200; WW to Bok, Jan. 22, 1921, WW Papers, Ser. 2, Box 201; Cummings, memorandum, Apr. 25, 1921, RSB Papers, Ser. I, Box 3; Glass to WW, Dec. 8, 1920, WW to Glass, Dec. 11, 1920, Glass Papers, Box 8.

CHAPTER 10

Epilogue: Wilson's legacy

Wilson's failure in the treaty fight left the United States without clear direction for its foreign policy. But those who shared his conception of internationalism overlooked the fact that the same problem would have confronted this nation even if he had succeeded. The League of Nations offered, at best, a framework for international relations; it did not provide answers to the difficult questions facing the great powers after the World War. The Covenant, under Articles 10 and 19, authorized the potentially contradictory alternatives of either enforcing or revising the Versailles Treaty. The choice remained open in Wilson's League. Rather than decide in 1919 whether to seek peace through collective sanctions or appeasement, the president wanted to retain both options for the future. The Covenant thus embodied his paradoxical idea of "progressive order" through international social control.

Wilson expected the new League to resolve the fundamental dilemma confronting the United States in the modern world. It would, he hoped, serve as an instrument of American control over foreign affairs, but without endangering national independence. It would allow the United States to provide global leadership without entangling itself in the Old World's diplomacy and wars. It would, in short, permit universal and unilateral tendencies to coexist harmoniously in American foreign relations. But pluralism, which prevented Wilson from achieving universal acceptance of his ideals and practices at Paris, continued to thwart fulfillment of his vision during the postwar years. At the same time, interdependence among nations precluded the United States from maintaining its traditional isolation from the Old World. This combination of pluralism and interdependence created the basic problems for the United States, and also for the League. Faced with this fundamental dilemma, Republican administrations from Harding's through Hoover's responded in a fashion similar to Wilson's. They, too, evidenced both unilateralism and universalism in their own versions of "independent internationalism." Unable either to control or to ignore the Old World, they struggled with the choice between enforcement and revision of the Versailles Treaty.[1]

In the 1930s, Adolf Hitler sharpened this dilemma for the United States, but he did not originate it. As he flagrantly challenged the Versailles peace, the alternatives of enforcement and revision became increasingly divergent. Whether to appease Nazi Germany or to resist Hitler's ambitions, if necessary by collective military action, emerged as one of the most crucial decisions for the United States during Franklin D. Roosevelt's presidency. Imperial Japan and Fascist Italy also presented similar problems for this nation. Hugh R. Wilson, the last American ambassador to Nazi Germany, still favored the revisionist alternative even after the outbreak of World War II in Europe. In contrast, William E. Dodd, his predecessor in Berlin, rejected appeasement after the Munich Conference of 1938. He blamed Republicans, especially Lodge, for creating the current crisis by their rejection of the League in 1919-1920. But Dodd himself had failed to recommend a viable policy for coping with the German problem during his own ambassadorship. Contributing to the revival of Wilsonian internationalism, he ignored the fact that the League, even if the United States had joined it, could not protect its members from aggression and also preserve international peace when a foe, such as Hitler's Germany, was willing to resort to war to change the status quo. That was the real difficulty for which President Wilson had never offered a solution. But Dodd, failing to comprehend or confront this dilemma, instead engaged in scapegoating. Like many other Americans during the 1930s, he searched for simple and inexpensive answers to the complex questions facing the United States in world affairs.[2]

Wilsonian internationalism enjoyed a revival in the United States during World War II. Witnessing the League's inability to halt the aggression of Japan in Asia, Italy in Africa, and Germany in Europe, many American leaders attributed these failures to the abstention of the United States from the international organization. The Japanese attack on Pearl Harbor convinced them that neutrality was no longer a viable option. Thinking in the dualistic categories of isolationism versus internationalism, these Americans typically concluded that the United States needed to provide global leadership to restore and preserve world peace. "Now at last," proclaimed

1 Joan Hoff Wilson, *American Business and Foreign Policy, 1920-1933* (Lexington, 1971), x; Ambrosius, "The United States and the Weimar Republic: America's Response to the German Problem," *Perspectives in American Diplomacy*, 78-104; Frank Costigliola, *Awkward Dominion: American Political, Economic, and Cultural Relations with Europe, 1919-1933* (Ithaca, 1984).

2 Hugh R. Wilson, *Diplomat Between Wars* (New York, 1941); Hugh R. Wilson, Jr., *A Career Diplomat, The Third Chapter: The Third Reich* (New York, 1960); William Edward Dodd, "The Dilemma of Modern Civilization," in Quincy Wright, ed., *Neutrality and Collective Security* (Chicago, 1936), 91-106; Arnold Offner, *American Appeasement: United States Foreign Policy and Germany, 1933-1938* (Cambridge, 1969); Robert Dallek, *Democrat and Diplomat: The Life of William E. Dodd* (New York, 1968), 171-317.

Vice President Henry A. Wallace, "the nations of the world have a second chance to erect a lasting structure of peace – a structure such as that which Woodrow Wilson sought to build but which crumbled away because the world was not yet ready." President Roosevelt, too, wanted the Allies, including the United States as well as Great Britain and Soviet Russia, to continue their cooperation after the war. "Bound together in solemn agreement that they themselves will not commit acts of aggression or conquest against any of their neighbors," he stated in 1943, "the United Nations can and must remain united for the maintenance of peace by preventing any attempt to rearm in Germany, in Japan, in Italy, or in any other nation which seeks to violate the Tenth Commandment, 'Thou shall not covet.'" He hoped to prevent future aggression and wars by establishing a new system of collective security.[3]

Like Wilson during World War I, Roosevelt adjusted to the realities of international politics by compromising with foreign leaders on specific issues. But by explaining his policy in the idealistic terms of liberal internationalism, he engendered false hope in the United States about the postwar era. He failed to prepare the American people for the limitations and frustrations that they would experience in the real world of pluralism and interdependence. After Roosevelt's death, President Harry S. Truman continued this same pattern of diplomatic leadership. Combining idealism and practicality, he, too, embraced Wilson's legacy as the intellectual foundation for American foreign relations. Addressing the San Francisco Conference, which founded the United Nations in June 1945, he told the delegates: "You have created a great instrument for peace and security and human progress in the world." He affirmed the willingness of the United States to join other nations in this new system of collective security. "By this Charter," Truman reminded the delegates, "you have given reality to the ideal of that great statesman of a generation ago – Woodrow Wilson." The triumph of Wilsonian internationalism seemed to offer the opportunity for freedom and prosperity in a global community of nations.[4]

Wilson's legacy continued to provide the assumptions undergirding Truman's foreign policy even after the Cold War shattered hope for "one world." The United States understood its difficulties with the Soviet Union within the context of its commitment to collective security. Interpreting Joseph Stalin's actions by analogy to Hitler's behavior before World War II, the president sought to apply the "lessons" he had learned during that earlier experience. In his major address on March 12, 1947, while proclaiming the Truman Doctrine, he linked his emerging policy of containment to

---

3 Robert A. Divine, *Second Chance: The Triumph of Internationalism in America During World War II* (New York, 1971), 79, 84; Bruce Kuklick, "History as a Way of Learning," *American Quarterly*, XXII (Fall 1970), 609-28; Thomas M. Campbell, *Masquerade Peace: America's UN Policy, 1944-1945* (Tallahassee, 1973), 131.

4 Harry S. Truman, *Public Papers of the Presidents of the United States: Harry S. Truman, 1945* (Washington, 1961), 138-44.

American obligations under the United Nations Charter: "The United Nations is designed to make possible lasting freedom and independence for its members. We shall not realize our objectives, however, unless we are willing to help free peoples to maintain their free institutions and their national integrity against aggressive movements that seek to impose upon them totalitarian regimes."[5]

To protect the United States and prevent a future world war, Truman firmly believed that he needed to avoid the mistakes of the interwar years. Rejecting the alternative of appeasement, he increasingly emphasized the military dimension of collective security. This conception of the American role in world affairs led him to the inescapable conclusion that the United States should intervene in Korea in June 1950 to halt communist aggression. "If this was allowed to go unchallenged," he recalled, "it would mean a third world war, just as similar incidents had brought on the second world war. It was also clear to me that the foundations and the principles of the United Nations were at stake unless this unprovoked attack on Korea could be stopped."[6]

Wilson's legacy, as interpreted in light of the experience of World War II, thus furnished the intellectual framework for American foreign policy during the Cold War. Although unable in this bipolar world to win universal acceptance of its own ideals and practices, the United States endeavored at least to prevent the Soviet Union from extending its influence over other nations which had not already come under its hegemony. American leaders, including Republican as well as Democratic presidents, sought to prevent communist aggression wherever it threatened. Their global policy of containment expressed the premises of liberal internationalism. By the 1960s the emergence of new nations in the so-called Third World began to change the character of international relations. The multipolarity of this increasingly diverse world altered the context in which Soviet-American rivalry continued. The United Nations reflected this change. "Due to the admission of so many new countries," observed Adlai E. Stevenson, whom President John F. Kennedy had just selected as ambassador, "the United States and the Western countries no longer control the United Nations. Our position is much more difficult and it will be my task to help maintain our position in these changing circumstances."[7] This continuing search for control through international organization thus characterized American diplomacy during the Cold War, as it had Wilson's statesmanship earlier in the century.

Erosion of American influence in the United Nations became apparent by

5   Ernest R. May, *"Lessons" of the Past: The Use and Misuse of History in American Foreign Policy* (New York, 1973), 43; Göran Rystad, *Prisoners of the Past? The Munich Syndrome and Makers of American Foreign Policy in the Cold War Era* (Lund, 1982), 24.

6   Harry S. Truman, *Memoirs* (New York, 1956), II, 378-79.

7   Richard P. Stebbins, *The United States in World Affairs, 1960* (New York, 1961), 357; Robert E. Osgood, "Woodrow Wilson, Collective Security, and the Lessons of History," *Confluence*, V (Winter 1957), 341-54; John Lewis Gaddis, *Strategies of Containment: A Critical Appraisal of Postwar American National Security Policy* (New York, 1982).

the 1960s and continued during subsequent decades. The emergence of Third World nations and the persistence of Cold War rivalries prevented the United States from fulfilling its conception of international social control. The reality of global interdependence evidenced a different pattern. Voting in the United Nations reflected the relative decline of American power in world affairs. Reacting to this trend, President Ronald Wilson Reagan criticized the United Nations for departing from its founders' original purpose. Reaffirming the earlier vision of Wilsonian internationalism, he challenged that body to "keep faith with the dreams that created this organization." He lamented that the United Nations was no longer pursuing its original goals of "civilized order" and "progress."[8]

American military intervention in Southeast Asia epitomized Wilson's legacy as understood in light of the World War II experience. In 1954, President Dwight D. Eisenhower reformulated the lesson of Munich in his analogy of falling dominoes. He feared that countries in Asia and the Pacific, like dominoes, would collapse one after another if Vietnam fell to communism. According to his domino theory, appeasement would invite more aggression and eventually a wider war.[9] Democratic presidents during the 1960s continued to believe in the domino theory and acted accordingly by expanding American involvement in Vietnam. As a universal principle, the lesson of Munich was presumably applicable everywhere. Kennedy began to apply this lesson in Vietnam before his assassination. In 1965, President Lyndon B. Johnson used the same rationale to explain the rapid escalation of American military participation in Vietnam. The logic of collective security drove the United States into the Vietnam War to avoid another world war.[10]

Johnson ardently embraced Wilson's legacy of liberal internationalism. He, too, believed American principles and practices were universally valid. His personality and statesmanship epitomized the search for control both at home and abroad. "When I first became President," he later explained, "I realized that if only I could take the next step and become dictator of the whole world, then I could really make things happen. Every hungry person would be fed, every ignorant child educated, every jobless man employed. And then I knew I could accomplish my greatest wish, the wish for eternal peace."[11] Like Wilson during World War I, Johnson justified the use of American armed forces in the Vietnam War by promising a new world order of prosperity and peace. This vision conformed, of course, to his own view of the United States. He, too, reconciled his internationalism with American

8 Department of State, *Realism, Strength, Negotiation: Key Foreign Policy Statements of the Reagan Administration* (Washington, D.C., Selected Documents No. 23, May 1984), 110; Ralph Kinney Bennett, "The Broken Promise of the United Nations," *Readers Digest* (Oct. 1983), 117-24.
9 Rystad, *Prisoners of the Past?*, 36, 39; F. M. Kail, *What Washington Said: Administration Rhetoric and the Vietnam War*, 1949-1969 (New York, 1973), 84-110; Townsend Hoopes, *The Devil and John Foster Dulles: The Diplomacy of the Eisenhower Era* (Boston, 1973).
10 Rystad, *Prisoners of the Past?*, 48-49, 56; May, *'Lessons' of the Past*, 114.
11 Doris Kearns, *Lyndon Johnson and the American Dream* (New York, 1976), 202.

nationalism. He failed, however, to recognize the limits of American power.[12]

Alternating between the intellectual twins of isolationism and internationalism, American policymakers still thought within Wilson's categories. Ignoring the advice of their realistic critics, they failed to escape from the limits of the American diplomatic tradition. Even when they adjusted somewhat to international realities during the 1970s, they never succeeded in formulating new concepts to replace the Cold War ideology. In the Vietnam War's aftermath, the United States finally abandoned the World War II dream of restoring the Versailles peace. President Gerald R. Ford and Secretary of State Henry Kissinger acknowledged in the Helsinki agreement of August 1975 that the boundaries of Europe were permanent. The European map of the interwar years would not be restored. By normalizing American diplomatic relations with the People's Republic of China at the beginning of 1979, President Jimmy Carter also accepted the revolutionary consequences of World War II in Asia.

These adjustments represented the culmination of initiatives taken earlier by President Richard M. Nixon. Assisted by Kissinger, he had withdrawn American armed forces from Vietnam, launched the era of détente in Soviet-American relations, and started the opening to China. Both Nixon and Kissinger advocated a balance-of-power policy, but their perspective was fundamentally different from the realism of Walter Lippmann, George F. Kennan, Hans Morgenthau or Norman A. Graebner. Their idea of "linkage" betrayed an underlying universalism, despite their professed willingness to accept diversity in the multipolar world. They combined an ideological rigidity with practical flexibility. The so-called realism of Nixon and Kissinger was actually closer to the cynicism which the theologian Reinhold Niebuhr had recognized as the reverse side of idealism.[13] Their vision of a new "structure of peace" was more Wilsonian than realistic. Both of them were obsessed with establishing their control at home and abroad, as the Nixon administration's reluctance to end American involvement in Vietnam and its complicity in the Watergate episode revealed. The relative decline of American power in world affairs, which defeat in Vietnam demonstrated, thus failed to produce a fundamentally new conception of foreign policy. Despite their partial adjustments to the real world, American statesmen still embraced Wilson's legacy.[14]

1 2   Frank Church, "Thoughts on the Limits to American Power," *New York Times* (Apr. 15, 1984), Sect. 4, p. 21.

1 3   Reinhold Niebuhr, *The Children of Light and the Children of Darkness: A Vindication of Democracy and a Critique of Its Traditional Defense* (New York, 1944), 162-63, 185; Ronald H. Stone, *Reinhold Niebuhr: Prophet to Politicians* (Washington, 1981); Richard Wightman Fox, *Reinhold Niebuhr: A Biography* (New York, 1985).

1 4   Garry Wills, *Nixon Agonistes: The Crisis of the Self-made Man* (Boston, 1970), 417-95; Robert Dallek, *The American Style of Foreign Policy: Cultural Politics and Foreign Affairs* (New York, 1983), 252-82; Norman A. Graebner, *The Age of Global Power: The United States Since 1939* (New York, 1979), 255-306;

The United States had not yet adopted a realistic policy for relating to the world of interdependence and pluralism. Instead, it gyrated between its isolationist and internationalist tendencies. While proclaiming the ideals of collective security, it acted unilaterally with its armed forces in Korea and Vietnam. To prevent another world war, it fought these limited wars against communist aggression. Seeking to make the world safe for democracy, both Democratic and Republican presidents authorized the Central Intelligence Agency to engage in covert activities in various countries. While proclaiming the goals of liberal internationalism as expressed in the United Nations Charter, American leaders often allowed their idealism to become in practice a kind of cynicism. Their style in foreign affairs continued to combine universalism and unilateralism. The search for control still characterized American policymakers. Their understanding of global interdependence assigned the predominant role to the United States. According to their conception of collective security, this nation should enjoy primacy over its allies as well as its enemies. Other nations might depend upon the United States, but it should not sacrifice its independence. In reality, however, the relative decline of American power made this nation increasingly dependent upon other countries for military defense as well as for markets and raw materials. This mutual interdependence among nations, along with plural-ism, frustrated the American search for control. Unfortunately, Wilson's legacy offered only inadequate guidance for the United States.[15]

The underlying problem of Wilson's legacy in American foreign relations stemmed from the fallacies of his intellectual framework. He hoped to achieve "progressive order" around the globe through the League of Nations. His conception of international social control presupposed the analogy between history and nature. Because of humankind's success in subduing nature by employing scientific methods, the prospect for establishing rational control over human affairs seemed similarly bright at the beginning of the twentieth century. This progressive faith undergirded Wilson's vision of a new world order. The idea of progress, based on his faith in God and confidence in science, permeated the understanding of history which he had developed as a scholar and expressed as a statesman. He projected his understanding of the American heritage onto the world in the form of his liberal internationalism. The whole experience of World War I, however, challenged the premises of Wilson's public philosophy. As Sigmund Freud noted in *Civilization and Its Discontents* (1929), the ability of people to control nature through science gave them the potential to destroy themselves. Science could produce bad as well as good results. "Men have gained control over the forces of nature to such an extent that with their help they would have no difficulty in exterminating one another to the last man," he concluded. "They know this, and hence comes a large part of their current unrest, their unhappiness and their mood of anxiety." Comprehending irrationality in human behavior, which the war had tragically evidenced, Freud recognized the human potential for evil. He rejected the optimism of Wilson's progressive faith. From his pessimistic view of human nature, he appreciated the irony of history. Freud's political and social thought, including the crude psychological study *Thomas Woodrow Wilson* (1966) which he coauthored with William C. Bullitt in the early 1930s, expressed his fundamentally different philosophy. Despite his personal prejudices against the American president and the serious limitations of this particular study, Freud identified a critical problem of the modern world which Wilson had not resolved or even understood.[16]

Humankind's capacity for using science to destroy itself, rather than to establish permanent peace as Wilson had hoped, became increasingly evident during the atomic age after 1945. Freud had seen in World War I the potential for exterminating the human species, but the proliferation of nuclear weapons brought this prospect even closer during the Cold War. Possession of these weapons by the United States and the Soviet Union, and by a growing number of other nations as well, posed the threat of what the journalist Jonathan Schell called "the second death." An all-out nuclear war might extinguish the human species – not merely kill vast numbers of persons. Superpowers now possessed the capacity, literally, to fight the war to end all wars. This grim prospect for the future appeared as an ironic twist on the hopeful promise of Wilson's earlier proclamation. Henry Adams had anticipated this ultimate consequence of scientific progress. During the American Civil War, he had observed: "Man has mounted science, and is now run away with it. I firmly believe that before many centuries more, science will be the master of man. The engines he will have invented will be beyond his strength to control. Some day science may have the existence of mankind in its power, and the human race commit suicide, by blowing up the world."[17]

Appreciation for the limits of science produced in the conservative Adams a profound skepticism about progress in human affairs. The radical Randolph Bourne, sharing this perspective, likewise doubted that social science could predict and control the future of history. Outside the mainstream of liberal culture in the United States, they both repudiated the progressive mentality which Wilson epitomized during the early twentieth century. Aware of the world's pluralism, Bourne rejected the idea of international social control. In his view, this Wilsonian vision of world peace through collective security presented a false promise. Adams and Bourne thus offered an intellectual

1 6   Sigmund Freud, *Civilization and Its Discontents* (1929; New York, 1961), 92; Paul Roazen, *Freud: Political and Social Thought* (New York, 1968).
1 7   Jonathan Schell, *The Fate of the Earth* (New York, 1982), 97-178; Alfred Kazin, "The Fascination of Henry Adams," *New Republic* (Aug. 1, 1983), 28.

alternative to Wilson's progressivism with their conservative and radical critiques. Other Americans later abandoned Wilson's liberal premises. The realistic thought of Lippmann, Niebuhr, Kennan, Morgenthau and Graebner similarly rejected his contribution to the American diplomatic tradition. These realists criticized the revival of Wilsonian internationalism during World War II and its manifestation in the orthodox Cold War ideology.[18]

All of these critics of Wilson and his legacy in American foreign relations pointed toward a redefinition of the role of the United States in world affairs. But his influence persisted. American policymakers continued to use Wilsonian categories in thinking about international affairs. Their idealism, however, often degenerated into cynicism, when hope succumbed to despair as a consequence of frustration in dealing with the modern world. Universalism and unilateralism still characterized their style in foreign affairs, which combined ideals with practicality. Just as President Wilson had failed to overcome the limitations of the American diplomatic tradition, so did subsequent foreign-policy leaders fail to surmount his legacy. Because the United States could neither ignore nor control the modern world, both traditional isolationism and Wilsonian internationalism provided unrealistic guidance for this nation. Throughout the twentieth century, instead of defining a realistic foreign policy, Americans sought to elude the fundamental dilemma arising from the combination of global interdependence and pluralism.

18 Walter Lippmann, *The Cold War: A Study in U.S. Foreign Policy* (New York, 1947); Steel, *Walter Lippmann and the American Century*, 404-584; Reinhold Niebuhr, *The Irony of American History* (New York, 1952); George F. Kennan, *Memoirs, 1925-1950* (Boston, 1967); George F. Kennan, *Memoirs, 1950-1963* (Boston, 1972); George F. Kennan, *The Cloud of Danger: Current Realities of American Foreign Policy* (Boston, 1977); George F. Kennan, *The Nuclear Delusion: Soviet-American Relations in the Atomic Age* (New York, 1983); Hans J. Morgenthau, *Scientific Man vs. Power Politics* (Chicago, 1946); Hans J. Morgenthau, *A New Foreign Policy for the United States* (New York, 1969); Norman A. Graebner, *America as a World Power: A Realist Appraisal from Wilson to Reagan* (Wilmington, 1984).

Bibliography

UNPUBLISHED DOCUMENTS

Bundesarchiv (Federal Archives), Koblenz, Germany: Akten der Reichskanzlei; Büro des Reichspräsidenten
Politisches Archiv des Auswärtigen Amts (Political Archives of the Foreign Office), Bonn, Germany: Auswärtiges Amt Weimar; Botschaft Washington, 4A34 (Friedensverhandlungen); Deutsche Friedensdelegation in Versailles; Handakten des Unterstaatssekretar [Hellmut] Toepffer; Weltkrieg 30 (Waffenstillstands- und Friedensverhandlungen); Weltkrieg 30 Geh. (Waffenstillstands- und Friedensverhandlungen)

UNPUBLISHED PRIVATE PAPERS

Alabama Department of Archives and History, Montgomery, Alabama: Oscar W. Underwood Papers
American Irish Historical Society, New York, New York: Daniel F. Cohalan Papers
Baker Library, Harvard University, Boston, Massachusetts: Thomas W. Lamont Papers
Beaverbrook Library (now in the House of Lords Record Office), London, England: David Lloyd George Papers
British Museum, London, England: Arthur J. Balfour Papers; Cecil of Chelwood Papers
Bundesarchiv (Federal Archives), Koblenz, Germany: Moritz Julius Bonn Papers; Matthias Erzberger Papers; Erich Koch-Weser Papers; Otto Landsberg Papers; Walther Schücking Papers; Wilhelm Solf Papers
Harvard University Archives, Cambridge, Massachusetts: A. Lawrence Lowell Papers
Herbert Hoover Presidential Library, West Branch, Iowa: Herbert Hoover Pre-Commerce Papers

Houghton Library, Harvard University, Cambridge, Massachusetts: League to Enforce Peace Papers
Indiana State Library, Indianapolis, Indiana: Will H. Hays Papers
Library of Congress, Washington, D.C.: Chandler P. Anderson Papers; Newton D. Baker Papers; Ray Stannard Baker Papers; Albert J. Beveridge Papers; Tasker Howard Bliss Papers; William E. Borah Papers; Albert Sidney Burleson Papers; Bainbridge Colby Papers; Josephus Daniels Papers; Gilbert M. Hitchcock Papers; Charles Evans Hughes Papers; Philander C. Knox Papers; Robert Lansing Papers; Breckinridge Long Papers; John J. Pershing Papers; Elihu Root Papers; William Howard Taft Papers; Joseph P. Tumulty Papers; Henry White Papers; Edith Bolling Wilson Papers; Woodrow Wilson Papers
Massachusetts Historical Society, Boston, Massachusetts: Henry Cabot Lodge Papers
Minnesota Historical Society, St. Paul, Minnesota: Frank B. Kellogg Papers
Nebraska State Historical Society, Lincoln, Nebraska: Gilbert M. Hitchcock Papers
Ohio Historical Society, Columbus, Ohio: Warren G. Harding Papers
University of Virginia Library, Charlottesville, Virginia: Carter Glass Papers
Yale University Library, New Haven, Connecticut: Gordon Auchincloss Papers; Edward M. House Papers; Vance C. McCormick Papers; Frank L. Polk Papers; William Wiseman Papers

PUBLISHED DOCUMENTS

Baker, Ray Stannard, and William E. Dodd, eds. *The Public Papers of Woodrow Wilson.* 6 vols. New York: Harper & Brothers, 1925-1927.
Bureau of the Census. *Historical Statistics of the United States: Colonial Times to 1957.* Washington: Government Printing Office, 1960.
Cronon, E. David, ed. *The Cabinet Diaries of Josephus Daniels, 1913-1921.* Lincoln: University of Nebraska Press, 1963.
Department of State. *Papers Relating to the Foreign Relations of the United States, 1916.* Supplement: *The World War.* Washington: Government Printing Office, 1929.
Department of State. *Papers Relating to the Foreign Relations of the United States, 1918.* Supplement 1: *The World War.* 2 vols. Washington: Government Printing Office, 1933.
Department of State. *Papers Relating to the Foreign Relations of the United States, 1919: The Paris Peace Conference,* I, III-VI, XI. Washington: Government Printing Office, 1942-1946.
Department of State. *Papers Relating to the Foreign Relations of the United States: The Lansing Papers, 1914-1920.* 2 vols. Washington: Government Printing Office, 1939-1940.
Department of State. *Realism, Strength, Negotiation: Key Foreign Policy Statements of the Reagan Administration.* Selected Documents No. 23, Washington, D.C., May 1984.
Great Britain. "Papers Respecting Negotiations for an Anglo-French Pact," Cmd. 2169, *House of Commons Sessional Papers,* Vol. 26. London: His Majesty's Stationery Office, 1924.
Hancock, W. K., and Jean van der Poel, eds. *Selections from the Smuts Papers,* IV. Cambridge: Cambridge University Press, 1966.

Johnson, Donald Bruce, and Kirk H. Porter, eds. *National Party Platforms,* 1840-1972. Urbana: University of Illinois Press, 1975.

Link, Arthur S., ed. *The Papers of Woodrow Wilson,* V-VIII, XII, XXVII-XXXVIII, XL-XLI. Princeton: Princeton University Press, 1968-1983.

Lodge, Henry Cabot, and A. Lawrence Lowell. "Joint Debate on the Covenant of Paris," *League of Nations,* II, No. 2 (Boston: World Peace Foundation, April 1919).

Mantoux, Paul. *Les Délibérations du Conseil des Quatre: 24 mars – 28 juin 1919,* I. Paris: Editions du Centre National de la Recherche Scientifique, 1955.

Marburg, Theodore, and Horace E. Flack, eds. *Taft Papers on League of Nations.* New York: Macmillan, 1920.

Miller, David Hunter. *My Diary: At the Conference of Paris.* New York: Appeal Publishing Company, 1924.

Miller, David Hunter. *The Drafting of the Covenant.* 2 vols. New York: G. P. Putnam's Sons, 1928.

Morison, Elting E., ed. *The Letters of Theodore Roosevelt,* VIII. Cambridge, Mass.: Harvard University Press, 1954.

Schulze, Hagen, ed. *Akten der Reichskanzlei, Weimarer Republik: Das Kabinett Scheidemann,* 13. *Februar bis 20. Juni 1919.* Boppard: Harold Boldt Verlag, 1971.

Truman, Harry S. *Public Papers of the Presidents of the United States: Harry S. Truman,* 1945. Washington: Government Printing Office, 1961.

U.S. Senate. *Congressional Record,* Vols. 56-59 (1918-1920).

U.S. Senate, Committee on Foreign Relations. *Proceedings of the Committee on Foreign Relations, United States Senate: From the Sixty-third Congress (Beginning April 7, 1913) to the Sixty-seventh Congress (Ending March 3, 1923).* Washington: Government Printing Office, 1925.

U.S. Senate, Committee on Foreign Relations. *Treaty of Peace with Germany: Hearings.* Document No. 106. Washington: Government Printing Office, 1919.

Woodward, E. L., and Rohan Butler, eds. *Documents on British Foreign Policy,* 1919-1939, First Series, V. London: Her Majesty's Stationery Office, 1954.

MEMOIRS

Adams, Henry. *The Education of Henry Adams: An Autobiography.* Boston: Houghton Mifflin, 1918.

Bernstorff, Count [Johann von]. *My Three Years in America.* New York: Charles Scribner's Sons, 1920.

Cecil, Robert. *A Great Experiment.* New York: Oxford University Press, 1941.

Clemenceau, Georges. *Grandeur and Misery of Victory.* New York: Harcourt, Brace, 1930.

Cox, James M. *Journey Through My Years.* New York: Simon & Schuster, 1946.

Erzberger, M[atthias]. *Erlebnisse im Weltkrieg.* Stuttgart: Deutsche Verlags-Anstalt, 1920.

George, David Lloyd. *Memoirs of the Peace Conference,* I. New Haven: Yale University Press, 1939.

Grey, Viscount, of Fallodon. *Twenty-five Years,* 1892-1916, II. London: Hodder & Stoughton, 1925.

Houston, David F. *Eight Years with Wilson's Cabinet:* 1913 *to* 1920, I. Garden City, N.Y.: Doubleday, Page, 1926.

Kennan, George F. *Memoirs,* 1925-1950. Boston: Little, Brown, 1967.

Kennan, George F. *Memoirs,* 1950-1963. Boston: Little, Brown, 1972.

Lodge, Henry Cabot. *The Senate and the League of Nations.* New York: Charles Scribner's Sons, 1925.

Ross, Edward Alsworth. *Seventy Years of It: An Autobiography.* New York: D. Appleton-Century, 1936.

Tardieu, André. *The Truth About the Treaty.* Indianapolis: Bobbs-Merrill, 1921.

Truman, Harry S. *Memoirs,* II. New York: Doubleday, 1956.

Tumulty, Joseph P. *Woodrow Wilson as I Know Him.* Garden City, N.Y.: Doubleday, Page, 1921.

Wilson, Edith Bolling. *My Memoirs.* Indianapolis: Bobbs-Merrill, 1938.

Wilson, Hugh R. *Diplomat Between Wars.* New York: Longmans, Green, 1941.

Wilson, Hugh R., Jr. *A Career Diplomat, The Third Chapter: The Third Reich.* New York: Vantage Press, 1960.

NEWSPAPERS

Gaelic American, Vols. XVI-XVII (1919-1920).

The Literary Digest, Vols. LX-LXIII (1919).

BOOKS

Adler, Selig. *The Isolationist Impulse: Its Twentieth Century Reaction.* New York: Free Press, 1957.

Bagby, Wesley M. *The Road to Normalcy: The Presidential Campaign and Election of* 1920. Baltimore: Johns Hopkins University Press, 1962.

Bailey, Thomas A. *Woodrow Wilson and the Great Betrayal.* New York: Macmillan, 1945.

Bailey, Thomas A. *Woodrow Wilson and the Lost Peace.* New York: Macmillan, 1944.

Barber, James David. *The Presidential Character: Predicting Performance in the White House.* Englewood Cliffs, N.J.: Prentice-Hall, 1972.

Barraclough, Geoffrey. *An Introduction to Contemporary History.* New York: Penguin Books, 1964.

Bartlett, Ruhl J. *The League to Enforce Peace.* Chapel Hill: University of North Carolina Press, 1944.

Berdahl, Clarence A. *War Powers of the Executive in the United States.* [Urbana: University of Illinois Press, 1921].

Billington, Ray Allen. *Frederick Jackson Turner: Historian, Scholar, Teacher.* New York: Oxford University Press, 1973.

Birnbaum, Karl E. *Peace Moves and U-Boat Warfare.* Stockholm: Almquist & Wiksell, 1958.

Blum, John M. *Joe Tumulty and the Wilson Era.* Boston: Houghton Mifflin, 1951.

Bourne, Randolph S., ed. *Towards an Enduring Peace: A Symposium of Peace Proposals and Programs, 1914-1916.* New York: American Association for International Conciliation, [1916].

Braeman, John. *Albert J. Beveridge: American Nationalist.* Chicago: University of Chicago Press, 1971.

Bragdon, Henry Wilkinson. *Woodrow Wilson: The Academic Years.* Cambridge, Mass.: Harvard University Press, 1967.

Briggs, Mitchell Pirie. *George D. Herron and the European Settlement.* Stanford, Calif.: Stanford University Press, 1932.

Brooks, Van Wyck. *Three Essays on America.* New York: E. P. Dutton, 1970.

Buehrig, Edward A. *Woodrow Wilson and the Balance of Power.* Bloomington: Indiana University Press, 1955.

Burner, David. *Herbert Hoover: A Public Life.* New York: Alfred A. Knopf, 1979.

Campbell, Thomas M. *Masquerade Peace: America's UN Policy, 1944-1945.* Tallahassee: Florida State University Press, 1973.

Carroll, F. M. *American Opinion and the Irish Question, 1910-23: A Study in Opinion and Policy.* New York: St. Martin's Press, 1978.

Clark, John Bates. *The Control of Trusts: An Argument in Favor of Curbing the Power of Monopoly by a Natural Method.* New York: Macmillan, 1901.

Claude, Inis L., Jr. *Power and International Relations.* New York: Random House, 1962.

Clements, Kendrick A. *William Jennings Bryan: Missionary Isolationist.* Knoxville: University of Tennessee Press, 1982.

Coben, Stanley. *A. Mitchell Palmer: Politician.* New York: Columbia University Press, 1963.

Cooley, Charles Horton. *Social Process.* New York: Charles Scribner's Sons, 1918.

Cooper, John Milton, Jr. *Walter Hines Page: The Southerner as American, 1855-1918.* Chapel Hill: University of North Carolina Press, 1977.

Cooper, John Milton, Jr. *The Warrior and the Priest: Woodrow Wilson and Theodore Roosevelt.* Cambridge, Mass.: Harvard University Press, 1983.

Corwin, Edward S. *The President's Control of Foreign Relations.* Princeton: Princeton University Press, 1917.

Costigliola, Frank. *Awkward Dominion: American Political, Economic, and Cultural Relations with Europe.* Ithaca, N.Y.: Cornell University Press, 1984.

Croly, Herbert. *The Promise of American Life* (1909). New York: Capricorn Books, 1964.

Crunden, Robert M. *Ministers of Reform: The Progressives' Achievement in American Civilization, 1889-1920.* New York: Basic Books, 1982.

Dallek, Robert. *The American Style of Foreign Policy: Cultural Politics and Foreign Affairs.* New York: Alfred A. Knopf, 1983.

Dallek, Robert. *Democrat and Diplomat: The Life of William E. Dodd.* New York: Oxford University Press, 1968.

Davis, Calvin DeArmond. *The United States and the Second Hague Peace Conference: American Diplomacy and International Organization, 1899-1914.* Durham, N.C.: Duke University Press, 1975.

DeBenedetti, Charles. *Origins of the Modern American Peace Movement, 1915-1929.* Millwood, N.Y.: KTO Press, 1978.

Divine, Robert A. *Second Chance: The Triumph of Internationalism in America During World War II.* New York: Atheneum, 1971.

Downes, Randolph C. *The Rise of Warren Gamaliel Harding, 1865-1920.* Columbus: Ohio State University Press, 1970.

Eckes, Alfred E., Jr. *The United States and the Global Struggle for Minerals.* Austin: University of Texas Press, 1979.

Egerton, George W. *Great Britain and the Creation of the League of Nations: Strategy, Politics, and International Organization, 1914-1919.* Chapel Hill: University of North Carolina Press, 1978.

Ferrell, Robert H. *Woodrow Wilson and World War I, 1917-1921.* New York: Harper & Row, 1985.

Fifield, Russell H. *Woodrow Wilson and the Far East: The Diplomacy of the Shantung Question.* Hamden, Conn.: Archon Books, 1965.

Fischer, Fritz. *Germany's Aims in the First World War.* New York: W. W. Norton, 1967.

Floto, Inga. *Colonel House in Paris: A Study of American Policy at the Paris Peace Conference, 1919.* Princeton: Princeton University Press, 1980.

Forcey, Charles. *The Crossroads of Liberalism: Croly, Weyl, Lippmann, and the Progressive Era, 1900-1925.* New York: Oxford University Press, 1961.

Fowler, W. B. *British-American Relations, 1917-1918: The Role of Sir William Wiseman.* Princeton: Princeton University Press, 1969.

Fox, Richard Wightman. *Reinhold Niebuhr: A Biography.* New York: Pantheon Books, 1985.

Freidel, Frank. *Franklin D. Roosevelt: The Ordeal.* Boston: Little, Brown, 1954.

Freud, Sigmund. *Civilization and Its Discontents* (1929). New York: W. W. Norton, 1961.

Freud, Sigmund, and William C. Bullitt. *Thomas Woodrow Wilson: A Psychological Study.* Boston: Houghton Mifflin, 1966.

Gaddis, John Lewis. *Strategies of Containment: A Critical Appraisal of Postwar American National Security Policy.* New York: Oxford University Press, 1982.

Gardner, Lloyd C. *Safe for Democracy: The Anglo-American Response to Revolution, 1913-1923.* New York: Oxford University Press, 1984.

Garraty, John A. *Henry Cabot Lodge: A Biography.* New York: Alfred A. Knopf, 1968.

Gatzke, Hans W. *Germany's Drive to the West: A Study of Germany's Western War Aims During the First World War.* Baltimore: Johns Hopkins University Press, 1966.

Gelfand, Lawrence E. *The Inquiry: American Preparations for Peace, 1917-1919.* New Haven: Yale University Press, 1963.

George, Alexander L., and Juliette L. George. *Woodrow Wilson and Colonel House: A Personality Study.* New York: Dover, 1964.

Giddings, Franklin Henry. *Democracy and Empire: Their Psychological, Economic and Moral Foundations.* New York: Macmillan, 1900.

Giddings, Franklin Henry. *The Responsible State: A Reexamination of Fundamental Political Doctrines in the Light of World War and the Menace of Anarchism.* Boston: Houghton Mifflin, 1918.

Giddings, Franklin Henry. *Studies in the Theory of Human Society.* New York: Macmillan, 1922.

Graebner, Norman A. *The Age of Global Power: The United States Since 1939.* New York: John Wiley & Sons, 1979.

Graebner, Norman A. *America as a World Power: A Realist Appraisal from Wilson to Reagan.* Wilmington: Scholarly Resources, 1984.

Graebner, Norman A., ed. *Ideas and Diplomacy: Readings in the Intellectual Tradition of American Foreign Policy*. New York: Oxford University Press, 1964.

Gregory, Ross. *Walter Hines Page: Ambassador to the Court of St. James's*. Lexington: University Press of Kentucky, 1970.

Harbaugh, William Henry. *The Life and Times of Theodore Roosevelt*. New York: Collier Books, 1963.

Herman, Sondra R. *Eleven Against War: Studies in American Internationalist Thought, 1898-1921*. Stanford, Calif.: Hoover Institution Press, 1969.

Herron, George D. *Woodrow Wilson and the World's Peace*. New York: Mitchell Kennerley, 1917.

Hilderbrand, Robert C. *Power and the People: Executive Management of Public Opinion in Foreign Affairs, 1897-1921*. Chapel Hill: University of North Carolina Press, 1981.

Hinsley, F. H. *Power and the Pursuit of Peace: Theory and Practice in the History of Relations Between States*. Cambridge: Cambridge University Press, 1963.

Hoopes, Townsend. *The Devil and John Foster Dulles: The Diplomacy of the Eisenhower Era*. Boston: Little, Brown, 1973.

Hopkins, Charles Howard. *The Rise of the Social Gospel in American Protestantism: 1865-1915*. New Haven: Yale University Press, 1940.

Hopkins, Raymond F., and Donald J. Puchala. *Global Food Interdependence: Challenge to American Foreign Policy*. New York: Columbia University Press, 1980.

Israel, Fred L. *Nevada's Key Pittman*. Lincoln: University of Nebraska Press, 1963.

Janowitz, Morris. *The Last Half-Century*. Chicago: University of Chicago Press, 1978.

Jessup, Philip C. *Elihu Root*, II. New York: Dodd, Mead, 1938.

Kail, F. M. *What Washington Said: Administration Rhetoric and the Vietnam War, 1949-1969*. New York: Harper & Row, 1973.

Karl, Barry D. *The Uneasy State: The United States from 1915 to 1945*. Chicago: University of Chicago Press, 1983.

Katz, Frederick. *The Secret War in Mexico: Europe, the United States, and the Mexican Revolution*. Chicago: University of Chicago Press, 1981.

Kearns, Doris. *Lyndon Johnson and the American Dream*. New York: New American Library, 1976.

Kennan, George F. *American Diplomacy, 1900-1950*. Chicago: University of Chicago Press, 1951.

Kennan, George F. *The Cloud of Danger: Current Realities of American Foreign Policy*. Boston: Little, Brown, 1977.

Kennan, George F. *The Decision to Intervene*. Princeton: Princeton University Press, 1958.

Kennan, George F. *The Nuclear Delusion: Soviet-American Relations in the Atomic Age*. New York: Pantheon Books, 1983.

Kennan, George F. *Russia Leaves the War*. Princeton: Princeton University Press, 1956.

Kennedy, David M. *Over Here: The First World War and American Society*. New York: Oxford University Press, 1980.

Kimmich, Christoph M. *Germany and the League of Nations*. Chicago: University of Chicago Press, 1976.

Kuehl, Warren F. *Seeking World Order: The United States and International Organization to 1920*. Nashville: Vanderbilt University Press, 1969.

Levin, N. Gordon, Jr. *Woodrow Wilson and World Politics: America's Response to War and Revolution.* New York: Oxford University Press, 1968.

Link, Arthur S. *The Higher Realism of Woodrow Wilson and Other Essays.* Nashville: Vanderbilt University Press, 1971.

Link, Arthur S. *Wilson, III: The Struggle for Neutrality, 1914-15.* Princeton: Princeton University Press, 1960.

Link, Arthur S. *Wilson, IV: Confusions and Crises, 1915-1916.* Princeton: Princeton University Press, 1964.

Link, Arthur S. *Wilson, V: Campaigns for Progressivism and Peace, 1916-1917.* Princeton: Princeton University Press, 1965.

Link, Arthur S. *Wilson the Diplomatist.* Baltimore: Johns Hopkins University Press, 1957.

Link, Arthur S. *Woodrow Wilson: Revolution, War, and Peace.* Arlington Heights, Ill.: AHM Publishing Corporation, 1979.

Link, Arthur S., ed. *Woodrow Wilson and a Revolutionary World, 1913-1921.* Chapel Hill: University of North Carolina Press, 1982.

Lippmann, Walter. *The Cold War: A Study in U.S. Foreign Policy.* New York: Harper & Row, 1947.

Lippmann, Walter. *Drift and Mastery: An Attempt to Diagnose the Current Unrest* (1914). Englewood Cliffs, N.J.: Prentice-Hall, 1961.

Lippmann, Walter. *Men of Destiny.* New York: Macmillan, 1927.

Livermore, Seward W. *Woodrow Wilson and the War Congress, 1916-18.* Seattle: University of Washington Press, 1966.

Lowitt, Richard. *George W. Norris: The Persistence of a Progressive, 1913-1933.* Urbana: University of Illinois Press, 1971.

Luebke, Frederick C. *Bonds of Loyalty: German-Americans and World War I.* DeKalb: Northern Illinois University Press, 1974.

McCoy, Donald R. *Calvin Coolidge: The Quiet President.* New York: Macmillan, 1967.

McDougall, Walter A. *France's Rhineland Diplomacy, 1914-1924: The Last Bid for a Balance of Power in Europe.* Princeton: Princeton University Press, 1978.

Maddox, Robert James. *William E. Borah and American Foreign Policy.* Baton Rouge: Louisiana State University Press, 1969.

Margulies, Herbert F. *Senator Lenroot of Wisconsin: A Political Biography, 1900-1929.* Columbia: University of Missouri Press, 1977.

Martin, Laurence W. *Peace Without Victory: Woodrow Wilson and the British Liberals.* New Haven: Yale University Press, 1958.

May, Ernest R. *"Lessons" of the Past: The Use and Misuse of History in American Foreign Policy.* New York: Oxford University Press, 1973.

May, Ernest R. *The World War and American Isolation, 1914-1917.* Cambridge, Mass.: Harvard University Press, 1959.

Mayer, Arno J. *Political Origins of the New Diplomacy, 1917-1918.* New Haven: Yale University Press, 1959.

Mayer, Arno J. *Politics and Diplomacy of Peacemaking: Containment and Counterrevolution at Versailles, 1918-1919.* New York: Alfred A. Knopf, 1967.

Morgenthau, Hans J. *In Defense of the National Interest: A Critical Examination of American Foreign Policy.* New York: Alfred A. Knopf, 1951.

Morgenthau, Hans J. *A New Foreign Policy for the United States.* New York: Frederick A. Praeger, 1969.

Morgenthau, Hans J. *Scientific Man vs. Power Politics*. Chicago: University of Chicago Press, 1946.

Mulder, John M. *Woodrow Wilson: The Years of Preparation*. Princeton: Princeton University Press, 1978.

Murray, Robert K. *Red Scare: A Study in National Hysteria, 1919-1920*. New York: McGraw-Hill, 1964.

Niebuhr, Reinhold. *The Children of Light and the Children of Darkness: A Vindication of Democracy and a Critique of Its Traditional Defense*. New York: Charles Scribner's Sons, 1944.

Niebuhr, Reinhold. *The Irony of American History*. New York: Charles Scribner's Sons, 1952.

Noble, David W. *Historians Against History: The Frontier Thesis and the National Covenant in American Historical Writing Since 1830*. Minneapolis: University of Minnesota Press, 1965.

Noble, David W. *The Progressive Mind, 1890-1917*. Chicago: Rand McNally, 1970.

Offner, Arnold. *American Appeasement: United States Foreign Policy and Germany, 1933-1938*. Cambridge, Mass.: Harvard University Press, 1969.

O'Grady, Joseph P. *The Immigrants' Influence on Wilson's Peace Policies*. Lexington: University Press of Kentucky, 1967.

Osborn, George C. *Woodrow Wilson: The Early Years*. Baton Rouge: Louisiana State University Press, 1968.

Osgood, Robert Endicott. *Ideals and Self-Interest in America's Foreign Relations: The Great Transformation of the Twentieth Century*. Chicago: University of Chicago Press, 1953.

Pringle, Henry F. *The Life and Times of William Howard Taft: A Biography*. Hamden, Conn.: Archon Books, 1964.

Pusey, Merlo J. *Charles Evans Hughes*, I. New York: Macmillan, 1951.

Resek, Carl, ed. *War and the Intellectuals: Essays by Randolph S. Bourne, 1915-1919*. New York: Harper & Row, 1964.

Roazen, Paul. *Freud: Political and Social Thought*. New York: Alfred A. Knopf, 1968.

Ross, Edward Alsworth. *Principles of Sociology*, Third Edition. New York: D. Appleton-Century, 1938.

Ross, Edward Alsworth. *Social Control: A Survey of the Foundations of Order*. New York: Macmillan, 1901.

Rothwell, V. H. *British War Aims and Peace Diplomacy, 1914-1918*. Oxford: Clarendon Press, 1971.

Rystad, Göran. *Prisoners of the Past? The Munich Syndrome and Makers of American Foreign Policy in the Cold War Era*. Lund: CWK Gleerup, 1982.

Schell, Jonathan. *The Fate of the Earth*. New York: Alfred A. Knopf, 1982.

Schwabe, Klaus. *Deutsche Revolution und Wilson Frieden: Die amerikanische und deutsche Friedensstrategie zwischen Ideologie und Machtpolitik 1918/19*. Düsseldorf: Droste Verlag, 1971.

Schwabe, Klaus. *Woodrow Wilson, Revolutionary Germany, and Peacemaking, 1918-1919: Missionary Diplomacy and the Realities of Power*. Chapel Hill: University of North Carolina Press, 1985.

Smith, Daniel M. *The Great Departure: The United States and World War I, 1914-1920*. New York: John Wiley & Sons, 1965.

Smith, Henry Nash. *Virgin Land: The American West as Symbol and Myth*. Cambridge, Mass.: Harvard University Press, 1950.

Smith, Rixey, and Norman Beasley. *Carter Glass: A Biography.* New York: Longmans, Green, 1939.

Smythe, Donald. *Pershing: General of the Armies.* Bloomington: Indiana University Press, 1986.

Stearns, Harold. *Liberalism in America: Its Origins, Its Temporary Collapse, Its Future.* New York: Boni & Liveright, 1919.

Stebbins, Richard P. *The United States in World Affairs, 1960.* New York: Vintage Books, 1961.

Steel, Ronald. *Walter Lippmann and the American Century.* Boston: Little, Brown, 1980.

Stevenson, D. *French War Aims Against Germany, 1914-1919.* Oxford: Clarendon Press, 1982.

Stone, Ralph. *The Irreconcilables: The Fight Against the League of Nations.* Lexington: University Press of Kentucky, 1970.

Stone, Ronald H. *Reinhold Niebuhr: Prophet to Politicians.* Washington, D.C.: University Press of America, 1981.

Stromberg, Roland N. *Collective Security and American Foreign Policy: From the League of Nations to NATO.* New York: Frederick A. Praeger, 1963.

Tansill, Charles Callan. *America and the Fight for Irish Freedom, 1866-1922.* New York: Devin-Adair, 1957.

Trask, David F. *Captains and Cabinets: Anglo-American Naval Relations, 1917-1918.* Columbia: University of Missouri Press, 1972.

Trask, David F. *The United States and the Supreme War Council: American War Aims and Inter-Allied Strategy, 1917-1918.* Middletown, Conn.: Wesleyan University Press, 1961.

Tuveson, Ernest Lee. *Redeemer Nation: The Idea of America's Millennial Role.* Chicago: University of Chicago Press, 1968.

Walworth, Arthur. *America's Moment, 1918: American Diplomacy at the End of World War I.* New York: W. W. Norton, 1977.

Weinstein, Edwin A. *Woodrow Wilson: A Medical and Psychological Biography.* Princeton: Princeton University Press, 1981.

Widenor, William C. *Henry Cabot Lodge and the Search for an American Foreign Policy.* Berkeley and Los Angeles: University of California Press, 1979.

Wiebe, Robert H. *The Search for Order: 1877-1920.* New York: Hill & Wang, 1967.

Wills, Garry. *Nixon Agonistes: The Crisis of the Self-made Man.* Boston: Houghton Mifflin, 1970.

Wilson, Joan Hoff. *American Business and Foreign Policy, 1920-1933.* Lexington: University Press of Kentucky, 1971.

Wilson, Woodrow. *Congressional Government: A Study in American Politics.* Boston: Houghton Mifflin, 1885.

Wilson, Woodrow. *Constitutional Government in the United States.* New York: Columbia University Press, 1908.

Wilson, Woodrow. *A History of the American People.* New York: Harper & Brothers, 1901.

Wilson, Woodrow. *The State: Elements of Historical and Practical Politics.* Boston: D. C. Heath, 1889.

Winkler, Henry R. *The League of Nations Movement in Great Britain, 1914-1919.* New Brunswick, N.J.: Rutgers University Press, 1952.

Wright, Quincy. *The Causes of War and the Conditions of Peace*. London: Longmans, Green, 1935.

Wright, Quincy. *The Control of American Foreign Relations*. New York: Macmillan, 1922.

Wright, Quincy. *Mandates Under the League of Nations*. Chicago: University of Chicago Press, 1930.

Wright, Quincy. *Problems of Stability and Progress in International Relations*. Berkeley: University of California Press, 1954.

Wright, Quincy, ed. *Neutrality and Collective Security*. Chicago: University of Chicago Press, 1936.

ARTICLES

Ambrosius, Lloyd E. "Ethnic Politics and German-American Relations After World War I: The Fight over the Versailles Treaty in the United States," in Hans L. Trefousse, ed., *Germany and America: Essays on Problems of International Relations and Immigration*. New York: Brooklyn College Press, 1980.

Ambrosius, Lloyd E. "The Orthodoxy of Revisionism: Woodrow Wilson and the New Left," *Diplomatic History*, I, No. 3 (Summer 1977), 199-214.

Ambrosius, Lloyd E. "Secret German-American Negotiations During the Paris Peace Conference," *Amerikastudien/American Studies*, XXIV, No. 2 (1979), 288-309.

Ambrosius, Lloyd E. "The United States and the Weimar Republic: America's Response to the German Problem," in Jules Davids, ed., *Perspectives in American Diplomacy: Essays on Europe, Latin America, China, and the Cold War*. New York: Arno Press, 1976.

Ambrosius, Lloyd E. "Wilson, Clemenceau and the German Problem at the Paris Peace Conference of 1919," *Rocky Mountain Social Science Journal*, XII, No. 2 (Apr. 1975), 69-79.

Ambrosius, Lloyd E. "Wilson, the Republicans, and French Security After World War I," *Journal of American History*, LIX, No. 2 (Sept. 1972), 341-52.

Ambrosius, Lloyd E. "Wilson's League of Nations," *Maryland Historical Magazine*, LXV (Winter 1970), 369-93.

Ambrosius, Lloyd E. "Woodrow Wilson and the Quest for Orderly Progress," in Norman A. Graebner, ed., *Traditions and Values: American Diplomacy, 1865-1945*. Lanham, Md.: University Press of America, 1985.

Ambrosius, Lloyd E. "Woodrow Wilson's Health and the Treaty Fight, 1919-1920," *International History Review*, IX, No. 1 (Feb. 1987), 73-84.

Bennett, Ralph Kinney. "The Broken Promise of the United Nations," *Readers Digest* (Oct. 1983), 117-24.

Boothe, Leon E. "Anglo-American Pro-League Groups Lead Wilson," *Mid-America*, LI, No. 2 (1969), 92-107.

Boothe, Leon E. "A Fettered Envoy: Lord Grey's Special Mission to the United States, 1919-1920," *Review of Politics*, XXXIII, No. 1 (Jan. 1971), 78-94.

Church, Frank. "Thoughts on the Limits to American Power," *New York Times* (Apr. 15, 1984), sect. 4, p. 21.

Clark, John Bates. "If This League Fails: The Alternative Is a League for War Dominated by Germany," *New York Times* (June 1, 1919), sect. 3, p. 2.

Clark, John Bates. "A Workable League," *New York Times* (Nov. 11, 1918), p. 14.

Coben, Stanley. "A Study in Nativism: The American Red Scare of 1919-20," *Political Science Quarterly*, LXXIX, No. 1 (March 1964), 52-75.

Cooper, John Milton, Jr. "The British Response to the House-Grey Memorandum: New Evidence and New Questions," *Journal of American History*, LIX, No. 4 (March 1973), 958-71.

Corwin, Edwin S. "Constitutional Law in 1919-1920, II," *American Political Science Review*, XV, No. 1 (Feb. 1921), 52-54.

Curry, George. "Woodrow Wilson, Jan Smuts, and the Versailles Settlement," *American Historical Review*, LXVI, No. 4 (July 1961), 968-86.

DeWitt, Howard A. "Hiram W. Johnson and Economic Opposition to Wilsonian Diplomacy: A Note," *The Pacific Historian*, XIX, No. 1 (Spring 1975), 15-23.

Duff, John F. "German-Americans and the Peace, 1918-1920," *American Jewish Historical Quarterly*, LIX (June 1970), 424-44.

Egerton, George W. "Britain and the 'Great Betrayal': Anglo-American Relations and the Struggle for United States Ratification of the Treaty of Versailles, 1919-1920," *The Historical Journal*, XXI, No. 4 (1978), 885-911.

Egerton, George W. "The Lloyd George Government and the Creation of the League of Nations," *American Historical Review*, LXXIX, No. 2 (Apr. 1974), 419-44.

[Einstein, Lewis]. "The United States and Anglo-German Rivalry," *The Living Age*, No. 3579 (Feb. 8, 1913), 323-32.

Everett, Helen. "Social Control," in Edwin R. A. Seligman, ed., *Encyclopaedia of the Social Sciences*. New York: Macmillan, 1931.

Farrell, John C. "John Dewey and World War I: Armageddon Tests a Liberal's Faith," *Perspectives in American History*, IX (1975), 299-340.

Floto, Inga. "Colonel House in Paris: The Fate of a Presidential Adviser," *American Studies in Scandinavia*, VI (1973-1974), 21-45.

George, Juliette L., and Alexander L. George. "Comments on 'Woodrow Wilson Re-examined: The Mind-Body Controversy Redux and Other Disputations,'" *Political Psychology*, IV, No. 2 (1983), 307-12.

George, Juliette L., and Alexander L. George. "*Woodrow Wilson and Colonel House*: A Reply to Weinstein, Anderson, and Link," *Political Science Quarterly*, XCVI, No. 4 (Winter 1981-1982), 641-65.

Giddings, Franklin H. "The Relation of Social Theory to Public Policy," *International Conciliation*, No. 58 (Sept. 1912), 3-13.

Giddings, Franklin H. "The United States Among Nations," *The Independent*, XCVIII (June 14, 1919), 399-400.

Giddings, Franklin H. "What Did It," *The Independent*, CIV (Nov. 20, 1920), 262-64.

Giddings, Franklin H. "What the War Was Worth," *The Independent*, IC (July 5, 1919), 16-17.

Gilderhus, Mark T. "Pan-American Initiatives: The Wilson Presidency and 'Regional Integration,' 1914-17," *Diplomatic History*, IV, No. 4 (Fall 1980), 409-23.

Gilderhus, Mark T. "Wilson, Carranza, and the Monroe Doctrine: A Question in Regional Organization," *Diplomatic History*, VII, No. 2 (Spring 1983), 103-15.

Graebner, Norman A. "America's Limited Power in the Contemporary World," *The Key Reporter*, XLVII (Spring 1982), 2-5.

Jeffreys-Jones, Rhodri. "Massachusetts Labour and the League of Nations Controversy, 1919," *Irish Historical Studies*, XIX, No. 76 (Sept. 1975), 396-416.

Kazin, Alfred. "The Fascination of Henry Adams," *The New Republic* (Aug. 1, 1983), 28.

Kernek, Sterling J. "Distractions of Peace During War: The Lloyd George Government's Reactions to Woodrow Wilson, December, 1916 – November, 1918," *Transactions of the American Philosophical Society*, New Series, Vol. 65, Part 2. Philadelphia: The American Philosophical Society, 1975.

Kuklick, Bruce. "History as a Way of Learning," *American Quarterly*, XXII (Fall 1970), 609-28.

Lauren, Paul Gordon. "Human Rights in History: Diplomacy and Racial Equality at the Paris Peace Conference," *Diplomatic History*, II, No. 3 (Summer 1978), 257-78.

Lazo, Dimitri D. "A Question of Loyalty: Robert Lansing and the Treaty of Versailles," *Diplomatic History*, IX, No. 1 (Winter 1985), 35-53.

Lewis, Thomas T. "Alternative Psychological Interpretations of Woodrow Wilson," *Mid-America*, LXV, No. 2 (Apr.-July 1983), 71-85.

Lowry, Bullitt. "Pershing and the Armistice," *Journal of American History*, LV, No. 2 (Sept. 1968), 281-91.

McCrum, Robert. "French Rhineland Policy at the Paris Peace Conference, 1919," *The Historical Journal*, XXI, No. 3 (1978), 623-48.

Marmor, Michael. "Comments on 'Woodrow Wilson Re-examined: The Mind-Body Controversy Redux and Other Disputations,'" *Political Psychology*, IV, No. 2 (1983), 325-27.

Marmor, Michael F. "Wilson, Strokes, and Zebras," *New England Journal of Medicine*, CCCVII, No. 9 (Aug. 26, 1982), 528-35.

Mervin, David. "Henry Cabot Lodge and the League of Nations," *Journal of American Studies*, IV, No. 2 (Feb. 1971), 201-14.

Osborn, George C. "Woodrow Wilson and Frederick Jackson Turner," *Proceedings of the New Jersey Historical Society*, LXXIV (July 1956), 208-29.

Osgood, Robert E. "Woodrow Wilson, Collective Security, and the Lessons of History," *Confluence*, V, No. 4 (Winter 1957), 341-54.

Patterson, David S. "The United States and the Origins of the World Court," *Political Science Quarterly*, XCI, No. 2 (Summer 1976), 279-95.

Post, Jerrold M. "Reply to the Three Comments on 'Woodrow Wilson Re-examined: The Mind-Body Controversy Redux and Other Disputations,'" *Political Psychology*, IV, No. 2 (1983), 329-31.

Post, Jerrold M. "Woodrow Wilson Re-examined: The Mind-Body Controversy Redux and Other Disputations," *Political Psychology*, IV, No. 2 (1983), 289-306.

Raffo, Peter. "The Anglo-American Preliminary Negotiations for a League of Nations," *Journal of Contemporary History*, IX, No. 4 (Oct. 1974), 153-76.

Redmond, Kent G. "Henry L. Stimson and the Question of League Membership," *The Historian*, XXV, No. 2 (Feb. 1963), 200-212.

Schwabe, Klaus. "Woodrow Wilson and Germany's Membership in the League of Nations, 1918-19," *Central European History*, VIII, No. 1 (March 1975), 3-22.

Smith, Daniel M. "National Interest and American Intervention, 1917: An Historiographical Appraisal," *Journal of American History*, LII, No. 1 (June 1965), 5-24.

"Social Control," *Papers and Proceedings, American Sociological Society*, XII. Chicago: University of Chicago Press, 1918.

Stephenson, Wendell H. "The Influence of Woodrow Wilson on Frederick Jackson Turner," *Agricultural History*, XIX (Oct. 1945), 250-53.

Stern, Sheldon M. "Henry Cabot Lodge and Louis A. Coolidge in Defense of American Sovereignty, 1898-1920," *Massachusetts Historical Society Proceedings*, LXXXVII (1975), 118-34.

Stevenson, David. "French War Aims and the American Challenge, 1914-1918," *The Historical Journal*, XXII, No. 4 (1979), 877-94.

Stromberg, Roland N. "Uncertainties and Obscurities About the League of Nations," *Journal of the History of Ideas*, XXXIII (1972), 139-54.

Trani, Eugene P. "Woodrow Wilson and the Decision to Intervene in Russia: A Reconsideration," *Journal of Modern History*, XLVIII, No. 3 (Sept. 1976), 440-61.

Trask, David F. "General Tasker Howard Bliss and the 'Sessions of the World,' 1919," *Transactions of the American Philosophical Society*, New Series, Vol. 56, Part 8. Philadelphia: The American Philosophical Society, 1966.

Trask, David F. "Woodrow Wilson and the Coordination of Force and Diplomacy," The Society for Historians of American Foreign Relations *Newsletter*, XII, No. 3 (Sept. 1981), 12-19.

Trask, David F. "Woodrow Wilson and the Reconciliation of Force and Diplomacy: 1917-1918," *Naval War College Review*, XXVII, No. 4 (Jan./Feb. 1975), 23-31.

Trow, Clifford W. "Woodrow Wilson and the Mexican Interventionist Movement of 1919," *Journal of American History*, LVIII, No. 1 (June 1971), 46-72.

Weaver, Judith L. "Edith Bolling Wilson as First Lady: A Study in the Power of Personality, 1919-1920," *Presidential Studies Quarterly*, XV, No. 1 (Winter 1985), 51-76.

Weinstein, Edwin A. "Comments on 'Woodrow Wilson Re-examined: The Mind-Body Controversy Redux and Other Disputations,'" *Political Psychology*, IV, No. 2 (1983), 313-24.

Weinstein, Edwin A. "Woodrow Wilson's Neurological Illness," *Journal of American History*, LVII, No. 2 (Sept. 1970), 324-51.

Weinstein, Edwin A., James William Anderson, and Arthur S. Link. "Woodrow Wilson's Political Personality: A Reappraisal," *Political Science Quarterly*, XCIII, No. 4 (Winter 1978), 585-98.

Williams, Joyce G. "The Resignation of Secretary of State Robert Lansing," *Diplomatic History*, III, No. 3 (Summer 1979), 337-43.

Wilson, Woodrow. "The Ideals of America," *Atlantic Monthly*, XC (Dec. 1902), 721-34.

Wilson, Woodrow. "The Making of the Nation," *Atlantic Monthly*, LXXX (July 1897), 1-14.

Wilson, Woodrow. "The Proper Perspective on American History," *The Forum*, XIX (June 1895), 544-59.

Wimer, Kurt. "Woodrow Wilson Tries Conciliation: An Effort That Failed," *The Historian*, XXV (Aug. 1963), 419-38.

Wimer, Kurt. "Woodrow Wilson's Plans to Enter the League of Nations Through an Executive Agreement," *Western Political Quarterly*, XI, No. 4 (Dec. 1958), 800-12.

Woodward, C. Vann. "The Age of Reinterpretation," *American Historical Review*, LXVI (Oct. 1960), 1-19.

Wright, Quincy. "The Control of Foreign Relations," *American Political Science Review*, XV, No. 1 (Feb. 1921), 1-26.

Wright, Quincy. "Effects of the League of Nations Covenant," *American Political Science Review*, XIII, No. 4 (Nov. 1919), 556-76.

Wright, Quincy. "Woodrow Wilson and the League of Nations," *Social Research*, XXIV, No. 1 (Spring 1957), 65-86.

Index